MAPPING THE SOCIAL LANDSCAPE

Readings in Sociology

Mapping the Social Landscape

Readings in Sociology

Second Edition

SUSAN J. FERGUSON
Grinnell College

MAYFIELD PUBLISHING COMPANY
Mountain View, California
London • Toronto

Library of Congress Cataloging-in-Publication Data
Mapping the social landscape : readings in sociology / [compiled by]
  Susan J. Ferguson.—2nd ed.
     p.   cm.
   ISBN 0-7674-0616-8
   1. Social institutions.   2. Socialization.   3. Equality.
  4. Social change.   5. Sociology.   I. Ferguson, Susan J.
  HM131.M333   1999
  301—dc21   98-36974
                                                    CIP

Manufactured in the United States of America

10 9 8 7 6 5 4 3

Mayfield Publishing Company
1280 Villa Street
Mountain View, California 94041

Sponsoring editor, Serina Beauparlant; *production,* Publishing Support Services; *manuscript editor,* Pam Suwinsky; *design manager,* Jean Mailander; *text designer,* Linda M. Robertson; *cover designer,* Diana Coe; *manufacturing manager,* Randy Hurst. The text was set in 10/12 Book Antiqua by G&S Typesetters, Inc., and printed on 45# Highland Plus by Malloy Lithographing, Inc.

Cover photos (top to bottom): © Andreas Rentsch/nonstock; VCG/FPG International; Oote Boe/nonstock; VCG/FPG International; © Andreas Bleckmann/nonstock.

With love to my grandmother, Edna Catherine Clark, who always believed that an education would open the doors of the world to me. She was right.

Preface

As the title suggests, *Mapping the Social Landscape* is about exploration and discovery. It means taking a closer look at a complex, ever-changing social world in which locations, pathways, and boundaries are not fixed. Because sociology describes and explains our social surroundings, it enables us to understand this shifting landscape. Thus, sociology is about discovering society and discovering ourselves. The purpose of this anthology is to introduce the discipline of sociology and to convey the excitement and the challenge of the sociological enterprise.

Although a number of readers in introductory sociology are already available for students, I have yet to find one that exposes students to the broad diversity of scholarship, perspectives, and authorship that exists within the field of sociology. This diversity goes beyond recognizing gender, racial-ethnic, and social class differences to acknowledging a plurality of voices and views within the discipline. Like other anthologies, this one includes classic works by authors such as Karl Marx, Emile Durkheim, Max Weber, W. E. B. Du Bois, C. Wright Mills, and Talcott Parsons; in addition, however, I have also drawn from a wide range of contemporary scholarship, some of which provides newer treatments of traditional concepts. This diversity of viewpoints and approaches should encourage students to evaluate and analyze the ideas and research findings presented.

In addition, because I find it invaluable in my own teaching to use examples from personal experiences to enable students to see the connection between "private troubles and public issues," as Mills phrased it, I have included in this collection a few personal narratives to help students comprehend how social forces affect individual lives. Thus, this anthology includes classic as well as contemporary writings, and the voices of other social scientists who render provocative sociological insights. The readings also exemplify functionalist, conflict, and symbolic interactionist perspectives and different types of research methodology. Each article is preceded by a brief headnote that sets the context within which the reader can seek to understand the sociological work. Thus, the selections communicate an enthusiasm for sociology while illustrating sociological concepts, theories, and methods.

During the last twenty-five years, sociology has benefited from a rich abundance of creative scholarship, but many of these original works have not been adequately presented in textbooks or readers. I believe an introductory anthology needs to reflect the new questions concerning research and theory within the discipline. Moreover, I find that students enjoy reading the actual research and words of sociologists. This anthology, therefore, includes many "cutting edge" pieces of sociological scholarship and some very recent publications by recognized social analysts. Current issues are examined, including the tattoo subculture, the mythopoetic men's movement, the effects of globalization, the political influence of corporate PACs, the anti-abortion movement, the rise of paramilitary subcultures, and environmental degradation. In essence, I have attempted, not to break new ground, but to compile a collection that provides a fresh, innovative look at the discipline of sociology.

Changes to the Second Edition

With this second edition, I maintain a balance of classical and contemporary readings. In addition to the classic pieces that appear in the first edition, I have added a few more classics, including Emile Durkheim's discussion of social facts, Max Weber's classic work on the protestant ethic and the spirit of capitalism, Talcott Parsons' view of the institution of medicine, and William Ogburn's theory of cultural lag. I also have added nineteen new selections of contemporary cutting-edge sociological research that illustrate analyses of timely social issues and the intersection between race, social class, and gender. Another new feature in the second edition is the development of a separate section on the social institution of health and medicine. In addition to the Talcott Parsons' reading mentioned above, this section also includes an article by Steven Epstein on AIDS and social activism, and a piece by David Karp on the experience of illness and taking anti-depressant drugs. Of course, for all of the readings, I have tried to choose selections that are interesting and accessible to students. Please note that I welcome feedback from professors and students on this edition of *Mapping the Social Landscape: Readings in Sociology*.

Printed Test Bank

I also have written an accompanying test manual that contains numerous examination and discussion questions for each reading. As the editor of this anthology, I developed these items with the goal of helping instructors test students' understanding of key sociological concepts and themes.

Acknowledgments

The completion of this book involved the labor and support of many people. I would like to begin by acknowledging the support of my colleagues in the sociology department at Grinnell College. I also am indebted to the Carnegie secretaries, Faun Black, Vicki Bunell, Patty Dale, and Karen Groves, for their time typing and xeroxing portions of the manuscript. My student library assistants, Alice Gates, Sarah Staveteig, and Adrienne Van der Valk, also need to be commended for carrying innumerable pounds of books between my office and the library. Moreover, I appreciate the help of Bertha Camacho, Heather Farber, Stephanie Jaros, Betsy McCallon, Michelle McManus, Emily Morse, Holly Pfitsch, Amy Reiter, and Sacha Steenhock in reading the page proofs. I also am grateful to Grinnell College for its generous research support.

Many sociologists reviewed earlier drafts of the manuscript and provided me with valuable observations. First and foremost, I want to acknowledge the early insights of Agnes Riedmann, who suggested several key pieces in the first draft. I also appreciate the suggestions for selections made by Joan Ferrante, Annette Lareau, and Michael Messner.

My special thanks go to Arnold Arluke, Northeastern University; Joanne M. Badagliacco, University of Kentucky; Gary L. Brock, Southwest Missouri State University; Tom Gerschick, Illinois State University; Thomas B. Gold, University of California at Berkeley; Jack Harkins, College of DuPage; Paul Kamolnick, East Tennessee State University; Peter Kivisto, Augustana College; Fred Kniss, Loyola University; Diane E. Levy, University of North Carolina at Wilmington; Peter Meiksins, Cleveland State University; Roslyn Arlin Mickelson, University of North Carolina at Charlotte; and Carol Ray, San Jose State University, for their feedback on the first edition of the manuscript. As a team of reviewers, your detailed comments were enormously helpful in the tightening and refining of the manuscript. And more important, your voices reflect the rich and varied experiences with teaching introductory sociology.

For the second edition, I would like to thank the following team of reviewers: Angela Danzi, State University of New York at Farmingdale; Diane Diamond, State University of New York at Stony Brook; Yvonne Downs, State University of New York at Fredonia; Kay Forest, Northern Illinois University; Bob Granfield, University of Denver; Susan Greenwood, University of Maine; Kate Hausbeck, University of Nevada at Las Vegas; Arthur J. Jipson, Miami University; James Jones, Mississippi State University; Carolyn A. Kapinus, Penn State University; J. Richard Kendrick, Jr., State University of New York at Cortland; M. Kris McIlwaine, University of Arizona; Kristy McNamara, Furman University; Tracy Ore, University of Illinois at Urbana; Denise Scott, State University of New York at Geneseo; Maynard Seider, Massachusetts College of Liberal Arts; Tom Soltis, Westmoreland Community College; Martha Thompson, Northeastern Illinois University; Huiying Wei-Arthus, Weber State University; Adam S. Weinberg, Colgate University; Amy S. Wharton, Washington State University; and John Zipp, University of Wisconsin at Milwaukee.

At Mayfield Publishing Company, I would like to recognize the creative and patient efforts of several individuals, including Mary Johnson, Amy

Reiter, Kimberly Russell, Jeanne M. Schreiber, Linda Toy, Pamela Trainer, and April Wells-Hayes. I also want to acknowledge the detailed work of the copyeditor, Pam Suwinsky, and the production management skills of Vicki Moran. My highest appreciation goes to Serina Beauparlant, the acquisitions editor. Serina, if I am a clutch hitter, then you are the phenomenal batting coach. I could not have asked for a more thoughtful and attentive sociology editor. Thank you.

Contents

Part V DEVIANCE, CRIME, AND SOCIAL CONTROL

Part VI SOCIAL INEQUALITY

Part VII   SOCIAL INSTITUTIONS

POWER AND POLITICS

THE ECONOMY AND WORK

About the Contributors

Nancy Abelmann (Reading #33) is an associate professor of anthropology at the University of Illinois, Urbana-Champaign. She and her co-author, John Lie, wrote *Blue Dreams: Korean Americans and the Los Angeles Riots* (1995), which is excerpted in this volume.

Elijah Anderson (Reading #8) is the Charles and William L. Day Professor of the Social Sciences, professor of sociology, and director of the Philadelphia Ethnography Project at the University of Pennsylvania. An expert on the sociology of black America, he is the author of the highly regarded sociological work *A Place on the Corner: Study of Black Streetcorner Men* (1978); numerous articles on the black experience, including "Of Old Heads and Young Boys: Notes on the Urban Black Experience" (1986), commissioned by the National Research Council's Committee on the Streets of Black Americans; "Sex Codes and Family Life among Inner-City Youth" (1989); and *The Code of the Streets*, which was the cover story in the May 1994 issue of the *Atlantic Monthly*. For his ethnographic study, *Streetwise: Race, Class, and Change in an Urban Community* (1990), he was honored with the Robert E. Park Award of the American Sociological Association. He has also won the Lindback Award for Distinguished Teaching at the University of Pennsylvania.

Dallas A. Blanchard (Reading #43) obtained his Ph.D. in the sociology of religion and social ethics from Boston University. Blanchard is a retired United Methodist minister, who pastored churches in racially changing communities in Alabama, Kentucky, Tennessee, and Rhode Island. During his seventeen years as a minister, Blanchard experienced the Selma–Montgomery March, the merging of white and black congregations, and numerous Ku Klux Klan confrontations. Blanchard has also served on the Alabama Advisory Committee to the U.S. Commission on Civil Rights. Currently, he is professor and chair of sociology at the University of West Florida.

Kathleen M. Blee (Reading #17) is professor of sociology at the University of Pittsburgh. Blee hopes that her research on the politics of racial hatred and religious bigotry might help in the development of effective strategies to counteract the growth of organized racism in the United States. She is presently studying the involvement of women in modern-day white supremacist movements, including the Ku Klux Klan and neo-Nazi and racist skinhead groups.

xix

Philippe Bourgois (Reading #21) is a research fellow at the San Francisco Urban Institute and associate professor of anthropology at San Francisco State University. He is the author of *Ethnicity at Work: Divided Labor on a Central American Banana Plantation* (1989), and also has co-edited two volumes on poverty and social unrest in Latin America.

Robert D. Bullard (Reading #55) is a Ware Professor of Sociology and director of the Environmental Justice Resource Center at Clark Atlanta University. He is the author of *Dumping in Dixie: Race, Class, and Environmental Quality* (1990), *Confronting Environmental Racism: Voices from the Grassroots* (1993), *Unequal Protection: Environmental Justice and Communities of Color* (1994), and *Residential Apartheid: The American Legacy* (1994).

Mary Beth Caschetta (Reading #28) is a treatment advocate for low-income HIV-positive women in New York City. A medical sociologist and lesbian feminist, she has published articles concerning women's health in the *Journal of the American Medical Women's Association*, the *Sex Information and Education Council of the U.S. Report*, the *New England Journal of Medicine*, and the Encyclopedia of Childbirth.

Mark Chaves (Reading #42) is an associate professor of sociology at the University of Arizona. He is the author of *Ordaining Women: Culture and Conflict in Religious Organizations* (1997). Most of Chaves' work spans the boundary between the sociology of religion and the sociology of organizations. He is currently working on the National Congregations Study, a survey sample of nationally representative religious congregations.

Dan Clawson (Reading #36) is a professor of sociology at the University of Massachusetts at Amherst. Clawson began studying campaign finance in the early 1980s in an attempt to figure out why and how politics shifted so decisively to conservatism. Business actions, he feels, are usually politically decisive but are generally neglected by students, the media, and many scholars. He is co-author of *Money Talks: Corporate PACs and Political Influence* (1992), which is excerpted in this volume.

Patricia Hill Collins (Reading #51) received her B.A. and Ph.D. degrees from Brandeis University and an M.A.T. degree from Harvard University. While her specialties in sociology include such diverse areas as sociology of knowledge, organizational theory, social stratification, and work and occupations, her research and scholarship have dealt primarily with issues of gender, race, and social class, specifically relating to African American women. Her first book, *Black Feminist Thought: Knowledge, Consciousness, and the Politics of Empowerment* (1990), has won many awards, including the C. Wright Mills Award. Her second book, *Race, Class, and Gender: An Anthology* (edited with Margaret Andersen) is widely used in undergraduate courses in the United States.

Peter W. Cookson, Jr. (Reading #48) is associate provost at Adelphi University. His current work centers on education reform and applying sociological principles to school policy. He is currently writing a book about education policy for Yale University Press.

Mary Crow Dog, nee Mary Brave Bird (Reading #47) grew up fatherless in a one-room cabin without plumbing or electricity, on a Sioux reservation in South Dakota. Her autobiography, *Lakota Woman* (1990), records her memories of growing up female and Native American on the impoverished margins of a racist mainstream America; it also celebrates her liberation from this legacy of despair through activist politics, Native American religion, and childbirth during the occupation of Wounded Knee in 1973. Her life history shows her determination against all odds to save herself in a world that has been hostile to America's First Peoples for centuries.

G. William Domhoff (Reading #23) received his education at Duke University, Kent State University, and the University of Miami. Domhoff says he never had any interest in politics or power in his mid-20s, when he already had finished a Ph.D. in psychology on the topic of dreams. He later became interested in the topic of the ruling class in America. He thinks studying both dreams and power is a nice counterbalance, and he teaches both subjects at the University of California, Santa Cruz, where he has been since 1965. Four of his books, *Who Rules America?* (1967), *The Higher Circles* (1970), *The Powers That Be* (1979), and *Who Rules America Now?* (1983), are among the top fifty best-sellers in sociology over the past forty years.

W. E. B. Du Bois (1868–1963) (Reading #31) was born in Great Barrington, Massachusetts. He studied at Fisk University before receiving his Ph.D. from Harvard in 1895. Du Bois was a leading social theorist on race issues in the United States, and his study, *The Philadelphia Negro* (1899), is considered to be a classic empirical sociological work. Another of his works, *Souls of Black Folk* (1903), stirred up controversy within the African American community. Du Bois went on to organize the Niagara Movement (1905–1910), which developed into the NAACP, and he also was active in the Pan-African movement. Du Bois moved to Ghana in 1961, where he died on August 27, 1963, the day of the civil rights march on Washington, D.C.

Emile Durkheim (1858–1917) (Reading #4) was born in Lorraine, France. He studied cultural anthropology before he began teaching pedagogy and social science at the University of Bordeaux in 1887. In 1902, he was appointed to the Sorbonne in Paris. Durkheim designed early courses around the concept of social solidarity, and he founded the *Annee Sociologique* in 1896 and served as its editor until 1913. His famous works include his dissertation, *The Division of Labor in Society* (1893), *Suicide* (1898), and *The Elementary Forms of the Religious Life* (1912). An excerpt from Durkheim's work, *Rules of Sociological Method* (1895), is in this volume. Durkheim's premature death in 1917, at the age of 59, was attributed to his grief from losing his son two years earlier.

Gwynne Dyer (Reading #14) is a freelance journalist who is the author and narrator of the PBS National Television Series, *War.* "Anybody's Son Will Do" is an excerpt from the book based on that series.

Kathryn Edin (Reading #26) is assistant professor of sociology at the University of Pennsylvania. She co-authored with Laura Lein, *Making Ends Meet: How Single Mothers Survive Welfare and Low-Wage Work* (1997), which is excerpted in this volume.

Friedrich Engels (1820–1895) (Reading #38) was born in Barmen, Germany. During his youth he studied mercantilism, jurisprudence, religion, and history. In 1842, Engels moved to Manchester where, during the 1840s, he published several articles that criticized social and political conditions in England. It was through his writing that he met Karl Marx; after corresponding, the two met in Paris during the fall of 1844. This meeting was the beginning of a loyal friendship and fruitful scholarly collaboration. Marx and Engels were co-authors of numerous works, including *The German Ideology* (1845–1846), and the *Manifesto of the Community Party* (1848); an excerpt of the latter work is included in this volume. Engels' most important work, *The Origin of the Family, Private Property, and the State* (1884), is a critical examination of the history of private property, the family, and the subjugation of women. As such, it is considered a fundamental work in feminist theory. Before dying of esophageal cancer in 1895, Engels devoted his last years to editing and defending Marx's final works, including *Capital.*

Steven Epstein (Reading #45) is an associate professor of sociology at the University of California, San Diego. The excerpt in this volume is from Epstein's book, *Impure Science: AIDS, Activism, and the Politics of Knowledge* (1996). This book is based upon Epstein's dissertation work, which won the American Sociological Association's award for best dissertation of the year. The book also is the winner of the C. Wright Mills Award of the Society for the Study of Social Problems (1997) and the Robert K. Merton Award of the American Sociological Association (1997).

Richard Erdoes (Reading #47) is the co-author of *Lame Deer: Seeker of Visions* (1972), *American Indian Myths and Legends* (1984), and the author of more than twenty other titles. His most recent work is *A.D. 1000: Living on the Brink of Apocalypse* (1995). He is an Austrian-born historian, ethnographer, and artist, and has contributed illustrations to many periodicals, including *Time, Life, Fortune, The New York Times, Smithsonian,* and *The Saturday Evening Post.* He was a finalist for the 1981 best Western nonfiction award by Western Writers of America for *Saloons of the Old West.* Erdoes has pursued the protection of indigenous people in North America throughout his life.

Yen Le Espiritu (Reading #30) is professor of ethnic studies at the University of California, San Diego, where she teaches Race and Ethnic Relations and Asian American Studies. She is the author of *Asian American Panethnicity:*

Bridging Institutions and Identities (1992), *Filipino American Lives* (1995), and *Asian American Women and Men: Labor, Laws, and Love* (1997). She also has served as the president of the Association of Asian American Studies and is a review editor of the *Journal of Asian American Studies*.

Joe R. Feagin (Reading #34) is a professor of sociology at the University of Florida. He does research mainly on gender and racial discrimination. He has completed a major research project on the discrimination faced by successful Black Americans, a major portion of which was published in 1994 as *Living with Racism: The Black Middle Class Experience*. He also has published a book, *White Racism: The Basics* (1995), with co-author Professor Hernan Vera, and has served as scholar-in-residence at the U.S. Commission on Civil Rights. For the 1998–1999 year, Feagin served as the president of the American Sociological Association.

Richard Flacks (Reading #56) is a professor of sociology at the University of California at Santa Barbara. As a graduate student, he participated in the founding of Students for a Democratic Society—the leading organization of the white new left. He did path-breaking research on the family backgrounds and socialization of student activists; among his many writings on the student movement of the sixties is the book, *Youth and Social Change* (1973). His study, with Jack Whalen, of the political fate of the sixties generation is described in their book, *Beyond Barricades* (1989). The article reprinted here continues his long-term effort to understand the potentials for radical democratic movement in the United States (an effort discussed in his book, *Making History: The American Left and the American Mind,* 1988).

Donna Gaines (Reading #2) is a journalist, cultural sociologist, and New York state certified social worker. As a features writer she has published in *Rolling Stone, Long Island Monthly, Spin, Newsday,* and *Contemporaries.* Her first book, *Teenage Wasteland: Suburbia's Dead-End Kids* (1990), is internationally acclaimed and required reading for university course lists in several disciplines. *Rolling Stone* declared *Teenage Wasteland* "the best book on youth culture." Gaines received her doctoral degree in sociology at the State University of New York at Stony Brook, December 1990. She is currently a senior fellow at the Institute for Cultural Studies in New York City.

Herbert J. Gans (Reading #25) states: "I came to America in 1940 as a refugee from Nazi Germany, and for the first few years here, my family and I were very poor: events that help to explain my later work. Being an immigrant evoked my lifelong curiosity about America and made me a sociologist; being a political refugee stimulated my concern with social injustice; and living in poverty helped create my enduring interest in doing something about it. This interest was furthered by the research done for my first book, *The Urban Villagers* (1962), which remains a popular undergraduate text; it is expressed once more in my ninth and latest book, *The War on the Poor: The Underclass and Antipoverty Policy* (1995)."

J. William Gibson (Reading #9) teaches sociology at California State University, Long Beach. He is the author of two books, *The Perfect War: Technowar in Vietnam* (1986) and *Warrior Dreams: Paramilitary Culture in Post-Vietnam America* (1994), which is excerpted in this volume. He also is the co-editor of *Making War/Making Peace: Social Foundations of Violent Conflict* (1989).

Robert Granfield (Reading #13) graduated from Northeastern University in 1989 and has been in the Department of Sociology at the University of Denver for six years. He developed an interest in the legal profession while he was in graduate school and initiated research on legal education that led to his dissertation and a book, *Making Elite Lawyers: Visions of Law at Harvard and Beyond* (1992). In addition to this work, he has published articles on the sociology of drugs, the products liability law, and social theory.

William Greider (Reading #37) is the national editor of *Rolling Stone* magazine. His books include *The Education of David Stockman and Other Americans* (1986); *Secrets of the Temple: How the Federal Reserve Runs the Country* (1987), which won the *Los Angeles Times* Book Prize; and *Who Will Tell the People: The Betrayal of American Democracy* (1992), which was nominated for a National Book Award. Greider's most recent book, *One World, Ready or Not: The Manic Logic of Global Capitalism* (1997), is excerpted in this volume. Greider lives in Washington, D.C.

C. Kirk Hadaway (Reading #42) is minister for research and evaluation at the United Church Board for Homeland Ministries (United Church of Christ) in Cleveland, Ohio. He is a sociologist (Ph.D. University of Massachusetts, Amherst) who conducts institutional and social research for the UCC. His current research involves studies of religious affiliation, church membership, and participation in several Western nations. He is the author of *What Can We Do about Church Dropouts?* (1990), and co-editor of *The Urban Challenge* (1982), a book on city churches. His most recent book is *Rerouting the Protestant Mainstream* (1995).

Arlie Russell Hochschild (Reading #52) is professor of sociology at the University of California at Berkeley. She has written extensively on the topic of gender, work, and family life. She is the author of *The Managed Heart: The Commercialization of Human Feeling* (1978), *The Second Shift: Working Parents and the Revolution at Home* (1989), and *The Time Bind: When Work Becomes Home and Home Becomes Work* (1997), which is excerpted in this volume.

Robert A. Hummer (Reading #22) is assistant professor of sociology at the University of Texas at Austin. His work currently centers on how social inequality influences the health and mortality levels of different populations. Outside of sociology, he loves to travel with his wife and three-year-old daughter, enjoys fishing, and tries to work in an occasional-to-regular dose of ESPN.

Martin Sanchez Jankowski (Reading #16) is a professor of sociology at the University of California at Berkeley. He authored *City Bound: Urban Life and Political Attitudes among Chicano Youth* (1986), and co-authored *Inequality by Design: Cracking the Bell Curve Myth* (1987). His most recent work, *Islands in the Street: Gangs and American Urban Society* (1991), is excerpted in this volume.

David A. Karp (Reading #46) is a professor of sociology at Boston College. Karp's book, *Speaking of Sadness: Depression, Disconnection, and the Meanings of Illness* (1996), is the winner of the 1996 Charles Horton Cooley Award from the Society for the Study of Symbolic Interaction. This work is excerpted in this volume.

Donald B. Kraybill (Reading #15) is a professor of sociology at Elizabethtown College in Elizabethtown, Pennsylvania. In addition to the excerpt in this volume from his book, *The Riddle of Amish Culture* (1989), Kraybill has published other books, including *Our Star-Spangled Faith* (1976) and *Perils of Professionalism, Facing Nuclear War* (1982). Kraybill's most recent book, *The Upside-Down Kingdom* (1990), is the winner of the National Religious Book Award.

Robin Leidner (Reading #40), associate professor of sociology at the University of Pennsylvania, was once a *Jeopardy!* champion. While researching *Fast Food, Fast Talk* (1993), she not only put in her time at McDonald's, but also found herself chanting, "I feel healthy! I feel happy! I feel TERRIFIC!" with a group of life insurance sales trainees. Before becoming a sociologist, she spent several years acting and writing for RIFT, the Rhode Island Feminist Theater.

Laura Lein (Reading #26) is senior lecturer in the Department of Anthropology and senior lecturer and research scientist in the School of Social Work at the University of Texas at Austin. She co-authored with Kathryn Edin, *Making Ends Meet: How Single Mothers Survive Welfare and Low-Wage Work* (1997), which is excerpted in this volume.

John Lie (Reading #33) is professor of sociology at the University of Illinois, Urbana-Champaign. He and his co-author, Nancy Abelmann, wrote *Blue Dreams: Korean Americans and the Los Angeles Riots* (1995), which is excerpted in this volume.

Judith Lorber (Reading #11) has taught courses in gender for twenty-five years at Brooklyn College and the Graduate Center, City University of New York, starting with Courtship and Marriage and ending with the Sociology of Gender. She is the author of *Women Physicians: Careers, Status and Power* (1984), and *Paradoxes of Gender* (1994), which is excerpted in this volume. In 1986 she founded a journal, *Gender & Society*, which is still going strong.

Penny Long Marler (Reading #42) is associate professor of religion and philosophy at Samford University in Birmingham, Alabama where she teaches sociology of religion, sociological theory, and congregational studies. She received her B.A. from Auburn University, her M.Div. and Ph.D. from Southern Baptist Theological Seminary, and her M.S.S.W. from the University of Louisville. She is co-author of *Being There* (1997), an ethnographic study of two American seminaries. Her current research deals with religious nominalism and an ecological approach to the transmission of religious belief and belonging.

Patricia Yancey Martin (Reading #22) teaches the sociology of gender, organizations, and work at Florida State University. Her interest in undergraduate student culture includes the social, service, and political organizations to which students belong. She has studied services provided for rape victims in 130 organizations in Florida and is currently interviewing men and women about gender and race-ethnicity in Fortune 500 companies that compete for markets, growth, and profits in a global capitalist economy.

Karl Marx (1818–1883) (Reading #38) was born in Trier in the Prussian Rhineland. He was a prodigy, receiving his doctorate in philosophy from the University of Jena at the age of twenty-three. Marx could not obtain a university position in Germany because of his association with the Young Hegelians, who were considered heretics. He left Germany in 1843, and after living in exile in Paris, Brussels, and Cologne, he moved his family to London. Marx devoted his life to the study of law, history, mortality, and the political economy. His scholarly work and brief employment as a journalist did not provide much income, so for most of his life, Marx was dependent on the financial help and friendship of Friedrich Engels. Together they collaborated on many works, including the *Manifesto of the Communist Party* (1848). Marx is known for his contributions to socialist thought, his synthesis of philosophical knowledge, and his theory of society and history. From his early works, such as the *Economic and Philosophic Manuscripts* (1844) to *Capital* (1867–1879), Marx has left a rich legacy of social thought.

Penelope A. McLorg (Reading #20) is a doctoral student in anthropology at Southern Illinois University at Carbondale. She is interested in the interplay between social and biological factors. Her recent publications involve eating disorders, infant feeding practices, and bone anatomy and measurement.

Michael Messner (Reading #12) played high school basketball, but then discovered as a college freshman that he was too short to play forward, too slow to play guard, but just the right size to warm the bench as his teammates played. Though today he still shoots some hoops, he spends the majority of his working hours as associate professor in the Department of Sociology and the Program for the Study of Women and Men in Society at the University of Southern California. Messner is the author of *Power at Play: Sports and the Problem of Masculinity* (1992), co-author of *Sex, Violence, and Power in Sports:*

Rethinking Masculinity (1994), and co-editor of *Men's Lives* (1995). He is the father of two young sons.

C. Wright Mills (Readings #1 and #35) was born in Waco, Texas. He received his Ph.D. in sociology from the University of Wisconsin and was professor of sociology at Columbia University. During his brief academic career, Mills became one of the best known and most controversial American sociologists. He believed that academics should be socially responsible and speak out against social injustice. He criticized social conditions through his works, the most famous of which are *White Collar: The American Middle Classes* (1951) and *The Power Elite* (1956); Reading 35 is excerpted from the latter of these. A selection from Mills' *The Sociological Imagination* (1959) also appears in this volume. Mills died of a coronary condition at the young age of 45.

Jeff B. Murray (Reading #7) is associate professor of marketing at the University of Arkansas. His research interests include the application of critical perspectives to consumer research and marketing. Recent publications include "The Critical Imagination: Emancipatory Interests in Consumer Research" in the *Journal of Consumer Research* (1991); "Using Critical Theory and Public Policy to Create the Reflexively Defiant Consumer" in the *American Behavioral Scientist* (1995); and "A Critical-Emancipatory Sociology of Knowledge: Reflections on the Social Construction of Consumer Research" in *Research in Consumer Behavior* (1997). His current research is focusing on the social construction of *style,* a diagnostic critique of Jean Baudrillard's early sociology. When Jeff is not writing and teaching, he enjoys hanging out with his partner, Deborah, and their son Seth.

Alan Neustadtl (Reading #36) is associate professor of sociology at the University of Maryland at College Park. He was drawn to studying campaign finance after reading books as an undergraduate by researchers like Floyd Hunter (*Community Power Structures*), C. Wright Mills (*The Power Elite*), and G. William Domhoff (*The Powers That Be* and *Bohemian Grove and Other Retreats*). He is co-author of *Money Talks: Corporate PACs and Political Influence* (1992), which is excerpted in this volume, and he has published research articles on political sociology in such journals as *American Sociological Review, American Journal of Sociology, Social Forces, Social Science Research,* and *Social Science Quarterly.*

William F. Ogburn (1886–1959) (Reading #53) received his Ph.D. in sociology from Columbia University in 1912. He taught sociology first at Reed College in Oregon, and was professor of sociology at Columbia from 1919 to 1927. He then moved to the University of Chicago where he taught until his retirement in 1951. Ogburn wrote several books, including *Social Change* (1922), *The Social Sciences and Their Interrelations* (1927), *American Marriage and Family Relationships* (1928), *Recent Social Trends* (1933), *Social Characteristics of Cities* (1937), and *The Social Effects of Aviation* (1946). He was editor or associate editor of at least four learned journals, and he published over two hundred articles in various periodicals. One of Ogburn's most important contributions to the discipline of sociology is his concept of cultural lag, which is excerpted in this volume.

Melvin L. Oliver (Reading #24) is on leave from his position as professor of sociology and policy studies at the University of California, Los Angeles. Currently, he is vice president of the Ford Foundation's program on Asset Building and Community Development Program. He was named the 1994 California Professor of the Year by the Carnegie Foundation. Oliver and Thomas M. Shapiro have been awarded the 1995 C. Wright Mills Award and the American Sociological Association's Distinguished Scholarly Publication Award for *Black Wealth/White Wealth: A New Perspective on Racial Inequality* (1995), which is excerpted in this volume.

Talcott Parsons (1902–1979) (Reading #44) studied economics in the United States and England before discovering the writings of Max Weber in Germany. Parsons translated several of Weber's works, including *The Protestant Ethic and the Spirit of Capitalism* (1905). After returning to the United States in 1927, Parsons began teaching in the economics department at Harvard University before joining, at the invitation of Pitirim Sorokin, the sociology department, where he remained until his retirement in 1973. Parsons' seminal work, *The Structure of Social Action* (1937), renewed attention to sociological theory and research, and during the 1940s and 1950s, Parsonian functionalism dominated American sociology. In 1951, Parsons published *The Social System*. Parsons served as chair of Harvard's Department of Social Relations from 1946 to 1956, and was president of the American Sociological Association in 1949. He died in 1979.

Caroline Hodges Persell (Reading #48) became aware of the profound social inequalities in the United States as a teenager, while riding the train through Harlem and Westchester County, New York. That interest led her to sociology; she is now a professor of sociology at New York University, where she has taught for more than twenty-five years. She particularly enjoys the very diverse students who attend NYU. When not teaching or doing sociological research, she enjoys her family, music, sports, and gardening.

George Ritzer (Reading #54) is an acknowledged expert in the field of social theory and the sociology of work and has served as chair of the American Sociological Association's Sections on Theoretical Sociology and Organizations and Occupations. A distinguished scholar-teacher at the University of Maryland, Professor Ritzer has been honored with that institution's Teaching Excellence award. Two of his most recent books include *Metatheorizing in Sociology* (1991) and *The McDonaldization of Society* (1995).

Mary Romero (Reading #3) lives in Tempe, Arizona. She is a professor at Arizona State University, where she teaches sociology in the Office of Chicana and Chicano Studies. Her study of Chicana domestics, *Maid in the U.S.A.* (1992), is excerpted in this volume. Romero is currently writing a book about the children of private household workers.

David L. Rosenhan (Reading #19) received his Ph.D. in psychology from Columbia University. His books include *Foundations of Abnormal Psychology*, with P. London (1968), *Theory and Research in Abnormal Psychology* (1969), and *Abnormal Psychology*, with Martin E. P. Seligman (1984). He is professor of psychology and law at Stanford University.

Barbara Katz Rothman (Reading #28) is professor of sociology at Baruch College and the Graduate Center of the City University of New York. She is the author of *The Tentative Pregnancy: Prenatal Diagnosis and the Future of Motherhood* (1986), a study of women's experiences with amniocentesis and selective abortion, and of *In Labor: Women and Power in the Birthplace* (1991), a comparison of the medical and midwifery models of childbirth. Her most recent works are *Recreating Motherhood: Ideology and Technology in a Patriarchal Society* (1989), a feminist analysis of changing ideas about motherhood in America, and *Centuries of Solace* (1992), with Wendy Simonds.

Lillian B. Rubin (Reading #32) is an internationally recognized author and social scientist who was born in Philadelphia, grew up in New York City, and moved to California as a young adult. Since receiving her doctorate in 1971, she has authored numerous books, including *Worlds of Pain: Life in the Working Class* (1976), *Intimate Strangers: Men and Women Together* (1983), and *Fall Down Seven Times, Get Up Eight* (1996), which presents case histories of people who have transcended very difficult paths. Rubin's 1994 book, *Families on the Fault Line: America's Working Class Speaks about the Family, the Economy, Race, and Ethnicity*, is excerpted in this volume. Rubin currently lives in San Francisco, where she is a practicing psychotherapist and Senior Research Fellow at the Institute for the Study of Social Change at the University of California, Berkeley.

Myra Sadker (Reading #29) was professor of education and dean of the School of Education at American University until 1995. *David Sadker* (Reading #29) is currently professor of education and director of the Master of Arts in Teaching Program at American University. They have co-authored five books, including *Teachers, Schools, and Society* (1997) and *Failing at Fairness: How Our Schools Cheat Girls* (1995), which is excerpted in this volume. More than fifty of their articles have appeared in *Phi Delta Kappan, Harvard Educational Review, Educational Leadership,* and other professional journals. Their research interests have focused on foundations of education, educational equity, teacher preparation, and curriculum. They also have conducted teaching and equity workshops for principals, teachers, and professors in over forty states and overseas.

Gabrielle Sándor (Reading #5) has written numerous feature articles for the journal *American Demographics.* The topics of her articles range from cleaning products and hearing aids to college costs and intermarriage. She currently lives in Ithaca, New York.

Michael Schwalbe (Reading #18) is an associate professor of sociology at North Carolina State University, where he teaches courses in social theory, social psychology, and inequality. He is the author of *The Sociologically Examined Life: Pieces of the Conversation* (1997), and *Unlocking the Iron Cage: The Men's Movement, Gender Politics, and American Culture* (1996), which is excerpted in this volume. Schwalbe also is the editor of the journal *Writing Sociology.*

Denise Scott (Reading #36) is an assistant professor of sociology at the State University of New York at Geneseo. Committed to the principles and practices of equal opportunity and justice, her current research focuses on class and gender inequality and issues of power. As an outgrowth of a larger project examining the political behavior of business, Scott's dissertation focused on women's involvement in corporate-government relations. She also is coauthor of *Money Talks: Corporate PACs and Political Influence* (1992), which is excerpted in this volume.

Thomas M. Shapiro (Reading #24) is a professor of sociology and anthropology at Northeastern University. Shapiro and Melvin L. Oliver have been awarded the 1995 C. Wright Mills Award and the American Sociological Association's Distinguished Scholarly Publication Award for *Black Wealth/ White Wealth: A New Perspective on Racial Inequality* (1995). Shapiro's other books include *Population Control Politics: Women, Sterilization, and Reproductive Choice* (1985), and *Great Divides: Readings in Social Inequality in the United States* (1998).

Melvin P. Sikes (Reading #34) is a clinical psychologist and consultant. He grew up in Gary, Indiana, where he worked in the steel mills until the war, when he served as one of the Tuskegee airmen. After the war, he attended the University of Chicago and earned a degree in clinical psychology. He has worked in private practice, taught at the Department of Educational Psychology at the University of Texas at Austin, was dean at several African American Colleges, practiced at a Veterans Administration hospital, and did work in drug and alcohol abuse programs, as well as in a Houston police training program. Sikes says that his goal for the book *Living with Racism: The Black Middle-Class Experience* (1994), excerpted in this volume, was not so much to fight racism as to help people understand how it affects them and to encourage them to uphold this country's principles of equality and justice.

Judith Stacey (Reading #50) is the Streisand Professor of Contemporary Gender Studies and professor of sociology at the University of Southern California, and has written and lectured extensively on the politics of family change. She is a founding member of the Council on Contemporary Families, a group committed to challenging the research and politics behind contemporary campaigns for family values. She is the author of *Brave New Families: Stories of Domestic Upheaval in Late Twentieth-Century America* (1990), and *In the Name of the Family: Rethinking Family Values in the Postmodern Age* (1996).

Diane E. Taub (Reading #20) is associate professor of sociology and associate dean at the College of Liberal Arts at Southern Illinois University at Carbondale (SIUC). Her publications primarily concern the sociology of deviance, with a focus on the experiences of women. She has received several teaching awards, including the 1994 SIUC Outstanding Teacher Award.

Haunani-Kay Trask (Reading #10) is descended from the Pi'ilani line of Maui and the Kahakumakaliua line of Kaua'i. Her books include *From a Native Daughter: Colonialism and Sovereignty in Hawai'i* (1993), which is excerpted in this volume, and *Light in a Crevice Never Seen* (1994). She co-produced the 1993 award-winning film *Act of War: The Overthrow of the Hawaiian Nation.* Trask is currently director of Hawaiian Studies at the University of Hawai'i at Manoa.

Guadalupe Valdés (Reading #49) is a professor in the School of Education and in the Department of Spanish and Portuguese at Stanford University. Valdés' ethnographic study, *Con Respeto: Bridging the Distances between Culturally Diverse Families and Schools* (1996), is excerpted in this volume.

Anne M. Velliquette (Reading #7) is a fourth-year marketing Ph.D. candidate at the University of Arkansas. Her current research interests involve issues related to symbolic consumer behavior, consumer subcultures, body adornment, and identity. Through her studies, Velliquette became interested in understanding how consumers accrue symbolic meaning and construct an identity with the products they consume. Focusing on one type of symbolic consumer behavior, her dissertation examines consumers' uses of tattoos in communicating individual and group identity. A piece of her research, "The New Tattoo Subculture," is co-written with Jeff B. Murray and excerpted in this volume.

Max Weber (1864–1920) (Reading #41) was born in Erfurt, Germany. Weber studied economics, history, and law at the University of Heidelberg before completing a Ph.D. thesis on medieval societies at the University of Berlin. In 1893, Weber was appointed to a chair in economics at the University of Freiburg, and in 1895, he transferred to the University of Heidelberg where he became a central figure among a group of scholars. Weber's most famous work, *The Protestant Ethic and the Spirit of Capitalism* (1905), is excerpted in this volume, and it reveals his concern for rationality and the modern world. Weber also extensively wrote on bureaucracies, politics, power, and authority. After years of struggling with mental health problems, Weber died at the age of 58.

Rose Weitz (Reading #6) is a professor of sociology at Arizona State University. She is the author of *The Sociology of Health, Illness, and Health Care: A Critical Approach* (1995), *Life with AIDS* (1991), which is excerpted in this volume, and co-author of *Labor Pains: Modern Midwives and Home Birth* (1988). Weitz, who has always believed that the personal is political, is a founding member and past chairperson of the Sociologists' AIDS Network, and is past-president of Sociologists for Women in Society.

Christine L. Williams (Reading #27) is associate professor of sociology at the University of Texas at Austin. Williams first became interested in the topic of gender and discrimination as a first-year college student in the 1970s, when she took a course entitled "The Sociology of Women." Back then, gender was considered something that affected only women. Today, most of her writings are about society's treatment of men and changing cultural definitions of masculinity. Her books include *Gender Differences at Work* (1989) and *"Doing Women's Work": Men in Non-traditional Occupations* (1993). The article in this volume was expanded into a book, *Still a Man's World*, published in 1995.

William Julius Wilson (Reading #39) was a professor at the University of Chicago for twenty-four years before becoming the Malcolm Wiener Professor of Social Policy at the John F. Kennedy School of Government, Harvard University. He is a MacArthur Prize Fellow and author of *The Declining Significance of Race* (1978) and *The Truly Disadvantaged* (1987). His most current book, *When Work Disappears: The World of the New Urban Poor* (1996), is excerpted in this volume. Wilson lives with his wife in Cambridge, Massachusetts.

Beverly H. Wright (Reading #55) is associate professor of sociology at Xavier University of Louisiana, and she directs the Deep South Center for Environmental Justice. Wright is a leading environmental justice scholar and advocate of university-community partnerships in addressing local environmental problems.

Tell me the landscape in which you live, and I will tell you who you are.

José Ortega y Gasset

PART I

The Sociological Perspective

1

THE PROMISE

C. WRIGHT MILLS

The initial three selections examine the sociological perspective. The first of these is an excerpt from C. Wright Mills' (1916–1962) acclaimed book, *The Sociological Imagination*. Since its original publication in 1959, this text has been a required reading for most introductory sociology students around the world. Mills' sociological imagination perspective not only compels the best sociological analyses but also enables the sociologist and the individual to distinguish between "personal troubles" and "public issues." By separating these phenomena, we can better comprehend the sources of and solutions to social problems.

Nowadays men often feel that their private lives are a series of traps. They sense that within their everyday worlds, they cannot overcome their troubles, and in this feeling, they are often quite correct: What ordinary men are directly aware of and what they try to do are bounded by the private orbits in which they live; their visions and their powers are limited to the close-up scenes of job, family, neighborhood; in other milieux, they move vicariously and remain spectators. And the more aware they become, however vaguely, of ambitions and of threats which transcend their immediate locales, the more trapped they seem to feel.

Underlying this sense of being trapped are seemingly impersonal changes in the very structure of continent-wide societies. The facts of contemporary history are also facts about the success and the failure of individual men and women. When a society is industrialized, a peasant becomes a worker; a feudal lord is liquidated or becomes a businessman. When classes rise or fall, a man is employed or unemployed; when the rate of investment goes up or down, a man takes new heart or goes broke. When wars happen, an insurance salesman becomes a rocket launcher; a store clerk, a radar man; a wife lives alone; a child grows up without a father. Neither the life of an individual nor the history of a society can be understood without understanding both.

Yet men do not usually define the troubles they endure in terms of historical change and institutional contradiction. The well-being they enjoy, they do not usually impute to the big ups and downs of the societies in which they live. Seldom aware of the intricate connection between the patterns of their own lives and the course of world history, ordinary men do not usually know what this connection means for the kinds of men they are becoming and for the kinds of history making in which they might take part. They do not possess the quality of mind essential to grasp the interplay of man and society, of biography and history, of self and world. They cannot cope with their personal troubles in such ways as to control the structural transformations that usually lie behind them.

Surely it is no wonder. In what period have so many men been so totally exposed at so fast a pace to such earthquakes of change? That Americans have not known such catastrophic changes as have the men and women of other societies is due to historical facts that are now quickly becoming "merely history." The history that now affects every man is world history. Within this scene and this period, in the course of a single generation, one-sixth of mankind is transformed from all that is feudal and backward into all that is modern, advanced, and fearful. Political colonies are freed; new and less visible forms of imperialism installed. Revolutions occur; men feel the intimate grip of new kinds of authority. Totalitarian societies rise and are smashed to bits—or succeed fabulously. After two centuries of ascendancy, capitalism is shown up as only one way to make society into an industrial apparatus. After two centuries of hope, even formal democracy is restricted to a quite small portion of mankind. Everywhere in the underdeveloped world, ancient ways of life are broken up and vague expectations become urgent demands. Everywhere in the overdeveloped world, the means of authority and of violence become total in scope and bureaucratic in form. Humanity itself now lies before us, the super-nation at either pole concentrating its most coordinated and massive efforts upon the preparation of World War Three.

The very shaping of history now outpaces the ability of men to orient themselves in accordance with cherished values. And which values? Even when they do not panic, men often sense that older ways of feeling and thinking have collapsed and that newer beginnings are ambiguous to the point of moral stasis. Is it any wonder that ordinary men feel they cannot cope with the larger worlds with which they are so suddenly confronted? That they cannot understand the meaning of their epoch for their own lives? That—in defense of selfhood—they become morally insensible, trying to remain altogether private men? Is it any wonder that they come to be possessed by a sense of the trap?

_____

It is not only information that they need—in this Age of Fact, information often dominates their attention and overwhelms their capacities to assimilate it. It is not only the skills of reason that they need—although their struggles to acquire these often exhaust their limited moral energy.

What they need, and what they feel they need, is a quality of mind that will help them to use information and to develop reason in order to achieve lucid summations of what is going on in the world and of what may be happening within themselves. It is this quality, I am going to contend, that journalists and scholars, artists and publics, scientists and editors are coming to expect of what may be called the sociological imagination.

_____

The sociological imagination enables its possessor to understand the larger historical scene in terms of its meaning for the inner life and the external career of a variety of individuals. It enables him to take into account how individuals, in the welter of their daily experience, often become falsely conscious of their social positions. Within that welter, the framework of modern society is sought, and within that framework the psychologies of a variety of men and women are formulated. By such means the personal uneasiness of individuals is focused upon explicit troubles and the indifference of publics is transformed into involvement with public issues.

The first fruit of this imagination—and the first lesson of the social science that embodies it—is the idea that the individual can understand his own experience and gauge his own fate only by locating himself within his period, that he can know his own chances in life only by becoming aware of those of all individuals in his circumstances. In many ways it is a terrible lesson; in many ways a magnificent one. We do not know the limits of man's capacities for supreme effort or willing degradation, for agony or glee, for pleasurable brutality or the sweetness of reason. But in our time we have come to know that the limits of "human nature" are frighteningly broad. We have come to know that every individual lives, from one generation to the next, in some society; that he lives out a biography, and that he lives it out within some historical sequence. By the fact of his living he contributes, however minutely, to the shaping of this society and to the course of its history, even as he is made by society and by its historical push and shove.

The sociological imagination enables us to grasp history and biography and the relations between the two within society. That is its task and its promise. To recognize this task and this promise is the mark of the classic social analyst. It is characteristic of Herbert Spencer—turgid, polysyllabic, comprehensive; of E. A. Ross—graceful, muckraking, upright; of Auguste Comte and Emile Durkheim; of the intricate and subtle Karl Mannheim. It is the quality of all that is intellectually excellent in Karl Marx; it is the clue to

Thorstein Veblen's brilliant and ironic insight, to Joseph Schumpeter's many-sided constructions of reality; it is the basis of the psychological sweep of W. E. H. Lecky no less than of the profundity and clarity of Max Weber. And it is the signal of what is best in contemporary studies of man and society.

No social study that does not come back to the problems of biography, of history and of their intersections within a society has completed its intellectual journey. Whatever the specific problems of the classic social analysts, however limited or however broad the features of social reality they have examined, those who have been imaginatively aware of the promise of their work have consistently asked three sorts of questions:

1. What is the structure of this particular society as a whole? What are its essential components, and how are they related to one another? How does it differ from other varieties of social order? Within it, what is the meaning of any particular feature for its continuance and for its change?
2. Where does this society stand in human history? What are the mechanics by which it is changing? What is its place within and its meaning for the development of humanity as a whole? How does any particular feature we are examining affect, and how is it affected by, the historical period in which it moves? And this period—what are its essential features? How does it differ from other periods? What are its characteristic ways of history making?
3. What varieties of men and women now prevail in this society and in this period? And what varieties are coming to prevail? In what ways are they selected and formed, liberated and repressed, made sensitive and blunted? What kinds of "human nature" are revealed in the conduct and character we observe in this society in this period? And what is the meaning for "human nature" of each and every feature of the society we are examining?

Whether the point of interest is a great power state or a minor literary mood, a family, a prison, a creed—these are the kinds of questions the best social analysts have asked. They are the intellectual pivots of classic studies of man in society—and they are the questions inevitably raised by any mind possessing the sociological imagination. For that imagination is the capacity to shift from one perspective to another—from the political to the psychological; from examination of a single family to comparative assessment of the national budgets of the world; from the theological school to the military establishment; from considerations of an oil industry to studies of contemporary poetry. It is the capacity to range from the most impersonal and remote transformations to the most intimate features of the human self—and to see the relations between the two. Back of its use there is always the urge to know the social and historical meaning of the individual in the society and in the period in which he has his quality and his being.

That, in brief, is why it is by means of the sociological imagination that men now hope to grasp what is going on in the world, and to understand what is happening in themselves as minute points of the intersections of biography and history within society. In large part, contemporary man's self-conscious view of himself as at least an outsider, if not a permanent stranger, rests upon an absorbed realization of social relativity and of the transformative power of history. The sociological imagination is the most fruitful form of this self-consciousness. By its use men whose mentalities have swept only a series of limited orbits often come to feel as if suddenly awakened in a house with which they had only supposed themselves to be familiar. Correctly or incorrectly, they often come to feel that they can now provide themselves with adequate summations, cohesive assessments, comprehensive orientations. Older decisions that once appeared sound now seem to them products of a mind unaccountably dense. Their capacity for astonishment is made lively again. They acquire a new way of thinking, they experience a transvaluation of values: in a word, by their reflection and by their sensibility, they realize the cultural meaning of the social sciences.

Perhaps the most fruitful distinction with which the sociological imagination works is between "the personal troubles of milieu" and "the public issues of social structure." This distinction is an essential tool of the sociological imagination and a feature of all classic work in social science.

Troubles occur within the character of the individual and within the range of his immediate relations with others; they have to do with his self and with those limited areas of social life of which he is directly and personally aware. Accordingly, the statement and the resolution of troubles properly lie within the individual as a biographical entity and within the scope of his immediate milieu—the social setting that is directly open to his personal experience and to some extent his willful activity. A trouble is a private matter: Values cherished by an individual are felt by him to be threatened.

Issues have to do with matters that transcend these local environments of the individual and the range of his inner life. They have to do with the organization of many such milieux into the institutions of a historical society as a whole, with the ways in which various milieux overlap and interpenetrate to form the larger structure of social and historical life. An issue is a public matter: Some value cherished by publics is felt to be threatened. Often there is a debate about what that value really is and about what it is that really threatens it. This debate is often without focus if only because it is the very nature of an issue, unlike even widespread trouble, that it cannot very well be defined in terms of the immediate and everyday environments of ordinary men. An issue, in fact, often involves a crisis in institutional arrangements, and often too it involves what Marxists call "contradictions" or "antagonisms."

In these terms, consider unemployment. When, in a city of 100,000, only one man is unemployed, that is his personal trouble, and for its relief we properly look to the character of the man, his skills, and his immediate opportunities.

But when in a nation of 50 million employees, 15 million men are unemployed, that is an issue, and we may not hope to find its solution within the range of opportunities open to any one individual. The very structure of opportunities has collapsed. Both the correct statement of the problem and the range of possible solutions require us to consider the economic and political institutions of the society, and not merely the personal situation and character of a scatter of individuals.

Consider war. The personal problem of war, when it occurs, may be how to survive it or how to die in it with honor; how to make money out of it; how to climb into the higher safety of the military apparatus; or how to contribute to the war's termination. In short, according to one's values, to find a set of milieux and within it to survive the war or make one's death in it meaningful. But the structural issues of war have to do with its causes; with what types of men it throws up into command; with its effects upon economic and political, family and religious institutions, with the unorganized irresponsibility of a world of nation-states.

Consider marriage. Inside a marriage a man and a woman may experience personal troubles, but when the divorce rate during the first four years of marriage is 250 out of every 1,000 attempts, this is an indication of a structural issue having to do with the institutions of marriage and the family and other institutions that bear upon them.

Or consider the metropolis—the horrible, beautiful, ugly, magnificent sprawl of the great city. For many upper-class people, the personal solution to "the problem of the city" is to have an apartment with private garage under it in the heart of the city, and forty miles out, a house by Henry Hill, garden by Garrett Eckbo, on a hundred acres of private land. In these two controlled environments—with a small staff at each end and a private helicopter connection—most people could solve many of the problems of personal milieux caused by the facts of the city. But all this, however splendid, does not solve the public issues that the structural fact of the city poses. What should be done with this wonderful monstrosity? Break it all up into scattered units, combining residence and work? Refurbish it as it stands? Or, after evacuation, dynamite it and build new cities according to new plans in new places? What should those plans be? And who is to decide and to accomplish whatever choice is made? These are structural issues; to confront them and to solve them requires us to consider political and economic issues that affect innumerable milieux.

Insofar as an economy is so arranged that slumps occur, the problem of unemployment becomes incapable of personal solution. Insofar as war is inherent in the nation-state system and in the uneven industrialization of the world, the ordinary individual in his restricted milieu will be powerless—with or without psychiatric aid—to solve the troubles this system or lack of system imposes upon him. Insofar as the family as an institution turns women into darling little slaves and men into their chief providers and unweaned dependents, the problem of a satisfactory marriage remains incapable of purely private solution. Insofar as the overdeveloped megalopolis and the overdeveloped automobile are built-in features of the overdeveloped society, the issues of urban living will not be solved by personal ingenuity and private wealth.

––––––

What we experience in various and specific milieux, I have noted, is often caused by structural changes. Accordingly, to understand the changes of many personal milieux we are required to look beyond them. And the number and variety of such structural changes increase as the institutions within which we live become more embracing and more intricately connected with one another. To be aware of the idea of social structure and to use it with sensibility is to be capable of tracing such linkages among a great variety of milieux. To be able to do that is to possess the sociological imagination.

2

––––––

TEENAGE WASTELAND
Suburbia's Dead-End Kids

DONNA GAINES

This reading by Donna Gaines (1990) is an example of sociological research that employs Mills' sociological imagination and, specifically, his distinction between personal troubles and public issues. As Gaines illustrates, when one teenager commits suicide it is a personal tragedy, but when groups of teenagers form a suicide pact and successfully carry it out, suicide becomes a matter of public concern. In order to explain adequately why this incident occurred, Gaines examines both the history and the biography of suburban teens.

In Bergenfield, New Jersey, on the morning of March 11, 1987, the bodies of four teenagers were discovered inside a 1977 rust-colored Chevrolet Camaro. The car, which belonged to Thomas Olton, was parked in an unused garage in the Foster Village garden apartment complex, behind the Foster Village Shopping Center. Two sisters, Lisa and Cheryl Burress, and their

––––––

friends, Thomas Rizzo and Thomas Olton, had died of carbon monoxide poisoning.

Lisa was 16, Cheryl was 17, and the boys were 19—they were suburban teens, turnpike kids like the ones in the town I live in. And thinking about them made me remember how it felt being a teenager too. I was horrified that it had come to this. I believed I understood why they did it, although it wasn't a feeling I could have put into words.

You could tell from the newspapers that they were rock and roll kids. The police had found a cassette tape cover of AC/DC's *If You Want Blood, You've Got It* near the bodies. Their friends were described as kids who listened to thrash metal, had shaggy haircuts, wore lots of black and leather. "Drop-outs," "druggies," the papers called them. Teenage suburban rockers whose lives revolved around their favorite bands and their friends. Youths who barely got by in school and at home and who did not impress authority figures in any remarkable way. Except as fuck-ups.

My friends, most of whom were born in the 1950s, felt the same way about the kids everyone called "burnouts." On the weekend following the suicides, a friend's band, the Grinders, were playing at My Father's Place, a Long Island club. That night the guys dedicated a song, "The Kids in the Basement," to the four teens from Bergenfield—"This is for the suicide kids." In the weeks following the suicide pact, a number of bands in the tri-state area also dedicated songs to them. Their deaths had hit close to home.

. . .

A week or two after the suicide pact, *The Village Voice* assigned me to go to Bergenfield. Now this was not a story I would've volunteered for. . . . But one day my editor at the *Voice* called to ask if I wanted to go to Bergenfield. She knew my background—that I knew suburbia, that I could talk to kids. By now I fully embraced the sociologist's ethical commitment to the "rights of the researched," and the social worker's vow of client confidentiality. As far as suicidal teenagers were concerned, I felt that if I couldn't help them, I didn't want to bother them.

But I was really pissed off at what I kept reading. How people in Bergenfield openly referred to the four kids as "troubled losers." Even after they were dead, nobody cut them any slack. "Burnouts," "druggies," "dropouts." Something was wrong. So I took the opportunity.

From the beginning, I believed that the Bergenfield suicides symbolized a tragic defeat for young people. Something was happening in the larger society that was not yet comprehended. Scholars spoke ominously of "the postmodern condition," "societal upheaval," "decay," "anomie." Meanwhile, American kids kept losing ground, showing all the symptoms of societal neglect. Many were left to fend for themselves, often with little success. The news got worse. Teenage suicides continued, and still nobody seemed to be getting the point.

Now, in trying to understand this event, I might have continued working within the established discourse on teenage suicide. I might have carried on the tradition of obscuring the bigger picture, psychologizing the Bergenfield suicide pact, interviewing the parents of the four youths, hounding their friends for the gory details. I might have spent my time probing school records, tracking down their teachers and shrinks for insights, focusing on their personal histories and intimate relationships. I might have searched out the individual motivations behind the words left in the note written and signed by each youth on the brown paper bag found with their bodies on March 11. But I did not.

Because the world has changed for today's kids. We also engaged in activities that adults called self-destructive. But for my generation, "doing it" meant having sex; for them, it means committing suicide.

"Teenage suicide" was a virtually nonexistent category prior to 1960. But between 1950 and 1980 it nearly tripled, and at the time of the Bergenfield suicide pact it was described as the second leading cause of death among America's young people; "accidents" were the first. The actual suicide rate among people aged 15 to 24—the statistical category for teenage suicide—is estimated to be even higher, underreported because of social stigma. Then there are the murky numbers derived from drug overdoses and car crashes, recorded as accidents. To date, there are more than 5,000 teen suicides annually, accounting for 12 percent of youth mortalities. An estimated 400,000 adolescents attempt suicide each year. While youth suicide rates leveled off by 1980, by mid-decade they began to increase again. Although they remained lower than adult suicide rates, the acceleration at which youth suicide rates increased was alarming. By 1987, we had books and articles detailing "copycat" and "cluster" suicides. Teenage suicide was now described as an epidemic.

Authors, experts, and scholars compiled the lists of kids' names, ages, dates, and possible motives. They generated predictive models: Rural and suburban white kids do it more often. Black kids in America's urban teenage wastelands are more likely to kill each other. Increasingly, alcohol and drugs are involved. In some cases adults have tried to identify the instigating factor as a lyric or a song—Judas Priest, Ozzy Osbourne. Or else a popular film about the subject—the suicide of a celebrity; too much media attention or not enough.

Some kids do it violently: drowning, hanging, slashing, jumping, or crashing. Firearms are still the most popular. Others prefer to go out more peacefully, by gas or drug overdose. Boys do it more than girls, though girls try it more often than boys. And it does not seem to matter if kids are rich or poor.

Throughout the 1980s, teenage suicide clusters appeared across the country—six or seven deaths, sometimes more, in a short period of time in a single community. In the boomtown of Plano, Texas. The fading factory town of Leominster, Massachusetts. At Bryan High School in a white, working-class suburb of Omaha, Nebraska. A series of domino suicides among Arapaho Indian youths at the Wind River Reservation in Wyoming. Six youth suicides in the county of Westchester, New York, in 1984; five in 1985 and seven in 1986.

Sometimes they were close friends who died together in pacts of two. In other cases, one followed shortly after the other, unable to survive apart. Then there were strangers who died alone, in separate incidents timed closely together.

The Bergenfield suicide pact of March 11 was alternately termed a "multiple-death pact," a "quadruple suicide," or simply a "pact," depending on where you read about it. Some people actually called it a *mass* suicide because the Bergenfield case reminded them of Jonestown, Guyana, in 1978, where over 900 followers of Jim Jones poisoned themselves, fearing their community would be destroyed.

As experts speculated over the deaths in Bergenfield, none could recall a teenage suicide pact involving four people dying together; *it was historically unique.*

I wondered, did the "burnouts" see themselves as a community under siege? Like Jim Jones's people, or the 960 Jews at Masada who jumped to their deaths rather than face defeat at the hands of the Romans? Were the "burnouts" of Bergenfield choosing death over surrender? Surrender to what? Were they martyrs? If so, what was their common cause?

Because the suicide pact was a *collective act,* it warrants a social explanation—a portrait of the "burnouts" in Bergenfield as actors within a particular social landscape.

For a long time now, the discourse of teenage suicide has been dominated by atomizing psychological and medical models. And so the larger picture of American youth as members of a distinctive generation with a unique collective biography, emerging at a particular moment in history, has been lost.

The starting-off point for this research, then, is a teenage suicide pact in an "upper-poor" white ethnic suburb in northern New Jersey. But, of course, the story did not begin and will not end in Bergenfield.

Yes, there were specific sociocultural patterns operating in Bergenfield through which a teenage suicide pact became objectively possible. Yes, there were particular conditions which influenced how the town reacted to the event. Yes, there were reasons—that unique constellation of circumstances congealed in the lives of the four youths in the years, weeks, and days prior to March 11—that made suicide seem like their best alternative.

Given the four youths' personal histories, their losses, their failures, their shattered dreams, the motivation to die in this way seems transparent. Yet, after the suicide pact, in towns across the country, on television and in the press, people asked, "Why did they do it?" But I went to Bergenfield with other questions.

This was a suicide pact that involved close friends who were by no accounts obsessed, star-crossed lovers. What would make four people want to die together? Why would they ask, in their collective suicide note, to be waked and buried together? Were they part of a suicide cult?

If not, what was the nature of the *social* bond that tied them so closely? What could be so intimately binding that in the early morning hours of March 11 not one of them could stop, step back from the pact they had made to say, "Wait, I can't do this"? Who were these kids that everybody called "burnouts"?

"Greasers," "hoods," "beats," "freaks," "hippies," "punks." From the 1950s onward, these groups have signified young people's refusal to cooperate. In the social order of the American high school, teens are expected to do what they are told—make the grade, win the prize, play the game. Kids who refuse have always found something else to do. Sometimes it kills them; sometimes it sets them free.

In the 1980s, as before, high school kids at the top were the "preps," "jocks," or "brains," depending on the region. In white suburban high schools in towns like Bergenfield, the "burnouts" are often the kids near the bottom—academically, economically, and socially.

To outsiders, they look tough, scruffy, poor, wild. Uninvolved in and unimpressed by convention, they create an alternative world, a retreat, a refuge. Some burnouts are proud; they "wave their freak flags high." They call themselves burnouts to flaunt their break with the existing order, as a form of resistance, a statement of refusal.

But the meaning changes when "burnout" is hurled by an outsider. Then it hurts. It's an insult. Everyone knows you don't call somebody a burnout to their face unless you are looking for a fight. At that point, the word becomes synonymous with "troubled loser," "druggie"—all the things the press and some residents of the town called the four kids who died together in Tommy Olton's Camaro.

How did kids in Bergenfield *become* "burnouts," I wondered. At what point were they identified as outcasts? Was this a labeling process or one of self-selection? What kinds of lives did they have? What resources were available for them? What choices did they have? What ties did these kids have to the world outside Bergenfield? Where did their particular subculture come from? Why in the 1980s, the Reagan years, in white, suburban America?

What were their hopes and fears? What did heavy metal, Satan, suicide, and long hair mean to them? Who were their heroes, their gods? What saved them and what betrayed them in the long, cold night?

And what was this "something evil in the air" that people spoke about? Were the kids in Bergenfield "possessed"? Was the suicide pact an act of cowardice by four "losers," or the final refuge of kids helplessly and hopelessly trapped? How different was Bergenfield from other towns?

Could kids be labeled to death? How much power did these labels have? I wanted to meet other kids in Bergenfield who were identified as "burnouts" to find out what it felt like to carry these labels. I wanted to understand the existential situation they operated in—not simply as hapless losers, help-less victims, or tragic martyrs, but also as *historical actors* determined in their choices, resistant, defiant.

Because the suicide pact in Bergenfield seemed to be a symptom of some-thing larger, a metaphor for something more universal, I moved on from there to other towns. For almost two years I spent my time reading thrash magazines, seeing shows, and hanging out with "burnouts" and "dirtbags" as well as kids who slip through such labels.

. . .

From the beginning, I decided I didn't want to dwell too much on the nega-tives. I wanted to understand how alienated kids survived, as well as how they were defeated. How did they maintain their humanity against what I now felt were impossible odds? I wondered. What keeps young people to-gether when the world they are told to trust no longer seems to work? What motivates them to be decent human beings when nobody seems to respect them or take them seriously?

. . .

Joe's[1] been up for more than a day already. He's fried, his clothes are getting crusty, and he points to his armpits and says he smells (he doesn't). He's broke, he misses his girlfriend. He says he can't make it without someone. His girlfriend dumped him last year. He's gone out with other girls, but it's not the same. And he knows he can't win in this town. He's got a bad name. What's the use. He's tried it at least six times. Once he gashed at his vein with an Army knife he picked up in Times Square. He strokes the scars.

Tonight, he says, he's going to a Bible study class. Some girl he met in-vited him. Shows me a God pamphlet, inspirational literature. He doesn't want anyone to know about this, though. He thought the Jesus girl was nice. He's meeting her at seven. Bobby comes back in the room with Nicky, look-ing for cigarettes.

Later in the living room Joe teases Doreen. Poking at her, he gets rough. Bobby monitors him. "Calm down, Joe." We are just sitting around playing music, smoking cigarettes. Fooling around. "Did you see those Jesus freaks down at Cooper's Pond the other day?" Randy laughs. Nicky tells Joe to for-get it. Jesus chicks won't just go with you; you have to date them for a long time, pretend you're serious about them. They don't fuck you right away. "It's not worth the bother."

Suicide comes up again. Joan and Susie have razor scars. The guys make Susie show me her freshly bandaged wrists. I look at her. She's such a beau-tiful girl. She's sitting there with her boyfriend, Randy, just fooling around. I ask her quietly, "Why are you doing this?" She smiles at me seductively. She doesn't say anything. What the fuck is this, erotic? Kicks? Romantic? I feel cold panic.

Nicky slashed his wrists when his old girlfriend moved out of state. His scars are much older. I motion to him about Susie. Discreetly he says, "It's best just to ignore it, don't pay too much attention." Throughout the afternoon I try every trick I know to get Susie to talk to me. She won't. She's shy, quiet; she's all inside herself.

And I really don't want to push too hard. The kids say they're already going nuts from all the suicide-prevention stuff. You can't panic. But I have to figure out if this is a cult, a fad, a hobby, or something I'm supposed to report to the police. I'm afraid to leave.

I wonder, do they know the difference between vertical and horizontal cuts? Don't their parents, their teachers, the cops, and neighbors see this shit going on? Maybe they feel as confused as I do. Maybe this is why they didn't see it coming here, and in the other towns. You can't exactly go around strip-searching teenagers to see if they have slash wounds.

. . .

After the suicide pact, parents complained that the kids really did need somewhere to go when school let out. The after-school activities were limited to academics, sports, or organized school clubs. Even with part-time after-school jobs, a number of the town's young people did not find the conventional activities offered by the town particularly intriguing.

But according to established adult reasoning, if you didn't get absorbed into the legitimate, established routine of social activity, you'd be left to burn out on street corners, killing time, getting wasted. It was impossible for anyone to imagine any autonomous activity that nonconforming youth en masse might enjoy that would not be self-destructive, potentially criminal, or meaningless.

Parents understood that the lack of "anything to do" often led to drug and alcohol abuse. Such concerns were aired at the volatile meeting in the auditorium of Bergenfield High School. It was agreed that the kids' complaint of "no place to go" had to be taken seriously. Ten years ago, in any suburban town, teenagers' complaints of "nothing to do" would have been met with adult annoyance. But not anymore.

In Bergenfield, teenage boredom could no longer be dismissed as the whining of spoiled suburban kids. Experts now claimed that national rates of teenage suicide were higher in suburbs and rural areas because of teen isolation and boredom. In Bergenfield adults articulated the fact that many local kids did hang out on street corners and in parks looking for drugs because things at home weren't too good.

Youngsters have always been cautioned by adults that the devil would make good use of their idle hands. But now they understood something else:

boredom led to drugs, and boredom could kill. Yet it was taken for granted that if you refused to be colonized, if you ventured beyond the boundaries circumscribed by adults, you were "looking for trouble." But in reality, it was adult organization of young people's social reality over the last few hundred years that had *created* this miserable situation: one's youth as wasted years. Being wasted and getting wasted. Adults often wasted kids' time with meaningless activities, warehousing them in school; kids in turn wasted their own time on drugs. Just to have something to do.

So by now whenever kids hang out, congregating in some unstructured setting, adults read *dangerousness*. Even if young people are talking about serious things, working out plans for the future, discussing life, jobs, adults just assume they are getting wasted. They are.

. . .

For the duration of my stay, in almost every encounter, the outcast members of Bergenfield's youth population would tell me these things: The cops are dicks, the school blows, the jocks suck, Billy Milano (lead singer of now defunct S.O.D.—Stormtroopers of Death) was from a nearby town, and Iron Maiden had dedicated "Wasted Years" to the Burress sisters the last time the band played Jersey. These were their cultural badges of honor, unknown to the adults.

Like many suburban towns, Bergenfield is occupationally mixed. Blue-collar aristocrats may make more money than college professors, and so one's local class identity is unclear. Schools claim to track kids in terms of "ability," and cliques are determined by subculture, style, participation, and refusal.

Because the myth of a democratized mass makes class lines in the suburbs of the United States so ambiguous to begin with, differences in status become the critical lines of demarcation. And in the mostly white, mainly Christian town of Bergenfield, where there are neither very rich nor very poor people, this sports thing became an important criterion for determining "who's who" among the young people.

The girls played this out, too, as they always have, deriving their status by involvement in school (as cheerleaders, in clubs, in the classroom). And just as important, by the boys they hung around with. They were defined by who they were, by what they wore, by where they were seen, and with whom.

Like any other "Other," the kids at the bottom, who everybody here simply called burnouts, were actually a conglomerate of several cliques—serious druggies, Deadheads, dirtbags, skinheads, metalheads, thrashers, and punks. Some were good students, from "good" families with money and prestige. In any other setting all of these people might have been bitter rivals, or at least very separate cliques. But here, thanks to the adults and the primacy of sports, they were all lumped together—united by virtue of a common enemy, the jocks.

. . .

For a bored, ignored, lonely kid, drug oblivion may offer immediate comfort; purpose and adventure in the place of everyday ennui. But soon it has a life of its own—at a psychic and a social level, the focus of your life becomes *getting high* (or *well* as some people describe it). Ironically, the whole miserable process often begins as a positive act of self-preservation.

Both the dirts and the burnt may understand how they are being fucked over and by whom. And while partying rituals may actually celebrate the refusal to play the game, neither group has a clue where to take it beyond the parking lot of 7-Eleven.

So they end up stranded in teenage wasteland. They devote their lives to their bands, to their friends, to partying; they live in the moment. They're going down in flames, taking literally the notion that "rust never sleeps," that it is "better to burn out than fade away." While left-leaning adults have valorized the politically minded punks and right-wing groups have engaged some fascistic skins, nobody really thinks too much about organizing dirts or burnouts. Law enforcement officials, special education teachers, and drug treatment facilities are the adults who are concerned with these kids.

Such wasted suburban kids are typically not politically "correct," nor do they constitute an identifiable segment of the industrial working class. They are not members of a specific racial or ethnic minority, and they have few political advocates. Only on the political issues of abortion and the death penalty for minors will wasted teenage girls and boys be likely to find adults in their corner.

Small in numbers, isolated in decaying suburbs, they aren't visible on any national scale until they are involved in something that really horrifies us, like a suicide pact, or parricide, or incest, or "satanic" sacrifice. For the most part, burnouts and dirtbags are anomic small town white boys and girls, just trying to get through the day. Their way of fighting back is to have enough fun to kill themselves before everything else does.

. . .

In the scheme of things average American kids who don't have rich or well-connected parents have had these choices: Play the game and try to get ahead. Do what your parents did—work yourself to death at a menial job and find solace in beer, God, or family. Or take risks, cut deals, or break the law. The Reagan years made it hard for kids to "put their noses to the grindstone" as their parents had. Like everyone, these people hoped for better lives. But they lived in an age of inflated expectations and diminishing returns. Big and fast money was everywhere, and ever out of reach. America now had an economy that worked sort of like a cocaine high—propped up by hot air and big debt. The substance was absent. People's lives were like that too, and at times they were crashing hard.

In the meantime, wherever you were, you could still dream of becoming spectacular. A special talent could be your ticket out. Long Island kids had role models in bands like the Crumbsuckers, Ludichrist, Twisted Sister, Steve Vai, and Pat Benatar. North Jersey was full of sports celebrities and rock millionaires—you grew up hoping you'd end up like Mike Tyson or Jon Bon Jovi. Or like Keith Richards, whose father worked in a factory; or Ozzy, who also came from a grim English factory town, a hero who escaped the drudge because he was spectacular. This was the hip version of the American dream.

Kids who go for the prize now understand there are only two choices—rise to the top or crash to the bottom. Many openly admit that they would rather end it all now than end up losers. The nine-to-five world, corporate grunt life, working at the same job for 30 years, that's not for them. They'd prefer to hold out until the last possibility and then just piss on it all. The big easy or the bottomless pit, but never the everyday drone. And as long as there are local heroes and stories, you can still believe you have a chance to emerge from the mass as something larger than life. You can still play the great lottery and dream.

Schools urge kids to make these choices as early as possible, in a variety of ways. In the terse words of the San Francisco hardcore band MDC, "There's no such thing as cheating in a loser's game." Many kids who start out as nobody from nowhere with nothing will end up that way. Nevertheless, everyone pretends that everything is possible if you give it your best shot. We actually believe it. While educators hope to be as efficient as possible in figuring out where unspectacular students can plug into the workforce, kids try to play at being one in a million, some way of shining, even if it's just for a while.

. . .

Girls get slightly different choices. They may hope to become spectacular by virtue of their talents and their beauty. Being the girlfriend of a guy in a band means you might get to live in his mansion someday if you stick it out with him during the lean years. You might just end up like Bon Jovi's high school sweetheart, or married to someone like Cinderella's lead singer—he married his hometown girlfriend and helped set her up in her own business. These are suburban fairy tales.

Around here, some girls who are beautiful and talented hope to become stars, too, like Long Island's local products Debbie Gibson and Taylor Dayne. Some hope to be like actress Heather Locklear and marry someone really hot like Motley Crüe's drummer, Tommy Lee. If you could just get to the right place at the right time.

But most people from New Jersey and Long Island or anywhere else in America don't end up rich and famous. They have some fun trying, though, and for a while life isn't bad at all.

Yet, if you are unspectacular—not too book-smart, of average looks and moderate creative ability—there have always been places for you. Much of your teachers' efforts will be devoted to your more promising peers, and so will your nation's resources. But your parents will explain to you that this is the way it is, and early on, you will know to expect very little from school.

There are still a few enclaves, reservations. The shop and crafting culture of your parents' class of origin is one pocket of refuge. In the vocational high school, your interests are rewarded, once you have allowed yourself to be dumped there. And if the skills you gather there don't really lead to anything much, there's always the military.

Even though half the kids in America today will never go to college, the country still acts as if they will. At least, most schools seem to be set up to prepare you for college. And if it's not what you can or want to do, their attitude is tough shit, it's your problem.

And your most devoted teachers at vocational high school will never tell you that the training you will get from them is barely enough to get your foot in the door. You picture yourself getting into something with a future only to find that your skills are obsolete, superficial, and the boss prefers people with more training, more experience, more promise. So you are stuck in dead-end "youth employment jobs," and now what?

According to the William T. Grant Commission on Work, Family and Citizenship, 20 million people between the ages of 16 and 24 are not likely to go to college. The "forgotten half," as youth advocates call them, will find jobs in service and retail. But the money is bad, only half that of typical manufacturing jobs. The good, stable jobs that don't require advanced training have been disappearing rapidly. From 1979 to 1985 the U.S.A. suffered a net loss of 1.7 million manufacturing jobs. What's left?

In my neighborhood, the shipping and warehousing jobs that guys like the Grinders took, hedging their bets against rock stardom, are now seen as "good jobs" by the younger guys at Metal 24. I am regularly asked to . . . "find out if they're hiring" down at [the] shipping company. Dead-end kids around here who aren't working with family are working "shit jobs."

The skills used in a typical "shit job" . . . involve slapping rancid butter on stale hard rolls, mopping the floor, selling Lotto tickets, making sure shelves and refrigerators are clean, sorting and stacking magazines, taking delivery on newspapers, and signing out videos. They are also advised to look out for shoplifters, to protect the register, and to be sure that the surveillance camera is running. Like most kids in shit jobs, they are most skilled at getting over on the boss and in developing strategies to ward off boredom. It is not unusual to see kids at the supermarket cash register or the mall clothing shop standing around with a glazed look in their eyes. And you will often hear them complain of boredom, tiredness, or whine, "I can't wait to get out of here." Usually, in shit jobs this is where it begins and ends. There aren't many alternatives.

Everywhere, such kids find getting into a union or having access to supervisory or managerial tracks hard to come by. Some forms of disinvestment are more obvious than others. In a company town, you will be somewhat clear about what is going on. At the end of the 1980s, the defense industry of Long Island seemed threatened; people feared that their lives would soon be devastated.

But the effect of a changing economic order on most kids only translates into scrambling for a new safety zone. It is mostly expressed as resentment against entrepreneurial foreigners (nonwhites) and as anomie—a vague sense of loss, then confusion about where they might fit in.

. . .

So where are we going? Some people fear we are polarizing into a two-class nation, rich and poor. More precisely, a privileged knowledge-producing class and a low-paid, low-status service class. It is in the public high school that this division of labor for an emergent postindustrial local economy is first articulated. At the top are the kids who will hold jobs in a highly competitive technological economic order, who will advance and be respected if they cooperate and excel.

At the bottom are kids with poor basic skills, short attention spans, limited emotional investment in the future. Also poor housing, poor nutrition, bad schooling, bad lives. And in their bad jobs they will face careers of unsatisfying part-time work, low pay, no benefits, and no opportunity for advancement.

There are the few possibilities offered by a relative—a coveted place in a union, a chance to join a small family business in a service trade, a spot in a small shop. In my neighborhood, kids dream of making a good score on the cop tests, working up from hostess to waitress. Most hang out in limbo hoping to get called for a job in the sheriff's department, or the parks, or sanitation. They're on all the lists, although they know the odds for getting called are slim. The lists are frozen, the screening process is endless.

Meantime they hold jobs for a few months here and there, or they work off the books, or at two bad jobs at once.

. . .

When he gave the eulogy at his godson's funeral, Tommy Olton's uncle Richard was quoted as saying, "When I held you in my arms at your baptism, I wanted it to be a fresh start, for you to be more complete than we had ever been ourselves, but I wonder if we expected too much. In thinking only of ourselves, maybe we passed down too great a burden."

Trans-historically, cross-culturally, humans have placed enormous burdens on their young. Sometimes these burdens have been primarily economic: The child contributes to the economy of the family or tribe. Sometimes the burden has been social—the child is a contribution to the immortality of our creed. Be fruitful and multiply.

But the spiritual burden we pass on to the child may be the most difficult to bear. We do expect them to fulfill an incompleteness in ourselves, in our world. Our children are our vehicle for the realization of unfulfilled human dreams: our class aspirations, our visions of social justice and world peace, of a better life on earth.

Faith in the child, in the next generation, helps get us through this life. Without this hope in the future *through the child* we could not endure slavery, torture, war, genocide, or even the ordinary, everyday grind of a "bad life." The child-as-myth is an empty slate upon which we carve our highest ideals. For human beings, the child is God, utopia, and the future incarnate. The Bergenfield suicide pact ruptured the sacred trust between the generations. It was a negation.

After I had been to Bergenfield people asked me, "Why did they do it?" People want to know in 25 words or less. But it's more complicated than that. I usually just say, "They had bad lives," and try to explain why these lives ended where, when, and how they did. But I still wonder, at what point are people pushed over the line?

On the surface the ending of the four kids' bad lives can be explained away by the "case history" approach. Three of the four had suicidal or self-destructive adult role models: the suicide of Tommy Olton's father, the drug-related death of the Burress sisters' father. Tommy Rizzo, along with his three friends, had experienced the recent loss of a beloved friend, Joe Major. Before Joe, the death of three other local "burnouts." Then there was the chronic drug and alcohol abuse, an acknowledged contributing factor in suicide. Families ruptured by divorce, death, estrangement. Failure at school.

But these explanations alone would not add up to a suicide pact among four kids. If they did, the teenage suicide rate would be much, much higher. The personal problems experienced by the four kids were severe, painful, but by the 1980s, they were no longer remarkable.

For a while I wondered if the excessive labeling process in Bergenfield was killing off the "burnouts." Essentially, their role, their collective identity in their town was that of the "nigger" or "Jew." Us and Them, the One and the Other. And once they were constituted as "burnouts" by the town's hegemonic order, the kids played out their assigned role as self-styled outcasts with irony, style, and verve.

Yes, Bergenfield was guilty of blaming the victim. But only slightly more guilty than any other town. Labeling, blaming the victim, and conferring rewards on more cooperative kids was cruel, but also not remarkable in the eighties.

As I felt from the beginning, the unusually cloying geography of Bergenfield seemed somehow implicated in the suicide pact. The landscape appeared even more circumscribed because of the "burnouts'" lack of legitimate space in the town: they were too old for the [roller skating] Rink, and the Building [an abandoned warehouse taken over by the teens] was available for criminal trespass only. Outcast, socially and spatially, for years the "burnouts" had been chased from corner to parking lot, and finally, to the garage bays of Foster Village. They were nomads, refugees in the town of their birth. *There was no place for them.* They felt unloved, unwanted, devalued, disregarded, and discarded.

But this little town, not even two miles long from north to south, was just a dot on a much larger map. It wasn't the whole world. Hip adults I know, friends who grew up feeling like outcasts in their hometown, were very sympathetic to the plight of the "burnouts." Yet even they often held out one last question, sometimes contemptuously: "Why didn't they *just leave*?" As if the four kids had failed even as outcasts. My friends found this confusing. "No matter how worthless the people who make the rules say you are, you don't have to play their game. You can always walk and not look back," they would argue. People who feel abject and weird in their hometown simply move away.

But that has always been a class privilege. The townies are the poor kids, the wounded street warriors who stay behind. And besides, escape was easier for everyone 20 years ago. American society had safety nets then that don't exist now—it's just not the same anymore.

During the eighties, dead-end kids—kids with personal problems and unspectacular talents living in punitive or indifferent towns with a sense of futility about life—became more common. There were lots of kids with bad lives. They didn't all commit suicide. But I believe that in another decade, Tommy Rizzo, Cheryl Burress, Tommy Olton, and Lisa Burress would not have "done it." They might have had more choices, or choices that really meant something to them. Teenage suicide won't go away until kids' bad lives do. Until there are other ways of moving out of bad lives, suicide will remain attractive.

NOTE

1. As I promised the kids I met hanging out on the streets of Bergen County and on Long Island, "No names, no pictures." Names such as "Joe," "Eddie," and "Doreen" are fictitious, changed to protect their privacy.

3

INTERSECTION OF BIOGRAPHY AND HISTORY
My Intellectual Journey

MARY ROMERO

This selection by sociologist Mary Romero is another example of Mills' sociological imagination. Romero explains how biography and history influenced her investigation of domestic service work done by Chicanas. In particular, Romero describes her research process, which involved reinterpreting her own and others' domestic service experiences within the larger work history of Mexican Americans and the devaluation of housework. This selection is from the introduction to Romero's 1992 book *Maid in the U.S.A.*, a study of domestic work and the social interactions between domestics and their employers.

When I was growing up many of the women whom I knew worked cleaning other people's houses. Domestic service was part of my taken-for-granted reality. Later, when I had my own place, I considered housework something you did before company came over. My first thought that domestic service and housework might be a serious research interest came as a result of a chance encounter with live-in domestics along the U.S.–Mexican border. Before beginning a teaching position at the University of Texas at El Paso, I stayed with a colleague while apartment hunting. My colleague had a live-in domestic to assist with housecleaning and cooking. Asking around, I learned that live-in maids were common in El Paso, even among apartment and condominium dwellers. The hiring of maids from Mexico was so common that locals referred to Monday as the border patrol's day off because the agents ignored the women crossing the border to return to their employers' homes after their weekend off. The practice of hiring undocumented Mexican women as domestics, many of whom were no older than fifteen, seemed strange to me. It was this strangeness that raised the topic of domestic service as a question and made problematic what had previously been taken for granted.

I must admit that I was shocked at my colleague's treatment of the 16-year-old domestic whom I will call Juanita. Only recently hired, Juanita was still adjusting to her new environment. She was extremely shy, and her timidity was made even worse by constant flirting from her employer. As far as I could see, every attempt Juanita made to converse was met with teasing so that the conversation could never evolve into a serious discussion. Her employer's sexist, paternalistic banter effectively silenced the domestic, kept her constantly on guard, and made it impossible for her to feel comfortable at work. For instance, when she informed the employer of a leaky faucet, he shot her a look of disdain, making it clear that she was overstepping her boundaries. I observed other encounters that clearly served to remind Juanita of her subservient place in her employer's home.

Although Juanita was of the same age as my colleague's oldest daughter and but a few years older than his two sons, she was treated differently from the other teenagers in the house. She was expected to share her bedroom with the ironing board, sewing machine, and other spare-room types of objects.[1] More importantly, she was assumed to have different wants and needs. I witnessed the following revealing exchange. Juanita was poor. She had not brought toiletries with her from Mexico. Since she had not yet been paid, she had to depend on her employer for necessities. Yet instead of offering her a small advance in her pay so she could purchase the items herself and giving her a ride to the nearby supermarket to select her own toiletries, the employer handled Juanita's request for toothbrush, toothpaste, shampoo, soap, and the like in the following manner. In the presence of all the family and the house guest, he made a list of the things she needed. Much teasing and joking accompanied the encounter. The employer shopped for her and purchased only generic brand items, which were a far cry from the brand-name products that filled the bathroom of his 16-year-old daughter. Juanita looked at the toothpaste, shampoo, and soap with confusion; she may never have seen generic products before, but she obviously knew that a distinction had been made.

One evening I walked into the kitchen as the employer's young sons were shouting orders at Juanita. They pointed to the dirty dishes on the table and pans in the sink and yelled "WASH!" "CLEAN!" Juanita stood frozen next to the kitchen door, angry and humiliated. Aware of possible repercussions for Juanita if I reprimanded my colleague's sons, I responded awkwardly by reallocating chores to everyone present. I announced that I would wash the dishes and the boys would clear the table. Juanita washed and dried dishes alongside me, and together we finished cleaning the kitchen. My colleague returned from his meeting to find us in the kitchen washing the last pan. The look on his face was more than enough to tell me that he was shocked to find his houseguest—and future colleague—washing dishes with the maid. His embarrassment at my behavior confirmed my suspicion that I had violated the normative expectations of class behavior within the home. He attempted to break the tension with a flirtatious and sexist remark to Juanita which served to excuse her from the kitchen and from any further discussion.

The conversation that followed revealed how my colleague chose to interpret my behavior. Immediately after Juanita's departure from the kitchen, he initiated a discussion about "Chicano radicals" and the Chicano movement. Although he was a foreign-born Latino, he expressed sympathy for *la causa*. Recalling the one Chicano graduate student he had known to obtain a Ph.D. in sociology, he gave several accounts of how the student's political behavior had disrupted the normal flow of university activity. Lowering his voice to a confidential whisper, he confessed to understanding why Marxist theory has become so popular among Chicano students. The tone of his comments and the examples that he chose made me realize that my "outrageous" behavior was explained, and thus excused, on the basis of my being one of those "Chicano radicals." He interpreted my washing dishes with his maid as a symbolic act; that is, I was affiliated with *los de abajo*.

My behavior had been comfortably defined without addressing the specific issue of maids. My colleague then further subsumed the topic under the rubric of "the servant problem" along the border. (His reaction was not unlike the attitude employers have displayed toward domestic service in the United States for the last hundred years.)[2] He began by providing me with chapter and verse about how he had aided Mexican women from Juarez by helping them cross the border and employing them in his home. He took further credit for introducing them to the appliances found in an American middle-class home. He shared several funny accounts about teaching country women from Mexico to use the vacuum cleaner, electric mixer, and microwave (remember the maid scene in the movie *El Norte*?) and implicitly blamed them for their inability to work comfortably around modern conveniences. For this "on-the-job training" and introduction to American culture, he complained, his generosity and goodwill had been rewarded by a high turnover rate. As his account continued, he assured me that most maids were simply working until they found a husband. In his experience they worked for a few months or less and then did not return to work on Monday morning after their first weekend off. Of course it never dawned on him that they may simply have found a job with better working conditions.

The following day, Juanita and I were alone in the house. As I mustered up my best Spanish, we shared information about our homes and families. After a few minutes of laughter about my simple sentence structure, Juanita lowered her head and in a sad, quiet voice told me how isolated and lonely she felt in this middle-class suburb literally within sight of Juarez. Her feelings were not the consequence of the work or of frustrations with modern appliances, nor did she complain about the absence of Mexican people in the neighborhood; her isolation and loneliness were in response to the norms and values surrounding domestic service. She described the situation quite clearly in expressing puzzlement over the social interactions she had with her employer's family: Why didn't her employer's children talk to her or include her in any of their activities when she wasn't working? Her reaction was not unlike that of Lillian Pettengill, who wrote about her two-year experience as a domestic in Philadelphia households at the turn of the century: "I feel my isolation alone in a big house full of people."[3]

Earlier in the day, Juanita had unsuccessfully tried to initiate a conversation with the 16-year-old daughter while she cleaned her room. She was of the same age as the daughter (who at that moment was in bed reading and watching TV because of menstrual cramps—a luxury the maid was not able to claim). She was rebuffed and ignored and felt that she became visible only when an order was given. Unable to live with this social isolation, she had already made up her mind not to return after her day off in Juarez. I observed the total impossibility of communication. The employer would never know why she left, and Juanita would not know that she would be considered simply another ungrateful Mexican whom he had tried to help.

After I returned to Denver, I thought a lot about the situations of Juanita and the other young undocumented Mexican women living in country club areas along the border. They worked long days in the intimacy of American middle-class homes but were starved for respect and positive social interaction. Curiously, the employers did not treat the domestics as "one of the family," nor did they consider themselves employers. Hiring a domestic was likely to be presented within the context of charity and good works; it was considered a matter of helping "these Mexican women" rather than recognized as a work issue.

I was bothered by my encounter along the border, not simply for the obvious humanitarian reasons, but because I too had once worked as a domestic, just as my mother, sister, relatives, and neighbors had. As a teenager, I cleaned houses with my mother on weekends and vacations. My own working experience as a domestic was limited because I had always been accompanied by my mother or sister instead of working alone. Since I was a day worker, my time in the employer's home was limited and I was able to return to my family and community each day. In Juanita's situation as a live-in domestic, there was no distinction between the time on and off work. I wondered whether domestic service had similarly affected my mother, sister, and neighbors. Had they too worked beyond the agreed-upon time? Did they have difficulty managing relationships with employers? I never worked alone and was spared the direct negotiations with employers. Instead, I cooperated with my mother or sister in completing the housecleaning as efficiently and quickly as possible.

I could not recall being yelled at by employers or their children, but I did remember anger, resentment, and the humiliation I had felt at kneeling to scrub other people's toilets while they gave step-by-step cleaning instructions. I remember feeling uncomfortable around employers' children who never acknowledged my presence except to question where I had placed their belongings after I had picked them up off the floor to vacuum. After all, my experience was foreign to them; at the age of 14 I worked as a domestic while they ran off to swimming, tennis, and piano lessons. Unlike Juanita, I preferred to remain invisible as I moved around the employer's house cleaning. Much later, I learned that the invisibility of workers in domestic service is a common characteristic of the occupation. Ruth Schwartz Cowan has commented on the historical aspect of invisibility:

> The history of domestic service in the United States is a vast, unresolved puzzle, because the social role "servant" so frequently carries with it the unspoken adjective *invisible*. In diaries and letters, the "invisible" servant becomes visible only when she departs employment ("Mary left today"). In statistical series, she appears only when she is employed full-time, on a live-in basis; or when she is willing to confess the nature of her employment to a census taker, and (especially since the Second World War) there have frequently been good reasons for such confessions to go unmade.[4]

Although I remained invisible to most of the employers' family members, the mothers, curiously enough, seldom let me move around the house invisibly, dusting the woodwork and vacuuming carpets. Instead, I was subjected to constant supervision and condescending observations about "what a good little girl I was, helping my mother clean house." After I had moved and cleaned behind a hide-a-bed and Lazy-boy chair, vacuumed three floors including two sets of stairs, and carried the vacuum cleaner up and downstairs twice because "little Johnny" was napping when I was cleaning the bedrooms—I certainly didn't feel like a "little girl helping mother." I felt like a domestic worker!

There were employers who attempted to draw parallels between my adolescent experience and their teenagers' behavior: they'd point to the messy bedrooms and claim, "Well, you're a teenager, you understand clothes, books, papers, and records on the floor." Even at 14, I knew that being sloppy and not picking up after yourself was a privilege. I had two brothers and three sisters. I didn't have my own bedroom but shared a room with my sisters. Not one of us would think of leaving our panties on the floor for the others to pick up. I didn't bother to set such employers straight but continued to clean in silence, knowing that at the end of the day I would get cash and confident that I would soon be old enough to work elsewhere.

Many years later, while attending graduate school, I returned to domestic service as an "off-the-record" means to supplement my income. Graduate fellowships and teaching assistantships locked me into a fixed income that frequently was not enough to cover my expenses.[5] So once again I worked alongside my mother for seven hours as we cleaned two houses. I earned about 50 dollars for the day. Housecleaning is strenuous work, and I returned home exhausted from climbing up and down stairs, bending over, rubbing, and scrubbing.

Returning to domestic service as a graduate student was awkward. I tried to reduce the status inconsistency in my life by electing to work only in houses from which families were absent during the day. If someone appeared while I worked, I ignored their presence as they did mine. Since working arrangements had been previously negotiated by my mother, I had limited face-to-face interactions with employers. Most of the employers knew I was a graduate student, and fortunately, most seemed reluctant to ask me too many questions. Our mutual silence served as a way to deal with the status inconsistency of a housewife with a B.A. hiring an ABD to clean her house.

I came to El Paso with all of these experiences unquestioned in my memory. My presuppositions about domestic service were called into question only after observing the more obviously exploitative situation in the border town. I saw how vulnerable undocumented women employed as live-in domestics are and what little recourse they have to improve their situation, short of finding another job. Experiencing Juanita's shame and disgust at my colleague's sons' behavior brought back a flood of memories that eventually influenced me to study the paid housework that I had once taken for granted. I began to wonder professionally about the Chicanas employed as domestics that I had known throughout my own life: how vulnerable were they to exploitation, racism, and sexism? Did their day work status and U.S. citizenship provide protection against degradation and humiliation? How did Chicanas go about establishing a labor arrangement within a society that marked them as racial and cultural inferiors? How did they deal with racial slurs and sexist remarks within their employers' homes? How did Chicanas attempt to negotiate social interactions and informal labor arrangements with employers and their families?

An Exploratory Study

The Research Process

Intending to compare my findings with the research on U.S. minority women employed as domestics, I chose to limit my study to Chicanas, that is, women of Mexican descent born and raised in the United States. Although many women born in Mexico and living in the United States consider themselves Chicanas, my sample did not include women born outside the United States. My major concern in making this distinction was to avoid bringing into the analysis immigration issues that increase the vulnerability of the women employed as domestics. I wanted to keep conditions as constant as possible to make comparisons with the experiences Judith Rollins, Bonnie Thornton Dill, and Soraya Moore Coley report among African American women and with Evelyn Nakano Glenn's study of Japanese American women.[6] In order to duplicate similar residential and citizenship characteristics of these studies, I restricted my sample to Chicanas living in Denver whose families had migrated from rural areas of New Mexico and Colorado. All of the women interviewed were U.S. citizens and lived in Denver most of their adult lives.

I began the project by soliciting the cooperation of current and former domestics from my own family. I relied on domestics to provide entree into informal networks. These networks turned out to be particularly crucial in gaining access to an occupation that is so much a part of the underground economy. My mother, sister, and sister-in-law agreed to be interviewed and to provide names of relatives, friends, and neighbors. I also identified Chicana domestics in the community with the assistance of outreach workers employed by local churches and social service agencies. The snowball sampling was achieved by asking each interviewee to recommend other Chicana domestics as potential interviewees.

The women were extremely cautious about offering the names of friends and relatives. In most cases, they contacted the person first and only then gave me the name and telephone number. This actually turned out to be quite helpful. Potential interviewees had already heard about my study from someone who had been interviewed. They had a general idea of the questions I was going to ask and in some cases a little background information about who I was. However, on three occasions, I called women to ask for an interview and was confronted with resistance and shame. The women expressed embarrassment at being identified by their work—as a "housekeeper" or "cleaning lady." I responded by sharing my research interests in the occupation and in the relationship between work and family. I also shared my previous experience as a domestic.[7] One woman argued with me for 20 minutes about conducting research on an occupation that was low status, suggesting instead that I study Chicana lawyers or doctors, that is, "another occupation that presents our people in a more positive light." Another woman denied ever having worked as a domestic even though several women, including her sister-in-law, had given me her name as someone currently employed as a domestic.

The stigma of domestic service was a problem during the interviews as well. From the outset, it was very important for each woman to establish herself as someone more than a private household worker. Conducting nonstructured, free-flowing, and open-ended interviews allowed the women to establish multiple identities, particularly diffuse family and community roles.

The interviews were conducted in the women's homes, usually while sitting in the living room or at the dining room table with the radio or television on in the background. Although family members peeked in, for the most part there were few interruptions other than an occasional telephone call. From time to time, the women called to their husbands in the other room to ask the name of a street where they had once lived or the year the oldest son had been born in order to figure out when they had left and returned to work. The average interview lasted two hours, but I often stayed to visit and chat long after the interview was over. They told me about their church activities and plans to remodel the house and asked me for my opinion on current Chicano politics. Some spread out blankets, tablecloths, and pillow covers to exhibit their needlework. They showed me pictures of their children and grandchildren, giving me a walking tour of living rooms and bedrooms where wedding and high school portraits hung. As each one was identified, I learned more about their lives.

I conducted 25 open-ended interviews with Chicanas living and working in the greater Denver metropolitan area. The most visible Chicano communities in Denver are in the low-income neighborhood located in the downtown area or in one of two working-class neighborhoods in the northern and western areas of the city. I interviewed women from each of these communities. I asked them to discuss their overall work histories, with particular emphasis on their experiences as domestics. I probed for detailed information on domestic work, including strategies for finding employers, definitions of appropriate and inappropriate tasks, the negotiation of working conditions, ways of doing housework efficiently, and the pros and cons of domestic service. The accounts included descriptions of the domestics' relationships with white middle-class mistresses and revealed Chicanas' attitudes toward their employers' lifestyles.

All of the interviewees' families of orientation were from northern New Mexico or southern Colorado, where many of them had lived and worked on small farms. Some of the women had arrived in Denver as children with their parents, others as young brides, and still others as single women to join siblings and cousins in Denver's barrios. Several women recalled annual migrations to northern Colorado to pick sugar beets, prior to their permanent relocation to Denver. In some cases, the women's entire families of orientation had migrated to Denver; in others, parents and siblings had either remained behind or migrated to other cities. Many older women had migrated with their husbands after World War II, and several younger women interviewed had arrived at the same time, as children. Women who had migrated as single adults typically had done so in the last 10 or 15 years. Now they were married and permanently living in Denver.

· · ·

Historical Background

After the Mexican American War, Mexicans were given the option to maintain their Mexican citizenship and leave the country or become U.S. citizens. Many reluctantly chose the latter in order to keep their homes. Although the Treaty of Guadalupe Hidalgo was supposed to guarantee land grant provisions to those who chose to remain in occupied territory, legal and illegal maneuvers were used to eliminate communal usage of land and natural resources. Between 1854 and 1930, an estimated 2,000,000 acres of private land and 1,700,000 acres of communal land were lost.[8] In the arid Southwest, small plots were insufficient to continue a subsistence-based farming economy, thus the members of the Hispano community were transformed from landowners to wage laborers. Enclosure of the common lands forced Mexicans from their former economic roles, "freed" Mexicans for wage labor, and established a racially stratified labor force in the Southwest.

As early as 1900, the Hispano farming and ranching communities of northern New Mexico and southern Colorado began to lose their population. A combination of push-pull factors conspired to force rural Hispanos off the land and attracted them to urban areas like Denver. Rural northern New Mexico and southern Colorado experienced drastic depopulation as adults left to find jobs. During the Depression, studies conducted in cooperation with the Works Progress Administration (WPA) noted the desperate situation:

> The Tewa Basin Study by the U.S. Department of Agriculture showed that in eleven Spanish-American villages containing 1,202 families, an average of 1,110 men went out of the villages to work for some part of each year prior to 1930. In 1934, only 157 men out of 1,202 families had found outside work.[9]

Migration in search of jobs became a way of life for many families. New Mexicans and southern Coloradans joined the migratory farm labor stream from Texas, California, and Mexico. World War II further depopulated the rural villages as people flocked to the cities in response to job openings in defense plants and related industries. Postwar migration from New Mexico was estimated to be one-fifth of the 1940 rural Chicano population.[10] This pattern continued in the following decades. For instance, Thomas Malone found that during the decade of the 1950s, only one of seven northern counties in New Mexico had not experienced a decrease in its former predominantly Spanish-speaking population.[11] By 1960, 61 percent of the population had been urbanized,[12] and between 1950 and 1960, an additional 24 percent left their rural communities.[13]

Perhaps because research on population movement among Chicanos has been so overwhelmingly concerned with emigration from Mexico, this type of internal population movement among Chicanos has not been well studied. What research is available has focused primarily on male workers and the relationship between urbanization and acculturation.[14] Chicanas have been either ignored or treated simply as family members—mothers, daughters, or wives, accompanying male relatives in search of work—rather than as wage earners in their own right. Nevertheless, for many women migration to an urban area made it necessary that they enter the labor market. Domestic service became a significant occupation in the experience.

Profile of Chicana Household Workers

Only the vaguest statistical data on Chicana private household workers are available; for the most part these workers remain a doubly hidden population. The reasons are themselves instructive. Domestic workers tend to be invisible because paid domestic work has not been one of the occupations recorded in social science surveys, and the U.S. Census Bureau uses a single code lumping together all private household workers, including launderers, cooks, housekeepers, child-care workers, cleaners, and servants. Even when statistics on domestics can be teased out of the census and labor data bases, they are marred by the common practice of underreporting work in the informal sector. Unlike some of the private household workers in the East, Chicana domestics are not unionized and remain outside the "counted" labor force. Many private household workers are not included in the statistics collected by the Department of Labor. The "job" involves an informal labor arrangement made between two people, and in many cases payment is simply a cash transaction that is never recorded with the Internal Revenue Service (IRS).

Governmental undercounting of Chicanos and Mexican immigrants in the United States further adds to the problem of determining the number of Chicanas and Mexicanas employed as private household workers. For many, domestic service is part of the underground economy, and employing undocumented workers is reported neither to the IRS nor to the Immigration and Naturalization Service (INS), thus making another source of statistical information unreliable. Chicanos continue to be an undercounted and obscure population. Problems with the categorization of domestics have been still further complicated by changing identifiers for the Mexican American population: Mexican, Spanish-speaking, Hispanic, Spanish-surnamed, and the like make it impossible to segment out the Chicano population.

The 25 Chicanas whom I interviewed included welfare recipients as well as working-class women, ranging in age from 29 to 68. Thirteen of the 25 women were between 29 and 45 years old. The remaining 12 were over 52 years old. All the women had children and the older women also had grandchildren. The smallest family consisted of one child, and the largest family had seven children. The average was three children. All but one of the women had been married. Five of the women were single heads of households, two of them were divorced, and the other three were single, separated, or widowed. The married women were currently living with husbands employed in blue-collar positions, such as construction and factory work. At the time of the interview, the women who were single heads of households were financially supporting no more than two children.

Educational backgrounds ranged from no schooling to completion of high school. Six women had completed high school, and seven had no high school experience, including one who had never attended school at all. The remaining 12 had at least a sixth-grade education. Although the least educated were the older women, eight of the women under 42 had not completed high school. The youngest woman with less than an eighth-grade education was 53 years old. The 12 women over 50 averaged eight years of schooling. Three of the high school graduates were in their early thirties, two were in their early forties, and one was 57 years old. Although one woman preferred to be interviewed in Spanish, all the women spoke English.

Work experience as a private household worker ranged from five months to 30 years. Women 50 years and older had worked in the occupation from eight to 30 years, while four of the women between the ages of 33 and 39 had worked as domestics for 12 years. Half of the women had worked for more than 10 years as private household workers. Only three women had worked as domestics prior to marriage; each of these women had worked in live-in situations in rural areas in Colorado. Several years later, after marriage and children, they returned as day workers. All the other women, however, had turned to nonresidential day work in response to a financial crisis; in the majority of cases, it was their first job after marriage and having children. Some of the women remained domestics throughout their lives, but others moved in and out of domestic work. Women who returned to domestic service after having other types of jobs usually did so following a period of unemployment.

The work histories revealed that domestic service was only one of several low-paying, low-status jobs the women had held during their lives. They had been hired as waitresses, laundresses, janitors, farmworkers, nurses aides, fast-food servers, cooks, dishwashers, receptionists, school aides, cashiers, baby-sitters, salesclerks, factory workers, and various types of line workers in poultry farms and car washes. Almost half of the women had worked as janitors in hospitals and office buildings or as hotel maids. About one-fourth of the women had held semiskilled and skilled positions such as beauticians, typists, and medical-record clerks. Six of the women had worked only as domestics.

Paid and Unpaid Domestic Work

In describing their daily routine activities, these Chicanas drew my attention to the interrelationship between paid and unpaid housework. As working women, Chicana private household workers face the "double day" or "second shift," but in their case both days consisted of the same types of tasks. Paid housework done for an employer was qualitatively different from housework done for their own families.

In the interviews, Chicanas described many complexities of domestic service. They explained how they used informal networks to find new employers for themselves and for relatives and friends. As they elaborated on the advantages and disadvantages of particular work arrangements and their reasons for refusing certain household tasks, I soon realized that these women not only knew a great deal about cleaning and maintaining homes, but they understood the influence of social relationships on household tasks. Analysis of the extensive planning and negotiation involved in the informal and underground arrangements of domestic service highlighted the significance of the social relationships surrounding housework.

Their work histories included detailed explanations of beginning, returning to, and continuing in domestic service. In the discussions, I began to understand the paradox of domestic service: On the one hand, cleaning houses is degrading and embarrassing; on the other, domestic service can be higher paying, more autonomous, and less dehumanizing than other low-status, low-skilled occupations. Previous jobs in the beet fields, fast-food restaurants, car washes, and turkey farms did not offer annual raises, vacations, or sick leave. Furthermore, these jobs forced employees to work long hours and to keep rigid time schedules, and they frequently occurred outside or in an unsafe work environment. Unlike the other options available, domestic service did have the potential for offering flexible work schedules and autonomy. In most cases, domestic service also paid much more. Although annual raises, vacation, and social security were not the norm for most Chicanas in domestic service, there remained the possibility that such benefits could be negotiated with employers. Furthermore, as former farmworkers, laundresses, and line workers, the women found freedom in domestic work from exposure to dangerous pesticides, poor ventilation, and other health risks. This paradox foreshadowed a critical theoretical issue, the importance of understanding the social process that constructs domestic service as a low-status occupation.

Stigma as a perceived occupational hazard of domestic service emerged during the initial contact and throughout most of the interviews. The stigma attached to domestic service punctuated the interviews. I knew that many women hid their paid household labor from the government, but I did not realize that this secrecy encompassed neighbors, friends, and even extended family members. Several women gave accounts that revealed their families' efforts to conceal their employment as domestics. Children frequently stated that their mothers "just did housework," which was ambiguous enough to define them as full-time homemakers and not necessarily as domestics.

Faced with limited job opportunities, Chicanas selected domestic service and actively sought to make the most of the situation. In comparison with other jobs they had held, domestic service usually paid more and offered greater flexibility in arranging the length of the workday and workweek. Although other jobs did not carry the stigma of servitude, workers were under constant supervision, and the work was similarly low status. Therefore, the women who chose domestic service over other low-paying, low-status jobs based their selection on the occupation that offered some possibility of control. Their challenge was to structure the work so as to reap the most benefits: pay, work hours, labor, and autonomy. Throughout the interviews, the women emphasized job flexibility as the major advantage of domestic service over previous jobs. Nonrigid work schedules allowed time to do their own housework and fulfill family obligations, such as caring for sick children or attending school functions. By stressing the benefits gained by doing day work, Chicanas diffused the low status in their work identities and emphasized their family and community identities. The ways in which they arranged both work and family revealed coping strategies used to deal with the stigma, and this drew me to analyze housework as a form of labor having both paid and unpaid manifestations.

The conventional social science separation of work and family is an analytical construct and is not found in the lived reality of Chicana domestics. Invariably the interviewees mixed and intertwined discussions of work and family. Moreover, the actual and practical relationships between work and family were explicit in their descriptions of daily activities: The reasons for seeking employment included the family's financial situation and the desire to raise its standard of living; earning extra money for the household was viewed as an extension of these women's roles as mothers and wives; arranging day work involved planning work hours around the children's school attendance, dentist and doctor appointments, and community and church activities; in some cases, young mothers even took their preschool-age children with them to work. The worlds of paid and unpaid housework were not disconnected in the lives of these women.

Attending to the importance of the relationship between paid and unpaid domestic work led me to ponder new questions about the dynamics of buying and selling household labor. How does housework differ when it is paid work? How does the housewife role change when part of her work is allocated to another woman? What is the range of employer-employee relationship in domestic service today? And is there a difference in the type of relationships developed by employed and unemployed women buying household labor?

The importance of attending to both paid and unpaid housework in researching domestic service became more apparent as I began presenting my research to academic audiences. When I read papers on the informal labor market or on family and community networks used to find work, some of my colleagues responded as women who employed domestics. Frequently question-and-answer sessions turned into a defense of such practices as hiring undocumented workers, not filing income taxes, or gift giving in lieu of raises and benefits. Although I was aware that as working women, many academics employed someone to clean their houses, I was not prepared for scholars and feminists to respond to my scholarly work as housewives or employers. I was also surprised to discover that many of the maternalistic practices traditionally found in domestic service were common practices in their homes. The recurring responses made me realize that my feminist colleagues had never considered their relationships with the "cleaning woman" on the same plane as those with secretaries, waitresses, or janitors; that is, they thought of the former more or less in terms of the mistress–maid relationship. When, through my research, I pointed out the contradiction, many still had difficulty thinking of their homes—the haven from the cruel academic world—as someone's workplace. Their overwhelming feelings of discomfort, guilt, and resentment, which sometimes came out as hostility, alerted me to the fact that something more was going on.

Although written over a decade ago, Margaret Mead's depiction of the middle-class woman's dilemma still seems to capture the contradictory feelings and attitudes that I hear among feminists today.

Traveling around the country, I meet a great many young wives and mothers who are struggling with the problem that seems to have no solution—how to hold down two full-time jobs at once. . . . As I listen I realize how many of them—guiltily but wistfully—yearn for the bygone days of servants. . . . They are guilty because they don't quite approve of anyone's working as a servant in someone else's home.[15]

In a society that espouses egalitarian values, we can expect yearnings "for the bygone days of servants" to be experienced as a contradiction. A century ago, Jane Addams discussed the awkward feelings and apprehensiveness academic women feel:

I should consider myself an unpardonable snob if, because a woman did my cooking, I should not hold myself ready to have her for my best friend, to drive, to read, to attend receptions with her, but that friendship might or might not come about, according to her nature and mine, just as it might or might not come about between me and my college colleague. On the other hand, I would consider myself very stupid if merely because a woman cooked my food and lived in my house I should insist upon having a friendship with her, whether her nature and mine responded to it or not. It would be folly to force the companionship of myself or my family upon her when doubtless she would vastly prefer the companionship of her own friends and her own family.[16]

In her book on black domestics and white employers in the South, Susan Tucker addresses the deeper psychological and class factors involved in hiring servants.

Most studies of domestic work maintain that the prime motivation for hiring a servant is the enhancement of the employer's image as a superior being. Yet, many women certainly must feel some discomfort, even when paying a decent wage, about the possibility of such a motivation. . . . There are many conflicting principles and traditions surrounding the employment of a socially and economically disadvantaged woman who goes daily into a wealthy home. One might feel discomfort if one were aware of any number of different types of ideas—feminist, egalitarian, religious.[17]

Domestic service must be studied because it raises a challenge to any feminist notion of "sisterhood." A growing number of employed middle- and upper-middle-class women escape the double-day syndrome by hiring poor women of color to do housework and child care. David Katzman underscored the class contradiction:

Middle-class women, the employers, gained freedom from family roles and household chores and assumed or confirmed social status by the employment of a servant. . . . The greater liberty of these middle-class women, however, was achieved at the expense of working-class women, who, forced to work, assumed the tasks beneath, distasteful to, or too demanding for the family members.[18]

Housework is ascribed on the basis of gender, and it is further divided along class lines and, in most cases, by race and ethnicity. Domestic service accentuates the contradiction of race and class in feminism, with privileged women of one class using the labor of another woman to escape aspects of sexism.

NOTES

1. The conditions I observed in El Paso were not much different from those described by D. Thompson in her 1960 article, "Are Women Bad Employers of Other Women," *Ladies Home Journal*: "Quarters for domestic help are usually ill placed for quiet. Almost invariably they open from pantry or kitchen, so that if a member of the family goes to get a snack at night he wakes up the occupant. And the live-in maid has nowhere to receive a caller except in the kitchen or one [of] those tiny rooms." "As a general rule anything was good enough for a maid's room. It became a catchall for furniture discarded from other parts of the house. One room was a cubicle too small for a regular-sized bed." Cited in Linda Martin and Kerry Segrave, *The Servant Problem: Domestic Workers in North America* (Jefferson, NC: McFarland, 1985), p. 25.

2. David Katzman addresses the "servant problem" in his historical study of domestic service, *Seven Days a Week: Women and Domestic Service in Industrializing America* (Chicago: University of Illinois Press, 1981). Defined by middle-class housewives, the problem includes both the shortage of servants available and the competency of women willing to enter domestic service. Employer's attitudes about domestics have been well documented in women's magazines. Katzman described the topic as "the bread and butter of women's magazines between the Civil War and World War I"; moreover, Martin and Segrave, *The Servant Problem*, illustrate the continuing presence of articles on the servant problem in women's magazines today.

3. Lillian Pettengill's account *Toilers of the Home: The Record of a College Woman's Experience As a Domestic Servant* (New York: Doubleday, 1903) is based on two years of employment in Philadelphia households.

4. Ruth Schwartz Cowan, *More Work for Mother: The Ironies of Household Technology from the Open Hearth to the Microwave* (New York: Basic Books, 1983), p. 228.

5. Earning money as domestic workers to pay college expenses not covered by scholarships is not that uncommon among other women of color in the United States. Trudier Harris interviewed several African American women public school and university college teachers about their college day experiences in domestic service. See *From Mammies to Militants: Domestics in Black American Literature* (Philadelphia: Temple University Press, 1982), pp. 5–6.

6. Judith Rollins, *Between Women: Domestics and Their Employers* (Philadelphia: Temple University Press, 1985); Bonnie Thornton Dill, "Across the Boundaries of Race and Class: An Exploration of the Relationship between Work and Family among Black Female Domestic Servants" (Ph.D. dissertation, New York University, 1979): Judith Rollins, "'Making Your Job Good Yourself': Domestic Service and the Construction of Personal Dignity," in *Women and the Politics of Empowerment*, ed. Ann Bookman and Sandra Morgen (Philadelphia: Temple University Press, 1988), pp. 33–52; Soraya Moore Coley, "'And Still I Rise': An Exploratory Study of Contemporary Black Private Household Workers" (Ph.D. dissertation,

Bryn Mawr College, 1981); Evelyn Nakano Glenn, *Issei, Nisei, War Brides: Three Generations of Japanese American Women in Domestic Service* (Philadelphia: Temple University Press, 1986).

7. In some cases, it was important to let women know that my own background had involved paid housework and that my mother and sister were currently employed full-time as private household workers. Sharing this information conveyed that my life had similarities to theirs and that I respected them. This sharing of information is similar to the concept of "reciprocity" (R. Wax, "Reciprocity in Field Work," in *Human Organization Research: Field Relationships and Techniques,* ed. R. N. Adams and J. J. Preiss [New York: Dorsey, 1960], pp. 90–98).

8. Clark Knowlton, "Changing Spanish-American Villages of Northern New Mexico," *Sociology and Social Research* 53 (1969): 455–75.

9. Nancie Gonzalez, *The Spanish-Americans of New Mexico* (Albuquerque: University of New Mexico Press, 1967), p. 123.

10. William W. Winnie, "The Hispanic People of New Mexico" (Master's thesis, University of Florida, 1955).

11. Thomas J. Malone, "Recent Demographic and Economic Changes in Northern New Mexico," *New Mexico Business* 17 (1964): 4–14.

12. Donald N. Barrett and Julian Samora, *The Movement of Spanish Youth from Rural to Urban Settings* (Washington, DC: National Committee for Children and Youth, 1963).

13. Clark Knowlton, "The Spanish Americans in New Mexico," *Sociology and Social Research* 45 (1961): 448–54.

14. See Paul A. Walter, "The Spanish-Speaking Community in New Mexico," *Sociology and Social Research* 24 (1939): 150–57; Thomas Weaver, "Social Structure, Change and Conflict in a New Mexico Village" (Ph.D. dissertation, University of California, 1965); Florence R. Kluckhohn and Fred L. Stodtbeck, *Variations in Value Orientations* (Evanston, IL: Row, Peterson, 1961); Frank Moore, "San Jose, 1946: A Study in Urbanization" (Master's thesis, University of New Mexico, 1947); Donald N. Barrett and Julian Samora, *The Movement of Spanish Youth* (Washington, DC: National Committee for Children and Youth, 1963).

15. Margaret Mead, "Household Help," *Redbook Magazine* (October 1976), pp. 42, 45, 47.

16. See page 545 of Jane Addams, "A Belated Industry," *American Journal of Sociology* 1 (1896): 536–50.

17. Susan Tucker, *Telling Memories among Southern Women: Domestic Workers and Their Employers in the Segregated South* (Baton Rouge: Louisiana State University Press, 1988), p. 231.

18. David Katzman, *Seven Days a Week* (Chicago: University of Illinois Press, 1981), pp. 269–70.

4

WHAT IS A SOCIAL FACT?

EMILE DURKHEIM

Most sociologists agree that the best way to learn about research is through the hands-on experience gained by conducting a study. The research process, examined in the next three readings, often turns up new questions and challenges for the researcher. One challenge has been to define exactly what it is that sociologists study; this question dates back to the earliest writings in sociology. An example of such early writing is the following selection by Emile Durkheim (1858–1917). Durkheim, who is considered to be one of the five founders of sociology, devoted his adult life to defining how this new discipline was different from the other social and natural sciences. This reading is taken from *The Rules of Sociological Method* (1895), in which Durkheim defines what the discipline of sociology is, and what sociologists study: *social facts*.

Before inquiring into the method suited to the study of social facts, it is important to know which facts are commonly called "social." This information is all the more necessary since the designation "social" is used with little precision. It is currently employed for practically all phenomena generally diffused within society, however small their social interest. But on that basis, there are, as it were, no human events that may not be called social. Each individual drinks, sleeps, eats, reasons; and it is to society's interest that these functions be exercised in an orderly manner. If, then, all these facts are counted as "social" facts, sociology would have no subject matter exclusively its own, and its domain would be confused with that of biology and psychology.

But in reality there is in every society a certain group of phenomena which may be differentiated from those studied by the other natural sciences. When I fulfil my obligations as brother, husband, or citizen, when I execute my contracts, I perform duties which are defined, externally to myself

---

· Reprinted with the permission of The Free Press, a division of Simon & Schuster, from *The Rules of Sociological Method* by Emile Durkheim, translated by Sarah A. Solovay and John H. Mueller. Edited by George E. G. Catlin. Copyright © 1938 by George E. G. Catlin; copyright renewed 1966 by Sarah A. Solovay, John H. Mueller, and George E. G. Catlin.

and my acts, in law and in custom. Even if they conform to my own sentiments and I feel their reality subjectively, such reality is still objective, for I did not create them; I merely inherited them through my education. How many times it happens, moreover, that we are ignorant of the details of the obligations incumbent upon us, and that in order to acquaint ourselves with them we must consult the law and its authorized interpreters! Similarly, the church member finds the beliefs and practices of his religious life ready-made at birth; their existence prior to his own implies their existence outside of himself. The system of signs I use to express my thought, the system of currency I employ to pay my debts, the instruments of credit I utilize in my commercial relations, the practices followed in my profession, etc., function independently of my own use of them. And these statements can be repeated for each member of society. Here, then, are ways of acting, thinking, and feeling that present the noteworthy property of existing outside the individual consciousness.

These types of conduct or thought are not only external to the individual but are, moreover, endowed with coercive power, by virtue of which they impose themselves upon him, independent of his individual will. Of course, when I fully consent and conform to them, this constraint is felt only slightly, if at all, and is therefore unnecessary. But it is, nonetheless, an intrinsic characteristic of these facts, the proof thereof being that it asserts itself as soon as I attempt to resist it. If I attempt to violate the law, it reacts against me so as to prevent my act before its accomplishment, or to nullify my violation by restoring the damage, if it is accomplished and reparable, or to make me expiate it if it cannot be compensated for otherwise.

In the case of purely moral maxims, the public conscience exercises a check on every act which offends it by means of the surveillance it exercises over the conduct of citizens, and the appropriate penalties at its disposal. In many cases the constraint is less violent, but nevertheless it always exists. If I do not submit to the conventions of society, if in my dress I do not conform to the customs observed in my country and in my class, the ridicule I provoke, the social isolation in which I am kept, produce, although in an attenuated form, the same effects as a punishment in the strict sense of the word. The constraint is nonetheless efficacious for being indirect. I am not obliged to speak French with my fellow countrymen nor to use the legal currency, but I cannot possibly do otherwise. If I tried to escape this necessity, my attempt would fail miserably. As an industrialist, I am free to apply the technical methods of former centuries; but by doing so, I should invite certain ruin. Even when I free myself from these rules and violate them successfully, I am always compelled to struggle with them. When finally overcome, they make their constraining power sufficiently felt by the resistance they offer. The enterprises of all innovators, including successful ones, come up against resistance of this kind.

Here, then, is a category of facts with very distinctive characteristics: it consists of ways of acting, thinking, and feeling, external to the individual, and endowed with a power of coercion, by reason of which they control him. These ways of thinking could not be confused with biological phenomena, since they consist of representations and of actions; nor with psychological phenomena, which exist only in the individual consciousness and through it. They constitute, thus, a new variety of phenomena; and it is to them exclusively that the term "social" ought to be applied. And this term fits them quite well, for it is clear that, since their source is not in the individual, their substratum can be no other than society, either the political society as a whole or some one of the partial groups it includes, such as religious denominations, political, literary, and occupational associations, etc. On the other hand, this term "social" applies to them exclusively, for it has a distinct meaning only if it designates exclusively the phenomena which are not included in any of the categories of facts that have already been established and classified. These ways of thinking and acting therefore constitute the proper domain of sociology. It is true that, when we define them with this word "constraint" we risk shocking the zealous partisans of absolute individualism. For those who profess the complete autonomy of the individual, man's dignity is diminished whenever he is made to feel that he is not completely self-determinant. It is generally accepted today, however, that most of our ideas and our tendencies are not developed by ourselves but come to us from without. How can they become a part of us except by imposing themselves upon us? This is the whole meaning of our definition. And it is generally accepted, moreover, that social constraint is not necessarily incompatible with the individual personality.

Since the examples that we have just cited (legal and moral regulations, religious faiths, financial systems, etc.) all consist of established beliefs and practices, one might be led to believe that social facts exist only where there is some social organization. But there are other facts without such crystallized form which have the same objectivity and the same ascendancy over the individual. These are called "social currents." Thus the great movements of enthusiasm, indignation, and pity in a crowd do not originate in any one of the particular individual consciousnesses. They come to each one of us from without and can carry us away in spite of ourselves. Of course, it may happen that, in abandoning myself to them unreservedly, I do not feel the pressure they exert upon me. But it is revealed as soon as I try to resist them. Let an individual attempt to oppose one of these collective manifestations, and the emotions that he denies will turn against him. Now, if this power of external coercion asserts itself so clearly in cases of resistance, it must exist also in the first mentioned cases, although we are unconscious of it. We are then victims of the illusion of having ourselves created that which actually forced itself from without. If the complacency with which we permit ourselves to be carried along conceals the pressure undergone, nevertheless it does not abolish it. Thus, air is no less heavy because we do not detect its weight. So, even if we ourselves have spontaneously contributed to the production of the common emotion, the impression we have received differs markedly from that which we would have experienced if we had been alone. Also, once the crowd has dispersed, that is, once these social influences have ceased to act upon us and we are alone again, the emotions which have passed through the mind appear strange to us, and we no longer recognize them as ours. We realize that these feelings have been impressed upon us to a much greater extent than they were created by us. It may even happen that they horrify us, so much were they contrary to our nature. Thus, a group of individuals, most of whom are perfectly inoffensive, may, when gathered in a crowd, be drawn into acts of atrocity. And what we say of these transitory outbursts applies similarly to those more permanent currents of opinion on religious, political, literary, or artistic matters which are constantly being formed around us, whether in society as a whole or in more limited circles.

To confirm this definition of the social fact by a characteristic illustration from common experience, one need only observe the manner in which children are brought up. Considering the facts as they are and as they have always been, it becomes immediately evident that all education is a continuous effort to impose on the child ways of seeing, feeling, and acting which he could not have arrived at spontaneously. From the very first hours of his life, we compel him to eat, drink, and sleep at regular hours; we constrain him to cleanliness, calmness, and obedience; later we exert pressure upon him in order that he may learn proper consideration for others, respect for customs and conventions, the need for work, etc. If, in time, this constraint ceases to be felt, it is because it gradually gives rise to habits and to internal tendencies that render constraint unnecessary; but nevertheless it is not abolished, for it is still the source from which these habits were derived. . . . What makes these facts particularly instructive is that the aim of education is, precisely, the socialization of the human being; the process of education, therefore, gives us in a nutshell the historical fashion in which the social being is constituted. This unremitting pressure to which the child is subjected is the very pressure of the social milieu which tends to fashion him in its own image, and of which parents and teachers are merely the representatives and intermediaries.

It follows that sociological phenomena cannot be defined by their universality. A thought which we find in every individual consciousness, a movement repeated by all individuals, is not thereby a social fact. If sociologists have been satisfied with defining them by this characteristic, it is because they confused them with what one might call their reincarnation in the individual. It is, however, the collective aspects of the beliefs, tendencies, and practices of a group that characterize truly social phenomena. As for the forms that the collective states assume when refracted in the individual, these are things of another sort. This duality is clearly demonstrated by the fact that these two orders of phenomena are frequently found dissociated from one another. Indeed, certain of these social manners of acting and thinking acquire, by reason of their repetition, a certain rigidity which on its own account crystallizes them, so to speak, and isolates them from the particular events which reflect them. They thus acquire a body, a tangible form, and constitute a reality in their own right, quite distinct from the individual facts which produce it. Collective habits are inherent not only in the successive acts which they determine but, by a privilege of which we find no example in the biological realm, they are given permanent expression in a formula which is repeated from mouth to mouth, transmitted by education, and fixed even in writing. Such is the origin and nature of legal and moral rules, popular aphorisms and proverbs, articles of faith wherein religious or political groups condense their beliefs, standards of taste established by literary schools, etc. None of these can be found entirely reproduced in the applications made of them by individuals, since they can exist even without being actually applied.

No doubt, this dissociation does not always manifest itself with equal distinctness, but its obvious existence in the important and numerous cases just cited is sufficient to prove that the social fact is a thing distinct from its individual manifestations. Moreover, even when this dissociation is not immediately apparent, it may often be disclosed by certain devices of method. Such dissociation is indispensable if one wishes to separate social facts from their alloys in order to observe them in a state of purity. Currents of opinion, with an intensity varying according to the time and place, impel certain groups either to more marriages, for example, or to more suicides, or to a higher or lower birthrate, etc. These currents are plainly social facts. At first sight they seem inseparable from the forms they take in individual cases. But statistics furnish us with the means of isolating them. They are, in fact, represented with considerable exactness by the rates of births, marriages, and suicides, that is, by the number obtained by dividing the average annual total of marriages, births, suicides, by the number of persons whose ages lie within the range in which marriages, births, and suicides occur. Since each of these figures contains all the individual cases indiscriminately, the individual circumstances which may have had a share in the production of the phenomenon are neutralized and, consequently, do not contribute to its determination. The average, then, expresses a certain state of the group mind (*l'âme collective*).

Such are social phenomena, when disentangled from all foreign matter. As for their individual manifestations, these are indeed, to a certain extent, social, since they partly reproduce a social model. Each of them also depends, and to a large extent, on the organopsychological constitution of the individual and on the particular circumstances in which he is placed. Thus they are not sociological phenomena in the strict sense of the word. They belong to two realms at once; one could call them socio-psychological. They interest the sociologist without constituting the immediate subject matter of sociology. There exist in the interior of organisms similar phenomena, compound in their nature, which form in their turn the subject matter of the "hybrid sciences," such as physiological chemistry, for example.

The objection may be raised that a phenomenon is collective only if it is common to all members of society, or at least to most of them—in other words, if it is truly general. This may be true; but it is general because it is collective (that is, more or less obligatory), and certainly not collective because general. It is a group condition repeated in the individual because it is imposed on him. It is to be found in each part because it exists in the whole, rather than in the whole because it exists in the parts. This becomes conspicuously evident in those beliefs and practices which are transmitted to us ready-made by previous generations; we receive and adopt them because, being both collective and ancient, they are invested with a particular authority that education has taught us to recognize and respect. It is, of course, true that a vast portion of our social culture is transmitted to us in this way; but even when the social fact is due in part to our direct collaboration, its nature is not different. A collective emotion which bursts forth suddenly and violently in a crowd does not express merely what all the individual sentiments had in common; it is something entirely different, as we have shown. It results from their being together, a product of the actions and reactions which take place between individual consciousnesses; and if each individual consciousness echoes the collective sentiment, it is by virtue of the special energy resident in its collective origin. If all hearts beat in unison, this is not the result of a spontaneous and preestablished harmony but rather because an identical force propels them in the same direction. Each is carried along by all.

We thus arrive at the point where we can formulate and delimit in a precise way the domain of sociology. It comprises only a limited group of phenomena. A social fact is to be recognized by the power of external coercion which it exercises or is capable of exercising over individuals, and the presence of this power may be recognized in its turn either by the existence of some specific sanction or by the resistance offered against every individual effort that tends to violate it. One can, however, define it also by its diffusion within the group, provided that, in conformity with our previous remarks, one takes care to add as a second and essential characteristic that its own existence is independent of the individual forms it assumes in its diffusion. This last criterion is perhaps, in certain cases, easier to apply than the preceding one. In fact, the constraint is easy to ascertain when it expresses itself externally by some direct reaction of society, as is the case in law, morals, beliefs, customs, and even fashions. But when it is only indirect, like the constraint which an economic organization exercises, it cannot always be so easily detected. Generality combined with externality may, then, be easier to establish. Moreover, this second definition is but another form of the first; for if a mode of behavior whose existence is external to individual consciousnesses becomes general, this can only be brought about by its being imposed upon them.

But these several phenomena present the same characteristic by which we defined the others. These "ways of existing" are imposed on the individual precisely in the same fashion as the "ways of acting" of which we have spoken. Indeed, when we wish to know how a society is divided politically, of what these divisions themselves are composed, and how complete is the fusion existing between them, we shall not achieve our purpose by physical inspection and by geographical observations; for these phenomena are social, even when they have some basis in physical nature. It is only by a study of public law that a comprehension of this organization is possible, for it is this law that determines the organization, as it equally determines our domestic and civil relations. This political organization is, then, no less obligatory than the social facts mentioned above. If the population crowds into our cities instead of scattering into the country, this is due to a trend of public opinion, a collective drive that imposes this concentration upon the individuals. We can no more choose the style of our houses than of our clothing—at least, both are equally obligatory. The channels of communication prescribe the direction of internal migrations and commerce, etc., and even their extent. Consequently, at the very most, it should be necessary to add to the list of phenomena which we have enumerated as presenting the distinctive criterion of a social fact only one additional category, "ways of existing," and as this enumeration was not meant to be rigorously exhaustive, the addition would not be absolutely necessary.

Such an addition is perhaps not necessary, for these "ways of existing" are only crystallized "ways of acting." The political structure of a society is merely the way in which its component segments have become accustomed to live with one another. If their relations are traditionally intimate, the segments tend to fuse with one another, or, in the contrary case, to retain their identity. The type of habitation imposed upon us is merely the way in which our contemporaries and our ancestors have been accustomed to construct their houses. The methods of communication are merely the channels which the regular currents of commerce and migrations have dug, by flowing in the same direction. To be sure, if the phenomena of a structural character alone presented this permanence, one might believe that they constituted a distinct species. A legal regulation is an arrangement no less permanent than a type of architecture, and yet the regulation is a "physiological" fact. A simple moral maxim is assuredly somewhat more malleable, but it is much more rigid than a simple professional custom or a fashion. There is thus a whole series of degrees without a break in continuity between the facts of the most articulated structure and those free currents of social life which are not yet definitely molded. The differences between them are, therefore, only differences in the degree of consolidation they present. Both are simply life, more or less crystallized. No doubt, it may be of some advantage to reserve the term "morphological" for those social facts which concern the social substratum, but only on condition of not overlooking the fact that they are of the same nature as the others. Our definition will then include the whole relevant range of facts if we say: *A social fact is every way of acting, fixed or not, capable of exercising on the individual an external constraint;* or again, *every way of acting which is general throughout a given society, while at the same time existing in its own right independent of its individual manifestations.*

5
───────

THE "OTHER" AMERICANS

GABRIELLE SÁNDOR

Social research is concerned with the definition and assessment of social phenomena. Many social concepts, such as racial identification, are difficult to study because of measurement problems. For example, this selection by Gabrielle Sándor illustrates how inaccurate the four racial categories of "white, black, Asian, and American Indian" are in the U.S. census. In 1990, over 10 million people refused to categorize themselves in one of those four categories. The implications of this situation are enormous because the government relies on census data to determine the efficacy of public policies, such as affirmative action and the Voting Rights Act. Thus, survey researchers are in a quandary because even though more detailed data on racial-ethnic differences are needed, race and ethnicity are social constructions and, therefore, difficult to measure.

Ada Nurie Pagán is a blonde, green-eyed, pale-skinned "person of color." When asked by affirmative action officers, she says that her race is Hispanic, Latina, or Puerto Rican. The Census Bureau would say that Hispanic origin is an ethnicity, not a race, so it classifies Ada as white. But Ada doesn't want to give that answer.

"I can't check a circle that labels me black, white, Asian, or American Indian, because I'm not any of those things," she says. "My sister and I have the same parents, but she's much darker than me. If it came down to choosing black or white, I'd have to choose white and she couldn't. That wouldn't make any sense."

Ada's confusion stems from the ambiguity in current definitions of race and ethnicity. The Census Bureau sees race and ethnicity as two different demographic characteristics and has separate questions on census forms and surveys. But the people who fill out the forms sometimes find the two concepts impossible to separate.

The result is much more than a problem for census takers. Ada's misgivings are part of a significant generation gap in attitudes toward race. The rules that govern government statistics on race and ethnicity are based on a 16-year-old definition, and young people like Ada live in a world where that definition seems arbitrary or even offensive.

TABLE 5.1   Interracial Marriages

The number of black and white interracial married couples has increased 78 percent since 1980. (number of marriages in thousands by type, percent of total married couples, 1980 and 1992; and percent change, 1980–92)

Race	1992 number	1992 percent	1980 number	1980 percent	percent change 1980–92
Total Married Couples	53,512	100.0%	49,714	100.0%	7.6%
Total Interracial Couples	1,161	2.2	651	1.3	78.3
Black / White Couples	246	0.5	167	0.3	47.3
White wife, black husband	163	0.3	122	0.2	33.6
Black wife, white husband	83	0.2	45	0.1	84.4
White Wife/Other-Race Husband (excluding black)	883	1.7	450	0.9	96.2
Black Wife/Other-Race Husband (excluding white)	32	0.1	34	0.1	−5.9

Source: Bureau of the Census, Marital Status and Living Arrangements; March 1992, *Current Population Reports,* Series P20–468.

People in their twenties today never saw sanctioned segregation. They read about the civil rights movement in history books, and they were taught in public schools that discrimination is wrong. Small wonder, then, that young adults are much more likely than older adults to object to racial categories or not to fit within them. In 1990, members of the "other race" category had a median age of about 24 years, compared with a national median of 33.

Some "other race" Americans are mixed-race children. Though relatively rare, they are often born to middle-class families that vote and organize. A larger share are recent immigrants to the U.S. They are likely to be young adults, and birth rates for most minority groups are higher than they are for non-Hispanic whites. As a result, younger Americans are more likely to be minorities.

Mixed-race children are also increasingly common, because the penalties once attached to interracial dating and marriage are slowly fading away. In 1991, 74 percent of Americans said that interracial marriage was acceptable for themselves or others, according to the Roper Organization, up from 70 percent who found it acceptable in 1986.

Nonwhite and Hispanic Americans will claim 28 percent of the total U.S. population in 2000, according to the Census Bureau. But at the same time, the share of minorities will be 36 percent among children under age 18 and 33 percent among young adults aged 18 to 34. If current trends continue, minorities will be approaching half of the total U.S. population as early as 2050. Today's children will be the first to see that society.

Four Categories

The conflict over racial statistics worries researchers. "The demand [for detailed data] is going in one direction, and the quality and consistency in counting is going the other way," says Greg Robinson, chief of population and analysis for the Census Bureau. "The quality of the race and ethnic data is deteriorating."

Young adults' attitudes toward race also raise important issues for businesses, because they clash with older rules. "Tolerance and diversity is absolutely the number-one shared value" of young adults, says Gwen Lipsky, MTV's senior vice president of research and planning. "They are much more [tolerant] than any previous generation."

But while young adults embrace tolerance and racial ambiguity, a rule requires federal agencies like the Census Bureau to fit all of their racial data into separate categories. The rule, known as Statistical Directive 15, was adopted in 1978 by the Office of Management and Budget (OMB). It creates four official racial categories—American Indian or Alaskan Native, Asian or Pacific Islander, black, and white. It also defines Hispanic origin as an ethnic category separate from race. The rule helps federal and state agencies share racial data, which are vital to affirmative action and other government programs.

The 1990 census questionnaire asked respondents to put themselves into a racial category and to indicate their ethnicity and ancestry elsewhere. Respondents who felt that they didn't fit into one of the four categories checked a box marked "other race." The number of people who checked that box increased 45 percent between the 1980 and 1990 censuses, to 9.8 million. That's about 1 in 25 Americans.

Most of the people who check "other race" probably have a clear racial identity, because 98 percent claim Hispanic origin on the ethnicity question. In other words, over 40 percent of the nation's 22 million Hispanics aren't willing to identify themselves as black or white.

"Most of them are probably indicating some version of multiracial," says Carlos Fernández, president of the Association of Multi-Ethnic Americans (AMEA) in San Francisco. "Mexicans, especially, regard themselves as mestizo—part Spanish, part indigenous. The large majority of Mexico is multiracial. It's almost the official culture. Mexico hasn't asked a race question on its census since 1921. So on the U.S. census, people who put Mexican for race know full well what it means. It's mestizo, and that is a racial designation, not a nationality."

Many Latin Americans trace the greatest part of their ancestry to native Indians, followed by Europeans and perhaps Africans. But the category on the U.S. census applies only to North American Indians, so a Hispanic person's choices usually come down to black or white. Ada Pagán, whose great-great-grandmother was black, passes as white. But she knows exactly what her dark-skinned sister is. She's "trigueña," which Ada translates as "brown."

Statistical Headache

In 1990, about 400,000 people who marked "other race" were not Hispanic. Though their numbers are small, they are the ones raising their voices the loudest against the census's race question. Many of the protestors may be parents in racially mixed marriages who confront an obvious problem when answering the race question for their children.

The statistical headaches over race get worse every year, as the number of interracial marriages continues to rise. Interracial marriages were illegal in some states until 1967, when the Supreme Court struck down antimiscegenation laws in the aptly titled case *Loving v. Virginia.* Since 1980, the number of black and white interracial married couples has increased from 651,000 to 1.2 million, according to the Census Bureau. Children born to parents of different races were more than 3 percent of births in 1990, according to the National Center for Health Statistics, up from 1 percent in 1968.

Unfortunately for survey designers, the race problem can't be solved simply by adding new categories for mestizos and multiracials. The reasons are a pair of statistical bugaboos called "primacy" and "recency" effects. Studies show that when respondents see a long list of choices on a written survey,

TABLE 5.2   Multiracial Babies

Forty percent of multiracial babies born in 1990 were black and white, up from 32 percent in 1970. (total live births to parents of different races and percent of all interracial live births, 1970–90)

Race	1990 number	1990 percent	1980 number	1980 percent	1970 number	1970 percent
Total Interracial Births	124,468	100.0%	73,596	100.0%	39,012	100.0%
Total Black/White Births	49,479	39.8	25,289	34.4	12,556	32.2
White mother/ black father	37,661	30.3	19,757	26.8	9,636	24.7
Black mother/ white father	11,818	9.5	5,532	7.5	2,920	7.5
White Mother/Other-Race Father (excluding black)	27,269	21.9	17,568	23.9	9,044	23.2
Black Mother/Other-Race Father (excluding white)	1,206	1.0	698	0.9	432	1.1
Other Interracial Births	46,514	37.4	30,041	40.8	16,980	43.5

Note: Does not include births for which the race of the mother or father is unknown.

Source: National Center for Health Statistics.

they are likely to pick the first choice that might apply to them instead of reading through the whole list. The reverse is true of telephone surveys, when people tend to pick the last choice. The more categories on the list, the more these effects complicate the results.

"We couldn't possibly get every person's idea of their race into the question," says Robert Tortora, associate director for statistical design, methodology and standards at the Census Bureau. "There would be all kinds of methodological effects, and the logistics of it are daunting." Tortora agrees that there are problems with the ways race and ethnicity are currently measured, and he does see changes coming. "Basically, what you're asking is a person's judgment of their race or ethnicity. And since we don't have precise definitions of every possible category, people's perceptions of themselves and their answers can change from census to census."

Race statistics can become muddled in many ways. In 1970, for example, about 1 million residents of midwestern and southern states mistakenly identified themselves as Central or South Americans because they were confused by the census form. Such goofs are relatively easy to correct. When someone writes "German" for their race, for example, they are automatically reassigned to the "white" category by a census computer.

When "other race" is what the person meant to write, the result is a quiet tug-of-war between the respondent's preferences and Statistical Directive 15. If a person won't fit themselves into one of the four racial categories designated by the OMB, a census computer does it for them. Usually, computers scan other answers on the same form and assign the person to the category that seems best. The stubborn few who check "other race," write in "biracial," and give two races are assigned the first race they report.

If someone checks "other race" and writes "Latino," the census's computers will check to see if any other household members designated a race. If no one in the household did, the bureau will check the forms of neighboring households who wrote their race as "Latino" and assign a race on that basis. This process, called "hot-decking," is considered fairly accurate on a nationwide basis. But it may be responsible for serious inaccuracies in neighborhood-level census data.

The Census Bureau says that the number of blacks of Hispanic origin in Los Angeles increased from 17,000 in 1980 to nearly 60,000 in 1990. But two local experts can find no evidence of the change, and they suspect computer error. Latinos in the city's South Central neighborhood may have ignored the race question, says James P. Allen, a geographer at Cal State Northridge. The nonrespondents were probably assigned a race based on the skin color of their neighbors, who are likely to be black, says sociologist David Heer of the University of Southern California. The overcount of blacks may have affected government funds and redistricting plans in L.A., and it doesn't stop there.

"This is a terribly important error," Allen told *Buzz* magazine. "I strongly believe it has happened in Miami, Houston, Chicago, and all cities where Latinos are migrating into black neighborhoods."

Young and Proud

With all of the confusion and the possibility of taking offense, some observers have wondered if collecting any racial statistics is a good idea. "As long as we differentiate, we will discriminate," writes Michael E. Tomlin, a professor of education at the University of Idaho, in a letter to *American Demographics* magazine. Tomlin describes himself as a native-born American of Scotch-Irish descent, but he refuses to answer any federal questions concerning ethnicity or race. "For our nation to truly earn its place as the land of the free," he continues, "we must free ourselves from placing others—and ourselves—in boxes."

Tomlin's objections might seem noble. But if he got his way, the federal government would have no way to fight racial discrimination. Racial data are used to enforce the Voting Rights Act, equal employment regulations, and affirmative action plans, to name just a few. These programs depend on a steady flow of data that conform to Statistical Directive 15, so they can be easily compared with data from other sources. State or federal agencies can ask for more detailed information on race, but the data must ultimately break down into the same four categories.

The OMB and Census Bureau are now reviewing Directive 15. Seven months of hearings in 1993 revealed three truths about racial statistics, according to Congressman Tom Sawyer, chairman of the House Subcommittee on Census. First, many people agree on the need to continue collecting ethnic and racial data. Second, the data must be uniform across the government. Third, racial categories must be relevant to the public, or the public won't cooperate.

Groups such as the Association of Multi-Ethnic Americans say that the way to restore relevance to racial data is to add a new multiracial category to Directive 15. "People ask, 'Why don't we eliminate all categories?'" says the AMEA's Carlos Fernández. "I say, that's nice, but you can't erase differences between people by ignoring them. When we get people from different communities intermarrying at a rate we would expect if there were no differences between them, then the categories will become irrelevant. Eventually it will happen."

6

PERSONAL REFLECTIONS ON RESEARCHING HIV DISEASE

ROSE WEITZ

Ethical questions concerning social research are a rather recent discussion in the history of social science. It wasn't until the 1960s and early 1970s that we began to question research protocols and the effects of social experiments on humans. This last reading, by Rose Weitz, in the social research section takes us inside the research world of one sociologist and reveals her ethical and legal concerns about studying persons with HIV/AIDS. This excerpt is taken from Weitz' 1991 book *Life With AIDS*.

During my "apprenticeship" as a sociologist, both during and after graduate school, I was taught how to review the literature, conduct interviews, analyze data, and the like. By the time I began this book, I had been out of graduate school and working as a sociologist for eight years. Nevertheless, in all those years, nothing I had read and no one I had studied with had taught me how to deal with the personal, legal, and ethical dilemmas I encountered while interviewing persons with HIV [human immunodeficiency virus] disease.

Personal Dilemmas

When I began this research, I expected it to be psychologically draining. In retrospect, however, I was terribly naive about the stresses I would encounter.

My most serious problem has been the unusually burdensome sense of responsibility this research created. Probably all researchers struggle with doubts about their abilities to do justice to their topics, particularly when others have provided financial support. However, the nature of my work has heightened this sense of responsibility enormously. If my research becomes widely read, it may affect health care policy and hence significantly affect many individuals' lives. Already, for example, I have testified to our Governor's Task Force on AIDS [acquired immune deficiency syndrome], and have learned that my testimony was influential in convincing the task force to oppose mandatory reporting of persons who test positive for HIV. More crucially, in terms of its personal emotional impact, many people I spoke with explicitly referred to their interviews as legacies. They participated in this project despite the emotional and sometimes physical pain it caused them because they believed I would use their stories to help others. Thus they gave me the responsibility of giving meaning to their lives and to their deaths.

I also have encountered personal difficulties in doing this research because it has made the inevitability of death and the possibility of disability far more salient for me. Early in the research, I realized that at each interview I automatically compared my age with that of the person I was interviewing. I was frequently disturbed to find that they were much younger than they looked and often younger than I. (I was 34 when I began this research.) Having to witness the pain of their lives was far more difficult than coping with the knowledge that they were dying, especially because the dying occurred out of my sight.

In addition to teaching me some truths about death and disability, the interviews also forced me to recognize the irrational nature of my own and others' response to potential contagion. To control my fears during interviews with those who have HIV disease, I often found myself repeating silently a calming litany about how HIV is and isn't transmitted. Meanwhile, I had to calm the fears of friends and acquaintances who wondered whether I had become a source of contagion. All I could do was to provide information about HIV, which they might or might not choose to assimilate. Fortunately, no one proved irrationally fearful.

Legal Dilemmas

I initially became involved in research on HIV disease after hearing a lecture about how the government is restricting the civil liberties of persons with this illness. These restrictions include deporting noncitizens and quarantining those judged a danger to themselves or others. I was therefore sensitized to the potential legal problems before I began this research. This was an issue from the start because Arizona law requires all health care workers to report to the state any person who has HIV disease at any stage. According to the state department of health services, I could legally be required to report anyone I interviewed (several of whom told me they had not been reported by their doctors). Moreover, an important recent case had confirmed that sociologists' rights to protect their data against subpoenas is not as strong as the right granted to physicians or lawyers.[1] Consequently, and recognizing that reporting someone could jeopardize their civil rights, I was unusually concerned about protecting the confidentiality of my records.

The need for confidentiality produced some unexpected difficulties. I wanted to make it easy for persons with HIV disease who were considering participating in this research to reach me, because I assumed that any difficulty might diminish their willingness to do so. However, I could not give out my home phone number because my housemate might listen to our answering machine and unintentionally hear a message meant only for me. Similarly, I could not write names, addresses, or phone numbers in the pocket calendar that I use to organize my life because I could not risk having the calendar subpoenaed and losing all my other daily records.

Ironically, my chief worry was protecting the signed "informed consent forms" that my university's research ethics committee required me to obtain from each person I interviewed. When I initially raised this issue with the committee, we were unable to reach an agreement on an alternative that would not require individuals to sign their names. (When, in 1989, I began interviewing persons with HIV disease again, however, we agreed that instead of having each sign a consent form, I would begin each interview by reading a statement about informed consent and would tape both my statement and their response.)

Ethical Dilemmas

Early in my training as a sociologist, I learned the value of informed consent. Translating this principle into action, however, requires more than simply presenting potential interviewees with a description of one's purposes and research methods. While interviewing persons with HIV disease, I soon discovered that many assumed that I was a counselor, worked for one of the community organizations that helps persons with HIV disease, or was a lesbian. I then had to decide how much responsibility I had to correct their assumptions, particularly when they were not explicit. Should I have assumed that they understood what a sociologist was, or should I have carefully differentiated sociology from social work? If an individual commented that I did not wear a wedding ring, should I have assumed that they were searching for a polite way of asking if I was a lesbian? How many times should I have stopped a given interview to explain that I did not work for a community organization, if the person I was interviewing did not understand the first time I explained?

Truly informed consent was even more rare among those who felt they could not afford to refuse to participate. Despite my disclaimers, many individuals obviously believed I worked for either the state or a community organization for persons with HIV disease. As a result, they may have feared that they would jeopardize their access to services if they did not participate. Even if they believed they would not be punished for lack of cooperation, they may still have believed they would be rewarded for helping. Several, for example, mentioned that they wanted their physicians to consider them exemplary patients so that the physicians would remember them when choosing patients for experimental treatment programs.

Truly free consent was even less likely in interviewing individuals who were in jail or prison. Because of the connection between HIV and drug use, many persons with HIV disease are imprisoned. As a result, I initially pursued the possibility of contacting persons with HIV disease through the health department of the state prison system. My first contacts with prison officials seemed promising. Even more than other persons with HIV disease, however, prisoners might have felt that they would be punished if they refused to participate. Moreover, I would have had no way to keep the administration from knowing who had refused, because I would have had to arrange the interviews through prison officials. Consequently, I was relieved when negotiations fell through.

Finally, I faced a broad range of ethical dilemmas when either the persons I interviewed or I myself viewed me as an information or counseling source. Often persons I interviewed asked me questions about the disease, drugs, or doctors. Similarly, I frequently encountered persons with HIV disease whose knowledge of their illness was clearly deficient. I then had to decide whether to answer their questions even if doing so might jeopardize my relationship with influential physicians (who, for example, had not provided information about the side effects of certain drugs). Similarly, I had to decide whether to correct individuals' information if not asked. These questions posed minimal problems compared to those generated by implicit or explicit pleas for counseling. I had no answer for the individual who asked me how to convince her uninfected husband to use condoms. Nor was it clear to me how to respond when individuals told me that their disease was punishment for sins, or that they felt suicidal, or that their greatest grief was losing their children but they would not contact them for fear of infecting them. Saying nothing did not feel ethical to me. Yet saying something required me to break professional norms for sociological research.

Searching for Solutions

The legal dilemmas posed by this research presented the fewest difficulties, because the problems and solutions were purely practical. To avoid writing confidential information in my usual daily calendar, I began carrying a small notepad with me. As is typical in this sort of research, all my records and tapes were number-coded, and all identifying information was removed from the transcripts and resulting publications. I recorded data on individuals' age, marital status, occupation, and the like separately from the taped interviews, so that persons who transcribed the tapes would not have that information. I hoped that this would make it more difficult for the transcriptionist to recognize the person I was interviewing, should the transcriptionist happen to know him or her. All papers with names or addresses were kept in one less-than-obvious location and have now been destroyed. In addition, I decided that if I were subpoenaed, I would refuse to turn over the information. (Of course, such a decision is easy to make in the abstract and I cannot predict what I might have done if actually faced with a jail sentence for contempt of court.) Finally, when some individuals, far from desiring confidentiality, told me that they would like me to use their real names in this "legacy" we were creating, I decided not to do so because the potential "stigma fallout" seemed an unfair burden to thrust on unsuspecting friends and relatives.

The remaining problems had no easy answers. I tried to answer all questions, whether direct or indirect, asked by those I interviewed. I also tried to clarify their understanding of such things as sociology versus social work and working *with* versus working *for* a community organization. If someone still seemed not to understand after two or three attempts at explaining, I did not pursue the matter.

When it came to a choice between being ethical and being "sociological," I went with ethical every time. I felt a strong moral obligation to answer any question I was asked and to provide needed information even when not asked directly. I did try to wait until after the individual had finished stating his views before interjecting any information. And I occasionally requested that individuals not tell their doctors that I was their source.

Similarly, I believe it is wrong to listen to a person's feelings of guilt and self-deprecation without attempting to alleviate those feelings. Thus if a person told me he felt horribly stupid for not using "safe sex" until a couple of years ago, I heard him out and then gently suggested that until recently no one knew how HIV was transmitted. I also volunteered suggestions about sources of information and social support when it seemed warranted. I realize that these tactics may have diminished my credibility as a researcher, but I thought that was less important than diminishing my credibility as a person.

Finally, I did whatever I could to maintain my own mental health, because I realized I would be of little use to anyone if I allowed myself to burn out. So I tried to restrict my contacts with those who have HIV disease to interviews. This tactic proved insufficient on two notable occasions—once when the family of someone I interviewed, recognizing that the interview had been an important experience for their relative, asked me if I would visit him on his deathbed, and the second time when students asked me to speak at a memorial vigil for an alumnus who had recently died of HIV disease. Finishing this research, especially given my fairly pessimistic predictions for the future, has been made much more difficult because I now have one good friend with HIV disease.

For my sanity's sake, I was grateful that at the time I was conducting most of these interviews I had no friends in high-risk groups (so far as I knew), that I did not know what any of the people I interviewed were like before their illness, and that I did not have to see them as their health deteriorated. For this reason I was very reluctant to do follow-up interviews, even though I knew they would provide invaluable data; it took many months of soul searching before I felt able to do so. Similarly, for a long time I avoided taking any steps that would have committed me to continuing this research for more than a year at a time. Knowing that my commitment was finite made it far more manageable psychologically.

I also learned the hard way that it was much more difficult emotionally for me to interview women than to interview men, because I identified so much more strongly with the women. The summer I began interviewing women was the summer I began having nightmares about contracting HIV disease. Fortunately for my mental health, although not for my research project, few women with HIV disease were available for interviews in Arizona.

To protect my mental and physical health, I tried always to schedule my interviews so that I would have time for exercise afterward, and tried to satisfy my worries with popcorn rather than chocolate. I calmed other new anxieties by updating my will, obtaining disability insurance, and giving a friend a medical power of attorney. I also soon lost most of my inhibitions about discussing the research and my attendant emotions, for I learned that it helped to share the burden. I remember vividly one afternoon when I stopped a casual acquaintance in a supermarket and harangued him for about 40 minutes with my troubles. He felt worse afterward, but I felt much better.

Undoubtedly many other researchers have coped with similar problems over the years. Unfortunately, norms for professional conduct do not allow easy and open discussion with colleagues about either psychological or ethical problems, while the rarity of lawsuits leaves few of us sensitized to legal issues. As a result, many universities provide excellent technical training in research skills, but few prepare students for dealing with these nontechnical but equally crucial difficulties. I am sure that I reinvented the wheel in my attempts to deal with these dilemmas, but I found few good places to read about—let alone discuss—my concerns. In the long run, the usual stresses of research on HIV disease may have at least one serendipitous effect, if they pressure scholars to begin tackling these issues openly.

NOTE

1. I subsequently learned, however, that sociologists' rights are greater in circumstances such as my own where the researcher consistently has emphasized to subjects that the data will be kept confidential and has established procedures to ensure this. See Ronald Bayer, Carol Levine, and Thomas H. Murray, 1984, "Guidelines for Confidentiality in Research on AIDS," *IRB: A Review of Human Subjects Research* 6:1–7.

PART II

Culture

7

THE NEW TATTOO SUBCULTURE

ANNE M. VELLIQUETTE • JEFF B. MURRAY

Culture is defined as the shared ways of a human social group. This definition includes the ways of thinking, understanding, and feeling that have
been gained through common experience in social groups and are passed on
from one generation to another. Thus culture reflects the social patterns of
thought, emotions, and practices that arise from social interaction within a
given society. In this reading, the first of four to explore culture, Anne Velliquette and Jeff Murray explore the social and symbolic meanings of body
adornment in the new tattoo subculture. In particular, this ethnographic
study investigates what tattoos, as cultural objects, signify for both the tattooist (the service provider) and the tattooee (the client).

*In the past, what you were determined what you looked like. Today, what you
choose to look like expresses who—or indeed what—you would like to be. The
choice is yours.*

—TED POLHEMUS

Humans are the only known species that deliberately alters its appearance through the customization of our bodies (Randall and Polhemus 1996). At the most basic level, we get up every morning and
make decisions about what to wear. The customization of our bodies, however, goes far beyond the clothing we choose to wear as a "second skin" (Randall and Polhemus 1996:79). At the surface level, our skin can be tattooed,
pierced, branded, scarred, and adorned with jewelry, cosmetics, and various
articles of clothing. Our hair can also be creatively modified and adorned. Beyond redefining our surface appearance, we can also alter the body's actual
shape through techniques such as body building and plastic surgery. In all
cultures, human beings spend time and effort customizing the body strictly
for the sake of appearance (Randall and Polhemus 1996). This customization

---

Reprinted by permission from Anne M. Velliquette and Jeff B. Murray.

often involves not only time and energy, but pain and discomfort (Myers 1992; Randall and Polhemus 1996). This leads to an engaging question: Why do human beings of all cultures alter their natural inherited appearance?

In most societies, the likely reason for altering the body is that such alteration provides a vehicle for self-expression (Finkelstein 1991; Randall and Polhemus 1996; Velliquette, Murray, and Creyer 1997). Permanent as well as temporary forms of body adornment may signify a wide array of symbolic meanings. For example, permanent forms of body decoration (e.g., tattoos, piercings, and scarification) have been known to represent emblems of accomplishment, group membership, social status, personal identity, or a willingness to endure pain in order to please a lover (Bohannan 1988; Drewal 1988; Gathercole 1988; Gritton 1988; Sanders 1988; Velliquette et al. 1997). Temporary forms of body adornment also provide an invaluable means of self-expression. Our personal choice in clothing, hairstyle, body shape, and use of objects may display various identity features such as gender, status, values, interests, and a particular approach to life. Clearly, body adornment has become a way for human beings to present their desired self-image to others (Blumer 1969; Finkelstein 1991; Goffman 1959). Thus, understanding the way that individuals use nonverbal signs and symbols to construct, revise, and maintain symbolic meaning is important for the construction of self-identity.

Focusing on one type of body adornment, this article presents an ethnographic account of symbolic meaning as expressed by two segments of the *New Tattoo Subculture*,[1] the tattooist (the service provider) and the tattooee (the client). Although it is difficult to assess the number of people participating in the new tattoo subculture, it has been estimated that 12 to 20 million Americans have joined the ranks of the tattooed (Blouin 1996; Velliquette et al. 1997). This is not surprising given that in 1996, tattoo studios were among the top six growth businesses in the United States (American Business Information, Inc. 1996; Velliquette et al. 1997). During the 1990s, observers have also witnessed sharp increases in the sale of tattoo ink, books, magazines, videos, special clothing designed to show off the decorated body, and other tattoo-related odds and ends, as well as the expansion of tattoo associations and conventions, the growth of state regulations, and an increase in the number of advertisements featuring tattooed models and celebrities (Ball 1996; Blouin 1996; Krakow 1994; Peterson 1996).

Tattooing's recent popularity, as well as the increased interest in the tattoo as popular culture (e.g., Gap and Polo Ads featuring tattoos, and a tattooed Barbie doll by Mattel), leads to some interesting research questions. What is it about the tattoo as a cultural object that draws people to participate in this subculture? In what ways is the tattoo used as a form of expression? What is involved in the experience of acquiring a tattoo? What transpires during the service interaction between the tattooist and tattooee? To address these questions, we begin with a brief discussion of the literature on tattooing as an art form, its rich history, and its cultural and subcultural roots. Next, we summarize the ethnographic method used for data collection. Following this summary, we offer an ethnographic account of the tattoo subculture in order to demonstrate the symbolic nature of the act of tattooing. We draw from our own experiences and observations (including fieldwork at two tattoo studios, a tattoo museum/archive, and a tattoo convention) to illustrate ways in which the tattoo is used as a form of expression. We also consider the process itself via interactions between tattooists and their clients. Finally, we consider emergent aspects of this research that may further illustrate what has been described as the New Tattoo Subculture.

Tattooing: Yesterday and Today

Tattoo is a word loaded with rich visual associations summoning images that range from circus sideshow freaks or tribal warriors to WWII sailors, the Holocaust, street gangs, criminals, or the more recent association of media stars and athletes (Velliquette et al. 1997). With such vivid associations spanning across decades, it becomes clear that tattoos have a long and fascinating history. . . . The practice of tattooing is one of the oldest art forms discovered by archaeologists (Ball 1996; Randall and Polhemus 1996). The word *tattoo* is derived from the Tahitian word *ta-tu* meaning "to strike." A *ta* was a sharp, jagged piece of antler or bone. Different types of bones or *tas* were used to create different designs by tapping or pushing ink, usually made from vegetable or fruit dyes, into the flesh (Ball 1996; Randall and Polhemus 1996). Because it is usually only the bones and not the skin of our distant ancestors that remain intact, it is impossible to determine just how old the tattoo really is. The oldest irrefutable evidence of tattooing entered the archaeological record only a few years ago, when the complete body of an Iceman was found frozen in a glacier in the Alps. Some 5,000 years old, this ancient hunter's body was adorned with 15 tattoos (Randall and Polhemus 1996). In order to appreciate the history of tattooing, one must appreciate its social logic and functions.

The social-symbolic role that tattoos have played in society varies a great deal, depending on factors such as historical period, geography, economic development, innovation, and cultural diffusion. In ancient societies, tattoos, as well as other forms of permanent body modification, were most commonly associated with permanency in one's life (e.g., gender and maturity), lifelong social connections (e.g., tribe membership), or a celebrated appearance style that showed considerable continuity through dozens of generations (Randall and Polhemus 1996; Sanders 1988). The permanency of the tattoo symbolized premodern society's need for social integration, order, and stability (Randall and Polhemus 1996). . . . The current trend in tattooing has been explained as serving a number of social-symbolic roles: as a mark of affiliation to express group commitment and belonging (e.g., the logo worn by Harley Davidson riders), as a mark of personal identity (e.g., a symbol that represents a unique personal experience), as a mark of resistance (e.g., a symbol that violates consumption codes), or as a mark of identity change (e.g., a symbol that emulates a media image) (Randall and Polhemus 1996; Sanders 1988; Velliquette et al. 1997).

The recent popular interest in tattoos, along with remarkable changes in the practices and styles of tattooing, has attracted a number of new artists, some of them classically trained at prestigious art institutes (e.g., the tattoo artist Jamie Summers; see Rubin 1988:256). The role the artist/tattooist plays becomes an important part of this "Tattoo Renaissance" (Rubin 1988:233). The tattooist engages in *impression management*[2] to set the stage for an artistic service encounter. For example, the tattooist sets an artistic tone by impressing upon the client that her shop is a studio, that her work is art, and that her identity is an artist (Sanders 1989). Thus tattooists who view themselves as artists are continually engaged in legitimation talk in order to neutralize the stigma that has been historically associated with tattooing (Sanders 1989). As tattoo artists legitimize their work as art, it seems that they in turn decrease the stigma for the consumer. This increased recognition of tattooing as an art form has not only led to its development as a creative medium for some artists, it has also led to a new creative form of expression for the consumer (Rubin 1988; Velliquette et al. 1997). The consumer engages in experiential consumption, and through negotiated order with the artist, the consumer embarks upon a symbolic journey where the choice in artist, design, colors, and body location are all linked to the consumer's personal experiences and sense of identity (Sanders 1988).

In summary, a review of literature suggests two central a priori themes: *collective legitimization*, and *self-identity*. These themes are not mutually exclusive, but rather are intertwined analytical categories that are useful for the framework of discovery. Further, to allow for a discussion of several aspects of interaction, several "sensitizing concepts" are introduced within each theme (Blumer 1969:147–48).

. . .

Ethnographic Method and Setting

Tattooing is one topic that "demands a plunge into the waters, not a comfortable observer's beach chair at the side of the ocean" (Steward 1990:198). According to Blumer (1969) and Hebdige (1979), immersion in the field (or hovering close) produces some of the most compelling and evocative accounts of subculture and human interaction. Given the symbolic complexity associated with the artist-client interaction, the choice of design, and the act of becoming tattooed, we decided to use ethnographic interviews and participant observation as our primary data gathering techniques.

We collected the majority of the text for this study over a six-month period in 1996. We returned to the field in 1997 for approximately two to three months in order to follow up on questions regarding support for both *a priori* and emerging themes grounded in the data. The text consists of over 400 pages of typed fieldnotes composed immediately after each participant observation in the everyday activities of two tattoo studios. Generally, we spent two to four hours at a time, at least once a week, in one of the studios, helping to maintain files of tattoo designs, working behind the front desk, sitting with customers as they were tattooed, assisting with some technical procedures, interviewing customers, and interviewing artists when they were not tattooing. . . . In addition to participating in the studios, we collected fieldnotes and took photographs at a 1996 national tattoo convention and two tattoo artwork museum gallery exhibitions. Further, in order to gain more historical appreciation, we traveled to the Tattoo Archive in Berkeley, California. The Tattoo Archive is a national museum of tattoo history and collectibles. We spent four days collecting relevant information and interviewing the curator.

Although the primary goal of ethnography is immersion in the lifeworlds and everyday experiences of a group of people, the researcher inevitably remains an outsider (Emerson, Fretz, and Shaw 1995). Since both "outsider" and "insider" perspectives are important in this type of research (Rubin 1988:11, n. 2), we decided to reinforce an insider's perspective by becoming tattooed. I (first author) chose a *cat* (ankle) for my first tattoo and a *butterfly* (lower front hip) for my second. . . . I carefully recorded the details of this experience in a private journal. These notes also became part of the text.

. . .

Findings from the Field

As expected, we found support for many of the *collective legitimization* issues that had been discussed in previous literature on tattooing. For example, we found that tattooists often tried to convince their clients that tattooing is an art form and that "tattoos aren't just for bikers anymore" (fieldnotes January 31, 1996). The tattooists worked hard to legitimize their field of work by becoming certified, referring to themselves as artists, attending national tattoo conventions, showing their work at local art galleries, and studying other artists in the field. The artists often conversed about different tattoo artists' reputations in the field, often ranking them in terms of their favorites. . . . The artists also discussed how bored they get with customer-requested designs that do not allow them to use their creative, artistic talent. One artist referred to these simplistic, uncreative designs as "cartoon characters." This artist hated these simple designs because she felt "like a kid coloring in a coloring book. . . . Something you do when you're five years old" (fieldnotes April 15, 1997).

The artist says to me, "The owner is tired of doing the small cartoon characters like the tazmanian devil. . . . She hates doing that shit. She is into the big pieces that she can really get creative with. . . . You know, custom work." (fieldnotes April 9, 1997)

We also found that the artists worked hard to impress upon their clients that their studios were clean and met all of the health department's regulations. Several neutralization tactics were employed by the artists to change the perceptions of those individuals who viewed tattooing as deviant and tattoo shops as dirty, underground holes where deviants hung out. The following passage represents an attempt to neutralize the tattooing experience:

The male artist calls the Irish man back to the room and I stay to watch. The artist sits him down in the chair and shows him the needles that will be used. The artist tells him they are clean, new needles and that they are sealed in the bags. I ask the artist to repeat what he said and he says, "I like to let the customers see that the needles are new and sterile. I would want to see that if I were the customer." The artist then cuts open the sealed bags to get the needles out. (fieldnotes March 1, 1997)

The owners of the tattoo studios worked hard to legitimize their businesses further by creating a clinical atmosphere. For example, in the client rooms where tattooing took place, there were several glass jars on the counter filled with supplies (e.g., cotton, disposable razors, gauze), paper towels, antiseptic cleaning sprays, lotions, ointments, and tattooing equipment (e.g., guns, disposable ink trays, and ink). Some of the equipment was displayed on the wall (e.g., pliers and parts to the gun). There were also boxes of surgical gloves on the counter, a washing sink, and a hazardous waste container for disposal of needles and other infectious material. The room had an appearance similar to that of a doctor's office.

Although the tattoo artists employed these neutralization tactics, a certain amount of stigma remained, as viewed and expressed by a few informants. One informant described how he thought others would react to his tattoos in his profession: "I know it is not totally acceptable. I would catch crap if I ever showed up here in the future to teach with my tattoos hanging out. . . . They would lay down and die!" (fieldnotes April 17, 1997). Several customers stated that there are levels of social acceptance for various kinds of tattoos. One informant explained how the sun design she wanted on her hip was more socially acceptable than a skull and crossbones on a person's chest. To further illustrate the stigma associated with tattoos, we provide the following quoted passage:

I want to get it where I can cover it up. You know, so my mom won't see it. My mom hates tattoos. She lives in a place where she associates all tattoos with gang members. (fieldnotes March 1, 1997)

As discussed in the literature, collective legitimization is a process of *impression management* (Goffman 1959). Early in the ethnography, it became apparent that, in many respects, tattooists are performers. We often observed tattooists putting on a public display of professionalism. For example, tattooists often impressed upon their clients that they were artistic, friendly, and most of all technically competent and sterile. The following passage is representative of this theme:

> The artist and I continue to talk and she tells me "I was so nervous when I had to do my first tongue piercing." She then tells me she was shaking when she did it which made the guy nervous. Then the artist said, "You really have to pretend like you know what the hell you are doing." (fieldnotes February 15, 1997)

Within the studio setting, we observed the tattooists spending their time in two different regions: the front stage and the back stage areas of the shop. In the front stage, "permanent cosmetic/tattoo artist" certificates were hung on the wall in the lobby. The walls in the lobby area were covered with photographs of tattoos given to previous clients: the best and most unique work made the "wall." The wall attracted customers who were entering the shop and added to the credibility of the artists. Also included in the front stage region were the rooms where clients became tattooed. In the front stage region, including both the lobby and the tattoo rooms, we often observed tattooists engaging in what Goffman (1959:80) refers to as "team performance."

> The artist is finishing a large, colorful, elaborate design with a horse, clouds, and moon on a woman's arm. The artist calls the other artist in to come and look at the work. The female artist says, "This design is a dual effort between me and _____." The male artist had done the outline the week before and now the female artist was adding color. They were both happy with the results of their work. They complimented one another's artistic work (telling each other how good they were) in front of the client. (fieldnotes March 1, 1997)

Another important concept related to impression management is emotion management. The artists often managed their emotions when in the presence of clients. The artists typically refrained from displaying disappointment, anger, disgust, or impatience when interacting with their customers.

> A guy came in looking for someone to quote him a price on some touch-up work. The owner asked him where he got the tattoo done and he replied, "By a friend of mine in Oklahoma City. He is a paraplegic and he does real good work. I just don't want to have to drive to OK City to have it touched up." After he left the owner said, "He thought that was a good tattoo?" She then said, "It was hard not to laugh!! You really have to control yourself from laughing in situations like that." (fieldnotes March 28, 1997)

The tattooists usually segregated their audiences by keeping conversations like this one within the circle of the other artists. However, a few instances were observed where this segregation did not take place and customers were allowed to hear backstage talk:

> The male artist assists this time on a tongue piercing. The owner talks to the male artist about piercing and tells him the first time she did a navel, she was extremely nervous. She says this in front of the customer as if he is not there. She then says "The only way to really practice is to just get in there and do one." The customer then asks with a nervous tone of voice, "Is this your first one?" He says this with surprise and anxiety. She said, "Oh no, I have done many, I am just saying that this is really the only way to get used to it." The male artist then tells the guy (as if to calm him down), "Everything we are using on you is sterile." The guy sits still as the two artists pierce his tongue and the client's friend and I watch. (field-notes March 19, 1997)

In the tattoo studio, the artists attempted to gain and maintain control during the service encounter by *negotiating order* (Strauss 1990). The artists claimed that the average client's lack of experience and knowledge necessitated the need for the artist to be in control at all times to ensure a successful interaction.

. . .

As we observed, most negotiations appeared to go smoothly during artist–client interactions. A working consensus was usually achieved, because most clients seemed to realize the artist's role as the expert in the situation.

> The female customer then said, "It is not the pain I am worried about. . . . I just want to know where it will look best." The owner replies, "Well, ankles are a nice place because the skin is so smooth and tight there, so it is easier to tattoo a nice design on the ankle. The skin is stretched tight on the ankle unlike the spongy skin of the breast, stomach, back or hip area." The owner then also tells her that the "shoulders [back] make a nice canvas as well." The artist refers to the skin as canvas for the ink. . . . The girl continues to ask the owner for advice on colors, size, and location. (field-notes February 15, 1997)

It appeared to us that most interactions were controlled by the artists. It was discovered rather quickly that the customer is literally in the tattooist's hands.

> The artist didn't like the way she had drawn the leaf. She said she had kind of made a mistake when tattooing it. I asked her about making mistakes. She said, "It happens. . . . When you make a mistake, you just cover it up. The customer won't ever know." I thought about this and realized that the customer usually can't see what is going on up-close during the process and that they probably wouldn't know if a mistake had been made. (fieldnotes February 22, 1997)

Although most interactions and negotiations went smoothly, there were instances where this was not the case. The artists labeled the clients involved in the unsuccessful interactions as "bad clients" and the customers involved in the successful interactions as "good clients." The following passages provide examples of "bad clients" as defined by the artists:

> The owner explains, "This chick came in the other day for a navel piercing and she had the dirtiest belly button I had ever seen! It took me five minutes to pick all of the shit out of it! I thought about charging her extra just for that!" (fieldnotes April 9, 1997)

> The artist defines bad customers: "The ones where price is the most important thing. . . . The customers that will let you run with it and do whatever you want to, those are the great ones. . . . Unfortunately there aren't many of those. . . . Most people say, "I can only afford 50 dollars' worth." I sometimes give them a few free colors just to make it look better. . . . The whiny ones are bad too, when you step on your pedal and you're not even touching them and they are like, 'Ow! Quit!' you know. . . . You just feel like slapping them." (fieldnotes April 15, 1997)

. . .

It was very common for customers to bring friends with them for support during the tattooing procedure. The social support often helped the potential client with such decisions as choice of design, size, colors, and body location. Friends offered further support by engaging in conversation to keep the client's mind off the painful procedure. We also observed this type of conversational support between the artists and their clients. One artist described how she felt this conversational support was part of the job:

> *You get to talk to a lot of people. Sitting there with them for an hour or an hour and a half, you get to talking and make new friends. We're actually like bartenders you know, people cry on our shoulder. . . . You usually know their life story by the time they leave.* (fieldnotes April 15, 1997)

The second *a priori* theme identified in the literature reveals how tattoos are used to reinforce one's *self-identity*. We discovered that the use of tattoos to express one's inner self was probably the most commonly stated motivation for acquiring a tattoo. In this context, the tattoo becomes an extension of the person, symbolizing the person's narrative story. One informant described how becoming tattooed "is more of a reflection of who you think you are" (fieldnotes April 17, 1997). As one artist explained, "The tattoo is already there inside those who really want it, it is already a part of them, the tattoo artist just brings it out." (fieldnotes July 12, 1996)

. . .

One of the informants, who had acquired tattoos from 35 different artists, described his tattoos as a "scrapbook" symbolizing his life story:

> I asked him if there was one he favored or if any particular one had great meaning. He said, "They all do." He told me that he considers his tattoo art work "his personal scrapbook." Each and every tattoo reminds the informant of a person, place, time or period in his life. A personal scrapbook of one's life or self. (fieldnotes July 12, 1996)

During the ethnography, we discovered that customers choose tattoos to represent who they are in different ways. Some choose symbols for personal distinction, whereas others choose symbols for integration purposes. Both cases contributed to an expression of identity: the former case seemed to represent one's personal identity whereas the latter case represented one's social identity. One informant described how tattoos distinguish him from others in a crowd (and help create a sense of personal identity):

> *When you make the decision, 'I'm going to be a person with a tattoo,' you know you are different from most people. . . . Just the bottom line, standing in the line at Wal-Mart, I know I'm different. . . . It is fun being different, it is even more fun being more different.* (fieldnotes April 17, 1997)

Other examples from interviews in which the tattoo symbolized the owner's personal identity include a Mickey Mouse tattooed to the informant's arm because his grandfather called him "Mickey"; a butterfly tattooed to the client's hip symbolizing her given name; a rattlesnake design chosen in memory of being bitten and almost dying; a rose tattooed on the wrist for every child born and a butterfly tattooed on the ankle for every family member who had died; and a cat design that reflected a woman's long history of living with and loving cats. There were other instances where the design seemed to represent the client's social identity (integration):

> Back at the counter, a young man (30s) with an Irish accent comes in and asks to see the hog file. The owner asks him to clarify what kind of hog and he says, "You know, a razorback." Shortly after that remark he says, "I am not getting a hog because of THE Razorbacks basketball team, the hog is part of my family crest. It looks just like the razorback, only it's not running. . . . It is just standing there." I ask him where he is from and he says "Dublin." He then tells me that every family name has a crest and that his has the hog in the design. (fieldnotes March 1, 1997)

Often the process of becoming tattooed could be explained as experiential consumption (Holbrook and Hirschman 1982), where the event was tied to a meaningful experience. The following passages are representative of this concept:

> The two girls who were best friends got matching tattoos on vacation in Mexico to bond their friendship. I ask her why the tribal piece and she

says, "I don't know, we didn't really care what the design was. . . . We just wanted something simple . . . to represent our friendship." (fieldnotes April 15, 1997)

A young woman comes in (WF 20) with her mother to get a tattoo of a moon and fairy. She tells me that she had drawn the design herself. This will be her fourth tattoo as she has gotten one every year for her birthday since she was 16 years old. (fieldnotes March 19, 1997)

As discovered in this ethnography, tattoos are consumed for many different reasons. Most informants agreed, however, that tattoos are a form of self-expression, a way to communicate to others some aspect of the wearer's self-identity.

. . .

Discussion and Conclusions

The preceding review of literature and ethnographic account suggests some feasible answers to the research questions stated in the introduction: What is it about the tattoo as a cultural object that draws people to participate in the tattoo subculture? In what ways is the tattoo used as a form of expression? What is involved in the experience of acquiring a tattoo? What transpires during the service interaction between the tattooist and tattooee? The a priori and emergent themes suggest that there are many reasons why individuals are drawn to participate in the new tattoo subculture. A subculture "signifies a way of life of a group of people" and is "characterized by interaction, continuity, and outsider and insider definitions of distinctiveness" (Prus 1996: 85). The tattoo subculture is no different in that the tattoo as a cultural object attracts people who want to express difference as well as integration. In this realm, the tattoo indicates the separate domains to which its wearers belong, while it expresses unity and connects otherwise diverse domains. For example, as we discovered in this ethnography, the tattoo was a common bond among all informants regardless of social class or background. Further, the tattoo was a form of distinction, separating the informants from the rest of society, or the non-tattooed.

Another reason that members are drawn to this subculture can be attributed to the phenomenon of certain objects becoming so firmly associated with an individual that they are understood as literal extensions of that individual's being. The tattoo as a cultural object is a "document that describes our past, an image that reflects our present, and a sign that calls us into the future" (Richardson 1989). Informants used tattoos to express symbolically the meanings they attached to themselves from past, present, and future perspectives. In other words, tattoos were used both to reflect one's past or current identity and to construct and revise one's future identity. Two of the most important themes used to represent this idea are *self-identity* and *simulated self*. Following the ideas presented under the self-identity theme, most informants used the tattoo to express the inner self; "to bring a little bit or a lot of their inner self out for others to see" (fieldnotes March 31, 1996). In this sense, tattoos were extensions of self-conceptions. In contrast, with the simulated self, informants believed that by adopting a symbol, they were changing their images and becoming someone different.

We conclude by stating that it is important and most "useful to examine subcultures by understanding the identities people achieve as participants, the activities deemed consequential in that context, the bonds participants develop with one another, and the sorts of commitments the people involved make with respect to the setting at hand" (Prus 1996:85). This study has achieved such a thorough examination of the new tattoo subculture. If the implications of the examples surveyed in this research can be summarized into a single idea, that idea would be the importance of cultural objects in constituting culture and human relations. Cultural artifacts, such as the tattoo, have properties and tendencies that in an era where material culture is rapidly increasing, deserve to be investigated in their own right.

NOTES

1. The modifier *New* signifies the recent expansion of popular interest in tattooing as a form of marking identity (Krakow 1994; Lautman 1994; Randall and Polhemus 1996; Velliquette et al. 1997).
2. Erving Goffman (1959) argues that in everyday life, there is a clear understanding that first impressions are important and seldom overlooked. Those in service occupations have many motives for trying to control the impression they present during the service encounter. This process is called *impression management.*

REFERENCES

American Business Information, Inc. 1996. "1996 Business Changes Report." Omaha, NE: Marketing Research Division. Jeff Ferris, Project Manager.

Ball, Keith, ed. 1996. "Skin and Bones: Tools of the Trade." *Tattoo* 82 (June): 76–79.

Blouin, Melissa, ed. 1996. "Tattoo You: Health Experts Worried about Artful Trend." *Northwest Arkansas Times*, July 14, p. C4.

Blumer, Herbert. 1969. *Symbolic Interactionism: Perspective and Method.* Englewood Cliffs, NJ: Prentice-Hall.

Bohannan, Paul. 1988. "Beauty and Scarification amongst the Tiv." Pp. 77–82 in *Marks of Civilization,* edited by Arnold Rubin. Los Angeles: Museum of Cultural History.

Drewal, Henry John. 1988. "Beauty and Being: Aesthetics and Ontology in Yoruba Body Art." Pp. 83–96 in *Marks of Civilization,* edited by Arnold Rubin. Los Angeles: Museum of Cultural History.

Emerson, Robert M., Rachael I. Fretz, and Linda L. Shaw. 1995. *Writing Ethnographic Fieldnotes.* Chicago: University of Chicago Press.

Finkelstein, Joanne. 1991. *The Fashioned Self.* Philadelphia: Temple University Press.

Gathercole, Peter. 1988. "Contexts of Maori Moko." Pp. 171–78 in *Marks of Civilization,* edited by Arnold Rubin. Los Angeles: Museum of Cultural History.

Goffman, Erving. 1959. *The Presentation of Self in Everyday Life.* New York: Doubleday.

Gritton, Joy. 1988. "Labrets and Tattooing in Native Alaska." Pp. 181–90 in *Marks of Civilization,* edited by Arnold Rubin. Los Angeles: Museum of Cultural History.

Hebdige, Dick. 1979. *Subculture: The Meaning of Style.* New York: Routledge.

Holbrook, Morris B. and Elizabeth C. Hirschman. 1982. "The Experiential Aspects of Consumption: Consumer Fantasies, Feelings, and Fun." *Journal of Consumer Research* 9 (September): 132–40.

Krakow, Amy. 1994. *Total Tattoo Book.* New York: Warner Books.

Lautman, Victoria. 1994. *The New Tattoo.* New York, London, and Paris: Abbeville Press.

Myers, James. 1992. "Nonmainstream Body Modification: Genital Piercing, Branding, Burning, and Cutting." *Journal of Contemporary Ethnography* 21(3): 267–306.

Peterson, Andrea. 1996. "Parents Spur Laws against Tattoos for Kids." *Wall Street Journal,* September, B1–B2.

Prus, Robert. 1996. *Symbolic Interaction and Ethnographic Research: Intersubjectivity and the Study of Human Lived Experience.* Albany, NY: State University of New York Press.

Randall, Housk and Ted Polhemus. 1996. *The Customized Body.* London and New York: Serpent's Tail.

Rubin, Arnold. 1988. "The Tattoo Renaissance." Pp. 233–62 in *Marks of Civilization,* Arnold Rubin. Los Angeles: Museum of Cultural History.

Sanders, Clinton R. 1988. "Drill and Frill: Client Choice, Client Typologies, and Interactional Control in Commercial Tattoo Settings." Pp. 219–33 in *Marks of Civilization,* edited by Arnold Rubin. Los Angeles: Museum of Cultural History.

———. 1989. "Organizational Constraints on Tattoo Images: A Sociological Analysis of Artistic Style." Pp. 232–41 in *The Meaning of Things,* edited by Ian Hodder. London: Unwin Hyman.

Steward, Samuel M. 1990. *Bad Boys and Tough Tattoos: A Social History of the Tattoo with Gangs, Sailors, and Street Corner Punks, 1950–1965.* New York: Harrington Park Press.

Velliquette, Anne M., Jeff B. Murray, and Elizabeth H. Creyer. Forthcoming. "The Tattoo Renaissance: An Ethnographic Account of Symbolic Consumer Behavior." *Advances in Consumer Research.*

8

THE CODE OF THE STREETS

ELIJAH ANDERSON

In this selection, adapted from *Streetwise: Race, Class, and Change in an Urban Community* (1990), Elijah Anderson demonstrates how cultural values create new standards for behavior. Anderson analyzes the social norms governing street behavior and violence in the inner city. The resulting "code" is a complex system of norms, dress, rituals, and expected behavior. In order to survive within the subculture of the inner city, children and adults must learn the code and adapt their lives accordingly.

Of all the problems besetting the poor inner-city black community, none is more pressing than that of interpersonal violence and aggression. It wreaks havoc daily with the lives of community residents and increasingly spills over into downtown and residential middle-class areas. Muggings, burglaries, carjackings, and drug-related shootings, all of which may leave their victims or innocent bystanders dead, are now common enough to concern all urban and many suburban residents. The inclination to violence springs from the circumstances of life among the ghetto poor—the lack of jobs that pay a living wage, the stigma of race, the fallout from rampant drug use and drug trafficking, and the resulting alienation and lack of hope for the future.

Simply living in such an environment places young people at special risk of falling victim to aggressive behavior. Although there are often forces in the community which can counteract the negative influences, by far the most powerful being a strong, loving, "decent" (as inner-city residents put it) family committed to middle-class values, the despair is pervasive enough to have spawned an oppositional culture, that of "the streets," whose norms are often consciously opposed to those of mainstream society. These two orientations—decent and street—socially organize the community, and their coexistence has important consequences for residents, particularly children growing up in the inner city. Above all, this environment means that even youngsters whose home lives reflect mainstream values—and the majority of homes in the community do—must be able to handle themselves in a street-oriented environment.

From *The Code of the Streets*. Originally in *The Atlantic Monthly* 273, no. 5 (May 1994): 81–94. Copyright © 1994 by Elijah Anderson. Reprinted with the permission of W. W. Norton & Company, Inc.

This is because the street culture has evolved what may be called a code of the streets, which amounts to a set of informal rules governing interpersonal public behavior, including violence. The rules prescribe both a proper comportment and a proper way to respond if challenged. They regulate the use of violence and so allow those who are inclined to aggression to precipitate violent encounters in an approved way. The rules have been established and are enforced mainly by the street-oriented, but on the streets the distinction between street and decent is often irrelevant; everybody knows that if the rules are violated, there are penalties. Knowledge of the code is thus largely defensive; it is literally necessary for operating in public. Therefore, even though families with a decency orientation are usually opposed to the values of the code, they often reluctantly encourage their children's familiarity with it to enable them to negotiate the inner-city environment.

At the heart of the code is the issue of respect—loosely defined as being treated "right," or granted the deference one deserves. However, in the troublesome public environment of the inner city, as people increasingly feel buffeted by forces beyond their control, what one deserves in the way of respect becomes more and more problematic and uncertain. This in turn further opens the issue of respect to sometimes intense interpersonal negotiation. In the street culture, especially among young people, respect is viewed as almost an external entity that is hard-won but easily lost, and so must constantly be guarded. The rules of the code in fact provide a framework for negotiating respect. The person whose very appearance—including his clothing, demeanor, and way of moving—deters transgressions feels that he possesses, and may be considered by others to possess, a measure of respect. With the right amount of respect, for instance, he can avoid "being bothered" in public. If he is bothered, not only may he be in physical danger but he has been disgraced or "dissed" (disrespected). Many of the forms that dissing can take might seem petty to middle-class people (maintaining eye contact for too long, for example), but to those invested in the street code, these actions become serious indications of the other person's intentions. Consequently, such people become very sensitive to advances and slights, which could well serve as warnings of imminent physical confrontation.

This hard reality can be traced to the profound sense of alienation from mainstream society and its institutions felt by many poor inner-city black people, particularly the young. The code of the streets is actually a cultural adaptation to a profound lack of faith in the police and the judicial system. The police are most often seen as representing the dominant white society and not caring to protect inner-city residents. When called, they may not respond, which is one reason many residents feel they must be prepared to take extraordinary measures to defend themselves and their loved ones against those who are inclined to aggression. Lack of police accountability has in fact been incorporated into the status system: The person who is believed capable of "taking care of himself" is accorded a certain deference, which translates into a sense of physical and psychological control. Thus the street code emerges where the influence of the police ends and personal responsibility for one's safety is felt to begin. Exacerbated by the proliferation of drugs and easy access to guns, this volatile situation results in the ability of the street-oriented minority (or those who effectively "go for bad") to dominate the public spaces.

Decent and Street Families

Although almost everyone in poor inner-city neighborhoods is struggling financially and therefore feels a certain distance from the rest of America, the decent and the street family in a real sense represent two poles of value orientation, two contrasting conceptual categories. The labels "decent" and "street," which the residents themselves use, amount to evaluative judgments that confer status on local residents. The labeling is often the result of a social contest among individuals and families of the neighborhood. Individuals of the two orientations often coexist in the same extended family. Decent residents judge themselves to be so while judging others to be of the street, and street individuals often present themselves as decent, drawing distinctions between themselves and other people. In addition, there is quite a bit of circumstantial behavior—that is, one person may at different times exhibit both decent and street orientations, depending on the circumstances. Although these designations result from so much social jockeying, there do exist concrete features that define each conceptual category.

Generally, so-called decent families tend to accept mainstream values more fully and attempt to instill them in their children. Whether married couples with children or single-parent (usually female) households, they are generally "working poor" and so tend to be better off financially than their street-oriented neighbors. They value hard work and self-reliance and are willing to sacrifice for their children. Because they have a certain amount of faith in mainstream society, they harbor hopes for a better future for their children, if not for themselves. Many of them go to church and take a strong interest in their children's schooling. Rather than dwelling on the real hardships and inequities facing them, many such decent people, particularly the increasing number of grandmothers raising grandchildren, see their difficult situation as a test from God and derive great support from their faith and from the church community.

Extremely aware of the problematic and often dangerous environment in which they reside, decent parents tend to be strict in their child-rearing practices, encouraging children to respect authority and walk a straight moral line. They have an almost obsessive concern about trouble of any kind and remind their children to be on the lookout for people and situations that might lead to it. At the same time, they are themselves polite and considerate of others, and teach their children to be the same way. At home, at work, and in church, they strive hard to maintain a positive mental attitude and a spirit of cooperation.

So-called street parents, in contrast, often show a lack of consideration for other people and have a rather superficial sense of family and community. Though they may love their children, many of them are unable to cope with the physical and emotional demands of parenthood and find it difficult to reconcile their needs with those of their children. These families, who are more fully invested in the code of the streets than the decent people are, may aggressively socialize their children into it in a normative way. They believe in the code and judge themselves and others according to its values.

. . .

Campaigning for Respect

[The] realities of inner-city life are largely absorbed on the streets. At an early age, often even before they start school, children from street-oriented homes gravitate to the streets, where they "hang"—socialize with their peers. Children from these generally permissive homes have a great deal of latitude and are allowed to "rip and run" up and down the street. They often come home from school, put their books down, and go right back out the door. On school nights eight- and nine-year-olds remain out until nine or ten o'clock (and teenagers typically come in whenever they want to). On the streets they play in groups that often become the source of their primary social bonds. Children from decent homes tend to be more carefully supervised and are thus likely to have curfews and to be taught how to stay out of trouble.

When decent and street kids come together, a kind of social shuffle occurs in which children have a chance to go either way. Tension builds as a child comes to realize that he must choose an orientation. The kind of home he comes from influences but does not determine the way he will ultimately turn out—although it is unlikely that a child from a thoroughly street-oriented family will easily absorb decent values on the streets. Youths who emerge from street-oriented families but develop a decency orientation almost always learn those values in another setting—in school, in a youth group, in church. Often it is the result of their involvement with a caring "old head" (adult role model).

In the street, through their play, children pour their individual life experiences into a common knowledge pool, affirming, confirming, and elaborating on what they have observed in the home and matching their skills against those of others. And they learn to fight. Even small children test one another, pushing and shoving, and are ready to hit other children over circumstances not to their liking. In turn, they are readily hit by other children, and the child who is toughest prevails. Thus the violent resolution of disputes, the hitting and cursing, gains social reinforcement. The child in effect is initiated into a system that is really a way of campaigning for respect.

In addition, younger children witness the disputes of older children, which are often resolved through cursing and abusive talk, if not aggression or outright violence. They see that one child succumbs to the greater physical and mental abilities of the other. They are also alert and attentive witnesses to the verbal and physical fights of adults, after which they compare notes and share their interpretations of the event. In almost every case the victor is the person who physically won the altercation, and this person often enjoys the esteem and respect of onlookers. These experiences reinforce the lessons the children have learned at home: Might makes right, and toughness is a virtue, while humility is not. In effect they learn the social meaning of fighting. When it is left virtually unchallenged, this understanding becomes an ever more important part of the child's working conception of the world. Over time the code of the streets becomes refined.

Those street-oriented adults with whom children come in contact—including mothers, fathers, brothers, sisters, boyfriends, cousins, neighbors, and friends—help them along in forming this understanding by verbalizing the messages they are getting through experience: "Watch your back." "Protect yourself." "Don't punk out." "If somebody messes with you, you got to pay them back." "If someone disses you, you got to straighten them out." Many parents actually impose sanctions if a child is not sufficiently aggressive. For example, if a child loses a fight and comes home upset, the parent might respond, "Don't you come in here crying that somebody beat you up; you better get back out there and whup his ass. I didn't raise no punks! Get back out there and whup his ass. If you don't whup his ass, I'll whup your ass when you come home." Thus the child obtains reinforcement for being tough and showing nerve.

While fighting, some children cry as though they are doing something they are ambivalent about. The fight may be against their wishes, yet they may feel constrained to fight or face the consequences—not just from peers but also from caretakers or parents, who may administer another beating if they back down. Some adults recall receiving such lessons from their own parents and justify repeating them to their children as a way to toughen them up. Looking capable of taking care of oneself as a form of self-defense is a dominant theme among both street-oriented and decent adults who worry about the safety of their children. There is thus at times a convergence in their child-rearing practices, although the rationales behind them may differ.

Self-Image Based on "Juice"

By the time they are teenagers, most youths have either internalized the code of the streets or at least learned the need to comport themselves in accordance with its rules, which chiefly have to do with interpersonal communication. The code revolves around the presentation of self. Its basic requirement is the display of a certain predisposition to violence. Accordingly, one's bearing must send the unmistakable if sometimes subtle message to "the next person" in public that one is capable of violence and mayhem when the situation requires it, that one can take care of oneself. The nature of this communication is largely determined by the demands of the circumstances but can include facial expressions, gait, and verbal expressions—all of which are geared mainly to deterring aggression. Physical appearance, including clothes, jewelry, and grooming, also plays an important part in how a person is viewed; to be respected, it is important to have the right look.

Even so, there are no guarantees against challenges because there are always people around looking for a fight to increase their share of respect— or "juice," as it is sometimes called on the street. Moreover, if a person is assaulted, it is important, not only in the eyes of his opponent but also in the eyes of his "running buddies," for him to avenge himself. Otherwise he risks being "tried" (challenged) or "moved on" by any number of others. To maintain his honor he must show he is not someone to be "messed with" or "dissed." In general, the person must "keep himself straight" by managing his position of respect among others; this involves in part his self-image, which is shaped by what he thinks others are thinking of him in relation to his peers.

Objects play an important and complicated role in establishing self-image. Jackets, sneakers, gold jewelry, reflect not just a person's taste, which tends to be tightly regulated among adolescents of all social classes, but also a willingness to possess things that may require defending. A boy wearing a fashionable, expensive jacket, for example, is vulnerable to attack by another who covets the jacket and either cannot afford to buy one or wants the added satisfaction of depriving someone else of his. However, if the boy forgoes the desirable jacket and wears one that isn't "hip," he runs the risk of being teased and possibly even assaulted as an unworthy person. To be allowed to hang with certain prestigious crowds, a boy must wear a different set of expensive clothes—sneakers and athletic suit—every day. Not to be able to do so might make him appear socially deficient. The youth comes to covet such items— especially when he sees easy prey wearing them.

In acquiring valued things, therefore, a person shores up his identity— but since it is an identity based on having things, it is highly precarious. This very precariousness gives a heightened sense of urgency to staying even with peers, with whom the person is actually competing. Young men and women who are able to command respect through their presentation of self—by allowing their possessions and their body language to speak for them—may not have to campaign for regard but may, rather, gain it by the force of their manner. Those who are unable to command respect in this way must actively campaign for it—and are thus particularly alive to slights.

One way of campaigning for status is by taking the possessions of others. In this context, seemingly ordinary objects can become trophies imbued with symbolic value that far exceeds their monetary worth. Possession of the trophy can symbolize the ability to violate somebody—to "get in his face," to take something of value from him, to "dis" him, and thus to enhance one's own worth by stealing someone else's. The trophy does not have to be something material. It can be another person's sense of honor, snatched away with a derogatory remark. It can be the outcome of a fight. It can be the imposition of a certain standard, such as a girl's getting herself recognized as the most beautiful. Material things, however, fit easily into the pattern. Sneakers, a pistol, even somebody else's girlfriend, can become a trophy. When a person can take something from another and then flaunt it, he gains a certain regard by being the owner, or the controller, of that thing. But this display of ownership can then provoke other people to challenge him. This game of who controls what is thus constantly being played out on inner-city streets, and the trophy—extrinsic or intrinsic, tangible or intangible—identifies the current winner.

An important aspect of this often violent give-and-take is its zero-sum quality. That is, the extent to which one person can raise himself up depends on his ability to put another person down. This underscores the alienation that permeates the inner-city ghetto community. There is a generalized sense that very little respect is to be had, and therefore everyone competes to get what affirmation he can of the little that is available. The craving for respect that results gives people thin skins. Shows of deference by others can be highly soothing, contributing to a sense of security, comfort, self-confidence, and self-respect. Transgressions by others which go unanswered diminish these feelings and are believed to encourage further transgressions. Hence one must be ever vigilant against the transgressions of others or even *appearing* as if transgressions will be tolerated. Among young people, whose sense of self-esteem is particularly vulnerable, there is an especially heightened concern with being disrespected. Many inner-city young men in particular crave respect to such a degree that they will risk their lives to attain and maintain it.

The issue of respect is thus closely tied to whether a person has an inclination to be violent, even as a victim. In the wider society people may not feel required to retaliate physically after an attack, even though they are aware that they have been degraded or taken advantage of. They may feel a great need to defend themselves *during* an attack, or to behave in such a way as to deter aggression (middle-class people certainly can and do become victims of street-oriented youths), but they are much more likely than street-oriented people to feel that they can walk away from a possible altercation with their self-esteem intact. Some people may even have the strength of character to flee, without any thought that their self-respect or esteem will be diminished.

In impoverished inner-city black communities, however, particularly among young males and perhaps increasingly among females, such flight would be extremely difficult. To run away would likely leave one's self-esteem in tatters. Hence people often feel constrained not only to stand up and at least attempt to resist during an assault but also to "pay back"—to seek revenge—after a successful assault on their person. This may include going to get a weapon or even getting relatives involved. Their very identity and self-respect, their honor, is often intricately tied up with the way they perform on the streets during and after such encounters. This outlook reflects the circumscribed opportunities of the inner-city poor. Generally people outside the ghetto have other ways of gaining status and regard, and thus do not feel so dependent on such physical displays.

By Trial of Manhood

On the street, among males these concerns about things and identity have come to be expressed in the concept of "manhood." Manhood in the inner city means taking the prerogatives of men with respect to strangers, other men, and women—being distinguished as a man. It implies physicality and a certain ruthlessness. Regard and respect are associated with this concept in large part because of its practical application: If others have little or no regard for a person's manhood, his very life and those of his loved ones could be in jeopardy. But there is a chicken-and-egg aspect to this situation: One's physical safety is more likely to be jeopardized in public *because* manhood is associated with respect. In other words, an existential link has been created between the idea of manhood and one's self-esteem, so that it has become hard to say which is primary. For many inner-city youths, manhood and respect are flip sides of the same coin; physical and psychological well-being are inseparable, and both require a sense of control, of being in charge.

The operating assumption is that a man, especially a real man, knows what other men know—the code of the streets. And if one is not a real man, one is somehow diminished as a person, and there are certain valued things one simply does not deserve. There is thus believed to be a certain justice to the code, since it is considered that everyone has the opportunity to know it. Implicit in this is that everybody is held responsible for being familiar with the code. If the victim of a mugging, for example, does not know the code and so responds "wrong," the perpetrator may feel justified even in killing him and may feel no remorse. He may think, "Too bad, but it's his fault. He should have known better."

So when a person ventures outside, he must adopt the code—a kind of shield, really—to prevent others from "messing with" him. In these circumstances it is easy for people to think they are being tried or tested by others even when this is not the case. For it is sensed that something extremely valuable is at stake in every interaction, and people are encouraged to rise to the occasion, particularly with strangers. For people who are unfamiliar with the code—generally people who live outside the inner city—the concern with respect in the most ordinary interactions can be frightening and incomprehensible. But for those who are invested in the code, the clear object of their demeanor is to discourage strangers from even thinking about testing their manhood. And the sense of power that attends the ability to deter others can be alluring even to those who know the code without being heavily invested in it—the decent inner-city youths. Thus a boy who has been leading a basically decent life can, in trying circumstances, suddenly resort to deadly force.

Central to the issue of manhood is the widespread belief that one of the most effective ways of gaining respect is to manifest "nerve." Nerve is shown when one takes another person's possessions (the more valuable the better), "messes with" someone's woman, throws the first punch, "gets in someone's face," or pulls a trigger. Its proper display helps on the spot to check others who would violate one's person and also helps to build a reputation that works to prevent future challenges. But since such a show of nerve is a forceful expression of disrespect toward the person on the receiving end, the victim may be greatly offended and seek to retaliate with equal or greater force. A display of nerve, therefore, can easily provoke a life-threatening response, and the background knowledge of that possibility has often been incorporated into the concept of nerve.

True nerve exposes a lack of fear of dying. Many feel that it is acceptable to risk dying over the principle of respect. In fact, among the hard-core street-oriented, the clear risk of violent death may be preferable to being "dissed" by another. The youths who have internalized this attitude and convincingly display it in their public bearing are among the most threatening people of all, for it is commonly assumed that they fear no man. As the people of the community say, "They are the baddest dudes on the street." They often lead an existential life that may acquire meaning only when they are faced with the possibility of imminent death. Not to be afraid to die is by implication to have few compunctions about taking another's life. Not to be afraid to die is the quid pro quo of being able to take somebody else's life— for the right reasons, if the situation demands it. When others believe this is one's position, it gives one a real sense of power on the streets. Such credibility is what many inner-city youths strive to achieve, whether they are decent or street-oriented, both because of its practical defensive value and because of the positive way it makes them feel about themselves. The difference between the decent and the street-oriented youth is often that the decent youth makes a conscious decision to appear tough and manly; in another setting—with teachers, say, or at his part-time job—he can be polite and deferential. The street-oriented youth, on the other hand, has made the concept of manhood a part of his very identity; he has difficulty manipulating it—it often controls him.

Girls and Boys

Increasingly, teenage girls are mimicking the boys and trying to have their own version of "manhood." Their goal is the same—to get respect, to be recognized as capable of setting or maintaining a certain standard. They try to achieve this end in the ways that have been established by the boys, including posturing, abusive language, and the use of violence to resolve disputes, but the issues for the girls are different. Although conflicts over turf and status exist among the girls, the majority of disputes seem rooted in assessments of beauty (which girl in a group is "the cutest"), competition over boyfriends, and attempts to regulate other people's knowledge of and opinions about a girl's behavior or that of someone close to her, especially her mother.

A major cause of conflicts among girls is "he say, she say." This practice begins in the early school years and continues through high school. It occurs when "people," particularly girls, talk about others, thus putting their "business in the streets." Usually one girl will say something negative about another in the group, most often behind the person's back. The remark will then get back to the person talked about. She may retaliate or her friends may feel required to "take up for" her. In essence this is a form of group gossiping in which individuals are negatively assessed and evaluated. As with much gossip, the things said may or may not be true, but the point is that such imputations can cast aspersions on a person's good name. The accused is required to defend herself against the slander, which can result in arguments and fights, often over little of real substance. Here again is the problem of low self-esteem, which encourages youngsters to be highly sensitive to slights and to be vulnerable to feeling easily "dissed." To avenge the dissing, a fight is usually necessary.

Because boys are believed to control violence, girls tend to defer to them in situations of conflict. Often if a girl is attacked or feels slighted, she will get a brother, uncle, or cousin to do her fighting for her. Increasingly, however, girls are doing their own fighting and are even asking their male relatives to teach them how to fight. Some girls form groups that attack other girls or take things from them. A hard-core segment of inner-city girls inclined toward violence seems to be developing. As one 13-year-old girl in a detention center for youths who have committed violent acts told me, "To get people to leave you alone, you gotta fight. Talking don't always get you out of stuff." One major difference between girls and boys: Girls rarely use guns. Their fights are therefore not life-or-death struggles. Girls are not often willing to put their lives on the line for "manhood." The ultimate form of respect on the male-dominated inner-city street is thus reserved for men.

"Going for Bad"

In the most fearsome youths such a cavalier attitude toward death grows out of a very limited view of life. Many are uncertain about how long they are going to live and believe they could die violently at any time. They accept this fate; they live on the edge. Their manner conveys the message that nothing intimidates them; whatever turn the encounter takes, they maintain their attack—rather like a pit bull, whose spirit many such boys admire. The demonstration of such tenacity "shows heart" and earns their respect.

This fearlessness has implications for law enforcement. Many street-oriented boys are much more concerned about the threat of "justice" at the hands of a peer than at the hands of the police. Moreover, many feel not only that they have little to lose by going to prison but that they have something to gain. The toughening-up one experiences in prison can actually enhance one's reputation on the streets. Hence the system loses influence over the hard core who are without jobs, with little perceptible stake in the system. If mainstream society has done nothing *for* them, they counter by making sure it can do nothing *to* them.

At the same time, however, a competing view maintains that the true nerve consists in backing down, walking away from a fight, and going on with one's business. One fights only in self-defense. This view emerges from the decent philosophy that life is precious, and it is an important part of the socialization process common in decent homes. It discourages violence as the primary means of resolving disputes and encourages youngsters to accept nonviolence and talk as confrontational strategies. But "if the deal goes down," self-defense is greatly encouraged. When there is enough positive support for this orientation, either in the home or among one's peers, then nonviolence has a chance to prevail. But it prevails at the cost of relinquishing a claim to being bad and tough, and therefore sets a young person up as at the very least alienated from street-oriented peers and quite possibly a target of derision or even violence.

Although the nonviolent orientation rarely overcomes the impulse to strike back in an encounter, it does introduce a certain confusion and so can prompt a measure of soul-searching, or even profound ambivalence. Did the person back down with his respect intact or did he back down only to be judged a "punk"—a person lacking manhood? Should he or she have acted? Should he or she have hit the other person in the mouth? These questions beset many young men and women during public confrontations. What is the "right" thing to do? In the quest for honor, respect, and local status—which few young people are uninterested in—common sense most often prevails, which leads many to opt for the tough approach, enacting their own particular versions of the display of nerve. The presentation of oneself as rough and tough is very often quite acceptable until one is tested. And then that presentation may help the person pass the test, because it will cause fewer questions to be asked about what he did and why. It is hard for a person to explain why he lost the fight or why he backed down. Hence many will strive to appear to "go for bad," while hoping they will never be tested. But when they are tested, the outcome of the situation may quickly be out of their hands, as they become wrapped up in the circumstances of the moment.

An Oppositional Culture

The attitudes of the wider society are deeply implicated in the code of the streets. Most people in inner-city communities are not totally invested in the code, but the significant minority of hard-core street youths who are have to maintain the code in order to establish reputations, because they have— or feel they have—few other ways to assert themselves. For these young people the standards of the street code are the only game in town. The extent to which some children—particularly those who through upbringing have become most alienated and those lacking in strong and conventional social support—experience, feel, and internalize racist rejection and contempt from mainstream society may strongly encourage them to express contempt for the more conventional society in turn. In dealing with this contempt and rejection, some youngsters will consciously invest themselves and their considerable mental resources in what amounts to an oppositional culture to preserve themselves and their self-respect. Once they do, any respect they might be able to garner in the wider system pales in comparison with the re- spect available in the local system; thus they often lose interest in even at- tempting to negotiate the mainstream system.

At the same time, many less alienated young blacks have assumed a street-oriented demeanor as a way of expressing their blackness while really embracing a much more moderate way of life; they, too want a nonviolent set- ting in which to live and raise a family. These decent people are trying hard to be part of the mainstream culture, but the racism, real and perceived, that they encounter helps to legitimate the oppositional culture. And so on occa- sion they adopt street behavior. In fact, depending on the demands of the sit- uation, many people in the community slip back and forth between decent and street behavior.

A vicious cycle has thus been formed. The hopelessness and alienation many young inner-city black men and women feel, largely as a result of en- demic joblessness and persistent racism, fuels the violence they engage in. This violence serves to confirm the negative feelings many whites and some middle-class blacks harbor toward the ghetto poor, further legitimating the oppositional culture and the code of the streets in the eyes of many poor young blacks. Unless this cycle is broken, attitudes on both sides will become increasingly entrenched, and the violence, which claims victims black and white, poor and affluent, will only escalate.

9

WARRIOR DREAMS
Violence and Manhood in Post-Vietnam America

J. WILLIAM GIBSON

Sociologists are interested in how culture limits our free choice and shapes social interaction. Because each of us is born into a particular culture that has certain norms and values, our personal values and life expectations are profoundly influenced by our culture. For example, what are the values of American culture? Many scholars agree that dominant U.S. values are achievement, Judeo-Christian morals, material comfort, patriotism, and individualism. Contrast these dominant culture values with those expressed by men who are active in the paramilitary culture. What are the values and expected behaviors of men involved in paramilitary groups? The following reading by J. William Gibson is excerpted from his 1994 book of the same title, and it takes us inside this subculture to reveal the beliefs, practices, and rituals of men who join paramilitary groups.

We couldn't see them, but we could hear their bugles sound the call. The Communist battalions were organizing for a predawn assault. Captain Kokalis smiled wickedly; he'd been through this before. A "human wave" assault composed of thousands of enemy soldiers was headed our way. The captain ordered the remaining soldiers in his command to check their .30- and .50-caliber machine guns. Earlier in the night, the demolitions squad attached to our unit had planted mines and explosive charges for hundreds of meters in front of our position.

And then it began. At a thousand meters, the soldiers emerged screaming from the gray-blue fog. "Fire!" yelled Captain Kokalis. The gun crews opened up with short bursts of three to seven rounds; their bullets struck meat. Everywhere I could see, clusters of Communist troops were falling by the second. But the wave still surged forward. At 500 meters, Kokalis passed the word to his gunners to increase their rate of fire to longer strings of 10 to 20 rounds. Sergeant Donovan, the demolitions squad leader, began to reap the harvest from the night's planting. Massive explosions ripped through the Communist troops. Fire and smoke blasted into the dawn sky. It was as if the human wave had hit a submerged reef; as the dying fell, wide gaps appeared in the line where casualties could no longer be replaced.

But still they kept coming, hundreds of men, each and every one bent on taking the American position and wiping us out. As the Communists reached 100 meters, Kokalis gave one more command. Every machine gun in our platoon went to its maximum rate of sustained full-automatic frenzy, sounding like chain saws that just keep cutting and cutting.

And then it was over. The attack subsided into a flat sea of Communist dead. No Americans had been killed or wounded. We were happy to be alive, proud of our victory. We only wondered if our ears would ever stop ringing and if we would ever again smell anything other than the bittersweet aroma of burning gunpowder. . . .

Although an astonishing triumph was achieved that day, no historian will ever find a record of this battle in the hundreds of volumes and thousands of official reports written about the Korean or Vietnam war. Nor was the blood spilt part of a covert operation in Afghanistan or some unnamed country in Africa, Asia, or Latin America.

No, this battle was fought inside the United States, a few miles north of Las Vegas, in September 1986. It was a purely *imaginary* battle, a dream of victory staged as part of the *Soldier of Fortune* [*SOF*] magazine's annual convention. The audience of several hundred men, women, and children, together with reporters and a camera crew from CBS News, sat in bleachers behind half a dozen medium and heavy machine guns owned by civilians. Peter G. Kokalis, *SOF*'s firearms editor, set the scene for the audience and asked them to imagine that the sandy brushland of the Desert Sportsman Rifle and Pistol Club was really a killing zone for incoming Communist troops. Kokalis was a seasoned storyteller; he'd given this performance before. When the fantasy battle was over, the fans went wild with applause. Kokalis picked up a microphone, praised Donovan (another *SOF* staff member)—"He was responsible for that whole damn Communist bunker that went up"—and told the parents in the audience to buy "claymores [anti-personnel land mines] and other good shit for the kids." A marvelous actor who knew what his audience wanted, Kokalis sneered, "Did you get that, CBS, on your videocam? Screw you knee-jerk liberals."[1]

The shoot-out and victory over Communist forces conducted at the Desert Sportsman Rifle and Pistol Club was but one battle in a cultural or imaginary "New War" that had been going on since the late 1960s and early 1970s. The bitter controversies surrounding the Vietnam War had discredited the old American ideal of the masculine warrior hero for much of the public. But in 1971, when Clint Eastwood made the transition from playing cowboys in old *Rawhide* reruns and spaghetti westerns to portraying San Francisco police detective Harry Callahan in *Dirty Harry*, the warrior hero returned in full force. His backup arrived in 1974 when Charles Bronson appeared in *Death Wish*, the story of a mild-mannered, middle-aged architect in New York City who, after his wife is murdered and his daughter is raped and driven insane, finds new meaning in life through an endless war of revenge against street punks.

In the 1980s, Rambo and his friends made their assault. The experience of John Rambo, a former Green Beret, was the paradigmatic story of the decade. In *First Blood* (1982), he burns down a small Oregon town while suffering hallucinatory flashbacks to his service in Vietnam. Three years later, in *Rambo: First Blood, Part 2*, he is taken off a prison chain gang by his former commanding officer in Vietnam and asked to perform a special reconnaissance mission to find suspected American POWs in Laos, in exchange for a presidential pardon. His only question: "Do we get to win this time?" And indeed, Rambo does win. Betrayed by the CIA bureaucrat in charge of the mission, Rambo fights the Russians and Vietnamese by himself and brings the POWs back home.

Hundreds of similar films celebrating the victory of good men over bad through armed combat were made during the late 1970s and 1980s. Many were directed by major Hollywood directors and starred well-known actors. Elaborate special effects and exotic film locations added tens of millions to production costs. And for every large-budget film, there were scores of cheaper formula films employing lesser-known actors and production crews. Often these "action-adventure" films had only brief theatrical releases in major markets. Instead, they made their money in smaller cities and towns, in sales to Europe and the Third World, and most of all, in the sale of video-cassettes to rental stores. Movie producers could even turn a profit on "video-only" releases; action-adventure films were the largest category of video rentals in the 1980s.

At the same time, Tom Clancy became a star in the publishing world. His book *The Hunt for Red October* (1984) told the story of the Soviet Navy's most erudite submarine commander, Captain Markus Ramius, and his effort to defect to the United States with the Soviets' premier missile-firing submarine. *Red Storm Rising* (1986) followed, an epic of World War III framed as a high-tech conventional war against the Soviet Union. Clancy's novels all featured Jack Ryan, Ph.D., a former Marine captain in Vietnam turned academic naval historian who returns to duty as a CIA analyst and repeatedly stumbles into life-and-death struggles in which the fate of the world rests on his prowess. All were best-sellers.

President Reagan, Secretary of the Navy John Lehman, and many other high officials applauded Clancy and his hero. Soon the author had a multi-million-dollar contract for a whole series of novels, movie deals with Paramount, and a new part-time job as a foreign-policy expert writing op-ed pieces for the *Washington Post*, the *Los Angeles Times*, and other influential newspapers around the country. His success motivated dozens of authors, mostly active-duty or retired military men, to take up the genre. The "techno-thriller" was born.

At a slightly lower level in the literary establishment, the same publishing houses that marketed women's romance novels on grocery and drugstore paperback racks rapidly expanded their collections of pulp fiction for men. Most were written like hard-core pornography, except that inch-by-inch descriptions of penises entering vaginas were replaced by equally graphic portrayals of bullets, grenade fragments, and knives shredding flesh: "He tried to grab the handle of the commando knife, but the terrorist pushed down on the butt, raised the point and yanked the knife upward through the muscle tissue and guts. It ripped intestines, spilling blood and gore."[2] A minimum of 20 but sometimes as many as 120 such graphically described killings occurred in each 200-to-250-page paperback. Most series came out four times a year with domestic print runs of 60,000 to 250,000 copies. More than a dozen different comic books with titles like *Punisher, Vigilante,* and *Scout* followed suit with clones of the novels.

Along with the novels and comics came a new kind of periodical which replaced the older adventure magazines for men, such as *True* and *Argosy,* that had folded in the 1960s. Robert K. Brown, a former captain in the U.S. Army Special Forces during the Vietnam War, founded *Soldier of Fortune: The Journal of Professional Adventurers* in the spring of 1975, just before the fall of Saigon. *SOF's* position was explicit from the start: The independent warrior must step in to fill the dangerous void created by the American failure in Vietnam. By the mid-1980s *SOF* was reaching 35,000 subscribers, had newsstand sales of another 150,000, and was being passed around to at least twice as many readers.[3]

Half a dozen new warrior magazines soon entered the market. Some, like *Eagle, New Breed,* and *Gung-Ho,* tried to copy the *SOF* editorial package—a strategy that ultimately failed. But most developed their own particular pitch. *Combat Handguns* focused on pistols for would-be gunfighters. *American Survival Guide* advertised and reviewed everything needed for "the good life" after the end of civilization (except birth control devices—too many Mormon subscribers, the editor said), while *S.W.A.T.* found its way to men who idealized these elite police teams and who were worried about home defense against "multiple intruders."

During the same period, sales of military weapons took off. Colt offered two semiautomatic versions of the M16 used by U.S. soldiers in Vietnam (a full-size rifle and a shorter-barreled carbine with collapsible stock). European armories exported their latest products, accompanied by sophisticated advertising campaigns in *SOF* and the more mainstream gun magazines. Israeli Defense Industries put a longer, 16-inch barrel on the Uzi submachine gun (to make it legal) and sold it as a semiautomatic carbine. And the Communist countries of Eastern Europe, together with the People's Republic of China, jumped into the market with the devil's own favorite hardware, the infamous AK47. The AK sold in the United States was the semiautomatic version of the assault rifle used by the victorious Communists in Vietnam and by all kinds of radical movements and terrorist organizations around the world. It retailed for $300 to $400, half the price of an Uzi or an AR-15; complete with three 30-round magazines, cleaning kit, and bayonet, it was truly a bargain.

To feed these hungry guns, munitions manufacturing packaged new "generic" brands of military ammo at discount prices, often selling them in cases of 500 or 1,000 rounds. New lines of aftermarket accessories offered parts for full-automatic conversions, improved flash-hiders, scopes, folding stocks, and scores of other goodies. In 1989, the U.S. Bureau of Alcohol, Tobacco and Firearms (ATF) estimated that two to three million military-style rifles had been sold in this country since the Vietnam War. The Bureau released these figures in response to the public outcry over a series of mass murders committed by psychotics armed with assault rifles.

But the Bureau's statistics tell only part of the story. In less than two decades, millions of American men had purchased combat rifles, pistols, and shotguns and began training to fight their own personal wars. Elite combat shooting schools teaching the most modern techniques and often costing $500 to over $1,000 in tuition alone were attended not only by soldiers and police but by increasing numbers of civilians as well. Hundreds of new indoor pistol-shooting ranges opened for business in old warehouses and shopping malls around the country, locations ideal for city dwellers and suburbanites.

A new game of "tag" blurred the line between play and actual violence: men got the opportunity to hunt and shoot other men without killing them or risking death themselves. The National Survival Game was invented in 1981 by two old friends, one a screenwriter for the weight-lifting sagas that gave Arnold Schwarzenegger his first starring roles, and the other a former member of the Army's Long Range Reconnaissance Patrol (LRRP) in Vietnam.[4] Later called paintball because it utilized guns firing balls of watercolor paint, by 1987 the game was being played by at least fifty thousand people (mostly men) each weekend on both outdoor and indoor battlefields scattered across the nation. Players wore hard-plastic face masks intended to resemble those of ancient tribal warriors and dressed from head to toe in camouflage clothes imported by specialty stores from military outfitters around the world. The object of the game was to capture the opposing team's flag, inflicting the highest possible body count along the way.

One major park out in the Mojave Desert 70 miles southeast of Los Angeles was named Sat Cong Village. *Sat Cong* is a slang Vietnamese phrase meaning "Kill Communists" that had been popularized by the CIA as part of its psychological-warfare program. Sat Cong Village employed an attractive Asian woman to rent the guns, sell the paintballs, and collect the $20 entrance fee. Players had their choice of playing fields: Vietnam, Cambodia, or Nicaragua. On the Nicaragua field, the owner built a full-size facsimile of the crashed C-47 cargo plane contracted by Lieutenant Colonel Oliver North to supply the contras. The scene even had three parachutes hanging from trees; the only thing missing was the sole survivor of the crash, Eugene Hasenfus.

The 1980s, then, saw the emergence of a highly energized culture of war and the warrior. For all its varied manifestations, a few common features stood out. The New War culture was not so much military as paramilitary. The new warrior hero was only occasionally portrayed as a member of a conventional military or law enforcement unit; typically, he fought alone or with a small, elite group of fellow warriors. Moreover, by separating the warrior from his traditional state-sanctioned occupations—policeman or soldier—the New War culture presented the warrior role as the ideal identity for *all* men. Bankers, professors, factory workers, and postal clerks could all transcend their regular stations in life and prepare for heroic battle against the enemies of society.

To many people, this new fascination with warriors and weapons seemed a terribly bad joke. The major newspapers and magazines that arbitrate what is to be taken seriously in American society scoffed at the attempts to resurrect the warrior hero. Movie critics were particularly disdainful of Stallone's Rambo films. *Rambo: First Blood, Part 2* was called "narcissistic jingoism" by *The New Yorker* and "hare-brained" by the *Wall Street Journal*. The *Washington Post* even intoned that "Sly's body looks fine. Now can't you come up with a workout for his soul?"

But in dismissing Rambo so quickly and contemptuously, commentators failed to notice the true significance of the emerging paramilitary culture. They missed the fact that quite a few people were not writing Rambo off as a complete joke; behind the Indian bandanna, necklace, and bulging muscles, a new culture hero affirmed such traditional American values as self-reliance, honesty, courage, and concern for fellow citizens. Rambo was a worker and a former enlisted man, not a smooth-talking professional. That so many seemingly well-to-do, sophisticated liberals hated him for both his politics and his uncouthness only added to his glory. Further, in their emphasis on Stallone's clownishness the commentators failed to see not only how widespread paramilitary culture had become but also its relation to the historical moment in which it arose.

Indeed, paramilitary culture can be understood only when it is placed in relation to the Vietnam War. America's failure to win that war was a truly profound blow. The nation's long, proud tradition of military victories, from the Revolutionary War through the century-long battles against the Indians to World Wars I and II, had finally come to an end. Politically, the defeat in Vietnam meant that the post–World War II era of overwhelming American political and military power in international affairs, the era that in 1945 *Time* magazine publisher Henry Luce had prophesied would be the "American Century," was over after only 30 years. No longer could U.S. diplomacy wield the big stick of military intervention as a ready threat—a significant part of the American public would no longer support such interventions, and the rest of the world knew it.

Moreover, besides eroding U.S. influence internationally, the defeat had subtle but serious effects on the American psyche. America has always celebrated war and the warrior. Our long, unbroken record of military victories has been crucially important both to the national identity and to the personal identity of many Americans—particularly men. The historian Richard Slotkin locates a primary "cultural archetype" of the nation in the story of a heroic warrior whose victories over the enemy symbolically affirm the country's fundamental goodness and power; we win our wars because, morally, we deserve to win. Clearly, the archetypical pattern Slotkin calls "regeneration through violence" was broken with the defeat in Vietnam.[5] The result was a massive disjunction in American culture, a crisis of self-image: If Americans were no longer winners, then who were they?

This disruption of cultural identity was amplified by other social transformations. During the 1960s, the civil rights and ethnic pride movements won many victories in their challenges to racial oppression. Also, during the 1970s and 1980s, the United States experienced massive waves of immigration from Mexico, Central America, Vietnam, Cambodia, Korea, and Taiwan. Whites, no longer secure in their power abroad, also lost their unquestionable dominance at home; for the first time, many began to feel that they too were just another hyphenated ethnic group, the Anglo-Americans.

Extraordinary economic changes also marked the 1970s and 1980s. U.S. manufacturing strength declined substantially; staggering trade deficits with other countries and the chronic federal budget deficits shifted the United States from creditor to debtor nation. The post–World War II American Dream—which promised a combination of technological progress and social reforms, together with high employment rates, rising wages, widespread home ownership, and ever increasing consumer options—no longer seemed a likely prospect for the great majority. At the same time, the rise in crime rates, particularly because of drug abuse and its accompanying violence, made people feel more powerless than ever.

While the public world dominated by men seemed to come apart, the private world of family life also felt the shocks. The feminist movement challenged formerly exclusive male domains, not only in the labor market and in many areas of political and social life but in the home as well. Customary male behavior was no longer acceptable in either private relationships or public policy. Feminism was widely experienced by men as a profound threat to their identity. Men had to change, but to what? No one knew for sure what a "good man" was anymore.

It is hardly surprising, then, that American men—lacking confidence in the government and the economy, troubled by the changing relations between the sexes, uncertain of their identity or their future—began to *dream*, to fantasize about the powers and features of another kind of man who could retake and reorder the world. And the hero of all these dreams was the paramilitary warrior. In the New War he fights the battles of Vietnam a thousand times, each time winning decisively. Terrorists and drug dealers are blasted into oblivion. Illegal aliens inside the United States and the hordes of nonwhites in the Third World are returned by force to their proper place. Women are revealed as dangerous temptresses who have to be mastered, avoided, or terminated.

Obviously these dreams represented a flight from the present and a rejection and denial of events of the preceding 20 years. But they also indicated a more profound and severe distress. The whole modern world was damned as unacceptable. Unable to find a rational way to face the tasks of rebuilding society and reinventing themselves, men instead sought refuge in myths from both America's frontier past and ancient times. Indeed, the fundamental narratives that shape paramilitary culture and its New War fantasies are often nothing but reinterpretations or reworkings of archaic warrior myths.

In ancient societies, the most important stories a people told about themselves concerned how the physical universe came into existence, how their ancestors first came to live in this universe, and how the gods, the universe, and society were related to one another. These cosmogonic, or creation, myths frequently posit a violent conflict between the good forces of order and the evil forces dedicated to the perpetuation of primordial chaos.[6] After the war in which the gods defeat the evil ones, they establish the "sacred order," in which all of the society's most important values are fully embodied. Some creation myths focus primarily on the sacred order and on the deeds of the gods and goddesses in paradise. Other myths, however, focus on the battles between the heroes and villains that lead up to the founding.[7] In these myths it is war and the warrior that are most sacred. American paramilitary culture borrows from both kinds of stories, but mostly from this second, more violent, type.

In either case, the presence, if not the outright predominance, of archaic male myths at the moment of crisis indicates just how far American men jumped psychically when faced with the declining power of their identities and organizations. The always-precarious balance in modern society between secular institutions and ways of thinking on the one hand and older patterns of belief informed by myth and ritual on the other tilted decisively in the direction of myth. The crisis revealed that at some deep, unconscious level these ancient male creation myths live on in the psyche of many men and that the images and tales from this mythic world of warriors and war still shape men's fantasies about who they are as men, their commitments to each other and to women, and their relationships to society and the state.

———

The imaginary New War that men created is a coherent mythical universe, formed by the repetition of key features in thousands of novels, magazines, films, and advertisements. As the sociologist Will Wright points out, the component elements of myth work to create a common "theoretical idea of a social order."[8] These New War stories about heroic warriors and their evil adversaries are ways of arguing about what is wrong with the modern world and what needs to be done to make society well again. . . .

War games took these fantasies one step further and allowed men to act on their desires in paramilitary games and theme parks that one would-be warrior described as "better than Disneyland." Here, away from the ordinary routines of world and family life, men could meet, mingle, and share their warrior dreams. Three major types of imaginary war zones developed: the National Survival Game, or paintball; the annual *Soldier of Fortune* convention in Las Vegas; and combat shooting schools and firing ranges. In these special environments, the gods of war could be summoned for games played along the edges of violence.

Finally, the imaginary New War turned into the real nightmares of "War Zone America." Since the 1970s, a number of racist groups, religious sects, mercenaries, and madmen have literally lived their own versions of the New War. At the same time, as hundreds of thousands of military-style rifles have entered the domestic gun market and become the weapon of choice for some killers, the gun-control debate has escalated to a new level. And not surprisingly, the myths of the New War have profoundly influenced several presidential administrations, affecting both those leaders who make military policy decisions and the lower-ranking personnel who carry out covert and overt operations.

Only at the surface level, then, has paramilitary culture been merely a matter of the "stupid" movies and novels consumed by the great unwashed lower-middle and working classes, or of the murderous actions of a few demented, "deviant" men. In truth, there is nothing superficial or marginal about the New War that has been fought in American popular culture since the 1970s. It is a war about basics: power, sex, race, and alienation. Contrary to the *Washington Post* review, Rambo was no shallow muscle man but the emblem of a movement that at the very least wanted to reverse the previous 20 years of American history and take back all the symbolic territory that had been lost. The vast proliferation of warrior fantasies represented an attempt to reaffirm the national identity. But it was also a larger volcanic upheaval of archaic myths, an outcropping whose entire structural formation plunges into deep historical, cultural, and psychological territories. These territories have kept us chained to war as a way of life; they have infused individual men, national political and military leaders, and society with a deep attraction to both imaginary and real violence. This terrain must be explored, mapped, and understood if it is ever to be transformed.

NOTES

1. Peter G. Kokalis, speaking at the *Soldier of Fortune* firepower demonstration at the Desert Sportsman Rifle and Pistol Club, Las Vegas, Nevada, September 20, 1986.
2. Gar Wilson, *The Fury Bombs*, vol. 5 of *Phoenix Force* (Toronto: Worldwide Library, 1983), p. 30.
3. *SOF* regularly hired the firm of Starch, Inra, Hopper to study their readership. A condensed version of their 1986 report, from which these figures were taken, was made available to the press at the September 1986 *SOF* convention in Las Vegas.
4. Lionel Atwill, *Survival Game: Airgun National Manual* (New London, NH: The National Survival Game, Inc., 1987), pp. 22–30.
5. Richard Slotkin, *Regeneration through Violence: The Mythology of the American Frontier, 1660–1860* (Middletown, CT: Wesleyan University Press, 1973).

6. Mircea Eliade, *Myth and Reality,* trans. Willard R. Trask (New York: Harper & Row, 1963).
7. Richard Stivers, *Evil in Modern Myth and Ritual* (Athens: University of Georgia Press, 1982).
8. Will Wright, *Sixguns and Society: A Structural Study of the Western* (Berkeley: University of California Press, 1975), p. 20.

10

LOVELY HULA HANDS
Corporate Tourism and the Prostitution of Hawaiian Culture

HAUNANI-KAY TRASK

Many U.S. racial-ethnic groups, including Native Americans, Latinos, and African Americans, have experienced cultural exploitation. Exploitation occurs when aspects of a subculture, such as its beliefs, rituals, and social customs, are commodified and marketed without the cultural group's permission. This selection by Haunani-Kay Trask explores the cultural commodification and exploitation of Hawaiian culture. Trask argues that several aspects of Polynesian and Hawaiian cultures, including their language, dress, and dance forms, have been marketed as products for the mass consumption of tourists. This excerpt is taken from Trask's 1993 book, *From a Native Daughter: Colonialism and Sovereignty in Hawai'i.*

I am certain that most, if not all, Americans have heard of Hawai'i and have wished, at some time in their lives, to visit my native land. But I doubt that the history of how Hawai'i came to be territorially incorporated, and economically, politically, and culturally subordinated to the United States is known to most Americans. Nor is it common knowledge that Hawaiians have been struggling for over 20 years to achieve a land base and some form of political sovereignty on the same level as American Indians. Finally, I would imagine that most Americans could not place Hawai'i or any other Pacific island on a map of the Pacific. But despite all this appalling ignorance, five million Americans will vacation in my homeland this year *and* the next, and so on into the foreseeable capitalist future. Such are the intended privi-

From *From a Native Daughter: Colonialism and Sovereignty in Hawai'i,* pp. 179–81, 183–84, 184–87. Reprinted with the permission of Common Courage Press.

leges of the so-called American standard of living: ignorance of, and yet power over, one's relations to native peoples.

Thanks to postwar American imperialism, the ideology that the United States has no overseas colonies and is, in fact, the champion of self-determination the world over holds no greater sway than in the United States itself. To most Americans, then, Hawai'i is *theirs:* to use, to take, and, above all, to fantasize about long after the experience.

Just five hours away by plane from California, Hawai'i is a thousand light years away in fantasy. Mostly a state of mind, Hawai'i is the image of escape from the rawness and violence of daily American life. Hawai'i—the word, the vision, the sound in the mind—is the fragrance and feel of soft kindness. Above all, Hawai'i is "she," the Western image of the native "female" in her magical allure. And if luck prevails, some of "her" will rub off on you, the visitor.

This fictional Hawai'i comes out of the depths of Western sexual sickness which demands a dark, sin-free native for instant gratification between imperialist wars. The attraction of Hawai'i is stimulated by slick Hollywood movies, saccharine Andy Williams music, and the constant psychological deprivations of maniacal American life. Tourists flock to my native land for escape, but they are escaping into a state of mind while participating in the destruction of a host people in a native place.

To Hawaiians, daily life is neither soft nor kind. In fact, the political, economic, and cultural reality for most Hawaiians is hard, ugly, and cruel.

In Hawai'i, the destruction of our land and the prostitution of our culture are planned and executed by multinational corporations (both foreign-based and Hawai'i-based), by huge landowners (like the missionary-descended Castle and Cook—of Dole Pineapple fame—and others) and by collaborationist state and county governments. The ideological gloss that claims tourism to be our economic savior and the "natural" result of Hawaiian culture is manufactured by ad agencies (like the state supported Hawai'i Visitors' Bureau) and tour companies (many of which are owned by the airlines), and spewed out to the public through complicitous cultural engines like film, television and radio, and the daily newspapers. As for the local labor unions, both rank and file and management clamor for more tourists while the construction industry lobbies incessantly for larger resorts.

. . .

My use of the word *tourism* in the Hawai'i context refers to a mass-based, corporately controlled industry that is both vertically and horizontally integrated such that one multinational corporation owns an airline, the tour buses that transport tourists to the corporation-owned hotel where they eat in a corporation-owned restaurant, play golf and "experience" Hawai'i on corporation-owned recreation areas, and eventually consider buying a second home built on corporation land. Profits, in this case, are mostly repatriated back to the home country. In Hawai'i, these "home" countries are Japan, Taiwan, Hong Kong, Canada, Australia, and the United States. . . .

. . .

With this as a background on tourism, I want to move now into the area of cultural prostitution. "Prostitution" in this context refers to the entire institution which defines a woman (and by extension the "female") as an object of degraded and victimized sexual value for use and exchange through the medium of money. The "prostitute" is then a woman who sells her sexual capacities and is seen, thereby, to possess and reproduce them at will, that is, by her very "nature." The prostitute and the institution which creates and maintains her are, of course, of patriarchal origin. The pimp is the conduit of exchange, managing the commodity that is the prostitute while acting as the guard at the entry and exit gates, making sure the prostitute behaves as a prostitute by fulfilling her sexual–economic functions. The victims participate in their victimization with enormous ranges of feeling, including resistance and complicity, but the force and continuity of the institution are shaped by men.

There is much more to prostitution than my sketch reveals but this must suffice for I am interested in using the largest sense of this term as a metaphor in understanding what has happened to Hawaiian culture. My purpose is not to exact detail or fashion a model but to convey the utter degradation of our culture and our people under corporate tourism by employing "prostitution" as an analytic category.

Finally, I have chosen four areas of Hawaiian culture to examine: our homeland, or *one hānau* that is Hawai'i, our lands and fisheries, the outlying seas and the heavens; our language and dance; our familial relationships; and our women.

Nā Mea Hawai'i—Things Hawaiian

The *mo'ōlelo,* or history of Hawaiians, is to be found in our genealogies. From our great cosmogonic genealogy, the *Kumulipo,* derives the Hawaiian identity. The "essential lesson" of this genealogy is "the interrelatedness of the Hawaiian world, and the inseparability of its constituent parts." Thus, "the genealogy of the land, the gods, chiefs, and people intertwine one with the other, and with all aspects of the universe."[1]

In the *mo'ōlelo* of Papa and Wākea, earth-mother and sky-father, our islands are born; Hawai'i, Maui, O'ahu, Kaua'i, and Ni'ihau. From their human offspring came the *taro* plant and from the taro came the Hawaiian people. The lessons of our genealogy are that human beings have a familial relationship to land and to the *taro,* our elder siblings or *kua'ana.*

In Hawai'i, as in all of Polynesia, younger siblings must serve and honor elder siblings who, in turn, must feed and care for their younger siblings. Therefore, Hawaiians must cultivate and husband the land which will feed and provide for the Hawaiian people. This relationship of people to land is called *mālama 'āina* or *aloha 'āina*, care and love of the land.

When people and land work together harmoniously, the balance that results is called *pono*. In Hawaiian society, the *ali'i* or chiefs were required to maintain order, abundance of food, and good government. The *maka'āinana* or common people worked the land and fed the chiefs; the *ali'i* organized production and appeased the gods.

Today, *mālama 'āina* is called stewardship by some, although that word does not convey spiritual and genealogical connections. Nevertheless, to love and make the land flourish is a Hawaiian value. *'Āina*, one of the words for land, means *that which feeds*. *Kama'āina*, a term for native-born people, means *child of the land*. Thus is the Hawaiian relationship to land both familial and reciprocal.

Our deities are also of the land: Pele is our volcano, Kāne and Lono our fertile valleys and plains, Kanaloa our ocean and all that lives within it, and so on with the 40,000 and 400,000 gods of Hawai'i. Our whole universe, physical and metaphysical, is divine.

Within this world, the older people or *kūpuna* are to cherish those who are younger, the *mo'opuna*. Unstinting generosity is a value and of high status. Social connections between our people are through *aloha*, simply translated as love but carrying with it a profoundly Hawaiian sense that is, again, familial and genealogical. Hawaiians feel *aloha* for Hawai'i whence they come and for their Hawaiian kin upon whom they depend. It is nearly impossible to feel or practice *aloha* for something that is not familial. This is why we extend familial relations to those few non-natives whom we feel understand and can reciprocate our *aloha*. But *aloha* is freely given and freely returned, it is not and cannot be demanded, or commanded. Above all, *aloha* is a cultural feeling and practice that works among the people and between the people and their land.

The significance and meaning of *aloha* underscores the centrality of the Hawaiian language or *'ōlelo* to the culture. *'Ōlelo* means both language and tongue; *mo'ōlelo*, or history, is that which comes from the tongue, that is, a story. *Haole* or white people say we have oral history, but what we have are stories passed on through the generations. These are different from the *haole* sense of history. To Hawaiians in traditional society, language had tremendous power, thus the phrase, *i ka 'ōlelo ke ola; i ka 'ōlelo ka make*—in language is life, in language is death.

After nearly 2,000 years of speaking Hawaiian, our people suffered the near extinction of our language through its banning by the American-imposed government in 1896. In 1900, Hawai'i became a territory of the United States. All schools, government operations and official transactions were thereafter conducted in English, despite the fact that most people, including non-natives, still spoke Hawaiian at the turn of the century.

Since 1970, *'ōlelo Hawai'i,* or the Hawaiian language, has undergone a tremendous revival, including the rise of language immersion schools. The state of Hawai'i now has two official languages, Hawaiian and English, and the call for Hawaiian language speakers and teachers grows louder by the day.[2]

Along with the flowering of Hawaiian language has come a flowering of Hawaiian dance, especially in its ancient form, called *hula kahiko.* Dance academies, known as *hālau,* have proliferated throughout Hawai'i as have *kumu hula,* or dance masters, and formal competitions where all-night presentations continue for three or four days to throngs of appreciative listeners. Indeed, among Pacific Islanders, Hawaiian dance is considered one of the finest Polynesian art forms today.

Of course, the cultural revitalization that Hawaiians are now experiencing and transmitting to their children is as much a *repudiation* of colonization by so-called Western civilization in its American form as it is a *reclamation* of our past and our own ways of life. This is why cultural revitalization is often resisted and disparaged by anthropologists and others: they see very clearly that its political effect is de-colonization of the mind. Thus our rejection of the nuclear family as the basic unit of society and of individualism as the best form of human expression infuriates social workers, the churches, the legal system, and educators. Hawaiians continue to have allegedly "illegitimate" children, to *hānai* or adopt both children and adults outside of sanctioned Western legal concepts, to hold and use land and water in a collective form rather than a private property form, and to proscribe the notion and the value that one person should strive to surpass and therefore outshine all others.

All these Hawaiian values can be grouped under the idea of *'ohana,* loosely translated as family, but more accurately imagined as a group of both closely and distantly related people who share nearly everything, from land and food to children and status. Sharing is central to this value since it prevents individual decline. Of course, poverty is not thereby avoided, it is only shared with everyone in the unit. The *'ohana* works effectively when the *kua'ana* relationship (elder sibling/younger sibling reciprocity) is practiced.

Finally, within the *'ohana,* our women are considered the lifegivers of the nation, and are accorded the respect and honor this status conveys. Our young women, like our young people in general, are the *pua,* or flower of our *lāhui,* or our nation. The renowned beauty of our women, especially their sexual beauty, is not considered a commodity to be hoarded by fathers and brothers but an attribute of our people. Culturally, Hawaiians are very open and free about sexual relationships, although Christianity and organized religion have done much to damage these traditional sexual values.

With this understanding of what it means to be Hawaiian, I want to move now to the prostitution of our culture by tourism.

Hawai'i itself is the female object of degraded and victimized sexual value. Our *'āina,* or lands, are not any longer the source of food and shelter, but the source of money. Land is now called real estate; rather than our mother, *Papa.* The American relationship of people to land is that of exploiter to exploited. Beautiful areas, once sacred to my people, are now expensive resorts; shorelines where net fishing, seaweed gathering, and crabbing occurred are more and more the exclusive domain of recreational activities: sunbathing, windsurfing, jet skiing. Now, even access to beaches near hotels is strictly regulated or denied to the local public altogether.

The phrase, *mālama 'āina*—to care for the land—is used by government officials to sell new projects and to convince the locals that hotels can be built with a concern for "ecology." Hotel historians, like hotel doctors, are stationed in-house to soothe the visitors' stay with the pablum of invented myths and tales of the "primitive."

High schools and hotels adopt each other and funnel teenagers through major resorts for guided tours from kitchens to gardens to honeymoon suites in preparation for postsecondary jobs in the lowest-paid industry in the state. In the meantime, tourist appreciation kits and movies are distributed through the state department of education to all elementary schools. One film, unashamedly titled "What's in it for Me?," was devised to convince locals that tourism is, as the newspapers never tire of saying, "the only game in town."

Of course, all this hype is necessary to hide the truth about tourism, the awful exploitative truth that the industry is the major cause of environmental degradation, low wages, land dispossession, and the highest cost of living in the United States.

While this propaganda is churned out to local residents, the commercialization of Hawaiian culture proceeds with calls for more sensitive marketing of our native values and practices. After all, a prostitute is only as good as her income-producing talents. These talents, in Hawaiian terms, are the *hula;* the generosity, or *aloha,* of our people; the *u'i* or youthful beauty of our women and men; and the continuing allure of our lands and waters, that is, of our place, Hawai'i.

The selling of these talents must produce income. And the function of tourism and the state of Hawai'i is to convert these attributes into profits.

The first requirement is the transformation of the product, or the cultural attribute, much as a woman must be transformed to look like a prostitute, that is, someone who is complicitous in her own commodification. Thus *hula* dancers wear clownlike make-up, don costumes from a mix of Polynesian cultures, and behave in a manner that is smutty and salacious rather than powerfully erotic. The distance between the smutty and the erotic is precisely the distance between Western culture and Hawaiian culture. In the hotel version of the *hula,* the sacredness of the dance has completely evaporated while the athleticism and sexual expression have been packaged like ornaments. The purpose is entertainment for profit rather than a joyful and truly Hawaiian celebration of human and divine nature.

But let us look at an example that is representative of literally hundreds of images that litter the pages of scores of tourist publications. From an Aloha Airlines booklet—shamelessly called the "Spirit of Aloha"—there is a characteristic portrayal of commodified *hula* dancers, one male and one female. The costuming of the female is more South Pacific—the Cook Islands and Tahiti—while that of the male is more Hawaiian. (He wears a Hawaiian loincloth called a *malo.*) The ad smugly asserts the hotel dinner service as a *lū'au,* a Hawaiian feast (which is misspelled) with a continuously open bar, lavish "island" buffet, and "thrilling" Polynesian revue. Needless to say, Hawaiians did not drink alcohol, eat "island" buffets, or participate in "thrilling" revues before the advent of white people in our islands.

But back to the advertisement. Lahaina, the location of the resort and once the capital of Hawai'i, is called "royal" because of its past association with our *ali'i,* or chiefs. Far from being royal today, Lahaina is sadly inundated by California yuppies, drug addicts, and valley girls.

The male figure in the background is muscular, partially clothed, and unsmiling. Apparently, he is supposed to convey an image of Polynesian sexuality that is both enticing and threatening. The white women in the audience can marvel at this physique and still remain safely distant. Like the black American male, this Polynesian man is a fantasy animal. He casts a slightly malevolent glance at our costumed maiden whose body posture and barely covered breasts contradict the innocent smile on her face.

Finally, the "wondrous allure" referred to in the ad applies to more than just the dancers in their performances; the physical beauty of Hawai'i "alive under the stars" is the larger reference.

In this little grotesquerie, the falseness and commercialism fairly scream out from the page. Our language, our dance, our young people, even our customs of eating are used to ensnare tourists. And the price is only a paltry $39.95, not much for two thousand years of culture. Of course, the hotel will rake in tens of thousands of dollars on just the *lū'au* alone. And our young couple will make a pittance.

The rest of the magazine, like most tourist propaganda, commodifies virtually every part of Hawai'i: mountains, beaches, coastlines, rivers, flowers, our volcano goddess, Pele, reefs and fish, rural Hawaiian communities, even Hawaiian activists.

The point, of course, is that everything in Hawai'i can be yours, that is, you the tourist, the non-native, the visitor. The place, the people, the culture, even our identity as a "native" people is for sale. Thus, the magazine, like the airline that prints it, is called *Aloha.* The use of this word in a capitalist context is so far removed from any Hawaiian cultural sense that it is, literally, meaningless.

Thus, Hawai'i, like a lovely woman, is there for the taking. Those with only a little money get a brief encounter; those with a lot of money, like the Japanese, get more. The state and counties will give tax breaks, build infrastructure, and have the governor personally welcome tourists to ensure they keep coming. Just as the pimp regulates prices and guards the commodity of the prostitute, so the state bargains with developers for access to Hawaiian land and culture. Who builds the biggest resorts to attract the most affluent tourists gets the best deal: more hotel rooms, golf courses, and restaurants approved. Permits are fast-tracked, height and density limits are suspended, new groundwater sources are miraculously found.

Hawaiians, meanwhile, have little choice in all this. We can fill up the unemployment lines, enter the military, work in the tourist industry, or leave Hawai'i. Increasingly, Hawaiians are leaving, not by choice but out of economic necessity.

Our people who work in the industry—dancers, waiters, singers, valets, gardeners, housekeepers, bartenders, and even a few managers—make between $10,000 and $25,000 a year, an impossible salary for a family in Hawai'i. Psychologically, our young people have begun to think of tourism as the only employment opportunity, trapped as they are by the lack of alternatives. For our young women, modeling is a "cleaner" job when compared to waiting on tables, or dancing in a weekly revue, but modeling feeds on tourism and the commodification of Hawaiian women. In the end, the entire employment scene is shaped by tourism.

Despite their exploitation, Hawaiians' participation in tourism raises the problem of complicity. Because wages are so low and advancement so rare, whatever complicity exists is secondary to the economic hopelessness that drives Hawaiians into the industry. Refusing to contribute to the commercialization of one's culture becomes a peripheral concern when unemployment looms.

Of course, many Hawaiians do not see tourism as part of their colonization. Thus tourism is viewed as providing jobs, not as a form of cultural prostitution. Even those who have some glimmer of critical consciousness don't generally agree that the tourist industry prostitutes Hawaiian culture. To me, this is a measure of the depth of our mental oppression: We can't understand our own cultural degradation because we are living it. As colonized people, we are colonized to the extent that we are unaware of our oppression. When awareness begins, then so too does de-colonization. Judging by the growing resistance to new hotels, to geothermal energy and manganese nodule mining which would supplement the tourist industry, and to increases in the sheer number of tourists, I would say that de-colonization has begun, but we have many more stages to negotiate on our path to sovereignty.

My brief excursion into the prostitution of Hawaiian culture has done no more than give an overview. Now that you have heard a native view, let me just leave this thought behind. If you are thinking of visiting my homeland, please don't. We don't want or need any more tourists, and we certainly don't like them. If you want to help our cause, pass this message on to your friends.

NOTES

Author's Note: "Lovely Hula Hands" is the title of a famous and very saccharine song written by a *haole* who fell in love with Hawai'i in the pre-statehood era. It embodies the worst romanticized views of *hula* dancers and Hawaiian culture in general.

1. Lilikalā Kame'eleihiwa, *Native Land and Foreign Desires* (Honolulu: Bishop Museum Press, 1992), p. 2.
2. See Larry Kimura, 1983. "Native Hawaiian Culture," in *Native Hawaiians Study Commission Report,* Vol. 1 (Washington, DC: U.S. Department of the Interior), pp. 173–97.

PART III

Socialization

11

"NIGHT TO HIS DAY"

The Social Construction of Gender

JUDITH LORBER

In this and the following three selections, we examine socialization, the process of learning cultural values and norms. *Socialization* refers to those social processes through which an individual becomes integrated into a social group by learning the group's culture and his or her roles in that group. It is largely through this process that an individual's concept of self is formed. Thus, socialization teaches us the cultural norms, values, and skills necessary to survive in society. Socialization also enables us to form social identities and an awareness about ourselves as individuals. The following reading by Judith Lorber is taken from her book *Paradoxes of Gender* (1993). Here, Lorber examines socialization and how we learn our gender identities following birth.

[Gethenians] do not see each other as men or women. This is almost impossible for our imagination to accept. What is the first question we ask about a newborn baby?

—URSULA LE GUIN

Talking about gender for most people is the equivalent of fish talking about water. Gender is so much the routine ground of everyday activities that questioning its taken-for-granted assumptions and presuppositions is like thinking about whether the sun will come up.[1] Gender is so pervasive that in our society we assume it is bred into our genes. Most people find it hard to believe that gender is constantly created and re-created out of human interaction, out of social life, and is the texture and order of that social life. Yet gender, like culture, is a human production that depends on everyone constantly "doing gender" (West and Zimmerman 1987).

And everyone "does gender" without thinking about it. Today, on the subway, I saw a well-dressed man with a year-old child in a stroller. Yesterday, on a bus, I saw a man with a tiny baby in a carrier on his chest. Seeing men taking care of small children in public is increasingly common—at least in New York City. But both men were quite obviously stared at—and smiled at, approvingly. Everyone was doing gender—the men who were changing the role of fathers and the other passengers, who were applauding them silently. But there was more gendering going on that probably fewer people noticed. The baby was wearing a white crocheted cap and white clothes. You couldn't tell if it was a boy or a girl. The child in the stroller was wearing a dark blue T-shirt and dark print pants. As they started to leave the train, the father put a Yankee baseball cap on the child's head. Ah, a boy, I thought. Then I noticed the gleam of tiny earrings in the child's ears, and as they got off, I saw the little flowered sneakers and lace-trimmed socks. Not a boy after all. Gender done.

Gender is such a familiar part of daily life that it usually takes a deliberate disruption of our expectations of how women and men are supposed to act to pay attention to how it is produced. Gender signs and signals are so ubiquitous that we usually fail to note them—unless they are missing or ambiguous. Then we are uncomfortable until we have successfully placed the other person in a gender status; otherwise, we feel socially dislocated. In our society, in addition to man and woman, the status can be *transvestite* (a person who dresses in opposite-gender clothes) and *transsexual* (a person who has had sex-change surgery). Transvestites and transsexuals carefully construct their gender status by dressing, speaking, walking, gesturing in the ways prescribed for women or men—whichever they want to be taken for—and so does any "normal" person.

For the individual, gender construction starts with assignment to a sex category on the basis of what the genitalia look like at birth.[2] Then babies are dressed or adorned in a way that displays the category because parents don't want to be constantly asked whether their baby is a girl or a boy. A sex category becomes a gender status through naming, dress, and the use of other gender markers. Once a child's gender is evident, others treat those in one gender differently from those in the other, and the children respond to the different treatment by feeling different and behaving differently. As soon as they can talk, they start to refer to themselves as members of their gender. Sex doesn't come into play again until puberty, but by that time, sexual feelings and desires and practices have been shaped by gendered norms and expectations. Adolescent boys and girls approach and avoid each other in an elaborately scripted and gendered mating dance. Parenting is gendered, with different expectations for mothers and for fathers, and people of different genders work at different kinds of jobs. The work adults do as mothers and fathers and as low-level workers and high-level bosses, shapes women's and men's life experiences, and these experiences produce different feelings, consciousness, relationships, skills—ways of being that we call feminine or masculine.[3] All of these processes constitute the social construction of gender.

Gendered roles change—today fathers are taking care of little children, girls and boys are wearing unisex clothing and getting the same education, women and men are working at the same jobs. Although many traditional social groups are quite strict about maintaining gender differences, in other social groups they seem to be blurring. Then why the one-year-old's earrings? Why is it still so important to mark a child as a girl or a boy, to make sure she is not taken for a boy or he for a girl? What would happen if they were? They would, quite literally, have changed places in their social world.

To explain why gendering is done from birth, constantly and by everyone, we have to look not only at the way individuals experience gender but at gender as a social institution. As a social institution, gender is one of the major ways that human beings organize their lives. Human society depends on a predictable division of labor, a designated allocation of scarce goods, assigned responsibility for children and others who cannot care for themselves, common values and their systematic transmission to new members, legitimate leadership, music, art, stories, games, and other symbolic productions. One way of choosing people for the different tasks of society is on the basis of their talents, motivations, and competence—their demonstrated achievements. The other way is on the basis of gender, race, ethnicity—ascribed membership in a category of people. Although societies vary in the extent to which they use one or the other of these ways of allocating people to work and to carry out other responsibilities, every society uses gender and age grades. Every society classifies people as "girl and boy children," "girls and boys ready to be married," and "fully adult women and men," constructs similarities among them and differences between them, and assigns them to different roles and responsibilities. Personality characteristics, feelings, motivations, and ambitions flow from these different life experiences so that the members of these different groups become different kinds of people. The process of gendering and its outcome are legitimated by religion, law, science, and the society's entire set of values.

. . .

Western society's values legitimate gendering by claiming that it all comes from physiology—female and male procreative differences. But gender and sex are not equivalent, and gender as a social construction does not flow automatically from genitalia and reproductive organs, the main physiological differences of females and males. In the construction of ascribed social statuses, physiological differences such as sex, stage of development, color of skin, and size are crude markers. They are not the source of the social statuses of gender, age grade, and race. Social statuses are carefully constructed through prescribed processes of teaching, learning, emulation, and enforcement.

Whatever genes, hormones, and biological evolution contribute to human social institutions is materially as well as qualitatively transformed by social
practices. Every social institution has a material base, but culture and social
practices transform that base into something with qualitatively different patterns and constraints. The economy is much more than producing food and
goods and distributing them to eaters and users; family and kinship are not
the equivalent of having sex and procreating; morals and religions cannot
be equated with the fears and ecstasies of the brain; language goes far beyond
the sounds produced by tongue and larynx. No one eats "money" or "credit";
the concepts of "god" and "angels" are the subjects of theological disquisi-
tions; not only words but objects, such as their flag, "speak" to the citizens of
a country.

Similarly, gender cannot be equated with biological and physiological
differences between human females and males. The building blocks of gender are *socially constructed statuses*. Western societies have only two genders,
"man" and "woman." Some societies have three genders—men, women, and
berdaches or *hijras* or *xaniths*. Berdaches, hijras, and xaniths are biological males
who behave, dress, work, and are treated in most respects as social women;
they are therefore not men, nor are they female women; they are, in our language, "male women." [4] There are African and American Indian societies that
have a gender status called *manly hearted women*—biological females who
work, marry, and parent as men; their social status is "female men" (Amadiume 1987; Blackwood 1984). They do not have to behave or dress as men to
have the social responsibilities and prerogatives of husbands and fathers;
what makes them men is enough wealth to buy a wife.

Modern Western societies' *transsexuals* and *transvestites* are the nearest
equivalent of these crossover genders, but they are not institutionalized as
third genders (Bolin 1987). Transsexuals are biological males and females
who have sex-change operations to alter their genitalia. They do so in order
to bring their physical anatomy in congruence with the way they want to live
and with their own sense of gender identity. They do not become a third gender; they change genders. Transvestites are males who live as women and females who live as men but do not intend to have sex-change surgery. Their
dress, appearance, and mannerisms fall within the range of what is expected
from members of the opposite gender, so that they "pass." They also change
genders, sometimes temporarily, some for most of their lives. Transvestite
women have fought in wars as men soldiers as recently as the nineteenth century; some married women, and others went back to being women and married men once the war was over. [5] Some were discovered when their wounds
were treated; others not until they died. In order to work as a jazz musician,
a man's occupation, Billy Tipton, a woman, lived most of her life as a man.
She died recently at 74, leaving a wife and three adopted sons for whom she
was husband and father, and musicians with whom she had played and traveled, for whom she was "one of the boys" (*New York Times* 1989). [6] There have

been many other such occurrences of women passing as men to do more prestigious or lucrative men's work (Matthaei 1982:192–93).[7]

Genders, therefore, are not attached to a biological substratum. Gender boundaries are breachable, and individual and socially organized shifts from one gender to another call attention to "cultural, social, or aesthetic dissonances" (Garber 1992:16). These odd or deviant or third genders show us what we ordinarily take for granted—that people have to learn to be women and men. Men who cross-dress for performances or for pleasure often learn from women's magazines how to "do femininity" convincingly (Garber 1992: 41–51). Because transvestism is direct evidence of how gender is constructed, Marjorie Garber claims it has "extraordinary power . . . to disrupt, expose, and challenge, putting in question the very notion of the 'original' and of stable identity" (1992:16).

Gender Bending

It is difficult to see how gender is constructed because we take it for granted that it's all biology, or hormones, or human nature. The differences between women and men seem to be self-evident, and we think they would occur no matter what society did. But in actuality, human females and males are physiologically more similar in appearance than are the two sexes of many species of animals and are more alike than different in traits and behavior (Epstein 1988). Without the deliberate use of gendered clothing, hairstyles, jewelry, and cosmetics, women and men would look far more alike.[8] Even societies that do not cover women's breasts have gender-identifying clothing, scarification, jewelry, and hairstyles.

The ease with which many transvestite women pass as men and transvestite men as women is corroborated by the common gender misidentification in Westernized societies of people in jeans, T-shirts, and sneakers. Men with long hair may be addressed as "miss," and women with short hair are often taken for men unless they offset the potential ambiguity with deliberate gender markers (Devor 1987, 1989). Jan Morris, in *Conundrum,* an autobiographical account of events just before and just after a sex-change operation, described how easy it was to shift back and forth from being a man to being a woman when testing how it would feel to change gender status. During this time, Morris still had a penis and wore more or less unisex clothing; the context alone made the man and the woman:

> Sometimes the arena of my ambivalence was uncomfortably small. At the Travellers' Club, for example, I was obviously known as a man of sorts—women were only allowed on the premises at all during a few hours of the day, and even then were hidden away as far as possible in lesser rooms or alcoves. But I had another club, only a few hundred yards away,

where I was known only as a woman, and often I went directly from one to the other, imperceptibly changing roles on the way—"Cheerio, sir," the porter would say at one club, and "Hello, madam," the porter would greet me at the other. (1975:132)

Gender shifts are actually a common phenomenon in public roles as well. Queen Elizabeth II of England bore children, but when she went to Saudi Arabia on a state visit, she was considered an honorary man so that she could confer and dine with the men who were heads of a state that forbids unrelated men and women to have face-to-unveiled face contact. In contemporary Egypt, lower-class women who run restaurants or shops dress in men's clothing and engage in unfeminine aggressive behavior, and middle-class educated women of professional or managerial status can take positions of authority (Rugh 1986:131). In these situations, there is an important status change: These women are treated by the others in the situation as if they are men. From their own point of view, they are still women. From the social perspective, however, they are men.[9]

In many cultures, gender bending is prevalent in theater or dance—the Japanese kabuki are men actors who play both women and men; in Shakespeare's theater company, there were no actresses—Juliet and Lady Macbeth were played by boys. Shakespeare's comedies are full of witty comments on gender shifts. Women characters frequently masquerade as young men, and other women characters fall in love with them; the boys playing these masquerading women, meanwhile, are acting out pining for the love of men characters.[10] . . .

. . .

But despite the ease with which gender boundaries can be traversed in work, in social relationships, and in cultural productions, gender statuses remain. Transvestites and transsexuals do not challenge the social construction of gender. Their goal is to be feminine women and masculine men (Kando 1973). Those who do not want to change their anatomy but do want to change their gender behavior fare less well in establishing their social identity. . . .

. . .

Paradoxically, then, bending gender rules and passing between genders does not erode but rather preserves gender boundaries. In societies with only two genders, the gender dichotomy is not disturbed by transvestites, because others feel that a transvestite is only transitorily ambiguous—is "really a man or woman underneath." After sex-change surgery, transsexuals end up in a conventional gender status—a "man" or a "woman" with the appropriate genitals (Eichler 1989). When women dress as men for business reasons, they are indicating that in that situation, they want to be treated the way men are treated; when they dress as women, they want to be treated as women:

By their male dress, female entrepreneurs signal their desire to suspend the expectations of accepted feminine conduct without losing respect and reputation. By wearing what is "unattractive" they signify that they are not intending to display their physical charms while engaging in public activity. Their loud, aggressive banter contrasts with the modest demeanor that attracts men. . . . Overt signalling of a suspension of the rules preserves normal conduct from eroding expectations. (Rugh 1986:131)

For Individuals, Gender Means Sameness

Although the possible combinations of genitalia, body shapes, clothing, mannerisms, sexuality, and roles could produce infinite varieties in human beings, the social institution of gender depends on the production and maintenance of a limited number of gender statuses and of making the members of these statuses similar to each other. Individuals are born sexed but not gendered, and they have to be taught to be masculine or feminine.[11] As Simone de Beauvoir said: "One is not born, but rather becomes, a woman . . . ; it is civilization as a whole that produces this creature . . . which is described as feminine" ([1949] 1953:267).

Children learn to walk, talk, and gesture the way their social group says girls and boys should. Ray Birdwhistell, in his analysis of body motion as human communication, calls these learned gender displays *tertiary* sex characteristics and argues that they are needed to distinguish genders because humans are a weakly dimorphic species—their only sex markers are genitalia (1970:39–46). Clothing, paradoxically, often hides the sex but displays the gender.

In early childhood, humans develop gendered personality structures and sexual orientations through their interactions with parents of the same and opposite gender. As adolescents, they conduct their sexual behavior according to gendered scripts. Schools, parents, peers, and the mass media guide young people into gendered work and family roles. As adults, they take on a gendered social status in their society's stratification system. Gender is thus both ascribed and achieved (West and Zimmerman 1987).

The achievement of gender was most dramatically revealed in a case of an accidental transsexual—a baby boy whose penis was destroyed in the course of a botched circumcision when he was seven months old (Money and Ehrhardt 1972:118–23). The child's sex category was changed to "female," and a vagina was surgically constructed when the child was 17 months old. The parents were advised that they could successfully raise the child, one of identical twins, as a girl. Physicians assured them that the child was too young to have formed a gender identity. Children's sense of which gender they belong to usually develops around the age of three, at the time that they start to group objects and recognize that the people around them also fit into categories—big, little; pink-skinned, brown-skinned; boys, girls. Three has also been the age when children's appearance is ritually gendered, usually by cutting a boy's hair or dressing him in distinctively masculine clothing. In Victorian times, English boys wore dresses up to the age of three, when they were put into short pants (Garber 1992:1–2).

The parents of the accidental transsexual bent over backward to feminize the child—and succeeded. Frilly dresses, hair ribbons, and jewelry created a pride in looks, neatness, and "daintiness." More significant, the child's dominance was also feminized:

> The girl had many tomboyish traits, such as abundant physical energy, a high level of activity, stubbornness, and being often the dominant one in a girls' group. Her mother tried to modify her tomboyishness: ". . . I teach her to be more polite and quiet. I always wanted those virtues. I never did manage, but I'm going to try to manage them to—my daughter—to be more quiet and ladylike." From the beginning the girl had been the dominant twin. By age of three, her dominance over her brother was, as her mother described it, that of a mother hen. The boy in turn took up for his sister, if anyone threatened her. (Money and Ehrhardt 1972:122)

This child was not a tomboy because of male genes or hormones; according to her mother, she herself had also been a tomboy. What the mother had learned poorly while growing up as a "natural" female she insisted that her physically reconstructed son-daughter learn well. For both mother and child, the social construction of gender overrode any possibly inborn traits.

People go along with the imposition of gender norms because the weight of morality as well as immediate social pressure enforces them. Consider how many instructions for properly gendered behavior are packed into this mother's admonition to her daughter: "This is how to hem a dress when you see the hem coming down and so to prevent yourself from looking like the slut I know you are so bent on becoming" (Kincaid 1978).

Gender norms are inscribed in the way people move, gesture, and even eat. In one African society, men were supposed to eat with their "whole mouth, wholeheartedly, and not, like women, just with the lips, that is half-heartedly, with reservation and restraint" (Bourdieu [1980] 1990:70). Men and women in this society learned to walk in ways that proclaimed their different positions in the society:

> The manly man . . . stands up straight into the face of the person he approaches, or wishes to welcome. Ever on the alert, because ever threatened, he misses nothing of what happens around him. . . . Conversely, a well brought-up woman . . . is expected to walk with a slight stoop, avoiding every misplaced movement of her body, her head or her arms, looking down, keeping her eyes on the spot where she will next put her foot, especially if she happens to have to walk past the men's assembly. (p. 70)

Many cultures go beyond clothing, gestures, and demeanor in gendering children. They inscribe gender directly into bodies. In traditional Chinese society, mothers bound their daughters' feet into three-inch stumps to enhance their sexual attractiveness. Jewish fathers circumcise their infant sons to show their covenant with God. Women in African societies remove the clitoris of prepubescent girls, scrape their labia, and make the lips grow together to preserve their chastity and ensure their marriageability. In Western societies, women augment their breast size with silicone and reconstruct their faces with cosmetic surgery to conform to cultural ideals of feminine beauty. . . .

. . .

Most parents create a gendered world for their newborn by naming, birth announcements, and dress. Children's relationships with same-gendered and different-gendered caretakers structure their self-identifications and personalities. Through cognitive development, children extract and apply to their own actions the appropriate behavior for those who belong in their own gender, as well as race, religion, ethnic group, and social class, rejecting what is not appropriate. If their social categories are highly valued, they value themselves highly; if their social categories are low status, they lose self-esteem (Chodorow 1974). Many feminist parents who want to raise androgynous children soon lose their children to the pull of gendered norms (Gordon 1990: 87–90). My son attended a carefully nonsexist elementary school, which didn't even have girls' and boys' bathrooms. When he was seven or eight years old, I attended a class play about "squares" and "circles" and their need for each other and noticed that all the girl squares and circles wore makeup, but none of the boy squares and circles did. I asked the teacher about it after the play, and she said, "Bobby said he was not going to wear makeup, and he is a powerful child, so none of the boys would either." In a long discussion about conformity, my son confronted me with the question of who the conformists were, the boys who followed their leader or the girls who listened to the woman teacher. In actuality, they both were, because they both followed same-gender leaders and acted in gender-appropriate ways. (Actors may wear makeup, but real boys don't.)

For human beings there is no essential femaleness and maleness, femininity or masculinity, womanhood or manhood, but once gender is ascribed, the social order constructs and holds individuals to strongly gendered norms and expectations. Individuals may vary on many of the components of gender and may shift genders temporarily or permanently, but they must fit into the limited number of gender statuses their society recognizes. In the process, they re-create their society's version of women and men: "If we do gender appropriately, we simultaneously sustain, reproduce, and render legitimate the institutional arrangements. . . . If we fail to do gender appropriately, we as individuals—not the institutional arrangements—may be called to account (for our character, motives, and predispositions)" (West and Zimmerman 1987:146).

The gendered practices of everyday life reproduce a society's view of how women and men should act (Bourdieu [1980] 1990). Gendered social arrangements are justified by religion and cultural productions and backed by law, but the most powerful means of sustaining the moral hegemony of the dominant gender ideology is that the process is made invisible; any possible alternatives are virtually unthinkable (Foucault 1972; Gramsci 1971).[12]

For Society, Gender Means Difference

The pervasiveness of gender as a way of structuring social life demands that gender statuses be clearly differentiated. Varied talents, sexual preferences, identities, personalities, interests, and ways of interacting fragment the individual's bodily and social experiences. Nonetheless, these are organized in Western cultures into two and only two socially and legally recognized gender statuses, "man" and "woman."[13] In the social construction of gender, it does not matter what men and women actually do; it does not even matter if they do exactly the same thing. The social institution of gender insists only that what they do is *perceived* as different.

If men and women are doing the same tasks, they are usually spatially segregated to maintain gender separation, and often the tasks are given different job titles as well, such as executive secretary and administrative assistant (Reskin 1988). If the differences between women and men begin to blur, society's "sameness taboo" goes into action (Rubin 1975:178). At a rock and roll dance at West Point in 1976, the year women were admitted to the prestigious military academy for the first time, the school's administrators "were reportedly perturbed by the sight of mirror-image couples dancing in short hair and dress gray trousers," and a rule was established that women cadets could dance at these events only if they wore skirts (Barkalow and Raab 1990:53).[14] Women recruits in the U.S. Marine Corps are required to wear makeup—at a minimum, lipstick and eye shadow—and they have to take classes in makeup, hair care, poise, and etiquette. This feminization is part of a deliberate policy of making them clearly distinguishable from men Marines. Christine Williams quotes a 25-year-old woman drill instructor as saying: "A lot of the recruits who come here don't wear makeup; they're tomboyish or athletic. A lot of them have the preconceived idea that going into the military means they can still be a tomboy. They don't realize that you are a *Woman* Marine" (1989:76–77).[15]

If gender differences were genetic, physiological, or hormonal, gender bending and gender ambiguity would occur only in hermaphrodites, who are born with chromosomes and genitalia that are not clearly female or male. Since gender differences are socially constructed, all men and all women can enact the behavior of the other, because they know the other's social script:

"'Man' and 'woman' are at once empty and overflowing categories. Empty because they have no ultimate, transcendental meaning. Overflowing because even when they appear to be fixed, they still contain within them alternative, denied, or suppressed definitions" (Scott 1988:49). Nonetheless, though individuals may be able to shift gender statuses, the gender boundaries have to hold, or the whole gendered social order will come crashing down.

Paradoxically, it is the social importance of gender statuses and their external markers—clothing, mannerisms, and spatial segregation—that makes gender bending or gender crossing possible—or even necessary. The social viability of differentiated gender statuses produces the need or desire to shift statuses. Without gender differentiation, transvestism and transsexuality would be meaningless. You couldn't dress in the opposite gender's clothing if all clothing were unisex. There would be no need to reconstruct genitalia to match identity if interests and lifestyles were not gendered. There would be no need for women to pass as men to do certain kinds of work if jobs were not typed as "women's work" and "men's work." Women would not have to dress as men in public life in order to give orders or aggressively bargain with customers.

Gender boundaries are preserved when transsexuals create congruous autobiographies of always having felt like what they are now. The transvestite's story also "recuperates social and sexual norms" (Garber 1992:69). In the transvestite's normalized narrative, he or she "is 'compelled' by social and economic forces to disguise himself or herself in order to get a job, escape repression, or gain artistic or political 'freedom'" (Garber 1992:70). The "true identity," when revealed, causes amazement over how easily and successfully the person passed as a member of the opposite gender, not a suspicion that gender itself is something of a put-on.

NOTES

1. Gender is, in Erving Goffman's words, an aspect of *Felicity's Condition:* "any arrangement which leads us to judge an individual's . . . acts not to be a manifestation of strangeness. Behind Felicity's Condition is our sense of what it is to be sane" (1983, p. 27). Also see Bem 1993; Frye 1983, pp. 17–40; Goffman 1977.
2. In cases of ambiguity in countries with modern medicine, surgery is usually performed to make the genitalia more clearly male or female.
3. See J. Butler 1990 for an analysis of how doing gender *is* gender identity.
4. On the hijras of India, see Nanda 1990; on the xaniths of Oman, Wikan 1982, pp. 168–86; on the American Indian berdaches, W. L. Williams 1986. Other societies that have similar institutionalized third-gender men are the Koniag of Alaska, the Tanala of Madagascar, the Mesakin of Nuba, and the Chukchee of Siberia (Wikan 1982, p. 170).
5. Durova 1989; Freeman and Bond 1992; Wheelwright 1989.
6. Gender segregation of work in popular music still has not changed very much, according to Groce and Cooper 1990, despite considerable androgyny in some very popular figures. See Garber 1992 on the androgyny. She discusses Tipton on pp. 67–70.

7. In the nineteenth century, not only did these women get men's wages, but they also "had male privileges and could do all manner of things other women could not: open a bank account, write checks, own property, go anywhere unaccompanied, vote in elections" (Faderman 1991, p. 44).

8. When unisex clothing and men wearing long hair came into vogue in the United States in the mid-1960s, beards and mustaches for men also came into style again as gender identifications.

9. For other accounts of women being treated as men in Islamic countries, as well as accounts of women and men cross-dressing in these countries, see Garber 1992, pp. 304–52.

10. Dollimore 1986; Garber 1992, pp. 32–40; Greenblatt 1987, pp. 66–93; Howard 1988. For Renaissance accounts of sexual relations with women and men of ambiguous sex, see Lacqueur 1990, pp. 134–39. For modern accounts of women passing as men that other women find sexually attractive, see Devor 1989, pp. 136–37; Wheelwright 1989, pp. 53–59.

11. For an account of how a potential man-to-woman transsexual learned to be feminine, see Garfinkel 1967, pp. 116–85, 285–88. For a gloss on this account that points out how, throughout his encounters with Agnes, Garfinkel failed to see how he himself was constructing his own masculinity, see Rogers 1992.

12. The concepts of moral hegemony, the effects of everyday activities (praxis) on thought and personality, and the necessity of consciousness of these processes before political change can occur are all based on Marx's analysis of class relations.

13. Other societies recognize more than two categories, but usually no more than three or four (Jacobs and Roberts 1989).

14. Carol Barkalow's book has a photograph of 11 first-year West Pointers in a math class, who are dressed in regulation pants, shirts, and sweaters, with short haircuts. The caption challenges the reader to locate the only woman in the room.

15. The taboo on males and females looking alike reflects the U.S. military's homophobia (Bérubé 1989). If you can't tell those with a penis from those with a vagina, how are you going to determine whether their sexual interest is heterosexual or homosexual unless you watch them having sexual relations?

REFERENCES

Amadiume, Ifi. 1987. *Male Daughters, Female Husbands: Gender and Sex in an African Society.* London: Zed Books.

Barkalow, Carol, with Andrea Raab. 1990. *In the Men's House.* New York: Poseidon Press.

Beauvoir, Simone de. [1949] 1953. *The Second Sex,* translated by H. M. Parshley. New York: Knopf.

Bem, Sandra Lipsitz. 1993. *The Lenses of Gender: Transforming the Debate on Sexual Inequality.* New Haven, CT: Yale University Press.

Bérubé, Allan. 1989. "Marching to a Different Drummer: Gay and Lesbian GIs in World War II." In *Hidden from History: Reclaiming the Gay and Lesbian Past,* edited by Martin Bauml Duberman, Martha Vicinus, and George Chauncey, Jr. New York: New American Library.

Birdwhistell, Ray L. 1970. *Kinesics and Context: Essays on Body Motion Communication.* Philadelphia: University of Pennsylvania Press.

Blackwood, Evelyn. 1984. "Sexuality and Gender in Certain Native American Tribes: The Case of Cross-Gender Females." *Signs* 10:27–42.

Bolin, Anne. 1987. "Transsexualism and the Limits of Traditional Analysis." *American Behavior Scientist* 31:41–65.

Bourdieu, Pierre. [1980] 1990. *The Logic of Practice.* Stanford, CA: Stanford University Press.

—— and Jean-Claude Passeron. [1970] 1977. *Reproduction in Education, Society and Culture,* translated by Richard Nice. Newbury Park, CA: Sage.

Butler, Judith. 1990. *Gender Trouble: Feminism and the Subversion of Identity.* New York: Routledge.

Chodorow, Nancy. 1974. "Family Structure and Feminine Personality." In *Woman, Culture and Society,* edited by Michelle Zimbalist Rosaldo and Louise Lamphere. Stanford, CA: Stanford University Press.

Devor, Holly. 1987. "Gender Blending Females: Women and Sometimes Men." *American Behavior Scientist* 31:12–40.

——. 1989. *Gender Blending: Confronting the Limits of Duality.* Bloomington: University of Indiana Press.

Dollimore, Jonathan. 1986. "Subjectivity, Sexuality, and Transgression: The Jacobean Connection." *Renaissance Drama,* n.s. 17:53–81.

Durova, Nadezhda. 1989. *The Cavalry Maiden: Journals of a Russian Officer in the Napoleonic Wars,* translated by Mary Fleming Zirin. Bloomington: Indiana University Press.

Eichler, Margrit. 1989. "Sex Change Operations: The Last Bulwark of the Double Standard." In *Feminist Frontiers II,* edited by Laurel Richardson and Verta Taylor. New York: Random House.

Epstein, C. F. 1988. *Deceptive Distinctions: Sex, Gender and the Social Order.* New Haven, CT: Yale University Press.

Faderman, Lillian. 1991. *Odd Girls and Twilight Lovers: A History of Lesbian Life in Twentieth-Century America.* New York: Columbia University Press.

Foucault, Michel. 1972. *The Archeology of Knowledge and the Discourse on Language,* translated by A. M. Sheridan Smith. New York: Pantheon.

Freeman, Lucy and Alma Halbert Bond. 1992. *America's First Woman Warrior: The Courage of Deborah Sampson.* New York: Paragon.

Frye, Marilyn. 1983. *The Politics of Reality: Essays in Feminist Theory.* Trumansburg, NY: Crossing Press.

Garber, Marjorie. 1992. *Vested Interests: Cross-Dressing and Cultural Anxiety.* New York: Routledge.

Garfinkel, Harold. 1967. *Studies in Ethnomethodology.* Englewood Cliffs, NJ: Prentice-Hall.

Goffman, Erving. 1977. "The Arrangement between the Sexes." *Theory and Society* 4:301–33.

——. 1983. "Felicity's Condition." *American Journal of Sociology* 89:1–53.

Gordon, Tuula. 1990. *Feminist Mothers.* New York: New York University Press.

Gramsci, Antonio. 1971. *Selections from the Prison Notebooks,* translated and edited by Quintin Hoare and Geoffrey Nowell Smith. New York: International Publishers.

Greenblatt, Stephen. 1987. *Shakespearean Negotiations: The Circulation of Social Energy in Renaissance England.* Berkeley: University of California Press.

Groce, Stephen B. and Margaret Cooper. 1990. "Just Me and the Boys? Women in Local-Level Rock and Roll." *Gender & Society* 4:220–29.

Howard, Jean E. 1988. "Crossdressing, the Theater, and Gender Struggle in Early Modern England." *Shakespeare Quarterly* 39:418–41.

Jacobs, Sue-Ellen and Christine Roberts. 1989. "Sex, Sexuality, Gender, and Gender Variance." In *Gender and Anthropology,* edited by Sandra Morgen. Washington, DC: American Anthropological Association.

Kando, Thomas. 1973. *Sex Change: The Achievement of Gender Identity among Feminized Transsexuals*. Springfield, IL: Charles C. Thomas.

Kincaid, Jamaica. June 26, 1978. "Girl." *The New Yorker*.

Lacqueur, Thomas. 1990. *Making Sex: Body and Gender from the Greeks to Freud*. Cambridge, MA: Harvard University Press.

Matthaei, Julie A. 1982. *An Economic History of Woman's Work in America*. New York: Schocken.

Money, John and Anke A. Ehrhardt. 1972. *Man and Woman, Boy and Girl*. Baltimore, MD: Johns Hopkins University Press.

Morris, Jan. 1975. *Conundrum*. New York: Signet.

Nanda, Serena. 1990. *Neither Man nor Woman: The Hijiras of India*. Belmont, CA: Wadsworth.

New York Times. February 2, 1989. "Musician's Death at 74 Reveals He Was a Woman."

Reskin, Barbara F. 1988. "Bringing the Men Back In: Sex Differentiation and the Devaluation of Women's Work." *Gender & Society* 2:58–81.

Rogers, Mary R. 1992. "They Were All Passing: Agnes, Garfinkel, and Company." *Gender & Society* 6:169–91.

Rubin, Gayle. 1975. "The Traffic in Women: Notes on the Political Economy of Sex." In *Toward an Anthropology of Women*, edited by Rayna Rapp Reiter. New York: Monthly Review Press.

Rugh, Andrea B. 1986. *Reveal and Conceal: Dress in Contemporary Egypt*. Syracuse, NY: Syracuse University Press.

Scott, Joan Wallach. 1988. *Gender and the Politics of History*. New York: Columbia University Press.

West, Candace and Don Zimmerman. 1987. "Doing Gender." *Gender & Society* 1:125–51.

Wheelwright, Julie. 1989. *Amazons and Military Maids: Women Who Cross-Dressed in Pursuit of Life, Liberty and Happiness*. London: Pandora Press.

Wikan, Unni. 1982. *Behind the Veil in Arabia: Women in Oman*. Baltimore, MD: Johns Hopkins University Press.

Williams, Christine L. 1989. *Gender Differences at Work: Women and Men in Nontraditional Occupations*. Berkeley: University of California Press.

Williams, Walter L. 1986. *The Spirit and the Flesh: Sexual Diversity in American Indian Culture*. Boston: Beacon Press.

12

BOYHOOD, ORGANIZED SPORTS, AND THE CONSTRUCTION OF MASCULINITIES

MICHAEL MESSNER

An important point about socialization is that societal values, identities, and social roles are learned and *not* instinctual. We have to learn the norms and behaviors our society expects from us. In this reading, published in 1990, Michael Messner challenges the notion that gender identity formation is biological or natural. Instead, Messner examines how masculinity is learned through socialization, especially through the participation of boys and men in organized sports.

I view gender identity not as a "thing" that people "have," but rather as a *process of construction* that develops, comes into crisis, and changes as a person interacts with the social world. Through this perspective, it becomes possible to speak of "gendering" identities rather than "masculinity" or "femininity" as relatively fixed identities or statuses.

There is an agency in this construction: People are not passively shaped by their social environment. As recent feminist analyses of the construction of feminine gender identity have pointed out, girls and women are implicated in the construction of their own identities and personalities, both in terms of the ways that they participate in their own subordination and the ways that they resist subordination (Benjamin 1988; Haug 1987). Yet this self-construction is not a fully conscious process. There are also deeply woven, unconscious motivations, fears, and anxieties at work here. So, too, in the construction of masculinity. Levinson et al. (1978) have argued that masculine identity is neither fully "formed" by the social context, nor is it "caused" by some internal dynamic put into place during infancy. Instead, it is shaped and constructed through the interaction between the internal and the social. The internal gendering identity may set developmental "tasks," may create thresholds of anxiety and ambivalence, yet it is only through a concrete examination of people's interactions with others within social institutions that we can begin to understand both the similarities and differences in the construction of gender identities.

In this study I explore and interpret the meanings that males themselves attribute to their boyhood participation in organized sport. In what ways do males construct masculine identities within the institution of organized

From *Journal of Contemporary Ethnology* 18, no. 4 (January 1990): 416–44. Copyright © 1990 by Sage Publications, Inc. Reprinted with the permission of the publishers.

sports? In what ways do class and racial differences mediate this relationship and perhaps lead to the construction of different meanings, and perhaps different masculinities? And what are some of the problems and contradictions within these constructions of masculinity?

Description of Research

Between 1983 and 1985, I conducted interviews with 30 male former athletes. Most of the men I interviewed had played the (U.S.) "major sports"—football, basketball, baseball, track. At the time of the interview, each had been retired from playing organized sports for at least five years. Their ages ranged from 21 to 48, with the median, 33; 14 were black, 14 were white, and two were Hispanic; 15 of the 16 black and Hispanic men had come from poor or working-class families, while the majority (9 of 14) of the white men had come from middle-class or professional families. All had at some time in their lives based their identities largely on their roles as athletes and could therefore be said to have had "athletic careers." Twelve had played organized sports through high school, 11 through college, and seven had been professional athletes. Though the sample was not randomly selected, an effort was made to see that the sample had a range of difference in terms of race and social class backgrounds, and that there was some variety in terms of age, types of sports played, and levels of success in athletic careers. Without exception, each man contacted agreed to be interviewed.

The tape-recorded interviews were semistructured and took from one and one-half to six hours, with most taking about three hours. I asked each man to talk about four broad eras in his life: (1) his earliest experiences with sports in boyhood, (2) his athletic career, (3) retirement or disengagement from the athletic career, and (4) life after the athletic career. In each era, I focused the interview on the meanings of "success and failure," and on the boy's/man's relationships with family, with other males, with women, and with his own body.

In collecting what amounted to life histories of these men, my overarching purpose was to use feminist theories of masculine gender identity to explore how masculinity develops and changes as boys and men interact within the socially constructed world of organized sports. In addition to using the data to move toward some generalizations about the relationship between "masculinity and sport," I was also concerned with sorting out some of the variations among boys, based on class and racial inequalities, that led them to relate differently to athletic careers. I divided my sample into two comparison groups. The first group was made up of 10 men from higher-status backgrounds, primarily white, middle-class, and professional families. The second group was made up of 20 men from lower-status backgrounds, primarily minority, poor, and working-class families.

Boyhood and the Promise of Sports

Zane Grey once said, "All boys love baseball. If they don't they're not real boys" (as cited in Kimmel 1990). This is, of course, an ideological statement: In fact, some boys do *not* love baseball, or any other sports, for that matter. There are millions of males who at an early age are rejected by, become alienated from, or lose interest in organized sports. Yet all boys are, to a greater or lesser extent, judged according to their ability, or lack of ability, in competitive sports (Eitzen 1975; Sabo 1985). In this study I focus on those males who did become athletes—males who eventually poured thousands of hours into the development of specific physical skills. It is in boyhood that we can discover the roots of their commitment to athletic careers.

How did organized sports come to play such a central role in these boy's lives? When asked to recall how and why they initially got into playing sports, many of the men interviewed for this study seemed a bit puzzled: After all, playing sports was "just the thing to do." A 42-year-old black man who had played college basketball put it this way:

> *It was just what you did. It's kind of like, you went to school, you played athletics, and if you didn't, there was something wrong with you. It was just like brushing your teeth: It's just what you did. It's part of your existence.*

Spending one's time playing sports with other boys seemed as natural as the cycle of the seasons: baseball in the spring and summer, football in the fall, basketball in the winter—and then it was time to get out the old baseball glove and begin again. As a black 35-year-old former professional football star said:

> *I'd say when I wasn't in school, 95 percent of the time was spent in the park playing. It was the only thing to do. It just came as natural.*

And a black, 34-year-old professional basketball player explained his early experiences in sports:

> *My principal and teacher said, "Now if you work at this you might be pretty damned good." So it was more or less a community thing—everybody in the community said, "Boy, if you work hard and keep your nose clean, you gonna be good." Cause it was natural instinct.*

"It was natural instinct." "I was a natural." Several athletes used words such as these to explain their early attraction to sports. But certainly there is nothing "natural" about throwing a ball through a hoop, hitting a ball with a bat, or jumping over hurdles. A boy, for instance, may have amazingly dexterous inborn hand-eye coordination, but this does not predispose him to a career of hitting baseballs any more than it predisposes him to a life as a brain surgeon. When one listens closely to what these men said about their early experiences in sports, it becomes clear that their adoption of the self-definition of "natural athlete" was the result of what Connell (1990) has called "a collective practice" that constructs masculinities. The boyhood development of masculine identity and status—truly problematic in a society that offers no official rite of passage into adulthood—results from a process of interaction with people and social institutions. Thus, in discussing early motivations in sports, men commonly talk of the importance of relationships with family members, peers, and the broader community.

Family Influences

Though most of the men in this study spoke of their mothers with love, respect, even reverence, their descriptions of their earliest experiences in sports are stories of an exclusively male world. The existence of older brothers or uncles who served as teachers and athletic role models—as well as sources of competition for attention and status within the family—was very common. An older brother, uncle, or even close friend of the family who was a successful athlete appears to have acted as a sort of standard of achievement against whom to measure oneself. A 34-year-old black man who had been a three-sport star in high school said:

> *My uncles—my Uncle Harold went to the Detroit Tigers, played pro ball—all of 'em, everybody played sports, so I wanted to be better than anybody else. I knew that everybody in this town knew them—their names were something. I wanted my name to be just like theirs.*

Similarly, a black 41-year-old former professional football player recalled:

> *I was the younger of three brothers and everybody played sports, so consequently I was more or less forced into it. 'Cause one brother was always better than the next brother and then I came along and had to show them that I was just as good as them. My oldest brother was an all-city ballplayer, then my other brother comes along he's all-city and all-state, and then I have to come along.*

For some, attempting to emulate or surpass the athletic accomplishments of older male family members created pressures that were difficult to deal with. A 33-year-old white man explained that he was a good athlete during boyhood, but the constant awareness that his two older brothers had been better made it difficult for him to feel good about himself, or to have fun in sports:

> *I had this sort of reputation that I followed from the playgrounds through grade school, and through high school. I followed these guys who were all-conference and all-state.*

Most of these men, however, saw their relationship with their athletic older brothers and uncles in a positive light; it was within these relationships that they gained experience and developed motivations that gave them a competitive "edge" within their same-aged peer group. As a 33-year-old black man describes his earliest athletic experiences:

> *My brothers were role models. I wanted to prove—especially to my brothers—that I had heart, you know, that I was a man.*

When asked, "What did it mean to you to be 'a man' at that age?" he replied:

> *Well, it meant that I didn't want to be a so-called scaredy-cat. You want to hit a guy even though he's bigger than you to show that, you know, you've got this macho image. I remember that at that young an age, that feeling was exciting to me. And that carried over, and as I got older, I got better and I began to look around me and see, well hey! I'm competitive with these guys, even though I'm younger, you know? And then of course all the compliments come—and I began to notice a change, even in my parents—especially in my father—he was proud of that, and that was very important to me. He was extremely important. . . . He showed me more affection, now that I think of it.*

As this man's words suggest, if men talk of their older brothers and uncles mostly as role models, teachers, and "names" to emulate, their talk of their relationships with their fathers is more deeply layered and complex. Athletic skills and competition for status may often be learned from older brothers, but it is in boys' relationships with fathers that we find many of the keys to the emotional salience of sports in the development of masculine identity.

Relationships with Fathers

The fact that boys' introductions to organized sports are often made by fathers who might otherwise be absent or emotionally distant adds a powerful emotional charge to these early experiences (Osherson 1986). Although playing organized sports eventually came to feel "natural" for all of the men interviewed in this study, many needed to be "exposed" to sports, or even gently "pushed" by their fathers to become involved in activities like Little League baseball. A white, 33-year-old man explained:

> *I still remember it like it was yesterday—Dad and I driving up in his truck, and I had my glove and my hat and all that—and I said, "Dad, I don't want to do it." He says, "What?" I says, "I don't want to do it." I was nervous. That I might fail. And he says, "Don't be silly. Lookit: There's Joey and Petey and all your friends out there." And so Dad says, "You're gonna do it, come on." And in my memory he's never said that about anything else; he just knew I needed a little kick in the pants and I'd do it. And once you're out there and you see all the other kids making errors and stuff, and you know you're better than those guys, you know: Maybe I do belong here. As it turned out, Little League was a good experience.*

Some who were similarly "pushed" by their fathers were not so successful as the aforementioned man had been in Little League baseball, and thus the experience was not altogether a joyous affair. One 34-year-old white man, for instance, said he "inherited" his interest in sports from his father, who started playing catch with him at the age of four. Once he got into Little League, he felt pressured by his father, one of the coaches, who expected him to be the star of the team:

> I'd go 0-for-four sometimes, strike out three times in a Little League game, and I'd dread the ride home. I'd come home and he'd say, "Go in the bathroom and swing the bat in the mirror for an hour," to get my swing level. . . . It didn't help much, though, I'd go out and strike out three or four times again the next game too [laughs ironically].

When asked if he had been concerned with having his father's approval, he responded:

> Failure in his eyes? Yeah, I always thought that he wanted me to get some kind of [athletic] scholarship. I guess I was afraid of him when I was a kid. He didn't hit that much, but he had a rage about him—he'd rage, and that voice would just rattle you.

Similarly, a 24-year-old black man described his awe of his father's physical power and presence, and his sense of inadequacy in attempting to emulate him:

> My father had a voice that sounded like rolling thunder. Whether it was intentional on his part or not, I don't know, but my father gave me a sense, an image of him being the most powerful being on earth, and that no matter what I ever did I would never come close to him. . . . There were definite feelings of physical inadequacy that I couldn't work around.

It is interesting to note how these feelings of physical inadequacy relative to the father lived on as part of this young man's permanent internalized image. He eventually became a "feared" high school football player and broke school records in weight-lifting.

. . .

Using sports activities as a means of identifying with and "living up to" the power and status of one's father was not always such a painful and difficult task for the men I interviewed. Most did not describe fathers who "pushed" them to become sports stars. The relationship between their athletic strivings and their identification with their fathers was more subtle. A 48-year-old black man, for instance, explained that he was not pushed into sports by his father, but was aware from an early age of the community status his father had gained through sports. He saw his own athletic accomplishments as a way to connect with and emulate his father:

I wanted to play baseball because my father had been quite a good baseball player in the Negro leagues before baseball was integrated, and so he was kind of a model for me. I remember, quite young, going to a baseball game he was in—this was before the war and all—I remember being in the stands with my mother and seeing him on first base, and being aware of the crowd. . . . I was aware of people's confidence in him as a serious baseball player. I don't think my father ever said anything to me like "play sports." . . . [But] I knew he would like it if I did well. . . . His admiration was important. . . . He mattered.

. . .

First experiences in sports might often come through relationships with brothers or other male relatives, and the early emotional salience of sports was often directly related to a boy's relationship with his father. The sense of commitment that these young boys eventually made to the development of athletic careers is best explained as a process of development of masculine gender identity and status in relation to same-sex peers.

Masculine Identity and Early Commitment to Sports

When many of the men in this study said that during childhood they played sports because "it's just what everybody did," they of course meant that it was just what *boys* did. They were introduced to organized sports by older brothers and fathers, and once involved, found themselves playing within an exclusively male world. Though the separate (and unequal) gendered worlds of boys and girls came to appear as "natural," they were in fact socially constructed. Thorne's observations of children's activities in schools indicated that rather than "naturally" constituting "separate gendered cultures," there is considerable interaction between boys and girls in classrooms and on playgrounds. When adults set up legitimate contact between boys and girls, Thorne observed, this usually results in "relaxed interactions." But when activities in the classroom or on the playground are presented to children as sex-segregated activities and gender is marked by teachers and other adults ("boys line up here, girls over there"), "gender boundaries are heightened, and mixed-sex interaction becomes an explicit arena of risk" (Thorne 1986: 70). Thus sex-segregated activities such as organized sports as structured by adults, provide the context in which gendered identities and separate "gendered cultures" develop and come to appear natural. For the boys in this study, it became "natural" to equate masculinity with competition, physical strength, and skills. Girls simply did not (could not, it was believed) participate in these activities.

Yet it is not simply the separation of children, by adults, into separate activities that explains why many boys came to feel such a strong connection with sports activities, while so few girls did. As I listened to men recall their earliest experiences in organized sports, I heard them talk of insecurity, lone-liness, and especially a need to connect with other people as a primary moti-vation in their early sports strivings. As a 42-year-old white man stated, "The most important thing was just being out there with the rest of the guys—being friends." Another 32-year-old interviewee was born in Mexico and moved to the United States at a fairly young age. He never knew his father, and his mother died when he was only nine years old. Suddenly he felt root-less, and threw himself into sports. His initial motivations, however, do not appear to be based on a need to compete and win:

> *Actually, what I think sports did for me is it brought me into kind of an instant family. By being on a Little League team, or even just playing with all kinds of different kids in the neighborhood, it brought what I really wanted, which was some kind of closeness. It was just being there, and being friends.*

Clearly, what these boys needed and craved was that which was most problematic for them: connection and unity with other people. But why do these young males find *organized sports* such an attractive context in which to establish "a kind of closeness" with others? . . . For the boy who both seeks and fears attachment with others, the rule-bound structure of organized sports can promise to be a safe place in which to seek nonintimate attachment with others within a context that maintains clear boundaries, distance, and separation.

Competitive Structures and Conditional Self-Worth

Young boys may initially find that sports gives them the opportunity to ex-perience "some kind of closeness" with others, but the structure of sports and athletic careers often undermines the possibility of boys learning to tran-scend their fears of intimacy, thus becoming able to develop truly close and intimate relationships with others (Kidd 1990; Messner 1987). The sports world is extremely hierarchical, and an incredible amount of importance is placed on winning, on "being number one." For instance, a few years ago I observed a basketball camp put on for boys by a professional basketball coach and his staff. The youngest boys, about eight years old (who could barely reach the basket with their shots) played a brief scrimmage. After-ward, the coaches lined them up in a row in front of the older boys who were sitting in the grandstands. One by one, the coach would stand behind each boy, put his hand on the boy's head (much in the manner of a priestly bene-diction), and the older boys in the stands would applaud and cheer, louder or softer, depending on how well or poorly the young boy was judged to have performed. The two or three boys who were clearly the exceptional players looked confident that they would receive the praise they were due. Most of the boys, though, had expressions ranging from puzzlement to thinly disguised terror on their faces as they awaited the judgments of the older boys.

This kind of experience teaches boys that it is not "just being out there with the guys—being friends," that ensures the kind of attention and connection that they crave; it is being *better* than the other guys—*beating* them—that is the key to acceptance. Most of the boys in this study did have some early successes in sports, and thus their ambivalent need for connection with others was met, at least for a time. But the institution of sport tends to encourage the development of what Schafer (1975) has called "conditional self-worth" in boys. As boys become aware that acceptance by others is contingent upon being good—a "winner"—narrow definitions of success, based upon performance and winning become increasingly important to them. A 33-year-old black man said that by the time he was in his early teens

> *it was expected of me to do well in all my contests—I mean by my coaches, my peers, and my family. So I in turn expected to do well, and if I didn't do well, then I'd be very disappointed.*

The man from Mexico, discussed above, who said that he had sought "some kind of closeness" in his early sports experiences began to notice in his early teens that if he played well, was a *winner*, he would get attention from others:

> *It got to the point where I started realizing, noticing that people were always there for me, backing me all the time—sports got to be really fun because I always had some people there backing me. Finally my oldest brother started going to all my games, even though I had never really seen who he was [laughs]—after the game, you know, we never really saw each other, but he was at all my baseball games, and it seemed like we shared a kind of closeness there, but only in those situations. Off the field, when I wasn't in uniform, he was never around.*

By high school, he said, he felt "up against the wall." Sports hadn't delivered what he had hoped it would, but he thought if he just tried harder, won one more championship trophy, he would get the attention he truly craved. Despite his efforts, this attention was not forthcoming. And, sadly, the pressures he had put on himself to excel in sports had taken most of the fun out of playing.

For many of the men in this study, throughout boyhood and into adolescence, this conscious striving for successful achievement became the primary means through which they sought connection with other people (Messner 1987). But it is important to recognize that young males' internalized ambivalences about intimacy do not fully determine the contours and directions of their lives. Masculinity continues to develop through interaction with the social world—and because boys from different backgrounds are interacting with substantially different familial, educational, and other institutions, these differences will lead them to make different choices and define situations in different ways. Next, I examine the differences in the ways that boys from higher- and lower-status families and communities related to organized sports.

Status Differences and Commitments to Sports

In discussing early attractions to sports, the experiences of boys from higher- and lower-status backgrounds are quite similar. Both groups indicate the importance of fathers and older brothers in introducing them to sports. Both groups speak of the joys of receiving attention and acceptance among family and peers for early successes in sports. Note the similarities, for instance, in the following descriptions of boyhood athletic experiences of two men. First, a man born in a white, middle-class family:

> *I loved playing sports so much from a very early age because of early exposure. A lot of the sports came easy at an early age, and because they did, and because you were successful at something, I think that you're inclined to strive for that gratification. It's like, if you're good, you like it, because it's instant gratification. I'm doing something that I'm good at and I'm gonna keep doing it.*

Second, a black man from a poor family:

> *Fortunately I had some athletic ability, and, quite naturally, once you start doing good in whatever it is—I don't care if it's jacks—you show off what you do. That's your ability, that's your blessing, so you show it off as much as you can.*

For boys from both groups, early exposure to sports, the discovery that they had some "ability," shortly followed by some sort of family, peer, and community recognition, all eventually led to the commitment of hundreds and thousands of hours playing, practicing, and dreaming of future stardom. Despite these similarities, there are also some identifiable differences that begin to explain the tendency of males from lower-status backgrounds to develop higher levels of commitment to sports careers. The most clear-cut difference was that while men from higher-status backgrounds are likely to describe their earliest athletic experiences and motivations almost exclusively in terms of immediate family, men from lower-status backgrounds more commonly describe the importance of a broader community context. For instance, a 46-year-old man who grew up in a "poor working class" black family in a small town in Arkansas explained:

> *In that community, at the age of third or fourth grade, if you're a male, they expect you to show some kind of inclination, some kind of skill in football or basketball. It was an expected thing, you know? My mom and my dad, they didn't push at all. It was the general environment.*

A 48-year-old man describes sports activities as a survival strategy in his poor black community:

> *Sports protected me from having to compete in gang stuff, or having to be good with my fists. If you were an athlete and got into the fist world, that was your business, and that was okay—but you didn't have to if you didn't want to. People would generally defer to you, give you your space away from trouble.*

A 35-year-old man who grew up in "a poor black ghetto" described his boyhood relationship to sports similarly:

> *Where I came from, either you were one of two things: You were in sports or you were out on the streets being a drug addict, or breaking into places. The guys who were in sports, we had it a little easier, because we were accepted by both groups. . . . So it worked out to my advantage, cause I didn't get into a lot of trouble—some trouble, but not a lot.*

The fact that boys in lower-status communities faced these kinds of realities gave salience to their developing athletic identities. In contrast, sports were important to boys from higher-status backgrounds, yet the middle-class environment seemed more secure, less threatening, and offered far more options. By the time most of these boys got into junior high or high school, many had made conscious decisions to shift their attentions away from athletic careers to educational and (nonathletic) career goals. A 32-year-old white college athletic director told me that he had seen his chance to pursue a pro baseball career as "pissing in the wind," and instead, focused on education. Similarly, a 33-year-old white dentist who was a three-sport star in high school, decided not to play sports in college so he could focus on getting into dental school. As he put it,

> *I think I kind of downgraded the stardom thing. I thought it was small potatoes. And sure, that's nice in high school and all that, but on a broad scale, I didn't think it amounted to all that much.*

This statement offers an important key to understanding the construction of masculine identity within a middle-class context. The status that this boy got through sports had been *very* important to him, yet he could see that "on a broad scale," this sort of status was "small potatoes." This sort of early recognition is more than a result of the oft-noted middle-class tendency to raise "future-oriented" children (Rubin 1976; Sennett and Cobb 1973). Perhaps more important, it is that the *kinds* of future orientations developed by boys from higher-status backgrounds are consistent with the middle-class context. These men's descriptions of their boyhoods reveal that they grew up immersed in a wide range of institutional frameworks, of which organized sports was just one. And—importantly—they could see that the status of adult males around them was clearly linked to their positions within various professions, public institutions, and bureaucratic organizations. It was clear that access to this sort of institutional status came through educational achievement, not athletic prowess. A 32-year-old black man who grew up in a professional-class family recalled that he had idolized Wilt Chamberlain and dreamed of being a pro basketball player, yet his father discouraged his athletic strivings:

> *He knew I liked the game. I loved the game. But basketball was not recommended; my dad would say, "That's a stereotyped image for black youth. . . . When your basketball is gone and finished, what are you gonna do? One day, you might get injured. What are you gonna look forward to?" He stressed education.*

Similarly, a 32-year-old man who was raised in a white, middle-class family, had found in sports a key means of gaining acceptance and connection in his peer group. Yet he was simultaneously developing an image of himself as a "smart student," and becoming aware of a wide range of nonsports life options:

> *My mother was constantly telling me how smart I was, how good I was, what a nice person I was, and giving me all sorts of positive strokes, and those positive strokes became a self-motivating kind of thing. I had this image of myself as smart, and I lived up to that image.*

It is not that parents of boys in lower-status families did not also encourage their boys to work hard in school. Several reported that their parents "stressed books first, sports second." It's just that the broader social context—education, economy, and community—was more likely to *narrow* lower-status boys' perceptions of real-life options, while boys from higher-status backgrounds faced an expanding world of options. For instance, with a different socioeconomic background, one 35-year-old black man might have become a great musician instead of a star professional football running back. But he did not. When he was a child, he said, he was most interested in music:

> *I wanted to be a drummer. But we couldn't afford drums. My dad couldn't go out and buy me a drum set or a guitar even—it was just one of those things; he was just trying to make ends meet.*

But he *could* afford, as could so many in his socioeconomic condition, to spend countless hours at the local park, where he was told by the park supervisor

> *that I was a natural—not only in gymnastics or baseball—whatever I did, I was a natural. He told me I shouldn't waste this talent, and so I immediately started watching the big guys then.*

In retrospect, this man had potential to be a musician or any number of things, but his environment limited his options to sports, and he made the best of it. Even within sports, he, like most boys in the ghetto, was limited:

We didn't have any tennis courts in the ghetto—we used to have a lot of tennis balls, but no racquets. I wonder today how good I might be in tennis if I had gotten a racquet in my hands at an early age.

It is within this limited structure of opportunity that many lower-status young boys found sports to be *the* place, rather than *a* place, within which to construct masculine identity, status, the relationships. A 36-year-old white man explained that his father left the family when he was very young and his mother faced a very difficult struggle to make ends meet. As his words suggest, the more limited a boy's options, and the more insecure his family situation, the more likely he is to make an early commitment to an athletic career:

I used to ride my bicycle to Little League practice—if I'd waited for someone to pick me up and take me to the ball park I'd have never played. I'd get to the ball park and all the other kids would have their dad bring them to practice or games. But I'd park my bike to the side and when it was over I'd get on it and go home. Sports was the way for me to move everything to the side—family problems, just all the embarrassments—and think about one thing, and that was sports. . . . In the third grade, when the teacher went around the classroom and asked everybody, "What do you want to be when you grow up?," I said, "I want to be a major league baseball player," and everybody laughed their heads off.

This man eventually did enjoy a major league baseball career. Most boys from lower-status backgrounds who make similar early commitments to athletic careers are not so successful. As stated earlier, the career structure of organized sports is highly competitive and hierarchical. In fact, the chances of attaining professional status in sports are approximately 4:100,000 for a white man, 2:100,000 for a black man, and 3:1 million for a Hispanic man in the United States (Leonard and Reyman 1988). Nevertheless, the immediate rewards (fun, status, attention), along with the constricted (nonsports) structure of opportunity, attract disproportionately large numbers of boys from lower-status backgrounds to athletic careers as their major means of constructing a masculine identity. These are the boys who later, as young men, had to struggle with "conditional self-worth," and, more often than not, occupational dead ends. Boys from higher-status backgrounds, on the other hand, bolstered their boyhood, adolescent, and early adult status through their athletic accomplishments. Their wider range of experiences and life chances led to an early shift away from sports careers as the major basis of identity (Messner 1989).

Conclusion

The conception of the masculinity-sports relationship developed here begins to illustrate the idea of an "elective affinity" between social structure and personality. Organized sports is a "gendered institution"—an institution constructed by gender relations. As such, its structure and values (rules, formal organization, sex composition, etc.), reflect dominant conceptions of masculinity and femininity. Organized sports is also a "gendering institution"—an institution that helps to construct the current gender order. Part of this construction of gender is accomplished through the "masculinizing" of male bodies and minds.

Yet boys do not come to their first experiences in organized sports as "blank slates," but arrive with already "gendering" identities due to early developmental experiences and previous socialization. I have suggested here that an important thread running through the development of masculine identity is males' ambivalence toward intimate unity with others. Those boys who experience early athletic successes find in the structure of organized sport an affinity with this masculine ambivalence toward intimacy: The rule-bound, competitive, hierarchical world of sport offers boys an attractive means of establishing an emotionally distant (and thus "safe") connection with others. Yet as boys begin to define themselves as "athletes," they must learn that in order to be accepted (to have connection) through sports, they must be winners. And in order to be winners, they must construct relationships with others (and with themselves) that are consistent with the competitive and hierarchical values and structure of the sports world. As a result, they often develop a "conditional self-worth" that leads them to construct more instrumental relationships with themselves and others. This ultimately exacerbates their difficulties in constructing intimate relationships with others. In effect, the interaction between the young male's preexisting internalized ambivalence toward intimacy with the competitive, hierarchical institution of sport has resulted in the construction of a masculine personality that is characterized by instrumental rationality, goal-orientation, and difficulties with intimate connection and expression (Messner 1987).

This theoretical line of inquiry invites us not simply to examine how social institutions "socialize" boys, but also to explore the ways that boys' already-gendering identities interact with social institutions (which, like organized sport, are themselves the product of gender relations). This study has also suggested that it is not some singular "masculinity" that is being constructed through athletic careers. It may be correct, from a psychoanalytic perspective, to suggest that all males bring ambivalences toward intimacy to their interactions with the world, but "the world" is a very different place for males from different racial and socioeconomic backgrounds. Because males have substantially different interactions with the world, based on class, race, and other differences and inequalities, we might expect the construction of masculinity to take on different meanings for boys and men from differing backgrounds (Messner 1989). Indeed, this study has suggested that boys from higher-status backgrounds face a much broader range of options than do their lower-status counterparts. As a result, athletic careers take on different meanings for these boys. Lower-status boys are likely to see athletic careers as *the* institutional context for the construction of their masculine status and identities, while higher-status males make an early shift away from athletic careers toward other institutions (usually education and nonsports careers). A key line of inquiry for future studies might begin by exploring this irony of sports careers: Despite the fact that "the athlete" is currently an example of an exemplary form of masculinity in public ideology, the vast majority of boys who become most committed to athletic careers are never well rewarded for their efforts. The fact that class and racial dynamics lead boys from higher-status backgrounds, unlike their lower-status counterparts, to move into nonsports careers illustrates how the construction of different kinds of masculinities is a key component of the overall construction of the gender order.

REFERENCES

Benjamin, J. 1988. *The Bonds of Love: Psychoanalysis, Feminism and the Problem of Domination.* New York: Pantheon.

Chodorow, N. 1978. *The Reproduction of Mothering.* Berkeley: University of California Press.

Connell, R. W. 1990. "An Iron Man: The Body and Some Contradictions of Hegemonic Masculinity." In *Sport, Men and the Gender Order: Critical Feminist Perspectives,* edited by M. A. Messner and D. F. Sabo. Champaign, IL: Human Kinetics.

Craib, I. 1987. "Masculinity and Male Dominance." *Sociological Review* 38:721–43.

Eitzen, D. S. 1975. "Athletics in the Status System of Male Adolescents: A Replication of Coleman's *The Adolescent Society.*" *Adolescence* 10:268–76.

Gilligan, C. 1982. *In a Different Voice: Psychological Theory and Women's Development.* Cambridge, MA: Harvard University Press.

Haug, F. 1987. *Female Sexualization.* London: Verso.

Kidd, B. 1990. "The Men's Cultural Centre: Sports and the Dynamic of Women's Oppression / Men's Repression." In *Sport, Men and the Gender Order: Critical Feminist Perspectives,* edited by M. A. Messner and D. F. Sabo. Champaign, IL: Human Kinetics.

Kimmel, M. S. 1990. "Baseball and the Reconstitution of American Masculinity: 1880–1920." In *Sport, Men and the Gender Order: Critical Feminist Perspectives,* edited by M. A. Messner and D. F. Sabo. Champaign, IL: Human Kinetics.

Leonard, W. M., II, and J. M. Reyman. 1988. "The Odds of Attaining Professional Athlete Status: Refining the Computations." *Sociology of Sport Journal* 5:162–69.

Lever, J. 1976. "Sex Differences in the Games Children Play." *Social Problems* 23:478–87.

Levinson, D. J. et al. 1978. *The Seasons of a Man's Life.* New York: Ballantine.

Lichterman, P. 1986. "Chodorow's Psychoanalytic Sociology: A Project Half-Completed." *California Sociologist* 9:147–66.

Messner, M. 1987. "The Meaning of Success: The Athletic Experience and the Development of Male Identity." Pp. 193–210 in *The Making of Masculinities: The New Men's Studies,* edited by H. Brod. Boston: Allyn & Unwin.

———. 1989. "Masculinities and Athletic Careers." *Gender and Society* 3:71–88.

Osherson, S. 1986. *Finding Our Fathers: How a Man's Life Is Shaped by His Relationship with His Father.* New York: Fawcett Columbine.

Piaget, J. H. 1965. *The Moral Judgement of the Child.* New York: Free Press.

Rubin, L. B. 1976. *Worlds of Pain: Life in the Working Class Family.* New York: Basic Books.

Sabo, D. 1985. "Sport, Patriarchy and Male Identity: New Questions about Men and Sport." *Arena Review* 9:2.

Schafer, W. E. 1975. "Sport and Male Sex Role Socialization." *Sport Sociology Bulletin* 4:47–54.

Sennett, R., and J. Cobb. 1973. *The Hidden Injuries of Class.* New York: Random House.

Thorne, B. 1986. "Girls and Boys Together . . . but Mostly Apart: Gender Arrangements in Elementary Schools." Pp. 167–84 in *Relationships and Development,* edited by W. W. Hartup and Z. Rubin. Hillsdale, NJ: Erlbaum.

13

MAKING IT BY FAKING IT
Working-Class Students in an Elite Academic Environment

ROBERT GRANFIELD

Learning an occupation is a common form of adult socialization. Occupational socialization occurs during formal education, during job training, and during time spent on the job. Every profession has a set of values that it wants its colleagues to embrace. For example, to become a doctor one needs to learn the skills and knowledge of practicing medicine as well as the attitudes and values of the medical profession. Medical students experience an intense period of professional socialization during the years, almost a decade, they spend in medical school and residency. Law students are socialized as well, and the following reading by Robert Granfield (1991) discusses how working-class students are socialized into elite law schools and into the legal profession.

R esearch on stigma has generated significant insights into the complex relationship between self and society. The legacy of Goffman's (1963) seminal work on the subject can be found in studies on alcoholism, mental illness, homosexuality, physical deformities, and juvenile delinquency. Even the literature on gender and racial inequality has benefited from an emphasis on stigma. Goffman's attention to the social processes of devaluation and the emerging self-concepts of discredited individuals not

From *Journal of Contemporary Ethnology* 20, no. 3 (October 1991): 331–51. Copyright © 1991 by Sage Publications, Inc. Reprinted with the permission of the publishers.

only created research opportunities for generations of sociologists but contributed to a humanistic ideology that viewed stigma assignment and its effects as unjust.

One of the most vibrant research programs that emerged from Goffman's classic work has been in the area of stigma management. A host of conceptual terms have been employed to describe the process through which discreditable individuals control information about themselves so as to manage their social identity. Concepts such as passing, deviance disavowal, accounts, disclaimers, and covering have often been used in analyzing accommodations and adjustments to deviance, as Pfuhl's (1986) review shows. These tactics, while offering rewards associated with being seen as normal, frequently contribute to psychological stress. Possessing what Goffman (1963:5) referred to as "undesired differentness" often has significant consequences for one's personal identity as well as for available life chances.

. . .

In this article, I focus on class stigma by examining a group of highly successful, upwardly mobile, working-class students who gained admission to a prestigious Ivy League law school in the East. While upward mobility from the working class occurs far less often within elite branches of the legal profession (Heinz and Laumann 1982; Smigel 1969) or corporate management (Useem and Karabel 1986), a certain amount of this type of mobility does take place. Working-class aspirants to the social elite, however, must accumulate cultural capital (Bourdieu and Passeron 1990; Cookson and Persell 1985) before they are able to transcend their status boundaries.

First, this article examines the ways in which working-class students experience a sense of differentness and marginality within the law school's elite environment. Next, I explore how these students react to their emerging class stigma by managing information about their backgrounds. I then demonstrate that the management strategies contribute to identity ambivalence and consider the secondary forms of adjustment students use to resolve this tension. Finally, I discuss why an analysis of social class can benefit from the insights forged by Goffman's work on stigma.

Setting and Methodology

The data analyzed for this article were collected as part of a much larger project associated with law school socialization (Granfield 1989). The subjects consist of students attending a prestigious, national law school in the eastern part of the United States. The school has had a long reputation of training lawyers who have become partners in major Wall Street law firms, Supreme Court judges, United States presidents and other politicians, heads of foundations, and . . . [have assumed many] other eminent leadership positions. Throughout the school's history, it has drawn mostly on the talents of high-status males. It was not until the second half of the twentieth century that women, minorities, and members of the lower classes were allowed admission into this esteemed institution (Abel 1989).

Most of the students attending the university at the time the study was being conducted were white and middle class.[1] The overwhelming majority are the sons and daughters of the professional-managerial class. Over 70 percent of those returning questionnaires had Ivy League or other highly prestigious educational credentials. As one would expect, fewer working-class students possessed such credentials.

A triangulated research design (Fielding and Fielding 1986) was used to collect the data. The first phase consisted of extensive fieldwork at the law school from 1985 to 1988, during which time I became a "peripheral member" (Adler and Adler 1987) in selected student groups. My activities while in the field consisted of attending classes with students, participating in their Moot Court[2] preparations, studying with students on campus, and at times, in their apartments, lunching with them, becoming involved in student demonstrations over job recruiting and faculty hiring, attending extracurricular lectures presented on campus, and participating in orientation exercises for first-year students. Throughout the entire fieldwork phase, I assumed both overt and covert roles. During the observation periods in classrooms, I recorded teacher-student interactions that occurred.

To supplement these observations, I conducted in-depth interviews with 103 law students at various stages in their training. Both personal interviews and small-group interviews with three or four students were recorded. The interviews lasted approximately two hours each and sought to identify the lived process through which law students experience legal training.

Finally, I administered a survey to 50 percent of the 1,540 students attending the law school. The survey examined their backgrounds, motives for attending law school, subjective perceptions of personal change, expectations about future practice, and evaluations of various substantive areas of practice. Over half (391) of the questionnaires were returned—a high rate of response for a survey of six pages requiring approximately 30 minutes of the respondent's time.

For this article, a subset of working-class students was selected for extensive analysis. Of the 103 students interviewed for the larger study, 23 came from working-class backgrounds, none of these from either the labor aristocracy or the unstable sectors of the working class. Typical parental occupations include postal worker, house painter, factory worker, fireman, dock worker, and carpenter. Many of these students were interviewed several times during their law school career. Many of the students selected for interviews were identified through questionnaires, while others were selected through the process of snowball sampling (Chadwick, Bahr, and Albrecht 1984).

Feeling Out of Place

Working-class students entered this elite educational institution with a great deal of class pride. This sense of class pride is reflected in the fact that a significantly larger proportion of working-class students reported entering law school for the purposes of contributing to social change than their non-working-class counterparts (see Granfield and Koenig 1990). That these students entered law school with the desire to help the downtrodden suggests that they identified with their working-class kin. In fact, students often credited their class background as being a motivating factor in their decision to pursue a career in social justice. One third-year student, whose father worked as a postal worker, recalled her parental influence:

> *I wanted a career in social justice. It seemed to me to be a good value for someone who wanted to leave this world a little better than they found it. My parents raised me with a sense that there are right things and wrong things and that maybe you ought to try to do some right things with your life.*

A second-year student said that he was influenced by the oppressive experiences that his father endured as a factory laborer. Coming to law school to pursue a career in a labor union, this student explained, "I was affected by my father who had a job as a machinist. My father believes that corporations have no decency. I would term it differently but we're talking about the same thing." Identifying with their working-class heritage produced not only a sense of pride but a system of values and ideals that greatly influenced their initial career objectives.

However, identification with the working class began to diminish soon after these students entered law school. Not long after arriving, most working-class students encountered an entirely new moral career. Although initially proud of their accomplishments, they soon came to define themselves as different and their backgrounds a burden. Lacking the appropriate cultural capital (Bourdieu 1984) associated with their more privileged counterparts, working-class students began to experience a crisis in competency. Phrases such as "the first semester makes you feel extremely incompetent," "the first year is like eating humble pie," and "I felt very small, powerless, and dumb" were almost universal among these working-class students. Some students felt embarrassed by their difficulty in using the elaborated speech codes (Bernstein 1977) associated with the middle class. One working-class woman said that she was very aware of using "proper" English, adding that "it makes me self-conscious when I use the wrong word or tense. I feel that if I had grown up in the middle class, I wouldn't have lapses. I have difficulty expressing thoughts while most other people here don't."

The recognition of their apparent differentness is perhaps best noted by examining the students' perception of stress associated with the first year of studies. Incoming working-class students reported significantly higher levels of personal stress than did their counterparts with more elite backgrounds. Much of this anxiety came from fears of academic inadequacy. Despite generally excellent college grades and their success in gaining admission to a nationally ranked law school, these students often worried that they did not measure up to the school's high standards. Nearly 62 percent of the first-year working-class students reported experiencing excessive grade pressure, compared to only 35 percent of those students from higher social class backgrounds.

In the words of Sennett and Cobb (1973), this lack of confidence is a "hidden injury of class," a psychological burden that working-class students experienced as they came to acquire the "identity beliefs" associated with middle-class society. While most students experience some degree of uncertainty and competency crisis during their first year, working-class students face the additional pressure of being cultural outsiders. Lacking manners of speech, attire, values, and experiences associated with their more privileged counterparts, even the most capable working-class student felt out of place:

> I had a real problem my first year because law and legal education are based on upper-middle-class values. The class debates had to do with profit maximization, law and economics, atomistic individualism. I remember in class we were talking about landlords' responsibility to maintain decent housing in rental apartments. Some people were saying that there were good reasons not to do this. Well, I think that's bullshit because I grew up with people who lived in apartments with rats, leaks, and roaches. I feel really different because I didn't grow up in suburbia.

Another student, a third-year working-class woman, felt marginalized because even her teachers assumed class homogeneity:

> I get sensitive about what professors have to say in class. I remember in a business class the professor seemed to assume that we all had fathers that worked in business and that we all understood about family investments. He said, "You're all pretty much familiar with this because of your family background." I remember thinking, doesn't he think there's any people in this law school who come from a working-class background?

Such experiences contributed to a student's sense of living in an alien world. The social distance these students experienced early in their law school career produced considerable discomfort.

This discomfort grew more intense as they became increasingly immersed into this new elite world. Within a short span of time, these students began to experience a credential gap vis-à-vis other students who possessed more prestigious academic credentials. A first-year male student who attended a state school in the Midwest explained:

> I'm not like most people here. I didn't go to prestigious schools. I'm a bit of a minority here because of that. When I got here I was really intimidated by the fact of how many Yale and Harvard people there were here.

At times, working-class law students were even embarrassed by their spouse's lower status. One first-year student described how her husband's credential gap caused her some anxiety:

> *People would ask me what my husband did and I would say he works for Radio Shack. People would be surprised. That was hard. Lately, we haven't done as much with [law school] people.*

Thus students sometimes pruned contacts that would potentially result in stigma disclosure. In general, then, as working-class students progressed through law school, they began to adopt a view of themselves as different. The recognition of this difference subsequently led them to develop techniques of adjusting to their perceived secondary status.

Faking It

The management of identity has critical strategic importance not only for group affiliation and acceptance but for life chances. Stigma limits one's opportunities to participate in social life as a complete citizen, particularly so for those possessing gender or racial stigmas. However, because of the visibility of these stigmas, a person's adjustment to second-class citizenship is accomplished typically through either role engulfment in which a person accepts a spoiled identity (Schur 1971) or through direct confrontation where assignment of secondary status is itself challenged (Schur 1980). Rarely are these groups able to employ the concealment tactics typical among those groups whose stigma is not overtly visible.

Unlike gender or racial stigma, however, individuals often adjust to class stigma by learning to conceal their uniqueness. The practice of concealing one's class background, for instance, is not unusual. Certainly, members of the elite frequently learn that it is in "bad taste" to flaunt their privileged background and that it is more gracious to conceal their eminent social status (Baltzell 1958). Similarly, individuals who experience downward mobility often attempt to maintain their predecline image by concealing loss of status. Camouflaging unemployment in the world of management by using such terms as "consultant" and by doctoring résumés are ways that downwardly mobile executives "cover" their spoiled status (Newman 1988). Concealing one's social class circumstances and the stigma that may be associated with it assist individuals in dealing with any rejection and ostracism that may be forthcoming were the person's actual status known.

Initially, students who took pride in having accomplished upward mobility openly displayed a working-class presentation of self. Many went out of their way to maintain this presentation. One first-year student who grew up in a labor union family in New York explained that "I have consciously maintained my working-class image. I wear work shirts or old flannel shirts and blue jeans every day." During his first year, this student flaunted his working-class background, frequently also donning an old army jacket, hiking boots, and a wool hat. Identifying himself as part of the "proletarian left," he tried to remain isolated from what he referred to as the "elitist" law school community.

This attempt to remain situated in the working class, however, not only separated these students from the entire law school community but alienated them from groups that shared their ideological convictions. While much of the clothing worn by non-working-class students suggests resistance to being identified as a member of the elite, working-class students become increasingly aware of their differentness. Although these students identify with the working class, others, despite their appearance, possess traits and lifestyles that are often associated with more privileged groups (see Lurie 1983; Stone 1970). One first-year woman who described herself as "radical" complained that the other law school radicals were really "a bunch of upper-class white men." Subsequently, working-class students must disengage from their backgrounds if they desire to escape feeling discredited.

Working-class students disengaged from their previous identity by concealing their class backgrounds. Just as deviants seek to manage their identity by "passing" as nondeviants (Goffman 1963), these working-class law students often adopted identities that were associated with the more elite social classes.[3] Concealment allowed students to better participate in the culture of eminence that exists within the law school and reap available rewards.

This concealment meant, for instance, that students needed to acquire new dress codes. As Stone (1970) illustrated, appearance signifies identity and exercises a regulatory function over the responses of others. Such cultural codes pertaining to appearance often are used to exclude individuals from elite social positions (Bourdieu 1984; Jackell 1988; Lamont and Lareau 1988). Although working-class students lacked the cultural capital of higher social classes, they began to realize that they could successfully mimic their more privileged counterparts. Like undistinguished prep school students (Cookson and Persell 1985), working-class law students learned how to behave in an upper-class world, including how to dress for a new audience whose favorable appraisal they must cultivate. One second-year male discussed this process:

> *I remember going to buy suits here. I went to Brooks Brothers for two reasons. One, I don't own a suit. My father owns one suit, and it's not that good. Second, I think it's important to look good. A lot of my friends went to Brooks Brothers, and I feel it's worth it to do it right and not to have another hurdle to walk in and have the wrong thing on. It's all a big play act. . . . During my first year, I had no luck with interviews. I was in my own little world when I came here. I wished I had paid more attention to the dressing habits of second- and third-year students.*

Being in their own "working-class world" forced these students to begin recognizing the importance of different interpersonal skills. A second-year woman commented that

> *I have really begun to see the value of having good social skills. I think that is one of the ways that law firms weed out people. In order to get jobs you have to have those social skills. I'm real conscious of that when I go out on interviews now.*

The recognition among working-class students that they were able to imitate upper-class students increasingly encouraged them to conceal their backgrounds. One second-year student, whose father worked as a house painter, boasted of his mastery of "passing":

> *I generally don't tell people what my father does or what my mother does. I notice that I'm different, but it's not something other people here notice because I can fake it. They don't notice that I come from a blue-collar background.*

Paying attention to the impression that one presents becomes extremely important for the upwardly mobile working-class student.

These students were sometimes assisted in their performances by professional career counselors employed by the law school. These professionals gave students instructions on how to present themselves as full-fledged members of this elite community. Students were taught that unless they downplayed their social class background, the most lucrative opportunities would be denied them. A third-year woman from a working-class area in Boston recalled learning this new norm of presentation:

> *I'm sort of proud that I'm from South Boston and come from a working-class background. During my second year, however, I wasn't having much luck with my first interviews. I went to talk with my adviser about how to change my résumé a bit or how to present myself better. I told my adviser that on the interviews I was presenting myself as a slightly unusual person with a different background. We talked about that, and he told me that it probably wasn't a good idea to present myself as being a little unusual. I decided that he was right and began to play up that I was just like them. After that, the interviews and offers began rolling in. I began to realize that they [interviewers] really like people who are like themselves.*

Recognizing that job recruiters seek homogeneity is an important lesson that upwardly mobile working-class students must learn if they are to gain admission into high status and financially rewarding occupations.[4] Kanter (1977) demonstrated, for instance, that managers come to reward those who resemble themselves. More recently, Jackell (1988) documented how the failure of managers to "fit in" resulted in suspicion and subsequent exclusion from advancement. Fitting in is particularly important in prestigious law firms which tend to resemble the high-status clients they represent

(Abel 1989). During interviews, however, working-class law students faced a distinct disadvantage, as the interviewers who actively pursued new recruits rarely posed questions about the student's knowledge of law.[5] Most seemed intent on finding students who fit into the law firm's corporate structure. The entire recruitment process itself, from the initial interview to "fly out," represents ceremonial affirmation of these students' elite status in which they need only demonstrate their "social" competence. Working-class students typically found such interactions stressful. One third-year student explained her experiences:

> They [the recruiters] didn't test my knowledge of law. They were interested in finding out what kind of person I was and what my background was. I tried to avoid talking about that and instead stressed the kind of work I was interested in. I think that most firms want a person who they can mold, that fits into their firm.

Some of the most successful working-class students enjoyed the accolades bestowed on them because of their hard work and natural abilities. In speaking of her success, a third-year student on law review said that when she entered law school, it never occurred to her that she would clerk for the Supreme Court and then work for a major Wall Street law firm, adding that "once you begin doing well and move up the ladder and gain a whole new set of peers, then you begin to think about the possibilities." However, such success comes at a price, particularly for working-class students of color. Although having achieved success, many of these students continued to feel like outsiders. One such student, a third-year black male, reflected on what he considered the unfortunate aspects of affirmative action programs:

> I have mixed feelings about the law review because of its affirmative action policies. On the one hand, I think it's good that minorities are represented on the law review. On the other hand, there's a real stigma attached to it. Before law school, I achieved by my own abilities. On law review, I don't feel I get respect. I find myself working very hard and getting no respect. Other students don't work as hard. I spend a lot of time at the review because I don't want to turn in a bad assignment. I don't want them [other law review members] to think that I don't have what it takes.

Students who perceived themselves as outsiders frequently overcompensated for their failings because they felt judged by the "master status" associated with their social identity. This reaction to class stigma is typical among working-class students in educational institutions. In addition to developing their educational skills, working-class students are confronted with learning social skills as well. This makes succeeding particularly difficult for these students and is a task fraught with the fear of being discovered as incompetent (Sennett and Cobb 1973).

Ambivalence

Despite their maneuvers, these working-class students had difficulty transcending their previous identity. The attempt by these students to manage their stigma resulted in what Goffman (1963:107) termed "identity ambivalence." Working-class students who sought to exit their class background could neither embrace their group nor let it go. This ambivalence is often felt by working-class individuals who attain upward mobility into the professional-managerial class (Steinitz and Solomon 1986). Many experience the "stranger in paradise" syndrome, in which working-class individuals feel like virtual outsiders in middle-class occupations (Ryan and Sackrey 1984). Such experiences frequently lead to considerable identity conflict among working-class individuals who attempt to align themselves with the middle class.

The working-class law students in my sample typically experienced identity conflicts on their upward climb. Not only did they feel deceptive in their adjustment strategies, but many felt the additional burden of believing they had "sold out" their own class and were letting their group down. Like other stigmatized individuals who gain acceptance among dominant groups (Goffman 1963), these students often felt they were letting down their own group by representing elite interests. One third-year female student ruefully explained:

> *My brother keeps asking me whether I'm a Republican yet. He thought that after I finished law school I would go to work to help people, not work for one of those firms that do business. In a way, he's my conscience. Maybe he's right. I've got a conflict with what I'm doing. I came from the working class and wanted to do public interest law. I have decided not to do that. It's been a difficult decision for me. I'm not completely comfortable about working at a large firm.*

Another student, who grew up on welfare, expressed similar reservations about his impending career in law:

> *I'm not real happy about going to a large firm. I make lots of apologies. I'm still upset about the fact that my clients are real wealthy people, and it's not clear as to what the social utility of that will be.*

Like the previous example, this student experienced a form of self-alienation as a result of his identity ambivalence. Students often experience a sense of guilt as they transcend their working-class backgrounds. Such guilt, however, needs to be abated if these students are to successfully adjust to their new reference group and reduce the status conflict they experience. For these working-class students, making the primary adjustment to upward mobility required strategies of accommodation in personal attitudes regarding their relationship to members of less privileged social classes. Secondary identity adjustments were therefore critical in helping students mitigate the ambivalence they experienced over their own success and subsequent separation from the working class.

Resolving Ambivalence

Although accommodation strategies were typical throughout the entire student body,[6] working-class students at this law school were more likely to employ particular types of strategies to help manage their identity. Students sought to manage their ambivalence by remaining "ideologically" distanced from the very social class their elite law school credential had facilitated alignment with. Many of these students became deliberate role models, unreservedly immersing themselves in higher social classes for that specific purpose. Such adjustments might be thought of as political since they were intended to directly challenge the domination of social elites. A black working-class student described how his actions would benefit the less fortunate:

> *I get slammed for being a corporate tool. People feel that I have sold out. I'm irritated by that. For years, blacks have been treated as slaves, sharecroppers, or porters. So I think that whether I want to be a partner at Cravath or to be a NAACP defense attorney, either of these positions are politically correct. We need black people with money and power. I think that I can make significant contributions to black causes.*

For many students who experienced ambivalence, working in elite law firms was seen as the best way to help those they left behind. Other students redefined the value of large corporate law firms for the opportunities that such positions offered in contributing to social change. One third-year student suggested:

> *I used to think that social change would come about by being an activist. That's why I originally wanted to do public interest law. But you really can't accomplish much by doing this. The hiring partner at [a major New York law firm] convinced me that this is the only way to get things done. He served as the under secretary of state in the [former president's] administration. He made sense when he told me that if I wanted to contribute to social change I had to become an important person.*

Students became less convinced that directly serving the less-privileged social classes would effectively resolve the problems that concerned them. A third-year student explained how disenchanted she had become with public interest law:

> *I used to think that you could do good things for people. . . . I don't think that anymore. I'm no longer troubled by the idea of being a corporate lawyer as opposed to a public interest one. I'm still concerned about social problems like poverty or poor housing, but I'm not sure that being a public interest attorney*

is the way to resolve those things. The needs of the people that public interest lawyers serve are just beyond what I can do as an attorney. I think I can do more good for people if I commit myself to working with community groups or activities in the bar during my spare time.

The offering of such accounts helps students resolve the contradiction they experience by choosing a large law firm practice, as does the practical planning to use one's spare time (e.g., to do community activities). Unfortunately, given the structure of contemporary large law firms, spare time is a rarity (Nelson 1988; Spangler 1986). Adopting these new definitions regarding the pursuit of effective social change means that working-class students need not feel penitent over their upward mobility. Such strategies, of course, are attractive, as they suggest that the student is becoming elite not solely because he or she is striving for personal reward and success but as a means to best pursue the noble ideals of public service and social activism.

A more drastic accommodation involved avoidance of those who reminded working-class students of their social obligations toward helping the less fortunate. Just associating with individuals whose career path was geared toward helping the downtrodden caused considerable uneasiness in working-class students who had decided to enter large law firms. One third-year student said that he had begun to avoid law students who had retained their commitment to work with the poor:

It's taken for granted here that you can work for a large firm and still be a good person. The people who don't reinforce that message make me uncomfortable now. Frankly, that's why I'm not hanging out with the public interest people. They remind me of my own guilt.

In some cases, avoidance turned into open hostility. Another third-year student described how she now saw other students who remained committed to their ideals of helping the less fortunate: "They're so single-minded at times and I think a little naive. They've really pushed me away from wanting to do public interest work as a full-time occupation." Condemning her condemners helped this student neutralize the guilt she felt over working for a corporate law firm.

Conclusion

. . .

Upwardly mobile working-class students in this study, as well as in others, interpret and experience their social class from the perspective of stigma. However, since the stigma of being a member of the lower classes is thought to be just, upwardly mobile working-class students frequently construct identities in which they seek to escape the taint associated with their affiliation.

Overcoming this stigma is therefore considered an individual rather than a collective effort. As was demonstrated in this study, such efforts often involve managing one's identity in the ways that Goffman outlined. Research that explores identity struggles as they relate to class could offer further extensions of Goffman's comments on stigma. Such research also has potential value in contributing to our understanding of working-class movements in the United States. Indeed, exploring the experience of class from the perspective of stigma and its management could offer great insight into the social psychology of working-class disempowerment.

NOTES

Author's Note: Partial funding for this research was provided by the Woodrow Wilson Foundation.

1. The following are the percentage distributions of social class background on the random sample of questionnaire returnees I collected for the larger project: upper class (2.8), upper-middle (44.6), middle (30.0), lower-middle (8.0), working (13.1), and lower (0.5).

2. This is a first-year exercise in which students select a case to argue in front of a three-person panel consisting of a law professor, a third-year student, and an invited guest from the legal community. First-year students prepare their cases for several months in advance before formally presenting their oral argument.

3. Similar findings were reported by Domhoff and Zweigenhaft (1991) in which they described the experiences of black students who were enrolled in elite prep schools as a result of affirmative action.

4. Students are actively pursued. During the 1987 recruitment seasons at the law school, an average of 44 recruiters from commercial law firms conducted interviews with students each day. This represents nearly one law firm for each law student eligible to interview. In most cases, law firms are looking to hire more than one student.

5. A recent study of hiring policies among large law firms found that "personal characteristics" ranked second among the criteria for selecting new lawyers (see Buller and Beck-Dudley 1990).

6. Many students are confronted with identity conflicts that stem from the separation of personal values from professional roles. This is felt most among those students who entered law school with social activist ideals (for further discussion of this, see Granfield 1986, 1989, forthcoming).

REFERENCES

Abel, R. 1989. *American Lawyers.* New York: Oxford University Press.

Adler, P., and P. Adler. 1987. *Membership Roles in Field Research.* Newbury Park, CA: Sage.

Baltzell, E. D. 1958. *Philadelphia Gentlemen.* New York: Free Press.

Bernstein, B. 1977. *Class Codes and Control. Vol. 3: Towards a Theory of Educational Transmission.* London: Routledge & Kegan Paul.

Bourdieu, P. 1984. *Distinction: A Social Critique of the Judgment of Taste.* Cambridge, MA: Harvard University Press.

Bourdieu, P., and J. C. Passeron. 1990. *Reproduction in Education, Society and Culture.* London: Routledge & Kegan Paul.

Buller, P., and C. Beck-Dudley. 1990. "Performance, Policies and Personnel." *American Bar Association Journal* 76:94.

Chadwick, B., H. Bahr, and S. Albrecht. 1984. *Social Science Research Methods.* Englewood Cliffs, NJ: Prentice-Hall.

Cookson, P., and C. Persell. 1985. *Preparing for Power: America's Elite Boarding Schools.* New York: Basic Books.

Domhoff, G. W., and R. Zweigenhaft. 1991. *Blacks in the White Establishment: A Study of Race and Class in America.* New Haven, CT: Yale University Press.

Fielding, N., and J. Fielding. 1986. *Linking Data.* Beverly Hills, CA: Sage.

Goffman, E. 1963. *Stigma: Notes on the Management of Spoiled Identity.* Englewood Cliffs, NJ: Prentice-Hall.

Granfield, R. 1986. "Legal Education As Corporate Ideology: Student Adjustment to the Law School Experience." *Sociological Forum* 1:514–23.

———. 1989. "Making the Elite Lawyer: Culture and Ideology in Legal Education." Ph.D. dissertation, Northeastern University, Boston.

———. Forthcoming. *Making Elite Lawyers.* New York: Routledge, Chapman & Hall.

Granfield, R., and T. Koenig. 1990. "From Activism to Pro Bono: The Redirection of Working Class Altruism at Harvard Law School." *Critical Sociology* 17:57–80.

Heinz, J., and E. Laumann. 1982. *Chicago Lawyers: The Social Structure of the Bar.* New York: Russell Sage.

Jackell, R. 1988. *Moral Mazes: The World of the Corporate Manager.* New York: Oxford University Press.

Kanter, R. 1977. *Men and Women of the Corporation.* New York: Basic Books.

Lamont, M., and A. Lareau. 1988. "Cultural Capital: Allusions, Gaps and Glissandos in Recent Theoretical Development." *Sociological Theory* 6:153–68.

Lurie, A. 1983. *The Language of Clothes.* New York: Vintage.

Nelson, R. 1988. *Partners with Power: The Social Transformation of the Large Law Firm.* Berkeley: University of California Press.

Newman, K. 1988. *Falling from Grace: The Experience of Downward Mobility in the American Middle Class.* New York: Free Press.

Pfuhl, E. 1986. *The Deviance Process.* Belmont, CA: Wadsworth.

Ryan, J., and C. Sackrey. 1984. *Strangers in Paradise: Academics from the Working Class.* Boston: South End Press.

Schur, E. 1971. *Labeling Deviant Behavior.* New York: Harper & Row.

———. 1980. *The Politics of Deviance.* Englewood Cliffs, NJ: Prentice-Hall.

Sennett, R., and R. Cobb. 1973. *The Hidden Injuries of Class.* New York: Random House.

Smigel, E. 1969. *The Wall Street Lawyer.* Bloomington: Indiana University Press.

Spangler, E. 1986. *Lawyers for Hire: Salaried Professionals at Work.* New Haven, CT: Yale University Press.

Steinitz, V., and E. Solomon. 1986. *Starting Out: Class and Community in the Lives of Working Class Youth.* Philadelphia: Temple University Press.

Stone, G. 1970. "Appearance and the Self." Pp. 394–414 in *Social Psychology through Symbolic Interaction,* edited by G. Stone and H. Farberman. New York: Wiley.

Useem, M., and J. Karabel. 1986. "Paths to Corporate Management." *American Sociological Review* 51:184–200.

14

ANYBODY'S SON WILL DO

GWYNNE DYER

An important point about socialization is that if culture is learned, it also can be unlearned. Sociologists call this process *resocialization*. This situation occurs when an individual gives up one way of life and one set of values for another. Examples of resocialization include the experiences of new immigrants, of a person changing careers, of someone joining a feminist consciousness raising group, or of an individual undergoing a religious conversion, such as a nun entering a convent or a person being initiated into a cult. The following reading by Gwynne Dyer is from his 1985 book *War: Past, Present, and Future.* Here Dyer focuses on the resocialization civilians experience during military basic training.

You think about it and you know you're going to have to kill but you don't understand the implications of that, because in the society in which you've lived murder is the most heinous of crimes . . . and you are in a situation in which it's turned the other way round. . . . When you do actually kill someone the experience, my experience, was one of revulsion and disgust.

. . .

I was utterly terrified—petrified—but I knew there had to be a Japanese sniper in a small fishing shack near the shore. He was firing in the other direction at Marines in another battalion, but I knew as soon as he picked off the people there—there was a window on our side—that he would start picking us off. And there was nobody else to go . . . and so I ran towards the shack and broke in and found myself in an empty room.

. . .

There was a door which meant there was another room and the sniper was in that—and I just broke that down. I was just absolutely gripped by the fear that this man would expect me and would shoot me. But as it turned out he was in a sniper harness and he couldn't turn around fast enough. He was entangled in the harness so I shot him with a .45, and I felt remorse and shame.

*I can remember whispering foolishly, "I'm sorry" and then just throwing
up. . . . I threw up all over myself. It was a betrayal of what I'd been taught
since a child.*

—WILLIAM MANCHESTER

Yet he did kill the Japanese soldier, just as he had been trained to—the
revulsion only came afterward. And even after Manchester knew what
it was like to kill another human being, a young man like himself, he
went on trying to kill his "enemies" until the war was over. Like all the other
tens of millions of soldiers who had been taught from infancy that killing
was wrong, and had then been sent off to kill for their countries, he was almost helpless to disobey, for he had fallen into the hands of an institution so
powerful and so subtle that it could quickly reverse the moral training of a
lifetime.

The whole vast edifice of the military institution rests on its ability to obtain obedience from its members even unto death—and the killing of others.
It has enormous powers of compulsion at its command, of course, but all authority must be based ultimately on consent. The task of extracting that consent from its members has probably grown harder in recent times, for the gulf
between the military and the civilian worlds has undoubtedly widened:
Civilians no longer perceive the threat of violent death as an everyday hazard of existence, and the categories of people whom it is not morally permissible to kill have broadened to include (in peacetime) the entire human race.
Yet the armed forces of every country can still take almost any young male
civilian and turn him into a soldier with all the right reflexes and attitudes in
only a few weeks. Their recruits usually have no more than twenty years' experience of the world, most of it as children, while the armies have had all of
history to practice and perfect their techniques.

*Just think of how the soldier is treated. While still a child he is shut up in the bar-
racks. During his training he is always being knocked about. If he makes the least
mistake he is beaten, a burning blow on his body, another on his eye, perhaps his
head is laid open with a wound. He is battered and bruised with flogging. On the
march . . . they hang heavy loads round his neck like that of an ass.*

—Egyptian, ca. 1500 B.C.[1]

*The moment I talk to the new conscripts about the homeland I strike a land mine.
So I kept quiet. Instead I try to make soldiers of them. I give them hell from morning to sunset. They begin to curse me, curse the army, curse the state. Then they
begin to curse together, and become a truly cohesive group, a unit, a fighting
unit.*

—Israeli, ca. A.D. 1970[2]

All soldiers belong to the same profession, no matter what country they
serve, and it makes them different from everybody else. They have to be different, for their job is ultimately about killing and dying, and those things are

not a natural vocation for any human being. Yet all soldiers are born civilians. The method for turning young men into soldiers—people who kill other people and expose themselves to death—is basic training. It's essentially the same all over the world, and it always has been, because young men everywhere are pretty much alike.

Human beings are fairly malleable, especially when they are young, and in every young man there are attitudes for any army to work with: the inherited values and postures, more or less dimly recalled, of the tribal warriors who were once the model for every young boy to emulate. Civilization did not involve a sudden clean break in the way people behave, but merely the progressive distortion and redirection of all the ways in which people in the old tribal societies used to behave, and modern definitions of maleness still contain a great deal of the old warrior ethic. The anarchic machismo of the primitive warrior is not what modern armies really need in their soldiers, but it does provide them with promising raw material for the transformation they must work in their recruits.

Just how this transformation is wrought varies from time to time and from country to country. In totally militarized societies—ancient Sparta, the samurai class of medieval Japan, the areas controlled by organizations like the Eritrean People's Liberation Front today—it begins at puberty or before, when the young boy is immersed in a disciplined society in which only the military values are allowed to penetrate. In more sophisticated modern societies, the process is briefer and more concentrated, and the way it works is much more visible. It is, essentially, a conversion process in an almost religious sense—and as in all conversion phenomena, the emotions are far more important than the specific ideas.

. . .

Armies know this. It is their business to get men to fight, and they have had a long time to work out the best way of doing it. All of them pay lip service to the symbols and slogans of their political masters, though the amount of time they must devote to this activity varies from country to country. . . . Nor should it be thought that the armies are hypocritical—most of their members really do believe in their particular national symbols and slogans. But their secret is that they know these are not the things that sustain men in combat.

What really enables men to fight is their own self-respect, and a special kind of love that has nothing to do with sex or idealism. Very few men have died in battle, when the moment actually arrived, for the United States of America or for the sacred cause of Communism, or even for their homes and families; if they had any choice in the matter at all, they chose to die for each other and for their own vision of themselves.

. . .

The way armies produce this sense of brotherhood in a peacetime environment is basic training: a feat of psychological manipulation on the grand scale which has been so consistently successful and so universal that we fail to notice it as remarkable. In countries where the army must extract its recruits in their late teens, whether voluntarily or by conscription, from a civilian environment that does not share the military values, basic training involves a brief but intense period of indoctrination whose purpose is not really to teach the recruits basic military skills, but rather to change their values and their loyalties. "I guess you could say we brainwash them a little bit," admitted a U.S. Marine drill instructor, "but you know they're good people."

The duration and intensity of basic training, and even its major emphases, depend on what kind of society the recruits are coming from, and on what sort of military organization they are going to. It is obviously quicker to train men from a martial culture than from one in which the dominant values are civilian and commercial, and easier to deal with volunteers than with reluctant conscripts. Conscripts are not always unwilling, however; there are many instances in which the army is popular for economic reasons.

. . .

It's easier if you catch them young. You can train older men to be soldiers; it's done in every major war. But you can never get them to believe that they like it, which is the major reason armies try to get their recruits before they are 20. There are other reasons too, of course, like the physical fitness, lack of dependents, and economic dispensability of teenagers, that make armies prefer them, but the most important qualities teenagers bring to basic training are enthusiasm and naiveté. Many of them actively want the discipline and the closely structured environment that the armed forces will provide, so there is no need for the recruiters to deceive the kids about what will happen to them after they join.

> *There is discipline. There is drill. . . . When you are relying on your mates and they are relying on you, there's no room for slackness or sloppiness. If you're not prepared to accept the rules, you're better off where you are.*
> —British army recruiting advertisement, 1976

> *People are not born soldiers, they become soldiers. . . . And it should not begin at the moment a new recruit is enlisted into the ranks, but rather much earlier, at the time of the first signs of maturity, during the time of adolescent dreams.*
> —*Red Star* (Soviet army newspaper), 1973

Young civilians who have volunteered and have been accepted by the Marine Corps arrive at Parris Island, the Corps's East Coast facility for basic training, in a state of considerable excitement and apprehension: Most are aware that they are about to undergo an extraordinary and very difficult experience. But they do not make their own way to the base; rather they trickle in to Charleston airport on various flights throughout the day on which their training platoon is due to form, and are held there, in a state of suppressed but mounting nervous tension, until late in the evening. When the buses finally come to carry them the 76 miles to Parris Island, it is often after midnight—and this is not an administrative oversight. The shock treatment they are about to receive will work most efficiently if they are worn out and somewhat disoriented when they arrive.

The basic training organization is a machine, processing several thousand young men every month, and every facet and gear of it has been designed with the sole purpose of turning civilians into Marines as efficiently as possible. Provided it can have total control over their bodies and their environment for approximately three months, it can practically guarantee converts. Parris Island provides that controlled environment, and the recruits do not set foot outside it again until they graduate as Marine privates 11 weeks later.

They're allowed to call home, so long as it doesn't get out of hand—every three weeks or so they can call home and make sure everything's all right, if they haven't gotten a letter or there's a particular set of circumstances. If it's a case of an emergency call coming in, then they're allowed to accept that call; if not, one of my staff will take the message.

. . .

In some cases I'll get calls from parents who haven't quite gotten adjusted to the idea that their son had cut the strings—and in a lot of cases that's what they're doing. The military provides them with an opportunity to leave home but they're still in a rather secure environment.

—Captain Brassington, USMC

For the young recruits, basic training is the closest thing their society can offer to a formal rite of passage, and the institution probably stands in an unbroken line of descent from the lengthy ordeals by which young males in pre-civilized groups were initiated into the adult community of warriors. But in civilized societies it is a highly functional institution whose product is not anarchic warriors, but trained soldiers.

Basic training is not really about teaching people skills; it's about changing them, so that they can do things they wouldn't have dreamt of otherwise. It works by applying enormous physical and mental pressure to men who have been isolated from their normal civilian environment and placed in one where the only right way to think and behave is the way the Marine Corps wants them to. The key word the men who run the machine use to describe this process is *motivation*.

I can motivate a recruit and in third phase, if I tell him to jump off the third deck, he'll jump off the third deck. Like I said before, it's a captive audience and I can train that guy; I can get him to do anything I want him to do. . . . They're good kids and they're out to do the right thing. We get some bad kids, but you know, we weed those out. But as far as motivation—here, we can motivate them to do anything you want, in recruit training.

—USMC drill instructor, Parris Island

The first three days the raw recruits spend at Parris Island are actually relatively easy, though they are hustled and shouted at continuously. It is during this time that they are documented and inoculated, receive uniforms, and learn the basic orders of drill that will enable young Americans (who are not very accustomed to this aspect of life) to do everything simultaneously in large groups. But the most important thing that happens in "forming" is the surrender of the recruits' own clothes, their hair—all the physical evidence of their individual civilian identities.

During a period of only 72 hours, in which they are allowed little sleep, recruits lay aside their former lives in a series of hasty rituals (like being shaven to the scalp) whose symbolic significance is quite clear to them even though they are quite deliberately given absolutely no time for reflection, or any hint that they might have the option of turning back from their commitment. The men in charge of them know how delicate a tightrope they are walking, though, because at this stage the recruits are still newly caught civilians who have not yet made their ultimate inward submission to the discipline of the Corps.

Forming Day One makes me nervous. You've got a whole new mob of recruits, you know, 60 or 70 depending, and they don't know anything. You don't know what kind of a reaction you're going to get from the stress you're going to lay on them, and it just worries me the first day.

. . .

Things could happen, I'm not going to lie to you. Something might happen. A recruit might decide he doesn't want any part of this stuff and maybe take a poke at you or something like that. In a situation like that it's going to be a spur-of-the-moment thing and that worries me.

—USMC drill instructor

But it rarely happens. The frantic bustle of forming is designed to give the recruit no time to think about resisting what is happening to him. And so the recruits emerge from their initiation into the system, stripped of their civilian clothes, shorn of their hair, and deprived of whatever confidence in their own identity they may previously have had as 18-year-olds, like so many blanks ready to have the Marine identity impressed upon them.

The first stage in any conversion process is the destruction of an individual's former beliefs and confidence, and his reduction to a position of helplessness and need. It isn't really as drastic as all that, of course, for three days cannot cancel out 18 years; the inner thoughts and the basic character are not erased. But the recruits have already learned that the only acceptable behavior is to repress any unorthodox thoughts and to mimic the character the Marine Corps wants. Nor are they, on the whole, reluctant to do so, for they *want* to be Marines. From the moment they arrive at Parris Island, the vague notion that has been passed down for a thousand generations that masculinity means being a warrior becomes an explicit article of faith, relentlessly preached: To be a man means to be a Marine.

There are very few 18-year-old boys who do not have highly romanticized ideas of what it means to be a man, so the Marine Corps has plenty of buttons to push. And it starts pushing them on the first day of real training: The officer in charge of the formation appears before them for the first time, in full dress uniform with medals, and tells them how to become men.

> *The United States Marine Corps has 205 years of illustrious history to speak for itself. You have made the most important decision in your life . . . by signing your name, your life, your pledge to the Government of the United States, and even more importantly, to the United States Marine Corps—a brotherhood, an elite unit. In 10.3 weeks you are going to become a member of that history, those traditions, this organization—if you have what it takes.*

> . . .

> *All of you want to do that by virtue of your signing your name as a man. The Marine Corps says that we build men. Well, I'll go a little bit further. We develop the tools that you have—and everybody has those tools to a certain extent right now. We're going to give you the blueprints, and we are going to show you how to build a Marine. You've got to build a Marine—you understand?*
>
> —Captain Pingree, USMC

The recruits, gazing at him in awe and adoration, shout in unison, "Yes, sir!" just as they have been taught. They do it willingly, because they are volunteers—but even conscripts tend to have the romantic fervor of volunteers if they are only 18 years old. Basic training, whatever its hardships, is a quick way to become a man among men, with an undeniable status, and beyond the initial consent to undergo it, it doesn't even require any decisions.

> *I had just dropped out of high school and I wasn't doing much on the street except hanging out, as most teenagers would be doing. So they gave me an opportunity—a recruiter picked me up, gave me a good line, and said that I could make it in the Marines, that I have a future ahead of me. And since I was living with my parents, I figured that I could start my own life here and grow up a little.*
>
> —USMC recruit, 1982

I like the hand-to-hand combat and . . . things like that. It's a little rough going on me, and since I have a small frame I would like to become deadly, as I would put it. I like to have them words, especially the way they've been teaching me here.
—USMC recruit (from Brooklyn), Parris Island, 1982

The training, when it starts, seems impossibly demanding physically for most of the recruits—and then it gets harder week by week. There is a constant barrage of abuse and insults aimed at the recruits, with the deliberate purpose of breaking down their pride and so destroying their ability to resist the transformation of values and attitudes that the Corps intends them to undergo. At the same time the demands for constant alertness and for instant obedience are continuously stepped up, and the standards by which the dress and behavior of the recruits are judged become steadily more unforgiving. But it is all carefully calculated by the men who run the machine, who think and talk in terms of the stress they are placing on the recruits: "We take so many c.c.'s of stress and we administer it to each man—they should be a little bit scared and they should be unsure, but they're adjusting." The aim is to keep the training arduous but just within most of the recruits' capability to withstand. One of the most striking achievements of the drill instructors is to create and maintain the illusion that basic training is an extraordinary challenge, one that will set those who graduate apart from others, when in fact almost everyone can succeed.

There has been some preliminary weeding out of potential recruits even before they begin basic training, to eliminate the obviously unsuitable minority, and some people do "fail" basic training and get sent home, at least in peacetime. The standards of acceptable performance in the U.S. armed forces, for example, tend to rise and fall in inverse proportion to the number and quality of recruits available to fill the forces to the authorized manpower levels. (In 1980, about 15% of Marine recruits did not graduate from basic training.) But there are very few young men who cannot be turned into passable soldiers if the forces are willing to invest enough effort in it.

Not even physical violence is necessary to effect the transformation, though it has been used by most armies at most times.

It's not what it was 15 years ago down here. The Marine Corps still occupies the position of a tool which the society uses when it feels like that is a resort that they have to fall to. Our society changes as all societies do, and our society felt that through enlightened training methods we could still produce the same product—and when you examine it, they're right. . . . Our 100 c.c.'s of stress is really all we need, not two gallons of it, which is what used to be. . . . In some cases with some of the younger drill instructors it was more an initiation than it was an acute test, and so we introduced extra officers and we select our drill instructors to "fine-tune" it.
—Captain Brassington, USMC

There is, indeed, a good deal of fine-tuning in the roles that the men in charge of training any specific group of recruits assume. At the simplest level, there is a sort of "good cop–bad cop" manipulation of recruits' attitudes toward those applying the stress. The three younger drill instructors with a particular serial are quite close to them in age and unremittingly harsh in their demands for ever higher performance, but the senior drill instructor, a man almost old enough to be their father, plays a more benevolent and understanding part and is available for individual counseling. And generally offstage, but always looming in the background, is the company commander, an impossibly austere and almost godlike personage.

At least these are the images conveyed to the recruits, although of course all these men cooperate closely with an identical goal in view. It works: In the end they become not just role models and authority figures, but the focus of the recruits' developing loyalty to the organization.

I imagine there's some fear, especially in the beginning, because they don't know what to expect. . . . I think they hate you at first, at least for a week or two, but it turns to respect. . . . They're seeking discipline, they're seeking someone to take charge, 'cause at home they never got it. . . . They're looking to be told what to do and then someone is standing there enforcing what they tell them to do, and it's kind of like the father-and-son game, all the way through. They form a fatherly image of the DI whether they want to or not.

—Sergeant Carrington, USMC

Just the sheer physical exercise, administered in massive doses, soon has recruits feeling stronger and more competent than ever before. Inspections, often several times daily, quickly build up their ability to wear the uniform and carry themselves like real Marines, which is a considerable source of pride. The inspections also help to set up the pattern in the recruits of unquestioning submission to military authority: Standing stock-still, staring straight ahead, while somebody else examines you closely for faults is about as extreme a ritual act of submission as you can make with your clothes on.

But they are not submitting themselves merely to the abusive sergeant making unpleasant remarks about the hair in their nostrils. All around them are deliberate reminders—the flags and insignia displayed on parade, the military music, the marching formations and drill instructors' cadenced calls—of the idealized organization, the "brotherhood" to which they will be admitted as full members if they submit and conform. Nowhere in the armed forces are the military courtesies so elaborately observed, the staffs' uniforms so immaculate (some DIs change several times a day), and the ritual aspects of military life so highly visible as on a basic training establishment.

Even the seeming inanity of close-order drill has a practical role in the conversion process. It has been over a century since mass formations of men were of any use on the battlefield, but every army in the world still drills its troops, especially during basic training, because marching in formation, with every man moving his body in the same way at the same moment, is a direct physical way of learning two things a soldier must believe: that orders have to be obeyed automatically and instantly, and that you are no longer an individual, but part of a group.

The recruits' total identification with the other members of their unit is the most important lesson of all, and everything possible is done to foster it. They spend almost every waking moment together—a recruit alone is an anomaly to be looked into at once—and during most of that time they are enduring shared hardships. They also undergo collective punishments, often for the misdeed or omission of a single individual (talking in the ranks, a bed not swept under during barracks inspection), which is a highly effective way of suppressing any tendencies toward individualism. And, of course, the DIs place relentless emphasis on competition with other "serials" in training: There may be something infinitely pathetic to outsiders about a marching group of anonymous recruits chanting, "Lift your heads and hold them high, 3313 is a-passin' by," but it doesn't seem like that to the men in the ranks.

Nothing is quite so effective in building up a group's morale and solidarity, though, as a steady diet of small triumphs. Quite early in basic training, the recruits begin to do things that seem, at first sight, quite dangerous: descend by ropes from 50-foot towers, cross yawning gaps hand-over-hand on high wires (known as the Slide for Life, of course), and the like. The common denominator is that these activities are daunting but not really dangerous: The ropes will prevent anyone from falling to his death off the rappelling tower, and there is a pond of just the right depth—deep enough to cushion a falling man, but not deep enough that he is likely to drown—under the Slide for Life. The goal is not to kill recruits, but to build up their confidence as individuals and as a group by allowing them to overcome apparently frightening obstacles.

> *You have an enemy here at Parris Island. The enemy that you're going to have at Parris Island is in every one of us. It's in the form of cowardice. The most rewarding experience you're going to have in recruit training is standing on line every evening, and you'll be able to look into each other's eyes, and you'll be able to say to each other with your eyes: "By God, we've made it one more day! We've defeated the coward."*
>
> —Captain Pingree, USMC

> *Number on deck, sir, 45 . . . highly motivated, truly dedicated, rompin', stompin', bloodthirsty, kill-crazy United States Marine Corps recruits, SIR!*
>
> —Marine chant, Parris Island, 1982

If somebody does fail a particular test, he tends to be alone, for the hurdles are deliberately set low enough that most recruits can clear them if they try. In any large group of people there is usually a goat: someone whose intelligence or manner or lack of physical stamina marks him for failure and contempt. The competent drill instructor, without deliberately setting up this unfortunate individual for disgrace, will use his failure to strengthen the solidarity and confidence of the rest. When one hapless young man fell off the Slide for Life into the pond, for example, his drill instructor shouted the usual invective—"Well, get out of the water. Don't contaminate it all day"—and then delivered the payoff line: "Go back and change your clothes. You're useless to your unit now."

"Useless to your unit" is the key phrase, and all the recruits know that what it means is "useless *in battle*." The Marine drill instructors at Parris Island know exactly what they are doing to the recruits, and why. They are not rear-echelon people filling comfortable jobs, but the most dedicated and intelligent NCOs the Marine Corps can find; even now, many of them have combat experience. The Corps has a clear-eyed understanding of precisely what it is training its recruits for—combat—and it ensures that those who do the training keep that objective constantly in sight.

The DIs "stress" the recruits, feed them their daily ration of synthetic triumphs over apparent obstacles, and bear in mind all the time that the goal is to instill the foundations for the instinctive, selfless reactions and the fierce group loyalty that is what the recruits will need if they ever see combat. They are arch-manipulators, fully conscious of it, and utterly unashamed. These kids have signed up as Marines, and they could well see combat; this is the way they have to think if they want to live.

I've seen guys come to Vietnam from all over. They were all sorts of people that had been scared—some of them had been scared all their life and still scared. Some of them had been a country boy, city boys—you know, all different kinds of people—but when they got in combat they all reacted the same—99 percent of them reacted the same. . . . A lot of it is training here at Parris Island, but the other part of it is survival. They know if they don't conform—conform I call it, but if they don't react in the same way other people are reacting, they won't survive. That's just it. You know, if you don't react together, then nobody survives.

—USMC drill instructor, Parris Island, 1982

When I went to boot camp and did individual combat training they said if you walk into an ambush what you want to do is just do a right face—you just turn right or left, whichever way the fire is coming from, and assault. I said, "Man, that's crazy. I'd never do anything like that. It's stupid."

. . .

The first time we came under fire, on Hill 1044 in Operation Beauty Canyon in Laos, we did it automatically. Just like you look at your watch to see what time it is. We done a right face, assaulted the hill—a fortified position with concrete bunkers emplaced, machine guns, automatic weapons—and we took it. And we killed—I'd estimate probably 35 North Vietnamese soldiers in the assault, and we only lost three killed. I think it was about two or three, and about eight or ten wounded.

. . .

But you know, what they teach you, it doesn't faze you until it comes down to the time to use it, but it's in the back of your head, like, What do you do when you come to a stop sign? It's in the back of your head, and you react automatically.

—USMC sergeant, 1982

Combat is the ultimate reality that Marines—or any other soldiers, under any flag—have to deal with. Physical fitness, weapons training, battle drills, are all indispensable elements of basic training, and it is absolutely essential that the recruits learn the attitudes of group loyalty and interdependency which will be their sole hope of survival and success in combat. The training inculcates or fosters all of those things, and even by the halfway point in the 11-week course, the recruits are generally responding with enthusiasm to their tasks.

. . .

In basic training establishments, . . . the malleability is all one way: in the direction of submission to military authority and the internalization of military values. What a place like Parris Island produces when it is successful, as it usually is, is a soldier who will kill because that is his job.

NOTES

1. Leonard Cottrell, *The Warrior Pharaohs* (London: Evans Brothers, 1968).
2. Samuel Rolbart, *The Israeli Soldier* (New York: A. S. Barnes, 1970), p. 206.

PART IV

Groups and Social Structure

15

THE SOCIAL ARCHITECTURE OF AMISH SOCIETY

DONALD B. KRAYBILL

The following four selections explore groups and social structure. The basic components of social structure are the roles and social statuses of individuals. Over the course of a lifetime, people occupy numerous statuses and roles. A *status* is a social position an individual holds within a group or a social system. A *role* is a set of expectations about the behavior assigned to a particular social status. Each role helps to define the nature of interaction with others and contributes to social organization by creating patterns of interpersonal and group relationships. Because we modify our social roles more than we do our social statuses, roles are the dynamic aspect of social status. In the first reading, Donald Kraybill illustrates the social structure of Amish society. This excerpt is taken from Kraybill's 1989 book *The Riddle of Amish Culture.*

Our discipline thrives on the man walking behind the plow, not the man traveling by train all over the country trying to build a superstructure.

—Amish Farmer

Social Building Blocks

Social life is shaped not only by cultural beliefs and symbolic meanings but also by patterns of behavior. Societies, as well as buildings, have distinctive architectural styles. Like building blocks, social relations are arranged together in unique ways by different groups. In some societies males dominate, whereas in others females do, and in still others neither dominates.

Donald Kraybill. *The Riddle of Amish Culture,* pp. 69–84 and 90–93. © 1989 by The Johns Hopkins University Press. Reprinted with permission.

Each set of human arrangements has a structure, a distinctive social architecture. Growing up in an Amish family with dozens of first cousins nearby is quite different from living in a modern nuclear family with two cousins living 500 miles apart. Child-rearing practices in Amish families, where both parents usually work at home, differ radically from dual-career families whose children play in day-care centers. A society's architectural design shapes human behavior in profound ways. What features distinguish the social architecture of Amish society? What is the organizational shape of *Gelassenheit* [Amish culture]?

Demographic factors, birth rates, sex ratios, marital status, and family size are the building blocks of a society's social structure. . . . The Amish [in Lancaster County, Pennsylvania] are more likely than their neighbors to marry, live in larger households, terminate school earlier, and engage in farming. A striking feature of Amish society is the large proportion (53 percent) of people under the age of 18. With only 5 percent of its members over 65, Amish life tilts toward child rearing. Schools, rather than retirement villages, dominate the social landscape.

The individualization of modern society, characterized by spiraling percentages of single people and single-parent homes, is largely absent from Amish society. Whatever the Amish do, they do together. Only 7 percent of Amish households are single-person units, compared to 20 percent for Lancaster County. Virtually all of the single-person households adjoin other Amish homes. In fact, 43 percent of all households are on the same property as another Amish household. Many of these double homes are farmhouses with a smaller adjacent house for grandparents. Five people live in the average Amish household—nearly double the county rate of 2.8. The vast majority of Amish reside in a household with a half-dozen other people, or at least live adjacent to one. Moreover, additional members of the extended family live across the road or beyond the next field.

Age and Sex Roles

Age and sex roles are essential building blocks in Amish society. The Amish identify four stages of childhood: babies, little children, scholars, and young people.[1] The term *little children* is used for children between the time that they begin walking and until they begin school. Children between the ages of 6 and 15 are often called *scholars*. *Young people,* from mid-teens to marriage, explore their independence by joining informal youth groups that crisscross the settlement.

Social power increases with age. In a rural society where children follow the occupations of their parents, the elderly provide valuable advice. Younger generations turn to them for their expertise in treating an earache, making pie dough, training a horse, predicting a frost, buying a cow. In a slowly changing society, the seasoned judgment of wise elders is esteemed by younger members. This contrasts sharply with rapidly changing societies, in which children often teach new technological skills to their parents. The power of age also engulfs the Amish church, where the words of an older minister count more than those of a younger one. The chairman of the ordained leaders is traditionally the oldest bishop. Wisdom accumulated by experience, rather than professional or technical competence, is the wedge of power in Amish society.

While power increases progressively with age, sex role distinctions are also a prime source of inequality in Amish society. In the realm of church, work, and community, the male voice carries more influence than the female one. Age and sex combine to produce a patriarchal hierarchy that gives older men the most social clout and younger females the least.

Amish families are organized around traditional sex roles. As in most marriages, a variety of power equations emerges, depending on the personalities of the partners. For the most part, the Amish husband is seen as the spiritual head of the home. He is responsible for its religious welfare and has the final word on matters related to the church and the outside world. The husband's role requires him to deal with strangers that appear on the Amish homestead. Among farming families, husbands organize the farm operation and supervise the work of children in barns and fields. Some husbands assist their wives with gardening, lawn care, and child care, but others do little. Amish children are usually born at home with the assistance of a certified midwife. The husband is often nearby to welcome the new child.[2] One father was called a "good Christian husband" because "he starts and tends the fires in the stove and helps with the children." Husbands rarely help with household work—washing, cooking, canning, sewing, mending, cleaning. The visible authority of the husband varies by household, but Amish society is primarily patriarchal and vests final authority for moral and social life in the male role.

Feminism has not changed the role of Amishwomen. Amish wives believe that, in the divine order of things, they are expected to submit to their husband's authority, but that does not mean they are docile.[3] Entrusted with the responsibility of raising a large family, they become efficient managers. Married women rarely have full-time jobs outside the home. In fact, only 3 percent of married women hold part-time jobs away from home. Even with ample help from children, it is difficult to manage a household of eight or more people without electrical can openers, blenders, mixers, dishwashers, microwave ovens, clothes dryers. In addition to providing child care, the wife normally oversees the garden, preserves food, cooks, cleans, washes, sews, mends, supervises yard work. Many women mow their lawns with push mowers, without engines. Moreover, those who live on a farm often assist with barn chores, milking cows, gathering eggs, pulling tobacco plants in the spring, stripping leaves from tobacco stalks in the winter. The work is hard and the hours are long, but there is quiet satisfaction in nourishing thriving families, tending productive gardens, canning fruit, baking pies, sewing colorful quilts, and watching grandchildren find their place in the Amish world. There are also pleasant moments of reprieve, a quilting "frolic," a sale, a wedding, and, of course, perpetual visiting.

Women are able to vote in church business meetings and nominate men for ministerial duties. They do not, however, participate in the community's formal power structure as ordained leaders or as members of special committees. Virtually all Amish schoolteachers are single women, but they are also on the fringe of the formal leadership structure. Without the prod of economic forces, labor-saving changes have come more slowly in the kitchen than in the barn.

· · ·

One young woman described the tilted balance of power in detail:

> *The joke among us women is that the men make the rules so that's why more modern things are permitted in the barn than in the house. The women have no say in the rules. Actually, I think the main reason is the men make the living and we don't make a living in the house. So you have to go along with what they need out there.*

· · ·

It would be wrong to conclude that Amishwomen are discontent. They are not liberated by modern standards, but their roles are stable and well-defined. They know who they are and what is expected of them. One husband said: "A wife is not a servant; she is the queen and the husband is the king."

As self-employed people, Amish wives, ironically, have greater control over their work and daily affairs than do many modern women who hold full-time clerical and nonprofessional jobs. Unfettered by the pressure to succeed in a career, Amishwomen devote their energies to family living. And while their work is hard, it is *their* work and it brings as much, if not more, satisfaction than a professional career. The Amish see the professional woman as a negative role model, a distortion of God's created order. Their role models are other Amishwomen who have managed their families well. Happiness, after all, depends on one's values and social point of reference. Amishwomen succeed well in comparison with their reference group— other Amishwomen—and are relatively happy. Liberated women in modern society, often burdened by conflicting role expectations and strong pressures to excel professionally, may experience greater anxiety over their roles than unliberated Amishwomen.

Family Ties

When Amish leaders tally up the size of their churches, they count families instead of individuals.[4] The family, the keystone of Amish society, is large in size and influence. Amish youth marry between the ages of 22 and 25, on a Tuesday or Thursday in November, after the harvest season comes to a close. It is rare for someone under the age of 21 to be married. Marriage is highly esteemed, and raising a family is the professional career of Amish adults. Nine out of ten adults are married. Marriage vows are rarely broken. In extreme cases, couples may live apart, but divorce is taboo. Divorced people are automatically excommunicated.

Believing that birth control is tampering with God's will, couples yield to the law of nature and produce large families.[5] Including parents and children, the average family has 8.6 members, compared to the county norm of 3.3. By age 45, the typical Amishwoman has given birth to 7.1 children, whereas her modern neighbors average 2.8. Death and disease reduce the number, so completed families average 6.6 children. Slightly over 13 percent of Amish families have 10 or more children, and while Amish children are numerous, the expense of their upbringing is relatively low. There are no orthodontia payments, swimming pool memberships, tennis lessons, stereos, summer camps, sports cars, college tuitions, or designer clothes.[6] Amish children assume daily chores by 5 or 6 years of age, and their responsibilities in the barn and house grow rapidly. They are not seen as economic burdens but welcomed as blessings from the Lord and as members who will contribute their fair share to the family economy.

The power of the family extends beyond sheer numbers. The family's scope, influence, and control dwarfs that of the modern nuclear family. Amish life is spent in the context of the family. Social functions in modern families, from birth to death, from eating to leisure, are often staged outside the home. In contrast, Amish activities are anchored at home. Children are usually born there. They play at home, and school is within walking distance. By age 14, children work full-time at home. Amish children are taught by their extended family, not by television, babysitters, popular magazines, or nursery school teachers. Teen-age recreational activities, such as sledding, swimming, skating, baseball, volleyball, barn tag, and corner ball, are centered at or near home, without admission fees.

Young couples are married at home. Church services rotate from home to home. Meals are eaten at home. In recent years church leaders have urged families not to eat in restaurants. Social events, singings, "sisters' days," quilting parties, and work "frolics" are staged at home. Occasionally, small groups of men slip away for a day of deep-sea fishing or, on the sly, even play a game of golf, but the majority of Amish recreation is close to home and nature.[7] Adults work at home or nearby. Vacations to "get away from home" are rare, although some elderly couples vacation in Florida for several winter months.[8] Out-of-state travel by van, train, or bus for medical or business purposes often includes visiting in other settlements. These journeys are called "trips," not vacations.

Hair is cut at home. Many table games are homemade. The Amish do buy groceries and purchase commercial products, but much of their food and clothing is homemade. Instead of eating at a pizza shop or buying frozen pizza, Amish families make homemade pizza. Time and money spent on shopping trips are minuscule compared to the American norm. There are no visits to the health spa, pet parlor, hairdresser, car wash, or sports stadium, and thus there is more time for "home work" and "home play." Staying home is not a dreaded experience of isolation for the Amish. It means being immersed in the chatter, work, and play of the extended family. The Amish use modern medicines and health services, but they are more likely to rely on home remedies and visit the doctor only as a last resort. All of these centripetal forces pull the Amish homeward most of the time. Retirement occurs at home. Funerals are held at home, and the deceased are buried in nearby cemeteries.

There are, of course, trips to town for business, shopping, and errands, as well as for social events in the Amish community. But most dramas of Amish life are staged at home or in a nearby Amish home. The Amish have not allowed industrialization to oust major life functions from their home. In this regard, they have certainly not joined the modern world.

In sharp contrast to mobile contemporary families, Amish families are tied to a geographical area and anchored in a large extended family. Many Amish live on or within several miles of their childhood homestead. Others may live as far as 15 miles away. After a new family "settles down" in a residence after marriage, its members typically live there for the rest of their lives. Thus geographical and family roots are strong. A mother of six children explained that all of them live within Lancaster County and that she delights in visiting her 36 grandchildren at least once a month. Those living on the other side of her house she, of course, sees daily. With families averaging nearly seven children, it is not unusual for a couple to have 45 grandchildren. A typical child will have two dozen aunts and uncles and as many as 75 first cousins. Although some of these relatives are scattered on the settlement's fringe, many live within a few miles of home. To be Amish is to have a niche, a secure place in this network of relatives. Embroidered or painted rosters of the extended family hang on the walls of Amish homes—a constant reminder of the individual's notch in the family tree.

The Church District

The Amish families who live near one another form a church district or congregation—the chief social unit in Amish society beyond the family. The number of households per church district in the Lancaster settlement ranges from 20 to 46, with an average of 33. With many double households, the average district has about 20 extended family units. Some 76 adults and 87 youths under 18 years of age give the typical district a total of 163 people.[9] Church services are held in homes, and, as congregations grow, they divide. A district's geographical size varies with the density of the Amish population. On the edge of the Lancaster settlement, church districts stretch 12 miles from side to side, but they shrink dramatically in the settlement's hub. Families in the center of small districts are within a half-mile walk of other members.

Roads and streams frame the boundaries of most church districts. Like members of a traditional parish, the Amish participate in the church district that encircles their home. The members of a district worship together every other week. They often attend the services of adjoining congregations on the "off Sunday" of their congregation. The residents of one district, however, cannot become members of another one unless they move into its territory. There are no church buildings, and the homes of members become the gathering points not only for worship but also for socializing.

Because families live in close proximity, many members of a district are also blood relatives. Throughout the settlement six surnames—Stoltzfus, King, Fisher, Beiler, Esh, and Lapp—account for over 70 percent of the households.

· · ·

Kinship networks are thus rather dense both within and between church districts. One rural mail carrier had to distinguish among 60 Stoltzfus families. Moreover, he had three Amos E. Stoltzfuses and three Elam S. Stoltzfuses on the same route.

The district is the social and ceremonial unit around which the Amish world orbits. Self-contained and autonomous, the congregations are tied together by a network of bishops. Districts ordain their own leaders and, on the recommendation of their bishop, have the power to excommunicate members. Baptisms, weddings, and funerals take place within the district. Errant members must confess their sins publicly before other members. Local congregations under the leadership of their bishop vary in their interpretation of religious regulations. Decisions to aid other districts financially and to participate in community-wide Amish programs are made by the local district. Congregational votes are taken on recommendations brought by the bishop. Hostetler has aptly called this system a "patriarchal democracy."[10] Although each member has a vote, it is usually a vote to accept or reject the bishop's recommendation. The authority of the bishop brings compelling pressure to comply with proposed actions. Fellowship meals after worship services and other social activities, such as Sunday evening "singings," take place in the district. Hence members play, socialize, worship, and work together in a dense ethnic network. The church district is factory, church, club, family, and precinct all wrapped up into a neighborhood parish.

Leadership Roles

Leadership in each district is consolidated in three male roles: bishop, minister, and deacon. The leaders are viewed as servants of God and of the congregation. In fact, their German titles translate literally as "servant."[11] The bishop serves as the church's spiritual head and often presides over two districts.[12] One district is usually the bishop's "home base." Congregations meet every other week, and their bishop is able to attend each of their regular meetings. The bishop officiates at baptisms, weddings, communions, funerals, and members' meetings of the congregation. As spiritual head of the leadership team, he interprets and enforces church regulations. If disobedience or conflict arises, it is his responsibility to resolve it. Neighborhood, family, and church networks are often entangled in local controversies that require delicate diplomacy. The bishop is responsible for recommending excommunication or, as the case may be, the reinstatement of penitent members. While considerable authority is vested in the office of bishop, final decisions to excommunicate or reinstate members require a congregational vote. Diverse personality styles among the bishops lead to diverse interpretations of church rules. Some leaders are "open-minded," whereas others take firm doctrinaire positions. The bishop is the incarnate symbol of church authority. One member remarked that every time she sees a policeman, he "reminds me of the bishop." She added, however, that her bishop is a kind person, more concerned about the inner spiritual life of people than about external regulations.

. . .

The minister, or preacher, fills the second leadership role in the local district. A congregation of 75 members usually has two preachers and sometimes three, depending on their age and health. Preaching long, extemporaneous sermons in the worship service without the aid of notes is the minister's primary responsibility. Ministers also assist the bishop in giving spiritual direction and leadership to the congregation. Without professional credentials or training, the ministers are selected from within the congregation and serve unpaid for life, earning their own living by farming, carpentry, or other typical Amish occupations.

A deacon's public duties are limited to reading Scripture and leading prayers in the worship service. He supervises an "alms fund" for the needy in the congregation. He attends to the material needs of families in the congregation which require mutual aid. The deacon also assists with baptism and communion. Social control in the local district also hinges on the deacon's office. At the request of the bishop, the deacon, often accompanied by a minister, makes investigative visits to the homes of members who are flouting or violating church regulations. The outcome of the interview is reported to the bishop, who takes appropriate action. The deacon also carries messages of excommunication or reinstatement to members from the bishop. One bishop called this aspect of the deacon's role "the dirty work." The deacon represents the congregation when young couples plan to marry. The groom brings a church letter of "good standing" to the deacon of the bride's congregation, who then meets with her to verify the marriage plans. The bride's deacon then announces, or "publishes," their plans to the local congregation. The deacon does not arrange marriages, but he does symbolize the church's supervision of them.

The bishop, minister, and deacon form an informal "executive committee" that guides and coordinates the activities of the local district. During the first phase of the worship service, while the congregation is singing, this leadership team of four or five men meets for consultation. They decide who will preach the "main" sermon later that morning, and they also discuss other issues. Additional meetings are held as necessary. The power consolidated in the ordained leaders rests primarily with the bishop.

The Mobile Sanctuary

The rotation of worship services from home to home shapes Amish identity and forms the bedrock of their social organization. In the local area, the Old Order Amish are sometimes called House Amish, in contrast to the more liberal Church Amish, who worship in church buildings. While the Old Order Amish share some cultural traits with other plain people in the region, the Amish are *not* "meeting house people." Their mobile "sanctuary" distinguishes them from Old Order Mennonites, who worship in meeting houses but, like the Amish, drive horses and speak Pennsylvania Dutch. The Amish view a permanent church building or meeting house as a symbol of worldliness.

. . .

Worshipping in homes is a prudent way of limiting the size of Amish congregations. The physical size of houses controls the numerical size of church districts. It guarantees that each individual has a social home in a relatively small congregation. So while the Amish sanctuary floats, the individual is securely anchored. People are known by first name. Birthdays are remembered, and illnesses are public knowledge. In contrast, Moderns often anonymously float in and out of permanent sanctuaries. The mobile Amish sanctuary affirms the centrality of the family by keeping religious functions literally at home, integrated with family life. This is a radical departure from modern religion, with its specialized services in a sanctuary cut off from the other sectors of life.

The mobile meeting house not only assures individuals a secure niche in a small social unit but also enhances informal social control. Close ties in family networks place informal checks on social behavior. The mobile sanctuary assures that, on the average, members will visit the home of each family once a year. These annual visits, subtle inspection tours, stymie the proliferation of worldly appliances. The visits also shore up social cohesion and solidarity. How many people in a modern congregation have toured the homes of *all* other members in the past year?

The mobile sanctuary protests the sanctuaries of modern Christendom, which the Amish view as ostentatious displays of pride that point not heavenward, but earthward to the congregation's social prestige. The financial resources used by modern congregations for buildings, steeples, organs, and pastors are used by the Amish for mutual aid. With geographically determined boundaries, there is little need for evangelism. Expansion, fueled by biological growth, is not dependent on novel programs and modern facilities that compete with other churches. The Amish are baffled as to why Moderns build opulent homes but do not worship in them. Although Amish homes are not luxurious, they are used for worship, work, eating, and socializing. The mobile sanctuary, while not a public symbol, is deeply etched in Amish consciousness. Small, local, informal, lowly, and unpretentious, it is the structural embodiment of Gelassenheit—a major clue to the riddle of Amish survival.

The Organizational Chart

The organizational structure of Amish society is ambiguous. There are no headquarters, professionals, executive directors, or organizational charts. Kitchens, shops, barns, and home offices provide office space for this religious organization. The nebulous structure confounds outsiders. On one occasion, public officials in a heavily populated Amish township were distressed by rowdy Amish youth. Not knowing whom to contact in the Amish community, the township supervisors finally expressed their concern in a letter to an Amish layman who sometimes serves as public spokesman.[13] The vitality of Amish culture is a remarkable achievement, despite the lack of experts, corporate offices, memos, computers, and elaborate flow charts. Apart from schoolteachers, there are no paid church employees, let alone professional ones. Amish society is linked by a web of interpersonal ties which stretches across the community. How do the Amish manage to retain uniformity with nearly ninety loosely coupled church districts?

The solution to this riddle lies in the flat leadership structure. Each bishop typically serves two districts. The 75 adult members in each district are only one step away from the top of the church hierarchy. The flat, two-tier structure links grass-roots members directly to the citadel of power and has several benefits. Each bishop personally knows the members of his districts and in this way monitors the pulse of the community. Members feel a close tie to the central decision-making structure because their bishop attends bishops' meetings and may provide feedback on the discussion. The bishop, in turn, understands the larger concerns of all the bishops across the settlement and can personally enforce and explain church regulations to the members of his two districts. With some 150 members in both districts, he is able to regulate and monitor social change effectively on a first-name basis.

A seniority system based on age and tenure undergirds the power structure of the bishops. A young minister described the decision-making process among the bishops: "The five oldest have priority. It tends to point to the oldest one. If they want a final decision they say to him, 'Let's hear your decision.'" If health permits, the senior bishop presides over the bishops' meeting, as well as a ministers' meeting a few weeks later. The diplomatic skills of this highly esteemed elder statesman are critical for upholding harmony. A minister described the seniority system: "Many bishops have told me that they are going to the oldest bishop to ask for his advice on a certain issue. And he will not hesitate to give his opinion, based on Scripture. Then he will conclude and say, 'Don't do it that way just because I told you, go home and work with your church.' So it is not a dictatorship by any means; it works on a priority basis and a *submitting* basis" (emphasis added).

Twice each year, the bishops confer on problems, shape informal policies, and discuss social changes that threaten the church's welfare. A leaders' or ministers' meeting, involving bishops, ministers, and deacons, follows the bishops' meeting each fall and spring. This combined group of ordained leaders, numbering several hundred men, meets in a large home, shop, barn, or machinery shed. The bishops report on issues from their bishops' meeting and solicit the ministers' support. Other issues of concern or special problems are also handled. The leaders' meeting plays a significant role in maintaining cohesion and harmony across the settlement.

. . .

Many members credit the leaders' meeting as the key factor that enabled the Amish to avoid schisms and maintain uniformity despite a host of social changes in the past 20 years.

. . .

Architectural Summary

The social architecture of Amish society is small, compact, local, informal, and homogeneous—features that clash with the design of modern societies. Amish social structure embodies Gelassenheit and bolsters the groups' defensive strategy against worldliness. A brief synopsis of the distinctive features concludes our architectural tour.

1. *Small.* From egos to organizational units, Gelassenheit prefers small-scale things. The Amish realize that larger things bring specialization, dis-

tance, divisive subgroups, and often remove average people from power. Meeting in homes for worship limits the size of congregations. Ironically, this commitment to small-scale units makes individuals "big" in the sense that they are known intimately by a small, stable group. It is impossible to get lost in the crowd in an Amish congregation. The security and identity provided by small congregations lessen the pressure for individuals to "make it on their own." Small farms are preferable to large ones. Large craft and manufacturing shops are frowned upon. Big operators garner attention to themselves, establishing a threatening power base, and insult the egalitarian community with excessive wealth.

An Amish businessman explained:

> *My people look at a large business as a sign of greed. We're not supposed to engage in large businesses, and I'm right at the borderline now and maybe too large for Amish standards. The Old Order Amish don't like large exposed volume. You don't drive down the road and see big Harvestore silos sitting on Amish farms, you don't see one of these big thousand-foot chicken houses. I can easily tell you which are the Mennonite farms. They'll feed 200 head of cattle, have 50,000 chickens, and milk 120 cows. They're a notch completely ahead of us. We stop at the point of a herd of 50 cows, and 10,000 chickens. We farm with horses, so that we're satisfied with eighty acres of land, where a Mennonite, hey, he can't afford to pay $40,000 for a tractor and only farm eighty acres. He's got to farm half of the neighborhood to make it pay. Then he needs some bigger equipment, he needs a combine, and then he needs the whole bit. That also applies to business, and my business is just at the point right now where it's beyond where the Old Order Amish people think it should be. It's just too large.*

Another businessman expressed the fear of large organizations: "Our discipline thrives with a small group. Once you get into that big superstructure, it seems to gather momentum and you can't stop it." Criticizing the growing size of an Amish organization that the bishops curbed, he said: "It became self-serving, like a pyramid. Suppose we get a rotten egg leading it sometime? He can do more damage, and wreck in one year, what we built up in 20 years. That's why the bishops curbed it." The Amish have not reviewed the scientific literature describing the impact of size on social life but realize that, in the long run, the modern impulse for large-scale things could debilitate their community.

2. *Compact.* The Amish have resisted the modern tendency to specialize and separate social functions. Unlike most religions in modern society, Amish religion is not partitioned off from other activities. Work, play, child rearing, education, and worship, for the most part, are neither highly specialized nor separated from one another. The same circle of people interacting in family, neighborhood, church, school, leisure, and work blends these functions together in a compact network. Members of these overlapping circles share common values. The dense webs of social interaction decrease

privacy. Gossip, ridicule, and small talk become informal instruments of social control as networks crisscross, and, in the words of a member, "everybody knows everything about everyone else."

If modernity separates through specialization and mobility, it is not surprising to hear Amish pleas for social integration—"togetherness," "unity," and a "common mind." In a formal statement, the bishops admonished teenagers to stay home more on weekends and urged parents to have morning worship with their families as "a good way of staying together."[14] A young woman explained why the church frowns on central heating systems: "A space heater in the kitchen keeps the family together. Heating all the rooms would lead to everyone going off to their own rooms."

Another member described the compact structure of Amish society: "What is more scriptural than the closely knit Christian community, living together, working together, worshipping together, with its own church and own schools? Here the members know each other, work with and care for each other every day of the week."[15] A bishop, arguing against the use of modern combines to harvest wheat, said they would eliminate binding up sheaves of wheat during the summer harvest. This practice, he said, reminds members anew each year of how the church is bound in unity like a sheaf of wheat. These symbolic descriptions illustrate how the overlapping spheres of Amish life merge together in a compact structure that has remained immune from the fragmentation of modern life.

3. *Local.* Amish life is staged in a local arena. Largely cut off from mass communication, rapid transit, geographical mobility, and national organizations, Amish life revolves around the immediate neighborhood. Businessmen are often conversant about national affairs, but the dominant orientation is local, not cosmopolitan. Things close by are known, understood, and esteemed. Typical phrases in Amish writings—"home rule," "home community," "local home standards"—anchor the entire social system in the local church district. The local base of Amish interaction is poignantly described in an Amish view of education: "The one-room, one-teacher, community school near the child's home is the best possible type of elementary school. Here the boys and girls of a local community grow up and become neighbors among each other."[16]

4. *Informal.* With few contractual and formal relationships, Amish life is fused by informal ties and anchored in family networks, common traditions, uniform symbols, and a shared mistrust of the outside world. The informality of Amish society expresses itself in many ways. Social interaction is conducted on a first-name basis without titles. Oral communication takes precedence over written. Few written records are kept of the meetings of ordained leaders. Organizational procedures are dictated by oral tradition, not policy manuals and flow charts. Although each bishop wields considerable influence in his districts, the congregations are loosely coupled together by family networks rather than by formal policies.

5. *Homogeneous.* The conventional marks of social class, education, income, and occupation have little validity in Amish society. Ending school at eighth grade homogenizes educational achievement. Farming, the traditional vocation, levels the occupational structure. In recent years, shop owners and craftspeople have emerged as a new occupational grouping. Similar occupational and educational levels have minimized financial differences in the community in the past. Some Amish own several farms and display discreet traces of wealth in their choice of farm equipment and animals. Historically, however, the common agricultural base has homogenized wealth. Recent changes threaten the historic equality. Farms are typically valued at over $300,000, and it is not uncommon for an Amish business to have annual sales exceeding $1 million.

Thus the financial resources of farm and shop owners exceed that of shop workers, who earn hourly wages. High land values and new sources of revenue will likely, in the long run, disturb the egalitarian nature of Amish society. One member, describing a certain rural road, said: "Three Amish millionaires live up there, but they don't drive around in Cadillacs, own a summer home at the bay, or have a yacht." Wealth in Amish society is held modestly, not displayed conspicuously. Despite growing inequality, there is, at least on the surface, an attempt to maintain homogeneous symbols of faith and ethnicity. Both the well-to-do businessman and the farm laborer dress alike, drive a horse to church, and will be buried under similar gravestones. On the whole, the economic structure of Amish society is relatively flat, in contrast to the hierarchical class structure of postindustrial societies. In all of these ways, Amish architecture exudes an elegant simplicity—small, compact, local, informal, and homogeneous—that embodies Gelassenheit and partially explains the riddle of Amish survival.

NOTES

1. Hostetler, John A. 1980. *Amish Society.* 3rd ed. Baltimore: Johns Hopkins University Press, p. 173.

2. In the fifties and sixties, many Amish children were born in hospitals. Since 1980 most children are born at home, with the assistance of a certified midwife. Some are delivered in outpatient clinics and doctors' offices. For colorful descriptions of a midwife's and doctor's work among the Amish, see respectively, Armstrong, Penny and Sheryl Feldman. 1986. *A Midwife's Story.* New York: Arbor House; and Kaiser, Grace H. 1986. *Dr. Frau: A Woman Doctor among the Amish.* Intercourse, PA: Good Books.

3. The role of the Amish wife is described by the bishop in the wedding ceremony: "The man should know that God has appointed him as head of his woman, that he is to lead, rule and protect her lovingly." The wife "is to honor and respect him and be subject to him. . . . She shall be quiet . . . and take good care of the children and housekeeping." Wives are told to conduct themselves submissively and are asked to pledge to "live in subjection to their husband"; see *Handbuch fur Bischof (Handbook for Bishops).* 1978 [1935]. Translated by Noah G. Good. Gordonville, PA: Gordonville Print Shop.

4. Huntington (1981) has written an excellent essay on the Amish family. Huntington, Gertrude E. 1981. "The Amish Family." In *Ethnic Families in America: Patterns and Variations,* edited by Charles H. Mindel and Robert W. Habenstein. 2nd ed. New York: Elsevier Scientific. For a description of age roles in the Amish family, see Hostetler, John A. and Gertrude E. Huntington. 1971. *Children in Amish Society: Socialization and Community Education.* New York: Holt, Rinehart and Winston, pp. 12–34.

5. It is possible that some progressive Amish couples use artificial means of birth control. However, church leaders and most of the community would condemn such behavior as morally wrong. For a variety of reasons, older women sometimes undergo sterilization to prevent further births. The acceptance of sterilization represents a modernizing trend—a shift from fate to choice.

6. Orthodontia is considered superfluous and rarely used for aesthetic purposes; if they have serious dental problems, the Amish will undergo orthodontic treatment.

7. One Amish farmer has a homemade putting green hidden in a secluded section of his pasture where he can practice his golfing on the sly. Another Amishman occasionally flies in a private plane with a pilot friend. If such activities became public knowledge, they would likely trigger some form of discipline in the church.

8. Businessmen and their families and well-to-do retired farmers travel occasionally and sometimes take vacations or "trips." They may travel by bus, train, or rented van; air travel is prohibited. Some Amish in the Lancaster area routinely take a winter vacation in Florida. Amish from various parts of the United States congregate in Pinecraft Village, southeast of Sarasota. For a description of this small Amish village, see *Intelligencer Journal,* January 14, 1987.

9. A household is defined as a living area having separate eating facilities. Many extended families have two or three households in the same house.

10. Hostetler (1980, p. 111).

11. The leaders are called *Diener* (servant). The *Handbuch* (1978) identifies them as *Volliger Diener* (bishop), *Diener zum Buch* (minister, or servant, of the book), and *Armendiener* (deacon, or servant, to the poor). Their roles are described in the *Handbuch* (1978, pp. 29–33). Yoder (1987) provides an excellent review of the ordained offices and notes that the term *bishop* was not used by the Amish until the 1860s.

12. A bishop is not required by church polity to have two districts. Typically a bishop has a "home" district but often oversees a second district for several years until the congregation is ready to ordain its own bishop. In some instances, a bishop may oversee three districts and in other cases only one. A bishop usually is responsible for two districts.

13. Steering Committee. 1983. *Minutes of Old Order Amish Steering Committee.* Vol. 3, pp. 35–36. Gordonville, PA: Gordonville Print Shop.

14. *Ordnung Fier Zu Shaffen (Arbeiten) und Halten Unter Unsere Alte Amische Gemeinen und Junge Leut. Der Folgen ist Uberreinkommen bei die Lancaster County Bischofen.* (Working ordinances to be kept among our Old Order Amish churches and young people. The following was agreed on by the Lancaster County bishops). 1983. In *Minutes of the Old Order Amish Steering Committee from 1981–1986* 3:36–37. Translated by Noah G. Good. Gordonville, PA: Gordonville Print Shop.

15. Wagler, David. n.d. *Are All Things Lawful?* Aylmer, Ontario: Pathway Publishers, p. 7.

16. *Standards of the Old Order Amish and Old Order Mennonite Parochial and Vocational Schools of Pennsylvania.* 1981. Gordonville, PA: Gordonville Print Shop, p. 41.

16

GANG BUSINESS
Making Ends Meet

MARTIN SANCHEZ JANKOWSKI

This selection by Martin Sanchez Jankowski is excerpted from his book, *Islands in the Street: Gangs in American Urban Society* (1991). Sanchez Jankowski studies the *primary group* of social gangs that exist in urban settings across the United States. Examples of other primary groups are families, friendship cliques, sororities and fraternities, neighborhood coffee klatches, and small work groups. Thus, primary groups emerge when people live or work closely together. As this reading by Sanchez Jankowski shows, gangs are similar to other primary groups in that they are small, intimate, and informal. Sanchez Jankowski also argues that, contrary to the stereotype of gang culture, gangs have social values similar to those of other American groups, including a work ethic and an entrepreneurial spirit.

Cunning and deceit will serve a man better than force to rise from a base condition to great fortune.

——NICCOLÒ MACHIAVELLI, THE DISCOURSES (1517?)

If there is one theme that dominates most studies of gangs, it is that gangs are collectives of individuals who are social parasites, and that they are parasitic not only because they lack the skills to be productive members of society but, more important, because they lack the values, particularly the work ethic, that would guide them to be productive members of society.[1] However, one of the most striking factors I observed was how much the entrepreneurial spirit, which most Americans believe is the core of their productive culture, was a driving force in the worldview and behavior of gang members.[2] If entrepreneurial spirit denotes the desire to organize and manage business interests toward some end that results in the accumulation of capital, broadly defined, nearly all the gang members that I studied possessed, in varying degrees, five attributes that are either entrepreneurial in character or that reinforce entrepreneurial behavior.

The first of these entrepreneurial attitudes is competitiveness. Most gang

Martin Sanchez Jankowski: *Islands in the Street: Gangs and American Urban Society,* pp. 101–105, 119–126. Copyright © 1991 The Regents of the University of California. Reprinted by permission of the University of California Press.

members I spoke with expressed a strong sense of self-competence and a drive to compete with others. They believed in themselves as capable of achieving some level of economic success and saw competition as part of human nature and an opportunity to prove one's self-worth. This belief in oneself often took on a dogmatic character, especially for those individuals who had lost in some form of economic competition. The losers always had ready excuses that placed the blame on something other than their own personal inadequacy, thereby artificially reinforcing their feelings of competence in the face of defeat.[3]

Gang members' sense of competitiveness also reflected their general worldview that life operates under Social Darwinist principles. In the economic realm, they believed there is no ethical code that regulates business ventures, and this attitude exempted them from moral constraints on individual economic-oriented action.[4] The views of Danny provide a good example of this Social Darwinist outlook. Danny was a 20-year-old Irish gang member from Boston:

> *I don't worry about whether something is fair or not when I'm making a business deal. There is nothing fair or unfair, you just go about your business of trying to make a buck, and if someone feels you took advantage of him, he has only himself to blame. If someone took advantage of me, I wouldn't sit around bellyaching about it, I'd just go and try to get some of my money back. One just has to ask around here [the neighborhood] and you'd find that nobody expects that every time you're going to make a business deal, that it will be fair—you know, that the other guy is not going to be fair, hell, he is trying to make money, not trying to be fair. This is the way those big business assholes operate too! The whole thing [the system] operates this way.*

. . .

The second entrepreneurial attribute I observed is the desire and drive to accumulate money and material possessions. Karl Marx, of course, described this desire as the "profit motive" and attributed it primarily to the bourgeoisie.[5] There is a profit-motive element to the entrepreneurial values of gang members, but it differs significantly from Marx's analysis of the desire to accumulate material and capital for their own sake, largely divorced from the desire to improve one's material condition. Nor is gang members' ambition to accumulate material possessions related to a need for achievement, which the psychologist David McClelland identifies as more central to entrepreneurial behavior in certain individuals than the profit motive per se.[6] Rather, the entrepreneurial activity of gang members is predicated on their more basic understanding of what money can buy.[7] The ambition to accumulate capital and material possessions is related, in its initial stages (which can last for a considerable number of years), to the desire to improve the comfort of everyday living and the quality of leisure time.

This desire, of course, is shared by most people who live in low-income neighborhoods. Some of them resign themselves to the belief that they will never be able to secure their desires. Others attempt to improve their life situation by using various "incremental approaches," such as working in those jobs that are made available to them and saving their money, or attempting to learn higher-level occupational skills. In contrast, the entrepreneurs of low-income neighborhoods, especially those in gangs, attempt to improve their lives by becoming involved in a business venture, or a series of ventures, that has the potential to create large changes in their own or their family's socioeconomic condition.

The third attribute of entrepreneurial behavior prevalent in gangs is status-seeking. Mirroring the dominant values of the larger society, most gang members attempt to achieve some form of status with the acquisition of possessions. However, most of them cannot attain a high degree of status by accumulation alone. To merit high status among peers and in the community, gang members must try, although most will be unsuccessful, to accumulate a large number of possessions and be willing to share them. Once gang members have accumulated sufficient material possessions to provide themselves with a relative level of comfort or leisure above the minimal, they begin to seek the increase in status that generosity affords. (For philanthropic purposes, accumulating cash is preferable to accumulating possessions, because the more money one has, the more flexibility one has in giving away possessions.)

The fourth entrepreneurial attribute one finds among gang members is the ability to plan. Gang members spend an impressive amount of time planning activities that will bring them fortune and fame, or, at least, plenty of spending money in the short term. At their grandest, these plans have the character of dreams, but as the accounts of renowned business tycoons show, having big dreams has always been a hallmark of entrepreneurial endeavors.[8] At the other end of the spectrum are short-range plans (also called small scams) that members try to pull on one another, usually to secure a loan.

. . .

Gang members also engage in intermediary and long-range planning. A typical intermediary plan might concern modest efforts to steal some type of merchandise from warehouses, homes, or businesses. Because most of the sites they select are equipped with security systems, a more elaborate plan involving more time is needed than is the case for those internal gang scams just described. Long-range planning and organization, sometimes quite elaborate, are, as other studies have reported, at times executed with remarkable precision.[9]

Finally, the fifth entrepreneurial attribute common among gang members is the ability to undertake risks. Generally, young gang members (nine to fifteen years of age) do not understand risk as part of a risk-reward calculus, and for this age group, risk-taking is nearly always pursued for itself, as an element of what Thrasher calls the "sport motive,"[10] the desire to test oneself. As gang members get older, they gradually develop a more sophisticated understanding of risk-taking, realizing that a certain amount of risk is necessary to secure desired goals. Now they attempt to calculate the risk factors involved for nearly every venture, measuring the risk to their physical well-being, money, and freedom. Just like mainstream businessmen, they discover that risk tends to increase proportionally to the level of innovation undertaken to secure a particular financial objective. Most of these older gang members are willing to assume risks commensurate with the subjective "value" of their designated target, but they will not assume risks just for the sake of risk-taking.

· · ·

Economic Activity: Accumulating

With a few exceptions, nearly all the literature on gangs focuses on their economic delinquency.[11] This is a very misleading picture, however, for although gangs operate primarily in illegal markets, they also are involved in legal markets. Of the 37 gangs observed in the present study, 27 generated some percentage of their revenues through legitimate business activity. It is true that gangs do more of their business activity in the illegal markets, but none of them wants to be exclusively active in these markets.[12]

In the illegal market, gangs concentrate their economic activities primarily in goods, services, and recreation. In the area of goods, gangs have been heavily involved in accumulating and selling drugs, liquor, and various stolen products such as guns, auto parts, and assorted electronic equipment. These goods are sometimes bought and sold with the gang acting as the wholesaler and/or retailer. At other times, the gang actually produces the goods it sells. For example, while most gangs buy drugs or alcohol and retail them, a few gangs manufacture and market homemade drugs and moonshine liquor. Two gangs (one African-American and one Irish) in this study had purchased stills and sold their moonshine to people on the street, most of whom were derelicts, and to high school kids too young to buy liquor legally.[13] Three other gangs (two Puerto Rican and one Dominican) made a moonshine liquor from fermented fruit and sold it almost exclusively to teenagers. Both types of moonshine were very high in alcohol, always above one hundred proof. While sales of this liquor were not of the magnitude to create fortunes, these projects were quite surprisingly capable of generating substantial amounts of revenue.

The biggest money-maker and the one product nearly every gang tries to market is illegal drugs.[14] The position of the gang within the illegal drug market varies among gangs and between cities. In New York, the size of the gang and how long it has been in existence have a great deal to do with whether it will have access to drug suppliers. The older and larger gangs are able to buy drugs from suppliers and act as wholesalers to pushers. They shun acting as pushers (the lowest level of drug sales) themselves because there are greater risks and little, if any, commensurate increase in profit. In addition, because heroin use is forbidden within most gangs, the gang leaders prefer to establish attitudes oriented to the sale rather than the consumption of drugs within the organization. In the past, when the supply was controlled by the Italian Mafia, it was difficult for gangs to gain access to the quantity of drug supplies necessary to make a profit marketing them. In the past ten years, though, the Mafia has given way (in terms of drug supply) to African-American, Puerto Rican, and Mexican syndicates.[15] In addition, with the increased popularity of cocaine in New York, the African-American, Puerto Rican, and Dominican syndicates' connections to Latin American sources of cocaine supply rival, and in many cases surpass, those of Mafia figures.[16] With better access to supplies, gangs in New York have been able to establish a business attitude toward drugs and to capitalize on the opportunities that drugs now afford them.

Some gangs have developed alternative sources of supply. They do so in two ways. Some, particularly the Chicano gangs, have sought out pharmacies where an employee can be paid off to steal pills for the gang to sell on the street.[17] Other gangs, particularly in New York, but also some in Los Angeles, have established "drug mills" to produce synthetic drugs such as LSD (or more recently crack cocaine) for sale on the street. The more sophisticated drug mills, which are controlled by various organized crime families, manufacture a whole line of drugs for sale, including cut heroin, but gangs are almost never involved in them. Those gangs that have established a production facility for generating drugs, no matter how crude it may be, generate sizable sums of money. Whether a gang is able to establish a sophisticated production and distribution system for drug sales depends on the sophistication of the gang organization and the amount of capital available for start-up purposes.

Stolen guns are another popular and profitable product. Gangs sometimes steal guns and then redistribute them, but most often they buy them from wholesale gun peddlers and then resell them. Sometimes the gangs will buy up a small number of shotguns and then cut the barrel and stock down to about 13 to 15 inches in length and then sell them as "easily concealable." A prospective buyer can get whatever gun he wants if he is willing to pay the going price. In the present study, the Irish gangs have been, commercially speaking, the most involved with guns, often moving relatively large shipments, ranging from sawed-off shotguns to fully automatic rifles and pistols of the most sophisticated types.[18] It was reported that these guns were being moved, with the help of the Irish social clubs, to the Catholics of Northern Ireland for their struggle with the Protestants there. No matter what the destination, rather large sums of money were paid to the Irish gangs for their efforts in acquiring the weapons or in helping move them. Although all the gangs studied were involved in the sale of illegal guns, illegal gun sales constituted a larger proportion of the economic activities of Irish gangs than they did for the others.

Gangs in all three cities were also involved in the selling of car parts. All the parts sold were stolen, some stolen to fill special orders from customers and others stolen and reworked in members' home garages into customized parts for resale. Business was briskest in Los Angeles, where there is a large market, especially among the low-rider clientele, for customized auto parts.[19] The amount of money made from stolen auto parts varies according to the area, whether or not the gang has an agent to whom to sell the parts, and the types of parts sold. On the whole, revenues from stolen auto parts are not nearly as high as those from selling illegal drugs, guns, or liquor, and so less time is devoted by gangs to this activity.

Gangs' business activities also include a number of services, the three most common being protection, demolition (usually arson), and indirect participation in prostitution. Protection is the most common service, both because there is a demand for it in the low-income areas in which gangs operate and because the gangs find it the easiest service to deliver, since it requires little in the way of resources or training. Gangs offer both personal and business protection. Nearly all the gangs had developed a fee schedule according to the type of protection desired. Most, but certainly not all, of the protection services offered by the gangs in this study involved extortion. Usually the gang would go into a store and ask the owner if he felt he needed protection from being robbed. Since it was clear what was being suggested, the owner usually said yes and asked how much it would cost him. When dealing with naive owners, those who did not speak English very well or did not know American ghetto customs, or with owners who flatly resisted their services, the gang would take time to educate or persuade them to retain its services. In the case of the immigrants (most of whom were Asian or Near Eastern), the gang members would begin by explaining the situation, but usually such owners did not understand, and so the gang would demonstrate its point by sending members into the store to steal. Another tactic was to pay a dope addict to go in and rob the store. After such an incident occurred, the gang would return and ask the owner if he now needed protection. If he refused, the tactics were repeated, and almost all the owners were finally convinced. However, for those owners who understood and resisted from the start, more aggressive tactics were used, such as destruction of their premises or harassment of patrons. More often than not, continued pressure brought the desired result. However, it should be noted that in the vast majority of cases, no coercion was needed, because store owners in high-crime areas were, more often than not, happy to receive protection. As one owner said to me: "I would need to hire a protection company anyway, and frankly the gang provides much more protection than they could ever do."

Gangs also offer their services as enforcers to clients who need punishment administered to a third party. Small-time hustlers or loan sharks, for example, hired some gangs to administer physical coercion to borrowers delinquent in their repayments. More recently one gang offered and apparently was hired by a foreign government to undertake terrorist attacks against the government and people of the United States.[20] Although that was an extreme case, nearly all gangs seek enforcement contracts because the fee is usually high, few resources have to be committed, and relatively little in the way of planning (compared to other projects) is needed.

The permanent elimination of or damage to property is another service gangs offer. This more often than not involves arson, and the buildings hit are commonly dilapidated. The gangs' clients are either landlords who want to torch the building to get the insurance money or residents who are so frustrated by the landlord's unwillingness to provide the most basic services that they ask the gang to retaliate. In both cases, there is usually much preliminary discussion of the project within the gang. These service jobs require a good deal of discussion and planning because there is the potential to hurt someone living in the building or to create enormous hardship if people have no alternative place to live, and the gang will do almost anything to avoid injuring people in its community. The gangs of New York have had the most business along these lines, particularly in the South Bronx, but arson is a service offered in Detroit, Chicago, and Philadelphia as well. As one gang leader from the Bronx said:

> *You just don't bomb or torch any building that someone wants down. You got to find out who lives there, if they got another place to go, if they would be for takin' out the building and if they'd be OK with the folks [law enforcement authorities]. Then you got to get organized to get everybody out and sometimes that ain't many people and sometimes it is. If there is lots of people in the building, we'd just pass [refuse] on the job. . . . Now if we can work all these things out, we take the job and we deliver either a skeleton [outer walls are standing, but nothing else] or a cremation [just ashes].*

Many potential clients know that a gang will refuse to burn down a building in its neighborhood if some type of harm will come to residents of its community, and so they contract with a gang from another area to do the job. Such incidents always ignite a war not only between the affected gangs but also between the communities. Take the example of the Hornets, a gang from one borough in New York that had contracted to set on fire a building in another borough. Although no one was killed in the fire, a few people were slightly burned, and of course everyone who lived in the building became homeless. At the request of a number of residents, the Vandals, a gang from the affected area, began to investigate and found out who had contracted to torch the building and which gang had been responsible. Then, at the request of an overwhelming majority of the community, the Vandals retaliated by burning down a building in the culprit gang's community. Hipper, a 20-year-old member of the Vandals, said:

> *We got to protect our community, they depend on us and they want us to do*
> *something so this [the burning of an apartment building in the neighborhood]*
> *don't happen again. . . . We be torchin' one of their buildings. I hope this don't*
> *hurt anybody, but if we don't do this, they be back hurting the people in our com-*
> *munity and we definitely don't be letting that happen!*

This is an excellent example of the bond that exists between the community and the gang. There is the understanding, then, among the community that the gang is a resource that can be counted on, particularly in situations where some form of force is necessary. Likewise, the gang knows that its legitimacy and existence are tied to being integrated in and responsible to community needs.

Prostitution is one illegal service in which gangs do not, for the most part, become directly involved. Gangs will accept the job of protecting pimps and their women for a fee (fifteen, or 40 percent, of the gangs in this study had), and in this way they become indirectly associated with the prostitution business. Yet they generally avoid direct involvement because they feel protective of the females in their communities, and their organizations are wary of being accused by neighborhood residents of exposing female members of the community to the dangers associated with prostitution.

The last type of illegal ecomomic activity in which all of the gangs in the present study were involved has to do with providing recreation. Some gangs establish numbers games in their neighborhoods. One New York gang had rented what had been a small Chinese food take-out place and was running numbers from the back where the kitchen had once been. (When I first observed the place, I thought it was a Chinese take-out and even proposed we get some quick food from it, which met with much laughter from the members of the gang I was with.) This gang became so successful that it opened up two other numbers establishments. One had been a pizza place (and was made to look as though it still served pizza slices); the other was a small variety store, which still functioned in that capacity, but also housed the numbers game in the back rooms.

Setting up gambling rooms is another aspect of the recreation business. Eleven of the gangs (or 30 percent) rented small storefronts, bought tables and chairs, and ran poker and/or domino games. The gang would assume the role of the "house," receiving a commission for each game played. Some of the gangs bought slot machines and placed them in their gambling rooms. Five (or 14 percent) of the gangs had as many as fifteen machines available for use.

Finally, ten gangs (27 percent), primarily those with Latino members, rented old buildings and converted them to accommodate cockfights. The gang would charge each cock owner a fee for entering his bird and an entrance fee for each patron. All of these ventures could, at various times, generate significant amounts of capital. The exact amount would depend on how often they were closed by the police and how well the gang managed the competition in its marketplace.

Turning to the legal economic activities undertaken by gangs, I observed that two ran "mom and pop" stores that sold groceries, candy, and soft drinks. Three gangs had taken over abandoned apartment buildings, renovated them, and rented them very cheaply—not simply because the accommodations were rather stark, but also because the gang wanted to help the less fortunate members of its community. The gangs also used these buildings to house members who had nowhere else to live. Undertaken and governed by social as much as economic concerns, these apartment ventures did not generate much income.

Interestingly, the finances of these legal activities were quite tenuous. The gangs that operated small grocery stores experienced periodic failures during which the stores had to be closed until enough money could be acquired (from other sources) to either pay the increased rent, rebuild shelf stock, or make necessary repairs. For those gangs who operated apartment buildings, in every case observed, the absence of a deed to the building or the land forced the gang to relinquish its holdings to either the city or a new landlord who wanted to build some new structure. Though there was a plentiful supply of abandoned buildings, most gangs lost interest in the renovation-and-rental business because such projects always created a crisis in their capital flow, which in turn precipitated internal bickering and conflict.

Other legal economic activities undertaken by the gangs I studied were automobile and motorcycle repair shops, car parts (quasi junk yards), fruit stands, and hair shops (both barber and styling). However, most of these ventures contributed only very modest revenues to the gangs' treasuries. Furthermore, the gang leadership had difficulty keeping most of the legal economic activities functioning because the rank and file were, by and large, not terribly enthusiastic about such activities. Rank-and-file resistance to most of these activities was of three sorts: members did not want to commit regularly scheduled time to any specific ongoing operation; members felt that the legal activities involved considerable overhead costs that lowered the profit rate; and members calculated that the time required to realize a large profit was far too long when compared to illegal economic activity. Thus, when such projects were promoted by the gang leadership and undertaken by the rank and file, they were done under the rubric of community service aid projects. The comments of Pin, a 19-year-old African-American gang member from New York, are representative of this general position on legal economic activity:

> No, I don't go for those deals where we [the gang] run some kind of hotel out of an old building or run some repair shop or something like that. When you do that you can't make no money, or if you do make something it so small and takes so long to get it that it's just a waste of our [the gang's] money. But when the

leadership brings it up as a possibility, well, sometimes I vote for it because I figure you got to help the community, many of them [people in the community] say they sort of depend on our help in one way or another, so I always say this is one way to help the community and me and the brothers go along with it. But everybody knows you can't make no money on shit like this.

NOTES

1. Nearly all studies of gangs incorporate this theme into their analysis. One of the exceptions is Cloward and Ohlin, *Delinquency and Opportunity,* which argues that many delinquents have the same values as other members of American society. However, even Cloward and Ohlin incorporate some of the conventional argument by accepting the premise that gang members' skills to compete in the larger society have been retarded by a lack of opportunity.

2. See Charles Sabel, *Work and Politics* (Cambridge: Cambridge University Press, 1987), pp. 1–30, on the importance of worldviews in affecting the behavior of individuals in industrial organizations and politics.

3. David Matza mentions a comparable tendency among delinquents to deny guilt associated with wrongdoing when he discusses the delinquent's belief that he is nearly always the victim of a "bum rap" (see Matza, *Delinquency and Drift* [New Brunswick, N.J.: Transaction Books], pp. 108–10).

4. I use the term *economic oriented action* the way Weber does: "Action will be said to be 'economical oriented' so far as, according to its subjective meaning, it is concerned with the satisfaction of a desire for 'utilities' *(Nutzleistung)*" (Weber, *Economy and Society* 1:63).

5. See Karl Marx, *The Economic and Philosophical Manuscripts of 1844,* 4th rev. ed. (Moscow: Progress Publishers, 1974), p. 38.

6. See David C. McClelland, *The Achieving Society* (New York: Free Press, 1961), pp. 233–37.

7. See Lee Rainwater, *What Money Buys: Inequality and the Social Meanings of Income* (New York: Basic Books, 1974). Also see Richard P. Coleman and Lee Rainwater, *Social Standing in America: New Dimensions of Class* (New York: Basic Books, 1978), pp. 29–45.

8. See the accounts of successful entrepreneurs from poor families who dreamed of grandeur and became America's most renowned business tycoons in Matthew Josephson, *The Robber Barons: the Great American Capitalists 1861–1901* (New York: Harcourt, Brace & World, 1962), especially the chapter entitled "What Young Men Dream," pp. 32–49.

9. See Thrasher, *The Gang,* p. 86.

10. Ibid., p. 86.

11. Both the theoretical and empirical literature focus on the gang's criminal activity. For theoretical discussions, see Kornhauser, *Social Sources of Delinquency,* pp. 51–61. For empirical studies, see nearly all of the classic and contemporary work on gangs. A sample of this literature would include Thrasher, *The Gang;* Herman Schwendinger and Julia Schwendinger, *Adolescent Subcultures and Delinquency* (New York: Praeger, 1985); Cloward and Ohlin, *Delinquency and Opportunity;* Cohen, *Delinquent Boys.* Two exceptions are Horowitz, *Honor and the American Dream,* and Vigil, *Barrio Gangs.*

12. There are two factors that have encouraged gangs to be more active in illegal markets. First, gangs, like organized crime syndicates, attempt to become active in

many economic activities that are legal. However, because so much of the legal market is controlled by groups that have established themselves in strategic positions (because they entered that market a considerable time in the past), gangs have found it difficult at best to successfully penetrate many legal markets. Further, there are financial incentives that have encouraged gangs to operate in the illegal market. These include the fact that costs are relatively low, and while personal risk (in terms of being incarcerated and/or physically hurt) is rather high, high demand along with high risk can produce greater profit margins. Despite the fact that these two factors have encouraged gangs to be more active in the illegal market, it is important to emphasize that nearly all the gangs studied attempted to, and many did, conduct business in the legal market as well.

13. The Schwendingers indicate that "youthful tastes regulate the flow of goods and services in the [adolescent] market" and gangs do take advantage of these tastes. See Schwendinger and Schwendinger, *Adolescent Subcultures and Delinquency,* p. 286.

14. See Fagan, "Social Organization of Drug Use and Drug Dealing among Urban Gangs," pp. 633–67; and Jerome H. Skolnick, *Forum: The Social Structure of Street Drug Dealing* (Sacramento: Bureau of Criminal Statistics/Office of the Attorney General, 1989).

15. See Francis A. J. Ianni, *Black Mafia: Ethnic Succession in Organized Crime* (New York: Simon & Schuster, 1974). Also see Moore, *Homeboys,* pp. 86–92, 114–16.

16. See Peter Lupsha and K. Schlegel, "The Political Economy of Drug Trafficking: The Herrera Organization (Mexico and the United States)" (Paper Presented at the Latin American Studies Association, Philadelphia, 1979).

17. This paying off of employees for drug supplies began, according to Joan Moore, in Los Angeles in the 1940s and 1950s (see Moore, *Homeboys,* pp. 78–82).

18. These gangs can procure fully automatic M-16s, Ingrams, and Uzzis.

19. Low riders are people, nearly all of whom are of Mexican descent, who drive customized older automobiles (1950s and 1960s models are preferred), one of the characteristics being that the springs for each wheel are cut away so that the car rides very low to the ground. Some of these cars have hydraulic systems that can be inflated at the flip of a switch so that the car can ride low to the ground at one moment and at the normal level the next. For a discussion of the importance of customized automobiles in Los Angeles, especially among Chicano youth, see Schwendinger and Schwendinger, *Adolescent Subcultures and Delinquency,* pp. 234–45.

20. The El Rukn gang in Chicago was recently indicted and convicted of contracting with the Libyan government to carry out terrorist acts within the United States. See *Chicago Tribune,* 3, 4, 6, 7 November 1987.

REFERENCES

Cloward, Richard A. and Lloyd B. Ohlin, *Delinquency and Opportunity: A Theory of Delinquent Gangs.* New York: Free Press, 1960.

Cohen, Albert K. *Delinquent Boys: The Culture of the Gang.* Glencoe, IL: Free Press, 1955.

Coleman, Richard P. and Lee Rainwater. *Social Standing in America: New Dimensions of Class.* New York: Basic Books, 1978.

Fagan, Jeffery. "The Social Organization of Drug Use and Drug Dealing among Urban Gangs." *Criminology* 27, no. 4 (November 1989): 633–70.

Horowitz, Ruth. *Honor and the American Dream: Culture and Identity in a Chicano Community.* New Brunswick: Rutgers University Press, 1983.

Ianni, Francis, A. J. *Black Mafia: Ethnic Succession in Organized Crime*. New York: Simon & Schuster, 1974.

Josephson, Matthew. *The Robber Barons: The Great American Capitalists, 1861–1901*. New York: Harcourt, Brace & World, 1962.

Kornhauser, Ruth Rosner. *Social Sources of Delinquency: An Appraisal of Analytic Models*. Chicago: University of Chicago Press, 1978.

Lupsha, Peter, and K. Schlegel. "The Political Economy of Drug Trafficking: The Herrera Organization (Mexico and the United States)." Paper presented at a meeting of the Latin American Studies Association, Philadelphia, 1979.

McClelland, David C. *The Achieving Society*. New York: Free Press, 1961.

Marx, Karl. *The Economic and Philosophical Manuscripts of 1844*. 4th rev. ed. Moscow: Progress Publishers, 1974.

Matza, David. *Delinquency and Drift*. New Brunswick, N.J.: Transaction Books, 1990.

Moore, Joan W. *Homeboys: Gangs, Drugs, and Prisons in the Barrios of Los Angeles*. Philadelphia: Temple University Press, 1978.

———. "Isolation and Stigmatization in the Development of an Underclass: The Case of Chicano Gangs in East Los Angeles." *Social Problems* 33, no. 1 (October 1985): 1–12.

Rainwater, Lee. *Behind Ghetto Walls: Black Family Life in a Federal Slum*. Chicago: Aldine Press, 1970.

———. *What Money Buys: Inequality and the Social Meanings of Income*. New York: Basic Books, 1974.

Thrasher, Frederic. *The Gang: A Study of 1303 Gangs in Chicago*. Chicago: University of Chicago Press, 1928.

Vigil, James Diego. *Barrio Gangs: Street Life and Identity in Southern California*. Austin: University of Texas Press, 1988.

Weber, Max. *Economy and Society: An Outline of Interpretive Sociology*. Edited by Guenther Roth and Claus Wittich. Berkeley: University of California Press, 1978.

17

WOMEN OF THE KLAN
Organizing 100 Percent American Women

KATHLEEN M. BLEE

This reading by Kathleen Blee is an example of sociological research done with a secondary group. *Secondary groups* tend to be larger, less intimate, and more formal than primary groups. Moreover, most secondary groups are utilitarian in that they serve some function. Blee looks at the history of the Women's Ku Klux Klan (WKKK) and the group characteristics that distin-

From *Women of the Klan: Racism and Gender in the 1920s*, pp. 27–41. Copyright © 1991 by The Regents of the University of California. Reprinted with the permission of the University of California Press.

guish this organization from the all-male KKK. Blee finds that the WKKK had a particular social structure that enabled it to obtain a large membership in a short period of time. This excerpt is taken from Blee's 1991 book *Women of the Klan: Racism and Gender in the 1920s.*

J udge R. M. Mann of the second division circuit court in Little Rock, Arkansas, officially chartered the Women of the Ku Klux Klan on June 10, 1923. Its national headquarters were set up in a three-room office in the Ancient Order of United Workmen hall in Little Rock, Arkansas, at some distance from the male Klan's Atlanta headquarters to symbolize the purported independence of the new women's order from its male counterpart.[1]

Membership in the WKKK was open to white Gentile female native-born citizens over 18 years of age who owed no allegiance to any foreign government or sect, that is, who were not Catholic, Socialist, Communist, or so forth. Applicants were required to have been resident in a Klan jurisdiction for at least six months and to be endorsed by at least two Klanswomen or a WKKK kleagle or Imperial Commander. Klanswomen swore to investigate "carefully and personally" the qualifications and background of every candidate they proposed for office. Dues of $10 included one robe and helmet but did not apply to wives of men who were members of the original Klan or a similar organization during Reconstruction. The national offices of the WKKK were supported (in lavish style) by a portion of all dues; an Imperial Tax (a per capita assessment); profits from the sale of regalia, uniforms, stationery, jewelry, and costumes; and by interest and profits from investments.[2]

. . . The WKKK declared itself an organization "by women, for women, and of women [that] no man is exploiting for his individual gain." The structure of the new women's Klan, worked out in a meeting of WKKK leaders in Asheville, North Carolina, would focus on specific functions and each would have a corresponding task department. The major areas of work for the WKKK's initial efforts were Americanism, education, public amusements, legislation, child welfare and delinquency, citizenship, civics, law enforcement, disarmament, peace, and politics.[3]

. . .

The charter membership of the new WKKK numbered 125,000 women. Most lived in the Midwest, Northwest, and Ozarks region, strongholds of the KKK. Not satisfied with a membership drawn from among the wives, sisters, sweethearts, and mothers of Klansmen, [WKKK leaders] immediately embarked on a recruiting trip throughout the West and Northwest, increasing the WKKK's overall membership and giving the new organization visibility in other regions. [Leaders] also hired female field agents and kleagles who worked with KKK kleagles to bring the message of the women's Klan to all areas of the country. WKKK kleagles, initially often the wives and sisters of KKK officers, worked on a commission basis, retaining a percentage of the initiation dues collected from each new Klanswoman. Organizers used techniques proven effective in the men's Klan: they recruited through personal, family, and work contacts and held highly publicized open meetings to reach politically inactive women and women not from Klan families. In addition, WKKK kleagles worked to recruit women through existing organizations. Female nativist and patriotic societies, in particular, were courted by WKKK organizers who sought to persuade them to merge into the new national women's Klan organization.[4]

Organizers for the women's Klan were effective. Within four months, the WKKK claimed that its membership had doubled to 250,000. By November 1923, 36 states had chapters of the Women of the Ku Klux Klan. Throughout 1924 the WKKK continued to grow, accepting girls over 16 years old and chartering 50 locals a week in 1924. The following year an influential anti-Klan commentator declared that at least three million women had been initiated into the women's Klan. His estimate was no doubt inflated, perhaps by projecting from the recruitment successes of the strong Ohio and Indiana WKKK realms; indeed, modern scholars judge the entire 1920s Klan to have enrolled no more than three to five million members. It is clear, however, that the WKKK attracted a great many women within a short time.[5]

It is impossible to determine the exact number or location of WKKK chapters across the country in the absence of organizational records, but we can estimate the expansion of the women's Klan by examining the pages of Klan periodicals. During the mid-1920s the *Fellowship Forum* published news about WKKK chapters, women's rights organizations, and women's clubs—mingled with recipes and fashion tips. The September 1925 issue carried news from local WKKK chapters in 11 states: New York, Connecticut, Pennsylvania, Michigan, Ohio, Virginia, West Virginia, Kansas, Oklahoma, Texas, and Colorado. Most chapters were located in small towns; the exceptions were those of Oklahoma City and Norfolk. The following September, in 1926, the *Fellowship Forum* included news from WKKK chapters in 16 states: New York, Pennsylvania, Maryland, Virginia, Georgia, Florida, Illinois, Indiana, Ohio, Iowa, Minnesota, Wisconsin, Michigan, Nebraska, California, Washington, and in the District of Columbia as well. Again, most chapters were located outside major metropolitan areas although most members of the WKKK, as of the male Ku Klux Klan, probably resided in large or middle-sized cities. Other issues of the *Fellowship Forum* show a similar geographical dispersion of the women's Klan. Many chapters clustered in Pennsylvania, Ohio, Indiana, Michigan, and New York—states where the KKK was also strong—but chapters existed in the West, on the Atlantic Coast, and along the North-South border.[6]

· · ·

In chartering its new women's organization, the Klan emphasized the role of women as helpmates to Klansmen. Women's cooperation and assistance were needed, Klansmen insisted, to ensure that the political agenda of the men's Klan could be implemented. The KKK press talked often of the WKKK as its "women's auxiliary" and argued that the men's Klan had created the WKKK with the same ideals and principles as its father organization.[7]

Klansmen were unsure, however, about what Klan membership would mean for women. Women might be convenient symbols for mobilizing men into the Klan, but women's actual political participation was another matter. An early advertisement written by the KKK to solicit members for an organization of Klanswomen illustrates the men's ambivalence. Although it was a recruitment pitch for the WKKK, the advertisement also pointed to a fearful potential in political involvement to masculinize women. Many worry, the ad suggested, that "giving [women] the ballot would foster masculine boldness and restless independence, which might detract from the modesty and virtue of womanhood." To this dilemma, the KKK posed as a solution the creation of a separate organization for Klanswomen. The WKKK would allow women to be politically active without "sacrifice of that womanly dignity and modesty we all admire." The key to the delicate balancing act between a "masculine" and a "feminine" political involvement, according to the KKK, was acquiescence of Klanswomen in the political agenda of Klansmen. By adopting as a whole the Klan's agenda of support for white Protestantism, the English language, public schools, the Bible, and immigration restrictions, women could exercise their newly granted enfranchisement without relying on "masculine" traits of political judgment and strategizing.[8]

A related tactic of recruitment for the women's organization stressed women's political *potential*. Although ostensibly supporting women's involvement in politics, this approach emphasized women's ignorance and limited abilities in the political arena. Excluded from the world of political debate, white Protestant women had developed only a "moral influence" in politics. Their special roles in the family and home gave women good political instincts, the Klan argued, but not mature political judgment. Women now needed to be taught (by men) those principles and attitudes that the world of politics required: clear thinking, intelligence, and collective and individual responsibility for maintaining the principles of Anglo-Saxon Protestantism. Women might have gained the ballot by law, but the ability to use it intelligently required further education—an education the Klan was prepared to provide through its women's organization.

. . .

The WKKK advertised its ability to champion the goals of white womanhood as a standard recruiting tool for new members. Its Washington chapter, for example, argued that white Protestant native-born women had common political interests and would be more effective in pursuing those interests if they were politically organized. Their recruitment advertisement posed a number of questions for women to consider:

> *Are you interested in the welfare of our Nation?*
> *As an enfranchised woman are you interested in Better Government?*
> *Do you not wish for the protection of Pure Womanhood?*
> *Shall we uphold the sanctity of the American Home?*
> *Should we not interest ourselves in Better Education for our children?*
> *Do we not want American teachers in our American schools?*

"Patriotic women," those who answered these questions in the affirmative, were needed in the women's Klan. Protestant white women, the WKKK insisted, shared a concern for their children's education and the welfare of the country. It is the "duty of the American Mother" to stamp out vice and immorality in the nation. Joining the Klan was an effective avenue for the political work that white Protestant women needed to do.[9]

The Women's Klan

To understand the nature of the new women's Klan, we need to examine the beliefs, organizations, rituals, and activities of the WKKK in comparison with those of the men's order. But we must use caution in our comparison. When Klanswomen swore to uphold the "sanctity of the home and chastity of womanhood" they echoed the words, but not necessarily the sentiments, of their male Klan counterparts. Although a simple listing of WKKK and KKK principles and rituals would suggest that there was little difference between the two organizations, we must understand how these were interpreted and justified by each organization.

Beliefs

On one level, many principles of the new women's Klan appear identical to the racist and xenophobic politics of the first and second men's Klans. The WKKK supported militant patriotism, national quotas for immigration, racial segregation, and antimiscegenation laws. Klanswomen cited the need to safeguard the "eternal supremacy" of the white race against a "rising tide of color" and decried Catholic and Jewish influence in politics, the schools, the media, and the business world. [Lulu] Markwell [of Arkansas, the first Imperial Commander of the WKKK,] . . . saw the mission of the women's Klan as "fighting for the same principles as the Knights of the Ku Klux Klan," although she reserved for the WKKK a special interest in "work peculiar to women's organization, such as social welfare work [and] the prevention of juvenile delinquency."[10]

Like the men's Klan, the WKKK often used politically palatable symbols to present its agenda of nativism and racial hatred to the public. It called for separation of church from state when crusading against Roman Catholic political influence, for free public schools when seeking to destroy parochial schools, and for the purity of race when seeking racial segregation and restricted immigration. In private, the racial bigotry of the WKKK was fully as vicious as that of the KKK, as in Klanswomen's condemnation of "mulatto leaders forced to remain members of the negro group [who] aspire to white association because of their white blood [thus] boldly preaching racial equality."[11]

But if many of the WKKK's basic principles followed existing doctrines of the men's Klan, women and men did not always have a common perception of the problems that required Klan action. Klansmen of the 1920s denounced interracial marriage for its destructive genetic outcomes; their Klan forefathers fought interracial sexuality to maintain white men's sexual access to white and black women. Klanswomen, however, saw a different danger in miscegenation: the destruction of white marriages by untrustworthy white men who "betray their own kind."

In many cases, women and men in the Klan took different messages from common symbols. Klansmen praised womanhood to underscore the correctness of male supremacy; Klanswomen used the symbol to point out the inequities that women faced in society and politics. Klansmen sought political inspiration in the "great achievements" of white American Protestantism, but Klanswomen read history differently. Rather than mimicking the men's empty gestures of praise for "true American women" in the past, the WKKK complained that women had been excluded from public politics throughout most of this glorious history, even though "our mothers have ever been Klanswomen at heart, sharing with our fathers the progress and development of our country." Klanswomen embraced the KKK's racist, anti-Catholic, and anti-Semitic agenda and symbols of American womanhood but they used these to argue as well for equality for white Protestant women.[12]

Organization

For the most part the WKKK adopted the militaristic hierarchical style of the KKK. An Excellent Commander served as president, with a four-year term of office and responsibility for issuing, suspending, and revoking the charters of locals and realms (state organizations). Next in the chain of command was the klaliff (vice-president), who acted as presiding officer of the Imperial Klonvokation; the klokard (lecturer), responsible for disseminating Klankraft; and the kludd (chaplain), who presided over Klan ritual. Other major officers included the kligrapp (secretary), bonded for $25,000 to handle minor Klan funds; the Klabee (treasurer), bonded for $50,000 to handle major Klan funds; and the officers of Klan ritual and ceremony, including the kladd (conductor), klagoro (inner guard), klexter (outer guard), night hawk (in charge of candidates), klokan (investigator and auditor), and kourier (messenger).

Each realm or group of realms of the WKKK was organized by a Major Kleagle with subjurisdictions organized by minor kleagles and supervised by a series of Realm Commanders and Imperial Commanders. Upon retirement from office, Excellent Commanders became Klan Regents, Realm Commanders became Grand Regents, and Imperial Commanders became Imperial Regents. In keeping with the military arrangement of the WKKK, nearly all offices were subdivided into further levels of authority. The rank of kourier, for example, was subdivided into that of kourier private, corporal, sergeant, lieutenant, captain, major, and colonel. Ranks carried more than symbolic authority, as failure to obey the command of an officer was defined as insubordination and could bring harsh punishment.[13]

The similarity between the organization of the male and female Klans is significant. Consistently, WKKK denied that it was like the auxiliary of a fraternal association, "merely a social order for social purposes." Instead, Klanswomen embraced the mixture of individualism and deference to authority that characterized the male Klan. Like Klansmen, Klanswomen had at least ostensible opportunities to rise within the organization through individual effort and talent; both organizations used a strict command hierarchy. In this, the WKKK claimed to stand apart from the outside world that discouraged women from individual efforts and achievements. By valuing both obedience and individual effort, the WKKK would "inculcate patriotism, upbuild character, and develop true clannishness among women."[14]

Other features of the WKKK show the contrasting aspects of obedience and commonality that characterized the KKK. Like their male counterparts, Klanswomen typically wore white robes with masks and helmets, although some chapters used red robes. Masks were clearly intended to disguise the identity of Klanswomen in public, but the WKKK insisted that masks had only a symbolic purpose. Through masking Klanswomen hid their individuality as well as identity, exemplifying the Klan motto "not for self, but for others." Similar claims were made about Klan robes. Although in fact officers' robes had more colors and accoutrements, Klanswomen asserted that their robes symbolized the equality of all women within Klankraft. Robes set Klanswomen apart from the invidious world of social class distinctions in fashion, leveling the divisions of wealth so pervasive in alien society. "As we look upon a body of women robed in white we realize that we are on a common level of sisterhood and fraternal union."[15]

The detailed laws and regulations of the WKKK ensured obedience to authority. Women, no less than men, were expected to conduct themselves according to klannish principles. The WKKK treated as major offenses those of treason to the Klan, violating the oath of allegiance, disrespect of virtuous womanhood, violation of the U.S. Constitution, the "pollution" of Caucasian blood through miscegenation, and other acts unworthy of a Klanswoman.

Minor offenses included profane language or vulgarity during a klonklave, acts against the best interest of the Klan or a Klanswoman, and refusal or failure to obey the Excellent Commander. The Excellent Commander assessed penalties for minor offenses; a tribunal handled major offenses. Violators faced reprimand, suspension, banishment forever, or complete ostracism.

Ritual

At least as central as laws and hierarchy to both women's and men's Klans was an elaborate and intricate web of ceremonials, rites, and protocols designed to increase members' commitment to the order and to sharpen the distinctions between insiders and outsiders ("aliens"). Like the men's Klan, the WKKK used threatening, frightening, and challenging rituals to ensure loyalty and instill fear in its members. Both the WKKK and the KKK referred to themselves as "invisible empires," conveying the Klan's aspirations to universal jurisdiction. Secret klannish words gave members an immediate way to recognize sister and brother Klan members. In Klan ceremonies, days of the week were not Sunday, Monday, and so forth as in the alien world but were desperate, dreadful, desolate, doleful, dismal, deadly, and dark. Weeks of the month became weird, wonderful, wailing, weeping, and woeful. January through December were labeled appalling, frightful, sorrowful, mournful, horrible, terrible, alarming, furious, fearful, hideous, gloomy, and bloody.

The Klan changed historical time as well, setting it to the ascendancy of white Gentile Americans. The reign of Incarnation included all time up to the American Revolution. A first reign of Reincarnation lasted from the beginning of the revolutionary war until the organization of the first Ku Klux Klan in 1866. A second reign of Reincarnation extended from 1866 to 1872, the collapse of the first KKK. The third reign of Reincarnation began in 1915, the reorganization of the KKK, and extended from the present into the future.[16]

The naturalization klonklave was typical of women's Klan rituals. An altar was placed in the center of a room or in an open-air gathering place surrounded by stations with water, a Bible, a flag, and a sword. WKKK officers entered the klonklave, kissed the flag, proceeded to the altar, and saluted the Excellent Commander or other presiding officer, raising their masks to reveal their identities to this official. When all officers were assembled, the kladd certified that everyone present was a valid member of the WKKK. The entrance to the building or park was secured by the klexter and klagoro and then all masks were removed.

Once assembled, officers were questioned about the seven sacred symbols of Klankraft in a ritualized catechism oddly patterned after the catechism ritual of the Roman Catholic church. Each officer repeated a litany of symbols: the Bible (God), fiery cross (sacrifice and service), flag (U.S.

Constitution), sword (law enforcement and national defense), water (purity of life and unity of purpose), mask (secrecy, unselfishness, and banishment of individuality), and robe (purity and equality). Between each restatement of Klan doctrine, the audience and officers sang a Christian hymn.

During the naturalization ceremony, a klokard led the class of candidates through the oath of admission. Candidates swore that they were serious, qualified for admission, believers in klannishness, and willing to practice klannishness toward other Klanswomen and work for the eternal maintenance of white supremacy. Candidates then were greeted by officers and members and congratulated for their "womanly decision to forsake the world of selfishness and fraternal alienation and emigrate to the delectable bounds of the Invisible Empire and become its loyal citizens." At this point, the Excellent Commander conferred the obligation and oath of admission on the assembled candidates and baptized the new members by pouring water and saying:

> With this transparent, life-giving, powerful God-given fluid, more precious and far more significant than all the sacred oils of the ancients, I set you apart from the women of your daily association to the great and honorable task you have voluntarily allotted yourselves as citizens of the Invisible Empire, Women of the Ku Klux Klan. As Klanswomen, may your character be as transparent, your life purpose as powerful, your motive in all things as magnanimous and as pure, and your Klannishness as real and as faithful as the manifold drops herein.

As a quartet of Klanswomen sang and the assembly prayed, the klannish initiates responded with their own ritual. They dipped fingers in water and touched their shoulders, saying "In body," and their foreheads, saying "In mind," then waved their hands in the air, saying "In spirit," and made a circle above their heads saying "In life." The klokard then imparted the secret signs and words of the Klan. The ceremony closed with an opportunity to raise issues from the floor (probably an infrequent occurrence), followed by a restatement of the need for secrecy in the presence of aliens. The night hawk extinguished the fiery cross, the kludd performed a benediction, and the klonklave was declared closed.[17]

Ceremonies for higher levels in the WKKK followed a similar pattern, although more was required of the candidates. Acceptance into the second-degree obligation, the highest rank below officer level, required candidates to make pledges against slandering other Klanswomen or Klansmen, against materialism, and against selfishness and similar temptations. Candidates for advanced degrees also made greater pledges of duty, swearing that "when pleasure interferes with my duty as Klanswoman . . . I will set aside pleasure"; they affirmed their loyalty, vowing not to recommend "faithless, contemptuous, careless, or indifferent" women for advancement in the order.[18]

Activities

It is difficult to compare the political practices of the women's and men's Klans, as both varied considerably across the nation and over time but the national agendas of each organization give some indication of the differences. The political agenda of the men's Klan ranged from infiltration into legislative and judicial politics on the state, municipal, and county level to acts of violence and terroristic intimidation against Jews, Catholics, and blacks. Many Klansmen, though, used the KKK as primarily a male fraternity, a social club of like-minded white Protestants.[19]

The women's Klan similarly showed a range of activities and purposes. On a national level, the women's Klan worked to legitimate the violence and terrorism of the men's order. It published and distributed a detailed guide to the proper display of the American flag and a pocket-sized version of the U.S. Constitution and circulated a card reminding Protestants to attend church faithfully; each item prominently displayed the WKKK logo. The WKKK involved itself in national legislative politics, although without much success. It actively supported the creation of a federal Department of Education to bolster public schools and undermine parochial education and opposed U.S. membership in the World Court. Although it claimed to be interested in safeguarding white Protestant children and the home, the WKKK opposed a 1924 bill outlawing child labor on the grounds that it was "a Communistic, Bolshevistic scheme." That same year Klanswomen were active in blocking an attempt by anti-Klan forces to introduce a plank in the national Democratic party platform condemning the Ku Klux Klan.[20]

At times the women's Klan sought to portray itself as an organization of social work and social welfare. One national WKKK speaker announced that she left social work for the "broader field of Klankraft" because of the Klan's effectiveness in promoting morality and public welfare. Many chapters claimed to collect food and money for the needy, although these donations typically went to Klan families, often to families of Klan members arrested for rioting and vigilante activities. A powerful Florida WKKK chapter operated a free day nursery, charging that Catholic teachers had ruined the local public schools.[21]

Some WKKK chapters ran homes for wayward girls. These homes served two purposes: to protect the virtue of Protestant women who were tempted by a life of vice and to underscore the danger faced by delinquent girls placed in Catholic-controlled reform schools. The Shreveport, Louisiana, WKKK chapter, for example, based its fund-raising for a Protestant girls' home on the story of a woman whose unhappy fate it was to be sent to a Catholic reform home after being convicted of selling whiskey and prostituting her teenaged daughters.[22]

Another activity of many WKKK locals was the crusade against liquor and vice. WKKK chapters worked to "clean up" a motion picture industry in which they claimed Jewish owners spewed a steady diet of immoral sex onto the screen. Other chapters fought against liquor, as evidenced by the case of Myrtle Cook, a Klanswoman and president of the Vinton, Iowa, WCTU, who was assassinated for documenting the names of suspected bootleggers. In death, Cook was eulogized by Klanswomen and WCTU members alike; all business in Vinton was suspended for the two hours of the funeral.[23]

WKKK chapters in many states were active also in campaigns to prohibit prenuptial religious agreements about future children, bar interracial marriage, outlaw the Knights of Columbus (a Catholic fraternal society), remove Catholic encyclopedias from public schools, bar the use of Catholic contractors by public agencies, and exclude urban (i.e., Jewish and Catholic) vacationers in majority-Protestant suburban resorts.[24]

Some WKKK locals, though, functioned largely for the personal and financial success of their members. F. C. Dunn of Lansing, Michigan, made a fortune after introducing her invention, a new antiseptic powder, at a local WKKK meeting.[25]

Klanswomen tended not to be involved in physical violence and rioting, but there were exceptions. In the aftermath of a 1924 Klan riot in Wilkinsburg, Pennsylvania, Mamie H. Bittner, a 39-year-old mother of three children and member of the Homestead, Pennsylvania, WKKK testified that she, along with thousands of other Klanswomen paraded through town, carrying heavy maple riot clubs. Moreover, Bittner claimed that the WKKK was teaching its members to murder and kill in the interest of the Klan.[26]

The activities of the women's Klan were shaped largely by the existing political agenda of the men's Klan. It is not accurate, however, to portray the WKKK as a dependent auxiliary of the men's order. Klanswomen created a distinctive ideology and political agenda that infused the Klan's racist and nativist goals with ideas of equality between white Protestant women and men. The ideology and politics of Klanswomen and Klansmen were not identical, though at many points they were compatible. But women and men of the Klan movement sometimes found themselves in contention as women changed from symbols to actors in the Klan.

The difference between the women's and men's Klan grew from an underlying message in the symbol of white womanhood. By using gender and female sexual virtue as prime political symbols, the Klan shaped its identity through intensely masculinist themes, as an organization of real men. Clearly, this was an effective recruitment strategy for the first Klan. But in the 1920s, as both financial and political expediency and significant changes in women's political roles prompted the Klan to accept female members, an identity based on symbols of masculine exclusivity and supremacy became problematic. In addition, if Klansmen understood that defending white womanhood meant safeguarding white Protestant supremacy and male supremacy, many women heard the message differently. The WKKK embraced ideas of racial and religious privilege but rejected the messages of white female vulnerability. In its place Klanswomen substituted support for women's rights and a challenge to white men's political and economic domination.

NOTES

1. *Arkansas Gazette,* June 10, 1923, 1.
2. WKKK, *Constitution and Laws* (WKKK, 1927).
3. *Fellowship Forum,* Feb. 23, 1924, p. 6; Nov. 17, 1923, p. 6; *Imperial Night-Hawk,* Oct. 31, 1923, p. 1; Aug. 1, 1923, p. 8.
4. *The Truth;* also, *Fiery Cross,* July 13, 1923, p. 1; Sue Wilson Abbey ("The Ku Klux Klan in Arizona, 1921–25," *Journal of Arizona History* 14 [Spring 1973]: 10–30) discusses how Tom Akers was sent to organize the Phoenix, Arizona, chapter of the WKKK in 1923; Loucks, *The Ku Klux Klan in Pennsylvania,* pp. 150–56; *Arkansas Gazette,* June 10, 1925, p. 1.
5. *Arkansas Gazette,* Oct. 7, 1923, p. 12; see also *Imperial Night-Hawk,* Oct. 31, 1923, p. 1; *New York Times,* Nov. 7, 1923, p. 15; Kenneth Jackson, *The Ku Klux Klan;* William M. Likins, *The Ku Klux Klan, Its Rise and Fall; Patriotism Capitalized or Religion Turned into Gold* (privately published, 1925).
6. See Kenneth Jackson, *The Ku Klux Klan; Fellowship Forum,* 1924–1928.
7. *Imperial Night-Hawk,* June 13, 1923, p. 5; Aug. 8, 1923, p. 6.
8. *Fiery Cross,* Mar. 2, 1923, p. 4; *Fellowship Forum,* June 2, 1923, p. 8.
9. *Watcher on the Tower,* Sept. 15, 1923, p. 12.
10. *Imperial Night-Hawk,* June 20, 1923, p. 8.
11. WKKK, *Ideals of the Women of the Ku Klux Klan* (WKKK, 1923), pp. 2–3, 4–5; WKKK, *Women of America!,* pp. 6–7, 9–10, 13–14 (WKKK, ca. 1923); WKKK, *Kreed* (WKKK, ca. 1924).
12. WKKK, *Women of America!;* WKKK, *Constitution and Laws,* pp. 6–7; WKKK, *Kreed;* WKKK, *Ideals,* pp. 2–3, 4–5; *Imperial Night-Hawk,* June 20, 1923, p. 8; May 14, 1924, p. 7; advertisement in *Dawn,* Aug. 11, 1923, p. 2.
13. WKKK, *Constitution and Laws.* From statement by Victoria Rogers, Major Kleagle for the Realm of Illinois, in *Dawn,* Feb. 2, 1924, p. 12.
14. WKKK, *Women of America!*
15. WKKK, *Catalogue of Official Robes and Banners* (WKKK, ca. 1923); WKKK, *Kloran or Ritual of the WKKK* (WKKK, 1923).
16. WKKK, *Constitution and Laws.*
17. WKKK, *Kloran or Ritual of the WKKK.* The *New York Times* (Aug. 19, 1923, p. 2) has detailed coverage of a naturalization ceremony involving 700 members of the women's Klan in Allenwood, New Jersey.
18. WKKK, *Second Degree Obligation of the Women of the Ku Klux Klan* (WKKK, n.d.); see also WKKK, *Installation Ceremonies of the Women of the Ku Klux Klan* (WKKK, n.d.).
19. Hiram Evans, *The Menace* and *The Attitude of the Knights of the Ku Klux Klan toward the Roman Catholic Hierarchy* (KKK, ca. 1923).
20. WKKK, *Flag Book* (WKKK, 1923); Ku Klux Klan record collection (hereafter cited as KKK), Indiana State Library; WKKK, *U.S. Constitution* (WKKK, n.d.); *Fiery Cross,* Oct. 10, 1924, p. 5; *Fellowship Forum,* July 5, 1924, pp. 6–7.
21. *Fellowship Forum,* Sept. 19, 1925, p. 6; July 5, 1924; Mar. 3, 1926, p. 6. The anonymous speaker is identified only as a "Klan female speaker." January 1925 issues of the *Fellowship Forum* have other examples of such self-promotion, as does that of May 1, 1926, p. 7; see also Chalmers, *Hooded Americanism.*

22. *Imperial Night-Hawk,* May 9, 1923, p. 2; see also *New York Times,* July 11, 1926, p. 7.

23. *Arkansas Gazette,* Sept. 8, 1925, p. 1; *Fiery Cross,* Mar. 30, 1923, p. 5; *Fellowship Forum,* Jan. 24, 1925, p. 6; *New York Times,* Sept. 9, 1925, p. 1; Sept. 19, 1925, p. 20; Sept. 11, 1925, p. 5.

24. *New York Times,* June 3, 1923, sect.1, pt. 2, p. 8; *Fellowship Forum,* Jan. 24, 1925, p. 6; *New York Times,* Mar. 21, 1922, p. 6; Dec. 8, 1922, p. 9; *Imperial Night-Hawk,* May 9, 1923, p. 3; *Fiery Cross,* Oct. 10, 1924, p. 5; *Fellowship Forum,* Jan. 17, 1925, p. 6; July 5, 1924, p. 6. For a detailed analysis of the conflict over the Klan during the 1924 election, especially during the Democratic party convention, see Lee Allen, "The McAdoo Campaign for the Presidential Nomination of 1924," *Journal of Southern History* 29 (1963): 211–18; "The Klan and the Democrats," *Literary Digest,* June 14, 1924, pp. 12–13; Rice, *Ku Klux Klan;* Chalmers, *Hooded Americanism,* pp. 282–90.

25. *Fiery Cross,* July 18, 1924, p. 6. In an odd twist—"because of their affiliation with the KKK"—two women were excluded from the will of a third woman with whom they had lived for 16 years (will of Alice Reid, filed in surrogate's court in Brooklyn in 1928 and reported in the *New York Times,* Oct. 10, 1928, p. 16).

26. Testimony of Mamie H. Bittner in U.S. District Court for the Western District of Pennsylvania, *Knights of the Ku Klux Klan, Plaintiff, v. Rev. John F. Strayer et al., Defendants,* 1928 (Equity 1897 in National Archives–Philadelphia Branch; William M. Likins, *The Trail of the Serpent* (n.p., 1928), pp. 64–67.

18

THE SEARCH FOR *COMMUNITAS* IN THE MEN'S MOVEMENT

MICHAEL SCHWALBE

Communities are another social structure often studied by sociologists. This selection by Michael Schwalbe investigates the Mythopoetic Men's Movement and a type of community, called *communitas,* that the men in these groups try to create. Schwalbe spent three years investigating the mythopoetic men's movement, including doing participant observation, interviewing members, and studying the writings of current movement leaders. His work resulted in the book, *Unlocking the Iron Cage: The Men's Movement, Gender Politics and American Culture* (1996), which is excerpted here.

In the late 1980s and early 1990s, the commercial media discovered the mythopoetic men's movement. Newspapers, magazines, and television reported that thousands of middle-aged, middle-class white men were retreating to rustic settings to share their feelings, to cry, hug, drum, dance, tell poems and fairy tales, and enact primitive rituals. The men were supposedly trying to get in touch with the inner "wildman" and other masculine archetypes as urged by movement leader Robert Bly, a famous poet and author of the 1991 bestseller *Iron John*.[1] Mythopoetic activity was covered because it was offbeat, and so, not surprisingly, most stories played up its odd trappings. The serious side of the movement—its implicit critique of men's lives in American society—was not examined.

While most observers thought mythopoetic activity was harmless and silly, others saw it as dangerous. Feminist critics accused Bly and the mythopoetic men of nefarious doings at their all-male retreats: whining about men's relatively minor psychological troubles while ignoring the much greater oppression of other groups, especially women; "modernizing" rather than truly changing masculinity; retreating from tough political realities into boyish play; unfairly blaming mothers and wives for men's troubles; and reproducing sexism by using fairy tales and rituals from patriarchal cultures. Critics thus saw the mythopoetic movement as part of an antifeminist backlash, or as a New Age maneuver in the battle of the sexes.[2]

Much of the criticism of the movement was based on the same superficial stories fed to the public. More responsible critics at least read Bly's book, saw his 1990 PBS interview ("A Gathering of Men") with Bill Moyers, attended a retreat, or read other pieces of mythopoetic literature.[3] Even so, almost none of the criticism was based on firsthand knowledge of what the men involved in mythopoetic activity were thinking, feeling, and doing together. The men themselves either disappeared behind the inflated image of Bly, or critics presumed that there was no need to distinguish them from Bly. But while Bly was indeed the chief public figure of the movement and a main source of its philosophy, mythopoetic activity or, as the men themselves called it, "mythopoetic men's work," was much more than Robert Bly.

In the fall of 1990, before Bly's *Iron John* raised the visibility of the mythopoetic movement, I began a participant-observation study of a group of men, associated with a local men's center, who were engaged in mythopoetic activity. As a sociologist, I wanted to know how the men began doing "men's work" and how it was affecting them. I was especially interested in how it affected the meanings they gave to their identities as men. So from September 1990 to June 1993, I attended 128 meetings of various kinds; observed and participated in all manner of mythopoetic activities; attended events led by the movement's prominent teachers; read the movement's guiding literature; and interviewed 21 of the local men at length. The full account of my study appears elsewhere.[4]

Any sociologist who has studied a social movement from the inside will tell you that there is always more diversity within it than outsiders tend to see. This was true in the case of the mythopoetic men. As I was doing my research, people often asked me for a quick explanation of who the men were, what they were doing, and why—as if all the men were alike and one explanation would fit all. While there were commonalities of experience and outlook among the mythopoetic men, there were also significant differences. The men did not all experience the same troubles, want the same things, or think similarly about gender politics. It's important to recognize this diversity, since in writing about any group of people there is a tendency to make internal diversity disappear.

Two other points may aid understanding of the mythopoetic men. One is that, while they held Robert Bly in high esteem, they did not see him as an infallible guru. Most of the men knew that Bly could be obnoxious, that he tended to exaggerate, and that he liked to be the center of attention. It would be fair to say that the men saw him as wise, entertaining, charismatic, and challenging—but hardly without fault. Many of the men had equally high regard for other teachers in the mythopoetic movement, especially the Jungian psychologist James Hillman and the drummer/storyteller Michael Meade. Even so, the mythopoetic men were wary of leaders and did not want to be dependent on them. They believed that men could and should learn to do men's work on their own.

The second point is that many of the men rejected the label "movement" for what they were doing, since to them this implied central organization, the imposition of a doctrine, and political goals. It's true that mythopoetic activity was not centrally coordinated, overtly oriented to political goals, or restricted to those who swore allegiance to a particular set of beliefs. There was, however, an underlying philosophy (derived in large part from Jungian psychology), a "circuit-riding" group of teachers, a body of inspirational literature, nationally circulated publications, and many similarities of practice among the mythopoetic men's groups that had sprung up around the country. So, to add all this up and call it a movement is a legitimate convenience.

Many of the men also shared certain goals, which they sought to achieve through mythopoetic work. As individuals they sought the therapeutic goals of self-acceptance, greater self-confidence, and better knowledge of themselves as emotional beings. As a group they sought to revalue "man" as a moral identity; that is, they collectively sought to define "man" as an identity that implied positive moral qualities. Identity work of this kind, which was partly a response to feminist criticism of men's behavior, was accomplished through talk at gatherings and through the movement's literature. Much of what the men sought to accomplish thus had to do with their feelings about themselves as men.

It's important to see, however, that mythopoetic men's work was not just about sharing feelings, as if the men knew what they were feeling and then met to talk about it. Things were not so simple. Often the work itself aroused feelings that surprised the men. And these feelings were not always pleasant. But even unpleasant feelings were resources for fashioning a special kind of collective experience. It was this experience, which the anthropologist Victor Turner calls *communitas,* that the men sought to create at their gatherings. This was a rare and seductive experience for men in a highly bureaucratized society such as ours.

Community and *Communitas*

Most of the mythopoetic men were between the ages of 35 and 60. Nearly all were white, self-identified as heterosexual, and college educated. Most had good jobs, owned homes, and helped maintain families. They were, by and large, successful in conventional, middle-class terms. Yet the men said that living out this conventional script had left them, at midlife, feeling empty and dissatisfied. They found that the external trappings of success were not spiritually fulfilling. What's more, many of the men felt isolated, cut off from other men, except for competitive contexts such as the workplace. Hence, many described mythopoetic activity as part of an effort to create a community where they could interact with other men in a supportive, noncompetitive way.

But it was not exactly community that these men created through mythopoetic work. Although they did sometimes establish serious friendships and networks of support, the men did not enter into relations of material dependence upon each other, live in close proximity to each other, work together, or interact on a daily basis. Usually, the men who met at gatherings and in support groups went home to their separate lives. Thus, strictly speaking, it was not a true community they created. What the mythopoetic men sought and tried to create at their gatherings was both more and less than community. It was *communitas.*

Victor Turner, an anthropologist who studied tribal rituals, describes *communitas* as both a shared feeling-state and a way of relating. To create *communitas,* people must relate to each other outside the constraints of formally defined roles and statuses. As Turner describes it:

> Essentially, *communitas* is a relationship between concrete, historical, idiosyncratic individuals. These individuals are not segmentalized into roles and statuses but confront one another rather in the manner of Martin Buber's "I and Thou." Along with this direct, immediate, and total confirmation of human identities, there tends to go a model of society as a homogeneous, unstructured *communitas,* whose boundaries are ideally coterminous with those of the human species.[5]

Communitas, as Turner says, can happen when the force of roles and statuses is suspended; that is, when individuals in a group feel themselves to be equals and there are no other significant differences to impede feelings of communality. Although the mythopoetic men did not use the term *communitas,* they sought to relate to each other in the way that Turner describes as characteristic of *communitas*. At gatherings they tried to engage each other in a way that was unmediated by the roles they played in their everyday work lives. The men tried to practice this kind of relating by talking about the feelings they had, which they believed arose out of their common experiences as men.

Turner distinguishes three types of *communitas:* normative, ideological, and spontaneous or existential. Of these, it is spontaneous or existential *communitas* that the mythopoetic men sought to create. Turner says that spontaneous *communitas* is "richly charged with affects, mainly pleasurable ones," that it "has something 'magical' about it," and that in it there is "the feeling of endless power."[6] He compares hippies and tribesmen in a passage that could also apply to the mythopoetic men:

> The kind of *communitas* desired by tribesmen in their rites and by hippies in their "happenings" is not the pleasurable and effortless comradeship that can arise between friends, coworkers, or professional colleagues any day. What they seek is a transformative experience that goes to the root of each person's being and finds in that root something profoundly communal and shared.[7]

There are several ways in which Turner's description of spontaneous *communitas* fits mythopoetic activity. First, the men sought personal growth through their experiences of "connection," as they called it, at mythopoetic gatherings. A connection was a feeling of emotional communion with another man or group of men. Such connections were made when a story, poem, dance, ritual, or psychodramatic enactment brought up strong feelings in one or more men, and this in turn induced emotional responses in others. In these moments the men learned about their own complexity as emotional beings. The changes they sought were greater awareness of their feelings, more clarity about them, and better ability to use those feelings constructively.

The mythopoetic men also presumed it was possible to establish deep emotional connections with each other because they were all, at root, men. This presumption grew out of the Jungian psychology that informed mythopoetic activity. The idea was that all men possessed the same set of masculine archetypes that predisposed them to think, feel, and act in similar ways.[8] In Jungian terms, these masculine archetypes are parts of the collective unconscious, to which we are all linked by our common humanity. Thus all men, simply by virtue of being male, were presumed to possess similar masculine energies and masculine ways of feeling. Mythopoetic activities were aimed at bringing out or tapping into these energies and feelings so that men could connect based on them and thereby mutually reinvigorate themselves.

Turner's references to pleasurable affects and mysterious feelings of power are echoed in how the mythopoetic men described their experiences. Mythopoetic activity was enjoyable, the men said, because "It's just being with men in a way that's very deep and powerful"; "There's a tremendous energy that grows out of men getting together and connecting emotionally"; and "It just feels great to be there connecting with other men in a noncompetitive way." And, indeed, the feelings were often intense. As one man said during a talking circle at the end of a weekend retreat, "I feel there's so much love in this room right now it hurts." Men also said that going back to their ordinary lives after a gathering meant "coming down from an emotional high." I, too, experienced this transition from the warm, open, supportive, emotionally charged atmosphere of a gathering to the relatively chilly atmosphere of a large research university.

The success of a gathering was measured by the intensity of the emotion it evoked and the connections thereby established. A less successful gathering was one where the emotional intensity was low and the men did not make strong connections. At a small two-day gathering, one man commented somewhat sadly, "We've had some good sharing, but only once did I feel much happening to me. That was when B. was talking. I felt tears welling up. So there's a deeper level we could get to." This was said at the beginning of the final talking circle, in hopes of prompting a more emotional discussion before the gathering was over. In addition to showing the desire for *communitas*, this statement also shows that it took effort to achieve. Spontaneous *communitas* did not happen spontaneously.

Creating Spontaneous *Communitas*

Mythopoetic men's work was in large part the conversation work required to create spontaneous *communitas*. I'll explain here how this work was done, through talk and other means. It should be understood that not all gatherings were aimed as intently at creating the same degree of spontaneous *communitas*. Some gatherings were more "heady," in that they were devoted to discussion of a topic, such as fathering or men's health or men's friendships. Often there were moments of *communitas* at these kinds of meetings; but it was at the retreats—those that had an explicit mythopoetic or "inner work" theme—where the greatest efforts were made to produce *communitas*. Talk, ritual, and drumming were the chief means for doing this.

Forms of Talk

At mythopoetic gatherings, men often made personal statements that revealed something shameful, tragic, or emotionally disturbing about their lives. Such statements might be made by each man in turn at the beginning of a retreat, as part of saying why he was there, what he was feeling, and what he hoped to accomplish at the retreat. Before any statements were made, the leader of the retreat or gathering would remind the men of the rules to follow in making statements: speak briefly, speak from the heart (i.e., focus on feelings), and speak to the other men—who were supposed to listen intently, make no judgments, and give no advice. The idea was that the statements should bring the unrehearsed truth up from a man's gut, since this would stir feelings in him and move other men to speak their "belly truth."

A great deal of feeling was stirred up as men talked about troubled relationships with fathers; being sexually abused as children; struggling to overcome addictions; repressed anger over past hurts and betrayals; grief and sadness over irreplaceable losses; efforts to be better fathers to their children. When men choked up, wept, shook with fear, or raged as they spoke it induced strong feelings in other men in the group. The sequence in which personal statements were made amplified this effect. Men would often begin their remarks by saying, "What that [the previous statement] brings up for me is . . . ," or "I really identify with what ——— said, because . . ." The more disclosing, expressive, and moving a man's statement, the more likely it was to evoke from the other men heavy sighs, sympathetic "mmmms," or a loud chorus of "Ho!" (supposedly a Native American way of affirming that a man's statement has been heard and felt). If a statement seemed inauthentic or insufficiently revealing it might evoke little or no reaction. In this way the men reinforced a norm of making risky, revealing, and evocative statements.

Thus, the men were not only sharing feelings but, by virtue of how they talked, knitting those feelings together into a group mood. In this way they were also creating *communitas*. It is important, too, that the settings in which these statements were made were defined as "safe," meaning that, by agreement, the men were not there to compete with or judge each other, but to listen and provide support. Even so, there was an element of risk and a degree of anxiety associated with making personal statements, since the mythopoetic men, like most men in American society, were unused to sharing feelings of hurt and vulnerability with other men. This anxiety aided the achievement of *communitas* because it created a higher-than-usual level of emotional arousal to begin with. It also allowed the men immediately to identify with one another over being anxious. As Turner likewise noted: "Danger is one of the chief ingredients in the production of spontaneous *communitas*." [9]

In making personal statements and in their general conversation at gatherings, the men could not help but refer to people, events, and circumstances outside themselves that evoked the feelings they had. In doing this, the men were careful to add to their statements the disclaimer "for me," as in "For *me*, the Gulf War was very depressing." This disclaimer signified that the man speaking was talking about *his* feelings based on *his* perceptions of things, and he was making no presumptions about how other men should feel. The use of this disclaimer helped the men maintain the fellow-feeling they sought by avoiding arguments about what was true of the external world. The mythopoetic men wanted their feelings validated, not challenged. As long as each man spoke the truth from his heart, no one could say he was wrong.

Talk about fathers was another way the men achieved *communitas*. It worked because almost every man had a father to talk about, and those few who didn't could talk about not having fathers. So every man could participate. Father talk also worked because it brought up feelings of sadness and anger for many of the men, and thus created the necessary emotional charge. Because many of the men experienced their fathers as physically or emotionally absent, or in some way abusive, the men could identify with each other based on these common experiences. Father talk may have helped them to reach insights about their relationships to their fathers. But father talk went on to the extent it did because it was so useful for creating *communitas*.

Poems and fairy tales were also a staple part of mythopoetic activity.[10] Most of the time no commentary or discussion followed the reading or reciting of a poem. The men would just steep in the feelings the poem evoked. An especially stirring poem, like a moving personal statement, would elicit deep sighs, "mmmmm," "yeah," sometimes "Ho!", and, often, calls for the reader to "read it again!" And as with the personal statements, these responses, which were signs of shared feelings, served to turn the individual feelings into a collective mood, and thus helped to create *communitas*. When fairy tales were told, there usually was commentary and discussion in a form that also encouraged *communitas*.

When a story was told, the storyteller would usually instruct the men to look for an image that evoked strong feelings. That image, it was said, would be a man's "doorway into the story"—his way of discovering what the story could tell him about his life as a man. This is consistent with Turner's observation that the "concrete, personal imagist mode of thinking is highly characteristic of those in love with existential [or spontaneous] *communitas*, with the direct relation between man and man, and man and nature. Abstractions appear as hostile to live contact."[11] In the case of the mythopoetics, the emphasis on specific images grew out of Jungian psychology, according to which the psyche was best explored by working with emotionally evocative images.

After a story or part of a story was told, men would talk about the images that struck them and the feelings these images evoked. In a large group of men many different images might be mentioned. Sometimes men reacted strongly to the same image. Talking about the stories in this way created more chances for men to express feelings and to find that they shared feelings and experiences with other men. This was in part how feelings of isolation were overcome and connections were made. Again, the stories may have helped the men to better understand their lives. But it was *how* the stories were talked about that helped the men to experience the good feelings and mysterious power of spontaneous *communitas*.

Ritual

Ritual is different from routine. Routine is the repetition of a behavioral pattern, like brushing one's teeth every night before bed. Ritual involves the symbolic enactment of values, beliefs, or feelings. It is a way of making external, visible, and public things that are normally internal, invisible, and private. By doing this, members of a community create a shared reality, reaffirm their common embrace of certain beliefs and values, and thereby keep the community alive. Ritual can also be a way of acknowledging changes in community members or of actually inducing such changes. The mythopoetic men used ritual for the same purposes: to call up, express, and share their otherwise private feelings, and to make changes in themselves.

Not all gatherings were ritual gatherings, though most included some ritual elements. Those gatherings where an explicit attempt was made to create "ritual space" or "sacred space" usually began with a symbolic act of separation from the ordinary world. For example, sometimes men would dip their hands into a large bowl of water to symbolize a washing off of concerns and distractions linked to the outside world. Other times, at the outset of gatherings the "spirits of the four directions" (and sometimes of the earth and sky, too) would be invoked and asked to bring the men strength and wisdom. Still other times, the men would dance their way into the space where the meeting was to be held, while the men already inside drummed and chanted. The point was to perform some collective act to mark a boundary between outside life and the "ritual space."

The scene of a gathering also had to be properly set. Ritual gatherings were often held at rustic lodges, where various objects—candles, bird feathers, masks, antlers, strangely shaped driftwood, animal skulls—might be set up around the main meeting area. Sage was often burned (a practice called "smudging") to make the air pungent and to cleanse the ritual space for the action that was going to take place. Usually the leader or leaders of the gathering made sure these things were done. Again, the idea was to heighten the sense of separation from ordinary reality, to make the physical space where the gathering would take place seem special, and to draw the men together. This preparation was talked about in terms of "creating a container" that could safely hold the psychic energies about to be unleashed.

The separation from ordinary reality also helped the men let go of the concerns for status and power that influenced their interactions with other men in everyday life. In the ritual space, the men were supposed to be "present for each other" in a direct and immediate way, as equals, as "brothers," and not as inferiors and superiors. Defining the situation as one in which feelings and other psychic matters were the proper focus of attention and activity helped to create and sustain this sense of equality. Thus, the men seldom talked about their jobs, except to describe job-related troubles (and sometimes triumphs) in general terms. Too much talk about occupations would have introduced status concerns, which in turn would have corroded the sense of equality and brotherhood that fostered feelings of *communitas*.

Two examples can help show more concretely how the mythopoetic men used ritual to create *communitas*. One example is from a six-day gathering of about 120 men in a remote rural setting. At this gathering the men were divided into three clans: Trout, Ravens, and Lions. During the week each clan worked with a dance teacher to develop a dance of its own, a dance that would symbolize the spirit of the men in the clan. At the carnivale on the last night of the gathering, each clan was to share its dance with the rest of the men. One clan would drum while another danced and the third clan "witnessed."

The carnivale was held in a large, dimly lit lodge built of rough-cut logs. Many of the men wore the wildly decorated masks they had made earlier in the week. When their turn came, the 40 men in the Trout clan moved to the center of the room and formed a circle. The men stood for a few moments and then hunched down, extended their arms with their hands together in front of them, and began to dip and sway like fish swimming. Then half the men began moving to their right and half to their left, creating two flowing, interweaving circles. The Trout men also carried small stones, which they clicked together as they moved. About 30 men drummed as the Trout men danced. The rest of the men watched.

After a while the Trout men stopped and stood again, holding hands in a circle inside the larger circle of witnesses. They began a sweet and mournful African chant that they said was used to honor the passing away of loved ones. One by one, each of the Trout men moved to the center of their circle and put down the stones he was carrying. As he did so, he called out the name of a person or people whose passing he wished to honor. Another of the Trout men walked along the row of men standing in the outer ring and said, "We invite you to join us by putting a stone in the center of the circle to honor your dead." The drumming and chanting continued all the while.

At first a few, then more and more of the Raven and Lion men stepped outside to get stones. Each man as he returned went to the center of the circle, called the name of the dead he was honoring, put down a stone, and then stepped back. There was sadness in the men's voices as they spoke. This lent gravity to their acts and drew everyone into the ritual. By now all the men had picked up the chant and joined hands in one large circle. The sound filled the lodge. After about 20 minutes the chanting reached a lull—and then one man began to sing "Amazing Grace." Soon all the men joined in and again their voices rose in chorus and filled the lodge. When we finished singing we stood silent, looking at all the stones between us.

This example shows how a great deal of work went into creating spontaneous *communitas*. The dance was carefully choreographed and the stage was elaborately set (one could argue that the five days leading up to the carnivale were part of the stage setting). But later I talked to Trout men who said that they had planned the dance only up to the point of asking the other men to honor their dead. They were surprised by what happened after that, by how quickly and powerfully the other men were drawn in. No one had expected the surge of emotion and fellow-feeling that the ritual induced, especially when the men began to sing "Amazing Grace." Several men I talked to later cited this ritual as one of the most moving experiences they had had at a mythopoetic gathering.

Another example comes from a sweat-lodge ritual modeled on a traditional Native American practice.[12] In this case the lodge was tiny, consisting of a framework of saplings held together with twine upon which were draped several layers of old blankets and tarps. Before the frame was built, a fire pit was dug in the center of the spot on which the lodge stood. Although a lodge could be made bigger, here it was about ten feet in diameter and four feet high—big enough for a dozen men to squeeze in. From the outside it looked like a miniature domed stadium.

It was a drizzly 45-degree morning on the second day of a teacher-led weekend retreat. I was in the second group of 12 men who would go into the lodge together. This was the first "sweat" for all of us. The men in this group were almost giddy as we walked from the cabins to the shore of a small lake where the sweat lodge had been built. When we got there the men from the previous group had just finished.

The scene stopped us abruptly. Next to the lodge a large rock-rimmed fire was burning. A fierce, black-haired man with a beard stood by the fire, a five-foot staff in his hand. Some of the men who had just finished their sweat were standing waist-deep in the lake. Others were on shore hugging, their naked bodies still steaming in the cool air. Our moment of stunned silence ended when the leader of the retreat said to us, matter of factly, "Get undressed, stay quiet, keep your humility." We undressed and stashed our clothes under the nearby pine trees, out of the rain.

Before we entered the lodge, the teacher urged us to reflect on the specialness of the occasion and to approach it with seriousness. Upon entering the lodge through a small entry flap each man was to say, "all my relations," to remind himself of his connections to the earth, to his ancestors, and to the other men. Once we were inside, the teacher called for the fire tender to bring us fresh, red-hot rocks. As each rock was placed by shovel into the fire pit, we said in unison, "welcome Grandfather," again as symbolic acknowledgment of our connection to the earth. The teacher then burned sage on the rocks to scent the air. When he poured water on the rocks, the lodge became a sauna. The space was tightly packed, lit only by the glow of the rocks, and very hot. We were to do three sessions of ten to fifteen minutes each. Because of the intensity of the heat, a few men could not do all three sessions.

During one of the sessions, the teacher urged us to call upon the spirits of our ancestors from whom we wanted blessings. In the cacophony of voices it was hard to make out what was being said. Some men were calling the names of people not present. A few were doing what sounded like a Native American Indian chant learned from the movies. The man next to me was gobbling like a turkey. At first this all struck me as ridiculous. I looked around the lodge for signs of similar bemusement in other men's faces. Surely they couldn't be taking this seriously. But those whose faces I could see appeared absorbed in the experience. Some men seemed oddly distant, as if they were engaged in a conversation going on elsewhere.

Although I was still put off by the bogus chanting and baffled by the gobbling, I, too, began to feel drawn in. I found myself wanting to suspend disbelief and find some meaning in the ritual, no matter how culturally foreign it was. In large part this was because the teacher and the other men seemed to be taking it seriously. I certainly didn't want to ruin the experience for them by showing any sign of cynicism. These were men who had taken my feelings seriously during the retreat. I felt I owed them the same consideration in the sweat lodge.

In both examples, a carefully crafted set of appearances made *communitas* likely to happen. The physical props, the words and actions of the ritual leaders, and the sincere words and actions of some men evoked real feelings in others and drew them in.[13] Because it seemed that there were genuine emotions at stake, it would have taken a hard heart to show any sign of cynicism during the Trout dance or the sweat lodge. To do so would have risked hurting other men's feelings and dimming the glow of *communitas*. It would also have cut the cynic himself off from the good feelings and mysterious power being generated by these occasions. Whether or not everyone really "believed" in what was happening didn't matter. Appearances made it seem so, and to achieve the *communitas* they desired, all the men needed to do was to act on these appearances.

Another dynamic was at work in the case of the sweat lodge. On the face of it, the idea of late twentieth-century white men enacting a Native American sweat lodge ritual was absurd. And for most of these men, the idea of squatting naked, haunch to haunch, with other men would have been—within an everyday frame of reference—embarrassing and threatening to their identities as heterosexuals. Thus, to avoid feeling ridiculous, threatened, or embarrassed, the men had to stay focused on the form of the ritual and show no sign of doubting its content or propriety. Because there was such a gap between their everyday frame of reference and the ritual, the men had to exaggerate their absorption in the ritual reality just to keep a grip on it. In so doing the men truly did create a common focus and, again, the appearance that a serious collective spiritual activity was going on.

The sweat lodge example also illustrated how the creation of *communitas* was aided by literally stripping men of signs of their differences. In the sweat lodge, men were only men—as symbolized by their nakedness. As such they were also equals. When a small group of us spoke afterwards about the experience, one man said, "The closeness and physicality, and especially being naked, are what make it work. Everyone is just a man in there. You can't wear any merit badges."

Drumming

Next to Bly, the most widely recognized icon of the mythopoetic movement was the drum. Drumming was indeed an important part of mythopoetic activity. Some mythopoetic groups held gatherings just to drum, although the group I studied was more likely to mix drumming with other activities. Not all of the men drummed. A few didn't care for it; others preferred to use rattles or tambourines during drumming sessions. The most enthusiastic men had congas, African-styled djembes, or hand-held shaman's drums, though all manner of large and small folk drums appeared at gatherings. On one occasion a man used a five-gallon pail turned upside down.

Why did the mythopoetic men drum? Some of the men in the local group said that they began drumming after a visit by Michael Meade, a prominent teacher in the mythopoetic movement, who was skilled at using drumming to accompany his telling of folk tales. This is what inspired one man I interviewed:

> *Bly came and told his Iron John story and that was my first introduction to using stories as a way of illuminating dilemmas or emotional situations in your life. Michael Meade came the following year in the spring and introduced some drumming at that weekend. I just loved the energy of that right away. It just really opened me up. After drumming I felt wonderful. I liked the feeling of it and felt a connection with the mythopoetic [movement] ever since then, more to the drumming than to anything else.*

But on only a few occasions did any of the local men use drumming as accompaniment to story telling. Most of the drumming was done in groups, which varied in size from six to forty. And while the men who were better drummers might lead the group into a complex rhythm, often something samba-like, the drumming was usually free-form, leaderless, and simple.

The appeal of this activity had little to do with acquiring virtuosity at drumming. Rather, much of the appeal stemmed from the fact that the men could be bad drummers and still participate. It was, most importantly, another means to achieve *communitas*. Victor Turner notes that simple musical instruments are often used this way: "It is . . . fascinating to consider how expressions of *communitas* are culturally linked with simple wind instruments (flutes and harmonicas). Perhaps, in addition to their ready portability, it is their capacity to convey in music the quality of spontaneous human *communitas* that is responsible for this."[14] This was equally true of drums, which were also readily portable and required even less skill to play.

What the mythopoetic men say about their experiences drumming tells much about not only drumming, but about the *communitas* it helped create and about the mythopoetic experience in general. In another interview, a 48-year-old salesman spoke of drumming as both ordinary and special at the same time:

> *You can kind of lose yourself in it. It's like any hobby—fishing or playing ball or whatever. There is something that happens. You go into an altered state almost, hearing that music. At this national meeting in Minnesota a month ago the common thing was the drums. You could hear the beating of that drum. At break people would drum and we would dance. So it's this common bond.*

Put another way, drumming was an activity that gave men who were strangers a way to quickly feel comfortable and familiar with each other. Some of the mythopoetic men believed that men in general had a special facility for connecting with each other via nonverbal means. The way that men were able to quickly bond via drumming was seen as evidence of this.

Although the men were aware that drumming was not an activity limited to men, some clearly felt that it held a special appeal for them. Another man, a 33-year-old technical writer, said in an interview:

> *Drumming does something—connects me with men in ways that I can't understand, in the same way I've observed women who have babies connecting with each other. There's something in it that I don't participate in emotionally. In the same way, the drumming—society with other men—is emotionally important to men in ways that women don't understand. They can't.*

Some of the mythopoetic men's ideas about gender are exemplified by this statement. Many of them believed that women, no matter how empathic they might be, could not know what it was like to be a man, just as men could not know what it was like to be a woman. Hence, men needed the understanding and support that could come only from other men just as women needed the same things from other women.

For other men, drumming was both a communal and, sometimes, a personal, spiritual experience. A 42-year-old therapist told me:

> *There was one point where I was really deeply entranced just drumming and then all of a sudden I had this real powerful experience where I felt like I was on a hill, on some mountainside or some mountaintop, in some land far far away, in some time that was all time. And I was in the middle of my men, who were my brothers, who were all men. It was one of those powerful, mystical experiences where all of a sudden I felt planted in the community of men. And that changed my life, because I felt like I was a man among men in the community of men and we were drumming and the drum was in my bones and it was in my heartbeat and it was good.*

This statement captures in spirit, tone, and rhythm the experience that many of the men found in drumming. Even if they didn't report such flights of imagination, others said that drumming provided a similar sense of communality, of connection—*communitas.*

My own experience corroborates this. I found that when I would pick up a beat and help sustain it without thinking, the sense of being part of the group was strong. It was as if the sound testified to the reality of the group, and the rhythm testified to our connection. By drumming in synch each man attached himself to the group and to the other men in it. The men valued this also because the attachment was created by physical action rather than by talk, and because it seemed to happen at a nonrational level. Drumming thus helped the men to do two other things that mythopoetic philosophy called for: getting out of their heads and into feeling their bodies, and by-passing the rational ego that kept a lid on the archetypal masculine energies the men sought to tap.

Communitas and Politics

My point has been to show that much mythopoetic activity can be understood as a search for *communitas*. This experience was rare in these men's lives and precious on the occasions when it occurred. Sometimes the men talked about the activities at their gatherings as "inviting the sacred to happen." Particular forms of talk, the orchestration of ritual, and drumming were means to this end. Because *communitas* was so valuable to the men, there were also things they *avoided* doing to make *communitas* more likely to happen. One thing they avoided was serious talk about politics.

This is not to say that the men were apolitical. Most of the men I studied were well informed on social issues and supported progressive causes. They were also critical of the rapacious greed of big corporations, the duplicity and brutal militarism of Reagan and Bush, and the general oppressiveness of large bureaucracies. But there were two revealing ironies in the politics of the mythopoetic men. First, while they were critical of the behavior of corporations and government, they avoided saying that these institutions were run by men. Usually it was an unspecified, genderless "they" who were said to be responsible for destroying the environment or for turning all culture into mass marketable schlock. And second, while many of the men saw corporate power and greed as root problems in U.S. society, they were uninterested in collective action to address these problems. This is, as one might expect, because the white, middle-class mythopoetic men did not do so badly in reaping the material benefits of the economic system they occasionally criticized.

In other words, the men were selectively apolitical. They did not want to see that it was other *men* who were responsible for many of the social problems they witnessed and were sometimes affected by. To do so, and to talk about it, would have shattered the illusion of universal brotherhood among men that helped sustain feelings of *communitas*. Talk about power, politics, and inequality in the external world was incompatible with the search for *communitas,* because it would have led to arguments, or at least to intellectual discussions, rather than to warm emotional communion. When discussions at mythopoetic gatherings inadvertently turned political, disagreements surfaced and tensions arose; someone would usually say, "we're getting away from the important work here." Or, as one man said in trying to stop a conversation that was becoming an argument, "I think we're losing the power of the drums."

The mythopoetic men believed that engaging in political or sociological analysis would have led them away from their goals of self-acceptance, self-knowledge, emotional authenticity, and *communitas.* The men wanted to feel better about themselves as men, to learn about the feelings and psychic energies that churned within them, to live fuller and more authentic emotional lives, and to experience the pleasure and mysterious power of *communitas.* They did not want to compete over whose interpretation of social reality was correct. They wanted untroubled brotherhood in which their feelings were validated by other men, and in which their identities as men could be infused with new value.

Here can be seen both the power and limits of mythopoetic men's work. Through this work some men have begun to free themselves from the debilitating repression of emotion that was part of their socialization into traditional masculinity. Feminism provided the intellectual basis and political impetus for this critique of traditional masculinity, although the mythopoetics have difficulty appreciating this. Yet they deserve credit for developing a method that allows some men to explore and express more of the emotions that make them human. Mythopoetic men's work has also helped men to see how these emotions can be the basis for connections to men they might otherwise have feared, mistrusted, or felt compelled to compete with. And, to the extent that men begin to see that they don't have to live out traditional masculinity and can even cooperate to heal the damage it causes, mythopoetic men's work has progressive potential.

One problem is that the progressive potential of mythopoetic men's work is limited, because it leads men to think about gender and gender inequality in psychological or, at best, cultural terms. Mythopoetic men's work may open men to seeing things in themselves and help them make connections with each other, but it also blinds them to seeing important connections between themselves and society. For example, the mythopoetic men do not see that, in a male-supremacist society, there can be no innocent celebration of masculinity. In such a society the celebration of manhood and of masculinity—even if it is supposedly "deep" or "authentic" and thus a more fully human version of masculinity—reaffirms the lesser value of women, whether this is intended or not. The therapeutic focus of mythopoetic men's work—as done by a largely homogeneous group of middle-class white males—also blinds them to matters of class inequality and to the exploitation of working-class people and people of color by the elite white *men* who run the economy.

Yet mythopoetic men's work is a form of resistance to domination. It's not just an entertaining form of group therapy or collective whining over imagined wounds, or retrograde male bonding. These middle-class white men, who are not the ruling elites, are responding to the alienation and isolation that stem from living in a capitalist society that encourages people to be greedy, selfish, and predatory. Their goal of trying to awaken the human sensibilities that have been benumbed by an exploitive economy is subversive. But to get to the root of the problem men will have to do more than take modest risks among themselves to try to heal their psyches. They will have to take big risks in trying to abolish the race, class, and gender hierarchies that damage us all. They will have to learn to create *communitas* in struggles for justice.

NOTES

1. Robert Bly, *Iron John: A Book about Men* (Reading, MA: Addison-Wesley, 1990).
2. See Kay Leigh Hagan, editor, *Women Respond to the Men's Movement* (San Francisco: HarperCollins, 1992); Kenneth Clatterbaugh, *Contemporary Perspectives on Masculinity* (Boulder, CO: Westview, 1990), pp. 85–103; Susan Faludi, *Backlash: The Undeclared War against American Women* (New York: Crown, 1991), pp. 304–12; R. W. Connell, "Drumming Up the Wrong Tree," *Tikkun* vol. 7, no. 1 (1992): 31–36; Sharon Doubiago, "Enemy of the Mother: A Feminist Response to the Men's Movement," *Ms.* March/April (1992): 82–85; Fred Pelka, "Robert Bly and Iron John," *On the Issues* Summer (1991): 17–19, 39; Diane Johnson, "Something for the Boys," *New York Review of Books* January 16 (1992): 13–17.
3. For a sampling of other writings in the mythopoetic genre, see Robert Moore and Douglas Gillette, *King, Warrior, Magician, Lover: Rediscovering the Archetypes of the Mature Masculine* (New York: HarperCollins, 1990); Wayne Liebman, *Tending the Fire: The Ritual Men's Group* (St. Paul, MN: Ally, 1991); Christopher Harding, editor, *Wingspan: Inside the Men's Movement* (New York: St. Martin's, 1992).
4. Michael Schwalbe, *Unlocking the Iron Cage: The Men's Movement, Gender Politics, and American Culture* (New York: Oxford University Press, 1996).
5. Victor Turner, *The Ritual Process* (Ithaca, NY: Cornell, 1969), pp. 94–165.
6. Ibid., pp. 131–32.
7. Ibid., p. 139.
8. For an introduction to the basic concepts of Jungian psychology, see Calvin Hall and Vernon Nordby, *A Primer of Jungian Psychology* (New York: Penguin, 1973); or Frieda Fordham, *An Introduction to Jung's Psychology* (New York: Penguin, 1966). For more detail, see Edward C. Whitmont, *The Symbolic Quest* (Princeton, NJ: Princeton, 1991).
9. Turner, p. 154.
10. Many of the poems frequently read at mythopoetic gatherings are collected in Robert Bly, James Hillman, and Michael Meade (eds.), *The Rag and Bone Shop of the Heart* (New York: HarperCollins, 1992). Many of the fairy tales told at gatherings, including Bly's "Iron John," originally known as "Iron Hans," are taken from the Grimm brothers' collection.
11. Turner, p. 141.
12. A description of the sweat-lodge ritual can be found in Joseph Epes Brown (recorder and editor), *The Sacred Pipe: Black Elk's Account of the Seven Rites of the Oglala Sioux* (Norman, OK: Univ. of Oklahoma, 1953), pp. 31–43. This account was a source of inspiration for some of the mythopoetic men. See also William K. Powers, *Oglala Religion* (Lincoln, NE: Univ. of Nebraska, 1977).
13. Catherine Bell writes about how ritual "catches people up in its own terms" and provides a "resistant surface to casual disagreement." See Bell, *Ritual Theory, Ritual Practice* (New York: Oxford Univ. Press, 1992), pp. 214–15. Other observers have noted how the improvised rituals at mythopoetic gatherings had this power to draw the men in. See Richard Gilbert, "Revisiting the Psychology of Men: Robert Bly and the Mytho-Poetic Movement," *Journal of Humanistic Psychology* 32 (1992): 41–67.
14. Turner, p. 165.

PART V

Deviance, Crime, and Social Control

19

ON BEING SANE IN INSANE PLACES

DAVID L. ROSENHAN

Sociologists have a long-standing interest in the study of social deviance, which is explored in the next four readings. *Deviance* is the recognized violation of social norms. As norms cover a wide range of human behavior, deviant acts are plentiful in any society. Moreover, whether a person is labeled deviant depends on how others perceive, define, and respond to that person's behavior. In this selection, which was originally published in 1973, David L. Rosenhan explores the social deviance of mental illness and the consequences of labeling people "sane" or "insane."

If sanity and insanity exist . . . how shall we know them? The question is neither capricious nor itself insane. However much we may be personally convinced that we can tell the normal from the abnormal, the evidence is simply not compelling. It is commonplace, for example, to read about murder trials wherein eminent psychiatrists for the defense are contradicted by equally eminent psychiatrists for the prosecution on the matter of the defendant's sanity. More generally, there is a great deal of conflicting data on the reliability, utility, and meaning of such terms as *sanity, insanity, mental illness,* and *schizophrenia*.[1] Finally, as early as 1934, Benedict suggested that normality and abnormality are not universal.[2] What is viewed as normal in one culture may be seen as quite aberrant in another. Thus, notions of normality and abnormality may not be quite as accurate as people believe they are.

To raise questions regarding normality and abnormality is in no way to question the fact that some behaviors are deviant or odd. Murder is deviant. So, too, are hallucinations. Nor does raising such questions deny the existence of the personal anguish that is often associated with "mental illness." Anxiety and depression exist. Psychological suffering exists. But normality and abnormality, sanity and insanity, and the diagnoses that flow from them may be less substantive than many believe them to be.

From *Science* 179 (January 19, 1973):250–58. Copyright © 1973 by American Academy for the Advancement of Science. Reprinted with the permission of *Science*.

At its heart, the question of whether the sane can be distinguished from the insane (and whether degrees of insanity can be distinguished from each other) is a simple matter: Do the salient characteristics that lead to diagnoses reside in the patients themselves or in the environments and contexts in which observers find them? From Bleuler, through Kretchmer, through the formulations of the recently revised *Diagnostic and Statistical Manual* of the American Psychiatric Association, the belief has been strong that patients present symptoms, that those symptoms can be categorized, and, implicitly, that the sane are distinguishable from the insane. More recently, however, this belief has been questioned. Based in part on theoretical and anthropological considerations, but also on philosophical, legal, and therapeutic ones, the view has grown that psychological categorization of mental illness is useless at best and downright harmful, misleading, and pejorative at worst. Psychiatric diagnoses, in this view, are in the minds of the observers and are not valid summaries of characteristics displayed by the observed.[3, 4, 5]

Gains can be made in deciding which of these is more nearly accurate by getting normal people (that is, people who do not have, and have never suffered, symptoms of serious psychiatric disorders) admitted to psychiatric hospitals and then determining whether they were discovered to be sane and, if so, how. If the sanity of such pseudopatients were always detected, there would be *prima facie* evidence that a sane individual can be distinguished from the insane context in which he is found. Normality (and presumably abnormality) is distinct enough that it can be recognized wherever it occurs, for it is carried within the person. If, on the other hand, the sanity of the pseudopatients were never discovered, serious difficulties would arise for those who support traditional modes of psychiatric diagnosis. Given that the hospital staff was not incompetent, that the pseudopatient had been behaving as sanely as he had been outside of the hospital, and that it had never been previously suggested that he belonged in a psychiatric hospital, such an unlikely outcome would support the view that psychiatric diagnosis betrays little about the patient but much about the environment in which an observer finds him.

This article describes such an experiment. Eight sane people gained secret admission to twelve different hospitals.[6] Their diagnostic experiences constitute the data of the first part of this article; the remainder is devoted to a description of their experiences in psychiatric institutions. Too few psychiatrists and psychologists, even those who have worked in such hospitals, know what the experience is like. They rarely talk about it with former patients, perhaps because they distrust information coming from the previously insane. Those who have worked in psychiatric hospitals are likely to have adapted so thoroughly to the settings that they are insensitive to the impact of that experience. And while there have been occasional reports of researchers who submitted themselves to psychiatric hospitalization,[7] these researchers have commonly remained in the hospitals for short periods of time, often with the knowledge of the hospital staff. It is difficult to know the extent to which they were treated like patients or like research colleagues. Nevertheless, their reports about the inside of the psychiatric hospital have been valuable. This article extends those efforts.

Pseudopatients and Their Settings

The eight pseudopatients were a varied group. One was a psychology graduate student in his 20s. The remaining seven were older and "established." Among them were three psychologists, a pediatrician, a psychiatrist, a painter, and a housewife. Three pseudopatients were women, five were men. All of them employed pseudonyms, lest their alleged diagnoses embarrass them later. Those who were in mental health professions alleged another occupation in order to avoid the special attentions that might be accorded by staff, as a matter of courtesy or caution, to ailing colleagues.[8] With the exception of myself (I was the first pseudopatient and my presence was known to the hospital administrator and chief psychologist and, so far as I can tell, to them alone), the presence of pseudopatients and the nature of the research program were not known to the hospital staffs.[9]

The settings were similarly varied. In order to generalize the findings, admission into a variety of hospitals was sought. The 12 hospitals in the sample were located in five different states on the East and West coasts. Some were old and shabby, some were quite new. Some were research-oriented, others not. Some had good staff-patient ratios, others were quite understaffed. Only one was a strictly private hospital. All of the others were supported by state or federal funds, or in one instance, by university funds.

After calling the hospital for an appointment, the pseudopatient arrived at the admissions office complaining that he had been hearing voices. Asked what the voices said, he replied that they were often unclear, but as far as he could tell they said "empty," "hollow," and "thud." The voices were unfamiliar and were of the same sex as the pseudopatient. The choice of these symptoms was occasioned by their apparent similarity to existential symptoms. Such symptoms are alleged to arise from painful concerns about the perceived meaninglessness of one's life. It is as if the hallucinating person were saying, "My life is empty and hollow." The choice of these symptoms was also determined by the *absence* of a single report of existential psychoses in the literature.

Beyond alleging the symptoms and falsifying name, vocation, and employment, no further alterations of person, history, or circumstances were made. The significant events of the pseudopatient's life history were presented as they had actually occurred. Relationships with parents and siblings, with spouse and children, with people at work and in school, consistent with the aforementioned exceptions, were described as they were or had been. Frustrations and upsets were described along with joys and satisfactions. These facts are important to remember. If anything, they strongly biased the subsequent results in favor of detecting sanity, since none of their histories or current behaviors were seriously pathological in any way.

Immediately upon admission to the psychiatric ward, the pseudopatient ceased simulating *any* symptoms of abnormality. In some cases, there was a brief period of mild nervousness and anxiety, since none of the pseudopatients really believed that they would be admitted so easily. Indeed, their shared fear was that they would be immediately exposed as frauds and greatly embarrassed. Moreover, many of them had never visited a psychiatric ward; even those who had, nevertheless had some genuine fears about what might happen to them. Their nervousness, then, was quite appropriate to the novelty of the hospital setting, and it abated rapidly.

Apart from that short-lived nervousness, the pseudopatient behaved on the ward as he "normally" behaved. The pseudopatient spoke to patients and staff as he might ordinarily. Because there is uncommonly little to do on a psychiatric ward, he attempted to engage others in conversation. When asked by the staff how he was feeling, he indicated that he was fine, that he no longer experienced symptoms. He responded to instructions from attendants, to calls for medication (which was not swallowed), and to dining-hall instructions. Beyond such activities as were available to him on the admissions ward, he spent his time writing down his observations about the ward, its patients, and the staff. Initially these notes were written "secretly," but as it soon became clear that no one much cared, they were subsequently written on standard tablets of paper in such public places as the dayroom. No secret was made of these activities.

The pseudopatient, very much as a true psychiatric patient, entered a hospital with no foreknowledge of when he would be discharged. Each was told that he would have to get out by his own devices, essentially by convincing the staff that he was sane. The psychological stresses associated with hospitalization were considerable, and all but one of the pseudopatients desired to be discharged almost immediately after being admitted. They were, therefore, motivated not only to behave sanely, but to be paragons of cooperation. That their behavior was in no way disruptive is confirmed by nursing reports, which have been obtained on most of the patients. These reports uniformly indicate that the patients were "friendly," "cooperative," and "exhibited no abnormal indications."

The Normal Are Not Detectably Sane

Despite their public "show" of sanity, the pseudopatients were never detected. Admitted, except in one case, with a diagnosis of schizophrenia,[10] each was discharged with a diagnosis of schizophrenia "in remission." The label "in remission" should in no way be dismissed as a formality, for at no time during any hospitalization had any question been raised about any pseudopatient's simulation. Nor are there any indications in the hospital records that the pseudopatient's status was suspect. Rather, the evidence is strong that, once labeled schizophrenic, the pseudopatient was stuck with that label. If the pseudopatient was to be discharged, he must naturally be "in remission"; but he was not sane, nor, in the institution's view, had he ever been sane.

The uniform failure to recognize sanity cannot be attributed to the quality of the hospitals, for, although there were considerable variations among them, several are considered excellent. Nor can it be alleged that there was simply not enough time to observe the pseudopatients. Length of hospitalization ranged from seven to 52 days, with an average of 19 days. The pseudopatients were not, in fact, carefully observed, but this failure clearly speaks more to the traditions within psychiatric hospitals than to lack of opportunity.

Finally, it cannot be said that the failure to recognize the pseudopatients' sanity was due to the fact that they were not behaving sanely. While there was clearly some tension present in all of them, their daily visitors could detect no serious behavioral consequences—nor, indeed, could other patients. It was quite common for the patients to "detect" the pseudopatients' sanity. During the first three hospitalizations, when accurate counts were kept, 35 of a total of 118 patients on the admissions ward voiced their suspicions, some vigorously. "You're not crazy. You're a journalist, or a professor [referring to the continual note-taking]. You're checking up on the hospital." While most of the patients were reassured by the pseudopatient's insistence that he had been sick before he came in but was fine now, some continued to believe that the pseudopatient was sane throughout his hospitalization.[11] The fact that the patients often recognized normality when staff did not raises important questions.

Failure to detect sanity during the course of hospitalization may be due to the fact that physicians operate with a strong bias toward what statisticians call the type 2 error.[12] This is to say that physicians are more inclined to call a healthy person sick (a false positive, type 2) than a sick person healthy (a false negative, type 1). The reasons for this are not hard to find: It is clearly more dangerous to misdiagnose illness than health. Better to err on the side of caution, to suspect illness even among the healthy.

But what holds for medicine does not hold equally well for psychiatry. Medical illnesses, while unfortunate, are not commonly pejorative. Psychiatric diagnoses, on the contrary, carry with them personal, legal, and social stigmas.[13] It was therefore important to see whether the tendency toward diagnosing the sane insane could be reversed. The following experiment was arranged at a research and teaching hospital whose staff had heard these findings but doubted that such an error could occur in their hospital. The staff was informed that at some time during the following three months, one or more pseudopatients would attempt to be admitted into the psychiatric hospital. Each staff member was asked to rate each patient who presented himself at admissions or on the ward according to the likelihood that the patient was a pseudopatient. A 10-point scale was used, with a 1 and 2 reflecting high confidence that the patient was a pseudopatient.

Judgments were obtained on 193 patients who were admitted for psychiatric treatment. All staff who had had sustained contact with or primary responsibility for the patient—attendants, nurses, psychiatrists, physicians, and psychologists—were asked to make judgments. Forty-one patients were alleged, with high confidence, to be pseudopatients by at least one member of the staff. Twenty-three were considered suspect by at least one psychiatrist. Nineteen were suspected by one psychiatrist and one other staff member. Actually, no genuine pseudopatient (at least from my group) presented himself during this period.

The experiment is instructive. It indicates that the tendency to designate sane people as insane can be reversed when the stakes (in this case, prestige and diagnostic acumen) are high. But what can be said of the 19 people who were suspected of being "sane" by one psychiatrist and another staff member? Were these people truly "sane," or was it rather the case that in the course of avoiding the type 2 error the staff tended to make more errors of the first sort—calling the crazy "sane"? There is no way of knowing. But one thing is certain: Any diagnostic process that lends itself so readily to massive errors of this sort cannot be a very reliable one.

The Stickiness of Psychodiagnostic Labels

Beyond the tendency to call the healthy sick—a tendency that accounts better for diagnostic behavior on admission than it does for such behavior after a lengthy period of exposure—the data speak to the massive role of labeling in psychiatric assessment. Having once been labeled schizophrenic, there is nothing the pseudopatient can do to overcome the tag. The tag profoundly colors others' perceptions of him and his behavior.

From one viewpoint, these data are hardly surprising, for it has long been known that elements are given meaning by the context in which they occur. Gestalt psychology made this point vigorously, and Asch[14] demonstrated that there are "central" personality traits (such as "warm" versus "cold") which are so powerful that they markedly color the meaning of other information in forming an impression of a given personality.[15] "Insane," "schizophrenic," "manic-depressive," and "crazy" are probably among the most powerful of such central traits. Once a person is designated abnormal, all of his other behaviors and characteristics are colored by that label. Indeed, that label is so powerful that many of the pseudopatients' normal behaviors were overlooked entirely or profoundly misinterpreted. Some examples may clarify this issue.

Earlier I indicated that there were no changes in the pseudopatient's personal history and current status beyond those of name, employment, and, where necessary, vocation. Otherwise, a veridical description of personal history and circumstances was offered. Those circumstances were not psychotic. How were they made consonant with the diagnosis of psychosis? Or were those diagnoses modified in such a way as to bring them into accord with the circumstances of the pseudopatient's life, as described by him?

As far as I can determine, diagnoses were in no way affected by the relative health of the circumstances of a pseudopatient's life. Rather, the reverse occurred: The perception of his circumstances was shaped entirely by the diagnosis. A clear example of such translation is found in the case of a pseudopatient who had had a close relationship with his mother but was rather remote from his father during his early childhood. During adolescence and beyond, however, his father became a close friend, while his relationship with his mother cooled. His present relationship with his wife was characteristically close and warm. Apart from occasional angry exchanges, friction was minimal. The children had rarely been spanked. Surely there is nothing especially pathological about such a history. Indeed, many readers may see a similar pattern in their own experiences, with no markedly deleterious consequences. Observe, however, how such a history was translated in the psychopathological context, this from the case summary prepared after the patient was discharged.

> This white 39-year-old male . . . manifests a long history of considerable ambivalence in close relationships, which begins in early childhood. A warm relationship with his mother cools during adolescence. A distant relationship to his father is described as becoming very intense. Affective stability is absent. His attempts to control emotionality with his wife and children are punctuated by angry outbursts and, in the case of the children, spankings. And while he says that he has several good friends, one senses considerable ambivalence embedded in those relationships also.

The facts of the case were unintentionally distorted by the staff to achieve consistency with a popular theory of the dynamics of schizophrenic reaction.[16] Nothing of an ambivalent nature had been described in relations with parents, spouse, or friends. To the extent that ambivalence could be inferred, it was probably not greater than is found in all human relationships. It is true the pseudopatient's relationships with his parents changed over time, but in the ordinary context that would hardly be remarkable—indeed, it might very well be expected. Clearly, the meaning ascribed to his verbalizations (that is, ambivalence, affective instability) was determined by the diagnosis: schizophrenia. An entirely different meaning would have been ascribed if it were known that the man was "normal."

All pseudopatients took extensive notes publicly. Under ordinary circumstances, such behavior would have raised questions in the minds of observers, as, in fact, it did among patients. Indeed, it seemed so certain that the notes would elicit suspicion that elaborate precautions were taken to remove them from the ward each day. But the precautions proved needless. The closest any staff member came to questioning these notes occurred when one pseudopatient asked his physician what kind of medication he was receiving and began to write down the response. "You needn't write it," he was told gently. "If you have trouble remembering, just ask me again."

If no questions were asked of the pseudopatients, how was their writing interpreted? Nursing records for three patients indicate that the writing was seen as an aspect of their pathological behavior. "Patient engages in writing behavior" was the daily nursing comment on one of the pseudopatients who was never questioned about his writing. Given that the patient is in the hospital, he must be psychologically disturbed. And given that he is disturbed, continuous writing must be a behavioral manifestation of that disturbance, perhaps a subset of the compulsive behaviors that are sometimes correlated with schizophrenia.

One tacit characteristic of psychiatric diagnosis is that it locates the sources of aberration within the individual and only rarely within the complex of stimuli that surrounds him. Consequently, behaviors that are stimulated by the environment are commonly misattributed to the patient's disorder. For example, one kindly nurse found a pseudopatient pacing the long hospital corridors. "Nervous, Mr. X?" she asked. "No, bored," he said.

The notes kept by pseudopatients are full of patient behaviors that were misinterpreted by well-intentioned staff. Often enough, a patient would go "berserk" because he had, wittingly or unwittingly, been mistreated by, say, an attendant. A nurse coming upon the scene would rarely inquire even cursorily into the environmental stimuli of the patient's behavior. Rather, she assumed that his upset derived from his pathology, not from his present interactions with other staff members. Occasionally, the staff might assume that the patient's family (especially when they had recently visited) or other patients had stimulated the outburst. But never were the staff found to assume that one of themselves or the structure of the hospital had anything to do with a patient's behavior. One psychiatrist pointed to a group of patients who were sitting outside the cafeteria entrance half an hour before lunchtime. To a group of young residents he indicated that such behavior was characteristic of the oral-acquisitive nature of the syndrome. It seemed not to occur to him that there were very few things to anticipate in the psychiatric hospital besides eating.

A psychiatric label has a life and an influence of its own. Once the impression has been formed that the patient is schizophrenic, the expectation is that he will continue to be schizophrenic. When a sufficient amount of time has passed, during which the patient has done nothing bizarre, he is considered to be in remission and available for discharge. But the label endures beyond discharge, with the unconfirmed expectation that he will behave as a schizophrenic again. Such labels, conferred by mental health professionals, are as influential on the patient as they are on his relatives and friends, and it should not surprise anyone that the diagnosis acts on all of them as a self-fulfilling prophecy. Eventually, the patient himself accepts the diagnosis, with all of its surplus meanings and expectations, and behaves accordingly.[17]

The inferences to be made from these matters are quite simple. Much as Zigler and Phillips have demonstrated that there is enormous overlap in the symptoms presented by patients who have been variously diagnosed,[18] so there is enormous overlap in the behaviors of the sane and the insane. The sane are not "sane" all of the time. We lose our tempers "for no good reason." We are occasionally depressed or anxious, again for no good reason. And we may find it difficult to get along with one or another person—again for no reason that we can specify. Similarly, the insane are not always insane. Indeed, it was the impression of the pseudopatients while living with them that they were sane for long periods of time—that the bizarre behaviors upon which their diagnoses were allegedly predicated constituted only a small fraction of their total behavior. If it makes no sense to label ourselves permanently depressed on the basis of an occasional depression, then it takes evidence that is presently available to label all patients insane or schizophrenic on the basis of bizarre behaviors or cognitions. It seems more useful, as Mischel[19] has pointed out, to limit our discussions to *behaviors*, the stimuli that provoke them, and their correlates.

It is not known why powerful impressions of personality traits, such as "crazy" or "insane," arise. Conceivably, when the origins of and stimuli that give rise to a behavior are remote or unknown, or when the behavior strikes us as immutable, trait labels regarding the *behavior* arise. When, on the other hand, the origins and stimuli are known and available, discourse is limited to the behavior itself. Thus, I may hallucinate because I am sleeping, or I may hallucinate because I have ingested a peculiar drug. These are termed sleep-induced hallucinations, or dreams, and drug-induced hallucinations, respectively. But when the stimuli to my hallucinations are unknown, that is called craziness, or schizophrenia—as if that inference were somehow as illuminating as the others.

The Consequences of Labeling and Depersonalization

Whenever the ratio of what is known to what needs to be known approaches zero, we tend to invent "knowledge" and assume that we understand more than we actually do. We seem unable to acknowledge that we simply don't know. The needs for diagnosis and remediation of behavioral and emotional problems are enormous. But rather than acknowledge that we are just embarking on understanding, we continue to label patients "schizophrenic," "manic-depressive," and "insane," as if in those words we had captured the essence of understanding. The facts of the matter are that we have known for a long time that diagnoses are often not useful or reliable, but we have nevertheless continued to use them. We now know that we cannot distinguish insanity from sanity. It is depressing to consider how that information will be used.

Not merely depressing, but frightening. How many people, one wonders, are sane but not recognized as such in our psychiatric institutions? How many have been needlessly stripped of their privileges of citizenship, from the right to vote and drive to that of handling their own accounts? How many have feigned insanity in order to avoid the criminal consequences of their behavior, and conversely, how many would rather stand trial than live interminably in a psychiatric hospital—but are wrongly thought to be mentally ill? How many have been stigmatized by well-intentioned, but nevertheless erroneous, diagnoses? On the last point, recall again that a "type 2 error" in psychiatric diagnosis does not have the same consequences it does in medical diagnosis. A diagnosis of cancer that has been found to be in error is cause for celebration. But psychiatric diagnoses are rarely found to be in error. The label sticks, a mark of inadequacy forever.

NOTES

1. P. Ash, *Journal of Abnormal and Social Psychology* 44 (1949):272; A. T. Beck, *American Journal of Psychiatry* 119 (1962):210; A. T. Boisen, *Psychiatry* 2 (1938):233; J. Kreitman, *Journal of Mental Science* 107 (1961):876; N. Kreitman, P. Sainsbury, J. Morrisey, J. Towers, and J. Scrivener, *Journal of Mental Science* 107 (1961):887; H. O. Schmitt, and C. P. Fonda, *Journal of Abnormal Social Psychology* 52 (1956):262; W. Seeman, *Journal of Nervous Mental Disorders* 118 (1953):541. For analysis of these artifacts and summaries of the disputes, see J. Zubin, *Annual Review of Psychology* 18 (1967):373; L. Phillips and J. G. Draguns, *Annual Review of Psychology* 22 (1971): 447.

2. R. Benedict, *Journal of General Psychology* 10 (1934):59.

3. See in this regard Howard Becker, *Outsiders: Studies in the Sociology of Deviance* (New York: Free Press, 1963); B. M. Braginsky, D. D. Braginsky, and K. Ring, *Methods of Madness: The Mental Hospital As a Last Resort* (New York: Holt, Rinehart and Winston, 1969); G. M. Crocetti and P. V. Lemkau, *American Sociological Review* 30 (1965):577; Erving Goffman, *Behavior in Public Places* (New York: Free Press, 1964); R. D. Laing, *The Divided Self: A Study of Sanity and Madness* (Chicago: Quadrangle, 1960); D. L. Phillips, *American Sociological Review* 28 (1963):963; T. R. Sarbin, *Psychology Today* 6 (1972):18; E. Schur, *American Journal of Sociology* 75 (1969):309; Thomas Szasz, *The Myth of Mental Illness: Foundations of a Theory of Mental Illness* (New York: Hoeber Harper, 1963). For a critique of some of these views, see W. R. Gave, *American Sociological Review* 35 (1970):873.

4. Erving Goffman, *Asylums* (Garden City, NY: Doubleday, 1961).

5. T. J. Scheff, *Being Mentally Ill: A Sociological Theory* (Chicago: Aldine, 1966).

6. Data from a ninth pseudopatient are not incorporated in this report because, although his sanity went undetected, he falsified aspects of his personal history, including his marital status and parental relationships. His experimental behaviors therefore were not identical to those of the other pseudopatients.

7. A. Barry, *Bellevue Is a State of Mind* (New York: Harcourt Brace Jovanovich, 1971); I. Belknap, *Human Problems of a State Mental Hospital* (New York: McGraw-Hill, 1956); W. Caudill, F. C. Redlich, H. R. Gilmore, and E. B. Brody, *American Journal of*

Orthopsychiatry 22 (1952):314; A. R. Goldman, R. H. Bohr, and T. A. Steinberg, *Professional Psychology* 1 (1970):427; *Roche Report* 1, no. 13 (1971):8.

8. Beyond the personal difficulties that the pseudopatient is likely to experience in the hospital, there are legal and social ones that, combined, require considerable attention before entry. For example, once admitted to a psychiatric institution, it is difficult, if not impossible, to be discharged on short notice, state law to the contrary notwithstanding. I was not sensitive to these difficulties at the outset of the project, nor to the personal and situational emergencies that can arise, but later a writ of habeas corpus was prepared for each of the entering pseudopatients and an attorney was kept "on call" during every hospitalization. I am grateful to John Kaplan and Robert Bartels for legal advice and assistance in these matters.

9. However distasteful such concealment is, it was a necessary first step to examining these questions. Without concealment, there would have been no way to know how valid these experiences were; nor was there any way of knowing whether whatever detections occurred were a tribute to the diagnostic acumen of the staff or to the hospital's rumor network. Obviously, since my concerns are general ones that cut across individual hospitals and staffs, I have respected their anonymity and have eliminated clues that might lead to their identification.

10. Interestingly, of the 12 admissions, 11 were diagnosed as schizophrenic and one, with the identical symptomatology, as manic-depressive psychosis. This diagnosis has a more favorable prognosis, and it was given by the only private hospital in our sample. On the relations between social class and psychiatric diagnosis, see A. B. Hollinghead and F. C. Redlich, *Social Class and Mental Illness: A Community Study* (New York: Wiley, 1958).

11. It is possible, of course, that patients have quite broad latitudes in diagnosis and therefore are inclined to call many people sane, even those whose behavior is patently aberrant. However, although we have no hard data on this matter, it was our distinct impression that this was not the case. In many instances, patients not only singled us out for attention, but came to imitate our behaviors and styles.

12. Scheff, *Being Mentally Ill.*

13. J. Cumming and E. Cumming, *Community Mental Health* 1 (1965):135; A. Farina and K. Ring, *Journal of Abnormal Psychology* 40 (1965):47; H. E. Freeman and O. G. Simmons, *The Mental Patient Comes Home* (New York: Wiley, 1963); W. J. Johannsen, *Mental Hygiene* 53 (1969):218; A. S. Linsky, *Social Psychology* 5 (1970):166.

14. S. E. Asch, *Abnormal Social Psychology* 41 (1946):258; S. E. Asch, *Social Psychology* (New York: Prentice-Hall, 1952).

15. See also I. N. Mensch and J. Wishner, *Journal of Personality* 16 (1947):188; J. Wishner, *Psychological Review* 67 (1960):96; J. S. Bruner and K. R. Tagiuri in *Handbook of Social Psychology*, vol. 2, ed. G. Lindzey (Cambridge, MA: Addison-Wesley, 1954), pp. 634–54; J. S. Bruner, D. Shapiro, and R. Tagiuri in *Person Perception and Interpersonal Behavior,* ed. R. Tagiuri and L. Petrullo (Stanford, CA: Stanford University Press, 1958), pp. 277–88.

16. For an example of a similar self-fulfilling prophecy, in this instance dealing with the "central" trait of intelligence, see R. Rosenthal and L. Jacobson, *Pygmalion in the Classroom* (New York: Holt, Rinehart and Winston, 1968).

17. Scheff, *Being Mentally Ill.*

18. E. Zigler and L. Phillips, *Journal of Abnormal and Social Psychology* 63 (1961):69. See also R. K. Freudenberg and J. P. Robertson, *A.M.A. Archives of Neurological Psychiatry* 76 (1956):14.

19. W. Mischel, *Personality and Assessment* (New York: Wiley, 1968).

20

ANOREXIA NERVOSA AND BULIMIA
The Development of Deviant Identities

PENELOPE A. McLORG • DIANE E. TAUB

Symbolic interactionists claim that deviance is relative depending on the situation and who is perceiving the act of deviance. Thus, according to *labeling theory,* people label certain acts as deviant and others as normal. This reading by Penelope McLorg and Diane Taub further illustrates this subjective process of deviance identification. McLorg and Taub (1987) employ labeling theory to explain how eating disorders have become defined as deviant behaviors and how some young women acquire deviant identities by modifying their self-concepts to conform to the societal labels of a person with an eating disorder.

Introduction

Current appearance norms stipulate thinness for women and muscularity for men; these expectations, like any norms, entail rewards for compliance and negative sanctions for violations. Fear of being overweight—of being visually deviant—has led to a striving for thinness, especially among women. In the extreme, this avoidance of overweight engenders eating disorders, which themselves constitute deviance. Anorexia nervosa, or purposeful starvation, embodies visual as well as behavioral deviation; bulimia, binge-eating followed by vomiting and/or laxative abuse, is primarily behaviorally deviant.

Besides a fear of fatness, anorexics and bulimics exhibit distorted body images. In anorexia nervosa, a 20–25 percent loss of initial body weight occurs, resulting from self-starvation alone or in combination with excessive exercising, occasional binge-eating, vomiting and/or laxative abuse. Bulimia denotes cyclical (daily, weekly, for example) binge-eating followed by vomiting or laxative abuse; weight is normal or close to normal (Humphries et al. 1982). Common physical manifestations of these eating disorders include menstrual cessation or irregularities and electrolyte imbalances; among behavioral traits are depression, obsessions/compulsions, and anxiety (Russell 1979; Thompson and Schwartz 1982).

Increasingly prevalent in the past two decades, anorexia nervosa and bulimia have emerged as major health and social problems. Termed an epidemic on college campuses (Brody, as quoted in Schur 1984:76), bulimia affects 13 percent of college students (Halmi et al. 1981). Less prevalent, anorexia nervosa was diagnosed in 0.6 percent of students utilizing a university health center (Stangler and Printz 1980). However, the overall mortality rate of anorexia nervosa is 6 percent (Schwartz and Thompson 1981) to 20 percent (Humphries et al. 1982); bulimia appears to be less life-threatening (Russell 1979).

Particularly affecting certain demographic groups, eating disorders are most prevalent among young, white, affluent (upper-middle to upper class) women in modern, industrialized countries (Crisp 1977; Willi and Grossman 1983). Combining all of these risk factors (female sex, youth, high socio-economic status, and residence in an industrialized country), prevalence of anorexia nervosa in upper class English girls' schools is reported at 1 in 100 (Crisp et al. 1976). The age of onset for anorexia nervosa is bimodal at 14.5 and 18 years (Humphries et al. 1982); the most frequent age of onset for bulimia is 18 (Russell 1979).

Eating disorders have primarily been studied from psychological and medical perspectives.[1] Theories of etiology have generally fallen into three categories: the ego psychological (involving an impaired child-maternal environment); the family systems (implicating enmeshed, rigid families); and the endocrinological (involving a precipitating hormonal defect). Although relatively ignored in previous studies, the sociocultural components of anorexia nervosa and bulimia (the slimness norm and its agents of reinforcement, such as role models) have been postulated as accounting for the recent, dramatic increases in these disorders (Boskind-White 1985; Schwartz et al. 1982).[2]

Medical and psychological approaches to anorexia nervosa and bulimia obscure the social facets of the disorders and neglect the individuals' own definitions of their situations. Among the social processes involved in the development of an eating disorder is the sequence of conforming behavior, primary deviance, and secondary deviance. Societal reaction is the critical mediator affecting the movement through the deviant career (Becker 1973). Within a framework of labeling theory, this study focuses on the emergence of anorexic and bulimic identities, as well as on the consequences of being career deviants.

Methodology

Sampling and Procedures

Most research on eating disorders has utilized clinical subjects or nonclinical respondents completing questionnaires. Such studies can be criticized for simply counting and describing behaviors and/or neglecting the social construction of the disorders. Moreover, the work of clinicians is often limited by therapeutic orientation. Previous research may also have included individuals who were not in therapy on their own volition and who resisted admitting that they had an eating disorder.

Past studies thus disregard the intersubjective meanings respondents attach to their behavior and emphasize researchers' criteria for definition as anorexic or bulimic. In order to supplement these sampling and procedural designs, the present study utilizes participant observation of a group of self-defined anorexics and bulimics.[3] As the individuals had acknowledged their eating disorders, frank discussion and disclosure were facilitated.

Data are derived from a self-help group, BANISH, Bulimics/Anorexics in Self-Help, which met at a university in an urban center of the mid-South. Founded by one of the researchers (D.E.T.), BANISH was advertised in local newspapers as offering a group experience for individuals who were anorexic or bulimic. Despite the local advertisements, the campus location of the meeting may have selectively encouraged university students to attend. Nonetheless, in view of the modal age of onset and socioeconomic status of individuals with eating disorders, college students have been considered target populations (Crisp et al. 1976; Halmi et al. 1981).

The group's weekly two-hour meetings were observed for two years. During the course of this study, 30 individuals attended at least one of the meetings. Attendance at meetings was varied: Ten individuals came nearly every Sunday; five attended approximately twice a month; and the remaining 15 participated once a month or less frequently, often when their eating problems were "more severe" or "bizarre." The modal number of members at meetings was 12. The diversity in attendance was to be expected in self-help groups of anorexics and bulimics

> Most people's involvement will not be forever or even a long time. Most people get the support they need and drop out. Some take the time to help others after they themselves have been helped but even they may withdraw after a time. It is a natural and in many cases *necessary* process (emphasis in original). (American Anorexia and Bulimia Association 1983)

Modeled after Alcoholics Anonymous, BANISH allowed participants to discuss their backgrounds and experiences with others who empathized. For many members, the group constituted their only source of help; these respondents were reluctant to contact health professionals because of shame, embarrassment, or financial difficulties.

In addition to field notes from group meetings, records of other encounters with all members were maintained. Participants visited the office of one of the researchers (D.E.T.), called both researchers by phone, and invited them to their homes or out for a cup of coffee. Such interaction facilitated genuine communication and mutual trust. Even among the 15 individuals who did not attend the meetings regularly, contact was maintained with 10 members on a monthly basis.

Supplementing field notes were informal interviews with 15 group members, lasting from two to four hours. Because they appeared to represent more extensive experience with eating disorders, these interviewees were chosen to amplify their comments about the labeling process, made during group meetings. Conducted near the end of the two-year observation period, the interviews focused on what the respondents thought antedated and maintained their eating disorders. In addition, participants described others' reactions to their behaviors as well as their own interpretations of these reactions. To protect the confidentiality of individuals quoted in the study, pseudonyms are employed.

Description of Members

The demographic composite of the sample typifies what has been found in other studies (Crisp 1977; Fox and James 1976; Herzog 1982; Schlesier-Stropp 1984). Group members' ages ranged from 19 to 36, with the modal age being 21. The respondents were white, and all but one were female. The sole male and three of the females were anorexic; the remaining females were bulimic.[4]

Primarily composed of college students, the group included four nonstudents, three of whom had college degrees. Nearly all members derived from upper-middle or lower-upper-class households. Eighteen students and two nonstudents were never married and uninvolved in serious relationships; two nonstudents were married (one with two children); two students were divorced (one with two children); and six students were involved in serious relationships. The duration of eating disorders ranged from three to 15 years.

Conforming Behavior

In the backgrounds of most anorexics and bulimics, dieting figures prominently, beginning in the teen years (Crisp 1977; Johnson et al. 1982; Lacey et al. 1986). As dieters, these individuals are conformist in their adherence to the cultural norms emphasizing thinness (Garner et al. 1980; Schwartz et al. 1982). In our society, slim bodies are regarded as the most worthy and attractive; overweight is viewed as physically and morally unhealthy—"obscene," "lazy," "slothful," and "gluttonous" (DeJong 1980; Ritenbaugh 1982; Schwartz et al. 1982).

Among the agents of socialization promoting the slimness norm is advertising. Female models in newspaper, magazine, and television advertisements are uniformly slender. In addition, product names and slogans exploit the thin orientation; examples include "Ultra Slim Lipstick," "Miller Lite," and "Virginia Slims." While retaining pressures toward thinness, an Ayds commercial attempts a compromise for those wanting to savor food: "Ayds . . . so you can taste, chew, and enjoy, while you lose weight." Appealing particularly to women, a nationwide fast-food restaurant chain offers low-calorie selections, so individuals can have a "license to eat." In the latter two examples, the notion of enjoying food is combined with the message to be slim. Food and restaurant advertisements overall convey the pleasures of eating, whereas advertisements for other products, such as fashions and diet aids, reinforce the idea that fatness is undesirable.

Emphasis on being slim affects everyone in our culture, but it influences women especially because of society's traditional emphasis on women's appearance. The slimness norm and its concomitant narrow beauty standards exacerbate the objectification of women (Schur 1984). Women view themselves as visual entities and recognize that conforming to appearance expectations and "becoming attractive object[s] [are] role obligation[s]" (Laws, as quoted in Schur 1984:66). Demonstrating the beauty motivation behind dieting, a recent Nielson survey indicated that of the 56 percent of all women aged 24 to 54 who dieted during the previous year, 76 percent did so for cosmetic, rather than health, reasons (Schwartz et al. 1982). For most female group members, dieting was viewed as a means of gaining attractiveness and appeal to the opposite sex. The male respondent, as well, indicated that "when I was fat, girls didn't look at me, but when I got thinner, I was suddenly popular."

In addition to responding to the specter of obesity, individuals who develop anorexia nervosa and bulimia are conformist in their strong commitment to other conventional norms and goals. They consistently excel at school and work (Bruch 1981; Humphries et al. 1982; Russell 1979), maintaining high aspirations in both areas (Lacey et al. 1986; Theander 1970). Group members generally completed college-preparatory courses in high school, aware from an early age that they would strive for a college degree. Also, in college as well as high school, respondents joined honor societies and academic clubs.

Moreover, pre-anorexics and -bulimics display notable conventionality as "model children" (Humphries et al. 1982:199), "the pride and joy" of their parents (Bruch 1981:215), accommodating themselves to the wishes of others. Parents of these individuals emphasize conformity and value achievement (Bruch 1981). Respondents felt that perfect or near-perfect grades were expected of them; however, good grades were not rewarded by parents, because "A's" were common for these children. In addition, their parents suppressed conflicts, to preserve the image of the "all-American family" (Humphries et al. 1982). Group members reported that they seldom, if ever, heard their parents argue or raise their voices.

Also conformist in their affective ties, individuals who develop anorexia nervosa and bulimia are strongly, even excessively, attached to their parents. Respondents' families appeared close-knit, demonstrating palpable emotional ties. Several group members, for example, reported habitually calling home at prescribed times, whether or not they had any news. Such families have been termed "enmeshed" and "overprotective," displaying intense interaction and concern for members' welfare (Minuchin et al. 1978; Selvini-

Palazzoli 1978). These qualities could be viewed as marked conformity to the norm of familial closeness.[5]

Another element of notable conformity in the family milieu of pre-anorexics and -bulimics concerns eating, body weight and shape, and exercising (Humphries et al. 1982; Kalucy et al. 1977). Respondents reported their fathers' preoccupation with exercising and their mothers' engrossment in food preparation. When group members dieted and lost weight, they received an extraordinary amount of approval. Among the family, body size became a matter of "friendly rivalry." One bulimic informant recalled that she, her mother, and her coed sister all strived to wear a size 5, regardless of their heights and body frames. Subsequent to this study, the researchers learned that both the mother and sister had become bulimic.

As pre-anorexics and -bulimics, group members thus exhibited marked conformity to cultural norms of thinness, achievement, compliance, and parental attachment. Their families reinforced their conformity by adherence to norms of family closeness and weight and body shape consciousness.

Primary Deviance

Even with familial encouragement, respondents, like nearly all dieters (Chernin 1981), failed to maintain their lowered weights. Many cited their lack of willpower to eat only restricted foods. For the emerging anorexics and bulimics, extremes such as purposeful starvation or binging accompanied by vomiting and/or laxative abuse appeared as "obvious solutions" to the problem of retaining weight loss. Associated with these behaviors was a regained feeling of control in lives that had been disrupted by a major crisis. Group members' extreme weight-loss efforts operated as coping mechanisms for entering college, leaving home, or feeling rejected by the opposite sex.

The primary inducement for both eating adaptations was the drive for slimness: With slimness came more self-respect and a feeling of superiority over "unsuccessful dieters." Brian, for example, experienced a "power trip" upon consistent weight loss through starvation. Binges allowed the purging respondents to cope with stress through eating while maintaining a slim appearance. As former strict dieters, Teresa and Jennifer used binging and purging as an alternative to the constant self-denial of starvation. Acknowledging their parents' desires for them to be slim, most respondents still felt it was a conscious choice on their part to continue extreme weight-loss efforts. Being thin became the "most important thing" in their lives—their "greatest ambition."

In explaining the development of an anorexic or bulimic identity, Lemert's (1951, 1967) concept of primary deviance is salient. Primary deviance refers to a transitory period of norm violations which do not affect an individual's self-concept or performance of social roles. Although respondents were exhibiting anorexic or bulimic behavior, they did not consider themselves to be anorexic or bulimic.

At first, anorexics' significant others complimented their weight loss, expounding on their new "sleekness" and "good looks." Branch and Eurman (1980:631) also found anorexics' families and friends describing them as "well groomed," "neat," "fashionable," and "victorious." Not until the respondents approached emaciation did some parents or friends become concerned and withdraw their praise. Significant others also became increasingly aware of the anorexics' compulsive exercising, preoccupation with food preparation (but not consumption), and ritualistic eating patterns (such as cutting food into minute pieces and eating only certain foods at prescribed times).

For bulimics, friends or family members began to question how the respondents could eat such large amounts of food (often in excess of 10,000 calories a day) and stay slim. Significant others also noticed calluses across the bulimics' hands, which were caused by repeated inducement of vomiting. Several bulimics were "caught in the act," bent over commodes. Generally, friends and family required substantial evidence before believing that the respondents' binging or purging was no longer sporadic.

Secondary Deviance

Heightened awareness of group members' eating behavior ultimately led others to label the respondents "anorexic" or "bulimic." Respondents differed in their histories of being labeled and accepting the labels. Generally first termed anorexic by friends, family, or medical personnel, the anorexics initially vigorously denied the label. They felt they were not "anorexic enough," not skinny enough; Robin did not regard herself as having the "skeletal" appearance she associated with anorexia nervosa. These group members found it difficult to differentiate between socially approved modes of weight loss— eating less and exercising more—and the extremes of those behaviors. In fact, many of their activities—cheerleading, modeling, gymnastics, aerobics— reinforced their pursuit of thinness. Like other anorexics, Chris felt she was being "ultra-healthy," with "total control" over her body.

For several respondents, admitting they were anorexic followed the realization that their lives were disrupted by their eating disorder. Anorexics' inflexible eating patterns unsettled family meals and holiday gatherings. Their regimented lifestyle of compulsively scheduled activities—exercising, school, and meals—precluded any spontaneous social interactions. Realization of their adverse behaviors preceded the anorexics' acknowledgment of their subnormal body weight and size.

Contrasting with anorexics, the binge/purgers, when confronted, more readily admitted that they were bulimic and that their means of weight loss was "abnormal." Teresa, for example, knew "very well" that her bulimic behavior was "wrong and unhealthy," although "worth the physical risks." While the bulimics initially maintained that their purging was only a temporary weight-loss method, they eventually realized that their disorder represented a "loss of control." Although these respondents regretted the self-indulgence, "shame," and "wasted time," they acknowledged their growing dependence on binging and purging for weight management and stress regulation.

The application of anorexic or bulimic labels precipitated secondary deviance, wherein group members internalized these identities. Secondary deviance refers to norm violations which are a response to society's labeling: "secondary deviation . . . becomes a means of social defense, attack or adaptation to the overt and covert problems created by the societal reaction to primary deviance" (Lemert 1967:17). In contrast to primary deviance, secondary deviance is generally prolonged, alters the individual's self-concept, and affects the performance of his/her social roles.

As secondary deviants, respondents felt that their disorders "gave a purpose" to their lives. Nicole resisted attaining a normal weight because it was not "her"—she accepted her anorexic weight as her "true" weight. For Teresa, bulimia became a "companion"; and Julie felt "every aspect of her life," including time management and social activities, was affected by her bulimia. Group members' eating disorders became the salient element of their self-concepts, so that they related to familiar people and new acquaintances as anorexics or bulimics. For example, respondents regularly compared their body shapes and sizes with those of others. They also became sensitized to comments about their appearance, whether or not the remarks were made by someone aware of their eating disorder.

With their behavior increasingly attuned to their eating disorders, group members exhibited role engulfment (Schur 1971). Through accepting anorexic or bulimic identities, individuals centered activities around their deviant role, downgrading other social roles. Their obligations as students, family members, and friends became subordinate to their eating and exercising rituals. Socializing, for example, was gradually curtailed because it interfered with compulsive exercising, binging, or purging.

Labeled anorexic or bulimic, respondents were ascribed a new status with a different set of role expectations. Regardless of other positions the individuals occupied, their deviant status, or master status (Becker 1973; Hughes 1958), was identified before all others. Among group members, Nicole, who was known as the "school's brain," became known as the "school's anorexic." No longer viewed as conforming model individuals, some respondents were termed "starving waifs" or "pigs."

Because of their identities as deviants, anorexics' and bulimics' interactions with others were altered. Group members' eating habits were scrutinized by friends and family and used as a "catch-all" for everything negative that happened to them. Respondents felt self-conscious around individuals who knew of their disorders; for example, Robin imagined people "watching and whispering" behind her. In addition, group members believed others expected them to "act" anorexic or bulimic. Friends of some anorexic group members never offered them food or drink, assuming continued disinterest on the respondents' part. While being hospitalized, Denise felt she had to prove to others she was not still vomiting, by keeping her bathroom door open. Other bulimics, who lived in dormitories, were hesitant to use the restroom for normal purposes lest several friends be huddling at the door, listening for vomiting. In general, individuals interacted with the respondents largely on the basis of their eating disorder; in doing so, they reinforced anorexic and bulimic behaviors.

Bulimic respondents, whose weight-loss behavior was not generally detectable from their appearance, tried earnestly to hide their bulimia by binging and purging in secret. Their main purpose in concealment was to avoid the negative consequences of being known as a bulimic. For these individuals, bulimia connoted a "cop-out": Like "weak anorexics," bulimics pursued thinness but yielded to urges to eat. Respondents felt other people regarded bulimia as "gross" and had little sympathy for the sufferer. To avoid these stigmas or "spoiled identities," the bulimics shrouded their behaviors.

Distinguishing types of stigma, Goffman (1963) describes discredited (visible) stigmas and discreditable (invisible) stigmas. Bulimics, whose weight was approximately normal or even slightly elevated, harbored discreditable stigmas. Anorexics, on the other hand, suffered both discreditable and discredited stigmas—the latter due to their emaciated appearance. Certain anorexics were more reconciled than the bulimics to their stigmas: For Brian, the "stigma of anorexia was better than being fat." Common to the stigmatized individuals was an inability to interact spontaneously with others. Respondents were constantly on guard against topics of eating and body size.

Both anorexics and bulimics were held responsible by others for their behavior and presumed able to "get out of it if they tried." Many anorexics reported being told to "just eat more," while bulimics were enjoined to simply "stop eating so much." Such appeals were made without regard for the complexities of the problem. Ostracized by certain friends and family members, anorexics and bulimics felt increasingly isolated. For respondents, the self-help group presented a nonthreatening forum for discussing their disorders. Here, they found mutual understanding, empathy, and support. Many participants viewed BANISH as a haven from stigmatization by "others."

Group members, as secondary deviants, thus endured negative consequences, such as stigmatization, from being labeled. As they internalized the labels anorexic or bulimic, individuals' self-concepts were significantly influenced. When others interacted with the respondents on the basis of their eating disorders, anorexic or bulimic identities were encouraged. Moreover, group members' efforts to counteract the deviant labels were thwarted by their master status.

Discussion

Previous research on eating disorders has dwelt almost exclusively on medical and psychological facets. Although necessary for a comprehensive understanding of anorexia nervosa and bulimia, these approaches neglect the social processes involved. The phenomena of eating disorders transcend concrete disease entities and clinical diagnoses. Multifaceted and complex, anorexia nervosa and bulimia require a holistic research design, in which sociological insights must be included.

A limitation of medical and psychiatric studies, in particular, is researchers' use of a priori criteria in establishing salient variables. Rather than utilizing predetermined standards of inclusion, the present study allows respondents to construct their own reality. Concomitant to this innovative approach to eating disorders is the selection of a sample of self-admitted anorexics and bulimics. Individuals' perceptions of what it means to become anorexic or bulimic are explored. Although based on a small sample, findings can be used to guide researchers in other settings.

With only 5 to 10 percent of reported cases appearing in males (Crisp 1977; Stangler and Printz 1980), eating disorders are primarily a women's aberrance. The deviance of anorexia nervosa and bulimia is rooted in the visual objectification of women and attendant slimness norm. Indeed, purposeful starvation and binging and purging reinforce the notion that "a society gets the deviance it deserves" (Schur 1979:71). As recently noted (Schur 1984), the sociology of deviance has generally bypassed systematic studies of women's norm violations. Like male deviants, females endure label applications, internalizations, and fulfillments.

The social processes involved in developing anorexic or bulimic identities comprise the sequence of conforming behavior, primary deviance, and secondary deviance. With a background of exceptional adherence to conventional norms, especially the striving for thinness, respondents subsequently exhibit the primary deviance of starving or binging and purging. Societal reaction to these behaviors leads to secondary deviance, wherein respondents' self-concepts and master statuses become anorexic or bulimic. Within this framework of labeling theory, the persistence of eating disorders, as well as the effects of stigmatization, are elucidated.

Although during the course of this research some respondents alleviated their symptoms through psychiatric help or hospital treatment programs, no one was labeled "cured." An anorexic is considered recovered when weight is normal for two years; a bulimic is termed recovered after being symptom-free for one and one-half years (American Anorexia and Bulimia Association Newsletter 1985). Thus deviance disavowal (Schur 1971), or efforts after normalization to counteract deviant labels, remains a topic for future exploration.

NOTES

1. Although instructive, an integration of the medical, psychological, and socio-cultural perspectives on eating disorders is beyond the scope of this paper.
2. Exceptions to the neglect of sociocultural factors are discussions of sex-role social-ization in the development of eating disorders. Anorexics' girlish appearance has been interpreted as a rejection of femininity and womanhood (Bruch 1981; Orbach 1979, 1985). In contrast, bulimics have been characterized as over-conforming to traditional female sex roles (Boskind-Lodahl 1976).
3. Although a group experience for self-defined bulimics has been reported (Boskind-Lodahl 1976), the researcher, from the outset, focused on Gestalt and behaviorist techniques within a feminist orientation.
4. One explanation for fewer anorexics than bulimics in the sample is that, in the gen-eral population, anorexics are outnumbered by bulimics at 8 or 10 to 1 (Lawson, as reprinted in American Anorexia and Bulimia Association Newsletter 1985:1). The proportion of bulimics to anorexics in the sample is 6.5 to 1. In addition, compared to bulimics, anorexics may be less likely to attend a self-help group as they have a greater tendency to deny the existence of an eating problem (Humphries et al. 1982). However, the four anorexics in the present study were among the members who attended the meetings most often.
5. Interactions in the families of anorexics and bulimics might seem deviant in being inordinately close. However, in the larger societal context, the family members epitomize the norms of family cohesiveness. Perhaps unusual in their occurrence, these families are still within the realm of conformity. Humphries and colleagues (1982:202) refer to the "highly enmeshed and protective" family as part of the "idealized family myth."

REFERENCES

American Anorexia / Bulimia Association. 1983, April. Correspondence.
American Anorexia / Bulimia Association Newsletter. 1985. 8(3).
Becker, Howard S. 1973. *Outsiders*. New York: Free Press.
Boskind-Lodahl, Marlene. 1976. "Cinderella's Stepsisters: A Feminist Perspective on Anorexia Nervosa and Bulimia." *Signs, Journal of Women in Culture and Society* 2:342–56.
Boskind-White, Marlene. 1985. "Bulimarexia: A Sociocultural Perspective." Pp. 113–26 in *Theory and Treatment of Anorexia Nervosa and Bulimia: Biomedical, Sociocultural and Psychological Perspectives*, edited by S. W. Emmett. New York: Brunner / Mazel.
Branch, C. H. Hardin and Linda J. Eurman. 1980. "Social Attitudes toward Patients with Anorexia Nervosa." *American Journal of Psychiatry* 137:631–32.
Bruch, Hilda. 1981. "Developmental Considerations of Anorexia Nervosa and Obe-sity." *Canadian Journal of Psychiatry* 26:212–16.
Chernin, Kim. 1981. *The Obsession: Reflections on the Tyranny of Slenderness*. New York: Harper & Row.
Crisp, A. H. 1977. "The Prevalence of Anorexia Nervosa and Some of Its Associations in the General Population." *Advances in Psychosomatic Medicine* 9:38–47.
Crisp, A. H., R. L. Palmer, and R. S. Kalucy. 1976. "How Common Is Anorexia Ner-vosa? A Prevalence Study." *British Journal of Psychiatry* 128:549–54.
DeJong, William. 1980. "The Stigma of Obesity: The Consequences of Naive As-sumptions Concerning the Causes of Physical Deviance." *Journal of Health and So-cial Behavior* 21:75–87.
Fox, K. C. and N. McI. James. 1976. "Anorexia Nervosa: A Study of 44 Strictly Defined Cases." *New Zealand Medical Journal* 84:309–12.

Garner, David M., Paul E. Garfinkel, Donald Schwartz, and Michael Thompson. 1980. "Cultural Expectations of Thinness in Women." *Psychological Reports* 47:483–91.

Goffman, Erving. 1963. *Stigma*. Englewood Cliffs, NJ: Prentice-Hall.

Halmi, Katherine A., James R. Falk, and Estelle Schwartz. 1981. "Binge-Eating and Vomiting: A Survey of a College Population." *Psychological Medicine* 11:697–706.

Herzog, David B. 1982. "Bulimia: The Secretive Syndrome." *Psychosomatics* 23:481–83.

Hughes, Everett C. 1958. *Men and Their Work*. New York: Free Press.

Humphries, Laurie L., Sylvia Wrobel, and H. Thomas Wiegert. 1982. "Anorexia Nervosa." *American Family Physician* 26:199–204.

Johnson, Craig L., Marilyn K. Stuckey, Linda D. Lewis, and Donald M. Schwartz. 1982. "Bulimia: A Descriptive Survey of 316 Cases." *International Journal of Eating Disorders* 2(1):3–16.

Kalucy, R. S., A. H. Crisp, and Britta Harding. 1977. "A Study of 56 Families with Anorexia Nervosa." *British Journal of Medical Psychology* 50:381–95.

Lacey, Hubert J., Sian Coker, and S. A. Birtchnell. 1986. "Bulimia: Factors Associated with Its Etiology and Maintenance." *International Journal of Eating Disorders* 5:475–87.

Lemert, Edwin M. 1951. *Social Pathology*. New York: McGraw-Hill.

———. 1967. *Human Deviance, Social Problems and Social Control*. Englewood Cliffs, NJ: Prentice-Hall.

Minuchin, Salvador, Bernice L. Rosman, and Lester Baker. 1978. *Psychosomatic Families: Anorexia Nervosa in Context*. Cambridge, MA: Harvard University Press.

Orbach, Susie. 1979. *Fat Is a Feminist Issue*. New York: Berkeley.

———. 1985. "Visibility/Invisibility: Social Considerations in Anorexia Nervosa—a Feminist Perspective." Pp. 127–38 in *Theory and Treatment of Anorexia Nervosa and Bulimia: Biomedical, Sociocultural and Psychological Perspectives*, edited by S. W. Emmett. New York: Brunner/Mazel.

Ritenbaugh, Cheryl. 1982. "Obesity As a Culture-Bound Syndrome." *Culture, Medicine and Psychiatry* 6:347–61.

Russell, Gerald. 1979. "Bulimia Nervosa: An Ominous Variant of Anorexia Nervosa." *Psychological Medicine* 9:429–48.

Schlesier-Stropp, Barbara. 1984. "Bulimia: A Review of the Literature." *Psychological Bulletin* 95:247–57.

Schur, Edwin M. 1971. *Labeling Deviant Behavior*. New York: Harper & Row.

———. 1979. *Interpreting Deviance: A Sociological Introduction*. New York: Harper & Row.

———. 1984. *Labeling Women Deviant: Gender, Stigma, and Social Control*. New York: Random House.

Schwartz, Donald M. and Michael G. Thompson. 1981. "Do Anorectics Get Well? Current Research and Future Needs." *American Journal of Psychiatry* 138:319–23.

Schwartz, Donald M., Michael G. Thompson, and Craig L. Johnson. 1982. "Anorexia Nervosa and Bulimia: The Socio-Cultural Context." *International Journal of Eating Disorders* 1(3):20–36.

Selvini-Palazzoli, Mara. 1978. *Self-Starvation: From Individual to Family Therapy in the Treatment of Anorexia Nervosa*. New York: Jason Aronson.

Stangler, Ronnie S. and Adolph M. Printz. 1980. "DSM-III: Psychiatric Diagnosis in a University Population." *American Journal of Psychiatry* 137:937–40.

Theander, Sten. 1970. "Anorexia Nervosa." *Acta Psychiatrica Scandinavica Supplement* 214:24–31.

Thompson, Michael G. and Donald M. Schwartz. 1982. "Life Adjustment of Women with Anorexia Nervosa and Anorexic-like Behavior." *International Journal of Eating Disorders* 1(2):47–60.

Willi, Jurg and Samuel Grossman. 1983. "Epidemiology of Anorexia Nervosa in a Defined Region of Switzerland." *American Journal of Psychiatry* 140:564–67.

21

IN SEARCH OF RESPECT
Selling Crack in El Barrio

PHILIPPE BOURGOIS

One type of social deviance, according to sociologists, is crime. If deviance is the violation of a social norm, then a *crime* is the violation of social norms that have been made into laws. One type of crime that sociologists have long studied is illegal drug use. Why do segments of the population use and abuse illegal drugs? How can we explain the growing underground economy of illegal drugs? In this selection, taken from *In Search of Respect: Selling Crack in El Barrio* (1995), Philippe Bourgois takes us inside the crack economy in East Harlem, New York City. Bourgois spent three and a half years living in "El Barrio," where he came to know the residents and their day-to-day struggles for economic survival. Bourgois' ethnographic account of life and social marginalization in this inner-city neighborhood reveals that many social factors lead people to deal illegal drugs and other social barriers prevent them from reentering the legal economy.

I was forced into crack against my will. When I first moved to East Harlem—"El Barrio"—as a newlywed in the spring of 1985, I was looking for an inexpensive New York City apartment from which I could write about the experience of poverty and ethnic segregation in the heart of one of the most expensive cities in the world. I was interested in the political economy of inner-city street culture. I wanted to probe the Achilles' heel of the richest industrialized nation in the world by documenting how it imposes racial segregation and economic marginalization on so many of its Latino/a and African-American citizens.

My original subject was the entire underground (untaxed) economy, from curbside car repairing and baby-sitting to unlicensed off-track betting and drug dealing. I had never even heard of crack when I first arrived in the neighborhood—no one knew about this particular substance yet, because this brittle compound of cocaine and baking soda processed into efficiently smokable pellets was not yet available as a mass-marketed product. By the end of the year, however, most of my friends, neighbors and acquaintances had been swept into the multibillion-dollar crack cyclone: selling it, smoking it, fretting over it. I followed them, and I watched the murder rate in the projects opposite my crumbling tenement apartment spiral into one of the highest in Manhattan.

But this essay is not about crack, or drugs, per se. Substance abuse in the inner city is merely a symptom—and a vivid symbol—of deeper dynamics of social marginalization and alienation. Of course, on an immediately visible personal level, addiction and substance abuse are among the most immediate, brutal facts shaping daily life on the street. Most important, however, the two dozen street dealers and their families that I befriended were not interested in talking primarily about drugs. On the contrary, they wanted me to learn all about their daily struggles for subsistence and dignity at the poverty line.

Through the 1980s and 1990s, slightly more than one in three families in El Barrio have received public assistance. Female heads of these impoverished households have to supplement their meager checks in order to keep their children alive. Many are mothers who make extra money by baby-sitting their neighbors' children, or by housekeeping for a paying boarder. Others may bartend at one of the half-dozen social clubs and after-hours dancing spots scattered throughout the neighborhood. Some work "off the books" in their living rooms as seamstresses for garment contractors. Finally, many also find themselves obliged to establish amorous relationships with men who are willing to make cash contributions to their household expenses.

Male income-generating strategies in the underground economy are more publicly visible. Some men repair cars on the curb; others wait on stoops for unlicensed construction subcontractors to pick them up for fly-by-night demolition jobs or window renovation projects. Many sell "numbers"—the street's version of off-track betting. The most visible cohorts hawk "nickels and dimes" of one illegal drug or another. They are part of the most robust, multibillion-dollar sector of the booming underground economy. Cocaine and crack, in particular during the mid-1980s and through the early 1990s, followed by heroin in the mid-1990s, have become the fastest-growing—if not the only—equal-opportunity employers of men in Harlem. Retail drug sales easily outcompete other income-generating opportunities, whether legal or illegal.

Why should these young men and women take the subway to work minimum-wage jobs—or even double-minimum-wage jobs—in downtown offices when they can usually earn more, at least in the short run, by selling drugs on the street corner in front of their apartment or schoolyard? In fact, I am always surprised that so many inner-city men and women remain in the legal economy and work nine-to-five plus overtime, barely making ends meet. According to the 1990 Census of East Harlem, 48 percent of all males and 35 percent of females over 16 were employed in officially reported jobs, compared with a citywide average of 64 percent for men and 49 percent for women. In the census tracts surrounding my apartment, 53 percent of all men over 16 years of age (1,923 out of 3,647) and 28 percent of all women over 16 (1,307 out of 4,626) were working legally in officially censused jobs. An additional 17 percent of the civilian labor force was unemployed but actively looking for work, compared with 16 percent for El Barrio as a whole, and 9 percent for all of New York City.

"If I Was Working Legal . . ."

Street dealers tend to brag to outsiders and to themselves about how much money they make each night. In fact, their income is almost never as consistently high as they report it to be. Most street sellers, like my friend Primo (who, along with other friends and co-workers, allowed me to tape hundreds of hours of conversation with him over five years), are paid on a piece-rate commission basis. When converted into an hourly wage, this is often a relatively paltry sum. According to my calculations, the workers in the Game Room crackhouse, for example, averaged slightly less than double the legal minimum wage—between 7 and 8 dollars an hour. There were plenty of exceptional nights, however, when they made up to ten times minimum wage—and these are the nights they remember when they reminisce. They forget about all the other shifts when they were unable to work because of police raids, and they certainly do not count as forfeited working hours the nights they spent in jail.

This was brought home to me symbolically one night as Primo and his co-worker Caesar were shutting down the Game Room. Caesar unscrewed the fuses in the electrical box to disconnect the video games. Primo had finished stashing the leftover bundles of crack vials inside a hollowed-out live electrical socket and was counting the night's thick wad of receipts. I was struck by how thin the handful of bills was that he separated out and folded neatly into his personal billfold. Primo and Caesar then eagerly lowered the iron riot gates over the Game Room's windows and snapped shut the heavy Yale padlocks. They were moving with the smooth, hurried gestures of workers preparing to go home after an honest day's hard labor. Marveling at the universality in the body language of workers rushing at closing time, I felt an urge to compare the wages paid by this alternative economy. I grabbed Primo's wallet out of his back pocket, carefully giving a wide berth to the fatter wad in his front pocket that represented Ray's share of the night's income—and that could cost Primo his life if it were waylaid. Unexpectedly, I pulled out fifteen dollars' worth of food stamps along with two $20 bills. After an embarrassed giggle, Primo stammered that his mother had added him to her food-stamp allotment.

> *Primo:*   I gave my girl, Maria, half of it. I said, "Here take it, use it if you need it for whatever." And then the other half I still got it in my wallet for emergencies.

Like that, we always got a couple of dollars here and there, to survive with. Because tonight, straight cash, I only got garbage. Forty dollars! Do you believe that?

At the same time that wages can be relatively low in the crack economy, working conditions are often inferior to those in the legal economy. Aside from the obvious dangers of being shot, or of going to prison, the physical work space of most crackhouses is usually unpleasant. The infrastructure of the Game Room, for example, was much worse than that of any legal retail outfit in East Harlem: There was no bathroom, no running water, no telephone, no heat in the winter and no air conditioning in the summer. Primo occasionally complained:

> Everything that you see here [sweeping his arm at the scratched and dented video games, the walls with peeling paint, the floor slippery with litter, the filthy windows pasted over with ripped movie posters] is fucked up. It sucks, man [pointing at the red 40-watt bare bulb hanging from an exposed fixture in the middle of the room and exuding a sickly twilight].

Indeed, the only furnishings besides the video games were a few grimy milk crates and bent aluminum stools. Worse yet, a smell of urine and vomit usually permeated the locale. For a few months Primo was able to maintain a rudimentary sound system, but it was eventually beaten to a pulp during one of Caesar's drunken rages. Of course, the deficient infrastructure was only one part of the depressing working conditions.

> *Primo:* Plus I don't like to see people fucked up [handing over three vials to a nervously pacing customer]. This is fucked-up shit. I don't like this crack dealing. Word up.
>   [gunshots in the distance] Hear that?

In private, especially in the last few years of my residence, Primo admitted that he wanted to go back to the legal economy.

> *Primo:* I just fuck up the money here. I rather be legal.
> *Philippe:* But you wouldn't be the head man on the block with so many girlfriends.
> *Primo:* I might have women on my dick right now but I would be much cooler if I was working legal. I wouldn't be drinking and the coke wouldn't be there every night.
>   Plus if I was working legally I would have women on my dick too, because I would have money.
> *Philippe:* But you make more money here than you could ever make working legit.
> *Primo:* O.K. So you want the money but you really don't want to do the job.

I really hate it, man. Hate it! I hate the people! I hate the environment! I hate the whole shit, man! But it's like you get caught up with it.
You do it, and you say, "Ay, fuck it today!" Another day, another dollar.
[pointing at an emaciated customer who was just entering] But I don't
really, really think that I would have hoped that I can say I'm gonna be
richer one day. I can't say that. I think about it, but I'm just living day
to day.

If I was working legal, I wouldn't be hanging out so much. I
wouldn't be treating you. [pointing to the 16-ounce can of Colt 45 in
my hand] In a job, you know, my environment would change . . . totally. Cause I'd have different friends. Right after work I'd go out with
a co-worker, for lunch, for dinner. After work I may go home; I'm too
tired for hanging out—I know I gotta work tomorrow.

After working a legal job, I'm pretty sure I'd be good.

Burned in the FIRE Economy

The problem is that Primo's good intentions do not lead anywhere when
the only legal jobs he can compete for fail to provide him with a livable
wage. None of the crack dealers were explicitly conscious of the links between their limited options in the legal economy, their addiction to drugs and
their dependence on the crack economy for economic survival and personal
dignity. Nevertheless, all of Primo's colleagues and employees told stories of
rejecting what they considered to be intolerable working conditions at entry-
level jobs.

Most entered the legal labor market at exceptionally young ages. By the
time they were 12, they were bagging and delivering groceries at the supermarket for tips, stocking beer off the books in local bodegas or running errands. Before reaching 21, however, virtually none had fulfilled their early
childhood dreams of finding stable, well-paid legal work.

The problem is structural: From the 1950s through the 1980s second-
generation inner-city Puerto Ricans were trapped in the most vulnerable
niche of a factory-based economy that was rapidly being replaced by service
industries. Between 1950 and 1990, the proportion of factory jobs in New
York City decreased approximately threefold at the same time that service-
sector jobs doubled. The Department of City Planning calculates that more
than 800,000 industrial jobs were lost from the 1960s through the early 1990s,
while the total number of jobs in all categories remained more or less constant at 3.5 million.

Few scholars have noted the cultural dislocations of the new service
economy. These cultural clashes have been most pronounced in the office-
work service jobs that have multiplied because of the dramatic expansion of
the finance, real estate and insurance (FIRE) sector in New York City. Service

work in professional offices is the most dynamic place for ambitious inner-city youths to find entry-level jobs if they aspire to upward mobility. Employment as mailroom clerks, photocopiers and messengers in the highrise office corridors of the financial district propels many into a wrenching cultural confrontation with the upper-middle-class white world. Obedience to the norms of highrise, office-corridor culture is in direct contradiction to street culture's definitions of personal dignity especially for males who are socialized not to accept public subordination.

Most of the dealers have not completely withdrawn from the legal economy. On the contrary—they are precariously perched on its edge. Their poverty remains their only constant as they alternate between street-level crack dealing and just-above-minimum-wage legal employment. The working-class jobs they manage to find are objectively recognized to be among the least desirable in U.S. society; hence the following list of just a few of the jobs held by some of the Game Room regulars during the years I knew them: unlicensed asbestos remover, home attendant, street-corner flier distributor, deep-fat fry cook and night-shift security guard on the violent ward at the municipal hospital for the criminally insane.

The stable factory-worker incomes that might have allowed Caesar and Primo to support families have largely disappeared from the inner city. Perhaps if their social network had not been confined to the weakest sector of manufacturing in a period of rapid job loss, their teenage working-class dreams might have stabilized them long enough to enable them to adapt to the restructuring of the local economy. Instead, they find themselves propelled headlong into an explosive confrontation between their sense of cultural dignity versus the humiliating interpersonal subordination of service work.

Workers like Caesar and Primo appear inarticulate to their professional supervisors when they try to imitate the language of power in the workplace; they stumble pathetically over the enunciation of unfamiliar words. They cannot decipher the hastily scribbled instructions—rife with mysterious abbreviations—that are left for them by harried office managers on diminutive Post-its. The "common sense" of white-collar work is foreign to them; they do not, for example, understand the logic in filing triplicate copies of memos or for postdating invoices. When they attempt to improvise or show initiative, they fail miserably and instead appear inefficient—or even hostile—for failing to follow "clearly specified" instructions.

In the highrise office buildings of midtown Manhattan or Wall Street, newly employed inner-city high school dropouts suddenly realize they look like idiotic buffoons to the men and women for whom they work. But people like Primo and Caesar have not passively accepted their structural victimization. On the contrary, by embroiling themselves in the underground economy and proudly embracing street culture, they are seeking an alternative to their social marginalization. In the process, on a daily level, they become the actual agents administering their own destruction and their community's suffering.

Both Primo and Caesar experienced deep humiliation and insecurity in their attempts to penetrate the foreign, hostile world of highrise office corridors. Primo had bitter memories of being the mailroom clerk and errand boy at a now-defunct professional trade magazine. The only time he explicitly admitted to having experienced racism was when he described how he was treated at that particular work setting.

> *Primo:* I had a prejudiced boss. . . . When she was talking to people she would say, "He's illiterate," as if I was really that stupid that I couldn't understand what she was talking about.
>
> So what I did one day—you see they had this big dictionary right there on the desk, a big heavy motherfucker—so what I just did was open up the dictionary, and I just looked up the word, "illiterate." And that's when I saw what she was calling me.
>
> So she's saying that I'm stupid or something. I'm stupid! [pointing to himself with both thumbs and making a hulking face] "He doesn't know shit."

In contrast, in the underground economy Primo never had to risk this kind of threat to his self-worth.

> *Primo:*   Ray would never disrespect me that way; he wouldn't tell me that because he's illiterate too, plus I've got more education than him. I almost got a G.E.D.

The contemporary street sensitivity to being dissed immediately emerges in these memories of office humiliation. The machismo of street culture exacerbates the sense of insult experienced by men because the majority of office supervisors at the entry level are women. In the lowest recesses of New York City's FIRE sector, tens of thousands of messengers, photocopy machine operators and security guards serving the Fortune 500 companies are brusquely ordered about by young white executives—often female— who sometimes make bimonthly salaries superior to their underlings' yearly wages. The extraordinary wealth of Manhattan's financial district exacerbates the sense of sexist-racist insult associated with performing just-above-minimum-wage labor.

"I Don't Even Got a Dress Shirt"

Several months earlier, I had watched Primo drop out of a "motivational training" employment program in the basement of his mother's housing project, run by former heroin addicts who had just received a multimillion-dollar private sector grant for their innovative approach to training the "unemployable." Primo felt profoundly disrespected by the program, and he focused his discontent on the humiliation he faced because of his inappropriate wardrobe. The fundamental philosophy of such motivational job-training programs is that "these people have an attitude problem." They take a boot-camp approach to their unemployed clients, ripping their self-esteem apart during the first week in order to build them back up with an epiphanic realization that they want to find jobs as security guards, messengers and data-input clerks in just-above-minimum-wage service-sector positions. The program's highest success rate had been with middle-aged African-American women who wanted to terminate their relationship to welfare once their children leave home.

I originally had a "bad attitude" toward the premise of psychologically motivating and manipulating people to accept boring, poorly paid jobs. At the same time, however, the violence and self-destruction I was witnessing at the Game Room were convincing me that it is better to be exploited at work than to be outside the legal labor market. In any case, I persuaded Primo and a half-dozen of his Game Room associates to sign up for the program. Even Caesar was tempted to join.

None of the crack dealers lasted for more than three sessions. Primo was the first to drop out, after the first day. For several weeks he avoided talking about the experience. I repeatedly pressed him to explain why he "just didn't show up" at the sessions. Only after repeated badgering on my part did he finally express the deep sense of shame and vulnerability he experienced whenever he attempted to venture into the legal labor market.

> *Philippe:* Yo Primo, listen to me. I worry that there's something taking place that you're not aware of, in terms of yourself. Like the coke that you be sniffing all the time; it's like every night.
>
> *Primo:* What do you mean?
>
> *Philippe:* Like not showing up at the job training. You say it's just procrastination, but I'm scared it's something deeper that you're not dealing with. Like wanting to be partying all night, and sniffing. Maybe that's why you never went back.
>
> *Primo:* The truth though—listen Felipe—my biggest worry was the dress code, 'cause my gear is limited. I don't even got a dress shirt, I only got one pair of shoes, and you can't wear sneakers at that program. They wear ties too—don't they? Well, I ain't even got ties—I only got the one you lent me.
>
> I would've been there three weeks in the same gear. T-shirt and jeans. *Estoy jodido como un bón!* [I'm all fucked up like a bum!]
>
> *Philippe:* What the fuck kinda bullshit excuse are you talking about? Don't tell me you were thinking that shit. No one notices how people are dressed.
>
> *Primo:* Yo, Felipe, this is for real! Listen to me! I was thinking about that shit hard. Hell yeah!

Hell yes they would notice, because I would notice if somebody's wearing a fucked-up tie and shirt.

I don't want to be in a program all *abochornado* [bumlike]. I probably won't even concentrate, getting dissed, like . . . and being looked at like a sucker. Dirty jeans . . . or like old jeans, because I would have to wear jeans, 'cause I only got one slack. Word though! I only got two dress shirts and one of them is missing buttons.

I didn't want to tell you about that because it's like a poor excuse, but that was the only shit I was really thinking about. At the time I just said, "Well, I just don't show up."

And Felipe, I'm a stupid [very] skinny nigga'. So I have to be careful how I dress, otherwise people will think I be on the stem [a crack addict who smokes out of a glass-stem pipe].

Philippe: [nervously] Oh shit. I'm even skinnier than you. People must think I'm a total drug addict.

Primo: Don't worry. You're white.

Obviously, the problem is deeper than not having enough money to buy straight-world clothes. Racism and the other subtle badges of symbolic power are expressed through wardrobes and body language. Ultimately, Primo's biggest problem was that he had no idea of what clothes might be appropriate in the professional, service sector context. Like Caesar, he feared he might appear to be a buffoon on parade on the days when he was trying to dress up. He admitted that the precipitating factor in his decision not to go back to the job training program was when he overheard someone accusing Candy of "looking tacky" after she proudly inaugurated her new fancy clothes at the first class. As a matter of fact, Primo had thought she had looked elegant in her skintight, yellow jumpsuit when she came over to his apartment to display her new outfit proudly to him and his mother before going to class.

Isolating oneself in inner-city street culture removes any danger of having to face the humiliations Candy, Caesar, or Primo inevitably confront when they venture out of their social circle to try to find legal employment.

. . .

Conclusion

Ooh, Felipe! You make us sound like such sensitive crack dealers.
—Caesar [COMMENTING ON THE MANUSCRIPT]

There is no panacea for the suffering and self-destruction of the protagonists in these pages. Solutions to inner-city poverty and substance abuse framed in terms of public policy often appear naive or hopelessly idealistic. Given the dimensions of structural oppression in the United States, it is atheoretical to expect isolated policy initiatives, or even short-term political reforms, to remedy the plight of the poor in U.S. urban centers in the short or medium term. Racism and class segregation in the United States are shaped in too complex a mesh of political-economic structural forces, historical legacies, cultural imperatives, and individual actions to be susceptible to simple solutions.

There are also the inevitable limits of political feasibility. For a number of complicated historical and ideological reasons the United States simply lacks the political will to address poverty in any concerted manner. Nevertheless, I hope my presentation of the experience of social marginalization in El Barrio, as seen through the struggles for dignity and survival of Ray's crack dealers and their families, contributes on a concrete practical level to calling attention to the tragedy of persistent poverty and racial segregation in the urban United States. I cannot resign myself to the terrible irony that the richest industrialized nation on earth, and the greatest world power in history, confines so many of its citizens to poverty and to prison.

. . .

The increasing material and political powerlessness of the working poor in the United States needs to become a central concern. The concentration of poverty, substance abuse, and criminality within inner-city enclaves such as East Harlem is the product of state policy and free market forces that have inscribed spatially the rising levels of social inequality discussed earlier. More subtly, this urban decay expresses itself in the growing polarization around street culture in North America, giving rise to what some observers call a "crisis in U.S. race relations." Middle-class society and its elites increasingly have been able to disassociate themselves from the ethnically distinct, urban-based working poor and unemployed who inhabit the inner city. Budget cuts and fiscal austerity have accelerated the trend toward public sector breakdown in impoverished urban neighborhoods, while services improve, or at least stay the same, in Anglo-dominated, wealthy suburban communities.

The psychological-reductionist and cultural-essentialist analyses of social marginalization that pass for common sense in the United States frame solutions to racism and poverty around short-term interventions that target the "bad attitude" of individuals. The biggest sociological unit for most poverty policy intervention, for example, is the nuclear family. Job training programs emphasize attitude and personal empowerment. Seminars designed to promote multicultural sensitivity are fashionable in both public and private sector institutions. While these initiatives are not harmful, and might even help superficially on the margins, it is the institutionalized expression of racism—America's de facto apartheid and inner-city public sector breakdown—that government policy and private sector philanthropy need to address if anything is ever to change significantly in the long run.

In other words, to draw on a classic metaphor from sports, the United States needs to level its playing field. Concretely, this means that the garbage needs to be picked up, schools have to teach, and laws must be enforced, as effectively in Latino/a, African American, Asian, and Native American communities as they are in white, middle-class suburbs. There is nothing particularly complicated or subtle about remedying the unequal provision of public funds and services across class and ethnic lines. Hundreds of short-term policy and legal reforms immediately jump to mind: from tax reform—namely, taxing the home mortgages of the upper middle class, and exempting the federal and state transfer benefits of the poor—to streamlining access to social welfare benefits and democratizing educational institutions—namely, universal affordable health care coverage, free day care, equalizing per capita funding for schools and universities, and so on.

One message the crack dealers communicated clearly to me is that they are not driven solely by simple economic exigency. Like most humans on earth, in addition to material subsistence, they are also searching for dignity and fulfillment. In the Puerto Rican context this incorporates cultural definitions of *respeto* built around a personal concern for autonomy, self-assertion, and community within constantly changing social hierarchies of statuses based on kinship, age, and gender. Complex cultural and social dimensions that extend far beyond material and logistical requirements have to be addressed by poverty policies if the socially marginal in the United States are ever going to be able to demand, and earn, the respect that mainstream society needs to share with them for its own good. Specifically, this means evaluating how public policy initiatives and the more impersonal political economy forces of the larger society interact with rapidly changing cultural definitions of gender and family. Women, children, and the elderly constitute most of the poor in the United States. Public policy intervention consequently should prioritize the needs of women and children instead of marginalizing them. Most important, poor women should not be forced to seek desperate alliances with men in order to stay sheltered, fed, clothed, and healthy. Current welfare policy explicitly encourages mothers to seek men with unreported illegal income.

. . .

The painful symptoms of inner-city apartheid will continue to produce record numbers of substance abusers, violent criminals, and emotionally disabled and angry youths if nothing is done to reverse the trends in the United States since the late 1960s around rising relative poverty rates and escalating ethnic and class segregation.

Given the bleak perspectives for policy reform at the federal level, on the one hand, or for political mobilization in the U.S. inner city, on the other, my most immediate goal in this research is to humanize the public enemies of the United States without sanitizing or glamorizing them. In documenting the depths of personal pain that are inherent to the experience of persistent poverty and institutional racism, I hope to contribute to our understanding of the fundamental processes and dynamics of oppression in the United States. More subtly, I also want to place drug dealers and street-level criminals into their rightful position within the mainstream of U.S. society. They are not "exotic others" operating in an irrational netherworld. On the contrary, they are "made in America." Highly motivated, ambitious inner-city youths have been attracted to the rapidly expanding, multibillion-dollar drug economy during the 1980s and 1990s precisely because they believe in Horatio Alger's version of the American Dream.

Like most other people in the United States, drug dealers and street criminals are scrambling to obtain their piece of the pie as fast as possible. In fact, in their pursuit of success they are even following the minute details of the classical Yankee model for upward mobility. They are aggressively pursuing careers as private entrepreneurs; they take risks, work hard, and pray for good luck. They are the ultimate rugged individualists braving an unpredictable frontier where fortune, fame, and destruction are all just around the corner, and where the enemy is ruthlessly hunted down and shot. In the specifically Puerto Rican context, resistance to mainstream society's domination and pride in street culture identity resonates with a reinvented vision of the defiant jíbaro who refused to succumb to elite society's denigration under Spanish and U.S. colonialism. The hyper-urban reconstruction of a hip-hop version of the rural jíbaro represents the triumph of a newly constituted Puerto Rican cultural assertion among the most marginalized members of the Puerto Rican diaspora. The tragedy is that the material base for this determined search for cultural respect is confined to the street economy.

At the same time, there is nothing exotically Puerto Rican about the triumphs and failures of the protagonists of this study. On the contrary, "mainstream America" should be able to see itself in the characters presented on these pages and recognize the linkages. The inner city represents the United States' greatest domestic failing, hanging like a Damocles sword over the larger society. Ironically, the only force preventing this suspended sword from falling is that drug dealers, addicts, and street criminals internalize their rage and desperation. They direct their brutality against themselves and their immediate community rather than against their structural oppressors. From a comparative perspective, and in a historical context, the painful and prolonged self-destruction of people like Primo, Caesar, Candy, and their children is cruel and unnecessary. There is no technocratic solution. Any long-term paths out of the quagmire will have to address the structural and political economic roots, as well as the ideological and cultural roots of social marginalization. The first step out of the impasse, however, requires a fundamental ethical and political reevaluation of basic socioeconomic models and human values.

22

FRATERNITIES AND RAPE ON CAMPUS

PATRICIA YANCEY MARTIN • ROBERT A. HUMMER

Conflict theory suggests that, in our society, whom and what the label "deviant" is placed on is based primarily on relative power. Those who have more authority and control define what is "normal" and what is deviant. Moreover, conflict theorists argue that social norms, including laws, generally reflect the interests of the rich and powerful. Thus, historically, we have property laws to protect against the theft of property of the land-owning classes and domestic laws that protect the status of men, as patriarchs, within the family. The reading by Patricia Yancey Martin and Robert A. Hummer (1989) exemplifies this process, in which the privileged attempt to socially construct deviance and crime to their advantage. In particular, Martin and Hummer analyze the social norms and rituals of male fraternities that contribute to the high incidence of violence against women on many college campuses.

apes are perpetrated on dates, at parties, in chance encounters, and in specially planned circumstances. That group structure and processes, rather than individual values or characteristics, are the impetus for many rape episodes was documented by Blanchard (1959) 30 years ago (also see Geis 1971), yet sociologists have failed to pursue this theme (for an exception, see Chancer 1987). A recent review of research (Muehlenhard and Linton 1987) on sexual violence, or rape, devotes only a few pages to the situational contexts of rape events, and these are conceptualized as potential risk factors for individuals rather than qualities of rape-prone social contexts.

Many rapes, far more than come to the public's attention, occur in fraternity houses on college and university campuses, yet little research has analyzed fraternities at American colleges and universities as rape-prone contexts (cf. Ehrhart and Sandler 1985). Most of the research on fraternities reports on samples of individual fraternity men. One group of studies compares the values, attitudes, perceptions, family socioeconomic status, psychological traits (aggressiveness, dependence), and so on, of fraternity and nonfraternity men (Bohrnstedt 1969; Fox, Hodge, and Ward 1987; Kanin 1967; Lemire 1979; Miller 1973). A second group attempts to identify the effects of fraternity memberships over time on the values, attitudes, beliefs, or moral

From *Gender & Society* 3, No. 4 (December 1989):457–73. Copyright © 1989 by Sociologists for Women in Society. Reprinted with the permission of Sage Publications, Inc.

precepts of members (Hughes and Winston 1987; Marlowe and Auvenshine 1982; Miller 1973; Wilder, Hoyt, Doren, Hauck, and Zettle 1978; Wilder, Hoyt, Shurbeck, Wilder, and Carney 1986). With minor exceptions, little research addresses the group and organizational context of fraternities or the social construction of fraternity life (for exceptions, see Letchworth 1969; Longino and Kart 1973; Smith 1964).

Gary Tash, writing as an alumnus and trial attorney in his fraternity's magazine, claims that over 90 percent of all gang rapes on college campuses involve fraternity men (1988:2). Tash provides no evidence to substantiate this claim, but students of violence against women have been concerned with fraternity men's frequently reported involvement in rape episodes (Adams and Abarbanel 1988). Ehrhart and Sandler (1985) identify over 50 cases of gang rape on campus perpetrated by fraternity men, and their analysis points to many of the conditions that we discuss here. Their analysis is unique in focusing on conditions in fraternities that make gang rapes of women by fraternity men both feasible and probable. They identify excessive alcohol use, isolation from external monitoring, treatment of women as prey, use of pornography, approval of violence, and excessive concern with competition as precipitating conditions to gang rape (also see Merton 1985; Roark 1987).

The study reported here confirmed and complemented these findings by focusing on both conditions and processes. We examined dynamics associated with the social construction of fraternity life, with a focus on processes that foster the use of coercion, including rape, in fraternity men's relations with women. Our examination of men's social fraternities on college and university campuses as groups and organizations led us to conclude that fraternities are a physical and sociocultural context that encourages the sexual coercion of women. We make no claim that all fraternities are "bad" or that all fraternity men are rapists. Our observations indicated, however, that rape is especially probable in fraternities because of the kinds of organizations they are, the kinds of members they have, the practices their members engage in, and a virtual absence of university or community oversight. Analyses that lay blame for rapes by fraternity men on "peer pressure" are, we feel, overly simplistic (cf. Burkhart 1989; Walsh 1989). We suggest, rather, that fraternities create a sociocultural context in which the use of coercion in sexual relations with women is normative and in which the mechanisms to keep this pattern of behavior in check are minimal at best and absent at worst. We conclude that unless fraternities change in fundamental ways, little improvement can be expected.

Methodology

Our goal was to analyze the group and organizational practices and conditions that create in fraternities an abusive social context for women. We developed a conceptual framework from an initial case study of an alleged gang rape at Florida State University that involved four fraternity men and an 18-year-old coed. The group rape took place on the third floor of a fraternity house and ended with the "dumping" of the woman in the hallway of a neighboring fraternity house. According to newspaper accounts, the victim's blood-alcohol concentration, when she was discovered, was .349 percent, more than three times the legal limit for automobile driving and an almost lethal amount. One law enforcement officer reported that sexual intercourse occurred during the time the victim was unconscious: "She was in a life-threatening situation" (*Tallahassee Democrat* 1988b). When the victim was found, she was comatose and had suffered multiple scratches and abrasions. Crude words and a fraternity symbol had been written on her thighs (*Tampa Tribune* 1988). When law enforcement officials tried to investigate the case, fraternity members refused to cooperate. This led, eventually, to a five-year ban of the fraternity from campus by the university and by the fraternity's national organization.

In trying to understand how such an event could have occurred, and how a group of over 150 members (exact figures are unknown because the fraternity refused to provide a membership roster) could hold rank, deny knowledge of the event, and allegedly lie to a grand jury, we analyzed newspaper articles about the case and conducted open-ended interviews with a variety of respondents about the case and about fraternities, rapes, alcohol use, gender relations, and sexual activities on campus. Our data included over 100 newspaper articles on the initial gang rape case; open-ended interviews with Greek (social fraternity and sorority) and non-Greek (independent) students (N = 20); university administrators (N = 8, five men, three women); and alumni advisers to Greek organizations (N = 6). Open-ended interviews were held also with judges, public and private defense attorneys, victim advocates, and state prosecutors regarding the processing of sexual assault cases. Data were analyzed using the grounded theory method (Glaser 1978; Martin and Turner 1986). In the following analysis, concepts generated from the data analysis are integrated with the literature on men's social fraternities, sexual coercion, and related issues.

Fraternities and the Social Construction of Men and Masculinity

Our research indicated that fraternities are vitally concerned—more than with anything else—with masculinity (cf. Kanin 1967). They work hard to create a macho image and context and try to avoid any suggestion of "wimpishness," effeminacy, and homosexuality. Valued members display, or are willing to go along with, a narrow conception of masculinity that stresses competition, athleticism, dominance, winning, conflict, wealth, material possessions, willingness to drink alcohol, and sexual prowess vis-à-vis women.

Valued Qualities of Members

When fraternity members talked about the kind of pledges they prefer, a litany of stereotypical and narrowly masculine attributes and behaviors was recited and feminine or women-associated qualities and behaviors expressly denounced (cf. Merton 1985). Fraternities seek men who are "athletic," "big guys," good in intramural competition, "who can talk college sports." Males "who are willing to drink alcohol," "who drink socially," or "who can hold their liquor" are sought. Alcohol and activities associated with the recreational use of alcohol are cornerstones of fraternity social life. Nondrinkers are viewed with skepticism and rarely selected for membership.[1]

Fraternities try to avoid "geeks," nerds, and men said to give the fraternity a "wimpy" or "gay" reputation. Art, music, and humanities majors, majors in traditional women's fields (nursing, home economics, social work, education), men with long hair, and those whose appearance or dress violate current norms are rejected. Clean-cut, handsome men who dress well (are clean, neat, conforming, fashionable) are preferred. One sorority woman commented that "the top ranking fraternities have the best-looking guys."

One fraternity man, a senior, said his fraternity recruited "some big guys, very athletic" over a two-year period to help overcome its image of wimpiness. His fraternity had won the interfraternity competition for highest grade-point average several years running but was looked down on as "wimpy, dancy, even gay." With their bigger, more athletic recruits, "our reputation improved; we're a much more recognized fraternity now." Thus a fraternity's reputation and status depends on members' possession of stereotypically masculine qualities. Good grades, campus leadership, and community service are "nice" but masculinity dominance—for example, in athletic events, physical size of members, athleticism of members—counts most.

Certain social skills are valued. Men are sought who "have good personalities," are friendly, and "have the ability to relate to girls" (cf. Longino and Kart 1973). One fraternity man, a junior, said: "We watch a guy [a potential pledge] talk to women. . . . We want guys who can relate to girls." Assessing a pledge's ability to talk to women is, in part, a preoccupation with homosexuality and a conscious avoidance of men who seem to have effeminate manners or qualities. If a member is suspected of being gay, he is ostracized and informally drummed out of the fraternity. A fraternity with a reputation as wimpy or tolerant of gays is ridiculed and shunned by other fraternities. Militant heterosexuality is frequently used by men as a strategy to keep each other in line (Kimmel 1987).

Financial affluence or wealth, a male-associated value in American culture, is highly valued by fraternities. In accounting for why the fraternity involved in the gang rape that precipitated our research project had been recognized recently as "the best fraternity chapter in the United States," a university official said: "They were good-looking, a big fraternity, had lots of BMWs [expensive, German-made automobiles]." After the rape, newspaper stories described the fraternity members' affluence, noting the high number of members who owned expensive cars (*St. Petersburg Times* 1988).

The Status and Norms of Pledgeship

A pledge (sometimes called an associate member) is a new recruit who occupies a trial membership status for a specific period of time. The pledge period (typically ranging from 10 to 15 weeks) gives fraternity brothers an opportunity to assess and socialize new recruits. Pledges evaluate the fraternity also and decide if they want to become brothers. The socialization experience is structured partly through assignment of a Big Brother to each pledge. Big Brothers are expected to teach pledges how to become a brother and to support them as they progress through the trial membership period. Some pledges are repelled by the pledging experience, which can entail physical abuse; harsh discipline; and demands to be subordinate, follow orders, and engage in demeaning routines and activities, similar to those used by the military to "make men out of boys" during boot camp.

Characteristics of the pledge experience are rationalized by fraternity members as necessary to help pledges unite into a group, rely on each other, and join together against outsiders. The process is highly masculinist in execution as well as conception. A willingness to submit to authority, follow orders, and do as one is told is viewed as a sign of loyalty, togetherness, and unity. Fraternity pledges who find the pledge process offensive often drop out. Some do this by openly quitting, which can subject them to ridicule by brothers and other pledges, or they may deliberately fail to make the grades necessary for initiation or transfer schools and decline to reaffiliate with the fraternity on the new campus. One fraternity pledge who quit the fraternity he had pledged described the experience during pledgeship as follows:

> This one guy was always picking on me. No matter what I did, I was wrong. One night after dinner, he and two other guys called me and two other pledges into the chapter room. He said, "Here X, hold this 25 pound bag of ice at arms' length 'til I tell you to stop." I did it even though my arms and hands were killing me. When I asked if I could stop, he grabbed me around the throat and lifted me off the floor. I thought he would choke me to death. He cussed me and called me all kinds of names. He took one of my fingers and twisted it until it nearly broke. . . . I stayed in the fraternity for a few more days, but then I decided to quit. I hated it. Those guys are sick. They like seeing you suffer.

Fraternities' emphasis on toughness, withstanding pain and humiliation, obedience to superiors, and using physical force to obtain compliance contributes to an interpersonal style that deemphasizes caring and sensitivity but fosters intragroup trust and loyalty. If the least macho or most critical pledges drop out, those who remain may be more receptive to, and influenced by, masculinist values and practices that encourage the use of force in sexual relations with women and the covering up of such behavior (cf. Kanin 1967).

Norms and Dynamics of Brotherhood

Brother is the status occupied by fraternity men to indicate their relations to each other and their membership in a particular fraternity organization or group. Brother is a male-specific status; only males can become brothers, although women can become "Little Sisters," a form of pseudomembership. "Becoming a brother" is a rite of passage that follows the consistent and often lengthy display by pledges of appropriately masculine qualities and behaviors. Brothers have a quasi-familial relationship with each other, are normatively said to share bonds of closeness and support, and are sharply set off from nonmembers. Brotherhood is a loosely defined term used to represent the bonds that develop among fraternity members and the obligations and expectations incumbent upon them (cf. Marlowe and Auvenshine [1982] on fraternities' failure to encourage "moral development" in freshman pledges).

Some of our respondents talked about brotherhood in almost reverential terms, viewing it as the most valuable benefit of fraternity membership. One senior, a business-school major who had been affiliated with a fairly high-status fraternity throughout four years on campus, said:

> *Brotherhood spurs friendship for life, which I consider its best aspect, although I didn't see it that way when I joined. Brotherhood bonds and unites. It instills values of caring about one another, caring about community, caring about ourselves. The values and bonds [of brotherhood] continually develop over the four years [in college] while normal friendships come and go.*

Despite this idealization, most aspects of fraternity practice and conception are more mundane. Brotherhood often plays itself out as an overriding concern with masculinity and, by extension, femininity. As a consequence, fraternities comprise collectivities of highly masculinized men with attitudinal qualities and behavior norms that predispose them to sexual coercion of women (cf. Kanin 1967; Merton 1985; Rapaport and Burkhart 1983). The norms of masculinity are complemented by conceptions of women and femininity that are equally distorted and stereotyped and that may enhance the probability of women's exploitation (cf. Ehrhart and Sandler 1985; Sanday 1981, 1986).

Practices of Brotherhood

Practices associated with fraternity brotherhood that contribute to the sexual coercion of women include a preoccupation with loyalty, group protection and secrecy, use of alcohol as a weapon, involvement in violence and physical force, and an emphasis on competition and superiority.

Loyalty, Group Protection, and Secrecy Loyalty is a fraternity preoccupation. Members are reminded constantly to be loyal to the fraternity and to their brothers. Among other ways, loyalty is played out in practices of group protection and secrecy. The fraternity must be shielded from criticism.

Members are admonished to avoid getting the fraternity into trouble and to bring all problems "to the chapter" (local branch of a national social fraternity) rather than to outsiders. Fraternities try to protect themselves from close scrutiny and criticism by the Interfraternity Council (a quasi-governing body composed of representatives from all social fraternities on campus), their fraternity's national office, university officials, law enforcement, the media, and the public. Protection of the fraternity often takes precedence over what is procedurally, ethically, or legally correct. Numerous examples were related to us of fraternity brothers' lying to outsiders to "protect the fraternity."

Group protection was observed in the alleged gang rape with which we began our study. Except for one brother, a rapist who turned state's evidence, the entire remaining fraternity membership was accused by university and criminal justice officials of lying to protect the fraternity. Members consistently failed to cooperate even though the alleged crimes were felonies, involved only four men (two of whom were not even members of the local chapter), and the victim of the crime nearly died. According to a grand jury's findings, fraternity officers repeatedly broke appointments with law enforcement officials, refused to provide police with a list of members, and refused to cooperate with police and prosecutors investigating the case (*Florida Flambeau* 1988).

Secrecy is a priority value and practice in fraternities, partly because full-fledged membership is premised on it (for confirmation, see Ehrhart and Sandler 1985; Longino and Kart 1973; Roark 1987). Secrecy is also a boundary-maintaining mechanism, demarcating in-group from out-group, us from them. Secret rituals, handshakes, and mottoes are revealed to pledge brothers as they are initiated into full brotherhood. Since only brothers are supposed to know a fraternity's secrets, such knowledge affirms membership in the fraternity and separates a brother from others. Extending secrecy tactics from protection of private knowledge to protection of the fraternity from criticism is a predictable development. Our interviews indicated that individual members knew the difference between right and wrong, but fraternity norms that emphasize loyalty, group protection, and secrecy often overrode standards of ethical correctness.

Alcohol as Weapon   Alcohol use by fraternity men is normative. They use it on weekdays to relax after class and on weekends to "get drunk," "get crazy," and "get laid." The use of alcohol to obtain sex from women is pervasive—in other words, it is used as a weapon against sexual reluctance. According to several fraternity men whom we interviewed, alcohol is the major tool used to gain sexual mastery over women (cf. Adams and Abarbanel 1988; Ehrhart and Sandler 1985). One fraternity man, a 21-year-old senior, described alcohol to gain sex as follows: "There are girls that you know will fuck, then some you have to put some effort into it. . . . You have to buy them drinks or find out if she's drunk enough."

A similar strategy is used collectively. A fraternity man said that at parties with Little Sisters: "We provide them with 'hunch punch' and things get wild. We get them drunk and most of the guys end up with one." "'Hunch punch,'" he said, "is a girls' drink made up of overproof alcohol and powdered Kool-Aid, no water or anything, just ice. It's very strong. Two cups will do a number on a female." He had plans in the next academic term to surreptitiously give hunch punch to women in a "prim and proper" sorority because "having sex with prim and proper sorority girls is definitely a goal." These women are a challenge because they "won't openly consume alcohol and won't get openly drunk as hell." Their sororities have "standards committees" that forbid heavy drinking and easy sex.

In the gang rape case, our sources said that many fraternity men on campus believed the victim had a drinking problem and was thus an "easy make." According to newspaper accounts, she had been drinking alcohol on the evening she was raped; the lead assailant is alleged to have given her a bottle of wine after she arrived at his fraternity house. Portions of the rape occurred in a shower, and the victim was reportedly so drunk that her assailants had difficulty holding her in a standing position (*Tallahassee Democrat* 1988a). While raping her, her assailants repeatedly told her they were members of another fraternity under the apparent belief that she was too drunk to know the difference. Of course, if she was too drunk to know who they were, she was too drunk to consent to sex (cf. Allgeier 1986; Tash 1988).

One respondent told us that gang rapes were wrong and can get one expelled, but he seemed to see nothing wrong in sexual coercion one-on-one. He seemed unaware that the use of alcohol to obtain sex from a woman is grounds for a claim that a rape occurred (cf. Tash 1988). Few women on campus (who also may not know these grounds) report date rapes, however; so the odds of detection and punishment are slim for fraternity men who use alcohol for "seduction" purposes (cf. Byington and Keeter 1988; Merton 1985).

Violence and Physical Force Fraternity men have a history of violence (Ehrhart and Sandler 1985; Roark 1987). Their record of hazing, fighting, property destruction, and rape has caused them problems with insurance companies (Bradford 1986; Pressley 1987). Two university officials told us that fraternities "are the third riskiest property to insure behind toxic waste dumps and amusement parks." Fraternities are increasingly defendants in legal actions brought by pledges subjected to hazing (Meyer 1986; Pressley 1987) and by women who were raped by one or more members. In a recent alleged gang rape incident at another Florida university, prosecutors failed to file charges but the victim filed a civil suit against the fraternity nevertheless (*Tallahassee Democrat* 1989).

Competition and Superiority Interfraternity rivalry fosters in-group identification and out-group hostility. Fraternities stress pride of membership and superiority over other fraternities as major goals. Interfraternity rivalries take many forms, including competition for desirable pledges, size of pledge class, size of membership, size and appearance of fraternity house, superiority in intramural sports, highest grade-point averages, giving the best parties, gaining the best or most campus leadership roles, and, of great importance, attracting and displaying "good looking women." Rivalry is particularly intense over members, intramural sports, and women (cf. Messner 1989).

Fraternities' Commodification of Women

In claiming that women are treated by fraternities as commodities, we mean that fraternities knowingly, and intentionally, *use* women for their benefit. Fraternities use women as bait for new members, as servers of brothers' needs, and as sexual prey.

Women as Bait   Fashionable attractive women help a fraternity attract new members. As one fraternity man, a junior, said, "They are good bait." Beautiful, sociable women are believed to impress the right kind of pledges and give the impression that the fraternity can deliver this type of woman to its members. Photographs of shapely, attractive coeds are printed in fraternity brochures and videotapes that are distributed and shown to potential pledges. The women pictured are often dressed in bikinis, at the beach, and are pictured hugging the brothers of the fraternity. One university official says such recruitment materials give the message: "Hey, they're here for you, you can have whatever you want," and "We have the best-looking women. Join us and you can have them too." Another commented: "Something's wrong when males join an all-male organization as the best place to meet women. It's so illogical."

Fraternities compete in promising access to beautiful women. One fraternity man, a senior, commented that "the attraction of girls [i.e., a fraternity's success in attracting women] is a big status symbol for fraternities." One university official commented that the use of women as a recruiting tool is so well entrenched that fraternities that might be willing to forgo it say they cannot afford to unless other fraternities do so as well. One fraternity man said, "Look, if we don't have Little Sisters, the fraternities that do will get all the good pledges." Another said, "We won't have as good a rush [the period during which new members are assessed and selected] if we don't have these women around."

In displaying good-looking, attractive, skimpily dressed, nubile women to potential members, fraternities implicitly, and sometimes explicitly, promise sexual access to women. One fraternity man commented that "part of what being in a fraternity is all about is the sex" and explained how his fraternity uses Little Sisters to recruit new members:

> *We'll tell the sweetheart [the fraternity's term for Little Sister], "You're gorgeous; you can get him." We'll tell her to fake a scam and she'll hang all over him during a rush party, kiss him, and he thinks he's done wonderful and wants to join. The girls think it's great too. It's flattering for them.*

Women as Servers   The use of women as servers is exemplified in the Little Sister program. Little Sisters are undergraduate women who are rushed and selected in a manner parallel to the recruitment of fraternity men. They are affiliated with the fraternity in a formal but unofficial way and are able, indeed required, to wear the fraternity's Greek letters. Little Sisters are not full-fledged fraternity members, however; and fraternity national offices and most universities do not register or regulate them. Each fraternity has an officer called Little Sister Chairman who oversees their organizations and activities. The Little Sisters elect officers among themselves, pay monthly dues to the fraternity, and have well-defined roles. Their dues are used to pay for the fraternity's social events, and Little Sisters are expected to attend and hostess fraternity parties and hang around the house to make it a "nice place to be." One fraternity man, a senior, described Little Sisters this way: "They are very social girls, willing to join in, be affiliated with the group, devoted to the fraternity." Another member, a sophomore, said: "Their sole purpose is social—attend parties, attract new members, and 'take care' of the guys."

Our observations and interviews suggested that women selected by fraternities as Little Sisters are physically attractive, possess good social skills, and are willing to devote time and energy to the fraternity and its members. One undergraduate woman gave the following job description for Little Sisters to a campus newspaper:

> It's not just making appearances at all the parties but entails many more responsibilities. You're going to be expected to go to all the intramural games to cheer the brothers on, support and encourage the pledges, and just be around to bring some extra life to the house. [As a Little Sister] you have to agree to take on a new responsibility other than studying to maintain your grades and managing to keep your checkbook from bouncing. You have to make time to be a part of the fraternity and support the brothers in all they do. (*The Tomahawk* 1988)

The title of Little Sister reflects women's subordinate status; fraternity men in a parallel role are called Big Brothers. Big Brothers assist a sorority primarily with the physical work of sorority rushes, which, compared to fraternity rushes, are more formal, structured, and intensive. Sorority rushes take place in the daytime and fraternity rushes at night so fraternity men are free to help. According to one fraternity member, Little Sister status is a benefit to women because it gives them a social outlet and "the protection of the brothers." The gender-stereotypic conceptions and obligations of these Little Sister and Big Brother statuses indicate that fraternities and sororities promote a gender hierarchy on campus that fosters subordination and dependence in women, thus encouraging sexual exploitation and the belief that it is acceptable.

Women as Sexual Prey   Little Sisters are a sexual utility. Many Little Sisters do not belong to sororities and lack peer support for refraining from unwanted sexual relations. One fraternity man (whose fraternity has 65 members and 85 Little Sisters) told us they had recruited "wholesale" in the prior year to "gets lots of new women." The structural access to women that the Little Sister program provides and the absence of normative supports for refusing fraternity members' sexual advances may make women in this program particularly susceptible to coerced sexual encounters with fraternity men.

Access to women for sexual gratification is a presumed benefit of fraternity membership, promised in recruitment materials and strategies and through brothers' conversations with new recruits. One fraternity man said: "We always tell the guys you get sex all the time, there's always new girls. . . . After I became a Greek, I found out I could be with females at will." A university official told us that, based on his observations, "no one [i.e., fraternity men] on this campus wants to have 'relationships.' They just want to have fun [i.e., sex]." Fraternity men plan and execute strategies aimed at obtaining sexual gratification, and this occurs at both individual and collective levels.

Individual strategies include getting a woman drunk and spending a great deal of money on her. As for collective strategies, most of our undergraduate interviewees agreed that fraternity parties often culminate in sex and that this outcome is planned. One fraternity man said fraternity parties often involve sex and nudity and can "turn into orgies." Orgies may be planned in advance, such as the Bowery Ball party held by one fraternity. A former fraternity member said of this party:

> The entire idea behind this is sex. Both men and women come to the party wearing little or nothing. There are pornographic pinups on the walls and usually porno movies playing on the TV. The music carries sexual overtones. . . . They just get schnockered [drunk] and, in most cases, they also get laid.

When asked about the women who come to such a party, he said: "Some Little Sisters just won't go. . . . The girls who do are looking for a good time, girls who don't know what it is, things like that."

Other respondents denied that fraternity parties are orgies but said that sex is always talked about among the brothers and they all know "who each other is doing it with." One member said that most of the time, guys have sex with their girlfriends "but with socials, girlfriends aren't allowed to come and it's their [members'] big chance [to have sex with other women]." The use of alcohol to help get women into bed is a routine strategy at fraternity parties.

Conclusions

In general, our research indicated that the organization and membership of fraternities contribute heavily to coercive and often violent sex. Fraternity houses are occupied by same-sex (all men) and same-age (late teens, early 20s) peers whose maturity and judgment are often less than ideal. Yet fraternity houses are private dwellings that are mostly off-limits to, and away from scrutiny of, university and community representatives, with the result that fraternity house events seldom come to the attention of outsiders. Practices associated with the social construction of fraternity brotherhood emphasize a macho conception of men and masculinity, a narrow, stereotyped conception of women and femininity, and the treatment of women as commodities. Other practices contributing to coercive sexual relations and the cover-up of rapes include excessive alcohol use, competitiveness, and normative support for deviance and secrecy (cf. Bogal-Allbritten and Allbritten 1985; Kanin 1967).

Some fraternity practices exacerbate others. Brotherhood norms require "sticking together" regardless of right or wrong; thus rape episodes are unlikely to be stopped or reported to outsiders, even when witnesses disapprove. The ability to use alcohol without scrutiny by authorities and alcohol's frequent association with violence, including sexual coercion, facilitates rape in fraternity houses. Fraternity norms that emphasize the value of maleness and masculinity over femaleness and femininity and that elevate the status of men and lower the status of women in members' eyes undermine perceptions and treatment of women as persons who deserve consideration and care (cf. Ehrhart and Sandler 1985; Merton 1985).

Androgynous men and men with a broad range of interests and attributes are lost to fraternities through their recruitment practices. Masculinity of a narrow and stereotypical type helps create attitudes, norms, and practices that predispose fraternity men to coerce women sexually, both individually and collectively (Allgeier 1986; Hood 1989; Sanday 1981, 1986). Male athletes on campus may be similarly disposed for the same reasons (Kirshenbaum 1989; Telander and Sullivan 1989).

Research into the social contexts in which rape crimes occur and the social constructions associated with these contexts illumine rape dynamics on campus. Blanchard (1959) found that group rapes almost always have a leader who pushes others into the crime. He also found that the leader's latent homosexuality, desire to show off to his peers, or fear of failing to prove himself a man are frequently an impetus. Fraternity norms and practices contribute to the approval and use of sexual coercion as an accepted tactic in relations with women. Alcohol-induced compliance is normative, whereas, presumably, use of a knife, gun, or threat of bodily harm would not be because the woman who "drinks too much" is viewed as "causing her own rape" (cf. Ehrhart and Sandler 1985).

Our research led us to conclude that fraternity norms and practices influence members to view the sexual coercion of women, which is a felony crime, as sport, a contest, or a game (cf. Sato 1988). This sport is played not between men and women but between men and men. Women are the pawns or prey in the interfraternity rivalry game; they prove that a fraternity is successful or prestigious. The use of women in this way encourages fraternity men to see women as objects and sexual coercion as sport. Today's societal norms support young women's right to engage in sex at their discretion, and coercion is unnecessary in a mutually desired encounter. However, nubile young women say they prefer to be "in a relationship" to have sex while young men say they prefer to "get laid" without a commitment (Muehlenhard and Linton 1987). These differences may reflect, in part, American puritanism and men's fears of sexual intimacy or perhaps intimacy of any kind. In a fraternity context, getting sex without giving emotionally demonstrates "cool" masculinity. More important, it poses no threat to the bonding and loyalty of the fraternity brotherhood (cf. Farr 1988). Drinking large quantities of alcohol before having sex suggests that "scoring" rather than intrinsic sexual pleasure is a primary concern of fraternity men.

Unless fraternities' compositions, goals, structures, and practices change in fundamental ways, women on campus will continue to be sexual prey for fraternity men. As all-male enclaves dedicated to opposing faculty and administration and to cementing in-group ties, fraternity members eschew any hint of homosexuality. Their version of masculinity transforms women, and men with womanly characteristics, into the out-group. "Womanly men" are ostracized; feminine women are used to demonstrate members' masculinity. Encouraging renewed emphasis on their founding values (Longino and Kart 1973), service orientation and activities (Lemire 1979), or members' moral development (Marlowe and Auvenshine 1982) will have little effect on fraternities' treatment of women. A case for or against fraternities cannot be made by studying individual members. The fraternity qua group and organization is at issue. Located on campus along with many vulnerable women, embedded in a sexist society, and caught up in masculinist goals, practices, and values, fraternities' violation of women—including forcible rape—should come as no surprise.

NOTE

1. Recent bans by some universities on open-keg parties at fraternity houses have resulted in heavy drinking before coming to a party and an increase in drunkenness among those who attend. This may aggravate, rather than improve, the treatment of women by fraternity men at parties.

REFERENCES

Adams, Aileen and Gail Abarbanel. 1988. *Sexual Assault on Campus: What Colleges Can Do*. Santa Monica, CA: Rape Treatment Center.

Allgeier, Elizabeth. 1986. "Coercive versus Consensual Sexual Interactions." G. Stanley Hall Lecture to American Psychological Association Annual Meeting, Washington, DC, August.

Blanchard, W. H. 1959. "The Group Process in Gang Rape." *Journal of Social Psychology* 49:259–66.

Bogal-Allbritten, Rosemarie B., and William L. Allbritten. 1985. "The Hidden Victims: Courtship Violence among College Students." *Journal of College Student Personnel* 43:201–4.

Bohrnstedt, George W. 1969. "Conservatism, Authoritarianism and Religiosity of Fraternity Pledges." *Journal of College Student Personnel* 27:36–43.

Bradford, Michael. 1986. "Tight Market Dries Up Nightlife at University." *Business Insurance* (March 2):2, 6.

Burkhart, Barry. 1989. Comments in Seminar on Acquaintance/Date Rape Prevention: A National Video Teleconference, February 2.

Burkhart, Barry R. and Annette L. Stanton. 1985. "Sexual Aggression in Acquaintance Relationships." Pp. 43–65 in *Violence in Intimate Relationships,* edited by G. Russell. Englewood Cliffs, NJ: Spectrum.

Byington, Diane B., and Karen W. Keeter. 1988. "Assessing Needs of Sexual Assault Victims on a University Campus." Pp. 23–31 in *Student Services: Responding to Issues and Challenges.* Chapel Hill: University of North Carolina Press.

Chancer, Lynn S. 1987. "New Bedford, Massachusetts, March 6, 1983–March 22, 1984: The 'Before and After' of a Group Rape." *Gender & Society* 1:239–60.

Ehrhart, Julie K. and Bernice R. Sandler. 1985. *Campus Gang Rape: Party Games?* Washington, DC: Association of American Colleges.

Farr, K. A. 1988. "Dominance Bonding through the Good Old Boys Sociability Network." *Sex Roles* 18:259–77.

Florida Flambeau. "Pike Members Indicted in Rape." (May 19):1, 5.

Fox, Elaine, Charles Hodge, and Walter Ward. 1987. "A Comparison of Attitudes Held by Black and White Fraternity Members." *Journal of Negro Education* 56:521–34.

Geis, Gilbert. 1971. "Group Sexual Assaults." *Medical Aspects of Human Sexuality* 5:101–13.

Glaser, Barney G. 1978. *Theoretical Sensitivity: Advances in the Methodology of Grounded Theory.* Mill Valley, CA: Sociology Press.

Hood, Jane. 1989. "Why Our Society Is Rape-Prone." *New York Times,* May 16.

Hughes, Michael J. and Roger B. Winston, Jr. 1987. "Effects of Fraternity Membership on Interpersonal Values." *Journal of College Student Personnel* 45:405–11.

Kanin, Eugene J. 1967. "Reference Groups and Sex Conduct Norm Violations." *The Sociological Quarterly* 8:495–504.

Kimmel, Michael, ed. 1987. *Changing Men: New Directions in Research on Men and Masculinity.* Newbury Park, CA: Sage.

Kirshenbaum, Jerry. 1989. "Special Report, an American Disgrace: A Violent and Unprecedented Lawlessness Has Arisen among College Athletes in All Parts of the Country." *Sports Illustrated* (February 27):16–19.

Lemire, David. 1979. "One Investigation of the Stereotypes Associated with Fraternities and Sororities." *Journal of College Student Personnel* 37:54–57.

Letchworth, G. E. 1969. "Fraternities Now and in the Future." *Journal of College Student Personnel* 10:118–22.

Longino, Charles F., Jr. and Cary S. Kart. 1973. "The College Fraternity: An Assessment of Theory and Research." *Journal of College Student Personnel* 31:118–25.

Marlowe, Anne F. and Dwight C. Auvenshine. 1982. "Greek Membership: Its Impact on the Moral Development of College Freshmen." *Journal of College Student Personnel* 40:53–57.

Martin, Patricia Yancey and Barry A. Turner. 1986. "Grounded Theory and Organizational Research." *Journal of Applied Behavioral Science* 22:141–57.

Merton, Andrew. 1985. "On Competition and Class: Return to Brotherhood." *Ms.* (September):60–65, 121–22.

Messner, Michael. 1989. "Masculinities and Athletic Careers." *Gender & Society* 3:71–88.

Meyer, T. J. 1986. "Fight against Hazing Rituals Rages on Campuses." *Chronicle of Higher Education* (March 12):34–36.

Miller, Leonard D. 1973. "Distinctive Characteristics of Fraternity Members." *Journal of College Student Personnel* 31:126–28.

Muehlenhard, Charlene L. and Melaney A. Linton. 1987. "Date Rape and Sexual Aggression in Dating Situations: Incidence and Risk Factors." *Journal of Counseling Psychology* 34:186–96.

Pressley, Sue Anne. 1987. "Fraternity Hell Night Still Endures." *Washington Post* (August 11):B1.

Rapaport, Karen, and Barry R. Burkhart. 1983. "Personality and Attitudinal Characteristics of Sexually Coercive College Males." *Journal of Abnormal Psychology* 93:216–21.

Roark, Mary L. 1987. "Preventing Violence on College Campuses." *Journal of Counseling and Development* 65:367–70.

St. Petersburg Times. 1988. "A Greek Tragedy." (May 29):1F, 6F.

Sanday, Peggy Reeves. 1981. "The Socio-Cultural Context of Rape: A Cross-Cultural Study." *Journal of Social Issues* 37:5–27.

———. 1986. "Rape and the Silencing of the Feminine." Pp. 84–101 in *Rape,* edited by S. Tomaselli and R. Porter. Oxford: Basil Blackwell.

Sato, Ikuya. 1988. "Play Theory of Delinquency: Toward a General Theory of 'Action.'" *Symbolic Interaction* 11:191–212.

Smith, T. 1964. "Emergence and Maintenance of Fraternal Solidarity." *Pacific Sociological Review* 7:29–37.

Tallahassee Democrat. 1988a. "FSU Fraternity Brothers Charged" (April 27):1A, 12A.

———. 1988b. "FSU Interviewing Students about Alleged Rape" (April 24):1D.

———. 1989. "Woman Sues Stetson in Alleged Rape" (March 19):3B.

Tampa Tribune. 1988. "Fraternity Brothers Charged in Sexual Assault of FSU Coed." (April 27):6B.

Tash, Gary B. 1988. "Date Rape." *The Emerald of Sigma Pi Fraternity* 75(4):1–2.

Telander, Rick and Robert Sullivan. 1989. "Special Report, You Reap What You Sow." *Sports Illustrated* (February 27):20–34.

The Tomahawk. 1988. "A Look Back at Rush, a Mixture of Hard Work and Fun" (April/May):3D.

Walsh, Claire. 1989. Comments in Seminar on Acquaintance/Date Rape Prevention: A National Video Teleconference, February 2.

Wilder, David H., Arlyne E. Hoyt, Dennis M. Doren, William E. Hauck, and Robert D. Zettle. 1978. "The Impact of Fraternity and Sorority Membership on Values and Attitudes." *Journal of College Student Personnel* 36:445–49.

Wilder, David H., Arlyne E. Hoyt, Beth Shuster Shurbeck, Janet C. Wilder, and Patricia Imperatrice Carney. 1986. "Greek Affiliation and Attitude Change in College Students." *Journal of College Student Personnel* 44:510–19.

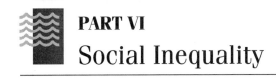

PART VI

Social Inequality

23

WHO RULES AMERICA?
The Corporate Community and the Upper Class

G. WILLIAM DOMHOFF

In the following four selections, we investigate social inequality that results from social class membership. *Social class* refers to categories of people who share common economic interests in a stratification system. Sociologists utilize various indicators to measure social class. For example, *socioeconomic status* (SES) is calculated using income, educational attainment, and occupational status. Sociologists also employ subjective indicators of social class, such as attitudes and values, class identification, and consumption patterns. This selection is taken from G. William Domhoff's 1998 book, *Who Rules America Now? Power and Politics in the Year 2000*. Using both subjective and objective indicators of social-class status, Domhoff finds that in addition to wealth, the upper class shares a distinctive lifestyle through participation in various social institutions. Domhoff argues that not only is there a cohesive upper class in the United States, but also that the upper class has a disproportionate share of power through their control over economic and political decision making in this country.

M ost Americans do not like the idea that there are social classes. Classes imply that people have relatively fixed stations in life. They fly in the face of beliefs about equality of opportunity and seem to ignore the evidence of upward social mobility. Even more, Americans tend to deny that social classes are based in wealth and occupational roles but then belie that denial through a fascination with rags-to-riches stories and the trappings of wealth.

. . .

If there is an American upper class, it must exist not merely as a collection of families who feel comfortable with each other and tend to exclude outsiders from their social activities. It must exist as a set of interrelated social institutions. That is, there must be patterned ways of organizing the lives of its members from infancy to old age that create a relatively unique style of life, and there must be mechanisms for socializing both the younger generation and new adult members who have risen from lower social levels. If the class is a reality, the names and faces may change somewhat over the years, but the social institutions that underlie the upper class must persist with remarkably little change over several generations. This emphasis on the institutionalized nature of the upper class, which reflects a long-standing empirical tradition in studies of it, is compatible with the theoretical focus of the "new institutionalists" within sociology and political science.

Four different types of empirical studies establish the existence of an interrelated set of social institutions, organizations, and social activities. They are historical case studies, quantitative studies of biographical directories, open-ended surveys of knowledgeable observers, and interview studies with members of the upper-middle and upper classes.

. . .

Prepping for Power

From infancy through young adulthood, members of the upper class receive a distinctive education. This education begins early in life in preschools that frequently are attached to a neighborhood church of high social status. Schooling continues during the elementary years at a local private school called a day school. During the adolescent years the student may remain at day school, but there is a strong chance that at least one or two years will be spent away from home at a boarding school in a quiet rural setting. Higher education will take place at one of a small number of heavily endowed private colleges and universities. Large and well-known Ivy League schools in the East and Stanford in the West head the list, followed by smaller Ivy League schools in the East and a handful of other small private schools in other parts of the country. Although some upper-class children may attend public high school if they live in a secluded suburban setting, or go to a state university if there is one of great esteem and tradition in their home state, the system of formal schooling is so insulated that many upper-class students never see the inside of a public school in all their years of education.

This separate educational system is important evidence for the distinctiveness of the mentality and life-style that exists within the upper class because schools play a large role in transmitting the class structure to their students. Surveying and summarizing a great many studies on schools in general, sociologist Randall Collins concludes: "Schools primarily teach vocabulary and inflection, styles of dress, aesthetic tastes, values and manners."[1] His statement takes on greater significance for studies of the upper class when it is added that only one percent of American teenagers attend independent private high schools of an upper-class nature.[2]

The training of upper-class children is not restricted to the formal school setting, however. Special classes, and even tutors, are a regular part of their extracurricular education. This informal education usually begins with dancing classes in the elementary years, which are seen as important for learning proper manners and the social graces. Tutoring in a foreign language may begin in the elementary years, and there are often lessons in horseback riding and music as well. The teen years find the children of the upper class in summer camps or on special travel tours, broadening their perspectives and polishing their social skills.

The linchpins in the upper-class educational system are the dozens of boarding schools founded in the last half of the nineteenth and the early part of the twentieth centuries. Baltzell concludes that these schools became "surrogate families" that played a major role "in creating an upper-class subculture on almost a national scale in America."[3] The role of boarding schools in providing connections to other upper-class social institutions is also important. As one informant explained to Ostrander in her interview study of upper-class women: "Where I went to boarding school, there were girls from all over the country, so I know people from all over. It's helpful when you move to a new city and want to get invited into the local social club."[4]

It is within these few hundred schools that are consciously modeled after their older and more austere British counterparts that a distinctive style of life is inculcated through such traditions as the initiatory hazing of beginning students, the wearing of school blazers or ties, compulsory attendance at chapel services, and participation in esoteric sports such as squash and crew. Even a different terminology is adopted to distinguish these schools from public schools. The principal is a headmaster or rector, the teachers are sometimes called masters, and the students are in forms, not grades. Great emphasis is placed on the building of "character." The role of the school in preparing the future leaders of America is emphasized through the speeches of the headmaster and the frequent mention of successful alumni. Thus, boarding schools are in many ways the kind of highly effective socializing agent that sociologist Erving Goffman calls "total institutions," isolating their members from the outside world and providing them with a set of routines and traditions that encompass most of their waking hours.[5] The end result is a feeling of separateness and superiority that comes from having survived a rigorous education. As a retired business leader told one of my research assistants: "At school we were made to feel somewhat better [than other people] because of our class. That existed, and I've always disliked it intensely. Unfortunately, I'm afraid some of these things rub off on one."[6]

Almost all graduates of private secondary schools go on to college, and almost all do so at prestigious universities. Graduates of the New England boarding schools, for example, historically found themselves at one of four large Ivy League universities: Harvard, Yale, Princeton, and Columbia. . . . Now many upper-class students attend a select handful of smaller private liberal arts colleges, most of which are in the East, but there are a few in the South and West as well.

Graduates of private schools outside of New England most frequently attend a prominent state university in their area, but a significant minority go to Eastern Ivy League and top private universities in other parts of the country. . . . A majority of private school graduates pursue careers in business, finance, or corporate law. For example, a classification of the occupations of a sample of the graduates of four private schools—St. Mark's, Groton, Hotchkiss, and Andover—showed that the most frequent occupation for all but the Andover graduates was some facet of finance and banking. Others became presidents of medium-size businesses or were partners in large corporate law firms. A small handful went to work as executives for major national corporations.[7]

. . .

Although finance, business, and law are the most typical occupations of upper-class males, there is no absence of physicians, architects, museum officials, and other professional occupations. This fact is demonstrated most systematically in Baltzell's study of Philadelphia: 39 percent of the Philadelphia architects and physicians listed in *Who's Who* for the early 1940s were also listed in the *Social Register,* as were 35 percent of the museum officials. These figures are close to the 51 percent for lawyers and the 42 percent for businessmen, although they are far below the 75 percent for bankers—clearly the most prestigious profession in Philadelphia at that time.[8]

. . .

From kindergarten through college, then, schooling is very different for members of the upper class and it teaches them to be distinctive in many ways. In a country where education is highly valued and nearly everyone attends public schools, this private system benefits primarily members of the upper class and provides one of the foundations for the old-boy and old-girl networks that will be with them throughout their lives.

Social Clubs

Just as private schools are a pervasive feature in the lives of upper-class children, so, too, are private social clubs a major point of orientation in the lives of upper-class adults. These clubs also play a role in differentiating members of the upper class from other members of society. According to Baltzell, "the club serves to place the adult members of society and their families within the social hierarchy." He quotes with approval the suggestion by historian Crane Brinton that the club "may perhaps be regarded as taking the place of those extensions of the family, such as the clan and the brotherhood, which have disappeared from advanced societies."[9] Conclusions similar to Baltzell's resulted from an interview study in Kansas City: "Ultimately, say upper-class Kansas Citians, social standing in their world reduces to one issue: where does an individual or family rank on the scale of private club memberships and informal cliques?"[10]

The clubs of the upper class are many and varied, ranging from family-oriented country clubs and downtown men's and women's clubs to highly specialized clubs for yacht owners, gardening enthusiasts, and fox hunters. Many families have memberships in several different types of clubs, but the days when most of the men by themselves were in a half dozen or more clubs faded before World War II. Downtown men's clubs originally were places for having lunch and dinner, and occasionally for attending an evening performance or a weekend party. But as upper-class families deserted the city for large suburban estates, a new kind of club, the country club, gradually took over some of these functions. The downtown club became almost entirely a luncheon club, a site to hold meetings, or a place to relax on a free afternoon. The country club, by contrast, became a haven for all members of the family. It offered social and sporting activities ranging from dances, parties, and banquets to golf, swimming, and tennis. Special group dinners were often arranged for all members on Thursday night—the traditional maid's night off across the United States.

Sporting activities are the basis for most of the specialized clubs of the upper class. The most visible are the yachting and sailing clubs, followed by the clubs for lawn tennis or squash. The most exotic are the several dozen fox hunting clubs. They have their primary strongholds in rolling countrysides from southern Pennsylvania down into Virginia, but they exist in other parts of the country as well. Riding to hounds in scarlet jackets and black boots, members of the upper class sustain over 130 hunts under the banner of the Masters of Fox Hounds Association. The intricate rituals and grand feasts accompanying the event, including the Blessing of the Hounds by an Episcopal bishop in the Eastern hunts, go back to the eighteenth century in the United States.[11]

Initiation fees, annual dues, and expenses vary from a few thousand dollars in downtown clubs to tens of thousands of dollars in some country clubs, but money is not the primary barrier in gaining membership to a club. Each club has a very rigorous screening process before accepting new members. Most require nomination by one or more active members, letters of recommendation from three to six members, and interviews with at least some members of the membership committee. Names of prospective members are sometimes posted in the clubhouse, so all members have an opportunity to make their feelings known to the membership committee. Negative votes by two or three members of what is typically a ten- to twenty-person committee often are enough to deny admission to the candidate. The carefulness with which new members are selected extends to a guarding of club membership lists, which are usually available only to club members. Older membership lists are sometimes given to libraries by members or their surviving spouses, but for most clubs there are no membership lists in the public domain.

Not every club member is an enthusiastic participant in the life of the club. Some belong out of tradition or a feeling of social necessity. One woman told Ostrander the following about her country club: "We don't feel we should withdraw our support even though we don't go much." Others mentioned a feeling of social pressure: "I've only been to [the club] once this year. I'm really a loner, but I feel I have to go and be pleasant even though I don't want to." Another volunteered: "I think half the members go because they like it and half because they think it's a social necessity."[12]

People of the upper class often belong to clubs in several cities, creating a nationwide pattern of overlapping memberships. These overlaps provide evidence for social cohesion within the upper class. An indication of the nature and extent of this overlapping is revealed by sociologist Philip Bonacich's study of membership lists for twenty clubs in several major cities across the country, including the Links in New York, the Century Association in New York, the Duquesne in Pittsburgh, the Chicago in Chicago, the Pacific Union in San Francisco, and the California in Los Angeles. Using his own original clustering technique based on Boolean algebra, his study revealed there was sufficient overlap among eighteen of the twenty clubs to form three regional groupings and a fourth group that provided a bridge between the two largest regional groups. The several dozen men who were in three or more of the clubs—most of them very wealthy people who also sat on several corporate boards—were especially important in creating the overall pattern. At the same time, the fact that these clubs often have from 1,000 to 2,000 members makes the percentage of overlap within this small number of clubs relatively small, ranging from as high as 20 to 30 percent between clubs in the same city to as low as 1 or 2 percent in clubs at opposite ends of the country.[13]

The overlap of this club network with corporate boards of directors provides evidence for the intertwining of the upper class and corporate community. In one study, the club memberships of the chairs and outside directors of the twenty largest industrial corporations were counted. The overlaps with upper-class clubs in general were ubiquitous, but the concentration of directors in a few clubs was especially notable. At least one director from twelve of the twenty corporations was a member of the Links Club, which Baltzell calls "the New York rendezvous of the national corporate establishment."[14] Seven of General Electric's directors were members, as were four from Chrysler, four from Westinghouse, three from IBM, and two from U.S. Steel. In addition to the Links, several other clubs had directors from four or more corporations. A study I did using membership lists from eleven prestigious clubs in different parts of the country confirmed and extended these findings. A majority of the top twenty-five corporations in every major sector of the economy had directors in at least one of these clubs, and several had many more.

. . .

There seems to be a great deal of truth to the earlier-cited suggestion by Crane Brinton that clubs may function within the upper class the way that the clan or brotherhood does in tribal societies. With their restrictive membership policies, initiatory rituals, private ceremonials, and great emphasis on tradition, clubs carry on the heritage of primitive secret societies. They create among their members an attitude of prideful exclusiveness that contributes greatly to an in-group feeling and a sense of fraternity within the upper class.

In concluding this discussion of . . . [social clubs and] the intersection of the upper class and corporate community, it needs to be stressed that the [social club] is not a place of power. No conspiracies are hatched there, nor anywhere else. Instead, it is a place where powerful people relax, make new acquaintances, and enjoy themselves. It is primarily a place of social bonding. The main sociological function of . . . [social] clubs is stated by sociologist Thomas Powell, based on his own interview study of members in upper-class clubs:

> The clubs are a repository of the values held by the upper-level prestige groups in the community and are a means by which these values are transferred to the business environment. The clubs are places in which the beliefs, problems, and values of the industrial organization are discussed and related to the other elements in the larger community. Clubs, therefore, are not only effective vehicles of informal communication, but also valuable centers where views are presented, ideas are modified, and new ideas emerge. Those in the interview sample were appreciative of this asset; in addition, they considered the club as a valuable place to combine social and business contacts.[15]

The Female Half of the Upper Class

During the late nineteenth and early twentieth centuries, women of the upper class carved out their own distinct roles within the context of male domination in business, finance, and law. They went to separate private schools, founded their own social clubs, and belonged to their own volunteer associations. As young women and party goers, they set the fashions for society. As older women and activists, they took charge of the nonprofit social welfare and cultural institutions of the society, serving as fund-raisers, philanthropists, and directors in a manner parallel to what their male counterparts did in business and politics. To prepare themselves for their leadership roles, in 1901 they created the Junior League to provide internships, role models, mutual support, and training in the management of meetings.

Due to the general social changes of the 1960s—and in particular the revival of the feminist movement—the socialization of wealthy young women has changed somewhat in recent decades. Many private schools are now coeducational. Their women graduates are encouraged to go to major four-year colleges rather than finishing schools. Women of the upper class are more likely to have careers; there are already two or three examples of women who have risen to the top of their family's business. They are also more likely to serve on corporate boards. Still, due to its emphasis on tradition, there may be even less gender equality in the upper class than there is in the professional stratum; it is not clear how much more equality will be attained.

The female half of the upper class has been studied by several sociologists. Their work provides an important window into the upper class and class consciousness in general as well as a portrait of the socialization of well-born women. But before focusing on their work, it is worthwhile to examine one unique institution of the upper class that has not changed very much in its long history—the debutante party that announces a young woman's coming of age and eligibility for marriage. It contains general lessons on class consciousness and the difficulties of maintaining traditional socializing institutions in a time of social unrest.

The Debutante Season

The debutante season is a series of parties, teas, and dances that culminates in one or more grand balls. It announces the arrival of young women of the upper class into adult society with the utmost of formality and elegance. These highly expensive rituals—in which great attention is lavished on every detail of the food, decorations, and entertainment—have a long history in the upper class. They made their first appearance in Philadelphia in 1748 and Charleston, South Carolina, in 1762, and they vary only slightly from city to city across the country. They are a central focus of the Christmas social season just about everywhere, but in some cities debutante balls are held in the spring as well.

Dozens of people are involved in planning the private parties that most debutantes have before the grand ball. Parents, with the help of upper-class women who work as social secretaries and social consultants, spend many hours with dress designers, caterers, florists, decorators, bandleaders, and champagne importers, deciding on just the right motif for their daughter's coming out. Most parties probably cost between $25,000 and $75,000, but sometimes the occasion is so extraordinary that it draws newspaper attention. Henry Ford II spent $250,000 on a debutante party for one of his daughters, hiring a Paris designer to redo the Country Club of Detroit in an eighteenth-century chateau motif and flying in 2 million magnolia boughs from Mississippi to cover the walls of the corridor leading to the reception room. A Texas oil and real estate family chartered a commercial jet airliner for a party that began in Dallas and ended with an all-night visit to the clubs in the French Quarter of New Orleans.[16]

The debutante balls themselves are usually sponsored by local social clubs. Sometimes there is an organization whose primary purpose is the selection of debutantes and the staging of the ball, such as the Saint Cecelia Society in Charleston, South Carolina, or the Allegro Club in Houston, Texas. Adding to the solemnity of the occasion, the selection of the season's debutantes is often made by the most prominent upper-class males in the city, often through such secret societies as the Veiled Prophet in St. Louis or the Mardi Gras krewes in New Orleans.

Proceeds from the balls are usually given to a prominent local charity sponsored by members of the upper class. "Doing something for charity makes the participants feel better about spending," explains Mrs. Stephen Van Rensselear Strong, a social press agent in New York and herself a member of the upper class.[17] It also makes at least part of the expense of the occasion tax deductible.

Evidence for the great traditional importance attached to the debut is to be found in the comments Ostrander received from women who thought the whole process unimportant but made their daughters go through it anyhow: "It think it's passé, and I don't care about it, but it's just something that's done," explained one woman. Another commented: "Her father wanted her to do it. We do have a family image to maintain. It was important to the grandparents, and I felt it was an obligation to her family to do it." When people begin to talk about doing something out of tradition or to uphold an image, Ostrander suggests, then the unspoken rules that dictate class-oriented behavior are being revealed through ritual behavior.[18]

Despite the great importance placed on the debut by upper-class parents, the debutante season came into considerable disfavor among young women as the social upheavals of the late 1960s and early 1970s reached their climax. This decline reveals that the reproduction of the upper class as a social class is an effort that must be made with each new generation. Although enough young women participated to keep the tradition alive, a significant minority refused to participate, which led to the cancellation of some balls and the curtailment of many others. Stories appeared on the women's pages across the country telling of debutantes who thought the whole process was "silly" or that the money should be given to a good cause. By 1973, however, the situation began to change again, and by the mid-1970s things were back to normal.[19]

The decline of the debutante season and its subsequent resurgence in times of domestic tranquility reveal very clearly that one of its latent functions is to help perpetuate the upper class from generation to generation. When the underlying values of the class were questioned by a few of its younger members, the institution went into decline. Attitudes toward such social institutions as the debutante ball are one indicator of whether adult members of the upper class have succeeded in insulating their children from the rest of society.

The Role of Volunteer

The most informative and intimate look at the adult lives of traditional upper-class women is provided in three different interview and observation studies, one on the East Coast, one in the Midwest, and one on the West Coast. They reveal the women to be both powerful and subservient, playing decision-making roles in numerous cultural and civic organizations but also accepting traditional roles at home vis-à-vis their husbands and children. By asking the women to describe a typical day and to explain which activities were most important to them, sociologists Arlene Daniels, Margot McLeod, and Susan Ostrander found that the role of community volunteer is a central preoccupation of upper-class women, having significance as a family tradition and as an opportunity to fulfill an obligation to the community. One elderly woman involved for several decades in both the arts and human services told Ostrander: "If you're privileged, you have a certain responsibility. This was part of my upbringing; it's a tradition, a pattern of life that my brothers and sisters do too." [20]

This volunteer role is institutionalized in the training programs and activities of a variety of service organizations, especially the Junior League, which is meant for women between 20 and 40 years of age, including some upwardly mobile professional women. "Voluntarism is crucial and the Junior League is the quintessence of volunteer work," said one woman. "Everything the League does improves the situation but doesn't rock the boat. It fits into existing institutions." [21]

Quite unexpectedly, Ostrander found that many of the women serving as volunteers, fund-raisers, and board members for charitable and civic organizations viewed their work as a protection of the American way of life against the further encroachment of government into areas of social welfare. Some even saw themselves as bulwarks against socialism. "There must always be people to do volunteer work," one said. "If you have a society where no one is willing, then you may as well have communism where it's all done by the government." Another commented: "It would mean that the government would take over, and it would all be regimented. If there are no volunteers, we would live in a completely managed society which is quite the opposite to our history of freedom." Another equated government support with socialism: "You'd have to go into government funds. That's socialism. The more we can keep independent and under private control, the better it is." [22]

Despite this emphasis on volunteer work, the women placed high value on family life. They arranged their schedules to be home when children came home from school (thirty of the thirty-eight in Ostrander's study had three or more children), and they emphasized that their primary concern was to provide a good home for their husbands. Several wanted to have greater decision-making power over their inherited wealth, but almost all wanted to take on the traditional roles of wife and mother, at least until their children were grown.

In recent years, thanks to the pressures on corporations from the women's movement, upper-class women have expanded their roles to include corporate directorships. A study of women in the corporate community by former sociologist Beth Ghiloni, now a corporate executive, found that 26 percent of all women directors had upper-class backgrounds, a figure very similar to overall findings for samples of predominantly male directors. The figure was even higher, about 71 percent, for the one-fifth of directors who described themselves as volunteers before joining corporate boards. Many of these women told Ghiloni that their contacts with male corporate leaders on the boards of women's colleges and cultural organizations led to their selection as corporate directors.[23]

Women of the upper class are in a paradoxical position. They are subordinate to male members of their class, but they nonetheless exercise important class power in some institutional arenas. They may or may not be fully satisfied with their ambiguous power status, but they bring an upper-class, antigovernment perspective to their exercise of power. There is thus class solidarity between men and women toward the rest of society. Commenting on the complex role of upper-class women, feminist scholar Catherine Stimson draws the following stark picture: "First they must do to class what gender has done to their work—render it invisible. Next, they must maintain the same class structure they have struggled to veil."[24]

Marriage and Family Continuity

The institution of marriage is as important in the upper class as it is in any level of American society, and it does not differ greatly from other levels in its patterns and rituals. Only the exclusive site of the occasion and the lavishness of the reception distinguish upper-class marriages. The prevailing wisdom within the upper class is that children should marry someone of their own social class. The women interviewed by Ostrander, for example, felt that marriage was difficult enough without differences in "interests" and "background," which seemed to be the code words for class in discussions of marriage. Marriages outside the class were seen as likely to end in divorce.[25]

The original purpose of the debutante season was to introduce the highly sheltered young women of the upper class to eligible marriage partners. It was an attempt to corral what Baltzell calls "the democratic whims of romantic love," which "often play havoc with class solidarity."[26] But the day when the debut could play such a role was long past, even by the 1940s. The function of directing romantic love into acceptable channels was taken over by fraternities and sororities, singles-only clubs, and exclusive summer resorts.

However, in spite of parental concerns and institutionalized efforts to provide proper marriage partners, some upper-class people marry members of the upper-middle and middle classes. Although there are no completely satisfactory studies, and none that are very recent, what information is available suggests that members of the upper class are no more likely to marry within their class than people of other social levels. The most frequently cited evidence on upper-class marriage patterns appears as part of biographical studies of prominent families. Though these studies demonstrate that a great many marriages take place within the class—and often between scions of very large fortunes—they also show that some marriages are to sons and daughters of middle-class professionals and managers. No systematic conclusions can be drawn from these examples.

Wedding announcements that appear in major newspapers provide another source of evidence on this question. In a study covering prominent wedding stories on the society pages on Sundays in June for two different years one decade apart, it was found that 70 percent of the grooms and 84 percent of the brides had attended a private secondary school. Two-thirds of the weddings involved at least one participant who was listed in the *Social Register,* with both bride and groom listed in the *Social Register* in 24 percent of the cases.[27] However, those who marry far below their station may be less likely to have wedding announcements prominently displayed, so such studies must be interpreted with caution.

A study that used the *Social Register* as its starting point may be indicative of rates of intermarriage within the upper class, but it is very limited in its scope and therefore can only be considered suggestive. It began with a compilation of all the marriages listed in the Philadelphia *Social Register* for 1940 and 1960. Since the decision to list these announcements may be a voluntary one, a check of the marriage announcements in the *Philadelphia Bulletin* for those years was made to see if there were any marriages involving listees in the *Social Register* that had not been included, but none was found. One in every three marriages for 1940 and one in five for 1961 involved partners who were both listed in the *Social Register.* When private-school attendance and social club membership as well as the *Social Register* were used as evidence for upper-class standing, the rate of intermarriage averaged 50 percent for the two years. This figure is very similar to that for other social levels.[28]

The general picture for social class and marriage in the United States is suggested in a statistical study of neighborhoods and marriage patterns in the San Francisco area. Its results are very similar to those of the Philadelphia study using the *Social Register.* Of eighty grooms randomly selected from the highest-level neighborhoods, court records showed that 51 percent married brides of a comparable level. The rest married women from middle-level neighborhoods; only one or two married women from lower-level residential areas. Conversely, 63 percent of eighty-one grooms from the lowest-level neighborhoods married women from comparable areas, with under 3 percent having brides from even the lower end of the group of top neighbor-hoods. Completing the picture, most of the eighty-two men from middle-level areas married women from the same types of neighborhoods, but about 10 percent married into higher-level neighborhoods. Patterns of intermar-riage, then, suggest both stability and some upward mobility through mar-riage into the upper class.[29]

Turning now to the continuity of the upper class, there is evidence that it is very great from generation to generation. This finding conflicts with the oft-repeated folk wisdom that there is a large turnover at the top of the American social ladder. Once in the upper class, families tend to stay there even as they are joined in each generation by new families and by middle-class brides and grooms who marry into their families. One study demon-strating this point began with a list of twelve families who were among the top wealthholders in Detroit for 1860, 1892, and 1902. After demonstrating their high social standing as well as their wealth, it traced their Detroit-based descendants to 1970. Nine of the twelve families still had members in the De-troit upper class; members from six of the families were directors of top cor-porations in the city. The study cast light on some of the reasons why the continuity is not even greater. One of the top wealthholders of 1860 had only one child, who in turn had no children. Another family dropped out of sight after the six children of the original 1860 wealthholder's only child went to court to divide the dwindling estate of $250,000 into six equal parts. A third family persisted into a fourth generation of four great-granddaughters, all of whom married outside of Detroit.[30]

. . .

Tracing the families of the steel executives into the twentieth century, John Ingham determined that most were listed in the *Social Register,* were mem-bers of the most exclusive social clubs, lived in expensive neighborhoods, and sent their children to Ivy League universities. He concludes that "there has been more continuity than change among the business elites and upper classes in America," and he contrasts his results with the claims made by sev-eral generations of impressionistic historians that there has been a decline of aristocracy, the rise of a new plutocracy, or a passing of the old order.[31]

. . .

It seems likely, then, that the American upper class is a mixture of old and new members. There is both continuity and social mobility, with the newer members being assimilated into the life-style of the class through participa-tion in the schools, clubs, and other social institutions described in this chap-ter. There may be some tensions between those newly arrived and those of established status—as novelists and journalists love to point out—but what they have in common soon outweighs their differences.[32]

NOTES

1. Randall Collins, "Functional and Conflict Theories of Educational Stratification," *American Sociological Review* 36 (1971):1010.

2. "Private Schools Search for a New Role," *National Observer* (August 26, 1968), p. 5. For an excellent account of major boarding schools, see Peter Cookson and Caroline Hodge Persell, *Preparing for Power: America's Elite Boarding Schools* (New York: Basic Books, 1985).

3. E. Digby Baltzell, *Philadelphia Gentlemen: The Making of a National Upper Class* (Glencoe, IL: Free Press, 1958), p. 339.

4. Susan Ostrander, *Women of the Upper Class* (Philadelphia: Temple University Press, 1984), p. 85.

5. Erving Goffman, *Asylums* (Chicago: Aldine, 1961).

6. Interview conducted for G. William Domhoff by research assistant Deborah Samuels, February 1975; see also Gary Tamkins, "Being Special: A Study of the Upper Class" (Ph.D. Dissertation, Northwestern University, 1974).

7. Steven Levine, "The Rise of the American Boarding Schools" (Senior Honors Thesis, Harvard University, 1975), pp. 128–30.

8. Baltzell, *Philadelphia Gentlemen*, pp. 51–65.

9. Baltzell, *Philadelphia Gentlemen*, p. 373.

10. Richard P. Coleman and Lee Rainwater, *Social Standing in America* (New York: Basic Books, 1978), p. 144.

11. Sophy Burnham, *The Landed Gentry* (New York: G. P. Putnam's Sons, 1978).

12. Ostrander, *Women of the Upper Class*, p. 104.

13. Philip Bonacich and G. William Domhoff, "Latent Classes and Group Membership," *Social Networks* 3 (1981).

14. G. William Domhoff, *Who Rules America?* (Englewood Cliffs, NJ: Prentice-Hall, 1967), p. 26; E. Digby Baltzell, *The Protestant Establishment*, op. cit., p. 371.

15. Thomas Powell, *Race, Religion, and the Promotion of the American Executive* (Columbus: Ohio State University Press, 1969), p. 50.

16. Gay Pauley, "Coming-Out Party: It's Back in Style," *Los Angeles Times* March 13, 1977, section 4, p. 22; "Debs Put Party on Jet," *San Francisco Chronicle* December 18, 1965, p. 2.

17. Pauley, "Coming-Out Party."

18. Ostrander, "Upper-Class Women: Class Consciousness As Conduct and Meaning," *Women of the Upper Class*, pp. 93–94; Ostrander, *Women of the Upper Class*, pp. 89–90.

19. "The Debut Tradition: A Subjective View of What It's All About," *New Orleans Times-Picayune* August 29, 1976, section 4, p. 13; Tia Gidnick, "On Being 18 in '78: Deb Balls Back in Fashion," *Los Angeles Times* November 24, 1978, part 4, p. 1; Virginia Lee Warren, "Many Young Socialites Want Simpler Debutante Party, or None," *New York Times* July 2, 1972, p. 34; Mary Lou Loper, "The Society Ball: Tradition in an Era of Change," *Los Angeles Times* October 28, 1973, part 4, p. 1.

20. Ostrander, *Women of the Upper Class*, pp. 128–29. For three other fine accounts of the volunteer work of upper-class women, see Arlene Daniels, *Invisible Careers* (Chicago: University of Chicago Press, 1988); Margot MacLeod, "Influential Women Volunteers" (paper presented to the meetings of the American Sociological Association, San Antonio, August 1984); and Margot MacLeod, "Older Generation, Younger Generation: Transition in Women Volunteers' Lives" (un-

published manuscript, 1987). For women's involvement in philanthropy and on the boards of nonprofit organizations, see Teresa Odendahl, *Charity Begins at Home: Generosity and Self-Interest among the Philanthropic Elite* (New York: Basic Books, 1990), and Teresa Odendahl and Michael O'Neill, eds., *Women and Power in the Nonprofit Sector* (San Francisco: Jossey-Bass, 1994). For in-depth interviews of both women and men philanthropists, see Francie Ostrower, *Why the Wealthy Give: The Culture of Elite Philanthropy* (Princeton, NJ: Princeton University Press, 1995).

21. Ostrander, *Women of the Upper Class*, pp. 113, 115.

22. Ostrander, "Upper-Class Women," p. 84; Ostrander, *Women of the Upper Class*, pp. 132–37.

23. Beth Ghiloni, "New Women of Power" (Ph.D. Dissertation, University of California, Santa Cruz, 1986), pp. 122, 159.

24. Daniels, *Invisible Careers*, p. x.

25. Ostrander, *Women of the Upper Class*, pp. 85–88.

26. Baltzell, *Philadelphia Gentlemen*, p. 26.

27. Paul M. Blumberg and P. W. Paul, "Continuities and Discontinuities in Upper-Class Marriages," *Journal of Marriage and the Family*, vol. 37, no. 1 (February 1975): 63–77; David L. Hatch and Mary A. Hatch, "Criteria of Social Status As Derived from Marriage Announcements in the *New York Times*," *American Sociological Review* 12 (August 1947): 396–403.

28. Lawrence Rosen and Robert R. Bell, "Mate Selection in the Upper Class," *Sociological Quarterly* 7 (Spring 1966): 157–66. I supplemented the original study by adding the information on schools and clubs.

29. Robert C. Tryon, "Identification of Social Areas by Cluster Analysis: A General Method with an Application to the San Francisco Bay Area," *University of California Publications in Psychology* 8 (1955); Robert C. Tryon, "Predicting Group Differences in Cluster Analysis: The Social Areas Problem," *Multivariate Behavioral Research* 2 (1967): 453–75.

30. T. D. Schuby, "Class Power, Kinship, and Social Cohesion: A Case Study of a Local Elite," *Sociological Focus* 8, no. 3 (August 1975): 243–55; Donald Davis, "The Price of Conspicuous Production: The Detroit Elite and the Automobile Industry, 1900–1933," *Journal of Social History* 16 (1982): 21–46.

31. John Ingham, *The Iron Barons* (Westport, CT: Greenwood Press, 1978), pp. 230–31. For the continuity of a more general sample of wealthy families, see Michael Allen, *The Founding Fortunes* (New York: Truman Talley Books, 1987).

32. For further evidence of the assimilation of new members into the upper class, see the study of the social affiliations and attitudes of the successful Jewish business owners who become part of the upper class by Richard L. Zweigenhaft and G. William Domhoff, *Jews in the Protestant Establishment* (New York: Praeger, 1982).

24

_____

BLACK WEALTH/WHITE WEALTH
A New Perspective on Racial Inequality

MELVIN L. OLIVER • THOMAS M. SHAPIRO

As G. William Domhoff argues in the previous selection, social classes do exist in America, and class distinctions can be observed through a variety of objective and subjective indicators. To understand social class relationships fully, however, sociologists also must examine racial-ethnic differences in the indicators of socioeconomic status. For example, data show persistent wealth discrepancies between African Americans and European Americans with similar achievements and credentials. Two sociologists, Melvin L. Oliver and Thomas M. Shapiro, examine this racial inequality in wealth in their study, *Black Wealth/White Wealth: A New Perspective on Racial Inequality* (1997). In the excerpt that follows, Oliver and Shapiro analyze state policies that currently and historically have curtailed opportunities for wealth accumulation among African Americans.

A frican Americans are vastly overrepresented among those Americans whose lives are the most economically and socially distressed. As William Julius Wilson has argued in *The Truly Disadvantaged,* "the most disadvantaged segments of the black urban community" have come to make up the majority of "that heterogeneous grouping of families and individuals who are outside the mainstream of the American occupational system," and who are euphemistically called the underclass.[1] With little or no access to jobs, trapped in poor areas with bad schools and little social and economic opportunity, members of the underclass resort to crime, drugs, and other forms of aberrant behavior to make a living and eke some degree of meaning out of their materially impoverished existence. Douglas Massey and Nancy Denton's *American Apartheid* has reinforced in our minds the crucial significance of racial segregation, which Lawrence Bobo calls the veritable "structural linchpin" of American racial inequality.[2]

These facts should not be in dispute. What is in dispute is our understanding of the source of such resounding levels of racial inequality. What factors were responsible for their creation and what are the sources of their continuation? Sociologists and social scientists have focused on either race or class or on some combination or interaction of the two as overriding factors responsible for racial inequality.

A focus on race suggests that race has had a unique cultural meaning in American society wherein blacks have been oppressed in such a way as to perpetuate their inferiority and second-class citizenship. Race in this context has a socially constructed meaning that is acted on by whites to purposefully limit and constrain the black population. The foundation of this social construction is the ideology of racism. Racism is a belief in the inherent inferiority of one race in relation to another. Racism both justifies and dictates the actions and institutional decisions that adversely affect the target group.[3]

Class explanations emphasize the relational positioning of blacks and whites in society and the differential access to power that accrues to the status of each group. Those classes with access to resources through the ownership or control of capital (in the Marxian variant) or through the occupational hierarchy (in the Weberian variant) are able to translate these resources into policies and structures through their access to power. In some cases this can be seen in the way in which those who control the economy also control the polity. In other cases it can be observed in the way in which institutional elites control institutions. In any case the class perspective emphasizes the relative positions of blacks and whites with respect to the ownership and control of the means of production and to access to valued occupational niches, both historically and contemporaneously. Because blacks have traditionally had access to few of these types of valued resources, they share an interest with the other have-nots. As Raymond Franklin notes in *Shadows of Race and Class,* "Ownership carries with it domination; its absence leads to subordination."[4] The subordinated and unequal status of African Americans, in the class perspective, grows out of the structured class divisions between blacks and a small minority of resource-rich and powerful whites.

Each of these perspectives has been successfully applied to understanding racial inequality. However, each also has major failings. The emphasis on race creates problems of evidence. Especially in the contemporary period, as William Wilson notes in *The Declining Significance of Race,* it is difficult to trace the enduring existence of racial inequality to an articulated ideology of racism. The trail of historical evidence proudly left in previous periods is made less evident by heightened sensitivity to legal sanctions and racial civility in language. Thus those who still emphasize race in the modern era speak of covert racism and use as evidence racial disparities in income, jobs, and housing. In fact, however, impersonal structural forces whose racial motivation cannot be ascertained are often the cause of the black disadvantage that observers identify. Likewise, class perspectives usually wash away any reference to race.[5] Moreover, the class-based analysis that blacks united with low-income white workers and other disadvantaged groups would be the most likely source of collective opposition to current social economic arrangements has given way to continued estrangement between these groups.[6] The materialist perspective that policy should address broad class groups as opposed to specific racial groups leaves the unique historical legacy of race untouched.

Despite these weaknesses it is imperative that race and class factors be taken into consideration in any attempt to understand contemporary racial inequality. It is clear, however, that a singular focus on one as opposed to another is counterproductive. Take, for example, earnings inequality. As economists assert, earnings are affected today more by class than by racial factors. Human capital attributes (such as education, experience, skills, etc.) that may result from historical disadvantages play an important role in the earnings gap between blacks and whites. But because of the unique position of black Americans, earnings must be viewed in relation to joblessness. If you do not have a job, you have no earnings. Here it is clear that race and class are important. As structural changes in the economy have occurred, blacks have been disproportionately disadvantaged. Such structural changes as the movement of entry-level jobs outside of the central city, the change in the economy from goods to service production, and the shift to higher skill levels have created a jobless black population.[7] Furthermore, increasing numbers of new entrants into the labor market find low-skill jobs below poverty wages that do not support a family. Nevertheless, race is important as well. Evidence from employers shows that negative racial attitudes about black workers are still motivating their hiring practices, particularly in reference to central-city blacks and in the service economy. In service jobs nonblacks are preferred over blacks, particularly black men, a preference that contributes to the low wages blacks earn, to high rates of joblessness, and thus to earnings inequality.[8]

Because of the way in which they reveal the effect of historical factors on contemporary processes, racial differences in wealth provide an important means of combining race and class arguments about racial inequality. We therefore turn to a theoretical discussion of wealth and race that develops aspects of traditional race and class arguments in an attempt to illuminate the processes that have led to wealth disparities between black and white Americans.

Toward a Sociology of Race and Wealth

A sociology of race and wealth must go beyond the traditional analysis of wealth that economists have elaborated. Economists begin with the assumption that wealth is a combination of inheritance, earnings, and savings and is enhanced by prudent consumption and investment patterns over a person's lifetime. Of course, individual variability in any of these factors depends on a whole set of other relationships that are sociologically relevant. Obviously one's inheritance depends on the family into which one is born. If one's family of origin is wealthy, one's chances of accumulating more wealth in a lifetime are greater. Earnings, the economists tell us, are a function of the productivity of our human capital: our education, experience, and skills. Since these are, at least in part, dependent on an investment in training activities, they can be acquired by means of inherited resources. Savings are a function of both our earning power and our consumption patterns. Spendthrifts will have little or no disposable income to save, while those who are frugal can find ways to put money aside. Those with high levels of human capital, who socially interact in the right circles, and who have knowledge of investment opportunities, will increase their wealth substantially more during their lifetime, than will those who are only thrifty. And since money usually grows over time, the earlier one starts and the longer one's money is invested, the more wealth one will be able to amass. Economists therefore explain differences in wealth accumulation by pointing to the lack of resources that blacks inherit compared to whites, their low investment in human capital, and their extravagant patterns of consumption.

Sociologists do not so much disagree with the economists' emphasis on these three factors and their relationship to human capital in explaining black-white differences in wealth; rather they are concerned that economists have not properly appreciated the social context in which the processes in question take place. Quite likely, formal models would accurately predict wealth differences. However, in the real world, an emphasis on these factors isolated from the social context misses the underlying reasons for why whites and blacks have displayed such strong differences in their ability to generate wealth. The major reason that blacks and whites differ in their ability to accumulate wealth is not only that they come from different class backgrounds or that their consumption patterns are different or that they fail to save at the same rate but that the structure of investment opportunity that blacks and whites face has been dramatically different. Work and wages play a smaller role in the accumulation of wealth than the prevailing discourse admits.

Blacks and whites have faced an opportunity to create wealth that has been structured by the intersection of class and race. Economists rightly note that blacks' lack of desirable human capital attributes places them at a disadvantage in the wealth accumulation process. However, those human capital deficiencies can be traced, in part, to barriers that denied blacks access to quality education, job training opportunities, jobs, and other work-related factors. Below we develop three concepts—the racialization of the state, the economic detour, and the sedimentation of racial inequality—to help us situate the distinct structures of investment opportunity that blacks and whites have faced in their attempts to generate wealth.

Racialization of the State

The context of one's opportunity to acquire land, build community, and generate wealth has been structured particularly by state policy. Slavery itself, the most constricting of social systems, was a result of state policy that gave blacks severely limited economic rights. Slaves were by law not able to own property or accumulate assets.[9] In contrast, no matter how poor whites were, they had the right—if they were males, that is—if not the ability, to buy land, enter into contracts, own businesses, and develop wealth assets that could build equity and economic self-sufficiency for themselves and their families. Some argue that it was the inability to participate in and develop a habit of savings during slavery that directly accounts for low wealth development among blacks today. Using a cultural argument, they assert that slaves developed a habit of excessive consumerism and not one of savings and thrift. This distorts the historical reality, however. While slaves were legally not able to amass wealth they did, in large numbers, acquire assets through thrift, intelligence, industry, and their owners' liberal paternalism. These assets were used to buy their own and their loved ones' freedom, however, and thus did not form the core of a material legacy that could be passed from generation to generation. Whites could use their wealth for the future; black slaves' savings could only buy the freedom that whites took for granted.

Slavery was only one of the racialized state policies that have inhibited the acquisition of assets for African Americans. . . . The homestead laws that opened up the East during colonial times and West during the nineteenth century created vastly different opportunities for black and white settlers. One commentator even suggests land grants "allowed three-fourths of America's colonial families to own their own farms."[10] Black settlers in California, the "Golden State," found that their claims for homestead status were not legally enforceable. Thus African Americans were largely barred from taking advantage of the nineteenth-century federal land-grant program.[11]

A centerpiece of the New Deal social legislation and a cornerstone of the modern welfare state, the old-age insurance program of the Social Security Act of 1935 virtually excluded African Americans and Latinos, for it exempted agricultural and domestic workers from coverage and marginalized low-wage workers.[12] As Gwendolyn Mink shows in "The Lady and the Tramp," men's benefits were tied to wages, military service, and unionism rather than to need or any notion of equality. Thus blacks were disadvantaged in New Deal legislation because they were historically less well paid, less fully employed, disproportionately ineligible for military service, and less fully unionized than white men. Minority workers were covered by social security and New Deal labor policies if employed in eligible occupations and if they earned the minimum amount required. Because minority wages were so low, minority workers fell disproportionately below the threshold for coverage in comparison to whites. In 1935, for example, 42 percent of black workers in occupations covered by social insurance did not earn enough to qualify for benefits compared to 22 percent for whites.[13]

Not only were blacks initially disadvantaged in their eligibility for social security, but they have disproportionately paid more into the system and received less. Because social security contributions are made on a flat rate and black workers earn less, as Jill Quadagno explains in *The Color of Welfare,* "black men were taxed on 100 percent of their income, on average, while white men earned a considerable amount of untaxed income." Black workers also earn lower retirement benefits. And benefits do not extend as long as for whites because their life span is shorter. Furthermore, since more black women are single, divorced, or separated, they cannot look forward to sharing a spouse's benefit. As Quadagno notes, again, the tax contributions of black working women "subsidize the benefits of white housewives."[14] In many ways social security is a model state program that allows families to preserve assets built over a lifetime. For African Americans, however, it is a different kind of model of state bias. Initially built on concessions made to white racial privilege in the South, the social security program today is a system in which blacks pay more to receive less. It is a prime example of how the political process and state policy build opportunities for asset accumulation sharply skewed along racial lines.

We now turn to three other instruments of state policy that we feel have been central to creating structured opportunities for whites to build assets while significantly curtailing access to those same opportunities among blacks. Sometimes the aim was blatantly racial; sometimes the racial intention was not clear. In both instances, however, the results have been explicitly racial. They are the Federal Housing Authority; the Supplementary Social Security Act, which laid the foundation for our present day Aid to Families with Dependent Children (AFDC); and the United States tax code. In each case state policies have created differential opportunities for blacks and whites to develop disposable income and to generate wealth.

FHA

As noted in earlier research, the development of low-interest, long-term mortgages backed by the federal government marked the appearance of a crucial opportunity for the average American family to generate a wealth stake. The purchase of a home has now become the primary mechanism for generating wealth. However, the FHA's conscious decision to channel loans away from the central city and to the suburbs has had a powerful effect on the creation of segregated housing in post–World War II America. George Lipsitz reports in "The Possessive Investment in Whiteness" that in the Los Angeles area of Boyle Heights, FHA appraisers denied home loans to prospective buyers because the neighborhood was "a melting pot area literally honeycombed with diverse and subversive elements."[15] Official government policy supported the prejudiced attitudes of private finance companies, realtors, appraisers, and a white public resistant to sharing social space with blacks.

The FHA's official handbook even went so far as to provide a model "restrictive covenant" that would pass court scrutiny to prospective white homebuyers. Such policies gave support to white neighborhoods like those in East Detroit in 1940. Concerned that blacks would move in, the Eastern

Detroit Realty Association sponsored a luncheon on "the benefits of an improvement association" where the speaker, a lawyer, lectured on how "to effect legal restrictions against the influx of colored residents into white communities."[16] He went on to present the elements needed to institute a legally enforceable restrictive covenant for "a district of two miles square." Such a task was too much for one man and would require an "organization" that could mobilize and gain the cooperation of "everyone in a subdivision." Imagine the hurdles that are placed in the path of blacks' attempts to move into white neighborhoods when communities, realtors, lawyers, and the federal government are all wholly united behind such restrictions!

Restrictive covenants and other "segregation markers" have been ruled unconstitutional in a number of important court cases. But the legacy of the FHA's contribution to racial residential segregation lives on in the inability of blacks to incorporate themselves into integrated neighborhoods in which the equity and demand for their homes is maintained. This is seen most clearly in the fact that black middle-class homeowners end up with less valuable homes even when their incomes are similar to those of whites. When black middle-class families pursue the American Dream in white neighborhoods adjacent to existing black communities, a familiar process occurs. As one study explains it:

> White households will begin to move out and those neighborhoods will tend to undergo complete racial transition or to "tip." Typically, when the percentage of blacks in a neighborhood increases to a relatively small amount, 10 to 20 percent, white demand for housing in the neighborhood will fall off and the neighborhood will tip toward segregation.[17]

Even though the neighborhood initially has high market value generated by the black demand for houses, as the segregation process kicks in, housing values rise at a slower rate. By the end of the racial transition housing prices have declined as white homeowners flee. Thus middle-class blacks encounter lower rates of home appreciation than do similar middle-class whites in all-white communities. As Raymond Franklin notes in *Shadows of Race and Class*, this is an example of how race and class considerations are involved in producing black-white wealth differentials. The "shadow" of class creates a situation of race. To quote Franklin:

> In sum, because there is a white fear of being inundated with lower-class black "hordes" who lack market capacities, it becomes necessary to prevent the entry of middle-class black families who have market capacities. In this way, middle-class blacks are discriminated against for purely racial reasons. . . . Given the "uncertainty inherent in racial integration and racial transition," white families—unwilling to risk falling property values—leave the area. This, of course, leads to falling prices, enabling poorer blacks' to enter the neighborhood "until segregation becomes complete."[18]

The impact of race and class is also channeled through institutional mechanisms that help to destabilize black communities. Insurance redlining begins to make it difficult and/or expensive for homes and businesses to secure coverage. City services begin to decline, contributing to blight. As the community declines, it becomes the center for antisocial activities: drug dealing, hanging out, and robbery and violence.[19] In this context the initial investment that the middle-class black family makes either stops growing or grows at a rate that is substantially lower than the rate at which a comparable investment made by a similarly well-off, middle-class white in an all-white community would gain in value. Racialized state policy contributed to this pattern, and the pattern continues unabated today.

AFDC

Within the public mind and according to the current political debate, AFDC has become synonymous with "welfare," even though it represents less than 10 percent of all assistance for the poor.[20] The small sums paid to women and their children are designed not to provide families a springboard for their future but to help them survive in a minimal way from day to day. When the initial legislation for AFDC was passed, few of its supporters envisioned a program that would serve large numbers of African American women and their children; the ideal recipient, according to Michael Katz in *In the Shadow of the Poor House,* "was a white widow and her young children." Until the mid-1960s states enforced this perception through the establishment of eligibility requirements that disproportionately excluded black women and their children. Southern states routinely deemed black women and their children as "unsuitable" for welfare by way of demeaning home inspections and searches. Northern states likewise created barriers that were directly targeted at black-female-headed families. They participated in "midnight raids" to discover whether a "man was in the house" or recomputed budgets to find clients ineligible and keep them off the rolls. Nonetheless, by the mid-1960s minorities were disproportionately beneficiaries of AFDC, despite intentions to the contrary. In 1988 while blacks and Hispanics made up only 44 percent of all women who headed households, they constituted 55 percent of all AFDC recipients.[21]

In exchange for modest and sometimes niggardly levels of income support, women must go through an "assets test" before they are eligible. Michael Sherraden describes it this way in his *Assets and the Poor:*

> The assets test requires that recipients have no more than minimal assets (usually $1,500, with home equity excluded) in order to become or remain eligible for the program. The asset test effectively prohibits recipients from accumulating savings.[22]

As a consequence, women enter welfare on the economic edge. They deplete almost all of their savings in order to become eligible for a program that will not provide more than a subsistence living. What little savings remain are usually drawn down to meet routine shortfalls and emergencies. The result is that AFDC has become for many women, especially African American women, a state-sponsored policy to encourage and maintain asset poverty.

To underscore the impact of AFDC's strictures let us draw the distinction between this program and Supplementary Security Income (SSI), a program that provides benefits for women and children whose spouses have died or become disabled after paying into social security. In contrast to AFDC benefits, SSI payments are generous. More important perhaps, eligibility for SSI does not require drawing down a family's assets as part of a "means test." The result, which is built into the structure of American welfare policy, is that "means tested" programs like AFDC and "non-means tested" social insurance programs like social security and SSI, in Michael Katz's words, have "preserved class distinctions" and "in no way redistribute income."[23] It is also an example of how the racialization of the state preserves and broadens the already deep wealth divisions between black and white.

The Internal Revenue Code

A substantial portion of state expenditures take the form of tax benefits, or "fiscal welfare." These benefits are hidden in the tax code as taxes individuals do not have to pay because the government has decided to encourage certain types of activity and behavior and not others. In *America: Who Really Pays the Taxes?* Donald Barlett and James Steele write that one of the most cherished privileges of the very rich and powerful resides in their ability to influence the tax code for their own benefit by protecting capital assets. Tax advantages may come in the form of different rates on certain types of income, tax deferral, or deductions, exclusions, and credits. Many are asset-based: if you own certain assets, you receive a tax break. In turn, these tax breaks directly help people accumulate financial and real assets. They benefit not only the wealthy but the broad middle class of homeowners and pension holders as well. More important, since blacks have fewer assets to begin with, the effect of the tax code's "fiscal welfare" is to limit the flow of tax relief to blacks and to redirect it to those who already have assets. The seemingly race-neutral tax code thus generates a racial effect that deepens rather than equalizes the economic gulf between blacks and whites.

Two examples will illustrate how the current functioning of the tax code represents yet another form of the "racialization of state policy." The *lower tax rates on capital gains* and the *deduction for home mortgages and real estate taxes,* we argue, flow differentially to blacks and whites because of the fact that blacks generally have fewer and different types of assets than whites with similar incomes.

For most of our nation's tax history the Internal Revenue Code has encouraged private investment by offering lower tax rates for income gained through "capital assets." This policy exists to encourage investment and further asset accumulation, not to provide more spendable income. In 1994, earned income in the top bracket was taxed at 39.6 percent, for example, while capital gains were taxed at 24 percent, a figure that can go as low as 14 percent. One has to be networked with accountants, tax advisers, investors, partners, and friends knowledgeable about where to channel money to take advantage of these breaks. Capital gains may be derived from the sale of stocks, bonds, commodities, and other assets. In 1989 the IRS reported that $150.2 billion in capital gains income was reported by taxpayers.[24] While this sounds like a lot of capital gains for everyone to divvy up, the lion's share (72 percent) went to individuals and families earning more than $100,000 yearly. These families represented only 1 percent of all tax filers. The remaining $42 billion in capital gains income was reported by only 7.2 million people with incomes of under $100,000 per year. This group represented only 6 percent of tax filers. Thus for more than nine of every ten tax filers (93 percent) no capital gains income was reported. Clearly then, the tax-reduction benefits on capital gains income are highly concentrated among the nation's wealthiest individuals and families. Thus it would follow that blacks, given their lower incomes and fewer assets, would be much less likely than whites to gain the tax advantage associated with capital gains. The black disadvantage becomes most obvious when one compares middle-class and higher-income blacks to whites at a similar level of earnings. Despite comparable incomes, middle-class blacks have fewer of their wealth holdings in capital-producing assets than similarly situated whites. Our data show that among high-earning families ($50,000 a year or more) 17 percent of whites' assets are in stocks, bonds, and mortgages versus 5.4 percent for blacks. Thus while race-neutral in intent, the current tax policy on capital gains provides disproportionate benefits to high-income whites, while limiting a major tax benefit to practically all African Americans.

Accessible to a larger group of Americans are those tax deductions, exclusions, and deferrals that the IRS provides to homeowners. Four IRS-mandated benefits can flow from home ownership: (1) the home mortgage interest deduction; (2) the deduction for local real estate taxes; (3) the avoidance of taxes on the sale of a home when it is "rolled over" into another residence; and, (4) the one-time permanent exclusion of up to $125,000 of profit on the sale of a home after the age of fifty-five. Put quite simply, since blacks are less likely to own homes, they are less likely to be able to take advantage of these benefits. Furthermore, since black homes are on average less expensive than white homes, blacks derive less benefit than whites when they do utilize these tax provisions. And finally, since most of the benefits in question here are available only when taxpayers itemize their deductions, there is a great deal of concern that many black taxpayers may not take advantage of the tax breaks they are eligible for because they file the short tax form. The stakes here are very high. The subsidy that goes to homeowners in the form of tax deductions for mortgage interest and property taxes alone comes to $54 billion, about $20 billion of which goes to the top 5 percent of taxpayers.[25]

These examples illustrate how the U.S. tax code channels benefits and encourages property and capital asset accumulation differentially by race. They are but a few of several examples that could have been used. Tax provisions pertaining to inheritance, gift income, alimony payments, pensions and Keogh accounts, and property appreciation, along with the marriage tax and the child-care credit on their face are not color coded, yet they carry with them the potential to channel benefits away from most blacks and toward some whites. State policy has racialized the opportunities for the development of wealth, creating and sustaining the existing patterns of wealth inequality and extending them into the future.

. . .

The Sedimentation of Racial Inequality

The disadvantaged status of contemporary African Americans cannot be divorced from the historical processes that undergird racial inequality. The past has a living effect on the present. We argue that the best indicator of this sedimentation of racial inequality is wealth. Wealth is one indicator of material disparity that captures the historical legacy of low wages, personal and organizational discrimination, and institutionalized racism. The low levels of wealth accumulation evidenced by current generations of black Americans best represent the position of blacks in the stratificational order of American society.

Each generation of blacks generally began life with few material assets and confronted a world that systematically thwarted any attempts to economically better their lives. In addition to the barriers that we have just described in connection with the racialization of state policy and the economic detour, blacks also faced other major obstacles in their quest for economic security. In the South, for example, as W. E. B. Du Bois notes in *Black Reconstruction in America,* blacks were tied to a system of peonage that kept them in debt virtually from cradle to grave. Schooling was segregated and unequally funded. Blacks in the smokestack industries of the North and the South were paid less and assigned to unskilled and dirty jobs.[26] The result was that generation after generation of blacks remained anchored to the lowest economic status in American society. The effect of this "generation after generation" of poverty and economic scarcity for the accumulation of wealth has been to "sediment" this kind of inequality into the social structure.

The sedimentation of inequality occurred because blacks had barriers thrown up against them in their quest for material self-sufficiency. Whites in general, but well-off whites in particular, were able to amass assets and use their secure economic status to pass their wealth from generation to generation. What is often not acknowledged is that the accumulation of wealth for some whites is ultimately tied to the poverty of wealth for most blacks.[27] Just as blacks have had "cumulative disadvantages," whites have had "cumulative advantages." Practically, every circumstance of bias and discrimination against blacks has produced a circumstance and opportunity of positive gain for whites. When black workers were paid less than white workers, white workers gained a benefit; when black businesses were confined to the segregated black market, white businesses received the benefit of diminished competition; when FHA policies denied loans to blacks, whites were the beneficiaries of the spectacular growth of good housing and housing equity in the suburbs. The cumulative effect of such a process has been to sediment blacks at the bottom of the social hierarchy and to artificially raise the relative position of some whites in society.

To understand the sedimentation of racial inequality, particularly with respect to wealth, is to acknowledge the way in which structural disadvantages have been layered one upon the other to produce black disadvantage and white privilege. Returning again to the Federal Housing Act of 1934, we may recall that the federal government placed its credit behind private loans to homebuyers, thus putting home ownership within the reach of millions of citizens for the first time. White homeowners who had taken advantage of FHA financing policies saw the value of their homes increase dramatically, especially during the 1970s when housing prices tripled.[28] As previously noted, the same FHA policies excluded blacks and segregated them into all-black areas that either were destroyed during urban renewal in the sixties or benefited only marginally from the inflation of the 1970s. Those who were locked out of the housing market by FHA policies and who later sought to become first-time homebuyers faced rising housing costs that curtailed their ability to purchase the kind of home they desired. The postwar generation of whites whose parents gained a foothold in the housing market through the FHA will harvest a bounteous inheritance in the years to come.[29] Thus the process of asset accumulation that began in the 1930s has become layered over and over by social and economic trends that magnify inequality over time and across generations.

NOTES

1. Wilson (1987, p. 8).
2. Bobo (1989, p. 307).
3. See Omi and Winant (1986).
4. Franklin (1991, p. xviii).
5. See Baran and Sweezy (1966) and Cox (1948).
6. See Hill (1977) and Jacobson (1968).
7. See Johnson and Oliver (1992); Kasarda (1988); and Wilson (1987).
8. See Kirschenman and Neckerman (1991).
9. See Butler (1991); Light (1972); and Myrdal (1944).
10. Anderson (1994, p. 123).
11. See Beasley (1919).
12. See Quadagno (1994, pp. 20–24).

13. Quadagno (1994, p. 161).
14. Ibid., p. 162.
15. Lipsitz (1995).
16. Thomas (1992, p. 140).
17. Mieszkowski and Syron (1979, p. 35).
18. Franklin (1991, p. 126).
19. See Skogan (1990).
20. See Rank (1994) and Stack (1974).
21. Sherraden (1991, p. 63).
22. Ibid., p. 64.
23. See Katz (1986, p. 247).
24. See Barlett and Steele (1992).
25. See Jackman and Jackman (1980); Ong and Grigsby (1988); and Horton and Thomas (1993).
26. See Jaynes (1986) and Lieberson (1980); Bloch (1969) and Bonacich (1976).
27. See Blauner (1972); Lipsitz (1995); and Thurow (1975).
28. See Adams (1988) and Stutz and Kartman (1982).
29. See Levy and Michel (1996).

REFERENCES

Adams, John. 1988. "Growth of U.S. Cities and Recent Trends in Urban Real Estate Values." Pp. 108–45 in *Cities and Their Vital Systems,* edited by J. H. Ausubel and R. Herman. Washington, DC: National Academy Press.

Anderson, Claud. 1994. *Black Labor, White Wealth: The Search for Power and Economic Justice.* Edgewood, MD: Duncan and Duncan.

Baran, Paul A. and Paul M. Sweezy. 1966. *Monopoly Capital.* New York: Monthly Review Press.

Barlett, Donald L. and James B. Steele. 1992. *America: What Went Wrong?* Kansas City: Andrews and McMeel.

———. 1994. *America: Who Really Pays the Taxes?* New York: Touchstone.

Beasley, Delilah. 1919. *Negro Trail Blazers of California.* Los Angeles: Times Mirror Print and Binding House.

Blauner, Bob. 1972. *Racial Oppression in America.* New York: Harper.

Bloch, Herman David. 1969. *The Circle of Discrimination: An Economic and Social Study of the Black Man in New York.* New York: New York University Press.

Bobo, Lawrence. 1989. "Keeping the Linchpin in Place: Testing the Multiple Sources of Opposition to Residential Integration." *Revue Internationale de Psychologie Sociale* 2:306–23.

Bonacich, Edna. 1976. "Advanced Capitalism and Black-White Relations in the United States: A Split Labor Market Interpretation." *American Sociological Review* 37:547–59.

Butler, John Sibley. 1991. *Entrepreneurship and Self-Help among Black Americans: A Reconsideration of Race and Economics.* Albany, NY: State University of New York Press.

Cox, Oliver C. 1948. *Caste, Race, and Class.* New York: Modern Reader Paperback.

Du Bois, W. E. B. 1935. *Black Reconstruction in America.* New York: Harcourt, Brace.

Franklin, Raymond S. 1991. *Shadows of Race and Class.* Minneapolis: University of Minnesota Press.

Hill, Herbert. 1977. *Black Labor and the American Legal System: Race, Work, and the Law.* Madison, WI: University of Wisconsin Press.

Horton, Hayward Derrick and Melvin E. Thomas. 1993. "Race, Class, and Family Structure: Differences in Housing Values for Black and White Homeowners." Unpublished manuscript.

Jackman, Mary R. and Robert W. Jackman. 1980. "Racial Inequalities in Home Ownership." *Social Forces* 58:1221–33.

Jacobson, Julius, ed. 1968. *The Negro and the American Labor Movement.* New York: Anchor.

Jaynes, Gerald D. 1986. *Branches without Roots: Genesis of the Black Working Class in the American South, 1862–1882.* New York: Oxford University Press.

Johnson, James H. and Melvin L. Oliver. 1992. "Structural Changes in the U.S. Economy and Black Male Joblessness: A Reassessment." Pp. 113–47 in *Urban Labor Markets and Job Opportunity,* edited by George Peterson and Wayne Vroman. Washington, DC: Urban Institute Press.

Kasarda, John D. 1988. "Jobs, Migration, and Emerging Urban Mismatches." Pp. 148–98 in *Urban Change and Poverty,* edited by M. G. H. McGeary and L. E. Lynn, Jr. Washington, DC: National Academy Press.

Katz, Michael. 1986. *In the Shadow of the Poor House: A Social History of Welfare in America.* New York: Basic Books.

Kirschenman, Joleen and Katherine Neckerman. 1991. "'We'd Love to Hire Them But': The Meaning of Race for Employers." Pp. 203–32 in *The Urban Underclass,* edited by Christopher Jencks and Paul Peterson. Washington, DC: Brookings Institution.

Levy, Frank S. and Richard Michel. 1996. "An Economic Bust for the Baby Boom." *Challenge,* March/April: 33–39.

Lieberson, Stanley. 1980. *A Piece of the Pie.* Berkeley: University of California Press.

Light, Ivan. 1972. *Ethnic Enterprise in America.* Berkeley: University of California Press.

Lipsitz, George. 1995. "The Possessive Investment in Whiteness: The 'White' Problem in American Studies." *American Quarterly,* Fall.

Massey, Douglas S. and Nancy A. Denton. 1993. *American Apartheid: Segregation and the Making of the Underclass.* Cambridge, MA: Harvard University Press.

Mieszkowski, Peter and Richard F. Syron. 1979. "Economic Explanations for Housing Segregation." *New England Economic Review,* November–December: 33–34.

Mink, Gwendolyn. 1990. "The Lady and the Tramp: Gender, Race, and the Origins of the American Welfare State." Pp. 92–122 in *Women, the State, and Welfare,* edited by Linda Gordon. Madison, WI: University of Wisconsin Press.

Myrdal, Gunnar. 1944. *An American Dilemma.* New York: Harper.

Omi, Michael and Howard Winant. 1986. *Racial Formation in the United States: From the 1960s to the 1980s.* New York: Routledge.

Ong, Pual and Eugene Grigsby, III. 1988. "Race and Life Cycle Effects on Home Ownership in Los Angeles, 1970 to 1980." *Urban Affairs Quarterly* 23:601–15.

Quadagno, Jill. 1994. *The Color of Welfare.* New York: Oxford University Press.

Rank, Mark R. 1994. *Living on the Edge: The Realities of Welfare in America.* New York: Columbia University Press.

Sherraden, Michael. 1991. *Assets and the Poor: A New American Welfare Policy.* New York: Sharpe.

Skogan, Wesley G. 1990. *Disorder and Decline: Crime and the Spiral of Decay in American Neighborhoods.* New York: Free Press.

Stack, Carol. 1974. *All Our Kin.* New York: Harper.

Stutz, Fred and A. E. Kartman. 1982. "Housing Affordability and Spatial Price Variation in the United States." *Economic Geography* 58:221–35.

Thomas, Richard Walter. 1992. *Life for Us Is What We Make It: Building Black Community in Detroit, 1915–1945.* Bloomington: Indiana University Press.

Thurow, Lester C. 1975. *Generating Inequality: Mechanisms of Distribution in the U.S. Economy.* New York: Basic Books.

Wilson, William J. 1978. *The Declining Significance of Race.* Chicago: University of Chicago Press.

———. 1987. *The Truly Disadvantaged.* Chicago: University of Chicago Press.

25

POSITIVE FUNCTIONS OF THE UNDESERVING POOR
Uses of the Underclass in America

HERBERT J. GANS

As the previous reading by Oliver and Shapiro demonstrated, the American Dream and the accumulation of wealth have been difficult to obtain for African Americans. They also have been impossible goals for the poor. Instead, the indigent struggle to meet the economic requirements of everyday survival. This 1994 article by Herbert J. Gans provides a functional analysis of poverty. Contrary to the conflict theory views presented in the readings by Domhoff and by Oliver and Shapiro, where power is the central characteristic of class relations, the functionalist view of social class is concerned with how stratification may benefit society. Utilizing this perspective, Gans outlines the benefits or functions that the poor serve in our society.

I. Introduction

Poverty, like any other social phenomenon, can be analyzed in terms of the *causes* which initiate and perpetuate it, but once it exists, it can also be studied in terms of the consequences or *functions* which follow. These functions can be both *positive* and *negative,* adaptive and destructive, depending on their nature and the people and interests affected.

Poverty has many negative functions (or dysfunctions), most for the poor themselves, but also for the nonpoor. Among those of most concern to

From *Koelner Zeitschrift für Soziologie und Soziolpsychologie,* Sonderheft No. 32, 48–62. Copyright © 1992 by Westdeutscher Verlag GmbH. Reprinted by permission from Westdeutscher Verlag GmbH.

both populations, perhaps the major one is that a small but visible proportion of poor people is involved in activities which threaten their physical safety, for example street crime, or which deviate from important norms claimed to be "mainstream," such as failing to work, bearing children in adolescence and out of wedlock, and being "dependent" on welfare. In times of high unemployment, illegal and even legal immigrants are added to this list for endangering the job opportunities of native-born Americans.

Furthermore, many better-off Americans believe that the number of poor people who behave in these ways is far larger than it actually is. More important, many think that poor people act as they do because of moral shortcomings that express themselves in lawlessness or in the rejection of mainstream norms. Like many other sociologists, however, I argue that the behavior patterns which concern the more fortunate classes are *poverty-related*, because they are, and have historically been, associated with poverty. After all, mugging is only practiced by the poor. They are in fact caused by poverty, although a variety of other causes must also be at work since most poor people are not involved in any of these activities, including mugging.

Because their criminal or disapproved behavior is ascribed to moral shortcomings, the poor people who resort to it are often classified as unworthy or *undeserving*. For example, even though the failure of poor young men (or women) to work may be the effect of a lack of jobs, they are frequently accused of laziness, and then judged undeserving. Likewise, even though poor young mothers may decide not to marry the fathers of their children, because they, being jobless, cannot support them, the women are still accused of violating conventional familial norms, and also judged undeserving. Moreover, once judged to be undeserving, poor people are then no longer thought to be deserving of public aid that is financially sufficient and secure enough to help them escape poverty.

Judgments of the poor as undeserving are not based on evidence, but derive from a stereotype, even if, like most others, it is a stereotype with a "kernel of truth" (e.g., the monopolization of street crime by the poor). . . . It is not difficult to understand why people, poor and more fortunate, are fearful of street crime committed by poor people, and even why the jobless poor and welfare recipients, like paupers before them, may be perceived as economic threats for not working and drawing on public funds, at least in bad economic times. Also, one can understand why other forms of poverty-related behavior, such as the early sexual activity of poor youngsters and the dramatic number of poor single-parent families are viewed as moral threats, since they violate norms thought to uphold the two-parent nuclear family and related normative bases of the social order. However, there would seem to be no inherent reason for exaggerating these threats, for example, in the case of welfare recipients who obtain only a tiny proportion of governmental expenditures, or more generally, by stereotyping poor people as undeserving without evidence of what they have and have not done, and why.

One reason, if not the only one, for the exaggeration and the stereotyping, and for the continued attractiveness of the concept of the undeserving poor itself, is that undeservingness has a number of *positive* functions for the better-off population. Some of these functions, or uses, are positive for everyone who is not poor, but most are positive for only some people, interest groups, and institutions, ranging from moderate income to wealthy ones. Needless to say, that undeservingness has uses for some people does not justify it; the existence of functions just helps to explain why it persists.

My notion of function, or empirically observable adaptive consequence, is adapted from the classic conceptual scheme of Robert K. Merton.[1] My analysis will concentrate on those positive functions which Merton conceptualized as *latent,* which are unrecognized and/or unintended, but with the proviso that the functions which are identified as latent would probably not be abolished once they were widely recognized. Positive functions are, after all, also benefits, and people are not necessarily ready to give up benefits, including unintended ones, even if they become aware of them.[2]

The rest of this article deals only with the functions of the poor labeled undeserving. It can also be read as a sequel to an earlier article, in which I analyzed the positive functions of poverty without distinguishing between the deserving and undeserving poor.[3]

II. Functions of the Undeserving Poor[4]

I will discuss five sets of positive functions: microsocial, economic, normative-cultural, political, and macrosocial, which I divide into 13 specific functions, although the sets are arbitrarily chosen and interrelated, and I could add many more functions. The functions are not listed in order of importance, for such a listing is not possible without empirical research on the various beneficiaries of undeservingness.

Two Microsocial Functions

1. *Risk reduction.* Perhaps the primary use of the idea of the undeserving poor, primary because it takes place at the microsocial scale of everyday life, is that it distances the labeled from those who label them. By stigmatizing people as undeserving, labelers protect themselves from the responsibility of having to associate with them, or even to treat them like moral equals, which reduces the risk of being hurt or angered by them. Risk reduction is a way of dealing with actual or imagined threats to physical safety, for example from people who might be muggers, or cultural threats attributed to poor youngsters or normative ones imagined to come from welfare recipients. All pejorative labels and stereotypes serve this function, which may help to explain why there are so many such labels.

2. *Scapegoating and displacement.* By being thought undeserving, the stig-

matized poor can be blamed for virtually any shortcoming of everyday life which can be credibly ascribed to them—violations of the laws of logic or social causation notwithstanding. Faulting the undeserving poor can also support the desire for revenge and punishment. In a society in which punishment is reserved for legislative, judicial, and penal institutions, *feelings* of revenge and punitiveness toward the undeserving poor supply at least some emotional satisfaction.

Since labeling poor people undeserving opens the door for nearly unlimited scapegoating, the labeled are also available to serve what I call the displacement function. Being too weak to object, the stigmatized poor can be accused of having caused social problems which they did not actually cause and can serve as cathartic objects on which better-off people can unload their own problems, as well as those of the economy, the polity, or of any other institution, for the shortcomings of which the poor can be blamed.

Whether societywide changes in the work ethic are displaced on to "shiftlessness," or economic stagnation on to "welfare dependency," the poor can be declared undeserving for what ails the more affluent. This may also help to explain why the national concern with poor Black unmarried mothers, although usually ascribed to the data presented in the 1965 Moynihan Report, did not gather steam until the beginning of the decline of the economy in the mid-1970s. Similarly, the furor about poor "babies having babies" waited for the awareness of rising adolescent sexual activity among the better-off classes in the 1980s—at which point rates of adolescent pregnancy among the poor had already declined. But when the country became ambivalent about the desirability of abortions, the issue was displaced on the poor by making it almost impossible for them to obtain abortions.

· · ·

Three Economic Functions

3. *Economic banishment and the reserve army of labor.* People who have successfully been labeled as undeserving can be banished from the formal labor market. If young people are designated "school dropouts," for example, they can also be thought to lack the needed work habits, such as proper adherence to the work ethic, and may not be offered jobs to begin with. Often, they are effectively banished from the labor market before entering it because employers imagine them to be poor workers simply because they are young, male, and Black.[5] Many ex-convicts are declared unemployable in similar fashion, and some become recidivists because they have no other choice but to go back to their criminal occupations.

Banishing the undeserving also makes room for immigrant workers, who may work for lower wages, are more deferential, and are more easily exploitable by being threatened with deportation. In addition, banishment helps to reduce the official jobless rate, a sometimes useful political function, especially if the banished drop so completely out of the labor force that they are not even available to be counted as "discouraged workers."

The economic banishment function is in many ways a replacement for the old reserve army of labor function, which played itself out when the undeserving poor could be hired as strikebreakers, as defense workers in the case of sudden wartime economic mobilization, as "hypothetical workers," who by their very presence could be used to depress the wages of other workers, or to put pressure on the unions not to make wage and other demands. Today, however, with a plentiful supply of immigrants, as well as a constantly growing number of banished workers who are becoming surplus labor, a reserve army is less rarely needed—and when needed, can be recruited from sources other than the undeserving poor.[6]

Welfare recipients may, however, turn out to continue to be a part of the reserve army. Currently, they are encouraged to stay out of the labor market by remaining eligible for the Medicaid benefits they need for their children only if they remain on welfare.[7] Should the Clinton administration welfare reform program become reality, however, welfare recipients, who will be required to work for the minimum wage or less, could exert pressure on the wages of the employed, thus bringing them right back into the reserve army.

4. *Supplying illegal goods.* The undeserving poor who are banished from other jobs remain eligible for work in the manufacture and sale of illegal goods, including drugs. Although it is estimated that 80 percent of all illegal drugs are sold to Whites who are not poor, the sellers are often people banished from the formal labor market.[8] Other suppliers of illegal goods include the illegal immigrants, considered undeserving in many American communities, who work for garment industry sweatshops manufacturing clothing under illegal conditions.

5. *Job creation.* Perhaps the most important economic function of the undeserving poor today is that their mere presence creates jobs for the better-off population, including professional ones. Since the undeserving poor are thought to be dangerous or improperly socialized, their behavior either has to be modified so that they act in socially approved ways, or they have to be isolated from the deserving sectors of society. The larger the number of people who are declared undeserving, the larger also the number of people needed to modify and isolate as well as control, guard, and care for them. Among these are the social workers, teachers, trainers, mentors, psychiatrists, doctors and their support staffs in juvenile training centers, "special" schools, drug treatment centers, and penal behavior modification institutions, as well as the police, prosecutors, defense attorneys, judges, court officers, probation personnel and others who constitute the criminal courts, and the guards and others who run the prisons.

Jobs created by the presence of the undeserving poor also include the massive bureaucracy of professionals, investigators, and clerks who administer welfare. Other jobs go to the officials who seek out poor fathers for child support monies they may or may not have, as well as the welfare office personnel needed to take recipients in violation of welfare rules off the rolls, and those needed to put them back on the rolls when they reapply. In fact, one can argue that some of the rules for supervising, controlling, and punishing the undeserving poor are more effective at performing the latent function of creating clerical and professional jobs for the better-off population than the manifest function of achieving their official goals.

More jobs are created in the social sciences and in journalism for conducting research about the undeserving poor and producing popular books, articles, and TV documentaries for the more fortunate who want to learn about them. The "job chain" should also be extended to the teachers and others who train those who serve, control, and study the undeserving poor.

In addition, the undeserving poor make jobs for what I call the salvation industries, religious, civil, or medical, which also try to modify the behavior of those stigmatized as undeserving. Not all such jobs are paid, for the undeserving poor also provide occasional targets for charity and thus offer volunteer jobs for those providing it—and paid jobs for the professional fundraisers who obtain most of the charitable funds these days. Among the most visible volunteers are the members of "cafe" and "high" society who organize and contribute to these benefits.[9]

Three Normative Functions

6. *Moral legitimation.* Undeservingness justifies the category of deservingness and thus supplies moral and political legitimacy, almost by definition, to the institutions and social structures that include the deserving and exclude the undeserving.[10] Of these structures, the most important is undoubtedly the class hierarchy, for the existence of an undeserving class or stratum legitimates the deserving classes, if not necessarily all of their class-related behavior.[11] The alleged immorality of the undeserving also gives a moral flavor to, and justification for, the class hierarchy, which may help to explain why upward mobility itself is so praiseworthy.[12]

7. *Norm reinforcement.* By violating, or being imagined as violating, a number of mainstream behavioral patterns and values, the undeserving poor help to reaffirm and reinforce the virtues of these patterns—and to do so visibly, since the violations by the undeserving are highly publicized. As Emile Durkheim pointed out nearly a century ago, norm violations and their punishments also provide an opportunity for preserving and reaffirming the norms. This is not insignificant, for norms sometimes disparaged as "motherhood" values gain new moral power when they are violated, and their violators are stigmatized.

If the undeserving poor can be imagined to be lazy, they help to reaffirm the Protestant work ethic; if poor single-parent families are publicly condemned, the two-parent family is once more legitimated as ideal. In the 1960s, middle-class morality was sometimes criticized as culturally parochial and therefore inappropriate for the poor, but since the 1980s, mainstream values have once more been regarded as vital sources of behavioral guidance for them.[13]

Enforcing the norms also contributes further to preserving them in another way, for one of the standard punishments of the undeserving poor for misbehaving—as well as a standard obligation in exchange for help—is practicing the mainstream norms, including those that the members of the mainstream may only be preaching, and that might die out if the poor were not required to incorporate them in their behavior. Old work rules that can no longer be enforced in the rest of the economy can be maintained in the regulations for workfare; old-fashioned austerity and thrift are built into the consumption patterns expected of welfare recipients. Economists like to argue that if the poor want to be deserving, they should take any kind of job, regardless of its low pay or demeaning character, reflecting a work ethic which economists themselves have never practiced.

Similarly, welfare recipients may be removed from the rolls if they are found to be living with a man—but the social worker who removes them has every right to cohabit and not lose his or her job. In most states, welfare recipients must observe rules of housecleaning and child care that middle-class people are free to ignore without being punished. While there are many norms and laws governing child care, only the poor are monitored to see if they obey these. Should they use more physical punishment on their children than social workers consider desirable, they can be charged with child neglect or abuse and can lose their children to foster care.[14]

The fact is that the defenders of such widely preached norms as hard work, thrift, monogamy, and moderation need people who can be accused, accurately or not, of being lazy, spendthrift, promiscuous, and immoderate. One reason that welfare recipients are a ready target for punitive legislation is that politicians, and most likely some of their constituents, imagine them to be enjoying leisure and an active sex life at public expense. Whether or not very many poor people actually behave in the ways that are judged undeserving is irrelevant if they can be imagined as doing so. Once imagining and stereotyping are allowed to take over, then judgments of undeservingness can be made without much concern for empirical accuracy. For example, in the 1990s, the idea that young men from poor single-parent families were highly likely to commit street crimes became so universal that the news media no longer needed to quote experts to affirm the accuracy of the charge.

Actually, most of the time most of the poor are as law abiding and observant of mainstream norms as are other Americans. Sometimes they are even more observant; thus the proportion of welfare recipients who cheat is always far below the percentage of taxpayers who do so.[15] Moreover, survey after survey has shown that the poor, including many street criminals and drug sellers, want to hold respectable jobs like everyone else, hope someday to live in the suburbs, and generally aspire to the same American dream as most moderate and middle-income Americans.[16]

8. *Supplying popular culture villains.* The undeserving poor have played a long-term role in supplying American popular culture with villains, allowing the producers of the culture both to reinforce further mainstream norms and to satisfy audience demands for revenge, notably by showing that crime and other norm violations do not pay. Street criminals are shown dead or alive in the hands of the police on local television news virtually every day, and more dramatically so in the crime and action movies and television series.

For many years before and after World War II, the criminal characters in Hollywood movies were often poor immigrants, frequently of Sicilian origin. Then they were complemented for some decades by communist spies and other Cold War enemies who were not poor, but even before the end of the Cold War, they were being replaced by Black and Hispanic drug dealers and gang leaders.

At the same time, however, the popular culture industry has also supplied music and other materials offering marketable cultural and political protest which does not reinforce mainstream norms, or at least not directly. Some of the creators and performers come from poor neighborhoods, however, and it may be that some rap music becomes commercially successful by displacing on ghetto musicians the cultural and political protest of record buyers from more affluent classes.[17]

Three Political Functions

9. *Institutionalized scapegoating.* The scapegoating of the undeserving poor mentioned in Function 2 above also extends to institutions which mistreat them. As a result, some of the responsibility for the existence of poverty, slums, unemployment, poor schools, and the like is taken off the shoulders of elected and appointed officials who are supposed to deal with these problems. For example, to the extent that educational experts decide that the children of the poor are learning disabled or that they are culturally or genetically inferior in intelligence, attempts to improve the schools can be put off or watered down.

To put it another way, the availability of institutional scapegoats both personalizes and exonerates social systems. The alleged laziness of the jobless and the anger aimed at beggars take the heat off the failure of the economy, and the imagined derelictions of slum dwellers and the homeless, off the housing industry. In effect, the undeserving poor are blamed both for their poverty and also for the absence of "political will" among the citizenry to do anything about it.

10. *Conservative power shifting.* Once poor people are considered undeserving, they also lose their political legitimacy and whatever little political influence they had before they were stigmatized. Some cannot vote, and many do not choose to vote or mobilize because they know politicians do not

listen to their demands. Elected officials might ignore them even if they voted or mobilized, because these officials and the larger polity cannot easily satisfy their demands for economic and other kinds of justice.[18] As a result, the political system is able to pay additional attention to the demands of more affluent constituents. It can therefore shift to the "right."

The same shift to the right also takes place ideologically. Although injustices of poverty help justify the existence of liberals and the more radical left, the undeserving poor themselves provide justification and opportunities for conservatives to attack their ideological enemies on their left. When liberals can be accused of favoring criminals over victims, their accusers can launch and legitimate incursions on the civil liberties and rights of the undeserving poor, and concurrently on the liberties and rights of defenders of the poor. Moreover, the undeservingness of the poor can be used to justify attacks on the welfare state. Charles Murray understood the essence of this ideological function when he argued that other welfare state legislation for the poor only increased the number of poor people.[19]

11. *Spatial purification.* Stigmatized populations are often used, deliberately or not, to stigmatize the areas in which they live, making such areas eligible for various kinds of purification. As a result, "underclass areas" can be torn down and their inhabitants moved to make room for more affluent residents or higher taxpayers.

However, such areas can also be used to isolate stigmatized poor people and facilities by selecting them as locations for homeless shelters, halfway houses for the mentally ill or for ex-convicts, drug treatment facilities, and even garbage dumps, which have been forced out of middle- and working-class areas following NIMBY (not in my backyard) protests. Drug dealers and other sellers of illegal goods also find a haven in areas stigmatized as underclass areas, partly because these supply some customers, but also because police protection in such areas is usually minimal enough to allow illegal activities without significant interference from the law.[20] In fact, municipalities would face major economic and political obstacles to their operations without stigmatized areas in which stigmatized people and activities can be located.

Two Macrosocial Functions

12. *Reproduction of stigma and the stigmatized.* For centuries now, undeservingness has given rise to policies and agencies which are manifestly set up to help the poor economically and otherwise to become deserving, but which actually prevent the undeserving poor from being freed of their stigma, and which also manage, unwittingly, to see to it that their children face the same obstacles.[21] In some instances, this process works so speedily that the children of the stigmatized face "anticipatory stigmatization," among them the children of welfare recipients who are frequently predicted to be unable to learn, to work, and to remain on the right side of the law even before they have been weaned.

If this outcome were planned deliberately, one could argue that politically and culturally dominant groups are reluctant to give up an easily accessible and always available scapegoat. In actuality, however, the reproduction function results unwittingly from other intended and seemingly popular practices. For example, the so-called War on Drugs, which has unsuccessfully sought to keep hard drugs out of the United States, but has meanwhile done little to provide drug treatment to addicts who want it, thereby aids the continuation of addiction, street crime, and a guaranteed prison population, not to mention the various disasters that visit the families of addicts and help to keep them poor.

The other major source of reproducing stigma and the stigmatized is the routine activities of the organizations which service welfare recipients, the homeless, and other stigmatized poor, and end up mistreating them.[22] For one thing, such agencies, whether they exist to supply employment to the poor or to help the homeless, are almost certain to be underfunded because of the powerlessness of their clientele. No organization has ever had the funds or power to buy, build, or rehabilitate housing for the homeless in sufficient number. Typically, they have been able to fund or carry out small demonstration projects.

In addition, organizations which serve stigmatized people often attract less well-trained and qualified staff than those with high-status clients, and if the clients are deemed undeserving, competence may become even less important in choosing staff.[23] Then too, helping organizations generally reflect the societal stratification hierarchy, which means that organizations with poor, low-status clients frequently treat them as undeserving. If they also fear some of their clients, they may not only withhold help, but attack the clients on a preemptive strike basis. Last but not least, the agencies that serve the undeserving poor are bureaucracies which operate by rules and regulations that routinize the work, encourage the stability and growth of the organizations, and serve the needs of their staffs before those of their clients.

When these factors are combined, as they often are, and become cumulative, as they often do, it should not be surprising that the organizations cut off escape routes from poverty not only for the clients, but in doing so, also make sure that some of their children remain poor as well.

13. *Extermination of the surplus.* In earlier times, when the living standards of all poor people were at or below subsistence, many died at an earlier age than the better off, thus performing the set of functions for the latter forever associated with Thomas Malthus. Standards of living, even for the very poor, have risen considerably in the last century, but even today, morbidity and mortality rates remain much higher among the poor than among moderate-income people. To put it another way, various social forces combine to do away with some of the people who have become surplus labor and are no longer needed by the economy.

Several of the killing illnesses and pathologies of the poor change over time; currently, they include AIDS, tuberculosis, hypertension, heart attacks, and cancer, as well as psychosis, substance abuse, street crime, injury and death during participation in the drug trade and other underworld activities, and intraclass homicide resulting from neighborhood conflicts over turf and "respect." Whether the poor people whose only problem is being unfairly stereotyped and stigmatized as undeserving die earlier than other poor people is not known.[24]

Moreover, these rates can be expected to remain high or even to rise as rates of unemployment—and of banishment from the labor force—rise, especially for the least skilled. Even the better-off jobless created by the downsizing of the 1990s blame themselves for their unemployment if they cannot eventually find new jobs, become depressed, and in some instances begin the same process of being extruded permanently from the labor market experienced by the least skilled of the jobless.

In effect, contemporary advanced capitalism may well have created the conditions for a new Malthusian hypothesis. In any case, the early departure of poor people from an economy and society which do not need them is useful for those who remain. Since the more fortunate classes have already developed a purposive blindness to the structural causes of unemployment and to the poverty-related causes of pathology and crime that follow, those who benefit from the current job erosion and the possible extermination of the surplus labor may not admit it consciously either. Nonetheless, those left over to compete for scarce jobs and other resources will have a somewhat easier time in the competition, thus assigning undeservingness a final positive function for the more fortunate members of society.[25]

III. Conclusion

I have described thirteen of the more important functions of the undeserving poor, enough to support my argument that both the idea of the undeserving poor and the stigmas with which some poor people are thus labeled may persist in part because they are useful in a variety of ways to the people who are not poor.

This analysis does not imply that undeservingness will or should persist. Whether it *will* persist is going to be determined by what happens to poverty in America. If it declines, poverty-related crime should also decline, and then fewer poor people will probably be described as undeserving. If poverty worsens, so will poverty-related crime, as well as the stereotyping and stigmatization of the poor, and any worsening of the country's economy is likely to add to the kinds and numbers of undeserving poor, if only because they make convenient and powerless scapegoats.

The functions that the undeserving poor play cannot, by themselves, perpetuate either poverty or undeservingness, for as I noted earlier, functions are not causes. For example, if huge numbers of additional unskilled workers should be needed, as they were for the World War II war effort, the undeserving poor will be welcomed back into the labor force, at least temporarily. Of course, institutions often try to survive once they have lost both their reasons for existence and their functions. Since the end of the Cold War, parts of the military-industrial establishment both in the United States and Russia have been campaigning for the maintenance of some Cold War forces and weapons to guarantee their own futures, but these establishments also supply jobs to their national economies, and in the United States, for the constituents of elected officials. Likewise, some of the institutions and interest groups that benefit from the existence of undeservingness, or from controlling the undeserving poor, may try to maintain undeservingness and its stigma. They may not even need to, for if Emile Durkheim was right, the decline of undeservingness would lead to the criminalization, or at least stigmatization, of new behavior patterns.

Whether applying the label of undeservingness to the poor *should* persist is a normative question which ought to be answered in the negative. Although people have a right to judge each other, that right does not extend to judging large numbers of people as a single group, with one common moral fault, or to stereotyping them without evidence either about their behavior or their values. Even if a case could be made for judging large cohorts of people as undeserving, these judgments should be distributed up and down the socioeconomic hierarchy, requiring Americans also to consider whether and how people in the working, middle, and upper classes are undeserving.

The same equality should extend to the punishment of crimes. Today, many Americans and courts still treat white-collar and upper-class criminals more leniently than poor ones. The public excuse given is that the street crime of the undeserving poor involves violence and thus injury or death, but as many students of white-collar and corporate crime have pointed out, these also hurt and kill people, and often in larger numbers, even if they do so less directly and perhaps less violently.

Changes also need to be made in the American conception of deviance, which like that of other countries, conflates people whose behavior is *different* with those whose behavior is socially *harmful*. Bearing children without marriage is a long-standing tradition among the poor. Born of necessity rather than preference, it is a poverty-related practice, but it is not, by itself, harmful, or at least not until it can be shown that either the children—or the moral sensibilities of the people who oppose illegitimacy—are significantly hurt. Poor single-parent families are hardly desirable, but as the lack of condemnation of more affluent single-parent families should suggest, the major problem of such families is not the number of parents, actual or surrogate, in the family, but its poverty.

Finally, because many of the poor are stereotyped unjustly as undeserving, scholars, writers, journalists, and others should launch a systematic and public effort to deconstruct and delegitimate the notion of the undeserving poor. This effort, which is necessary to make effective antipoverty programs politically acceptable again, should place the following five ideas on the public agenda and encourage discussion as well as dissemination of available research.

The five ideas, all discussed earlier in this article, are that (1) the criminal and deviant behavior among the poor is largely poverty related rather than the product of free choice based on distinctive values; (2) the undeservingness of the poor is an ancient stereotype, and like all stereotypes, it vastly exaggerates the actual dangers that stem from the poor; (3) poverty-related deviance is not necessarily harmful just because it does not accord with mainstream norms; (4) the notion of undeservingness survives in part because of the positive functions it has for the better-off population; and (5) the only certain way to eliminate both this notion and the functions is to eliminate poverty.[26]

NOTES

Author's Note: This is a revised version of an article first published in the *Koelner Zeitschrift fuer Soziologie und Sozialpsychologie,* Sonderheft No. 32, 1992, 48–62. It appears with the permission of the original publisher, Westdeutscher Verlag Gmbh, Opladen. I am grateful to Allan Silver for helpful comments on an earlier draft of this article.

1. Robert K. Merton, "Manifest and Latent Functions," in his *Social Theory and Social Structure: Toward the Codification of Social Research* (Glencoe, IL, 1949), chap. 1.
2. Actually, some of the functions that follow may in fact have been intended by some interest groups in society, but neither intended nor recognized by others, adding an interesting conceptual variation—and empirical question—to Merton's dichotomy.
3. Herbert J. Gans, "The Positive Functions of Poverty," *American Journal of Sociology* 78, no. 2 (1972):275–89. That article also had another purpose, to show that functional analysis could come to liberal or radical conclusions, to counter the charge commonly launched against functional analysis that it is inherently conservative or supportive of the status quo. That article, like its present complement, was a straightforward analysis, written sans irony, even though the analysis of latent functions often becomes a debunking exercise that can take on an unintentionally ironic tone.
4. For brevity's sake, I will hereafter refer to the undeserving poor instead of the poor labeled undeserving, but I always mean the latter.
5. Kathryn M. Neckerman and Joleen Kirschenman, "Hiring Strategies, Racial Bias and Inner-City Workers," *Social Problems* 38, no. 4 (1991):433–47.
6. Dahrendorf has suggested, surely with Marx's *Lumpenproletariat* in mind, that when the very poor are excluded from full citizenship, they can become "a reserve army for demonstrations . . . including soccer violence, race riots, and running battles with the police." Ralf Dahrendorf, *Law and Order* (London: Stevens, 1985), 107. He is writing with Europe in mind, however.
7. Consequently, they are part of the reserve army only if and when they also work off-the-books and in the informal economy. For the argument that recipients are permanently part of the reserve army, see Frances F. Piven and Richard A. Cloward, *Regulating the Poor: The Functions of Public Welfare,* 2d ed. (New York: Pantheon, 1993).
8. Ron Harris, "Blacks Feel Brunt of Drug War," *Los Angeles Times,* 22 April 1990, p. 1.

9. While most charity benefits target the deserving poor, they are also held for poor AIDS victims and the homeless, who are considered undeserving, at least by some members of the better-off classes. The undeserving poor who are served by these charities thus help to justify the continued existence of these upper-class "societies."

10. Since political legitimacy is involved here, these functions could also be listed among the political ones below.

11. That many of the undeserving poor, and literally those of the underclass, are also thought to be *declasse*, adds to the moral and political legitimacy of the rest of the class system.

12. Although Marxists might have been expected to complain that the notion of the undeserving poor enables the higher classes to create a split in the lower ones, in-stead Marxist theory creates a mirror image of the capitalist pattern. In declaring undeserving the owners of the means of production, and sometimes the entire bourgeoisie, the theorists ennobled the working class and the poor together with it. Nonetheless, Marx found it necessary to make room for the *Lumpenproletariat*, although for him if not all of his successors, its moral failures were largely deter-mined by the needs of Marxist ideology, just as those of the undeserving poor were shaped by capitalist ideology.

13. See Isabel Sawhill, "The Underclass: An Overview," *The Public Interest*, no. 96 (1989):3–15. For a contrary analysis, which finds and criticizes the acceptance of poverty-related deviance as normal, see Daniel P. Moynihan, "Defining Deviancy Down," *American Scholar* 62, no. 1 (1993):17–30.

14. Poor immigrants who still practice old-country discipline norms are particularly vulnerable to being accused of child abuse.

15. Teresa Funiciello, *Tyranny of Kindness: Dismantling the Welfare System to End Poverty in America* (New York: Atlantic Monthly Press, 1993), 60.

16. See Mark R. Rank, *Living on the Edge: The Realities of Welfare in America* (New York: Columbia University Press, 1994), 93.

17. A sizable proportion of the blues, country music, cowboy songs, and jazz of ear-lier eras was originally composed and played in prisons, brothels, and slum area taverns. It is probably not coincidental that as far back as the eighteenth century, at least, English "actors, fencers, jugglers, minstrels, and in fact all purveyors of amusements to common folk," were thought undeserving by the higher classes. Webb and Webb, *English Poor Law History*, 354.

18. In addition, the undeserving poor make a dangerous constituency. Politicians who say kind words about them or who act to represent their interests are likely to be attacked for their words and actions. Jesse Jackson was hardly the first na-tional politician to be criticized for being too favorable to the poor.

19. Charles Murray, *Losing Ground: American Social Policy, 1950–1980* (New York: Ba-sic Books, 1984). Myron Magnet went him one step better, blaming the increase in undeservingness also on various unnamed radicals associated with the conser-vative image of the 1960s. Myron Magnet, *The Dream and the Nightmare: The Six-ties' Legacy to the Underclass* (New York: Morrow, 1993).

20. Since even middle-class drug buyers are willing to travel to underclass areas for drugs, neighborhoods convenient to expressways and bridges that serve the sub-urbs often become major shopping centers for hard drugs.

21. It is well known that many policies and agencies reproduce the positions and sta-tuses of the people they are asked to raise, notably the public schools.

22. For some examples of the literature on client mistreatment, see Michael B. Katz, *In the Shadow of the Poor House: A Social History of Welfare in America* (New York:

Basic Books, 1986); Michael Lipsky, *Street Level Bureaucracy: Dilemmas of the Individual in Public Services* (New York: Russell Sage Foundation, 1980); Piven and Cloward, *Regulating the Poor*, chaps. 4 and 5; and for mistreatment of the homeless, Elliot Liebow, *Tell Them Who I Am: The Lives of Homeless Women* (New York: Free Press, 1993), chap. 4.

23. They may also attract young professionals with reforming or missionary impulses, but many of them either burn out or leave for financial reasons when they begin to raise families.

24. Poor Blacks and members of some racial minorities pay additional "health penalties" for being non-White.

25. Killing off the undeserving poor may conflict with the prior function (see Function 12) of reproducing them, but functional analysis describes consequences which do not have to be logically consistent. Moreover, since turning poor people into undeserving ones can be a first step toward eliminating them, Functions 12 and 13 may even be logically consistent.

26. A fuller discussion of policy proposals will appear in my forthcoming book, *Ending the War against the Poor*.

26

MAKING ENDS MEET
How Single Mothers Survive on a Welfare Check

KATHRYN EDIN • LAURA LEIN

Many Americans commonly assume that people on welfare are abusing the system by refusing to go to work and by having additional children in order to receive more welfare benefits. The reality is actually quite different, as Kathryn Edin and Laura Lein demonstrate in this reading. This selection, taken from their book *Making Ends Meet: How Single Mothers Survive Welfare and Low-Wage Work* (1997), shows how women spend their welfare checks each month. In this comprehensive study of impoverished women in four U.S. cities (Boston, Charleston, Chicago, and San Antonio), Edin and Lein interviewed 379 single mothers who were either welfare recipients or nonrecipients who held low-wage jobs. The selection that follows focuses on the 214 welfare-reliant mothers and their struggles to sustain their families each month.

---

long Minnesota's Highway 72—which runs between the Canadian border town of Rainy River and Bemidji, Minnesota—a large, crudely lettered billboard greets the southbound traveler:

WELCOME TO MINNESOTA
LAND OF 10,000 TAXES
BUT WELFARE PAYS GOOD

Antiwelfare sentiment is common among Minnesotans, who live in a state with high personal income taxes and cash welfare benefits substantially above the national median. But even in southern states, where cash welfare benefits are very low and taxes modest, citizens are likely to denigrate welfare. In 1990, about 40 percent of respondents in each region told interviewers from the National Opinion Research Center that the United States spends too much on welfare.[1] In 1994, another nationally representative survey found that 65 percent of Americans believed welfare spending was too high (Blendon et al. 1995).

Legislators recognize welfare's unpopularity. In the first half of the 1990s, several states cut benefits, and all let their value lag behind inflation. In addition, most states applied for federal waivers to experiment with benefit limitations or sanctions not allowed by the old federal rules. Some states established a "family cap," which denied additional cash to mothers who had another child while receiving welfare. In other states, mothers whose children were truant from school lost a portion of their cash grant. Furthermore, under the new federal rules, all states must limit the amount of time a mother spends on welfare to five years.

Public dissatisfaction with welfare persists despite the fact that cash benefits to welfare recipients have declined by more than 40 percent in real terms since the mid-1970s (Blank 1994:179). The reasons for the continuing public discontent throughout this period are complex, but probably rest on the widespread belief that the federal welfare entitlement perpetuated laziness and promiscuity (Bobo and Smith 1994; Page and Shapiro 1992).[2] Lazy women had babies to get money from the welfare system, the story went, and then let lazy boyfriends share their beds and live off their benefits. These lazy and immoral adults then raised lazy and immoral children, creating a vicious cycle of dependency.

Those who have promoted this view include the news media and talk show hosts, but social scientists also have contributed. The most widely known "scientific" argument was developed by Charles Murray, who in 1984 claimed that welfare actually makes the poor worse off. Federal welfare became too generous during the 1960s and 1970s, Murray argued, and began to reward unwed motherhood and indolence over marriage and jobs (Murray 1984). Social scientists spent much of the late 1980s attempting to discover whether Murray was right. Typically, economists judged the merits of the claim by estimating the disincentive effects of more or less generous state welfare benefits on work (for a review of this literature, see Moffitt 1992). Other researchers attempted to measure the effect of varying state benefits on marriage, divorce, and remarriage (Bane and Ellwood 1994).

The task we set for ourselves in this [article] is a more fundamental one. In order to assess whether any welfare program is too generous, one must compare its benefits to the cost of living faced by that program's recipients. An obvious starting point is to ask how much families headed by single mothers spend each month to make ends meet, and how that income compares with what they receive from welfare.

How Much Do Welfare-Reliant Mothers Spend?

In 1992, Donna Carson, a forty-year-old African American mother of two living in San Antonio, characterized herself as "ambitious and determined." She had spent most of her adult life playing by the rules. After high school graduation, she got a job and got married. She conceived her first child at age twenty-five, but her husband left before the child was born. Soon after her son's birth, she arranged for her mother to take care of him and went back to work. Because she did not have to pay for child care, her wages from her nurse's aide job combined with the child support she received from her ex-husband were enough to pay the bills. Ten years later, when she turned thirty-six, she had a second child. This time she was not married to the father. Carson's mother was willing to watch this child as well, so again she returned to work. Shortly thereafter, Carson's father's diabetes worsened and both of his legs were amputated. Her mother was overwhelmed by the tragedy and checked herself into a psychiatric hospital, leaving Carson to care for her two children and her disabled father alone. Seeing no other way out, she quit her job and turned to welfare. That was 1989.

Three years later, when we were talking with her, Carson was still on welfare, and her budget was tight. Her typical monthly expenditures were about $920 a month. One-third of that amount went to rent and utilities, another third went to food, and the rest went to cover her children's clothing, their school supplies, her transportation, and all the other things the family needed. Her combined monthly benefits from AFDC and food stamps, however, came to only $477.

Some months, she received a "pass through" child support payment of $50 from the father of her first child, who was legally obligated to pay. Although this payment did not reduce her AFDC benefits, her food stamps did go down by about $15 every time she received it. The father of her second child bypassed the formal child support system and paid her $60 directly each month. To get the rest of the money she needed, Carson took care of a working neighbor's child during the day. This neighbor could pay only $100 a month, but gave her the money in cash so that Carson's welfare caseworker could not detect the earnings and reduce her check. She got the rest of the

TABLE 26.1   **Monthly Expenses of 214 AFDC Recipients:
Means and Standard Deviations**

	Mean	SD
Housing costs	$213	$187
Food costs	262	112
Other necessities	336	176
Medical	18	43
Clothing	69	62
Transportation	62	83
Child care	7	32
Phone	31	35
Laundry/toiletries/cleaning supplies	52	31
Baby care	18	32
School supplies and fees	14	48
Appliance and furniture	17	39
Miscellaneous	47	59
Nonessentials	64	63
Entertainment	20	31
Cable TV	6	14
Cigarettes and alcohol	22	30
Eat out	13	27
Lottery costs	3	16
TOTAL EXPENSES	$876	$283

Source: Authors' calculations using Edin and Lein survival strategies data.
Note: The mean family size is 3.17 people. Numbers do not total due to rounding.

money she needed from her father, who paid her $250 in cash each month to care for him.

Though Carson had more personal tragedy than most, her budget was similar to that of most other welfare recipients we talked with. Table 26.1 gives the monthly expenses of the 214 welfare-reliant mothers we interviewed (and their 464 children). It shows that our respondents averaged $213 a month on housing, $262 on food, $336 on other necessary expenses, and $64 on items that were arguably not essential—a total of $876 for an average family of 3.17 people.[3]

Housing Expenses

The housing expenses of welfare-reliant families varied substantially. This variation depended on whether recipients paid market rent, had a housing subsidy in a public housing project or a private building (Section 8), or shared housing with a relative or friend. Donna Carson paid market rent, which in San Antonio was quite low but still higher than what most mothers pay in subsidized units. However, apartments that meet the physical criteria required for Section 8 tended to be in neighborhoods with less access to public transportation than the neighborhoods where housing projects were generally located, so these families usually had to maintain an automobile. Consequently, while public housing and Section 8 residents paid roughly the same amount for housing, Section 8 families spent far more for transportation.

In most cases, the welfare-reliant families who shared housing with a friend or relative were able to split the rent, utilities, telephone bill, and other household expenses. Thus, their expenses for rent and these other items were relatively low. About half of those who shared housing lived with one or both parents. The other half lived with siblings or friends. Mothers who lived with a parent usually made only token contributions toward the rent and took some portion of the responsibility for utilities and household maintenance. Most lived with their parents precisely because they could not afford to maintain their own households. Those who lived with a sibling or friend usually paid half of the household expenses. Sometimes, however, mothers "rented" only a portion of the living space (a single room, for example) and paid only a quarter or a third of the household costs.[4]

Food Expenses

Food expenditures averaged $262 a month for the welfare-reliant families we interviewed. This means that these mothers spent $19 per person on food in a typical week. This amount is nearly identical to the federal government's cheap food plan (the "thrifty food budget"), which uses as its base what poor mothers bought for their families in the 1950s and adjusts the prices in that "basket" for inflation each year (Ruggles 1990; Schwarz and Volgy 1992). The average weekly food stamp allotment for the families we interviewed, however, was slightly lower than this amount—$16 per person. This is because we oversampled mothers with housing subsidies to try to find mothers who could live on their benefits alone, and they do not qualify for the maximum amount of food stamps (food stamps are adjusted for living costs). This meant that the average mother had to cover $40 of food expenses each month with income from some source other than food stamps.[5]

Food stamp benefits also varied with family income, including cash welfare. In the lowest AFDC benefit states, therefore, families could receive up to $292 a month in food stamps for a family of three, or $21 per person per week in 1991, and families in these sites who reported no outside income received this maximum. Most found it sufficient to cover the bulk of their food expenditures. Families in states that paid more generous welfare benefits received roughly 30 cents less in food stamps for each additional dollar in cash welfare benefits. Because of this, hardly anyone who lived outside the South could pay their food bills with food stamps alone.[6] In San Antonio, food stamps covered 99 percent of respondents' average food expenditures; in

Charleston, 88 percent; in Chicago, 80 percent; and in high-benefit Boston, only 65 percent.

Other Expenses

Besides housing and food, clothing took the next biggest bite out of the average family's monthly budget, followed by transportation, laundry and toiletries, telephone charges, medical expenses, baby care, and appliance and furniture costs. On average, welfare-reliant mothers spent $69 a month on clothing. This means that the mothers with whom we spoke typically purchased $261 worth of shoes, coats, and other apparel for each family member in a year. Most of this was for their children, since children continually grow out of their clothing.

Welfare-reliant mothers employed a number of strategies to contain their clothing expenditures. Virtually all purchased some of their clothing at thrift or second-hand stores, and most scoured neighborhood yard sales. During our interviews, many mothers proudly showed us their second-hand buys: a barely worn pair of name-brand jeans or a winter coat that was practically new and only a bit too small. A mother's largest expense in the clothing category was for children's shoes. Children not only went through two or more pairs of shoes a year, but shoes in children's sizes and in good condition were seldom available at neighborhood thrift stores. Winter coats, hats, mittens, and boots were also expensive, and most children grew out of them every other winter. Thus in the winter months, clothing needs could become an added hardship. One mother told us,

> *In the winter months, I have had to keep my children at home on the really cold days because I didn't have warm enough clothes to dress them. I have learned to swallow my pride, though, and go to the second-hand shops and try to get the right kind of winter clothes for the boys.*

The welfare-reliant mothers we interviewed felt that second-hand clothing was acceptable for younger children, whose peers were still largely unconcerned with appearance. One mother told us,

> *For shopping I go to yard sales and the Salvation Army for Jay's clothes. Fortunately, he isn't the type of kid who always has to have Nike sneakers or he won't go to school. I get him K-Mart ones, or I go to the used clothes store [on] Belmont [Avenue]. I probably spend $200 a season on new clothes for him, but some of those he can wear from season to season.*

Other mothers reported that their older children—especially high school boys—felt they could not maintain their self-respect or the respect of their peers while wearing K-Mart shoes to school. Some mothers felt that if they did not purchase name-brand sneakers, an athletic jacket, or other popular items for their teenagers, their children might be lured into criminal activity so they could buy these items themselves:

> *My boy, he sees these kids that sell drugs. They can afford to buy these [tennis shoes] and he can't. So I have my little side-job and [I buy them for him]. You got to do it to keep them away from drugs, from the streets.*

One mother told us that in order to buy her child a $50 pair of tennis shoes, she ate only one meal a day for a month. The savings in her food bill were enough to cover the purchase of the shoes. Most mothers in her neighborhood did not feel it was necessary to go hungry to meet their children's clothing needs, because they could generate the extra cash in other ways, which we discuss later.

Mothers who bought new clothing generally had to put the clothing on layaway. They paid a small portion of the purchase price each month. Some others found professional shoplifters who would note the children's sizes, shoplift the clothing, and sell it for a fraction of the ticket price to the mother.

Transportation cost the average welfare-reliant family $62 a month. Families living in Charleston (where there was little access to public transportation) and families living outside central cities spent more because they had to maintain automobiles or pay for taxis. At the time of our interviews, welfare rules limited the value of a family's automobile to $2,500. This meant that mothers had older cars, which generally required more frequent repair and got poorer gas mileage. All of the states we studied had mandatory insurance laws, and respondents told us that minimum insurance coverage cost at least $40 a month. In addition, Chicago and metropolitan Boston required that families purchase city stickers to park on the street, and South Carolina taxed the value of a family's car each year.

Although mothers who had access to public transportation spent less than those mothers who maintained cars, bus and subway transportation cost the average mother who used it more than $60 a month. Few mothers lived in areas where they could walk to the laundromat or the grocery store. In neighborhoods that provided these amenities, rents were higher. Since few mothers could afford child care, a shopping trip required that mothers bring their children with them and pay the bus or subway fares for the older children as well (younger children often ride free).

Laundry, toiletries, and cleaning supplies also constituted a significant proportion of monthly expenses. Some mothers washed their clothing in the bathtub and let it air-dry in their apartment or outside. This is a time-consuming task, however, and mothers complained that their clothes did not get as clean as machine-washed clothing. A few mothers owned or rented their own washers and dryers, but most used local laundromats. Because most families' clothing stock was slim (for example, two or three pairs of pants for each person was typical), mothers usually washed their clothing once each week or more. Laundromat prices varied, but mothers seldom spent less than $6 for coin machines each time they visited the laundromat, for roughly three loads.

All told, the welfare-reliant mothers had to spend $23 in a typical month to wash and dry their clothing and an additional $29 on toiletries and cleaning supplies. Food stamps could not be used to purchase toiletries or cleaning supplies, so mothers had to pay for sponges, cleaning fluids, dishwashing liquid, hand and laundry soap, bleach, toilet paper, hair care products, deodorant, disposable razors, and feminine products with cash.

Ninety-two percent of our sample had telephone service for at least part of the year. On average, families spent $31 monthly on telephone charges. Twenty-six percent of the welfare recipients had their phone disconnected at least once during the past year because of nonpayment. When mothers ran short of money, they were usually more willing to do without a phone than to neglect rent, utilities, food, clothing, transportation, or other essentials. Basic service charges also varied widely by site. In San Antonio, where basic local service cost about $12 a month, families spent only $18 a month for phone-related costs. In all other sites, comparable service ranged from $20 to $25 a month, and families spent much more. These costs included not only charges for local and long-distance calls but connection and reconnection charges as well. Although not strictly necessary for a family's material well-being, mothers without telephones had a difficult time maintaining contact with welfare caseworkers and their children's schools. It was also more difficult to apply for jobs because prospective employers could not reach them to set up an interview. Some solved this dilemma by sharing a phone with a neighbor; messages left with neighbors, however, were not always promptly forwarded.

Medicaid, the government's health insurance program for low-income families, offered free emergency care and routine physician care. All the households in our welfare-reliant sample were covered by Medicaid. Over-the-counter medicines and other medical services, however, were not covered and constituted another $18 of the average welfare-reliant mother's monthly budget. These expenses included routine drugstore costs, such as those for pain relievers, cough syrup, adhesive bandages, vitamin tablets, or other medicines families frequently used. In addition, few state Medicaid programs pay for prescription birth control pills, abortions, antidepressants, or other mental health drugs. Nor do most Medicaid plans pay for dental care, except for emergency oral surgery.

Diapers and other baby care products cost an average welfare-reliant family $18 a month (37 percent of the welfare recipients in our sample had babies in diapers). Welfare-reliant mothers with infants and young toddlers typically received formula, milk, eggs, and cheese from WIC (Women's, Infant's, and Children's nutritional program). Most mothers told us, however, that they were usually one or two cans short of formula each month and had to purchase them at the grocery store. In addition, WIC does not provide disposable diapers, which constituted roughly 80 percent of the cash welfare-reliant mothers had to spend on baby care. Only a tiny minority of the mothers we interviewed used cloth diapers; although cheaper than disposables, cloth diapering was not practicable for mothers who relied on laundromats. In addition, mothers who used cloth diapers reported substantial up-front costs (they had to buy the diapers), and these mothers spent substantially more for laundry supplies than other mothers. Mothers also averaged $14 a month on school-related expenses and $7 a month on child care.

Appliances and furniture cost the typical family another $17 a month. Generally mothers purchased both new and used furniture and appliances with installment payments. Because they could not get bank credit, these mothers would often arrange credit at local thrift shops and "rent-to-own" furniture stores. Although local thrift stores did not generally apply finance charges to mothers' purchases (they usually held the item until it was fully paid for), rent-to-own furniture stores did. Because the latter stores charged very high interest rates and allowed long repayment periods, mothers sometimes ended up paying two to three times the actual value of the item. Meanwhile, mothers who missed a payment could have the furniture repossessed, losing whatever equity they had built up.

Miscellaneous items in the families' budgets included check-cashing fees and fees for money orders, debt service, burial insurance, and haircuts. These items totaled $47 in the average month.

Nonessentials

Entertainment cost the typical family $20 each month and was usually limited to video rentals; occasionally it included movies, trips to amusement parks, and travel (mothers sometimes sent their children to relatives during the summer). Mothers spent an average of $22 for cigarettes and alcohol each month, mostly on cigarettes. Mothers seldom bought their own alcohol, and those who drank depended on boyfriends, friends, and family members to pay for their drinks. This was also true for most mothers who used marijuana or other drugs. In addition, mothers spent an average of $3 a month for the lottery, $6 a month for cable television, and $13 a month to eat out. All told, the typical welfare-reliant family spent $64 a month on these unnecessary items, or about 7 percent of their total budget.[7] Although not physical necessities, the items met crucial psychological needs.

Although the mothers in our sample worried about day-to-day material survival, most saw survival as having broader "psychological" and "social" dimensions. One mother commented:

> You know, we live in such a materialistic world. Our welfare babies have needs and wants too. They see other kids going to the circus, having toys and stuff like that. You gotta do what you gotta do to make your kid feel normal. There is no way you can deprive your child.

This woman's statement captures a common sentiment among the welfare recipients we interviewed: children need to have an occasional treat, and mothers who refuse them may deprive their offspring of normalcy. Even among Mexican American mothers in San Antonio, who spent less than any of the other welfare-reliant mothers, one family in six paid a small monthly fee for a basic cable subscription. These mothers told us they saw the cable subscription as a cheap way of keeping their kids off the streets and out of trouble.

The mothers themselves needed an occasional boost too. Many reported that by spending small amounts on soda pop, cosmetics, cigarettes, alcohol, or the lottery, they avoided feeling like they were "completely on the bottom," or that their lives were "completely hopeless." When we asked respondents if they could do without them, they replied that these items gave them some measure of self-respect, and without them they would lose hope of bettering their situations:

> *I never buy for myself, only for my son. Well, I take that back. I allow myself two of what I guess you would call luxuries. Well, I guess three. First, I buy soda pop. I do not eat meals hardly ever, but I always have to have a can of Pepsi in my hand. I drink Pepsi nonstop. My boyfriend, he buys it for me by the case 'cause he knows how much I like it, and I guess it's the pop that gives me my energy for dealing with my son—you know, the sugar and caffeine and stuff.*
>
> *And then I treat myself to the cigarettes. Without the smoking, I would just worry all the time about how we was going to eat and would never relax. I feel like I deserve some little pleasure, you know, and so those cigarettes keep me up, keep me feeling that things aren't so bad.*
>
> *And the other thing is, I buy my cosmetics. I mean, I go around feeling so low all the time, and the makeup makes me feel, you know, better about myself. I feel like I'm not so poor when I can buy myself some cosmetics at the discount house.*

The few respondents who spent money on alcohol reported similar sentiments:

> *Oh, sometimes, you know, just to relax or somethin', I just go out and have a few. And when I'm really low, I sometimes go out and tie one on, if you know what I mean. Sometimes I think I'll go crazy all day in the house if I can't get out once in a while. I just couldn't take it.*

Although few mothers played the lottery with any regularity, those who did also viewed it as a sort of escape:

> *I just can't afford not to buy some tickets when the pot gets real big. I sometimes buy five tickets if I can afford it. I like to plan what I'm going to do with it, you know, fantasize and stuff—dream of what it would be like to own nice things and such.*

· · ·

Only one of our 214 mothers—an extremely frugal, publicly housed Boston-area resident—was able to meet her expenses with her welfare benefits. She made ends meet because she lived in an unusually generous state and spent nothing whatsoever on entertainment, alcohol, cigarettes, or the lottery; nothing on child care; nothing on school supplies (what the school did not provide, her son did not get); and nothing on furniture or appliances (she scavenged broken-down furniture from alleys). She spent nothing on transportation, since all her friends lived in the projects and she walked nearly everywhere she needed to go. She also spent very little on laundry because she washed clothes in the bathtub and let them air-dry. She spent little on clothing because she purchased the majority of the family's clothes (the few there were) at thrift stores. Finally, she spent nothing for Christmas, birthdays, or any other special occasion. No other respondent in *any* site made ends meet on so little. Since her child frequently went hungry, had only one change of clothes, and often missed school because he lacked adequate winter clothing, several of this woman's neighbors (whom we interviewed) had reported her to child protective services for neglect.

How Do Welfare-Reliant Mothers Make Ends Meet?

No one without substantial assets can spend more than they take in for long. The welfare-reliant women we interviewed had few savings, no IRA accounts, no stocks or bonds, and no valuable assets. If they had and if their caseworkers had known, they would have been ineligible for welfare. When they ran out of cash and food stamps, those who did not have a generous parent or boyfriend worked at regular or informal jobs. They also had to "work" the system, making sure that neither their earnings nor the contributions they received came to the attention of the welfare department. If they reported such income, their welfare checks would soon be reduced by almost the full amount of this income, leaving them as poor as before.

Table 26.2 shows that, on average, cash welfare, food stamps, and SSI covered only about three-fifths of welfare-reliant mothers' expenses.[8] A small amount also came from the earned income tax credit (EITC) for wages earned in the prior year. From our conversations with mothers, we learned that they made up the remaining gap by generating extra cash, garnering in-kind contributions, and purchasing stolen goods at below market value. We found it difficult to estimate, however, how much each mother saved by using the latter two techniques. Therefore, we only present figures for those strategies that generated extra cash.

Earnings from reported work, unreported work (off the books or under a false identity), or work in the underground economy (selling sex, drugs, or stolen goods) made up 15 percent of welfare-reliant mothers' total monthly income.[9] Another chunk (17 percent) came from members of their personal networks and went unreported. Agency-based contributions—usually cash

TABLE 26.2 Survival Strategies of 214 Welfare-Reliant Mothers

Variable	Amount of Income Generated Through Each Survival Strategy	Percentage of Total Budget	Percent of Mothers Engaging in Each Survival Strategy[a]
TOTAL EXPENSES	$876	100%	N/A
Housing costs	213	24	N/A
Food costs	262	30	N/A
Other necessities	336	39	N/A
Nonessentials	64	7	N/A
Welfare benefits	565	64	N/A
AFDC	307	35	100%
Food Stamps	222	25	95
SSI	36	4	9
EITC	3	2	7
Work-based strategies	128	15	46
Reported work	19	2	5
Unreported work	90	10	39
Underground work	19	2	8
Network-based strategies	151	17	77
Family and friends	62	7	46
Men	95	11	52
Boyfriends	56	6	29
Absent fathers	39	4	33
Covert system	33	4	23
Formal system	7	1	14
Agency-based strategies	37	4	31
TOTAL INCOME	$883	100%	N/A

[a]The sum of the percentages exceeds the total because some mothers engaged in more than one strategy.
Source: Authors' calculations using Edin and Lein survival strategies data.
Note: These income-generating strategies do not include in-kind contributions or purchasing goods illegally because these figures were difficult to estimate. Columns do not total due to rounding.

contributions, direct payment of mothers' bills, or the portion of student grants and loans that could be squeezed for extra household cash after paying for tuition and books—covered the last 4 percent of the average welfare-reliant mother's budget.

To get a clearer sense of how welfare-reliant mothers generated extra income, Table 26.2 also shows the degree to which mothers relied on various sources of income each month. By definition, all the mothers we coded as welfare-reliant received something from the AFDC program. Table 26.2 shows that almost all of them also received food stamps (95 percent), compared with 87 percent of welfare recipients nationwide (U.S. House of Representatives 1993:711).[10] Nine percent of the sample received SSI or payments for the care of foster children. Seven percent received money from the EITC because they reported income from work during the previous calendar year.

Table 26.2 gives further detail on how mothers' earnings from work contributed to their family budgets. Five percent worked in the formal economy at reported jobs, compared with 6 percent nationally (U.S. House of Representatives 1993:696). Others were also working and not reporting it. Approximately two-fifths (39 percent) worked off the books or under a false identity to generate additional income, and 8 percent worked in the underground economy selling sex, drugs, or stolen goods. (The percentages do not sum to 46 percent because some mothers engaged in more than one strategy.) Table 26.2 also shows that 77 percent of mothers were currently receiving covert contributions from family, boyfriends, or absent fathers in order to make ends meet.[11] Nearly half (46 percent) of welfare-reliant mothers relied on family and friends for financial help each month. Even more, 52 percent, received help from a man: 29 percent from boyfriends on a regular basis, 14 percent through the formal child support collection system, and 23 percent from the fathers of their children on a covert basis. In addition, 31 percent received cash, voucher, or direct assistance in paying a bill from a community group, charity, or student aid program.

Critics of welfare programs often suspect that low-income families cause their material poverty through poor money management (Heclo 1994). By comparing the expenses that our mothers reported, however, with those of the poorest income group in the Consumer Expenditure Survey (CES), we show that our welfare-reliant mothers spent substantially less than most American households in the early 1990s.[12]

. . .

Surviving on Welfare

Americans have long worried that welfare benefits are too generous. Many hear about high rates of out-of-wedlock births among the poor and conclude that welfare contributes to the problem. A more fundamental question is how do individual welfare recipients actually use the government support they receive? What standard of living do welfare benefits afford single mothers?

We have attempted to answer this question by interviewing 214 welfare-reliant mothers about what they spent to keep their families together. We also examined the level of welfare benefits available to the mothers. We found that for most welfare-reliant mothers food and shelter alone cost almost as much as these mothers received from the government. For more than one-third, food and housing costs exceeded their cash benefits, leaving no extra money for uncovered medical care, clothing, and other household expenses. When we added the costs of other necessities to the mothers' budgets, it was evident that virtually all welfare-reliant mothers experienced a wide gap between what they could get from welfare and what they needed to support their families. In fact, with only one exception, we met no welfare mother who was making ends meet on her government check alone. Mothers filled the gap through reported and unreported work and through handouts from family, friends, and agencies. . . . Finally, we asked the difficult question of whether welfare-reliant mothers' expenditures were truly necessary. We found that our mothers' budgets were far below the household budgets collected by the Consumer Expenditure Survey in 1991 for single-parent families. Our welfare-reliant mothers also spent less than the lowest income group the CES interviewed. Our conclusion is that the vast majority of our welfare-reliant mothers' expenses were at the very low end of widely shared national consumption norms.

Despite spending far more than their welfare benefits, many of the families we interviewed experienced serious material hardship. Variations in benefit levels had real consequences for welfare-reliant single mothers and their children. Lower benefits substantially increased material hardship as did having larger families. Life on welfare, it seems, was an exceedingly tenuous affair.[13] An articulate Chicago respondent put it this way:

> *I don't understand why [Public Aid is] punishing people who are poor if you want to mainstream them. If indeed, the idea is to segregate, to be biased, to create a widening gap between the haves and the have-nots, then the welfare system is working. If it is to provide basic needs, not just the financial but the psychological and social needs of every human being, then the system fails miserably.*

NOTES

1. In 1994, 49 percent of Americans thought that welfare programs discouraged people from working, and two-thirds believed that welfare encouraged women to have more children than they would have had if welfare were not available (Blendon et al. 1995).

2. These responses were gathered during the center's General Social Survey.

3. Due to rounding, these estimates do not total $876.

4. We did not include any teenage mothers living at home. Mothers under age eighteen constitute only a tiny portion of all mothers on the welfare rolls (U.S. House of Representatives 1995, table 10-27). We did interview seventeen teenage mothers and found that they paid almost none of their own bills because most of them lived rent-free with their mothers while they tried to finish school. Therefore, these teenage mothers could not construct a household budget.

5. Nor could families with housing subsidies, disability income, or reported outside income buy all of their food with food stamps.

6. There is a reduction in food stamp benefits as cash benefits rise.

7. In terms of nonnecessary spending, more than a third of families spent nothing whatsoever on entertainment during the previous year; two-thirds never ate out;

nearly half had spent nothing on cigarettes or alcohol during the year; and four-fifths had gone without cable television.

8. Four percent of all welfare-reliant families received either SSI or survivor's benefits (U.S. House of Representatives 1993, p. 719).

9. For those mothers who sold illegal drugs, a small personal supply was sometimes an in-kind benefit of the job.

10. These small differences are due to the fact that we did not interview any teenage recipients, who often lived with better-off family members and were thus not eligible for food stamps.

11. Fourteen percent had received payments through the Child Support Enforcement system in the last year, which was slightly above the national average of 12 percent for welfare recipients (U.S. Department of Health and Human Services 1990, p. 43).

12. This poorest income group included individuals and families reporting household incomes of less than $5,000 a year. Of course, this group spent far more than their reported income, and the CES could not account for the discrepancy.

13. Whereas Charles Murray (1984) portrayed an overly generous welfare system that kept the poor in poverty because it rewarded their indolence, mothers saw welfare as a stingy and punishing system that placed them and their children in a desperate economic predicament.

REFERENCES

Bane, Mary Jo and David T. Ellwood. 1983. "The Dynamics of Dependence: The Routes to Self-Sufficiency." Report supported by U.S. Department of Health and Human Services under Grant no. HHS-100-82-0038. Cambridge, MA: John F. Kennedy School of Government, Harvard University. Mimeo.

Blank, Rebecca M. 1994. "The Employment Strategy: Public Policies to Increase Work and Earnings." In *Confronting Poverty,* edited by Sheldon H. Danziger, Gary D. Sandefur, and Daniel H. Weinberg. Cambridge, MA: Harvard University Press; New York: Russell Sage Foundation.

Blendon, Robert J., Drew E. Altman, John Benson, Mollyann Brodie, Matt James, and Gerry Chervinsky. 1995. "The Public and the Welfare Reform Debate." *Archives of Pediatric and Adolescent Medicine* 149:1065–69.

Bobo, Lawrence and Ryan A. Smith. 1994. "Antipoverty Policy, Affirmative Action, and Racial Attitudes." In *Confronting Poverty,* edited by Sheldon H. Danziger, Gary D. Sandefur, and Daniel H. Weinberg. Cambridge, MA: Harvard University Press; New York: Russell Sage Foundation.

Heclo, Hugh. 1994. "Poverty Politics." In *Confronting Poverty,* edited by Sheldon H. Danziger, Gary D. Sandefur, and Daniel H. Weinberg. Cambridge, MA: Harvard University Press; New York: Russell Sage Foundation.

Moffitt, Robert. 1992. "Incentive Effects of the U.S. Welfare System: A Review." *Journal of Economic Literature* 30 (March):1–61.

Murray, Charles A. 1984. *Losing Ground: American Social Policy.* New York: Basic Books.

Page, Benjamin I. and Robert Y. Shapiro. 1992. *The Rational Public: Fifty Years of Trends in American's Policy Preferences.* Chicago: University of Chicago Press.

Ruggles, Patricia. 1990. *Drawing the Line: Alternative Poverty Measures and Their Implications.* Washington, DC: Urban Institute Press.

Schwarz, John E. and Thomas J. Volgy. 1992. "Social Support for Self-Reliance: The Politics of Making Work Pay." *American Prospect* 9 (Spring):67–73.

U.S. Department of Health and Human Services. 1990. *Child Support Enforcement.* Annual Report to Congress 92-3301. Washington, DC: U.S. Government Printing Office.

U.S. House of Representatives, Committee on Ways and Means. 1993. Overview of Entitlement Programs (Green Block). Washington, DC: U.S. Government Printing Office.

U.S. House of Representatives, Committee on Ways and Means. 1995. Overview of Entitlement Programs (Green Block). Washington, DC: U.S. Government Printing Office.

GENDER

27

THE GLASS ESCALATOR
Hidden Advantages for Men
in the "Female" Professions

CHRISTINE L. WILLIAMS

Gender stratification, examined in the next four selections, refers to those social systems in which socioeconomic resources and political power are distributed on the basis of one's sex and gender. In any social system, we can measure the gendered distribution of resources and rewards to see whether men or women have a higher social status. Objective indices of gender inequality include income, educational attainment, wealth, occupational status, mortality rates, and access to social institutions. Moreover, gender role socialization often reinforces gender inequality because men and women are expected to fulfill different family and occupational roles. Thus, in U.S. society, women traditionally are assigned the roles of homemaker, nurse, teacher, and secretary, which typically have less social status and lower salaries than male occupational roles. This 1992 article by Christine L. Williams is an analysis of what happens when men enter traditionally defined "female" occupations. Williams' in-depth interviews reveal the advantages and disadvantages experienced by male nurses, teachers, librarians, and social workers.

The sex segregation of the U.S. labor force is one of the most perplexing and tenacious problems in our society. Even though the proportion of men and women in the labor force is approaching parity (particularly

From *Social Problems* 39, no. 3 (August 1992):253–67. © 1992 by The Society for the Study of Social Problems. Reprinted by permission from Christine L. Williams.

for younger cohorts of workers) (U.S. Department of Labor 1991:18), men and women are still generally confined to predominantly single-sex occupations. Forty percent of men or women would have to change major occupational categories to achieve equal representation of men and women in all jobs (Reskin and Roos 1990:6), but even this figure underestimates the true degree of sex segregation. It is extremely rare to find specific jobs where equal numbers of men and women are engaged in the same activities in the same industries (Bielby and Baron 1984).

Most studies of sex segregation in the workforce have focused on women's experiences in male-dominated occupations. Both researchers and advocates for social change have focused on the barriers faced by women who try to integrate predominantly male fields. Few have looked at the "flipside" of occupational sex segregation: the exclusion of men from predominantly female occupations (exceptions include Schreiber 1979; Williams 1989; Zimmer 1988). But the fact is that men are less likely to enter female sextyped occupations than women are to enter male-dominated jobs (Jacobs 1989). Reskin and Roos, for example, were able to identify 33 occupations in which female representation increased by more than nine percentage points between 1970 and 1980, but only three occupations in which the proportion of men increased as radically (1990:20–21).

In this paper, I examine men's underrepresentation in four predominantly female occupations—nursing, librarianship, elementary school teaching, and social work. Throughout the twentieth century, these occupations have been identified with "women's work"—even though prior to the Civil War, men were more likely to be employed in these areas. These four occupations, often called the female "semi-professions" (Hodson and Sullivan 1990), today range from 5.5 percent male (in nursing) to 32 percent male (in social work). These percentages have not changed substantially in decades. In fact, two of these professions—librarianship and social work—have experienced declines in the proportions of men since 1975. Nursing is the only one of the four experiencing noticeable changes in sex composition, with the proportion of men increasing 80 percent between 1975 and 1990. Even so, men continue to be a tiny minority of all nurses.

. . .

Methods

I conducted in-depth interviews with 76 men and 23 women in four occupations from 1985 to 1991. Interviews were conducted in four metropolitan areas: San Francisco/Oakland, California; Austin, Texas; Boston, Massachusetts; and Phoenix, Arizona. These four areas were selected because they show considerable variation in the proportions of men in the four professions. For example, Austin has one of the highest percentages of men in nursing (7.7 percent), whereas Phoenix's percentage is one of the lowest (2.7 percent)

(U.S. Bureau of the Census 1980). The sample was generated using "snow-balling" techniques. Women were included in the sample to gauge their feelings and responses to men who enter "their" professions.

. . .

Discrimination in Hiring

Contrary to the experience of many women in the male-dominated professions, many of the men and women I spoke to indicated that there is a *preference* for hiring men in these four occupations. A Texas librarian at a junior high school said that his school district "would hire a male over a female."

> I: Why do you think that is?
>
> R: *Because there are so few, and the . . . ones that they do have, the library directors seem to really . . . think they're doing great jobs. I don't know, maybe they just feel they're being progressive or something, [but] I have had a real sense that they really appreciate having a male, particularly at the junior high. . . . As I said, when seven of us lost our jobs from the high schools and were redistributed, there were only four positions at junior high, and I got one of them. Three of the librarians, some who had been here longer than I had with the school district, were put down in elementary school as librarians. And I definitely think that being male made a difference in my being moved to the junior high rather than an elementary school.*

Many of the men perceived their token status as males in predominantly female occupations as an *advantage* in hiring and promotions. I asked an Arizona teacher whether his specialty (elementary special education) was an unusual area for men compared to other areas within education. He said,

> *Much more so. I am extremely marketable in special education. That's not why I got into the field. But I am extremely marketable because I am a man.*

In several cases, the more female-dominated the specialty, the greater the apparent preference for men. For example, when asked if he encountered any problem getting a job in pediatrics, a Massachusetts nurse said,

> *No, no, none. . . . I've heard this from managers and supervisory-type people with men in pediatrics: "It's nice to have a man because it's such a female-dominated profession."*

However, there were some exceptions to this preference for men in the most female-dominated specialties. In some cases, formal policies actually barred men from certain jobs. This was the case in some rural Texas school districts, which refused to hire men in the youngest grades (K–3). Some nurses also reported being excluded from positions in obstetrics and gynecology wards, a policy encountered more frequently in private Catholic hospitals.

But often the pressures keeping men out of certain specialties were more subtle than this. Some men described being "tracked" into practice areas within their professions which were considered more legitimate for men. For example, one Texas man described how he was pushed into administration and planning in social work, even though "I'm not interested in writing policy; I'm much more interested in research and clinical stuff." A nurse who is interested in pursuing graduate study in family and child health in Boston said he was dissuaded from entering the program specialty in favor of a concentration in "adult nursing." A kindergarten teacher described the difficulty of finding a job in his specialty after graduation: "I was recruited immediately to start getting into a track to become an administrator. And it was men who recruited me. It was men that ran the system at that time, especially in Los Angeles."

This tracking may bar men from the most female-identified specialties within these professions. But men are effectively being "kicked upstairs" in the process. Those specialties considered more legitimate practice areas for men also tend to be the most prestigious, better paying ones. A distinguished kindergarten teacher, who had been voted citywide "Teacher of the Year," told me that even though people were pleased to see him in the classroom, "there's been some encouragement to think about administration, and there's been some encouragement to think about teaching at the university level or something like that, or supervisory-type position." That is, despite his aptitude and interest in staying in the classroom, he felt pushed in the direction of administration.

The effect of this "tracking" is the opposite of that experienced by women in male-dominated occupations. Researchers have reported that many women encounter a "glass ceiling" in their efforts to scale organizational and professional hierarchies. That is, they are constrained by invisible barriers to promotion in their careers, caused mainly by sexist attitudes of men in the highest positions (Freeman 1990). In contrast to the "glass ceiling," many of the men I interviewed seem to encounter a "glass escalator." Often, despite their intentions, they face invisible pressures to move up in their professions. As if on a moving escalator, they must work to stay in place.

A public librarian specializing in children's collections (a heavily female-dominated concentration) described an encounter with this "escalator" in his very first job out of library school. In his first six-months' evaluation, his supervisors commended him for his good work in storytelling and related activities, but they criticized him for "not shooting high enough."

Seriously. That's literally what they were telling me. They assumed that because I was a male—and they told me this—and that I was being hired right out of graduate school, that somehow I wasn't doing the kind of management-oriented work that they thought I should be doing. And as a result, really they had a lot of bad marks, as it were, against me on my evaluation. And I said I couldn't believe this!

Throughout his 10-year career, he has had to struggle to remain in children's collections.

The glass escalator does not operate at all levels. In particular, men in academia reported some gender-based discrimination in the highest positions due to their universities' commitment to affirmative action. Two nursing professors reported that they felt their own chances of promotion to deanships were nil because their universities viewed the position of nursing dean as a guaranteed female appointment in an otherwise heavily male-dominated administration. One California social work professor reported his university canceled its search for a dean because no minority male or female candidates had been placed on their short list. It was rumored that other schools on campus were permitted to go forward with their searches—even though they also failed to put forward names of minority candidates—because the higher administration perceived it to be "easier" to fulfill affirmative action goals in the social work school. The interviews provide greater evidence of the "glass escalator" at work in the lower levels of these professions.

Of course, men's motivations also play a role in their advancement to higher professional positions. I do not mean to suggest that the men I talked to all resented the informal tracking they experienced. For many men, leaving the most female-identified areas of their professions helped them resolve internal conflicts involving their masculinity. One man left his job as a school social worker to work in a methadone drug treatment program not because he was encouraged to leave by his colleagues, but because "I think there was some macho shit there, to tell you the truth, because I remember feeling a little uncomfortable there . . . ; it didn't feel right to me." Another social worker, employed in the mental health services department of a large urban area in California, reflected on his move into administration:

> The more I think about it, through our discussion, I'm sure that's a large part of why I wound up in administration. It's okay for a man to do the administration. In fact, I don't know if I fully answered a question that you asked a little while ago about how did being male contribute to my advancing in the field. I was saying it wasn't because I got any special favoritism as a man, but . . . I think . . . because I'm a man, I felt a need to get into this kind of position. I may have worked harder toward it, may have competed harder for it, than most women would do, even women who think about doing administrative work.

Elsewhere I have speculated on the origins of men's tendency to define masculinity through single-sex work environments (Williams 1989). Clearly, personal ambition does play a role in accounting for men's movement into more "male-defined" arenas within these professions. But these occupations also structure opportunities for males independent of their individual desires or motives.

The interviews suggest that men's underrepresentation in these professions cannot be attributed to discrimination in hiring or promotions. Many of the men indicated that they received preferential treatment because they were men. Although men mentioned gender discrimination in the hiring process, for the most part they were channeled into the more "masculine" specialties within these professions, which ironically meant being "tracked" into better-paying and more prestigious specialties.

Supervisors and Colleagues: The Working Environment

Researchers claim that subtle forms of workplace discrimination push women out of male-dominated occupations (Jacobs 1989; Reskin and Hartmann 1986). In particular, women report feeling excluded from informal leadership and decision-making networks, and they sense hostility from their male co-workers, which makes them feel uncomfortable and unwanted (Carothers and Crull 1984). Respondents in this study were asked about their relationships with supervisors and female colleagues to ascertain whether men also experienced "poisoned" work environments when entering gender atypical occupations.

A major difference in the experience of men and women in nontraditional occupations is that men in these situations are far more likely to be supervised by a member of their own sex. In each of the four professions I studied, men are overrepresented in administrative and managerial capacities, or, as is the case of nursing, their positions in the organizational hierarchy are governed by men (Grimm and Stern 1974; Phenix 1987; Schmuck 1987; Williams 1989; York, Henley and Gamble 1987). Thus, unlike women who enter "male fields," the men in these professions often work under the direct supervision of other men.

Many of the men interviewed reported that they had good rapport with their male supervisors. Even in professional school, some men reported extremely close relationships with their male professors. For example, a Texas librarian described an unusually intimate association with two male professors in graduate school:

> *I can remember a lot of times in the classroom there would be discussions about a particular topic or issue, and the conversation would spill over into their office hours, after the class was over. And even though there were . . . a couple of the other women that had been in on the discussion, they weren't there. And I don't know if that was preferential or not . . . it certainly carried over into personal life as well. Not just at the school and that sort of thing. I mean, we would get together for dinner. . . .*

. . .

Other men reported similar closeness with their professors. A Texas psychotherapist recalled his relationships with his male professors in social work school:

I made it a point to make a golfing buddy with one of the guys that was in administration. He and I played golf a lot. He was the guy who kind of ran the research training, the research part of the master's program. Then there was a sociologist who ran the other part of the research program. He and I developed a good friendship.

This close mentoring by male professors contrasts with the reported experience of women in nontraditional occupations. Others have noted a lack of solidarity among women in nontraditional occupations. Writing about military academies, for example, Yoder describes the failure of token women to mentor succeeding generations of female cadets. She argues that women attempt to play down their gender difference from men because it is the source of scorn and derision.

> Because women felt unaccepted by their male colleagues, one of the last things they wanted to do was to emphasize their gender. Some women thought that, if they kept company with other women, this would highlight their gender and would further isolate them from male cadets. These women desperately wanted to be accepted as cadets, not as *women* cadets. Therefore, they did everything from not wearing skirts as an option with their uniforms to avoiding being a part of a group of women. (Yoder 1989:532)

Men in nontraditional occupations face a different scenario—their gender is construed as a *positive* difference. Therefore, they have an incentive to bond together and emphasize their distinctiveness from the female majority.

. . .

Openly gay men may encounter less favorable treatment at the hands of their supervisors. For example, a nurse in Texas stated that one of the physicians he worked with preferred to staff the operating room with male nurses exclusively—as long as they weren't gay. Stigma associated with homosexuality leads some men to enhance, or even exaggerate their "masculine" qualities, and may be another factor pushing men into more "acceptable" specialties for men.

Not all men who work in these occupations are supervised by men. Many of the men interviewed who had female bosses also reported high levels of acceptance—although levels of intimacy with women seemed lower than with other men. In some cases, however, men reported feeling shut out from decision making when the higher administration was constituted entirely by women. I asked an Arizona librarian whether men in the library profession were discriminated against in hiring because of their sex:

Professionally speaking, people go to considerable lengths to keep that kind of thing out of their [hiring] deliberations. Personally, is another matter. It's pretty common around here to talk about the "old girl network." This is one of the few libraries that I've had any intimate knowledge of which is actually controlled by women. . . . Most of the department heads and upper-level administrators are women. And there's an "old girl network" that works just like the "old boy network," except that the important conferences take place in the women's room rather than on the golf course. But the political mechanism is the same, the exclusion of the other sex from decision making is the same. The reasons are the same. It's somewhat discouraging. . . .

Although I did not interview many supervisors, I did include 23 women in my sample to ascertain their perspectives about the presence of men in their professions. All of the women I interviewed claimed to be supportive of their male colleagues, but some conveyed ambivalence. For example, a social work professor said she would like to see more men enter the social work profession, particularly in the clinical specialty (where they are underrepresented). Indeed, she favored affirmative action hiring guidelines for men in the profession. Yet, she resented the fact that her department hired "another white male" during a recent search.

. . .

Even outside work, most of the men interviewed said they felt fully accepted by their female colleagues. They were usually included in informal socializing occasions with the women—even though this frequently meant attending baby showers or Tupperware parties. Many said that they declined offers to attend these events because they were not interested in "women's things," although several others claimed to attend everything: The minority men I interviewed seemed to feel the least comfortable in these informal contexts. One social worker in Arizona was asked about socializing with his female colleagues:

> I: So in general, for example, if all the employees were going to get together to have a party, or celebrate a bridal shower or whatever, would you be invited along with the rest of the group?
> R: *They would invite me, I would say, somewhat reluctantly. Being a black male, working with all white females, it did cause some outside problems. So I didn't go to a lot of functions with them. . . .*
> I: You felt that there was some tension there on the level of your acceptance . . . ?
> R: *Yeah. It was OK working, but on the outside, personally, there was some tension there. It never came out, that they said, "Because of who you are we can't invite you" (laughs), and I wouldn't have done anything anyway. I would have probably respected them more for saying what was on their minds. But I never felt completely in with the group.*

Some single men also said they felt uncomfortable socializing with married female colleagues because it gave the "wrong impression." But in general, the men said that they felt very comfortable around their colleagues and described their work places as very congenial for men. It appears unlikely, therefore, that men's underrepresentation in these professions is due to hostility toward men on the part of supervisors or women workers.

Discrimination from "Outsiders"

The most compelling evidence of discrimination against men in these professions is related to their dealings with the public. Men often encounter negative stereotypes when they come into contact with clients or "outsiders"—people they meet outside of work. For instance, it is popularly assumed that male nurses are gay. Librarians encounter images of themselves as "wimpy" and asexual. Male social workers describe being typecast as "feminine" and "passive." Elementary school teachers are often confronted by suspicions that they are pedophiles. One kindergarten teacher described an experience that occurred early in his career, which was related to him years afterward by his principal:

> He indicated to me that parents had come to him and indicated to him that they had a problem with the fact that I was a male. . . . I recall almost exactly what he said. There were three specific concerns that the parents had: One parent said, "How can he love my child; he's a man." The second thing that I recall, he said the parent said, "He has a beard." And the third thing was, "Aren't you concerned about homosexuality?"

Such suspicions often cause men in all four professions to alter their work behavior to guard against sexual abuse charges, particularly in those specialties requiring intimate contact with women and children.

Men are very distressed by these negative stereotypes, which tend to undermine their self-esteem and to cause them to second-guess their motivations for entering these fields. A California teacher said,

> If I tell men that I don't know, that I'm meeting for the first time, that that's what I do, . . . sometimes there's a look on their faces that, you know, "Oh, couldn't get a real job?"

When asked if his wife, who is also an elementary school teacher, encounters the same kind of prejudice, he said,

> No, it's accepted because she's a woman. . . . I think people would see that as a . . . step up, you know. "Oh, you're not a housewife, you've got a career. That's great . . . that you're out there working. And you have a daughter, but you're still out there working. You decided not to stay home, and you went out there and got a job." Whereas for me, it's more like I'm supposed to be out working anyway, even though I'd rather be home with [my daughter].

Unlike women who enter traditionally male professions, men's movement into these jobs is perceived by the "outside world" as a step down in status. This particular form of discrimination may be most significant in explaining why men are underrepresented in these professions. Men who otherwise might show interest in and aptitudes for such careers are probably discouraged from pursuing them because of the negative popular stereotypes associated with the men who work in them. This is a crucial difference from the experience of women in nontraditional professions: "My daughter, the physician," resonates far more favorably in most people's ears than "my son, the nurse."

Many of the men in my sample identified the stigma of working in a female-identified occupation as the major barrier to more men entering their professions. However, for the most part, they claimed that these negative stereotypes were not a factor in their own decisions to join these occupations. Most respondents didn't consider entering these fields until well into adulthood, after working in some related occupation. Several social workers and librarians even claimed they were not aware that men were a minority in their chosen professions. Either they had no well-defined image or stereotype, or their contacts and mentors were predominantly men. For example, prior to entering library school, many librarians held part-time jobs in university libraries, where there are proportionally more men than in the profession generally. Nurses and elementary school teachers were more aware that mostly women worked in these jobs, and this was often a matter of some concern to them. However, their choices were ultimately legitimized by mentors, or by encouraging friends or family members who implicitly reassured them that entering these occupations would not typecast them as feminine. In some cases, men were told by recruiters there were special advancement opportunities for men in these fields, and they entered them expecting rapid promotion to administrative positions.

> *I:*   Did it ever concern you when you were making the decision to enter nursing school, the fact that it is a female-dominated profession?
> *R: Not really. I never saw myself working on the floor. I saw myself pretty much going into administration, just getting the background and then getting a job someplace as a supervisor and then working, getting up into administration.*

Because of the unique circumstances of their recruitment, many of the respondents did not view their occupational choices as inconsistent with a male gender role, and they generally avoided the negative stereotypes directed against men in these fields.

Indeed, many of the men I interviewed claimed that they did not encounter negative professional stereotypes until they had worked in these fields for several years. Popular prejudices can be damaging to self-esteem and probably push some men out of these professions altogether. Yet, ironically, they sometimes contribute to the "glass escalator" effect I have been describing. Men seem to encounter the most vituperative criticism from the public when they are in the most female-identified specialties. Public concerns sometimes result in their being shunted into more "legitimate" positions for men. A librarian formerly in charge of a branch library's children's collection, who now works in the reference department of the city's main library, describes his experience:

> *R: Some of the people [who frequented the branch library] complained that they didn't want to have a man doing the storytelling scenario. And I got transferred here to the central library in an equivalent job. . . . I thought that I did a good job. And I had been told by my supervisor that I was doing a good job.*
>
> *I: Have you ever considered filing some sort of lawsuit to get that other job back?*
>
> *R: Well, actually, the job I've gotten now . . . well, it's a reference librarian; it's what I wanted in the first place. I've got a whole lot more authority here. I'm also in charge of the circulation desk. And I've recently been promoted because of my new stature, so . . . no, I'm not considering trying to get that other job back.*

The negative stereotypes about men who do "women's work" can push men out of specific jobs. However, to the extent that they channel men into more "legitimate" practice areas, their effects can actually be positive. Instead of being a source of discrimination, these prejudices can add to the "glass escalator effect" by pressuring men to move *out* of the most female-identified areas, and *up* to those regarded more legitimate and prestigious for men.

Author's Note: This research was funded in part by a faculty grant from the University of Texas at Austin. I also acknowledge the support of the sociology departments of the University of California, Berkeley; Harvard University; and Arizona State University. I would like to thank Judy Auerbach, Martin Button, Robert Nye, Teresa Sullivan, Debra Umberson, Mary Waters, and the reviewers at *Social Problems* for their comments on earlier versions of this paper. © 1992 by the Society for the Study of Social Problems. Reprinted from *Social Problems,* Vol. 39, No. 3, August 1992, pp. 253–67 by permission.

REFERENCES

Bielby, William T. and James N. Baron. 1984. "A Woman's Place Is with Other Women: Sex Segregation within Organizations." Pp. 27–55 in *Sex Segregation in the Workplace: Trends, Explanations, Remedies,* edited by Barbara Reskin. Washington, DC: National Academy Press.

Carothers, Suzanne C. and Peggy Crull. 1984. "Contrasting Sexual Harassment in Female-Dominated and Male-Dominated Occupations." Pp. 220–27 in *My Troubles Are Going to Have Trouble with Me: Everyday Trials and Triumphs of Women Workers,* edited by Karen B. Sacks and Dorothy Remy. New Brunswick, NJ: Rutgers University Press.

Freeman, Sue J. M. 1990. *Managing Lives: Corporate Women and Social Change.* Amherst, MA: University of Massachusetts Press.

Grimm, James W. and Robert N. Stern. 1974. "Sex Roles and Internal Labor Market Structures: The Female Semi-Professions." *Social Problems* 21:690–705.

Hodson, Randy and Teresa Sullivan. 1990. *The Social Organization of Work.* Belmont, CA: Wadsworth Publishing Co.

Jacobs, Jerry. 1989. *Revolving Doors: Sex Segregation and Women's Careers.* Stanford, CA: Stanford University Press.

Phenix, Katherine. 1987. "The Status of Women Librarians." *Frontiers* 9:36–40.

Reskin, Barbara and Heidi Hartmann. 1986. *Women's Work, Men's Work: Sex Segregation on the Job.* Washington, DC: National Academy Press.

Reskin, Barbara and Patricia Roos. 1990. *Job Queues, Gender Queues: Explaining Women's Inroads into Male Occupations.* Philadelphia: Temple University Press.

Schmuck, Patricia A. 1987. "Women School Employees in the United States." Pp. 75–97 in *Women Educators: Employees of Schools in Western Counties,* edited by Patricia A. Schmuck. Albany: State University of New York Press.

Schreiber, Carol. 1979. *Men and Women in Transitional Occupations.* Cambridge, MA: MIT Press.

U.S. Bureau of the Census. 1980. *Detailed Population Characteristics,* vol. 1, Ch. D. Washington, DC: Government Printing Office.

U.S. Department of Labor. Bureau of Labor Statistics. 1991. *Employment and Earnings.* Washington, DC: Government Printing Office.

Williams, Christine L. 1989. *Gender Differences at Work: Women and Men in Nontraditional Occupations.* Berkeley: University of California Press.

Yoder, Janice D. 1989. "Women at West Point: Lessons for Token Women in Male-Dominated Occupations." Pp. 523–37 in *Women: A Feminist Perspective,* edited by Jo Freeman. Mountain View, CA: Mayfield Publishing Company.

York, Reginald O., H. Carl Henley, and Dorothy N. Gamble. 1987. "Sexual Discrimination in Social Work: Is It Salary or Advancement?" *Social Work* 32:336–40.

Zimmer, Lynn. 1988. "Tokenism and Women in the Workplace." *Social Problems* 35:64–77.

28

TREATING HEALTH
Women and Medicine

BARBARA KATZ ROTHMAN • MARY BETH CASCHETTA

Gender inequality has enormous consequences for women, men, and society. Gender inequality reinforces and perpetuates *sexism,* which is prejudice and discrimination against a person on the basis of his or her sex. The costs and consequences of sexism are extensive and include the wage gap, the feminization of poverty, high rates of female victimization as a result of male violence, and psychological and physical health problems in both women and men. This selection by Barbara Katz Rothman and Mary Beth Caschetta (1995) reveals the rampant sexism within the institution of medicine, both historically and currently. Specifically, the authors examine how the institution of medicine has defined and treated women and their illnesses differently from men and their illnesses.

Women are not only people: *Woman* is a subject one can specialize in within medicine. However, except for sex organs and reproduction, women have not been studied or treated adequately by the medical establishment. At the moment, when a woman enters the health delivery system, her body is essentially divided among specialists. Obstetricians and gynecologists, for example, are medicine's, and perhaps society's, generally recognized "experts" on the subject of women, though technically they provide care for only reproduction and the functioning of sex organs.[1] *Obstetrics* is the branch of medicine limited to the care of women during pregnancy, labor, and the time surrounding childbirth,[2] a practice that tried to supplant midwifery. *Gynecology* is the "science of the diseases of women, especially those affecting the sex organs."[3] Diseases that frequently affect women and do not involve the sex organs, such as thyroid disease, rheumatoid arthritis, adult-type diabetes, osteoporosis, and depression, have not been studied in women.[4] Conditions occurring more frequently in women of color, for example, hypertension, alcoholism, and cardiovascular diseases, have, until very recently, received no attention at all.

At its simplest, a medical specialty can be seen as arising out of preexisting needs. People have heart attacks: The medical specialty of cardiology develops. Or the amount of knowledge generated in a field grows so enormously that no one person can hope to master it all. Physicians then "carve out" their own areas of specialization. Increasing knowledge about cancer thus led to the specialty of, and the subspecialties within, oncology. By looking at the history of emerging specialties, their successes and failures, we can tell a lot about medical needs and knowledge. For instance, an attempt by urologists in 1891 to develop an "andrology" specialty for men came to nothing.[5] Technically, there is no "science" of the study of men, comparable to the specialties devoted to women and their reproductive functions. This may be because most of generalized medicine is already geared toward men and the male body, and women are treated as special cases in that they are different from men.

But the development of a medical specialty is not necessarily the creation of a key for an already existing lock. Medical needs do not necessarily predate the specialty, even though the specialty is presumably organized to meet those needs. This has been made quite clear in the work of Thomas Szasz on the expansion of medicine into such "social problem" areas as alcoholism, gambling, and suicide.[6] Medicine does not have "cures" for these problems, but by defining them in medical terms, as a sickness, the physician gains political control over the societal response: Punishment becomes "treatment," desired or not, successful or not. Similarly, medicine can be viewed as a tool in the political control over women's sexuality, childbirth, lactation, menopause, and general health and well-being. Such medical control has rarely been based on superior ability to deal with these concerns.

Exclusion of Women from Research

In 1985, the United States Public Health Service reported a general lack of research data on women and a limited understanding of women's general health needs.[7] Because menstrual cycles are said to constitute a separate variable affecting test results,[8] researchers have used menses as an excuse to exclude women from research. A woman's period "muddies" the research data, so to speak. Additionally, medical experts have been, and continue to be, reluctant to perform studies on women of childbearing age, because experimental treatments or procedures may affect their reproductive capabilities and/or a potential fetus.[9]

The exclusion of females from medical research is so institutionalized that even female rats are commonly excluded from early basic research, on which most medical decisions rest. The result of female exclusion from human research is that most medical recommendations made to the general population are extrapolated from the Caucasian male body.[10] Therefore, the original research on the ability of aspirin to prevent coronary artery disease was done exclusively on men,[11] although it had been known for some time

that heart disease is a leading killer of women. The original testing of antidepressant drugs on men[12] did not anticipate the fact that the constant doses appropriate for men may in women sometimes be too high or too low, due to
the natural hormonal changes during the menstrual cycle.[13]

As expected, this astounding lack of research concerning women's biology has enormous impact on the individual experiences of women seeking
care and results in inadequate health care. For instance, more women than
men die from heart disease each year, yet women with heart trouble are less
likely to receive treatment, even when symptoms clearly indicate severe
heart trouble exists.[14] And while lung cancer is the number-one cancer killer
of women, they are twice as likely as men *not* to be tested for lung cancer.[15]
Additionally, while AIDS is a leading killer of women in many urban areas,
the official definition of AIDS—which is actually a series of infections and
cancers that occur when the immune system is weakened by the human immunodeficiency virus (HIV)—did not originally include many of the HIV-
related conditions in women because what is known about HIV disease is derived principally from research on men.[16] Therefore, significant numbers of
women who die of HIV-related complications do so without an actual diagnosis of AIDS.[17]

The medical specialists clash over women and AIDS: Infectious disease
experts claim not to know about the gynecological infections and cancers of
HIV, and gynecologists claim not to understand the general manifestations of
HIV. Internists generally do not look for HIV infection in women. Therefore
undercounting of women in the epidemic is enormous: Women are denied
disability entitlements to which they are entitled; their illness goes mis-
diagnosed and untreated; and research efforts are skewed, distorting general
knowledge of the scope of the AIDS epidemic.

Problems with "Women" As a Medical Category

It is important to understand that the medical term *women* almost always
assumes white, middle-class females. The significance of this short-sighted
view of a diverse population is wide-reaching. For instance, biological racial
differences and socioeconomic impacts on illness are only now coming to
light, although they have long been suspected. Studies show that compared
to whites, Asians may achieve significantly higher blood serum levels when
given certain drugs; osteoporosis is more prevalent in white women; and
black women have a significantly higher rate of low birth weights, a fact often
blamed on inner-city socioeconomic status, yet Latina women in similar
inner-city situations birth far fewer low-weight babies.[18] Nonetheless, until
recently, medicine has ignored differences among real people, including gender and race.

Doctors, Midwives, and Other Struggles for Power

. . .

In the nineteenth and early twentieth centuries midwives and physicians were in direct competition for patients, and not only for their fees. Newer, more clinically oriented medical training demanded "teaching material," so that even immigrant and poor women were desired as patients.[19] The displacement of the midwife by the male obstetrician can be better understood in terms of this competition than as an ideological struggle or as "scientific advancement." Physicians, unlike the unorganized, disenfranchised midwives, had access to the power of the state through their professional associations. They were thus able to control licensing legislation, restricting the midwife's sphere of activity and imposing legal sanctions against her in state after state.[20]

The legislative changes were backed up by the medical establishment's attempt to win public disapproval for midwifery and support for obstetrics. Physicians accused midwives of ignorance and incompetence and attacked midwifery practices as "meddlesome." Rather than upgrading the practice of midwifery by teaching the skills physicians thought necessary, the profession of medicine refused to train women either as midwives or as physicians.[21] Physicians argued repeatedly that medicine was the appropriate profession to handle birth because "normal pregnancy and parturition are exceptions and to consider them to be normal physiologic conditions was a fallacy."[22] Childbirth was redefined as a medical rather than a social event, and the roles and care surrounding it were reorganized to suit medical needs.[23]

Once professional dominance was established in the area of childbirth, obstetrics rapidly expanded into the relatively more sophisticated area of gynecology. The great obstetricians of the nineteenth century were invariably gynecologists (and of course were all men).[24] Among other effects, this linking of obstetrics and gynecology further reinforced the obstetrical orientation toward pathology.

Medical Control and Women

One of the earliest uses of the developing field of gynecology was the overt social control of women through surgical removal of various sexual organs. Surgical removal of the clitoris (clitoridectomy) or, less dramatically, its foreskin (circumcision) and removal of the ovaries (oopherectomy or castration) were used to check women's "mental disorders." The first gynecologist to do a clitoridectomy was an Englishman, in 1858.[25] In England, the procedure was harshly criticized and was not repeated by others after the death of the originator in 1860. In America, however, clitoridectomies were done regularly from the late 1860s until at least 1904,[26] and then sporadically until as recently as the late 1940s.[27] The procedure was used to terminate sexual desire or sexual behavior, something deemed pathological in women. Circumcisions were done on women of all ages to stop masturbation up until at least 1937.[28]

More widespread than clitoridectomies or circumcisions were oopherectomies for psychological "disorders." Interestingly, the female gonads were removed not when women were "too female"—i.e., too passive or dependent—but when women were too masculine—assertive, aggressive, "unruly." Oopherectomies for "psychiatric" reasons were done in America between 1872 and 1946.[29] (By the 1940s, prefrontal lobotomies were gaining acceptance as psychosurgery.)

The developing medical control of women was not limited to extreme cures for psychiatric problems. The physical health and stability of even the most socially acceptable women were questioned. Simply by virtue of gender, women were (and are) subject to *illness labeling*.

One explanation for women's vulnerability to illness labeling lies in the functionalist approach to the sociology of health. Talcott Parsons has pointed out that it is a functional requirement of any social system that there be a basic level of health of its members.[30] Any definition of illness that is too lenient would disqualify too many people from fulfilling their functions and would impose severe strains on the social system. System changes, such as war, can make changes in standards of health and illness generally set for members. This works on an individual level as well, standards of health and illness being related to social demands: A mild headache will excuse a student from attending class but not from taking final exams. A logical extension of this is that the less valued a person's or group's contribution to society, the more easily are such people labeled ill.

Women are not always seen as functional members of society, as people doing important things. This has historically and cross-culturally been especially true of the women of the upper classes in patriarchal societies, where it is a mark of status for a man to be able to afford to keep a wife who is not performing any useful function. A clear, if horrifying, example of this is the traditional Chinese practice of foot-binding. By crippling girls, men were able to show that they could afford to have wives and daughters who did nothing. It is a particularly disturbing example of conspicuous consumption. In their historical analysis of the woman patient, *Complaints and Disorders*, Barbara Ehrenreich and Deirdre English speak of the European-American "lady of leisure" of the late nineteenth and early twentieth centuries. "She was the social ornament that proved a man's success; her idleness, her delicacy, her child-like ignorance of 'reality' gave a man the 'class' that money alone could not provide."[31]

Menstruation and the Body As Machine

The practice of creating physical deformity in women can be seen in our history as well. A woman researcher who studied menstrual problems among college women, between 1890 and 1920 found that women in the earlier period probably were somewhat incapacitated by menstruation, just as the gynecologists of the day were claiming. However, the researcher did not attribute the menstrual problems to women's "inherent disabilities" or "overgrowth of the intellect" as did the male physicians; she related it to dress styles. Women in the 1890s carried some 15 pounds of skirts and petticoats, hanging from a tightly corseted waist. As skirts got lighter and waists were allowed to be larger, menstruation ceased to be the problem it had been.[32] In the interest of science, women might try the experiment of buckling themselves into a painfully small belt and hanging a 15-pound weight from it. One might expect weakness, fatigue, shortness of breath, even fainting: all the physical symptoms of women's "inherent" disability. And consider further the effects of bleeding as a treatment for the problem.

It follows from Parsons' analysis that, in addition to suffering by created physical disabilities (the bound feet of the Chinese, the deforming corsetry of our own history), women were more easily *defined* as sick when they were not seen as functional social members. At the same time in our history that the upper-class women were "delicate," "sickly," and "frail," the working-class women were well enough to perform the physical labor of housework, both their own and that of the upper classes, as well as to work in the factories and fields. "However sick or tired working class women might have been, they certainly did not have the time or money to support a cult of invalidism. Employers gave no time off for pregnancy or recovery from childbirth, much less for menstrual periods, though the wives of these same employers often retired to bed on all these occasions."[33] The working-class women were seen as strong and healthy; for them, pregnancy, menstruation, and menopause were not allowed to be incapacitating.

These two factors—the treatment of the body as a machine and the lesser functional importance assigned to women—still account for much of the medical treatment of women. Contemporary physicians do not usually speak of the normal female reproductive functions as diseases. The exception, to be discussed below, is menopause. The other specifically female reproductive functions—menstruation, pregnancy, childbirth, and lactation—are regularly asserted in medical texts to be normal and healthy phenomena. However, these statements are made within the context of teaching the medical "management," "care," "supervision," and "treatment" of each of these "conditions."

Understood in limited mechanical terms, each of these normal female conditions or happenings is a complication or stress on an otherwise normal system. Medicine has fared no better than has any other discipline in developing a working model of women that does not take men as the comparative norm. For example, while menstruation is no longer viewed as a disease, it is seen as a complication in the female system, contrasted to the reputed biological stability of the supposedly noncycling male.[34] As recently as 1961, the *American Journal of Obstetrics and Gynecology* was still referring to women's "inherent disabilities" in explanations of menstruation:

> Women are known to suffer at least some inconvenience during certain phases of the reproductive cycle, and often with considerable mental and physical distress. Woman's awareness of her inherent disabilities is thought to create added mental and in turn physical changes in the total body response, and there result problems that concern the physician who must deal with them.[35]

Premenstrual syndrome (PMS) is probably the most recent and most stunning example of the construction of women's normal functions as disease. According to the medical model, PMS manifests as emotional, physical, and behavioral conditions, characterized by more than 150 "symptoms," any number of which a woman might "suffer" during a specific phase of her menstrual cycle. Symptoms are always negative and include the following, to name a few: tension, irritability, forgetfulness, depression, mood swings, anger, muscle pains, cramps, craving for sweets or alcohol, headaches, crying jags, panic attacks, suicidal depressions, and bouts of violent or abusive behavior.[36]

The cause of PMS is thought to be a physiologic abnormality or an abnormal response to normal hormonal changes during the seventh to tenth day before the menstrual period starts. However, the most current research shows that no such abnormalities could be consistently identified and linked to women who are diagnosed as having PMS.[37] Nonetheless, an abundance of hypotheses link PMS to medical causes. For instance, the syndrome has been attributed to an overproduction of estrogen, under- and overproduction of progesterone, a disturbance in the estrogen/progesterone balance, water retention, salt retention, an insulin imbalance, a liver malfunction, stress, and inadequate nutrition.[38] To accommodate "treatment" for the new medical condition, PMS clinics have sprung up across the United States, offering "diagnoses" of the syndrome by pelvic exam and blood tests that cost anywhere from $200 to $500.[39]

There is much debate about whether PMS is a true medical entity or a social phenomenon that medicalizes the menstrual cycle in order to enforce social control over women. Emily Martin explores current conceptions of women's role in society and women's bodies by examining accounts of the language used to describe PMS and its foremost "symptom," anger.[40] Martin writes:

> The problems of men in these accounts are caused by outside circumstances and other people (women). The problems of women are caused by their own internal failure, seen as a biological malfunction. What

is missing is any consideration of why, in Western societies, women might feel extreme rage at a time when their usual emotional controls are reduced.[41]

Pregnancy and the Mother-Host

Research on contraception displays mechanistic biases. The claim has been made that contraceptive research has concentrated on the female rather than the male because of the sheer number of potentially vulnerable links in the female chain of reproductive events.[42] Reproduction is clearly a more complicated process for the female than the male. While we might claim that it is safer to interfere in a simpler process, medicine has tended to view the number of points in the female reproductive process as distant entities. Reproduction is dealt with not as a complicated organic process but as a series of discrete points, like stations on an assembly line, with more for female than for male.

The alternative to taking the female system as a complication of the "basic" or "simpler" male system is of course to take female as the working norm. In this approach, a pregnant woman is compared only to pregnant women, a lactating breast compared only to other lactating breasts. Pregnancy and lactation are accepted not only as nominally healthy variations but as truly normal states. To take the example of pregnancy, women *are* pregnant; pregnancy is not something they "have" or "catch" or even "contain." It involves physical changes; these are not, as medical texts frequently call them, "symptoms" of pregnancy. Pregnancy is not a disease, and its changes are no more symptoms than the growth spurt and development of pubic hair are symptomatic of puberty. There may be diseases or complications of pregnancy, but the pregnancy itself is neither disease nor complication.

In contrast, medicine's working model of pregnancy is a woman with an insulated parasitic capsule growing inside. The pregnancy, while physically located within the woman, is still seen as external to her, not a part of her. The capsule within has been seen as virtually omniscient and omnipotent, reaching out and taking what it needs from the mother-host, at her expense if necessary, while protected from all that is bad or harmful.

The pregnancy, in this medical model, is almost entirely a mechanical event in the mother. She differs from the nonpregnant woman only in the presence of this thing growing inside her. Differences other than the mechanical are accordingly seen as symptoms to be treated, so that the woman can be kept as "normal" as possible through the "stress" of the pregnancy. Pregnancy in this model is not seen necessarily as inherently unhealthy, but it is frequently associated with changes other than the growth of the uterus and its contents, and these changes are seen as unhealthy. For example, hemoglobin (iron) is lower in pregnant women than nonpregnant, making pregnant women appear (by nonpregnant standards) anemic. They are then treated for this anemia with iron supplements. Water retention, or edema, is greater in pregnant women than nonpregnant ones, so pregnant women are treated with limits placed on their salt intake and with diuretics. Pregnant women tend to gain weight over that accounted for by the fetus, placenta, and amniotic fluid. They are treated for this weight gain with strict diets, sometimes even with "diet pills." And knowing that these changes are likely to occur in pregnant women, American doctors generally have tried to treat all pregnant women with iron supplements, with limits on salt and calorie intake, and sometimes with diuretics. This attempt to cure the symptoms has brought up not only strict diets to prevent normal weight gain and diuretics to prevent normal fluid retention but also the dangerous drugs, from thalidomide to Bendectin, to prevent nausea. Each of these "cures" has had devastating effects: fetal malformation, maternal and fetal illness, even death.

What is particularly important to note is that these "treatments" of entirely normal phenomena are frequently not perceived by the medical profession as interventions or disruptions. Rather, the physician sees himself as assisting nature, restoring the woman to normality. Janet Bogdan, in her study of the development of obstetrics, reports that in the 1800s, a noninterventionist physician, as opposed to a "regular" physician, would give a laboring woman some castor oil or milk of magnesia, catheterize her, bleed her a pint or so, administer ergot, and use poultices to blister her. "Any of these therapies would be administered in the interests of setting the parturient up for an easier, less painful labor and delivery, while still holding to the belief that the physician was letting nature take its course."[43] Dorothy Wertz says that medicine currently has redefined "natural childbirth," in response to consumer demand for it, to include any of the following techniques: spinal or epidural anesthesia, inhalation anesthesia in the second stage of labor, forceps, episiotomy, induced labor.[44] Each of these techniques increases the risks of childbirth for mothers and babies.[45] Under the title "Normal Delivery," an obstetric teaching film shows "the use of various drugs and procedures used to facilitate normal delivery." Another "Normal Delivery" film is "a demonstration of a normal, spontaneous delivery, including a paracervical block, episiotomy."

As the technologies of both "curing" and "diagnosis" grow more powerful, the danger increases. The extraordinary rise in cesarean sections starting in the 1970s in the United States provides a striking example of this. Refinements in anesthesiology, and to a lesser extent in surgery itself, have made the cesarean section a much safer procedure in recent years. While it is not, and cannot be, as safe as an unmedicated vaginal birth—a section is major abdominal surgery, and all anesthesia entails risk—it is unquestionably safer today than it was 20 or 40 years ago. Thus, the "cure" is more readily used. But what is the disease? The disease is labor, of course. While medicine now claims that pregnancy and labor are not diseases per se, they are always considered in terms of "riskiness": labor is at best "low risk" and is increasingly often defined as "high risk." At first only labors defined as high risk, but now even low-risk labors, are routinely being monitored electronically. The electronic fetal monitor has a belt that wraps around the pregnant belly, thus preventing normal walking and movement, and an electrode that goes into the vagina and literally screws into the top of the baby's head. Contractions, fetal heartbeat, and fetal scalp blood are all continuously monitored. With all of this diagnostic sophistication, "fetal distress" can be detected—and presumably cured, by cesarean section. The National Center for Health Services Research announced as far back as 1978 that electronic fetal monitoring may do more harm than good, citing among other things the dangers of the rapidly increasing cesarean section rate, but monitoring is still receiving widespread medical acceptance.[46]

Menopause and the End of the Femininity Index

The use of estrogens provides an even better example of how medicine views the body as a machine that can be "run" or managed without being changed. Estrogens are female hormones; in medicine they are seen as femininity in a jar. In the widely selling *Feminine Forever,* Dr. Robert A. Wilson, pushing "estrogen-replacement therapy" for all menopausal women, calls estrogen levels, as detected by examination of cells from the vagina, a woman's "femininity index."[47] As estrogen levels naturally drop off after menopause a woman, according to Wilson, is losing her femininity. Interestingly, estrogen levels are also quite low while a woman is breastfeeding, something not usually socially linked to a "loss of feminity."

Menopause remains the one normal female process that is still overtly referred to as a disease in the medical literature. To some physicians, menopause is a "deficiency disease," and the use of estrogens is restoring the woman to her "normal" condition. Here we must reconsider the question of women's functional importance in the social system. Middle-aged housewives have been called the last of the "ladies of leisure," having outlived their social usefulness as wife-mothers and having been allowed no alternatives. While oopherectomies and clitoridectomies are no longer being done on upper-class women as they were a hundred years ago, to cure all kinds of dubious ills, older women are having hysterectomies (surgical removal of the uterus) at alarming rates.[48] Much more typical of modern medicine, however, is the use of chemical rather than surgical "therapy." Because the social changes and demands for readjustment of middle age roughly coincide with the time of menopause, menopause becomes the "illness" for which women can be treated.

Estrogens have been used in virtually every stage of the female reproductive cycle, usually with the argument that they return the woman to normal or are a "natural" treatment. Estrogens are used to keep adolescent girls from getting "unnaturally" tall; to treat painful menstruation; as contraception, supposedly mimicking pregnancy; as a chemical abortion in the "morning after" pill; to replace supposedly missing hormones and thus to prevent miscarriages; to dry up milk and return women to the "normal" nonlactating state; and to return menopausal women to the "normal" cycling state. For all the claims of normality and natural treatment, at this writing approximately half of these uses of estrogens have been shown to cause cancer. The use of estrogens in pregnancy was the first to be proved carcinogenic: Daughters of women who had taken estrogens (notably DES, a synthetic estrogen) are at risk for the development of a rare cancer of the vagina.[49] The sequential birth-control pill was taken off the market as the danger of endometrial cancer (cancer of the lining of the uterus) became known,[50] and, similarly, estrogens taken in menopause have been shown to increase the risk of endometrial cancer by as much as 14 times after seven years of use.[51]

The model of the body as a machine that can be regulated, controlled, and managed by medical treatments is not working. "Femininity" or physical "femaleness" is not something that comes in a jar and can be manipulated. Nor are women accepting the relegation to secondary functional importance, as wives and mothers of men. In rejecting the viewpoint that women bear men's children for them, women are reclaiming their bodies. When pregnancy is seen not as the presence of a (man's) fetus in a woman but as a condition of the woman herself, attitudes toward contraception, infertility, abortion, and childbirth all change. When pregnancy is perceived as a condition of the woman, then abortion, for example, is primarily a response to that condition.

Changing Feminist Perspectives

In the 1970s, the reemergence of the feminist movement brought about a new focus on women and health that called attention to medicine's treatment of female patients. Women's health advocates rejected not only the "specialty treatment" offered women by the medical establishment but in fact the whole medical system. These women opted for methods of care outside of the system altogether and urged the mobilization of self-help groups, self-examinations, and women's clinics. Self-help and lay midwifery groups have worked, and continue to work, outside of the medical system, redefining women's health. They taught, and continue to teach, women how to examine their own bodies, not in the never-ending search for pathology in which physicians are trained, but to learn more about health.

Contemporary women's health advocates also reject the specialty care approach, but do so by emphasizing women's inclusion into the system. These new feminists, operating at a time separated from their foremothers by a decade of conservative politics and an ailing, underfunded health care system, demand access to primary medical attention for women of all classes, colors, and cultures. Additionally, they emphasize a need for women's general health care that is based on a sound scientific understanding of female biology. These health advocates are geared toward consumerism within medicine, seeking better medical care and access for a wider range of services and a more inclusive population of women. Better trained, more knowledge-able, and more humane health care workers are a high priority, as is care that is based on the realities of women's lives.

Demanding better access, however, may not address the problem that medical care in the United States consists of an overmedicalization of the fe-male body, a primary treatment focus on women's reproduction, and a gen-eral lack of information about female biology. And do we want physicians to be "treating" our health? Do we agree with what physicians consider to be illness in women? Do we want to urge comprehensive care that overmed-icalizes the female body? It is entirely possible for a woman to fit herself for a diaphragm, do a pap smear and a breast examination (all with help and in-struction if she needs it), and never adopt the patient role. It is also possible for a woman to go through a pregnancy and birth her baby with good, knowl-edgeable, caring help without becoming a patient under the supervision of a physician.

Women have been imbued with the medical model of women's bodies and health. And it is essential, whether working within or outside of the sys-tem, to redefine women in women's terms and to redefine physical normality within the context of the female body. This is not a problem unique to health. It is an essential feminist issue.

NOTES

1. Diana Scully and Pauline Bart, "A Funny Thing Happened on the Way to the Ori-fice: Women and Gynecology Textbooks," *American Journal of Sociology* 78 (1971): 1045–50.
2. *Gould Medical Dictionary*, 3rd ed. (New York: McGraw-Hill, 1972):1056.
3. *Gould Medical Dictionary*, p. 658.
4. Karen Johnson and Charlea Massion, "Why a Women's Medical Specialty?" *Ms.* 11, no. 3 (1991):68–69.
5. G. J. Barker-Benfield, *The Horrors of the Half-Known Life* (New York: Harper & Row, 1976).
6. Thomas Szasz, *The Theology of Medicine* (New York: Harper Colophon, 1977).
7. U.S. Public Health Service, "Women's Health: Report of the Public Health Service Task Force on Women's Health Issues," Washington, DC: U.S. Department of Health and Human Services, 1985.
8. A. Hamilton and C. Perry, "Sex Related Differences in Clinical Drug Response: Implications for Women's Health," *Medical Women's Association* 38 (1983):126–37.
9. Council on Ethical and Judicial Affairs of the American Medical Association, "Gender Disparities in Clinical Decision Making," *Journal of the American Medical Association* 266 (1991):559–62.
10. Paul Cotton, "Is There Still Too Much Extrapolation from Data on Middle-Aged White Men?" *Journal of the American Medical Association* 263 (1990):1049–50.
11. Joann E. Manson et al., "A Prospective Study of Aspirin Use and Primary Pre-vention of Cardiovascular Disease in Women," *Journal of the American Medical Association* 266 (1991):521–27.

12. A. Raskin, "Age-Sex Differences in Response to Antidepressant Drugs," *Journal of Nervous Mental Disease* 159 (1974):120–30.
13. Paul Cotton, "Examples Abound of Gaps in Medical Knowledge because of Groups Excluded from Scientific Study," *Journal of the American Medical Association* 263 (1990):1051–52.
14. N. K. Wenger, "Gender, Coronary Artery Disease, and Coronary Bypass Surgery," *Annals of Internal Medicine* 112 (1985):557–58.
15. Council on Ethical and Judicial Affairs of the American Medical Association, "Gender Disparities in Clinical Decision Making," *Journal of the American Medical Association* 266 (1991):559–62.
16. Howard Minkoff and Jack DeHovitz, "Care of Women Infected with the Human Immunodeficiency Virus," *Journal of the American Medical Association* 266 (1991): 2253–58.
17. Susan Chu et al., "Impact of the Human Immunodeficiency Virus Epidemic on Mortality in Women of Reproductive Age, United States," *Journal of the American Medical Association* 264 (1990):225–29.
18. Cotton, "Examples Abound," pp. 1051–52.
19. Barbara Ehrenreich and Deirdre English, *Witches, Midwives and Nurses* (Old Westbury, NY: Feminist Press, 1973), p. 33.
20. Datha Clapper Brack, "The Displacement of the Midwife: Male Domination in a Formerly Female Occupation" (unpublished, 1976).
21. Janet Carlisle Bogdan, "Nineteenth-Century Childbirth: Its Context and Meaning" (paper presented at the third Berkshire Conference on the History of Women, June 9–11, 1976), p. 8.
22. Frances E. Kobrin, "The American Midwife Controversy: A Crisis in Professionalization," *Bulletin of the History of Medicine* (1966):353.
23. Brack, "Displacement of the Midwife," p. 1.
24. Barker-Benfield, *The Horrors of the Half-Known Life*, p. 83.
25. Ibid., p. 120.
26. Ibid.
27. Barbara Ehrenreich and Deirdre English, *Complaints and Disorders* (Old Westbury, NY: Feminist Press, 1973).
28. Barker-Benfield, *The Horrors of the Half-Known Life*, p. 120.
29. Ibid., p. 121.
30. Talcott Parsons, "Definitions of Health and Illness in Light of American Value Systems," in *Patients, Physicians and Illnesses*, ed. E. Gartly Jaco (New York: Free Press, 1958).
31. Ehrenreich and English, *Complaints and Disorders*, p. 16.
32. Vern Bullough and Martha Voght, "Women, Menstruation and Nineteenth-Century Medicine" (paper presented at the 45th annual meeting of the American Association for the History of Medicine, 1972).
33. Ehrenreich and English, *Complaints and Disorders*, p. 47.
34. Estelle Ramey, "Men's Cycles (They Have Them Too, You Know)," *Ms.* (1972), pp. 8–14.
35. Milton Abramson and John R. Torghele, *American Journal of Obstetrics and Gynecology* (1961):223.
36. Lynda Madaras and Jane Paterson, M.D., *Womancare: A Gynecological Guide to Your Body* (New York: Avon Books, 1984), p. 601.

37. Peter J. Schmidt, M.D., Lynnette K. Nieman, et al., "Lack of Effect of Induced Menses on Symptoms in Women with Premenstrual Syndrome," *The Journal of the American Medical Association* 324, no. 17 (1991): 1174–79.
38. Madaras and Paterson, p. 604.
39. Ellen Switzer, "PMS, the Return of Raging Hormones," *Working Woman,* (October 1983), pp. 123–27.
40. Emily Martin, "Premenstrual Syndrome: Discipline, Work, Anger in Late Industrial Societies," in *Blood Magic: The Anthology of Menstruation,* ed. Thomas Buckley and Alma Gottlieb (Berkeley: University of California Press, 1988), pp. 161–81.
41. Ibid., 174.
42. Sheldon Segal, "Contraceptive Research: A Male Chauvinist Plot?" *Family Planning Perspectives* (July 1972), pp. 21–25.
43. Janet Carlisle Bogdan, "Nineteenth-Century Childbirth: The Politics of Reality" (paper presented at the 71st annual meeting of the American Sociological Association, 1976), p. 11.
44. Dorothy C. Wertz, "Childbirth As a Controlled Workspace: From Midwifery to Obstetrics" (paper presented at the 71st annual meeting of the American Sociological Association, 1976), p. 15.
45. Doris Haire, *The Cultural Warping of Childbirth* (Hillside, NJ: International Childbirth Education Association, 1972).
46. See Barbara Katz Rothman, *In Labor: Women and Power in the Birthplace* (New York: Norton, 1982), for a fuller discussion of the medicalization of the maternity cycle and developing alternatives.
47. Robert A. Wilson, *Feminine Forever* (New York: Pocket Books, 1968).
48. John Bunker, "Surgical Manpower," *New England Journal of Medicine* 282 (1970): 135–44.
49. Arthur Herbst, J. Ulfelder, and D. C. Poskanzer, "Adenocarcinoma of the Vagina," *New England Journal of Medicine* 284 (1971): 871–81.
50. Barbara Seaman and Gideon Seaman, *Women and the Crisis in Sex Hormones* (New York: Rawson Associates, 1977), p. 78.
51. Harry Ziel and William Finkle, "Estrogen Replacement Therapy," *New England Journal of Medicine* 293 (1975): 1167–70.

29

FAILING AT FAIRNESS
Hidden Lessons

MYRA SADKER • DAVID SADKER

Few social institutions mold the social environment as faithfully as schools do. The institution of education reinforces social inequality by teaching the dominant culture's values and biases. The following reading by Myra Sadker and David Sadker examines how the social institution of education has replicated social hierarchies that perpetuate gender inequality. In this excerpt, taken from their 1995 book, *Failing at Fairness: How Our Schools Cheat Girls*, they illustrate the gender biases that permeate the institution of education.

Sitting in the same classroom, reading the same textbook, listening to the same teacher, boys and girls receive very different educations. From grade school through graduate school female students are more likely to be invisible members of classrooms. Teachers interact with males more frequently, ask them better questions, and give them more precise and helpful feedback. Over the course of years the uneven distribution of teacher time, energy, attention, and talent, with boys getting the lion's share, takes its toll on girls. Since gender bias is not a noisy problem, most people are unaware of the secret sexist lessons and the quiet losses they engender.

Girls are the majority of our nation's schoolchildren, yet they are second-class educational citizens. The problems they face—loss of self-esteem, decline in achievement, and elimination of career options—are at the heart of the educational process. Until educational sexism is eradicated, more than half our children will be shortchanged and their gifts lost to society.

Award-winning author Susan Faludi discovered that backlash "is most powerful when it goes private, when it lodges inside a woman's mind and turns her vision inward, until she imagines the pressure is all in her head, until she begins to enforce the backlash too—on herself."[1] Psychological backlash internalized by adult women is a frightening concept, but what is even more terrifying is a curriculum of sexist school lessons becoming secret mind games played against female children, our daughters, tomorrow's women.

Reprinted with the permission of Scribner, a Division of Simon & Schuster, from *Failing at Fairness: How America's Schools Cheat Girls* by Myra Sadker and David Sadker. Copyright © 1994 by Myra Sadker and David Sadker.

After almost two decades of research grants and thousands of hours of classroom observation, we remain amazed at the stubborn persistence of these hidden sexist lessons. When we began our investigation of gender bias, we looked first in the classrooms of one of Washington, D.C.'s elite and expensive private schools. Uncertain of exactly what to look for, we wrote nothing down; we just observed. The classroom was a whirlwind of activity, so fast paced we could easily miss the quick but vital phrase or gesture, the insidious incident, the tiny inequity that held a world of meaning. As we watched, we had to push ourselves beyond the blind spots of socialization and gradually focus on the nature of the interaction between teacher and student. On the second day we saw our first example of sexism, a quick, jarring flash within the hectic pace of the school day:

Two second graders are kneeling beside a large box. They whisper excitedly to each other as they pull out wooden blocks, colored balls, counting sticks. So absorbed are these two small children in examining and sorting the materials, they are visibly startled by the teacher's impatient voice as she hovers over them. "Ann! Julia! Get your cotton-pickin' hands out of the math box. Move over so the boys can get in there and do their work."

Isolated here on the page of a book, this incident is not difficult to interpret. It becomes even more disturbing if you think of it with the teacher making a racial distinction. Picture Ann and Julia as African-American children moved away so white children can gain access to the math materials. If Ann and Julia's parents had observed this exchange, they might justifiably wonder whether their tuition dollars were well spent. But few parents actually watch teachers in action, and fewer still have learned to interpret the meaning behind fast-paced classroom events.

The incident unsettles, but it must be considered within the context of numerous interactions this harried teacher had that day. While she talked to the two girls, she was also keeping a wary eye on fourteen other active children. Unless you actually shadowed the teacher, stood right next to her as we did, you might not have seen or heard the event. After all, it lasted only a few seconds.

It took us almost a year to develop an observation system that would register the hundreds of daily classroom interactions, teasing out the gender bias embedded in them. Trained raters coded classrooms in math, reading, English, and social studies. They observed students from different racial and ethnic backgrounds. They saw lessons taught by women and by men, by teachers of different races. In short, they analyzed America's classrooms. By the end of the year we had thousands of observation sheets, and after another year of statistical analysis, we discovered a syntax of sexism so elusive that most teachers and students were completely unaware of its influence.[2]

Recently a producer of NBC's "Dateline" contacted us to learn more about our discovery that girls don't receive their fair share of education. Jane Pauley, the show's anchorwoman, wanted to visit classrooms, capture these covert sexist lessons on videotape, and expose them before a television audience. The task was to extricate sound bites of sexism from a fifth-grade classroom where the teacher, chosen to be the subject of the exposé, was aware she was being scrutinized for sex bias.

"Dateline" had been taping in her class for two days when we received a concerned phone call. "This is a fair teacher," the producer said. "How can we show sexism on our show when there's no gender bias in this teacher's class?" We drove to the NBC studio in Washington, D.C., and found two "Dateline" staffers, intelligent women concerned about fair treatment in school, sitting on the floor in a darkened room staring at the videotape of a fifth-grade class. "We've been playing this over and over. The teacher is terrific. There's no bias in her teaching. Come watch."

After about twenty minutes of viewing, we realized it was a case of déjà vu: The episodal sexist themes and recurring incidents were all too familiar. The teacher was terrific, but she was more effective for half of the students than she was for the other. She was, in fact, a classic example of the hundreds of skillful well-intentioned professionals we have seen who inadvertently teach boys better than girls.

We had forgotten how difficult it was to recognize subtle sexism before you learn how to look. It was as if the "Dateline" staff members were wearing blinders. We halted the tape, pointed out the sexist behaviors, related them to incidents in our research, and played the tape again. There is a classic "aha!" effect in education when people finally "get it." Once the hidden lessons of unconscious bias are understood, classrooms never look the same again to the trained observer.

Much of the unintentional gender bias in that fifth-grade class could not be shown in the short time allowed by television, but the sound bites of sexism were also there. "Dateline" chose to show a segregated math group: boys sitting on the teacher's right side and girls on her left. After giving the math book to a girl to hold open at the page of examples, the teacher turned her back to the girls and focused on the boys, teaching them actively and directly. Occasionally she turned to the girls' side, but only to read the examples in the book. This teacher, although aware that she was being observed for sexism, had unwittingly transformed the girls into passive spectators, an audience for the boys. All but one, that is: The girl holding the math book had become a prop.

"Dateline" also showed a lively discussion in the school library. With both girls' hands and boys' hands waving for attention, the librarian chose boy after boy to speak. In one interaction she peered through the forest of girls' hands waving directly in front of her to acknowledge the raised hand of a boy in the back of the room. Startled by the teacher's attention, the boy muttered, "I was just stretching."

The next day we discussed the show with future teachers, our students at The American University. They were bewildered. "Those teachers really were sexist. They didn't mean to be, but they were. How could that happen—with the cameras and everyone watching?" When we took those students into classrooms to discover the hidden lessons for themselves, they began to understand. It is difficult to detect sexism unless you know precisely how to observe. And if a lifetime of socialization makes it difficult to spot gender bias even when you're looking for it, how much harder it is to avoid the traps when you are the one doing the teaching.

Among Schoolchildren

Subtle sexism is visible to only the most astute readers of *Among Schoolchildren*, Tracy Kidder's chronicle of real-life educator Chris Zajac. A thirty-four-year-old teacher in Mt. Holyoke, Massachusetts, Mrs. Zajac is a no-nonsense veteran of the classroom. She does not allow her fifth-grade students to misbehave, forget to do their homework, or give up without trying their hardest. Underlying her strict exterior is a woman who cares about schoolchildren. Our students admired her dedication and respected her as a good human being, and it took several readings and discussions before they discovered her inadvertent gender bias. Then came the questions: Does Mrs. Zajac work harder teaching boys than girls? Does she know there is sex bias in her classroom?

These questions probably do not occur to most readers of *Among Schoolchildren* and might jolt both Chris Zajac and the author who so meticulously described the classroom. Here's how Tracy Kidder begins the story of a year in the life of this New England teacher:

> Mrs. Zajac wasn't born yesterday. She knows you didn't do your best work on this paper, Clarence. Don't you remember Mrs. Zajac saying that if you didn't do your best, she'd make you do it over? As for you, Claude, God forbid that you should ever need brain surgery. But Mrs. Zajac hopes that if you do, the doctor won't open up your head and walk off saying he's almost done, as you said when Mrs. Zajac asked you for your penmanship, which, by the way, looks like you did it and ran. Felipe, the reason you have hiccups is, your mouth is always open and the wind rushes in. You're in fifth grade now. So, Felipe, put a lock on it. Zip it up. Then go get a drink of water. Mrs. Zajac means business, Robert. The sooner you realize she never said everybody in the room has to do the work except for Robert, the sooner you'll get along with her. And . . . Clarence. Mrs. Zajac knows you didn't try. You don't just hand in junk to Mrs. Zajac. She's been teaching an awful lot of years. She didn't fall off the turnip cart yesterday. She told you she was an old-lady teacher." [3]

Swiftly, adroitly, Kidder introduces the main characters in the classroom—Clarence, Claude, Felipe, Robert, and back to Clarence, the boy in whom Mrs. Zajac invests most. But where are the girls?

As our students analyzed the book and actually examined who Mrs. Zajac was speaking to, they saw that page after page she spent time with the boys—disciplining them, struggling to help them understand, teaching them with all the energy and talent she could muster. In contrast, the pages that showed Mrs. Zajac working with girls were few and far between.

When we ask teachers at our workshops why they spend more time helping boys, they say, "Because boys need it more" or "Boys have trouble reading, writing, doing math. They can't even sit still. They need me more." In *Among Schoolchildren*, Chris Zajac feels that way, too. Kidder describes how she allows boys to take her over because she thinks they need her.

So teachers of good intention, such as Chris Zajac, respond to boys and teach them more actively, but their time and attention are not limitless. While the teachers are spending time with boys, the girls are being ignored and shortchanged. The only girl clearly realized in *Among Schoolchildren* is Judith, a child who is so alert that she has a vast English vocabulary even though her parents speak only Spanish. But while Judith is a girl of brilliant potential, she rarely reaps the benefit of Mrs. Zajac's active teaching attention. In fact, rather than trouble her teacher and claim time and attention for herself, Judith helps Mrs. Zajac, freeing her to work with the more demanding boys. Mrs. Zajac knows she isn't giving this talented girl what she needs and deserves: "If only I had more time," she thinks as she looks at Judith.

On a field trip to old Sturbridge Village, the children have segregated themselves by sex on the bus, with the boys claiming the back. In a moment of quiet reflection, Chris realizes that in her classroom "the boys rarely give her a chance to spend much time with her girls." She changes her seat, joins the girls, and sings jump rope songs with them for the remainder of the trip.[4]

But her time spent with the girls is short-lived—the length of the day-long field trip—and her recognition of the gender gap in time and attention is brief: a paragraph-long flash of understanding in a book of more than three hundred pages. On the whole, Chris Zajac does not invest her talent in girls. But nurturing children is not unlike tending a garden: Neglect, even when benign, is withering; time and attention bear fruit. Mrs. Zajac and other caring teachers across the country are unaware of the full impact of uneven treatment. They do not realize the high academic and emotional price many girls pay for being too good. Drawn from years of research, the episodes that follow demonstrate the sexist lessons taught daily in America's classrooms.[5] Pulled out of the numerous incidents in a school day, these inequities become enlarged, as if observed through a magnifying glass, so we can see clearly how they extinguish learning and shatter self-esteem. Imagine yourself in a sixth-grade science class like the one we observed in Maryland.

The teacher is writing a list of inventors and their discoveries on the board:

Elias Howe	sewing machine
Robert Fulton	steamboat
Thomas A. Edison	light bulb
James Otis	elevator

Alexander Graham Bell	telephone
Cyrus McCormick	reaper
Eli Whitney	cotton gin
Orville and Wilbur Wright	airplane

A girl raises her hand and asks, "It looks like all the inventors were men. Didn't women invent anything?" The teacher does not add any female inventors to the list, nor does he discuss new scholarship recognizing the involvement of women in inventions such as the cotton gin. He does not explain how hard it was in times past for women to obtain patents in their own names, and therefore we may never know how many female inventors are excluded from the pages of our history books. Instead he grins, winks, and says, "Sweetheart, don't worry about it. It's the same with famous writers and painters. It's the man's job to create things and the woman's job to look beautiful so she can inspire him." Several boys laugh. A few clown around by flexing their muscles as they exclaim, "Yes!" One girl rolls her eyes toward the ceiling and shakes her head in disgust. The incident lasts less than a minute, and the discussion of male inventors continues.

We sometimes ask our students at The American University to list twenty famous women from American history. There are only a few restrictions. They cannot include figures from sports or entertainment. Presidents' wives are not allowed unless they are clearly famous in their own right. Most students cannot do it. The seeds of their ignorance were sown in their earliest years of schooling.

In the 1970s, analyses of best-selling history books showed a biological oddity, a nation with only founding fathers.[6] More space was given to the six-shooter than to the women's suffrage movement. In fact, the typical history text gave only two sentences to enfranchising half the population. Science texts continued the picture of a one-gender world, with the exception of Marie Curie who was permitted to stand behind her husband and peer over his shoulder as he looked into a microscope. Today's history and science texts are better—but not much.[7]

At our workshops we ask teachers and parents to tell or write about any sexism they have seen in their schools. We have been collecting their stories for years.[8] A Utah teacher told us: "Last year I had my U.S. history class write biographies about famous Americans. When I collected all one hundred and fifty, I was dismayed to find only five on women. When I asked my kids why, they said they didn't know any famous women. When I examined their textbook more closely, I saw there were few females in it. And there were even fewer books on famous American women in our school library."

Teachers add to textbook bias when they produce sexist materials of their own. One parent described her efforts to stop a teacher-made worksheet that perpetuated stereotypes of yesteryear:

A few years ago my daughter came home upset over her grade. When I looked at her paper, I got more angry than she was. At the top of the worksheet were the faces of a man and a woman. At the bottom were different objects—nails, a saw, a sewing needle, thread, a hammer, a screwdriver, a broom. The directions said to draw a line from the woman to the objects that go with her. In our house my husband does the cooking and I do the repair work, so you can imagine what the lines on my daughter's paper looked like. There was a huge red F in the middle of her worksheet. I called the teacher right away. She was very understanding and assured me the F wouldn't count. A small victory, I thought, and forgot about it.

This year my son is in her class. Guess what he brought home last week. Same worksheet—same F. Nothing had changed at all.

When girls do not see themselves in the pages of textbooks, when teachers do not point out or confront the omissions, our daughters learn that to be female is to be an absent partner in the development of our nation. And when teachers add their stereotypes to the curriculum bias in books, the message becomes even more damaging.

In a 1992 survey in *Glamour*, 74 percent of those responding said that they had "a teacher who was biased against females or paid more attention to the boys." Math class was selected as the place where inequities were most likely to occur. Fifty-eight percent picked it as their most sexist subject. Physical education was second, and science came in third, selected by 47 percent of the respondents.[9] Women at our workshops recall remarks made by math and science teachers that years later still leave them upset and angry:

In my A.P. physics class in high school in 1984 there were only three girls and twenty-seven boys. The three girls, myself included, consistently scored at the top end of the scale. On one test I earned a 98. The next closest boy earned an 88. The teacher handed the tests back saying, "Boys, you are failing. These three pretty cookies are outscoring you guys on every test." He told the boys it was embarrassing for them to be beaten by a girl. He always referred to us (the girls) as "Cookie" or made our names sound very cutesy!

Sometimes the humiliating lessons come not from school policies, teachers, or books but from boys, the very individuals that adolescent girls most want to impress:

The New England high school was having an assembly during the last period on Friday, and the auditorium was packed with more than a thousand students, who were restless as they listened to announcements. A heavy, awkward tenth grader made her way across the stage to reach the microphone located in the center. As she walked, several male students made loud barking noises to signify she was a dog. Others oinked like pigs. Later a slender long-haired senior walked to the mike; she was greeted by catcalls and whistles. Nobody attempted to stop the demeaning and hurtful public evaluation of the appearance of these teenage girls.

Tolerated under the assumption that "boys will be boys" and hormone levels are high in high school, sexual harassment is a way of life in America's schools. While teachers and administrators look the other way, sexually denigrating comments, pinching, touching, and propositioning happen daily. Sensitive and insecure about their appearance, some girls are so intimidated they suffer in silence. Others fight back only to find this heightens the harassment. Many girls don't even realize they have a right to protest. And when they do come forward, bringing school sexual harassment into the open, it is often dealt with quickly and nervously; it is swept under the rug, turned aside, or even turned against the girl who had the courage to complain. A teacher at a workshop in Indiana told us: "In our school a girl was pinched on the derriere by two boys and verbally harassed. When she reported the incident to the principal, she was told that her dress was inappropriate and that she had asked for it."

Intimidating comments and offensive sexual jokes are even more common in college and sometimes are even made public as part of a classroom lecture and discussion. A female faculty member, teaching at a university that was historically all male, told us about one of the most popular teachers on campus, an economics professor:

> *He would show slides illustrating an economic theory and insert women in bikinis in the middle "to keep students interested." He illustrated different phases of the economic cycle by showing a slide of a woman's breast and pointed out how far away from the nipple each phase was. When a number of female students complained, the local newspaper supported the professor and criticized the "ultrasensitive coeds." That semester the university gave the professor the Teacher of the Year award.*

Although sexually harassing remarks, stories, and jokes occur only occasionally in classrooms, female silence is the norm. During our two-year study of colleges, our raters found that girls grow quieter as they grow older. In coeducational classes, college women are even less likely to participate in discussions than elementary and secondary school girls. In the typical college classroom, 45 percent of students do not speak; the majority of these voiceless students are women.[10]

Breaking the Sound Barrier

Women who have spent years learning the silence in elementary, secondary, and college classrooms have trouble regaining their voices. In our workshops we often set up a role play to demonstrate classroom sex bias. Four volunteers, two women and two men, are asked to pretend to be students in a middle school social studies lesson. They have no script; their only direction is to take a piece of paper with them as David, playing the part of the social studies teacher, ushers them to four chairs in front of the room. He tells the audience that he will condense all the research on sexism in the classroom into a ten-minute lesson, so the bias will look blatant, even overwhelming.

The job of the parents and teachers in the audience is to detect the different forms of egregious sexism. He begins the lesson.

"Today we're going to discuss the chapter in your book, 'The Gathering Clouds of War,' about the American Revolution. But first I'd like you to take out your homework so I can check it." David walks over to Sarah, the first student in the line of four. (In real life she is an English teacher at the local high school.)

"Let's see your paper, Sarah." He pauses to look it over. "Questions three and seven are not correct." Sarah looks concerned.

David moves to Peggy (who is a communications professor at a state college). "Oh, Peggy, Peggy, Peggy!" She looks up as everyone stares. David holds up Peggy's paper. "Would you all look at this. It is sooo neat. You print just like a typewriter. This is the kind of paper I like to put on the bulletin board for open school night." Peggy looks down, smiles, blushes, looks up wide-eyed, and bats her eyelashes. She is not faking or exaggerating these behaviors. Before our eyes she has returned to childhood as the stereotypical good girl with pretty penmanship. The lessons have been well learned.

Next David stops by Tony (who is a vocational education teacher) and looks at the blank paper he is holding. "Tony, you've missed questions three, seven, and eleven. I think you would do better on your assignments if you used the bold headings to guide your reading. I know you can get this if you try harder." Tony nods earnestly as David moves to Roy. Sarah, who missed questions three and seven, looks perplexed.

David scans Roy's paper and hands it back. "Roy, where's your homework?"

Roy (a college physics teacher) stammers, "Here it is," and again offers the blank paper that served as homework for the others in the role play.

"Roy, that's not your history homework. That's science." Roy still looks puzzled. "Trust me, Roy," David says. "No matter what you come up with, it won't be history homework. Now, where is it?"

"The dog ate it," Roy mutters, getting the picture and falling into the bad boy role.

Next David discusses revolutionary battles, military tactics, and male leaders—George Washington, John and Samuel Adams, Paul Revere, Benjamin Franklin, Thomas Jefferson, and more. He calls on Roy and Tony more than twenty times each. When they don't know the answer, he probes, jokes, challenges, offers hints. He calls on Sarah only twice. She misses both her questions because David gives her less than half a second to speak. After effusively praising Peggy's pretty paper, David never calls on her again. As the lesson progresses, Sarah's face takes on a sad, almost vacant expression. Peggy keeps on smiling.

When the scene of blatant sexism is over, many in the audience want to know how the two women felt.

"That was me all through school," Peggy blurts out. "I did very well. My work was neat. I was always prepared. I would have had the right answer if someone had called on me. But they never did."

"Why did you watch the two males get all the attention?" we ask. "If you weren't called on, why didn't you call out?"

"I tried. I just couldn't do it."

"Why? You weren't wearing a muzzle. The men were calling out."

"I know. I felt terrible. It reminded me of all those years in school when I wanted to say something but couldn't."

"What about you, Sarah?" we ask. "Why didn't you just shout out an answer?"

"It never occurred to me to do it," Sarah says, then pauses. "No, that's not true. I thought about it, but I didn't want to be out there where I might get laughed at or ridiculed."

David has taught this role play class hundreds and hundreds of times in workshops in big cities and small towns all across the United States. Each time he demonstrates sex bias by blatantly and offensively ignoring female students, and almost always the adult women, put back into the role of twelve-year-olds, sit and say nothing; once again they become the nice girls watching the boys in action. Inside they may feel sad or furious or relieved, but like Sarah and Peggy, they remain silent.

When women try to get into classroom interaction, they rarely act directly. Instead they doodle, write letters, pass notes, and wait for the teacher to notice them. In a California workshop one parent who was playing the part of a student developed an elaborate pantomime. She reached into her large purse, pulled out a file, and began to do her nails. When that failed to attract David's attention, she brought out a brush, makeup, and a mirror. But David continued to ignore her, talking only with the two males.

"I was so mad I wanted to hit you," the woman fumed at the end of the role play when she was invited to express her feelings.

"What did you do to show your anger?" David asked.

"I didn't do anything." Then she paused, realizing the passive-aggressive but ultimately powerless strategy she had pursued. "No, I did do something—my nails," she said sadly.

After hundreds of these role plays, we are still astonished at how quickly the veneer of adulthood melts away. Grown women and men replay behavior they learned as children at school. The role plays are always revealing—funny, sad, and sometimes they even have a troubling twist.

At a workshop for college students at a large university in the Midwest, one of the young women ignored in the role play did not exhibit the usual behavior of silence or passive hostility. Instead, in the middle of the workshop in front of her classmates, she began to sob. She explained later in private that as one of only a few girls in the university's agricultural program, she had been either ignored or harassed. That week in an over-enrolled course an instructor had announced, "There are too many students in this class. Everyone with ovaries—out!"

"What did you do?"

"What could I do? I left. Later I told my adviser about it. He was sympathetic but said if there was no room, I should consider another major."

Silent Losses

Each time a girl opens a book and reads a womanless history, she learns she is worth less. Each time the teacher passes over a girl to elicit the ideas and opinions of boys, that girl is conditioned to be silent and to defer. As teachers use their expertise to question, praise, probe, clarify, and correct boys, they help these male students sharpen ideas, refine their thinking, gain their voice, and achieve more. When female students are offered the leftovers of teacher time and attention, morsels of amorphous feedback, they achieve less.

Then girls and women learn to speak softly or not at all; to submerge honest feelings, withhold opinions, and defer to boys; to avoid math and science as male domains; to value neatness and quiet more than assertiveness and creativity; to emphasize appearance and hide intelligence. Through this curriculum in sexism they are turned into educational spectators instead of players; but education is not a spectator sport.

When blatantly sexual or sexist remarks become an accepted part of classroom conversation, female students are degraded. Sexual harassment in business and the military now causes shock waves and legal suits. Sexual harassment in schools is dismissed as normal and unavoidable "boys will be boys" behavior; but by being targeted, girls are being intimidated and caused to feel like members of an inferior class.

Like a thief in school, sexist lessons subvert education, twisting it into a system of socialization that robs potential. Consider this record of silent, devastating losses.[11]

- ▾ In the early grades girls are ahead of or equal to boys on almost every standardized measure of achievement and psychological well-being. By the time they graduate from high school or college, they have fallen back. Girls enter school ahead but leave behind.[12]
- ▾ In high school, girls score lower on the SAT and ACT tests, which are critical for college admission. The greatest gender gap is in the crucial areas of science and math.
- ▾ Girls score far lower on College Board Achievement tests, which are required by most of the highly selective colleges.
- ▾ Boys are much more likely to be awarded state and national college scholarships.
- ▾ The gap does not narrow in college. Women score lower on all sections of the Graduate Record Exam, which is necessary to enter many graduate programs.

▼ Women also trail on most tests needed to enter professional schools: the GMAT for business school, the LSAT for law school, and the MCAT for medical school.

▼ From elementary school through higher education, female students receive less active instruction, both in the quantity and in the quality of teacher time and attention.[13]

In addition to the loss of academic achievement, girls suffer other difficulties:

▼ Eating disorders among girls in middle and secondary schools and in college are rampant and increasing.[14]

▼ Incidents of school-based sexual harassment are now reported with alarming frequency.[15]

▼ One in ten teenage girls becomes pregnant each year. Unlike boys, when girls drop out, they usually stay out.[16]

▼ As girls go through school, their self-esteem plummets, and the danger of depression increases.[17]

▼ Economic penalties follow women after graduation. Careers that have a high percentage of female workers, such as teaching and nursing, are poorly paid. And even when women work in the same jobs as men, they earn less money. Most of America's poor live in households that are headed by women.

If the cure for cancer is forming in the mind of one of our daughters, it is less likely to become a reality than if it is forming in the mind of one of our sons. Until this changes, everybody loses.

NOTES

1. Susan Faludi, *Backlash: The Undeclared War against American Women* (New York: Crown, 1991), p. xxii.

2. Our first study, which analyzed gender bias in elementary and secondary classrooms, lasted more than three years and was funded by the National Institute of Education. The report submitted to the government was Myra Sadker and David Sadker, *Year 3: Final Report: Promoting Effectiveness in Classroom Instruction* (Washington, DC: National Institute of Education, 1984); Myra Sadker and David Sadker, "Sexism in the Schoolroom of the Eighties," *Psychology Today* (March 1985), pp. 54–57; Myra Sadker and David Sadker, "Sexism in the Classroom: From Grade School to Graduate School," *Phi Delta Kappan* 67, no. 7 (March 1986), pp. 512–15. We also reported this study as one of the contributing authors to Wellesley College Center for Research on Women, *How Schools Shortchange Girls: The AAUW Report* (Washington, DC: American Association of University Women Educational Foundation), 1992.

3. Tracy Kidder, *Among Schoolchildren* (Boston: Houghton Mifflin, 1989), p. 3.

4. Kidder, *Among Schoolchildren*, p. 262.

5. These episodes are drawn primarily from our three-year study of sex bias in elementary and secondary classrooms. They are also taken from classroom observations conducted as we supervised student teachers at The American University

and as we consulted with schools around the country and assessed their classrooms for gender bias.

6. Janice Law Trecker, "Women in U.S. History High School Textbooks," *Social Education* 35 (1971), pp. 249–60.

7. Lenore Weitzman and Diane Rizzo, *Biased Textbooks: Images of Males and Females in Elementary School Textbooks* (Washington, DC: Resource Center on Sex Roles in Education, 1976); Terry Saario, Carol Jacklin, and Carol Tittle, "Sex Role Stereotyping in the Public Schools," *Harvard Educational Review* 43, pp. 386–416; Women on Words and Images, *Dick and Jane As Victims: Sex Stereotyping in Children's Readers.* (Princeton, NJ: Carolingian Press, 1972).

8. For more than a decade we have offered workshops on gender bias for educators and parents around the country. At these workshops we have collected anecdotes and stories from students, teachers, and parents about sex bias that they faced at school.

9. "This Is What You Thought: Were Any of Your Teachers Biased against Females?" *Glamour* (August 1992), p. 157.

10. Following our three-year study of elementary and secondary classrooms, we conducted a two-year study of college classrooms and were sponsored by the Fund for the Improvement of Postsecondary Education. The project report submitted to the government was Myra Sadker and David Sadker, *Final Report: Project Effect (Effectiveness and Equity in College Teaching).* Washington, DC: Fund for the Improvement of Postsecondary Education, 1986; Myra Sadker and David Sadker, "Confronting Sexism in the College Classroom," in Susan, Gabriel, and Isaiah Smithson (eds.), *Gender in the Classroom: Power and Pedagogy* (Urbana: University of Illinois Press, 1990), pp. 176–87.

11. Myra Sadker, David Sadker, and Susan Klein, "The Issue of Gender in Elementary and Secondary Education," in Grant, Gerald (ed.), *Review of Research in Education,* vol. 17. (Washington, DC: American Educational Research Association, 1991); Wellesley College Center for Research on Women, *How Schools Shortchange Girls: The AAUW Report.*

12. Data documenting the loss of academic achievement were obtained from reports, tables, news releases, and studies issued by test publishers. The Educational Testing Service in Princeton, New Jersey, provided several reports and statistics related to the Preliminary Scholastic Aptitude Test, the Scholastic Aptitude Test, the Achievement tests, the Graduate Record Exam, and the Graduate Management Admissions Test. While the Graduate Record Exam data were from 1987–1988 (the most recently published), all other data reflected 1991 and 1992 test administrations. The American College Testing Program data were derived from a variety of profile and normative reports for 1990 and 1991 issued by American College Testing in Iowa City, Iowa.

Professional organizations and schools often contract with testing services to develop and administer their admissions tests. For example, the Medical College Admission Test (MCAT) is developed by ACT in Iowa City. For each of these admission tests the professional association responsible was contacted first, and it provided the requisite information. These organizations included the Association of American Medical Colleges, the Graduate Management Admissions Council, and the Law School Data Assembly Service.

13. Sadker and Sadker, *Year 3: Final Report;* Sadker and Sadker, *Final Report: Project Effect.*

14. K. L. Nagel and Karen H. Jones, "Sociological Factors in the Development of Eating Disorders," *Adolescence* 27 (Spring 1992), pp. 107–13; Claire Wiseman, James Gray, James Mosimann, and Anthony Ahrens, "Cultural Expectations of Thinness

in Women: An Update," *International Journal of Eating Disorders* 11, no. 1 (1992), pp. 85–89; Eric Button, "Self-Esteem in Girls Aged 11–12. Baseline Findings from a Planned Prospective Study of Vulnerability to Eating Disorders," *Journal of Adolescence* 13 (December 7, 1990):407–13.

15. Jean O'Gorman Hughes, and Bernice Sandler, *Peer Harassment: Hassles for Women on Campus.* (Washington, DC: Project on the Status and Education of Women, Association of American Colleges, 1988); Nan Stein, "Sexual Harassment in Schools," *The School Administrator* (January 1993), pp. 14–21.

16. Janice Earle, *Counselor/Advocates: Keeping Pregnant and Parenting Teens in School.* (Alexandria, VA: National Association of State Boards of Education, 1990).

17. A vast body of research documents girls' declining self-esteem at adolescence: Betty Allgood-Merten, Peter Lewinsohn, and Hyman Hops, "Sex Differences and Adolescent Depression," *Journal of Abnormal Psychology* 99, no. 1 (February 1990): 55–63; Herman Brutsaert, "Changing Sources of Self-Esteem among Girls and Boys in Secondary Schools," *Urban Education* 24, no. 4 (January 1990), pp. 432–39; Kevin Kelly, and LaVerne Jordan. "Effects of Academic Achievement and Gender on Academic and Social Self-Concept: A Replication Study," *Journal of Counseling and Development* 69 (November–December 1990):173–77; Keith Widaman, et al. "Differences in Adolescents' Self-Concept As a Function of Academic Level, Ethnicity, and Gender," *American Journal of Mental Retardation* 96, no. 4 (1992):387–404; Sheila Williams, and Rob McGee, "Adolescents' Self-Perceptions of Their Strengths," *Journal of Youth and Adolescence* 20, no. 3 (June 1991):325–37.

30

THE RACIAL CONSTRUCTION OF ASIAN AMERICAN WOMEN AND MEN

YEN LE ESPIRITU

When sociologists examine social inequality, they try to understand how different types of inequality interact and affect each other. For example, it is difficult to understand social class inequality without also examining racial and gender inequality. Similarly, it is difficult to understand gender oppression without also looking at the experiences of women and men in different social classes and racial-ethnic groups. In this selection, taken from *Asian American Women and Men: Labor, Laws, and Love* (1997), Yen Le Espiritu examines the interaction between race, social class, and gender in the treatment of

Yen Le Espiritu, *Asian American Woman and Men: Labor, Laws, and Love*, pp. 86–88, 90–102, 106–107, copyright © 1997 by Sage Publications, Inc. Reprinted by permission of Sage Publications, Inc.

Asian American women and men by the media and by the dominant culture. She finds that the cultural images of Asian Americans often contain sexual stereotypes, which are both racist and sexist, and they reinforce racial, patriarchal, and social class domination.

The slit-eyed, bucktooth Jap thrusting his bayonet, thirsty for blood. The inscrutable, wily Chinese detective with his taped eyelids and wispy moustache. The childlike, indolent Filipino houseboy. Always giggling. Bowing and scraping. Eager to please, but untrustworthy. The sexless, hairless Asian male. The servile, oversexed Asian female. The Geisha. The sultry, sarong-clad, South Seas maiden. The serpentine, cunning Dragon Lady. Mysterious and evil, eager to please. Effeminate. Untrustworthy. Yellow Peril. Fortune Cookie Psychic. Savage. Dogeater. Invisible. Mute. Faceless peasants breeding too many children. Gooks. Passive Japanese Americans obediently marching off to "relocation camps" during the Second World War.
—JESSICA HAGEDORN (1993:XXII)

Focusing on the material lives of Asian Americans, . . . [earlier research explored] . . . how racist and gendered immigration policies and labor conditions have worked in tandem to keep Asian Americans in an assigned, subordinate place. But as is evident from the stereotypes listed above, besides structural discrimination, Asian American men and women have been subject to ideological assaults. Focusing on the ideological dimension of Asian American oppression, this [article] examines the cultural symbols—or what Patricia Hill Collins called "controlling images" (1991:67–68)—generated by the dominant group to help justify the economic exploitation and social oppression of Asian American men and women over time. Writing on the objectification of black women, Collins observed that the exercise of political-economic domination by racial elites "always involves attempts to objectify the subordinate group" (1991:69). Transmitted through cultural institutions owned, controlled, or supported by various elites, these "controlling images" naturalize racism, sexism, and poverty by branding subordinate groups as alternatively inferior, threatening, or praiseworthy. These controlling images form part of a larger system of what Donald G. Baker referred to as "psychosocial dominance" (1983:37). Along with the threat and occasional use of violence, the psychosocial form of control conditions the subject minority to become the stereotype, to "live it, talk it, embrace it, measure group and individual worth in its terms, and believe it" (Chin & Chan 1972:66–67). In so doing, minority members reject their own individual and group identity and accept in its stead "a white supremacist complex that establishes the primacy of Euro-American cultural practices and social institutions" (Hamamoto 1994:2). But the objectification of Asian Americans as the exotic and inferior "other" has never been absolute. Asian Americans have always, but particularly since the 1960s, resisted race, class, and gender exploitation not only through political and economic struggles but also through cultural activism. My goal is to understand how the internalization and renunciation of these stereotypes have shaped sexual and gender politics within Asian America. In particular, I explore the conflicting politics of gender between Asian American men and women as they negotiate the difficult terrain of cultural nationalism—the construction of an antiassimilationist, native Asian American subject—and gender identities.

Yellow Peril, Charlie Chan, and Suzie Wong

A central aspect of racial exploitation centers on defining people of color as "the other" (Said 1979). The social construction of Asian American "otherness"—through such controlling images as the Yellow Peril, the model minority, the Dragon Lady, and the China Doll—is "the precondition for their cultural marginalization, political impotence, and psychic alienation from mainstream American society" (Hamamoto 1994:5). As indicated by these stereotypes, representations of gender and sexuality figure strongly in the articulation of racism. These racist stereotypes collapse gender and sexuality: Asian men have been constructed as hypermasculine, in the image of the "Yellow Peril," but also as effeminate, in the image of the "model minority," and Asian women have been depicted as superfeminine, in the image of the "China Doll," but also as castrating, in the image of the "Dragon Lady" (Mullings 1994:279–80; Okihiro 1995). As Mary Ann Doane suggested, sexuality is "indissociable from the effects of polarization and differentiation, often linking them to structures of power and domination" (1991:217). In the Asian American case, the gendering of ethnicity—the process whereby white ideology assigns selected gender characteristics to various ethnic "others"—cast Asian American men and women as simultaneously masculine and feminine but also as neither masculine nor feminine. On the one hand, as part of the Yellow Peril, Asian American men and women have been depicted as a *masculine* threat that needs to be contained. On the other hand, both sexes have been skewed toward the female side: an indication of the group's marginalization in U.S. society and its role as the compliant "model minority" in contemporary U.S. cultural ideology. Although an apparent disjunction, both the feminization and masculinization of Asian men and women exist to define and confirm the white man's superiority (Kim 1990).

. . .

The Racial Construction of Asian American Manhood

Like other men of color, Asian American men have been excluded from white-based cultural notions of the masculine. Whereas white men are depicted both as virile and as protectors of women, Asian men have been characterized both as asexual *and* as threats to white women. It is important to note the historical contexts of these seemingly divergent representations of Asian American manhood. The racist depictions of Asian men as "lascivious and predatory" were especially pronounced during the nativist movement against Asians at the turn of the century (Frankenberg 1993:75–76). The exclusion of Asian women from the United States and the subsequent establishment of bachelor societies eventually reversed the construction of Asian masculinity from "hypersexual" to "asexual" and even "homosexual." The contemporary model-minority stereotype further emasculates Asian American men as passive and malleable. Disseminated and perpetuated through the popular media, these stereotypes of the emasculated Asian male construct a reality in which social and economic discrimination against these men appears defensible. As an example, the desexualization of Asian men naturalized their inability to establish conjugal families in pre–World War II United States. Gliding over race-based exclusion laws that banned the immigration of most Asian women and antimiscegenation laws that prohibited men of color from marrying white women, these dual images of the eunuch and the rapist attributed the "womanless households" characteristic of prewar Asian America to Asian men's lack of sexual prowess and desirability.

A popular controlling image applied to Asian American men is that of the sinister Oriental—a brilliant, powerful villain who plots the destruction of Western civilization. Personified by the movie character of Dr. Fu Manchu, this Oriental mastermind combines Western science with Eastern magic and commands an army of devoted assassins (Hoppenstand 1983: 178). Though ruthless, Fu Manchu lacks masculine heterosexual prowess (Wang 1988:19), thus privileging heterosexuality. Frank Chin and Jeffrey Chan (1972), in a critique of the desexualization of Asian men in Western culture, described how the Fu Manchu character undermines Chinese American virility:

> Dr. Fu, a man wearing a long dress, batting his eyelashes, surrounded by muscular black servants in loin cloths, and with his habit of caressingly touching white men on the leg, wrist, and face with his long fingernails is not so much a threat as he is a frivolous offense to white manhood. (1972:60)

In another critique that glorifies male aggression, Frank Chin contrasted the neuterlike characteristics assigned to Asian men to the sexually aggressive images associated with other men of color: "Unlike the white stereotype of the evil black stud, Indian rapist, Mexican macho, the evil of the evil Dr. Fu Manchu was not sexual, but homosexual" (1972:66). However, Chin failed to note that as a homosexual, Dr. Fu (and by extension, Asian men) threatens and offends white masculinity—and therefore needs to be contained ideologically and destroyed physically.[1]

Whereas the evil Oriental stereotype marks Asian American men as the white man's enemy, the stereotype of the sexless Asian sidekick—Charlie

Chan, the Chinese laundryman, the Filipino houseboy—depicts Asian men as devoted and impotent, eager to please. William Wu reported that the Chinese servant "is the most important single image of the Chinese immigrants" in American fiction about Chinese Americans between 1850 and 1940 (1982:60). More recently, such diverse television programs as *Bachelor Father* (1957–1962), *Bonanza* (1959–1973), *Star Trek* (1966–1969), and *Falcon Crest* (1981–1990) all featured the stock Chinese bachelor domestic who dispenses sage advice to his superiors in addition to performing traditional female functions within the household (Hamamoto 1994:7). By trapping Chinese men (and by extension, Asian men) in the stereotypical "feminine" tasks of serving white men, American society erases the figure of the Asian "masculine" plantation worker in Hawaii or railroad construction worker in the western United States, thus perpetuating the myth of the androgynous and effeminate Asian man (Goellnicht 1992:198). This feminization, in turn, confines Asian immigrant men to the segment of the labor force that performs women's work.

The motion picture industry has been key in the construction of Asian men as sexual deviants. In a study of Asians in the U.S. motion pictures, Eugene Franklin Wong maintained that the movie industry filmically castrates Asian males to magnify the superior sexual status of white males (1978:27). As on-screen sexual rivals of whites, Asian males are neutralized, unable to sexually engage Asian women and prohibited from sexually engaging white women. By saving the white woman from sexual contact with the racial "other," the motion picture industry protects the Anglo-American, bourgeois male establishment from any challenges to its hegemony (Marchetti 1993:218). At the other extreme, the industry has exploited one of the most potent aspects of the Yellow Peril discourses—the sexual danger of contact between the races—by concocting a sexually threatening portrayal of the licentious and aggressive Yellow Man lusting after the White Woman (Marchetti 1993:3). Heedful of the larger society's taboos against Asian male-white female sexual union, white male actors donning "yellowface"—instead of Asian male actors—are used in these "love scenes." Nevertheless, the message of the perverse and animalistic Asian male attacking helpless white women is clear (Wong 1978). Though depicting sexual aggression, this image of the rapist, like that of the eunuch, casts Asian men as sexually undesirable. As Wong succinctly stated, in Asian male-white female relations, "There can be rape, but there cannot be romance" (1978:25). Thus, Asian males yield to the sexual superiority of the white males who are permitted filmically to maintain their sexual dominance over both white women and women of color. A young Vietnamese American man describes the damaging effect of these stereotypes on his self-image:

> Every day I was forced to look into a mirror created by white society and its media. As a young Asian man, I shrank before white eyes. I wasn't tall, I wasn't fair, I wasn't muscular, and so on. Combine that with the enor-

mous insecurities any pubescent teenager feels, and I have no difficulty in knowing now why I felt naked before a mass of white people. (Nguyen 1990:23)

White cultural and institutional racism against Asian males is also reflected in the motion picture industry's preoccupation with the death of Asians—a filmic solution to the threats of the Yellow Peril. In a perceptive analysis of Hollywood's view of Asians in films made from the 1930s to the 1960s, Tom Engelhardt (1976) described how Asians, like Native Americans, are seen by the movie industry as inhuman invaders, ripe for extermination. He argued that the theme of the nonhumanness of Asians prepares the audience to accept, without flinching, "the levelling and near-obliteration of three Asian areas in the course of three decades" (Engelhardt 1976:273). The industry's death theme, though applying to all Asians, is mainly focused on Asian males, with Asian females reserved for sexual purposes (Wong 1978:35). Especially in war films, Asian males, however advantageous their initial position, inevitably perish at the hands of the superior white males (Wong 1978:34).

The Racial Construction of Asian American Womanhood

Like Asian men, Asian women have been reduced to one-dimensional caricatures in Western representation. The condensation of Asian women's multiple differences into gross character types—mysterious, feminine, and nonwhite—obscures the social injustice of racial, class, and gender oppression (Marchetti 1993:71). Both Western film and literature promote dichotomous stereotypes of the Asian woman: Either she is the cunning Dragon Lady or the servile Lotus Blossom Baby (Tong 1994:197). Though connoting two extremes, these stereotypes are interrelated: Both eroticize Asian women as exotic "others"—sensuous, promiscuous, but untrustworthy. Whereas American popular culture denies "manhood" to Asian men, it endows Asian women with an excess of "womanhood," sexualizing them but also impugning their sexuality. In this process, both sexism and racism have been blended together to produce the sexualization of white racism (Wong 1978:260). Linking the controlling images of Asian men and women, Elaine Kim suggested that Asian women are portrayed as sexual for the same reason that men are asexual: "Both exist to define the white man's virility and the white man's superiority" (1990:70).

As the racialized exotic "others," Asian American women do not fit the white-constructed notions of the feminine. Whereas white women have been depicted as chaste and dependable, Asian women have been represented as promiscuous and untrustworthy. In a mirror image of the evil Fu Manchu, the Asian woman was portrayed as the castrating Dragon Lady who, while puffing on her foot-long cigarette holder, could poison a man as easily as she could seduce him. "With her talon-like six-inch fingernails, her skin-tight satin dress slit to the thigh," the Dragon Lady is desirable, deceitful, and dangerous (Ling 1990:11). In the 1924 film *The Thief of Baghdad,* Anna May Wong, a pioneer Chinese American actress, played a handmaid who employed treachery to help an evil Mongol prince attempt to win the hand of the Princess of Baghdad (Tajima 1989:309). In so doing, Wong unwittingly popularized a common Dragon Lady social type: treacherous women who are partners in crime with men of their own kind. The publication of *Daughter of Fu Manchu* (1931) firmly entrenched the Dragon Lady image in white consciousness. Carrying on her father's work as the champion of Asian hegemony over the white race, Fah Lo Sue exhibited, in the words of American studies scholar William F. Wu, "exotic sensuality, sexual availability to a white man, and a treacherous nature" (cited in Tong 1994:197). A few years later, in 1934, Milton Caniff inserted into his adventure comic strip *Terry and the Pirates* another version of the Dragon Lady who "combines all the best features of past moustache twirlers with the lure of the handsome wench" (Hoppenstand 1983:178). As such, Caniff's Dragon Lady fuses the image of the evil male Oriental mastermind with that of the Oriental prostitute first introduced some 50 years earlier in the dime novels.

At the opposite end of the spectrum is the Lotus Blossom stereotype, reincarnated throughout the years as the China Doll, the Geisha Girl, the War Bride, or the Vietnamese prostitute—many of whom are the spoils of the last three wars fought in Asia (Tajima 1989:309). Demure, diminutive, and deferential, the Lotus Blossom Baby is "modest, tittering behind her delicate ivory hand, eyes downcast, always walking ten steps behind her man, and, best of all, devot[ing] body and soul to serving him" (Ling 1990:11). Interchangeable in appearance and name, these women have no voice; their "nonlanguage" includes uninterpretable chattering, pidgin English, giggling, or silence (Tajima 1989). These stereotypes of Asian women as submissive and dainty sex objects not only have impeded women's economic mobility but also have fostered an enormous demand for X-rated films and pornographic materials featuring Asian women in bondage, for "Oriental" bathhouse workers in U.S. cities, and for Asian mail-order brides (Kim 1984:64).

Sexism, Racism, and Love

The racialization of Asian manhood and womanhood upholds white masculine hegemony. Cast as sexually available, Asian women become yet another possession of the white man. In motion pictures and network television programs, interracial sexuality, though rare, occurs principally between a white male and an Asian female. A combination of sexism and racism makes this form of miscegenation more acceptable: Race mixing between an Asian male and a white female would upset not only racial taboos but those that attend patriarchal authority as well (Hamamoto 1994:39). Whereas Asian men are depicted as either the threatening rapist or the impotent eunuch, white men are endowed with the masculine attributes with which to sexually attract the

Asian women. Such popular television shows as *Gunsmoke* (1955–1975) and *How the West Was Won* (1978–1979) clearly articulate the theme of Asian female sexual possession by the white male. In these shows, only white males have the prerogative to cross racial boundaries and to choose freely from among women of color as sex partners. Within a system of racial and gender oppression, the sexual possession of women and men of color by white men becomes yet another means of enforcing unequal power relations (Hamamoto 1994:46).

The preference for white male-Asian female is also prevalent in contemporary television news broadcasting, most recently in the 1993–1995 pairing of Dan Rather and Connie Chung as coanchors of the *CBS Evening News*. Today, virtually every major metropolitan market across the United States has at least one Asian American female newscaster (Hamamoto 1994:245). While female Asian American anchorpersons—Connie Chung, Tritia Toyota, Wendy Tokuda, and Emerald Yeh—are popular television news figures, there is a nearly total absence of Asian American men. Critics argue that this is so because the white male hiring establishment, and presumably the larger American public, feels more comfortable (i.e., less threatened) seeing a white male sitting next to a minority female at the anchor desk than the reverse. Stephen Tschida of WDBJ-TV (Roanoke, Virginia), one of only a handful of male Asian American television news anchors, was informed early in his career that he did not have the proper "look" to qualify for the anchorperson position. Other male broadcast news veterans have reported being passed over for younger, more beauteous, female Asian Americans (Hamamoto 1994:245). This gender imbalance sustains the construction of Asian American women as more successful, assimilated, attractive, and desirable than their male counterparts.

To win the love of white men, Asian women must reject not only Asian men but their entire culture. Many Hollywood narratives featuring romances between Anglo American men and Asian women follow the popular Pocahontas mythos: The Asian woman, out of devotion for her white American lover, betrays her own people and commits herself to the dominant white culture by dying, longing for, or going to live with her white husband in his country. For example, in the various versions of *Miss Saigon,* the contemporary version of *Madame Butterfly,* the tragic Vietnamese prostitute eternally longs for the white boy soldier who has long abandoned her and their son (Hagedorn 1993:xxii). These tales of interracial romance inevitably have a tragic ending. The Asian partner usually dies, thus providing a cinematic resolution to the moral lapse of the Westerner. The Pocahontas paradigm can be read as a narrative of salvation; the Asian woman is saved either spiritually or morally from the excesses of her own culture, just as she physically saves her Western lover from the moral degeneracy of her own people (Marchetti 1993:218). For Asian women, who are marginalized not only by gender but also by class, race, or ethnicity, the interracial romance narratives promise "the American Dream of abundance, protection, individual choice, and freedom from the strictures of a traditional society in the paternalistic name of heterosexual romance" (Marchetti 1993:91). These narratives also carry a covert political message, legitimizing a masculinized Anglo American rule over a submissive, feminized Asia. The motion picture *China Gate* (1957) by Samuel Fuller and the network television program *The Lady from Yesterday* (1985), for example, promote an image of Vietnam that legitimizes American rule. Seduced by images of U.S. abundance, a feminized Vietnam sacrifices herself for the possibility of future incorporation into America, the land of individual freedom and economic opportunities. Thus, the interracial tales function not only as a romantic defense of traditional female roles within the patriarchy but also as a political justification of American hegemony in Asia (Marchetti 1993:108).

Fetishized as the embodiment of perfect womanhood and genuine exotic femininity, Asian women are pitted against their more modern, emancipated Western sisters (Tajima 1989). In two popular motion pictures, *Love Is a Many-Splendored Thing* (1955) and *The World of Suzie Wong* (1960), the white women remain independent and potentially threatening, whereas both Suyin and Suzie give up their independence in the name of love. Thus, the white female characters are cast as calculating, suffocating, and thoroughly undesirable, whereas the Asian female characters are depicted as truly "feminine"—passive, subservient, dependent, and domestic. Implicitly, these films warn white women to embrace the socially constructed passive Asian beauty as the feminine ideal if they want to attract and keep a man. In pitting white women against Asian women, Hollywood affirms white male identity against the threat of emerging feminism and the concomitant changes in gender relations (Marchetti 1993:115–16). As Robyn Wiegman (1991) observed, the absorption of women of color into gender categories traditionally reserved for white women is "part of a broader program of hegemonic recuperation, a program that has as its main focus the reconstruction of white masculine power" (p. 320). It is also important to note that as the racialized exotic "other," Asian women do not replace but merely substitute for white women, and thus will be readily dismissed once the "real" mistress returns.

The controlling images of Asian men and Asian women, exaggerated out of all proportion in Western representation, have created resentment and tension between Asian American men and women. Given this cultural milieu, many American-born Asians do not think of other Asians in sexual terms (Fung 1994:163). In particular, due to the persistent desexualization of the Asian male, many Asian females do not perceive their ethnic counterparts as desirable marriage partners (Hamamoto 1992:42). In so doing, these women unwittingly enforce the Eurocentric gender ideology that objectifies both sexes and racializes all Asians (see Collins 1990:185–86). In a column to *Asian Week*, a weekly Asian American newspaper, Daniel Yoon (1993) reported that at a recent dinner discussion hosted by the Asian American Students Association at his college, the Asian American women in the room proceeded, one after another, to describe how "Asian American men were too passive, too weak, too boring, too traditional, too abusive, too domineering, too ugly, too greasy, too short, too . . . Asian. Several described how they preferred white men, and how they never had and never would date an Asian man" (p. 16). Partly as a result of the racist constructions of Asian American womanhood and manhood and their acceptance by Asian Americans, intermarriage patterns are high, with Asian American women intermarrying at a much higher rate than Asian American men.[2] Moreover, Asian women involved in intermarriage have usually married white partners (Agbayani-Siewert & Revilla 1995:156; Min 1995:22; Nishi 1995:128). In part, these intermarriage patterns reflect the sexualization of white racism that constructs white men as the most desirable sexual partners, frowns on Asian male-white women relations, and fetishizes Asian women as the embodiment of perfect womanhood. Viewed in this light, the high rate of outmarriage for Asian American women is the "material outcome of an interlocking system of sexism and racism" (Hamamoto 1992:42).[3]

Cultural Resistance: Reconstructing Our Own Images

"One day/I going to write/about you," wrote Lois-Ann Yamanaka (1993) in "Empty Heart" (p. 548). And Asian Americans did write—"to inscribe our faces on the blank pages and screens of America's hegemonic culture" (Kim 1993:xii). As a result, Asian Americans' objectification as the exotic aliens who are different from, and other than, Euro-Americans has never been absolute. Within the confines of race, class, and gender oppression, Asian Americans have maintained independent self-definitions, challenging controlling images and replacing them with Asian American standpoints. The civil rights and ethnic studies movements of the late 1960s were training grounds for Asian American cultural workers and the development of oppositional projects. Grounded in the U.S. black power movement and in anticolonial struggles of Third World countries, Asian American antihegemonic projects have been unified by a common goal of articulating cultural resistance. Given the historical distortions and misrepresentations of Asian Americans in mainstream media, most cultural projects produced by Asian American men and women perform the important tasks of correcting histories, shaping legacies, creating new cultures, constructing a politics of resistance, and opening spaces for the forcibly excluded (Kim 1993:xiii; Fung 1994:165).

Fighting the exoticization of Asian Americans has been central in the ongoing work of cultural resistance. As discussed above, Asian Americans, however rooted in this country, are represented as recent transplants from Asia or as bearers of an exotic culture. . . . Asian American cultural workers simply do not accept the exotic, one-dimensional caricatures of themselves in U.S. mass media. . . . Asian American cultural projects also deconstruct the myth of the benevolent United States promised to women and men from

Asia. . . . To reject the myth of a benevolent United States is also to refute ideological racism: the justification of inequalities through a set of controlling images that attribute physical and intellectual traits to racially defined groups (Hamamoto 1994:3). . . . Finally, Asian American cultural workers reject the narrative of salvation: the myth that Asian women (and a feminized Asia) are saved, through sexual relations with white men (and a masculinized United States), from the excesses of their own culture. Instead, they underscore the considerable potential for abuse in these inherently unequal relationships.

. . .

Conclusion

Ideological representations of gender and sexuality are central in the exercise and maintenance of racial, patriarchal, and class domination. In the Asian American case, this ideological racism has taken seemingly contrasting forms: Asian men have been cast as both hypersexual and asexual, and Asian women have been rendered both superfeminine and masculine. Although in apparent disjunction, both forms exist to define, maintain, and justify white male supremacy. The racialization of Asian American manhood and womanhood underscores the interconnections of race, gender, and class. As categories of difference, race and gender relations do not parallel but intersect and confirm each other, and it is the complicity among these categories of difference that enables U.S. elites to justify and maintain their cultural, social, and economic power. Responding to the ideological assaults on their gender identities, Asian American cultural workers have engaged in a wide range of oppositional projects to defend Asian American manhood and womanhood. In the process, some have embraced a masculinist cultural nationalism, a stance that marginalizes Asian American women and their needs. Though sensitive to the emasculation of Asian American men, Asian American feminists have pointed out that Asian American nationalism insists on a fixed masculinist identity, thus obscuring gender differences. Though divergent, both the nationalist and feminist positions advance the dichotomous stance of man or woman, gender or race or class, without recognizing the complex relationality of these categories of oppression. It is only when Asian Americans recognize the intersections of race, gender, and class that we can transform the existing hierarchical structure.

NOTES

1. I thank Mary Romero for pointing this out to me.
2. Filipino Americans provide an exception in that Filipino American men tend to intermarry as frequently as Filipina American women. This is partly so because they are more Americanized and have a relatively more egalitarian gender-role orientation than other Asian American men (Agbayani-Siewert & Revilla 1995:156).

3. In recent years, Asian Americans' rising consciousness, coupled with their phenomenal growth in certain regions of the United States, has led to a significant increase in inter-Asian marriages (e.g., Chinese Americans to Korean Americans). In a comparative analysis of the 1980 and 1990 Decennial Census, Larry Hajimi Shinigawa and Gin Young Pang (forthcoming) found a dramatic decrease of interracial marriages and a significant rise of inter-Asian marriages. In California (where 39% of all Asian Pacific Americans reside), inter-Asian marriages increased from 21.1% in 1980 to 64% in 1990 of all intermarriages for Asian American husbands, and from 10.8% to 45% for Asian American wives during the same time period.

REFERENCES

Agbayani-Siewart, Pauline, and Linda Revilla. 1995. "Filipino Americans." Pp. 134–68 in *Asian Americans: Contemporary Trends and Issues*, edited by P. G. Min. Thousand Oaks, CA: Sage.

Baker, Donald G. 1983. *Race, Ethnicity, and Power: A Comparative Study*. New York: Routledge.

Chin, Frank. 1972. "Confessions of the Chinatown Cowboy." *Bulletin of Concerned Asian Scholars* 4(3):66.

Chin, Frank and Chan, Jeffrey P. 1972. "Racist Love." Pp. 65–79 in *Seeing through Shuck*, edited by R. Kostelanetz. New York: Ballantine.

Collins, Patricia Hill. 1990. *Black Feminist Thought: Knowledge, Consciousness, and the Politics of Empowerment*. New York: Routledge.

Doane, Mary Ann. 1991. *Femme Fatales: Feminism, Film Theory, Psychoanalysis*. New York: Routledge.

Engelhardt, Tom. 1976. "Ambush at Kamikaze Pass." Pp. 270–79 in *Counterpoint: Perspectives on Asian America*, edited by E. Gee. Los Angeles: University of California at Los Angeles, Asian American Studies Center.

Frankenberg, Ruth. 1993. *White Women, Race Matters: The Social Construction of Whiteness*. Minneapolis: University of Minnesota Press.

Fung, R. 1994. "Seeing Yellow: Asian Identities in Film and Video." Pp. 161–71 in *The State of Asian America*, edited by K. Aguilar-San Juan. Boston: South End Press.

Goellnicht, D. C. 1992. "Tang Ao in America: Male Subject Positions in *China Men*." Pp. 191–212 in *Reading the Literatures of Asian America*, edited by S. G. Lim and A. Ling. Philadelphia: Temple University Press.

Hagedorn, J. 1993. "Introduction: 'Role of Dead Man Require Very Little Acting.'" Pp. xxi–xxx in *Charlie Chan Is Dead: An Anthology of Contemporary Asian American Fiction*, edited by J. Hagedorn. New York: Penguin.

Hamamoto, D. Y. 1992. "Kindred Spirits: The Contemporary Asian American Family on Television." *Amerasia Journal* 18(2):35–53.

———. 1994. *Monitored Peril: Asian Americans and the Politics of Representation*. Minneapolis: University of Minnesota Press.

Hoppenstand, G. 1983. "Yellow Devil Doctors and Opium Dens: A Survey of the Yellow Peril Stereotypes in Mass Media Entertainment." Pp. 171–85 in *The Popular Culture Reader*, edited by C. D. Geist and J. Nachbar. Bowling Green, OH: Bowling Green University Press.

Kim, E. 1984. "Asian American Writers: A Bibliographical Review." *American Studies International* 22:2.

———. 1990. "'Such Opposite Creatures': Men and Women in Asian American Literature." *Michigan Quarterly Review* 29:68–93.

———. 1993. "Preface." Pp. vii–xiv in *Charlie Chan Is Dead: An Anthology of Contemporary Asian American Fiction*, edited by J. Hagedorn. New York: Penguin.

Ling, A. 1990. *Between Worlds: Women Writers of Chinese Ancestry*. New York: Pergamon.

Marchetti, G. 1993. *Romance and the "Yellow Peril": Race, Sex, and Discursive Strategies in Hollywood Fiction.* Berkeley: University of California Press.

Min, P. G. 1995. "Korean Americans." Pp. 199–231 in *Asian Americans: Contemporary Trends and Issues,* edited by P. G. Min. Thousand Oaks, CA: Sage.

Mullings, L. 1994. "Images, Ideology, and Women of Color." Pp. 265–89 in *Women of Color in U.S. Society,* edited by M. B. Zinn and B. T. Dill. Philadelphia: Temple University Press.

Nguyen, V. 1990. "Growing Up in White America." *Asian Week* (December 7), p. 23.

Nishi, S. M. 1995. "Japanese Americans." Pp. 95–133 in *Asian Americans: Contemporary Trends and Issues,* edited by P. G. Min. Thousand Oaks, CA: Sage.

Okihiro, G. Y. 1995. "Reading Asian Bodies, Reading Anxieties." Paper presented at the University of California, San Diego Ethnic Studies Colloquium, La Jolla, CA. November.

Said, E. 1979. *Orientalism.* New York: Random House.

Tajima, R. 1989. "Lotus Blossoms Don't Bleed: Images of Asian Women." Pp. 308–17 in *Making Waves: An Anthology of Writings by and about Asian American Women,* edited by Asian Women United of California. Boston: Beacon.

Tong, B. 1994. *Unsubmissive Women: Chinese Prostitutes in Nineteenth-Century San Francisco.* Norman, OK: University of Oklahoma Press.

Wang, A. 1988. "Maxine Hong Kingston's Reclaiming of America: The Birthright of the Chinese American Male." *South Dakota Review* 26:18–29.

Wiegman, Robin. 1991. "Black Bodies/American Commodities: Gender, Race, and the Bourgeois Ideal in Contemporary Film." Pp. 308–28 in *Unspeakable Images: Ethnicity and the American Cinema,* edited by L. D. Friedman. Urbana: University of Illinois Press.

Wong, Eugene Franklin. 1978. *On Visual Media Racism: Asians in the American Motion Pictures.* New York: Arno.

Wu, William F. 1982. *The Yellow Peril: Chinese Americans in American Fiction, 1850–1940.* Hamden, CT: Archon.

Yamanaka, Lois-Ann. 1993. "Empty Heart." Pp. 544–50 in *Charlie Chan Is Dead: An Anthology of Contemporary Asian American Fiction,* edited by J. Hagedorn. New York: Penguin.

Yoon, D. D. 1993. "Asian American Male: Wimp or What?" *Asian Week* (November 26), p. 16.

31

THE PROBLEM OF THE TWENTIETH CENTURY IS THE PROBLEM OF THE COLOR LINE

W. E. B. Du Bois

Race and ethnicity are the topics explored in the next four selections. This reading by W. E. B. Du Bois, "The Problem of the Twentieth Century Is the Problem of the Color Line," describes the U.S. system of racial apartheid. Du Bois, a well-known sociologist, wrote the first essay based on that title in 1901. In this selection, written in 1950, Du Bois analyzes the changing patterns of racial relations since the turn of the century. Even though some progress had been made in fifty years, Du Bois concludes that the color line is still visible in everyday life in America.

We are just finishing the first half of the twentieth century. I remember its birth in 1901. There was the usual discussion as to whether the century began in 1900 or 1901; but, of course, 1901 was correct. We expected great things . . . peace; the season of war among nations had passed; progress was the order . . . everything going forward to bigger and better things. And then, not so openly expressed, but even more firmly believed, the rule of white Europe and America over black, brown, and yellow peoples.

I was 32 years of age in 1901, married, and a father, and teaching at Atlanta University with a program covering a hundred years of study and investigation into the condition of American Negroes. Our subject of study at that time was education: the college-bred Negro in 1900, the Negro common school in 1901. My own attitude toward the twentieth century was expressed in an article which I wrote in the *Atlantic Monthly* in 1901. It said:

The problem of the Twentieth Century is the problem of the color-line . . . I have seen a land right merry with the sun, where children sing, and rolling hills lie like passioned women wanton with harvest. And there in the King's Highway sat, and sits, a figure veiled and bowed, by which the

From *Pittsburgh Courier* (January 14, 1950). Copyright © 1950 by the Pittsburgh Courier Publishing Co. Reprinted with permission of the Estate of W. E. B. Du Bois.

Traveler's footsteps hasten as they go. On the tainted air broods fair. Three centuries' thought have been the raising and unveiling of that bowed human soul; and now behold, my fellows, a century now for the duty and the deed! The problem of the Twentieth Century is the problem of the color-line.

This is what we hoped, to this we Negroes looked forward; peace, progress and the breaking of the color line. What has been the result? We know it all too well . . . war, hate, the revolt of the colored peoples and the fear of more war.

In the meantime, where are we; those 15,000,000 citizens of the United States who are descended from the slaves, brought here between 1600 and 1900? We formed in 1901, a separate group because of legal enslavement and emancipation into caste conditions, with the attendant poverty, ignorance, disease, and crime. We were an inner group and not an integral part of the American nation; but we were exerting ourselves to fight for integration.

The burden of our fight was in seven different lines. We wanted education; we wanted particularly the right to vote and civil rights; we wanted work with adequate wage; housing, without segregation or slums; a free press to fight our battles, and (although in those days we dare not say it) social equality.

In 1901 our education was in perilous condition, despite what we and our white friends had done for 30 years. The Atlanta University Conference said in its resolutions of 1901:

> We call the attention of the nation to the fact that less than one million of the three million Negro children of school age are at present regularly attending school, and these attend a session which lasts only a few months. We are today deliberately rearing millions of our citizens in ignorance and at the same time limiting the rights of citizenship by educational qualifications. This is unjust.

More particularly in civil rights, we were oppressed. We not only did not get justice in the courts, but we were subject to peculiar and galling sorts of injustice in daily life. In the latter half of the nineteenth century, where we first get something like statistics, no less than 3,000 Negroes were lynched without trial. And in addition to that we were subject continuously to mob violence and judicial lynching.

In political life we had, for 25 years, been disfranchised by violence, law, and public opinion. The 14th and 15th amendments were deliberately violated and the literature of the day in book, pamphlet, and daily press, was widely of opinion that the Negro was not ready for the ballot, could not use it intelligently, and that no action was called for to stop his political power from being exercised by Southern whites like Tillman and Vardaman.

We did not have the right or opportunity to work at an income which would sustain a decent and modern standard of life. Because of a past of chattel slavery, we were for the most part common laborers and servants, and a very considerable proportion were still unable to leave the plantations where they worked all their lives for next to nothing.

There were a few who were educated for the professions and we had many good artisans; that number was not increasing as it should have been, nor were new artisans being adequately trained. Industrial training was popular, but funds to implement it were too limited, and we were excluded from unions and the new mass industry.

We were housed in slums and segregated districts where crime and disease multiplied, and when we tried to move to better and healthier quarters we were met by segregation ordinance if not by mobs. We not only had no social equality, but we did not openly ask for it. It seemed a shameful thing to beg people to receive us as equals and as human beings; that was something we argued "that came and could not be fetched." And that meant not simply that we could not marry white women or legitimize mulatto bastards, but we could not stop in a decent hotel, nor eat in a public restaurant nor attend the theater, nor accept an invitation to a private white home, nor travel in a decent railway coach. When the "public" was invited, this did not include us and admission to colleges often involved special consideration if not blunt refusal.

Finally we had poor press . . . a few struggling papers with little news and inadequately expressed opinion, with small circulation or influence and almost no advertising.

This was our plight in 1901. It was discouraging, but not hopeless. There is no question but that we had made progress, and there also was no doubt but what that progress was not enough to satisfy us or to settle our problems.

We could look back on a quarter century of struggle which had its results. We had schools; we had teachers; a few had forced themselves into the leading colleges and were tolerated if not welcomed. We voted in Northern cities, owned many decent homes and were fighting for further progress. Leaders like Booker Washington had perceived wide popular approval and a Negro literature had begun to appear.

But what we needed was organized effort along the whole front, based on broad lines of complete emancipation. This came with the Niagara Movement in 1906 and the NAACP in 1909. In 1910 came the *Crisis* magazine and the real battle was on.

What have we gained and accomplished? The advance has not been equal on all fronts, nor complete on any. We have not progressed with closed ranks like a trained army, but rather with serried and broken ranks, with wide gaps and even temporary retreats. But we have advanced. Of that there can be no atom of doubt.

First of all in education; most Negro children today are in school and most adults can read and write. Unfortunately this literacy is not as great as the census says. The draft showed that at least a third of our youth are illiterate. But education is steadily rising. Six thousand bachelor degrees are awarded to Negroes each year and doctorates in philosophy and medicine are not uncommon. Nevertheless as a group, American Negroes are still in the lower ranks of learning and adaptability to modern conditions. They do not read widely, their travel is limited and their experience through contact with the modern world is curtailed by law and custom.

Secondly, in civil rights, the Negro has perhaps made his greatest advance. Mob violence and lynching have markedly decreased. Three thousand Negroes were lynched in the last half of the nineteenth century and five hundred in the first half of the twentieth. Today lynching is comparatively rare. Mob violence also has decreased, but is still in evidence, and summary and unjust court proceedings have taken the place of open and illegal acts. But the Negro has established, in the courts, his legal citizenship and his right to be included in the Bill of Rights. The question still remains of "equal but separate" public accommodations, and that is being attacked. Even the institution of "jim-crow" in travel is tottering. The infraction of the marriage situation by law and custom is yet to be brought before the courts and public opinion in a forcible way.

Third, the right to vote on the part of the Negro is being gradually established under the 14th and 15th amendments. It was not really until 1915 that the Supreme Court upheld this right of Negro citizens and even today the penalties of the 14th amendment have never been enforced. There are 7,000,000 possible voters among American Negroes and of these it is a question if more than 2,000,000 actually cast their votes. This is partly from the national inertia, which keeps half of all American voters away from the polls; but even more from the question as to what practical ends the Negro shall cast his vote.

He is thinking usually in terms of what he can do by voting to better his condition and he seldom gets a chance to vote on this matter. On the wider implications of political democracy he has not yet entered; particularly he does not see the economic foundations of present civilization and the necessity of his attacking the rule of corporate wealth in order to free the labor group to which he belongs.

Fourth, there is the question of occupation. There are our submerged classes of farm labor and tenants: our city laborers, washerwomen and scrubwomen and the mass of lower-paid servants. These classes still form a majority of American Negroes and they are on the edge of poverty, with the ignorance, disease, and crime that always accompany such poverty.

If we measure the median income of Americans, it is $3,000 for whites and $2,000 for Negroes. In Southern cities, seven percent of the white families and 30 percent of the colored families receive less than $1,000 a year. On the other hand, the class differentiation by income among Negroes is notable: the number of semiskilled and skilled artisans has increased or will as membership in labor unions. Professional men have increased, especially teachers and less notably, physicians, dentists, and lawyers.

The number of Negroes in business has increased; mostly in small retail businesses, but to a considerable extent in enterprises like insurance, real estate and small banking, where the color line gives Negroes certain advantages and where, too, there is a certain element of gambling. Also beyond the line of gambling, numbers of Negroes have made small fortunes in antisocial enterprises. All this means that there has arisen in the Negro group a distinct stratification from poor to rich. Recently I polled 450 Negro families belonging to a select organization 45 years old. Of these families, 127 received over $10,000 a year and a score of these over $25,000; 200 families received from $5,000 to $10,000 a year and 86 less than $5,000.

This is the start of a tendency which will grow; we are beginning to follow the American pattern of accumulating individual wealth and of considering that this will eventually settle the race problem. On the other hand, the whole trend of the thought of our age is toward social welfare; the prevention of poverty by more equitable distribution of wealth, and business for general welfare rather than private profit. There are few signs that these ideals are guiding Negro development today. We seem to be adopting increasingly the ideal of American culture.

Housing has, of course, been a point of bitter pressure among Negroes, because the attempt to segregate the race in its living conditions has not only kept the more fortunate ones from progress, but it has confined vast numbers of Negro people to the very parts of cities and country districts where they have fewest opportunities and least social contacts. They must live largely in slums, in contact with criminals and with fewest of the social advantages of government and human contact. The fight against segregation has been carried on in the courts and shows much progress against city ordinances, against covenants which make segregation hereditary.

Literature and art have made progress among Negroes, but with curious handicaps. An art expression is normally evoked by the conscious and unconscious demand of people for portrayal of their own emotion and experience. But in the case of the American Negroes, the audience, which embodies the demand and which pays sometimes enormous price for satisfaction, is not the Negro group, but the white group. And the pattern of what the white group wants does not necessarily agree with the natural desire of Negroes.

The whole of Negro literature is therefore curiously divided. We have writers who have written, not really about Negroes, but about the things which white people, and not the highest class of whites, like to hear about Negroes. And those who have expressed what the Negro himself thinks and feels, are those whose books sell to few, even of their own people; and whom most folk do not know. This has not made for the authentic literature which the early part of this century seemed to promise. To be sure, it can be said that American literature today has a considerable amount of Negro expression and influence, although not as much as once we hoped.

Despite all this we have an increasing number of excellent Negro writers who make the promise for the future great by their real accomplishment. We have done something in sculpture and painting, but in drama and music we have markedly advanced. All the world listens to our singers, sings our music, and dances to our rhythms.

In science, our handicaps are still great. Turner, a great entomologist, was worked to death for lack of laboratory, just never had the recognition he richly deserved; and Carver was prisoner of his inferiority complex. Notwithstanding this, our real accomplishment in biology and medicine; in history and law; and in the social sciences has been notable and widely acclaimed. To this in no little degree is due our physical survival, our falling death rate, and our increased confidence in our selves and in our destiny.

The expression of Negro wish and desire through a free press has greatly improved as compared with 1900. We have a half dozen large weekly papers with circulations of a hundred thousand or more. Their news coverage is immense, even if not discriminating. But here again, the influence of the American press on us has been devastating. The predominance of advertising over opinion, the desire for income rather than literary excellence and the use of deliberate propaganda, has made our press less of a power than it could be, and leaves wide chance for improvement in the future.

In comparison with other institutions, the Negro church during the twentieth century has lost ground. It is no longer the dominating influence that it used to be, the center of social activity and of economic experiment. Nevertheless, it is still a powerful institution in the lives of a numerical majority of American Negroes if not upon the dominant intellectual classes. There has been a considerable increase in organized work for social progress through the church, but there has also been a large increase of expenditure for buildings, furnishings, and salaries; and it is not easy to find any increase in moral stamina or conscientious discrimination within church circles.

The scandal of deliberate bribery in election of bishops and in the holding of positions in the churches without a hierarchy has been widespread. It is a critical problem now as to just what part in the future the church among Negroes is going to hold.

Finally there comes the question of social equality, which, despite efforts on the part of thinkers, white and black, is after all the main and fundamental problem of race in the United States. Unless a human being is going to have all human rights, including not only work, but friendship, and if mutually desired, marriage and children, unless these avenues are open and free, there can be no real equality and no cultural integration.

It has hitherto seemed utterly impossible that any such solution of the Negro problem in America could take place. The situation was quite similar to the problem of the lower classes of laborers, serfs and servants in European nations during the sixteenth, seventeenth, and eighteenth centuries. All nations had to consist of two separate parts and the only relations between them was employment and philanthropy.

That problem has been partly solved by modern democracy, but modern democracy cannot succeed unless the peoples of different races and religions are also integrated into the democratic whole. Against this, large numbers of

Americans have always fought and are still fighting, but the progress despite this has been notable. There are places in the United States, especially in large cities like New York and Chicago, where the social differences between the races has, to a large extent, been nullified and there is a meeting on terms of equality which would have been thought impossible a half century ago.

On the other hand, in the South, despite religion, education, and reason, the color line, although perhaps shaken, still stands, stark and unbending, and to the minds of most good people, eternal. Here lies the area of the last battle for the complete rights of American Negroes.

Within the race itself today there are disquieting signs. The effort of Negroes to become Americans of equal status with other Americans is leading them to a state of mind by which they not only accept what is good in America, but what is bad and threatening so long as the Negro can share equally. This is peculiarly dangerous at this epoch in the development of world culture.

After two world wars of unprecedented loss of life, cruelty, and destruction, we are faced by the fact that the industrial organization of our present civilization has in it something fundamentally wrong. It went to pieces in the first world war because of the determination of certain great powers excluded from world rule to share in that rule, by acquisition of the labor and materials of colonial peoples. The attempt to recover from the cataclysm resulted in the collapse of our industrial system, and a second world war.

In spite of the propaganda which has gone on, which represents America as the leading democratic state, we Negroes know perfectly well, and ought to know even better than most, that America is not a successful democracy and that until it is, it is going to drag down the world. This nation is ruled by corporate wealth to a degree which is frightening. One thousand persons own the United States and their power outweighs the voice of the mass of American citizens. This must be cured, not by revolution, not by war and violence, but by reason and knowledge.

Most of the world is today turning toward the welfare state; turning against the idea of production for individual profit toward the idea of production for use and for the welfare of the mass of citizens. No matter how difficult such a course is, it is the only course that is going to save the world and this we American Negroes have got to realize.

We may find it easy now to get publicity, reward, and attention by going along with the reactionary propaganda and war hysteria which is convulsing this nation, but in the long run America will not thank its black children if they help it go the wrong way, or retard its progress.

32

"IS THIS A WHITE COUNTRY, OR WHAT?"

LILLIAN B. RUBIN

In this reading, Lillian Rubin presents her findings of racial hostility among working-class white ethnics. Rubin finds that the "color line" has been redefined to include immigrants and all people of color. Using interviews and document analysis, Rubin compares the anti-immigrant, racist beliefs of her respondents with actual demographic data on immigration and social opportunities in the United States. This excerpt is taken from Rubin's 1994 book *Families on the Fault Line: America's Working Class Speaks about the Family, the Economy, Race, and Ethnicity.*

"They're letting all these coloreds come in and soon there won't be any place left for white people," broods Tim Walsh, a 33-year-old white construction worker. "It makes you wonder: Is this a white country, or what?"

It's a question that nags at white America, one perhaps that's articulated most often and most clearly by the men and women of the working class. For it's they who feel most vulnerable, who have suffered the economic contractions of recent decades most keenly, who see the new immigrants most clearly as direct competitors for their jobs.

It's not whites alone who stew about immigrants. Native-born blacks, too, fear the newcomers nearly as much as whites—and for the same economic reasons. But for whites the issue is compounded by race, by the fact that the newcomers are primarily people of color. For them, therefore, their economic anxieties have combined with the changing face of America to create a profound uneasiness about immigration—a theme that was sounded by nearly 90 percent of the whites I met, even by those who are themselves first-generation, albeit well-assimilated, immigrants.

Sometimes they spoke about this in response to my questions; equally often the subject of immigration arose spontaneously as people gave voice to their concerns. But because the new immigrants are predominantly people of color, the discourse was almost always cast in terms of race as well as immigration, with the talk slipping from immigration to race and back again as if these are not two separate phenomena. "If we keep letting all them for-eigners in, pretty soon there'll be more of them than us and then what will this country be like?" Tim's wife, Mary Anne, frets. "I mean, this is *our* coun-try, but the way things are going, white people will be the minority in our own country. Now does that make any sense?"

Such fears are not new. Americans have always worried about the strangers who came to our shores, fearing that they would corrupt our soci-ety, dilute our culture, debase our values. So I remind Mary Anne, "When your ancestors came here, people also thought we were allowing too many foreigners into the country. Yet those earlier immigrants were successfully in-tegrated into the American society. What's different now?"

"Oh, it's different, all right," she replies without hesitation. "When my people came, the immigrants were all white. That makes a big difference."

"Why do you think that's so?"

"I don't know; it just is, that's all. Look at the black people; they've been here a long time, and they still don't live like us—stealing and drugs and having all those babies."

"But you were talking about immigrants. Now you're talking about blacks, and they're not immigrants."

"Yeah, I know," she replies with a shrug. "But they're different, and there's enough problems with them, so we don't need any more. With all these other people coming here now, we just have more trouble. They don't talk English; and they think different from us, things like that."

Listening to Mary Anne's words I was reminded again how little we Americans look to history for its lessons, how impoverished is our historical memory. For, in fact, being white didn't make "a big difference" for many of those earlier immigrants. The dark-skinned Italians and the eastern Euro-pean Jews who came in the late nineteenth and early twentieth centuries didn't look very white to the fair-skinned Americans who were here then. Indeed, the same people we now call white—Italians, Jews, Irish—were seen as another race at that time. Not black or Asian, it's true, but an alien other, a race apart, although one that didn't have a clearly defined name. Moreover, the racist fears and fantasies of native-born Americans were far less con-tained then than they are now, largely because there were few social con-straints on their expression.

When, during the nineteenth century, for example, some Italians were taken for blacks and lynched in the South, the incidents passed virtually un-noticed. And if Mary Anne and Tim Walsh, both of Irish ancestry, had come to this country during the great Irish immigration of that period, they would have found themselves defined as an inferior race and described with the same language that was used to characterize blacks: "low-browed and sav-age, grovelling and bestial, lazy and wild, simian and sensual."[1] Not only during that period but for a long time afterward as well, the U.S. Census Bu-reau counted the Irish as a distinct and separate group, much as it does today with the category it labels "Hispanic."

But there are two important differences between then and now, differences that can be summed up in a few words: the economy and race. Then, a growing industrial economy meant that there were plenty of jobs for both immigrant and native workers, something that can't be said for the contracting economy in which we live today. True, the arrival of the immigrants, who were more readily exploitable than native workers, put Americans at a disadvantage and created discord between the two groups. Nevertheless, work was available for both.

Then, too, the immigrants—no matter how they were labeled, no matter how reviled they may have been—were ultimately assimilable, if for no other reason than that they were white. As they began to lose their alien ways, it became possible for native Americans to see in the white ethnics of yesteryear a reflection of themselves. Once this shift in perception occurred, it was possible for the nation to incorporate them, to take them in, chew them up, digest them, and spit them out as Americans—with subcultural variations not always to the liking of those who hoped to control the manners and mores of the day, to be sure, but still recognizably white Americans.

Today's immigrants, however, are the racial other in a deep and profound way. It's true that race is not a fixed category, that it's no less an *idea* today than it was yesterday. And it's also possible, as I have already suggested, that we may be witness to social transformation from race to ethnicity among some of the most assimilated—read: middle-class—Asians and Latinos. But even if so, there's a long way to go before that metamorphosis is realized. Meanwhile, the immigrants of this era not only bring their own language and culture, they are also people of color—men, women, and children whose skin tones are different and whose characteristic features set them apart and justify the racial categories we lock them into.[2] And integrating masses of people of color into a society where race consciousness lies at the very heart of our central nervous system raises a whole new set of anxieties and tensions.

It's not surprising, therefore, that racial dissension has increased so sharply in recent years. What is surprising, however, is the passion for ethnicity and the preoccupation with ethnic identification among whites that seems suddenly to have burst upon the public scene. . . .

. . .

What does being German, Irish, French, Russian, Polish mean to someone who is an American? It's undoubtedly different for recent immigrants than for those who have been here for generations. But even for a relative newcomer, the inexorable process of becoming an American changes the meaning of ethnic identification and its hold on the internal life of the individual. Nowhere have I seen this shift more eloquently described than in a recent op-ed piece published in the *New York Times*. The author, a Vietnamese refugee writing on the day when Vietnamese either celebrate or mourn the fall of Saigon, depending on which side of the conflict they were on, writes:

> Although I sometimes mourn the loss of home and land, it's the American landscape and what it offers that solidify my hyphenated identity. . . . Assimilation, education, the English language, the American 'I'—these have carried me and many others further from that beloved tropical country than the C-130 ever could. . . . When did this happen? Who knows? One night, America quietly seeps in and takes hold of one's mind and body, and the Vietnamese soul of sorrows slowly fades away. In the morning, the Vietnamese American speaks a new language of materialism: his vocabulary includes terms like career choices, down payment, escrow, overtime.[3]

A new language emerges, but it lives, at least for another generation, alongside the old one; Vietnamese, yes, but also American, with a newly developed sense of self and possibility—an identity that continues to grow stronger with each succeeding generation. It's a process we have seen repeated throughout the history of American immigration. The American world reaches into the immigrant communities and shapes and changes the people who live in them.[4] By the second generation, ethnic identity already is attenuated; by the third, it usually has receded as a deeply meaningful part of life.

Residential segregation, occupational concentration, and a common language and culture—these historically have been the basis for ethnic solidarity and identification. As strangers in a new land, immigrants banded together, bound by their native tongue and shared culture. The sense of affinity they felt in these urban communities was natural; they were a touch of home, of the old country, of ways they understood. Once within their boundaries, they could feel whole again, sheltered from the ridicule and revulsion with which they were greeted by those who came before them. For whatever the myth about America's welcoming arms, nativist sentiment has nearly always been high and the anti-immigrant segment of the population large and noisy.

Ethnic solidarity and identity in America, then, were the consequence of the shared history each group brought with it, combined with the social and psychological experience of establishing themselves in the new land. But powerful as these were, the connections among the members of the group were heightened and sustained by the occupational concentration that followed—the Irish in the police departments of cities like Boston and San Francisco, for example, the Jews in New York City's garment industry, the east central Europeans in the mills and mines of western Pennsylvania.[5]

As each ethnic group moved into the labor force, its members often became concentrated in a particular occupation, largely because they were helped to find jobs there by those who went before them. For employers, this ethnic homogeneity made sense. They didn't have to cope with a babel of different languages, and they could count on the older workers to train the newcomers and keep them in line. For workers, there were advantages as well. It meant that they not only had compatible workmates, but that they weren't alone as they faced the jeers and contempt of their American-born counterparts. And perhaps most important, as more and more ethnic peers filled the available jobs, they began to develop some small measure of control in the workplace.

The same pattern of occupational concentration that was characteristic of yesterday's immigrant groups exists among the new immigrants today, and for the same reasons. The Cubans in Florida and the Dominicans in New York,[6] the various Asian groups in San Francisco, the Koreans in Los Angeles and New York—all continue to live in ethnic neighborhoods; all use the networks established there to find their way into the American labor force.[7]

For the white working-class ethnics whose immigrant past is little more than part of family lore, the occupational, residential, and linguistic chain has been broken. This is not to say that white ethnicity has ceased to be an observable phenomenon in American life. Cities like New York, Chicago, and San Francisco still have white ethnic districts that influence their culture, especially around food preferences and eating habits. But as in San Francisco's North Beach or New York's Little Italy, the people who once created vibrant neighborhoods, where a distinct subculture and language remained vividly alive, long ago moved out and left behind only the remnants of the commercial life of the old community. As such transformations took place, ethnicity became largely a private matter, a distant part of the family heritage that had little to do with the ongoing life of the family or community.

What, then, are we to make of the claims to ethnic identity that have become so prominent in recent years? Herbert Gans has called this identification "symbolic ethnicity"—that is, ethnicity that's invoked or not as the individual chooses.[8] Symbolic ethnicity, according to Gans, has little impact on a person's daily life and, because it is not connected to ethnic structures or activities—except for something like the wearing of the green on St. Patrick's Day—it makes no real contribution to ethnic solidarity or community.

The description is accurate. But it's a mistake to dismiss ethnic identification, even if only symbolic, as relatively meaningless. Symbols, after all, become symbolic precisely because they have meaning. In this case, the symbol has meaning at two levels: One is the personal and psychological, the other is the social and political.

At the personal level, in a nation as large and diverse as ours—a nation that defines itself by its immigrant past, where the metaphor for our national identity has been the melting pot—defining oneself in the context of an ethnic group is comforting. It provides a sense of belonging to some recognizable and manageable collectivity—an affiliation that has meaning because it's connected to the family where, when we were small children, we first learned about our relationship to the group. As Vilma Janowski, a

24-year-old first-generation Polish-American who came here as a child put it: "Knowing there's other people like you is really nice. It's like having a big family, even if you don't ever really see them. It's just nice to know they're there. Besides, if I said I was American, what would it mean? Nobody's just American."

Which is true. Being an American is different from being French or Dutch or any number of other nationalities because, except for Native Americans, there's no such thing as an American without a hyphen somewhere in the past. To identify with the front end of that hyphen is to maintain a connection—however tenuous, illusory, or sentimentalized—with our roots. It sets us apart from others, allows us the fantasy of uniqueness—a quest given particular urgency by a psychological culture that increasingly emphasizes the development of the self and personal history. Paradoxically, however, it also gives us a sense of belonging—of being one with others like ourselves—that helps to overcome some of the isolation of modern life.

But these psychological meanings have developed renewed force in recent years because of two significant sociopolitical events. The first was the civil rights movement with its call for racial equality. The second was the change in the immigration laws, which, for the first time in nearly half a century, allowed masses of immigrants to enter the country.

It was easy for northern whites to support the early demands of the civil rights movement when blacks were asking for the desegregation of buses and drinking fountains in the South. But supporting the black drive to end discrimination in jobs, housing, and education in the urban North was quite another matter—especially among those white ethnics whose hold on the ladder of mobility was tenuous at best and with whom blacks would be most likely to compete, whether in the job market, the neighborhood, or the classroom. As the courts and legislatures around the country began to honor some black claims for redress of past injustices, white hackles began to rise.

It wasn't black demands alone that fed the apprehensions of whites, however. In the background of the black civil rights drive, there stood a growing chorus of voices, as other racial groups—Asian Americans, Latinos, and Native Americans—joined the public fray to seek remedy for their own grievances. At the same time that these home-grown groups were making their voices heard and, not incidentally, affirming their distinctive cultural heritages and calling for public acknowledgment of them, the second great wave of immigration in this century washed across our shores.

After having closed the gates to mass immigration with the National Origins Act of 1924, Congress opened them again when it passed the Immigration Act of 1965.[9] This act, which was a series of amendments to the McCarran-Walter Act of 1952, essentially jettisoned the national origins provisions of earlier law and substituted overall hemisphere caps. The bill, according to immigration historian Roger Daniels, "changed the whole course of American immigration history" and left the door open for a vast increase in the numbers of immigrants.[10]

More striking than the increase in numbers has been the character of the new immigrants. Instead of the large numbers of western Europeans whom the sponsors had expected to take advantage of the new policy, it has been the people of Asia, Latin America, and the Caribbean who rushed to the boats. "It is doubtful if any drafter or supporter of the 1965 act envisaged this result," writes Daniels.[11] In fact, when members of Lyndon Johnson's administration, under whose tenure the bill became law, testified before Congress, they assured the legislators and the nation that few Asians would come in under the new law.[12]

This is a fascinating example of the unintended consequences of a political act. The change in the law was sponsored by northern Democrats who sought to appeal to their white ethnic constituencies by opening the gates to their countrymen once again—that is, to the people of eastern and southern Europe whom the 1924 law had kept out for nearly half a century. But those same white ethnics punished the Democratic Party by defecting to the Republicans during the Reagan-Bush years, a defection that was at least partly related to their anger about the new immigrants and the changing racial balance of urban America.

During the decade of the 1980s, 2.5 million immigrants from Asian countries were admitted to the United States, an increase of more than 450 percent over the years between 1961 and 1970, when the number was slightly less than half a million. In 1990 alone, nearly as many Asian immigrants—one-third of a million—entered the country as came during the entire decade of the 1960s. Other groups show similarly noteworthy increases. Close to three-quarters of a million documented Mexicans crossed the border in the single year of 1990, compared to less than half a million during all of the 1960s. Central American immigration, too, climbed from just under one hundred thousand between 1961 and 1970 to more than triple that number during the 1980s. And immigrants from the Caribbean, who numbered a little more than half a million during the 1960s, increased to over three-quarters of a million in the years between 1981 and 1989.[13]

Despite these large increases and the perception that we are awash with new immigrants, it's worth noting that they are a much smaller proportion of the total population today, 6.2 percent, than they were in 1920, when they were a hefty 13.2 percent of all U.S. residents.[14] But the fact that most immigrants today are people of color gives them greater visibility than ever before.

Suddenly, the nation's urban landscape has been colored in ways unknown before. In 1970, the California cities that were the site of the original research for *Worlds of Pain* were almost exclusively white. Twenty years later, the 1990 census reports that their minority populations range from 54 to 69 percent. In the nation at large, the same census shows nearly one in four Americans with African, Asian, Latino, or Native American ancestry, up from one in five in 1980.[15] So dramatic is this shift that whites of European descent now make up just over two-thirds of the population in New York State, while in California they number only 57 percent. In cities like New York, San Francisco, and Los Angeles whites are a minority—accounting for 38, 47, and 37 percent of residents, respectively. Twenty years ago the white population in all these cities was over 75 percent.[16]

The increased visibility of other racial groups has focused whites more self-consciously than ever on their own racial identification. Until the new immigration shifted the complexion of the land so perceptibly, whites didn't think of themselves as white in the same way that Chinese know they're Chinese and African Americans know they're black. Being white was simply a fact of life, one that didn't require any public statement, since it was the definitive social value against which all others were measured. "It's like everything's changed and I don't know what happened," complains Marianne Bardolino. "All of a sudden you have to be thinking all the time about these race things. I don't remember growing up thinking about being white like I think about it now. I'm not saying I didn't know there was coloreds and whites; it's just that I didn't go along thinking, *Gee, I'm a white person.* I never thought about it at all. But now with all the different colored people around, you have to think about it because they're thinking about it all the time."

"You say you feel pushed now to think about being white, but I'm not sure I understand why. What's changed?" I ask.

"I told you," she replies quickly, a small smile covering her impatience with my question. "It's because they think about what they are, and they want things their way, so now I have to think about what I am and what's good for me and my kids." She pauses briefly to let her thoughts catch up with her tongue, then continues. "I mean, if somebody's always yelling at you about being black or Asian or something, then it makes you think about being white. Like, they want the kids in school to learn about their culture, so then I think about being white and being Italian and say: What about my culture? If they're going to teach about theirs, what about mine?"

To which America's racial minorities respond with bewilderment. "I don't understand what white people want," says Gwen Tomalson. "They say if black kids are going to learn about black culture in school, then white people want their kids to learn about white culture. I don't get it. What do they think kids have been learning about all these years? It's all about white people and how they live and what they accomplished. When I was in school you wouldn't have thought black people existed for all our books ever said about us."

As for the charge that they're "thinking about race all the time," as Marianne Bardolino complains, people of color insist that they're forced into it by a white world that never lets them forget. "If you're Chinese, you can't forget it, even if you want to, because there's always something that reminds you," Carol Kwan's husband, Andrew, remarks tartly. "I mean, if Chinese kids get good grades and get into the university, everybody's worried and you read about it in the papers."

While there's little doubt that racial anxieties are at the center of white concerns, our historic nativism also plays a part in escalating white alarm. The new immigrants bring with them a language and an ethnic culture that's vividly expressed wherever they congregate. And it's this also, the constant reminder of an alien presence from which whites are excluded, that's so troublesome to them.

The nativist impulse isn't, of course, given to the white working class alone. But for those in the upper reaches of the class and status hierarchy—those whose children go to private schools, whose closest contact with public transportation is the taxicab—the immigrant population supplies a source of cheap labor, whether as nannies for their children, maids in their households, or workers in their businesses. They may grouse and complain that "nobody speaks English anymore," just as working-class people do. But for the people who use immigrant labor, legal or illegal, there's a payoff for the inconvenience—a payoff that doesn't exist for the families in this study but that sometimes costs them dearly.[17] For while it may be true that American workers aren't eager for many of the jobs immigrants are willing to take, it's also true that the presence of a large immigrant population—especially those who come from developing countries where living standards are far below our own—helps to make these jobs undesirable by keeping wages depressed well below what most American workers are willing to accept.[18]

Indeed, the economic basis of our immigration policies too often gets lost in the lore that we are a land that says to the world, "Give me your tired, your poor, your huddled masses, yearning to breathe free."[19] I don't mean to suggest that our humane impulses are a fiction, only that the reality is far more complex than Emma Lazarus' poem suggests. The massive immigration of the nineteenth and early twentieth centuries didn't just happen spontaneously. America may have been known as the land of opportunity to the Europeans who dreamed of coming here—a country where, as my parents once believed, the streets were lined with gold. But they believed these things because that's how America was sold by the agents who spread out across the face of Europe to recruit workers—men and women who were needed to keep the machines of our developing industrial society running and who, at the same time, gave the new industries a steady supply of hungry workers willing to work for wages well below those of native-born Americans.

The enormous number of immigrants who arrived during that period accomplished both those ends. In doing so, they set the stage for a long history of antipathy to foreign workers. For today, also, one function of the new immigrants is to keep our industries competitive in a global economy. Which simply is another way of saying that they serve to depress the wages of native American workers.

It's not surprising, therefore, that working-class women and men speak so angrily about the recent influx of immigrants. They not only see their jobs and their way of life threatened, they feel bruised and assaulted by an environment that seems suddenly to have turned color and in which they feel like strangers in their own land. So they chafe and complain: "They come here to take advantage of us, but they don't really want to learn our ways," Beverly Sowell, a 33-year-old white electronics assembler, grumbles irritably. "They live different than us; it's like another world how they live. And they're so clannish. They keep to themselves, and they don't even *try* to learn English. You go on the bus these days and you might as well be in a foreign country; everybody's talking some other language, you know, Chinese or Spanish or something. Lots of them have been here a long time, too, but they don't care; they just want to take what they can get."

But their complaints reveal an interesting paradox, an illuminating glimpse into the contradictions that beset native-born Americans in their relations with those who seek refuge here. On the one hand, they scorn the immigrants; on the other, they protest because they "keep to themselves." It's the same contradiction that dominates black–white relations. Whites refuse to integrate blacks but are outraged when they stop knocking at the door, when they move to sustain the separation on their own terms—in black theme houses on campuses, for example, or in the newly developing black middle-class suburbs.

I wondered, as I listened to Beverly Sowell and others like her, why the same people who find the lifeways and languages of our foreign-born population offensive also care whether they "keep to themselves."

"Because like I said, they just shouldn't, that's all," Beverly says stubbornly. "If they're going to come here, they should be willing to learn our ways—you know what I mean, be real Americans. That's what my grandparents did, and that's what they should do."

"But your grandparents probably lived in an immigrant neighborhood when they first came here, too," I remind her.

"It was different," she insists. "I don't know why; it was. They wanted to be Americans; these here people now, I don't think they do. They just want to take advantage of this country."

She stops, thinks for a moment, then continues, "Right now it's awful in this country. Their kids come into the schools, and it's a big mess. There's not enough money for our kids to get a decent education, and we have to spend money to teach their kids English. It makes me mad. I went to public school, but I have to send my kids to Catholic school because now on top of the black kids, there's all these foreign kids who don't speak English. What kind of an education can kids get in a school like that? Something's wrong when plain old American kids can't go to their own schools.

"Everything's changed, and it doesn't make sense. Maybe you get it, but I don't. We can't take care of our own people and we keep bringing more and more foreigners in. Look at all the homeless. Why do we need more people here when our own people haven't got a place to sleep?"

"Why do we need more people here?"—a question Americans have asked for two centuries now. Historically, efforts to curb immigration have come during economic downturns, which suggests that when times are good, when American workers feel confident about their future, they're likely to be more generous in sharing their good fortune with foreigners. But when the economy falters, as it did in the 1990s, and workers worry about having to compete for jobs with people whose standard of living is well below their own, resistance to immigration rises. "Don't get me wrong; I've got nothing against these people," Tim Walsh demurs. "But they don't talk English, and they're used to a lot less, so they can work for less money than guys like me can. I see it all the time; they get hired and some white guy gets left out."

It's this confluence of forces—the racial and cultural diversity of our new immigrant population; the claims on the resources of the nation now being made by those minorities who, for generations, have called America their home; the failure of some of our basic institutions to serve the needs of our people; the contracting economy, which threatens the mobility aspirations of working-class families—all these have come together to leave white workers feeling as if everyone else is getting a piece of the action while they get nothing. "I feel like white people are left out in the cold," protests Diane Johnson, a 28-year-old white single mother who believes she lost a job as a bus driver to a black woman. "First it's the blacks; now it's all those other colored people, and it's like everything always goes their way. It seems like a white person doesn't have a chance anymore. It's like the squeaky wheel gets the grease, and they've been squeaking and we haven't," she concludes angrily.

Until recently, whites didn't need to think about having to "squeak"—at least not specifically as whites. They have, of course, organized and squeaked at various times in the past—sometimes as ethnic groups, sometimes as workers. But not as whites. As whites they have been the dominant group, the favored ones, the ones who could count on getting the job when people of color could not. Now suddenly there are others—not just individual others but identifiable groups, people who share a history, a language, a culture, even a color—who lay claim to some of the rights and privileges that formerly had been labeled "for whites only." And whites react as if they've been betrayed, as if a sacred promise has been broken. They're white, aren't they? They're *real* Americans, aren't they? This is their country, isn't it?

NOTES

1. David R. Roediger, *The Wages of Whiteness* (New York: Verso, 1991), p. 133.
2. I'm aware that many Americans who have none of the characteristic features associated with their African heritage are still defined as black. This is one reason why I characterize race as an idea, not a fact. Nevertheless, the main point I am making here still holds—that is, the visible racial character of a people makes a difference in whether white Americans see them as assimilable or not.
3. *New York Times,* April 30, 1993.
4. For an excellent historical portrayal of the formation of ethnic communities among the east central European immigrants in Pennsylvania, the development of ethnic identity, and the process of Americanization, see Ewa Morawska, *For Bread with Butter* (New York: Cambridge University Press, 1985).

5. Ibid.

6. Alejandro Portes and Ruben G. Rumbaut, *Immigrant America* (Berkeley: University of California Press, 1990).

7. One need only walk the streets of New York to see the concentration of Koreans in the corner markets and the nail care salons that dot the city's landscape.

   In San Francisco the Cambodians now own most of the donut shops in the city. It all started when, after working in such a shop, an enterprising young Cambodian combined the family resources and opened his own store and bakery. He now has 20 shops and has been instrumental in helping his countrymen open more, all of them buying their donuts from his bakery.

8. Herbert Gans, "Symbolic Ethnicity: The Future of Ethnic Groups and Cultures in America," *Ethnic and Racial Studies* 2 (1979):1–18.

9. Despite nativist protests, immigration had proceeded unchecked by government regulation until the end of the nineteenth century. The first serious attempt to restrict immigration came in 1882 when, responding to the clamor about the growing immigration of Chinese laborers to California and other western states, Congress passed the Chinese Exclusion Act. But European immigration remained unimpeded. In the years between 1880 and 1924, twenty-four million newcomers arrived on these shores, most of them eastern and southern Europeans, all bringing their own language and culture, and all the target of pervasive bigotry and exploitation by native-born Americans. By the early part of the twentieth century, anti-immigration sentiments grew strong enough to gain congressional attention once again. The result was the National Origins Act of 1924, which established the quota system that sharply limited immigration, especially from the countries of southern and eastern Europe.

10. Roger Daniels, *Coming to America: A History of Immigration and Ethnicity in American Life* (New York: HarperCollins, 1990), pp. 338–44.

11. Daniels, *Coming to America,* p. 341, writes further, "In his Liberty Island speech Lyndon Johnson stressed the fact that he was redressing the wrong done [by the McCarran-Walter Act] to those 'from southern or eastern Europe,' and although he did mention 'developing continents,' there was no other reference to Asian or Third World immigration."

12. For a further review of the Immigration Act of 1965, see chapter 13 (pp. 328–49) of *Coming to America.*

13. *Statistical Abstract,* U.S. Bureau of the Census (1992), Table 8, p. 11.

14. *Statistical Abstract,* U.S. Bureau of the Census (1992), Table 45, p. 42.

15. *Statistical Abstract,* U.S. Bureau of the Census (1992), Table 18, p. 18, and Table 26, p. 24.

16. U.S. Bureau of the Census, *Population Reports,* 1970 and 1990. Cited in Mike Davis, "The Body Count," *Crossroads* (June 1993). The difference in the racial composition of New York and San Francisco explains, at least in part, why black–white tensions are so much higher in New York City than they are in San Francisco. In New York, 38 percent of the population is now white, 30 percent black, 25 percent Hispanic, and 7 percent Asian. In San Francisco, whites make up 47 percent of the residents, blacks 11 percent, Hispanics 14 percent, and Asians 29 percent. Thus, blacks in New York reflect the kind of critical mass that generally sparks racial prejudices, fears, and conflicts. True, San Francisco's Asian population—three in ten of the city's residents—also form that kind of critical and noticeable mass. But whatever the American prejudice against Asians, and however much it has been acted out in the past, Asians do not stir the same kind of fear and hatred in white hearts as do blacks.

17. Zoë Baird, the first woman ever to be nominated to be attorney general of the United States, was forced to withdraw when it became known that she and her husband had hired an illegal immigrant as a nanny for their three-year-old child. The public indignation that followed the revelation came largely from people who were furious that, in a time of high unemployment, American workers were bypassed in favor of cheaper foreign labor.

18. This is now beginning to happen in more skilled jobs as well. In California's Silicon Valley, for example, software programmers and others are being displaced by Indian workers, people who are trained in India and recruited to work here because they are willing to do so for lower wages than similarly skilled Americans (*San Francisco Examiner,* February 14, 1993).

19. From Emma Lazarus' "The New Colossus," inscribed at the base of the Statue of Liberty in New York's harbor, the gateway through which most of the immigrants from Europe passed as they came in search of a new life.

33

BLUE DREAMS
Korean Americans and the Los Angeles Riots

NANCY ABELMANN • JOHN LIE

Race is a creation of culture that reflects social distinctions and power. To say that race is a social construction, however, does not mean that race is not real. Many people believe in the existence of discrete biological racial categories. Sociologists are concerned not only with how race and ethnicity are defined, but also with the consequences of those distinctions. One important aspect in the social construction of race and ethnicity is how the media defines and frames race-ethnicity and racial problems. The following reading by Nancy Abelmann and John Lie examines how the media "framed" the 1992 Los Angeles riots as an interethnic conflict between Korean Americans and African Americans. Their analysis shows how problematic these media frames of race issues are for race relations in the United States. This selection is excerpted from Abelmann and Lie's 1995 book *Blue Dreams: Korean Americans and the Los Angeles Riots.*

As the complex realities of the multiethnic L.A. riots came to the surface, the media fixated on the conflict between African Americans and Korean Americans.[1] Their mutual animosity became an article of faith. The *Los Angeles Business Journal* reported: "The feelings of many in the black community toward Koreans had become comparable to that of a vanquished populace to the occupying army" (McNelis-Ahern 1992:4). Simultaneously, as Harold Meyerson explained: "Many within the Korean community conceal a raging anti-black animus behind a wafer-thin veneer of peace rhetoric" (1992:2). The looming "race war" prompted Jeff Yang to observe: "The broadest barrage turned the L.A. riots into a sensationalistic Tale of Two Tapes: Rodney King versus Soon Ja Du, the 'killer Korean shop-keeper'" (1992:47). Instances of the "Black–Korean conflict" beyond Los Angeles, ranging from episodes in Spike Lee's film *Do the Right Thing* to the well-publicized boycott of a Korean American grocer in Flatbush, New York, suggested that it might be a nationwide phenomenon.

Here we criticize the "Black–Korean conflict" frame of the L.A. riots and examine its ideological context. We realize that challenging its explanatory power or noting its ideological construction does not fully explain particular instances of African American–Korean American tension. The reality of individual anger and passionate prejudices held by some African Americans and Korean Americans toward each other cannot be denied. Nor do we wish to dismiss vitriolic expressions of dislike and distrust broadcast in the media simply as articulations of dominant ideologies. Nonetheless, we advance two interrelated arguments against the "Black–Korean conflict." First, we argue that it reifies both African Americans and Korean Americans, and the instances of conflict between them. In other words, it homogenizes diverse peoples and phenomena and thus elides alternative interpretations. Second, and more important, we trace the ideological currents that bolster the "Black–Korean conflict" as a depiction of the two groups as antipodal minorities: the Asian American model minority epitomized by Korean entrepreneurial success and the urban underclass represented by the impoverished African American community. These two portraits constitute flip sides of the same ideological coin, which presumes that the United States is an open society with no systematic barriers to success. The same constellation of factors—culture, attitudes, and family structure—is used to explain the success and failure of each group. We locate the sources of this ideology in the conservative climate of the 1980s in particular and in the idea of the American dream in general. The ideological construction and constitution of the "Black–Korean conflict" should alert us to the dangers of emphasizing this interethnic conflict.

. . .

The Reification of the Interethnic Conflict

Before we explore the ideological roots of the "Black–Korean conflict," let us consider its descriptive and explanatory problems. The "Black–Korean conflict" reifies both African Americans and Korean Americans and the conflict itself. In so doing, the interethnic conflict becomes a ready-made explanation for diverse phenomena and diverts our attention from other events and explanations.

The media disseminates ready-made stereotypes as truths about the two groups. All African Americans are not poor, nor do they constitute a homogeneous or cohesive group. Similarly, neither are all Korean Americans shopkeepers nor do they constitute a unified community, even within the narrow perimeters of Koreatown. Multiethnic South Central Los Angeles and Koreatown belie simple ethnic generalizations. We must, therefore, beware of presuming widespread interethnic animosity from individual expressions of anger and prejudice by people in particular social positions.

Beyond promoting overgeneralizations concerning each group, the frame reifies the conflict itself. Uncritical acceptance of the frame leads to descriptive and explanatory errors. In narrating a set scenario depicting warring factions of Korean American merchants against African American residents, distinct events, with different causes and characteristics, become instantiations of the same conflict. In effect, the "Black–Korean conflict" frame acts as an ex post facto explanation; disparate events are treated under the same rubric. Consider, for example, a 1990 boycott in New York. Although ostensibly a case of "Black–Korean conflict," the reality in Brooklyn was not the same as that in South Central Los Angeles. The initial conflict arose between recent Haitian immigrants and a Korean American shopkeeper (Rieder 1990). Although long-term African American residents of South Central Los Angeles and recent Haitian immigrants in Brooklyn are both black within the American racial framework, it would be a mistake to consider them in the same category. In this regard, we should note that in Miami, for instance, people speak of the "Black–Haitian conflict" (Portes and Stepick 1993:190–92).

The interethnic conflict frame leads to explanations, which, in keeping with the prior reifications of each group, locate the conflict's cause in each group's characteristics. Rather than focusing on the broader political economic context, the presumed interethnic conflict pits one homogenized group against another. Consider the hypothetical case of a Korean American shopkeeper who fires an African American employee. In the dominant media frame, the individual case may stimulate a narrative about the "Black–Korean conflict" and explanations based on different interpersonal interaction styles or cultural characteristics. Yet the case may be nothing more than an employer laying off an employee—a product of capitalist social relations rather than interethnic conflict.

The presumed existence of the "Black–Korean conflict" blinds us to a number of inconvenient facts. If there were seething hatred between the two groups, then one might have expected some instances of interethnic killing during the riots. Yet there were no such documented cases. More crucially, the ground zero of the 1992 upheaval was the verdict in the Rodney King beating. African Americans' anger was primarily directed against white racism and the attack on the "black body" (Turner 1993:207–208). Most immediate reactions as well as later reflections by African American writers rarely mentioned Korean Americans (Cleage 1993:123–27; Wiley 1993: 82–91; Alan-Williams 1994:169–73). During the riots: "People took up chants proposing alternative targets. 'Beverly Hills!' shouted one cluster. 'Parker Center' (Los Angeles Police Department headquarters), yelled another" (Meyerson 1992:2; see also Ward 1992). Pamela Franklin told the *New York Times:* "The looting and violence was the only way angry blacks in Los Angeles had left to express their bitterness to whites. She said the destruction should be carried to Beverly Hills" (Marriott 1992:A11). Rioters and looters were unable to go to Beverly Hills because of police protection and logistical difficulties, not lack of intention. Hence Korean Americans focused not on African American rioting or looting but, rather, on the state's abandonment of Koreatown and South Central Los Angeles during the riots.

The "Black–Korean conflict" also averts our gaze from interethnic conflicts that have *prima facie* plausibility. African Americans and Latinos, especially recent Central American immigrants, compete for employment, housing, and political power. Thus one might expect a potent interethnic conflict between African Americans and Latinos—the so-called "Black–Brown conflict" (Oliver and Johnson 1984:75–84; Miles 1992; Skerry 1993:83–86). Korean Americans, in contrast, do not generally compete with African Americans, particularly in South Central Los Angeles, for manufacturing or service jobs. Very few Korean Americans live in South Central Los Angeles, and therefore they do not vie for existing housing stock or struggle over political power and representation.

Alternatively, we might have expected more media coverage of the "Korean–Latino conflict," especially given that so many Latinos work for Korean American businesses and industries. As we have noted, the majority of rioters and looters arrested were Latinos; recall the second-generation Korean American's shock over the looting in Koreatown carried out by his Latino neighbors and acquaintances.

Our intention is not to initiate discourses on the "Black–Latino conflict" or the "Korean–Latino conflict" but to question the salience of the "Black–Korean conflict." Indeed, we might ask why the media did not seize on the "Korean–white conflict," given that European Americans also looted Koreatown stores. The African American novelist Ishmael Reed queries: "Why doesn't the looting and burning of Korean stores by whites in Koreatown— which was witnessed by Pacifica Radio's Kwazi Nkrumah—indicate a bias of whites toward Koreans?" (1993:44).

The Antipodal Minorities

Why should the "Black–Korean conflict" emerge as a central phenomenon in the reporting on the 1992 L.A. riots? We argue that the "Black–Korean conflict" is deeply rooted in American ideologies.

Media reports on the "Black–Korean conflict" often highlight different customs and interpersonal interaction styles as the source of friction between Korean American merchants and African American customers (Stewart 1989, 1993; Cheng and Espiritu 1989:525–28). Korean American merchants are said to avoid eye contact, slam the change on the countertop, fail to make small talk, and, in general, refuse to assimilate to American cultural norms.[2] The journalist C. Connie Kang explains: "In the Confucian-steeped Korean culture, a smile is reserved for family members and close friends. . . . Expressions such as 'thank you' and 'excuse me' are used sparingly."[3] A source even more likely than Confucian legacies, however, is the experience of living in Seoul, which, as one of the world's most densely populated and rapidly urbanized cities, has not been congenial to refined manners. At worst, Korean American merchants are depicted as rude, racist, and rapacious. In turn, African American customers are said not to understand Korean cultural norms and to act in such a way as to offend Korean American merchants. H. Andrew Kim writes: "Blacks have little understanding of Korean merchants, who are in constant fear of being robbed or shot, while going through the massive readjustment to a strange culture, customs and language" (*Korea Times* 1992:6).

The concept of culture generally denotes a constellation of attributes, transient and intransigent, that distinguishes one group from another—for example, the French from the German. Cultural characteristics may be easily transferable—a Korean may become inordinately fond of truffles, a French person may acquire a taste for *kimch'i*, a spicy Korean dish—or more intransigent: values and world views often do not translate or transplant well across cultures. Both the transient and the intransigent aspects of culture are used to characterize the conflict between African Americans and Korean Americans.

The focus on transient aspects of culture mandates cosmetic changes in order to achieve interethnic reconciliation. From this perspective, better understanding, promoted through mutual recognition and interethnic interaction, would solve the problem. The stress on transient cultural attributes leads the *New York Times* to celebrate New York's "admirable example" (that is, its lack of rioting and looting after the L.A. riots) as the result of the Human Rights Commission's providing "sensitivity training to Korean merchants and the black community on how to prevent tensions and what to do when problems occur."[4] Seminars, furthermore, teach Korean American merchants to "smile more frequently" and African American leaders are invited on tours of South Korea (Martin 1993). Though commendable, these steps provide superficial solutions. After all, smiling Korean American merchants and understanding African American customers leave both groups in the same place they were in to begin with: Korean Americans as merchants and African Americans as customers.

Many commentators therefore seek deeper causes of the conflict and argue that the two groups manifest contrasting values, attitudes, and behavior—intransigent cultural differences. Accounts emphasizing intransigent aspects of culture highlight Korean Americans' education, hard work, and family solidarity as corollaries of the Confucian ethos and their supposed corresponding absence among African Americans. These contrasting cultural constructs are used to explain the different success rates of Korean Americans and African Americans.

At the heart of the interethnic contrast lies the Korean American entrepreneur—independent and diligent—who embodies the promise of capitalism and the free enterprise system. The *Economist* writes: "The Koreans have a remarkable business bent. . . . They are also capitalists. In short, they are model American citizens" (Grimond 1982). Edward Norden waxes enthusiastic about a Korean American shop owner, Roy Kim: "Kim's story . . . was the usual one for [Korean Americans] who had set up in South-Central. He stepped off the plane with $100 in his pocket, and by mobilizing his family, joining a *kye* [rotating credit association], and working fifteen-hour days for fifteen years, put enough money aside to buy a mortgaged house in the suburbs" (1992:33).

In contrast to the entrepreneurial heroism of Korean Americans, African Americans cut a pathetic figure in this ideological fabric. Norden is indignant about an African American activist who faults the larger society: "So why not found bigger, stronger, more aggressive black banks with the black money out there, or the black version of the *kye,* the hybrid lottery and savings-and-loan scheme to which masses of KAs [Korean Americans] belong? . . . Or why not mobilize families . . . to run mom-and-pop shops for fifteen hours a day in place of KAs [Korean Americans]?" (1992:38). The contrast is drawn more starkly regarding their relationship to welfare. "It's rare for Korean immigrants to go on the dole, even in the beginning. For these people [after the riots] it was shameful to have to prove, in triplicate, not only that the livelihoods they had created had been destroyed, but that they had no savings, no insurance, and no close relatives working" (1992:35). Korean Americans, in this line of argument, are exemplary for not relying on welfare.[5]

According to these accounts, not only do Korean American merchants exhibit the virtues of rugged individualism and make a mockery of racism and welfare, but they rely on familial and communal resources. Jim Sleeper proclaims:

> Many of the Koreans get their business going because they have a sense of responsibility to each other. They pool their limited resources to "stake" one another—in a way we don't see happening even with these African Americans who make it out of the ghettos. . . . It's just so obvious

that family units are critical to success. Inner-city black communities do not have the social structure to sustain the bonds of trust that are needed to "stake" one another and sustain that kind of family output.[6]

In these accounts, Korean Americans and African Americans are polar opposites.

The contrast is most insistently articulated by conservative commentators.

[It] was permissible to explain black antagonism toward Koreans in Los Angeles in terms of "anger" over Soon Ja Du, the Korean shopkeeper who, having shot and killed a 15 year old black girl named Latasha Harlins who had assaulted her, was then released by a judge. But it was impermissible to note that 25 Korean merchants had been murdered in the ghetto in the last two years. It was permissible to mention that blacks were "frustrated" by Korean economic success. It was impermissible to specify that this rise was based on 14 hour work days, personal sacrifice often approaching indenture, and family solidarity. (*Heterodoxy* 1992:10).

In lionizing the Korean American shopkeepers, the polemic simultaneously belittles African American charges of racism and discrimination: "The Koreans had given the lie to fantasies about racism and its discontents on which black leadership has come to depend. . . . They were a living refutation, right there in South Central Los Angeles, of the notion that job equals chump, an argument against the narcotic of self-pity and the whine of victimhood which has become the elevator music of the ghetto."[7]

In these narratives, Korean American entrepreneurs personify the values of individual responsibility and family solidarity, while African Americans stand for welfare dependence and family dissolution. These views appear to be widespread. Neil Saari wrote to *Time* that "the intense attacks directed at the Koreans were unmistakably racist. Instead of burning them out, Los Angeles' African Americans would do well to study and copy the Koreans' work ethic and family solidarity" (1992:10). Or, as one "white man" told the *Los Angeles Times*: "I'm so goddamn mad. Let these people burn their own stuff down. If you don't like the Koreans, why don't you go get your own grocery store, mister?" (*Los Angeles Times* 1992c, pt. iii, p. 6). Max Kerstein, publisher of the *Beverage Bulletin*, wrote: "It is a sad commentary when honest, hard-working citizens of our city face criminals within our society bent on destruction, injury, death and hate. Of all the people who suffered those terrible losses [during the riots], the Korean community felt the devastation and ruin more than anyone else" (1992:18).

In summary, many accounts depict African Americans and Korean Americans as antipodal minorities. The comparison highlights the contrasting portrait of each group in the 1980s: Korean Americans as a model minority and African Americans as an urban underclass.

. . .

The American Dream: Capitalism, Race, and Community

The celebration of the model minority and the denigration of the urban underclass reflected and basked in the conservative climate of the 1980s, a decade of both greed and denial, during which the rich grew richer and the poor grew poorer (Mattera 1990). Kevin Phillips writes: "The 1980s were the triumph of upper America—an ostentatious celebration of wealth, the political ascendancy of the richest third of the population and a glorification of capitalism, free markets and finance" (1991:xvii). The unfettered pursuit of profit became fashionable; capitalist theologians such as George Gilder and Charles Murray celebrated the entrepreneurial spirit of U.S. capitalism and simultaneously absolved the system of any problems. Concomitant with the unleashing of the greed motive was the denial of its costs. As Haynes Johnson (1991) entitled his book on the Reagan years, the United States seemed to be "sleepwalking through history."[8] While the United States was gradually losing its claim as the premier economic power in the world, the momentary euphoria of the Gulf War victory symbolized, while the Rodney King beating epitomized the underside of, the decade of self-congratulation.[9]

It is in this context that we need to understand the popularity of the underclass thesis, as well as its foil, the successful model minority. The underlying message is that people succeed or fail in spite of external constraints and contexts. The self-evident successes of Asian Americans, in the absence of government support, supposedly controvert the claim that more welfare or antiracist remedies are necessary to alleviate inner-city poverty.

The categories of the model minority and the urban underclass became ubiquitous in the 1980s because of their affinity with the dominant ideological movement. Their popularity, however, is not a temporary aberration. Rather, the archaeology of the dominant ideological current in the United States suggests their venerable provenance—the ideal of the American dream. Its principal tenet is that the United States is essentially an open society in which everyone can achieve her or his dream. A corollary of the belief is a series of assumptions about the nature of the economy, race, and community in the United States.

. . .

The American dream denotes a belief in the United States as a land of opportunity in which no major obstacles exist to individual success. Unlike in the Old World or the Third World, individuals are liberated and unleashed from their pre-American fetters to pursue their vision of happiness.[10] Inequalities and divides of class, gender, and race are ultimately meaningless; rugged individualism reigns supreme in this social view. Put simply, people with talent and who work hard succeed, while others do not. Those who fail, then, have no one to blame but themselves.[11]

The American dream is an individualistic ideology. The projected economic order is *laissez-faire* capitalism, in which sovereign individuals compete with one another to pursue material gains. In this vision, the entrepreneur, relying essentially on ingenuity and hard work, represents the iconic figure of success.[12] In turn, social welfare programs are never legitimate except as expressions of collective "charity" to the "truly needy." Michael Katz comments in *The Undeserving Poor* (1989) that there is a long tradition of sequestering the comfortable middle-class "us" from the morally inferior and impoverished "them." The moral primacy of work and its flip side, the ethical castigation of the "lazy" poor, is a deeply ingrained Americanism, a civilization founded on the rejection of European aristocrats and the denigration of African slaves (Shklar 1991, chap. 2; see also Rodgers 1978). In this line of thought, people on welfare are, almost by definition, morally suspect; the very concept of social welfare carries a pejorative connotation. When the Reagan and Bush administrations castigated the moral standing of welfare recipients, they were expressing a conservative reading of the American dream ideology.[13] In 1987 Reagan said of welfare: "It is time to reform this outdated social dinosaur and finally break the poverty trap."[14]

The celebration of the individual often entails the neglect of the collective and systematic constraints. Class is eschewed in public discourse.[15] Racism, sexism, or other forms of systematic discrimination neither explain nor justify existing inequalities. The refutation of racism constitutes, as we have suggested, one of the appeals of the model minority thesis.[16] One terminus of the denial of racism is universal "ethnicization." In effect, everyone becomes an "ethnic" in the United States. Richard Alba argues: "The thrust of European-American identity is to defend the individualistic view of the American system, because it portrays the system as open to those who are willing to work hard and pull themselves over barriers of poverty and discrimination" (1990:317). Charges of racism lose force if all ethnicities are considered to have struggled their way toward equality and prosperity under the same conditions.[17]

Finally, the American dream offers a particular social vision (Baritz 1989). The outline of a good society is constituted by two pillars: the family as a "haven in a heartless world" and the community that upholds the individualist ethos. In this vision, "home" is the nurturing environment, while the larger "community" protects the "home." The family is a sacred institution in the ideal of the American dream. Essentially, the home is a "haven" where individuals are nourished and protected; it is an incubator and protector of individuality.[18] The community is inseparable from the family.[19] Reagan, for example, spoke of America's "bedrock, its communities where neighbors help one another" (Reich 1991:277). In turn, the idealized environment of the ideal family in modern America is suburbia. "The central symbol of the nearly perfected America . . . was the suburban family. Suburbia meant more than physical comfort; it embodied a long-held American dream of a happy, secure family life" (Skolnick 1991:2). "Bourgeois utopias" of American suburbia became the ideal community (Fishman 1987; see also Hayden 1984 and Jackson 1985). In contrast, urban life represents an undesirable ideal. The city, with its disorders and dangers, represents a demonized environment. In the cacophony and heterogeneity of city life, deviant social relations and institutions proliferate.[20] More prosaically, the city is where the "community," understood in all its suburban splendor, breaks down; in cities, strange languages, foods, and peoples coexist. The city is, moreover, racialized and poor. Instead of individual achievement, there is sloth and dependence (on government welfare); instead of family values, there is deviance; instead of suburban *communitas,* there is urban anomie; and, finally, instead of "real" Americans, there are minorities.[21] The city—particularly the inner city—is the racialized "other" of the American dream.

The American dream thus projects a vision of the United States where individual initiatives and efforts determine success and failure, racism is not a serious affliction, and the family and the community exist to nurture sovereign individuals.

The social reality of the contemporary United States contradicts the idealized vision of the American dream. The world of entrepreneurial capitalism, for example, occupies a relatively small, if surprisingly persistent, part of the contemporary United States economy. The global economy of the late twentieth century is dominated by large corporations and large governments. It is via corporations and professions, not classical entrepreneurship, that most Americans seek material comfort in affluent suburbs. The free market ideology, however, celebrates nineteenth-century entrepreneurial capitalism, while ignoring the reality of twentieth-century corporate capitalism.[22] To be sure, instances of individual success continue to exist, but it would be egregious to deny the predominance of large corporations in the contemporary economy.

The individualism articulated in the American dream downplays systemic barriers to individual success, such as racism. Such a view misses not only racism's historical ferocity against African Americans—Jim Crow laws that rendered them virtually an "untouchable" caste into the 1960s in some regions of the United States—but also its contemporary, albeit weakening, force.[23]

The ideal of the nuclear family, similarly, diverges from the reality of most U.S. households. Many people of all ethnicities live in a variety of "nontraditional" households.[24] In addition, a generation of women's movements and feminist writings have noted the dysfunctions of the patriarchal nuclear family (Thorne 1992). Similarly, in spite of the celebration of the suburbs and the denigration of the city, people's concrete living patterns and ideals complicate this simple dichotomy. One principal trend, for example, has been the gentrification and renewal of urban centers (Zukin 1991). More important, many people abhor the isolation, anomie, and homogeneity of suburbs. Most American suburbs are not places, in Reagan's idealized imagery, "where neighbors help one another," but instead resemble the stereotyped cold and impersonal city.

The American dream presents a problematic ideal of individual life and community. More crucially for our purpose, however, the constellation of attitudes and institutions that constitutes the American dream has found a powerful articulation in the contrast between the model minority and the urban underclass: Korean Americans embody the American dream, while African Americans betray its promise. The ideological constitution and construction of the "Black–Korean conflict" should alert us not only to the importance of the broader political economy but also to the necessity of rethinking dominant American ideologies.

We cannot make sense of the heterogeneous voices of both conflict and cooperation, racism and solidarity, unless we see that they are the very ground on which ideologies work. In particular, an attempt to understand Korean American responses to the riots and the "Black–Korean conflict" requires us to consider their transnational context and their heterogeneity. In so doing, we place American ideologies on trial. The complexities and contradictions of Korean American responses—indeed, the gritty reality of individual immigrant lives—require nothing less than an appreciation of themes at the heart of this research.

NOTES

1. There is by now a growing literature on the "Black–Korean conflict"; see, for example, E. Chang (1990, 1993a, 1993b); Abelmann (1991); Ahn (1991); Chen (1991); S. Kim (1991); Min (1991b); Yi (1992); S. K. Cho (1993); and E. H. Kim (1993b). For literary works, see Lew (1993) and Min (1994).

2. Eui-Young Yu notes: "Korean shoppers think that non-Korean markets are more courteous, less expensive, carry more fresh vegetables, and have more choices" (1990a, p. 106).

3. Shaw (1990), p. A31. Edward Chang (1990, p. 244) asserts that Korean Americans "tend to be very cold toward people they do not know" and hence "there is a tendency . . . to disrespect their black customers."

4. *New York Times* (1992a). One effort forces individuals to crystallize and articulate "a compilation of negative, false stereotypes" about others (Njeri 1993, p. 22).

5. Charles Murray states: "The rhetoric had always proclaimed that affirmative action was needed to help minorities who were disadvantaged by the white majority. But Asians refused to exhibit the symptoms of disadvantage" (1992a, p. 32).

6. In *Tikkun* (1992), p. 42. In *The Closest of Strangers,* Sleeper writes: "Yet one 'means' never mentioned [by African American activists] is the recruitment and training of a few hundred young blacks prepared to work fifteen hours a day at low wages and in close family units, as the Koreans do, in order to pay their debts to immigrant lending societies [rotating credit associations]" (1990, p. 208).

7. *Heterodoxy* (1992), p. 10. In a similar vein, Midge Decter (1992, pp. 21–22) charges that the "refusal of empathy with the Los Angeles Koreans on the part of America's liberal publicists has very deep roots," which include their advocacy of social welfare: "Assuming responsibility for one's life, for one's everyday choices as well as for one's moral conduct, is a practice that has been eroding in American life for a long, long time."

8. On Reagan, see the indispensable work by Wills (1987). The best metaphor of denial comes from neurophysiologist Oliver Sachs: "Aphasiacs . . . experience an elevated understanding of . . . the quality of speech that communicates an inner meaning rather than the mere assemblage of words. One cannot lie to an aphasiac because he cannot comprehend your words, and so is not deceived by them. . . . An aphasiac perceives the verisimilitude of a speaker's voice and cannot suspend disbelief. Reagan's 'grimaces, the histrionisms, the false gestures, and above all, the false tones and cadences of the voice . . . rang false for these immensely sensitive patients.' . . . Normal audiences, 'aided doubtless by our wish to be fooled,' were indeed well and truly fooled.' The president's cunning and 'deceptive' use of words and tones assured that 'only the brain-damaged remained intact, undeceived'" (Schaller 1992, p. 59).

9. See, for example, Shapiro (1992). Stephen Graubard polemicizes: "The United States has become a victim of years of self-neglect, self-delusion, and self-praise. Once a quintessential model of a progressive society, it has become dowdy and old-fashioned, losing appreciation of its one remaining substantial resource—the heterogeneity of its people" (1992, p. 187).

10. Kluegel and Smith (1986, p. 52) conclude their survey of ordinary Americans' beliefs about inequality thus: "A clear majority of the American population subscribes, largely undeservedly, to the characterization of America as the 'land of opportunity.'"

11. "The belief that all men, in accordance with certain rules, but exclusively by their own efforts, can make of their own lives what they will has been widely popularized for well over a century" (Weiss 1969, p. 3). See also Lipset (1979), p. 2.

12. Bellah and his colleagues note: "The self-sufficient entrepreneur, competitive, tough, and freed by wealth from external constraints, was one new American character" (1985, p. 44).

13. As Piven and Cloward (1993, chap. 11) argue, the anti-welfare ideology also functions to discipline workers.

14. Schwarz and Volgy (1992), p. 133. Although the transformation of social welfare into a social evil marked a tremendous shift in the terrain of political debate from the 1960s and 1970s, when Great Society programs and the alleviation of poverty were nearly consensual goals for U.S. citizens, the moral-philosophical foundation of social welfare in the United States remains less than secure and legitimate (see Katz 1989, chap. 3). Indeed, what Theodore Marmor and his colleagues call the "opportunity-insurance" state, which U.S. citizens broadly support, suffers from its conflation with the maligned welfare state (Marmor, Mashaw, and Harvey 1990, p. 49).

15. Benjamin DeMott writes: "America as a classless society is, finally, a deceit, and today, as yesterday, the deceit causes fearful moral and social damage" (1990, p. 12). Americans may be, however, class conscious in some ways; see Vanneman and Cannon (1987).

16. Indeed, neoconservative writers, especially in the 1980s, were emphatic on this point: to blame the lack of progress by some African Americans on racism was not only empirically wrong but morally objectionable. In so doing, they attempted to

stem the tide of progressive "racial" legislation initiated by the civil rights movement of the 1950s and 1960s. Two African American intellectuals particularly influential in the 1980s articulated the ultimate irrelevance of race. Denying the
impact of racism, the economist Thomas Sowell notes: "The presence of Jewish
and Japanese Americans at the top of the income rankings must undermine any
simplistic theory that discrimination is an overwhelming determinant of socioeconomic position" (1981b, p. 126). In his best-selling book *Ethnic America,* Sowell
argues further that "perhaps the most striking difference among ethnic groups is
in their attitudes toward learning and self-improvement" (1981a, p. 280). In other
words, racism explains little of the disproportionate poverty experienced by
African Americans. In another version of this argument, Shelby Steele highlights
the fault with explaining African American problems with reference to racism. He
writes: "Hard work, education, individual initiative, stable family life, property
ownership—those have always been the means by which ethnic groups have
moved ahead in America" (1990, p. 108).

17. Universal ethnicity also accentuates the irreducible import of culture in the sense
that Michael Novak wrote: "Emotions, instincts, memory, imagination, passions,
and ways of perceiving are passed on to us in ways we do not choose, and in
ways so thick with life that they lie far beyond the power of consciousness (let
alone of analytical and verbal reason) thoroughly to master, totally to alter. We
are, in a word, ineffably ethnic in our values and our actions" (1972, p. xvi). Our
"ineffably ethnic" self exists as a crucial precondition for the cultural explanation
of ethnic groups' success and failure.

18. The shift from the older patriarchal norm to the new individualist ideal occurred
as early as the late eighteenth century. Helena Wall writes: "Colonial society began by deferring to the needs of the community and ended by deferring to the
rights of the individual" (1990, p. vii). The new ideal "was understood to be affectionate, voluntaristic, and private" (p. 138).

19. Claude Fischer writes: "Americans of the Left and of the Right esteem the local
community. It rests in the pantheon of American civil religion paradoxically close
to that supreme value, individualism. In our ideology, the locality is, following
the family, the premier locus for 'community,' in the fullest sense of solidarity,
commitment, and intimacy" (1991, p. 79). See also Gans (1988), p. 64.

20. Lewis Lapham notes: "The idea of a great city never has occupied a comfortable
place in the American imagination. Much of the country's political and literary
history suggests that the city stands as a metaphor for depravity—the port of
entry for things foreign and obnoxious" (1992, p. 4). See also White and White
(1962).

21. The political scientist Edward Banfield writes: "The most conspicuous fact of life
in the city is racial division. . . . The residential suburbs are mostly white—often
'lily-white'; the central cities, especially their older, more deteriorated parts, and
above all their slums, are predominantly or entirely black" (1974, p. 77).

22. "Voices still trumpeting the nineteenth-century medley of stable independence
and dynamic entrepreneurship have a patently disingenuous ring. The largest
conglomerates regularly advertise their similarity to small business" (Berthoff
1980, pp. 42–43).

23. See, for example, Burstein (1985), p. 1. As Cornel West describes: "The chronic refusal of most Americans to understand the sheer absurdity that confronts human
beings of African descent in this country—the incessant assaults on black intelligence, beauty, character, and possibility—is not simply a matter of defending
white-skin privilege. It also bespeaks a reluctance to look squarely at the brutal
side and tragic dimension of the American past and present" (1991, p. 35). See also
Shklar (1991); Gould (1992); T. Morrison (1992); and Sundquist (1993).

24. Arlene Skolnick writes: "Contrary to the homogeneous, idealized family portrayed in the sitcoms, the most distinctive feature of American family life has always been its diversity" (1991, p. 3). She (pp. 51–54) also notes that the 1950s was
in fact the "deviant decade." See also Coontz (1992).

REFERENCES

Abelmann, Nancy. 1991. "Transgressing Headlines: Reporting Race in the African
American/Korean American Conflicts." Paper presented at the Association for
Asian Studies meeting, New Orleans, LA.

Ahn, Choong Sik. 1991. "An Alternative Approach to the Racial Conflict between Korean Small Business Owners and the Black-American Community in the New York
Area." Pp. 49–55 in *The Korean-American Community*, edited by Tae-Hwan Kwak
and Seong Hyong Lee.

Alan-Williams, Gregory. 1994. *A Gathering of Heroes: Reflections on Rage and Responsibility—a Memoir of the Los Angeles Riots*. Chicago: Academy Chicago.

Alba, Richard. 1990. *Ethnic Identity: The Transformation of White America*. New Haven,
CT: Yale University Press.

Banfield, Edward C. 1974. *The Unheavenly City Revisited*. Boston: Little, Brown.

Baritz, Loren. 1989. *The Good Life: The Meaning of Success for the American Middle Class*.
New York: Knopf.

Bellah, Robert, et al. 1985. *Habits of the Heart: Individualism and Commitment in American Life*. Berkeley: University of California Press.

Berthoff, Rowland. 1980. "Independence and Enterprise: Small Business in the American Dream." Pp. 28–48 in *Small Business in American Life*, edited by Stuart W.
Bruchey. New York: Columbia University Press.

Burstein, Paul. 1985. *Discrimination, Jobs, and Politics: The Struggle for Equal Employment
Opportunity in the United States since the New Deal*. Chicago: University of Chicago
Press.

Chang, Edward T. 1990. "New Urban Crisis: Korean–Black Conflicts in Los Angeles."
Ph.D. dissertation, University of California, Berkeley.

———. 1993a. *Hug'in: Kudul un nugunji* [Blacks: Who Are They?]. Seoul: Han'guk
Kyongje Sinmunsa.

———. 1993b. "America's First Multiethnic 'Riots.'" Pp. 101–17 in *The State of Asian
America*, edited by Karin Aguilar-San Juan. Boston: South End Press.

Chen, Elsa Y. 1991. "Black-Led Boycotts of Korean-Owned Grocery Stores." B.A. Thesis, Princeton University.

Cheng, Lucie and Yen Espiritu. 1989. "Korean Businesses in Black and Hispanic
Neighborhoods: A Study of Intergroup Relations." *Sociological Perspectives* (32):
521–34.

Cho, Soon Kyong. 1985. "The Labor Process and Capital Mobility: The Limits of the
New International Division of Labor." *Politics and Society* (14):185–22.

Cleage, Pearl. 1993. *Deals with the Devil and Other Reasons to Riot*. New York: Harper
and Row.

Coontz, Stephanie. 1992. *The Way We Never Were: American Families and the Nostalgia
Trap*. New York: Basic Books.

DeMott, Benjamin. 1990. *The Imperial Middle: Why Americans Can't Think Straight about
Class*. New York: William Morrow.

Fischer, Claude S. 1991. "Ambivalent Communities: How Americans Understand
Their Localities." Pp. 79–90 in *America at Century's End*, edited by Alan Wolfe.
Berkeley: University of California Press.

Fishman, Robert. 1987. *Bourgeois Utopias: The Rise and Fall of Suburbia*. New York:
Basic Books.

Gans, Herbert J. 1988. *Middle American Individualism: The Future of Liberal Democracy.* New York: Free Press.

Gould, Mark. 1992. "The New Racism in the United States Society." Pp. 154–74 in *The Dynamics of Social Systems,* edited by P. Colomy. London: Sage.

Graubard, Stephen R. 1992. *Mr. Bush's War: Adventures in the Politics of Illusion.* New York: Hill and Wang.

Grimond, John. 1982. "Somewhere Serious: Los Angeles—a Survey." *Economist,* April 3, special survey section.

Hayden, Delores. 1984. *Redesigning the American Dream: The Future of Housing, Work, and Family Life.* New York: Norton.

Heterodoxy. 1992. June.

Jackson, Kenneth T. 1985. *Crabgrass Frontier: The Suburbanization of the United States.* New York: Oxford University Press.

Johnson, Haynes. 1991. *Sleepwalking through History: America in the Reagan Years.* New York: Norton.

Katz, Michael B. 1989. *The Undeserving Poor: From the War on Poverty to the War on Welfare.* New York: Pantheon.

Kerstein, Max. 1992. "Rebuilding Anew." *KAGRO Newsletter* 3(5/6):18.

Kim, Elaine H. 1993. "Creating a Third Space." *Bay Guardian,* March 10, pp. 31ff.

Kim, Shin. 1991. "Conceptualization of Inter-minority Group Conflict: Conflict between Korean Entrepreneurs and Black Local Residents." Pp. 29–48 in *The Korean-American Community,* edited by Tae-Hwan Kwak and Seong Hyong Lee.

Kluegel, James R. and Eliot R. Smith. 1986. *Beliefs about Inequality: Americans' Views of What Is and What Ought to Be.* New York: Aldine de Gruyter.

Lapham, Lewis. 1992. "Notebook: City Lights." *Harper's Magazine,* July, pp. 4–6.

"Letters to Ted Koppel." *Korea Times,* May 11, 1992, p. 7.

Lew, Walter. 1993. "Black Korea." Pp. 230–35 in *Charlie Chan Is Dead,* edited by J. Hagedorn. New York: Penguin.

Lipset, Seymour Martin. 1979. *The First New Nation: The United States in Historical and Comparative Perspective.* 2nd ed. New York: Norton.

Marmor, Theodore R., Jerry L. Mashaw, and Philip L. Harvey. 1990. *America's Misunderstood Welfare State: Persistent Myths, Enduring Realities.* New York: Basic Books.

Marriott, Michael. 1992. "Fire of Anguish and Rage as Random Violence Spreads across Los Angeles." *New York Times,* May 1, p. A11.

Martin, Douglas. 1993. "Seeking New Ties and Clout, Korean Grocers Join Voices." *New York Times,* March 22, pp. A1ff.

Mattera, Philip. 1990. *Prosperity Lost: How a Decade of Greed Has Eroded Our Standard of Living and Endangered Our Children's Future.* Reading, MA: Addison-Wesley.

McNelis-Ahern, Margaret. 1992. "Agenda for Action." Pp. 12–15 in *Beyond the Ashes,* edited by the *Los Angeles Business Journal.*

Meyerson, Harold. 1992. "Casualties of the Los Angeles Riot." *In These Times,* May 13–19, p. 2.

Miles, Jack. 1992. "Blacks vs. Browns." *Atlantic,* October, pp. 41–61.

Min, Katherine. 1994. "K-Boy and 2 Bad." *TriQuarterly* (89):38–51.

Min, Pyong Gap. 1991. "Korean Immigrants' Small Business Activities and Korean–Black Interracial Conflicts." Pp. 13–28 in *The Korean-American Community,* edited by Tae-Hwan Kwak and Seong Hyong Lee.

Morrison, Toni. 1992. *Playing in the Dark: Whiteness and the Literary Imagination.* Cambridge, MA: Harvard University Press.

Murray, Charles. 1992. "Causes, Root Causes, and Cures." *National Review,* June 8, pp. 30–32.

Njeri, Itabara. 1993. "The Conquest of Hate." *Los Angeles Times Magazine,* April 25, pp. 20–21.

Norden, Edward. 1992. "South-Central Korea: Post-Riot L.A." *American Spectator,* September, pp. 33–40.

Novak, Michael. 1972. *The Rise of the Unmeltable Ethnics: Politics and Culture in the Seventies.* New York: Macmillan.

Oliver, Melvin L., and James H. Johnson, Jr. 1984. "Inter-Ethnic Conflict in an Urban Ghetto: The Case of Blacks and Latinos in Los Angeles." *Research in Social Movements, Conflict, and Change* (6):57–94.

Phillips, Kevin. 1991. *The Politics of Rich and Poor: Wealth and the American Electorate in the Reagan Aftermath.* 2nd ed. New York: Harper Perennial.

Piven, Frances Fox and Richard A. Cloward. 1993. *Regulating the Poor: The Functions of Public Welfare,* updated ed. New York: Vintage.

Portes, Alejandro and Alex Stepick. 1993. *City on the Edge: The Transformation of Miami.* Berkeley: University of California Press.

Reed, Ishmael. 1993. *Airing Dirty Laundry.* Reading, MA: Addison-Wesley.

Reich, Robert B. 1991. *The Work of Nations: Preparing Ourselves for Twenty-First Century Capitalism.* New York: Knopf.

Rieder, Jonathan. 1990. "Trouble in Store." *New Republic,* July 2, pp. 16–20.

Rodgers, Daniel. 1978. *The Work Ethic in Industrial America, 1850–1920.* Chicago: University of Chicago Press.

Saari, Neil. 1992. "Letter." *Time,* June 1, p. 10.

Schaller, Michael. 1992. *Reckoning with Reagan: America and Its President in the 1980s.* New York: Oxford University Press.

Schwarz, John E. and Thomas J. Volgy. 1992. *The Forgotten Americans: Thirty Million Working Poor in the Land of Opportunity.* New York: Norton.

Shapiro, Andrew L. 1992. *We're Number One.* New York: Vintage.

Shaw, David. 1990. "Asian-Americans Chafe against Stereotype of 'Model Citizen.'" *Los Angeles Times,* Dec. 11, p. A31.

Shklar, Judith N. 1991. *American Citizenship: The Quest for Inclusion.* Cambridge, MA: Harvard University Press.

Skerry, Peter. 1993. *Mexican-Americans: The Ambivalent Minority.* New York: Free Press.

Skolnick, Arlene. 1991. *Embattled Paradise: The American Family in an Age of Uncertainty.* New York: Basic Books.

Sleeper, Jim. 1990. *The Closest of Strangers: Liberalism and the Politics of Race in New York.* New York: Norton.

Sowell, Thomas. 1981a. *Ethnic America: A History.* New York: Basic Books.

———. 1981b. *Markets and Minorities.* New York: Basic Books.

Steele, Shelby. 1990. *The Content of Our Character: A New Vision of Race in America.* New York: St. Martin's Press.

Stewart, Ellen. 1989. "Ethnic Cultural Diversity: An Interpretive Study of Cultural Differences and Communication Styles between Korean Merchants/Employees and Black Patrons in South Los Angeles." M.A. Thesis, California State University, Los Angeles.

Sundquist, Eric J. 1993. *To Wake the Nations: Race in the Making of American Literature.* Cambridge, MA: Harvard University Press.

Thorne, Barrie. 1992. "Feminism and the Family: Two Decades of Thought." Pp. 3–30 in *Rethinking the Family: Some Feminist Questions,* rev. ed., edited by Barrie Thorne and Marilyn Yalom. Boston: Northeastern University Press.

Turner, Patricia A. 1993. *I Heard It through the Grapevine: Rumor in African-American Culture.* Berkeley: University of California Press.

"Understanding the Riots," parts 1–5. *Los Angeles Times,* May 11–16, 1992.

Vanneman, Reeve, and Lynn Weber Cannon. 1987. *The American Perception of Class.* Philadelphia: Temple University Press.

Wall, Helena M. 1990. *Fierce Communion: Family and Community in Early America*. Cambridge, MA: Harvard University Press.

Ward, Arvli. 1992. "Twenty-Four Hours in the Life of the Rebellion." *Nommo*, May–June, pp. 18ff.

Weiss, Richard. 1969. *The American Myth of Success: From Horatio Alger to Norman Vincent Peale*. New York: Basic Books.

West, Cornel. 1991. "On Black Rage." *Village Voice*, Sept. 17, pp. 35–36.

White, Morton and Lucia White. 1962. *The Intellectual versus the City: From Thomas Jefferson to Frank Lloyd Wright*. Cambridge, MA: Harvard University Press.

Wiley, Ralph. 1993. *What Black People Should Do Now: Dispatches from Near the Vanguard*. New York: Ballantine.

Wills, Garry. 1987. *Reagan's America: Innocents at Home*. Garden City, NY: Doubleday.

Yang, Jeff. 1992. "Shooting Back." *Village Voice*, May 19, pp. 47–48.

Yi, Jeongduk. 1992. "Social Order and Protest: Black Boycotts against Korean Shopkeepers in Poor New York City Neighborhoods." Paper presented at the meeting of the American Anthropological Association, Chicago, IL.

Yu, Eui-Young. 1990. *Korean Community Profile: Life and Consumer Patterns*. Los Angeles: Korea Times.

Zukin, Sharon. 1991. "Hollow Center: U.S. Cities in the Global Era." Pp. 245–61 in *America at Century's End*, edited by Alan Wolfe. Berkeley: University of California Press.

34

NAVIGATING PUBLIC PLACES

JOE R. FEAGIN • MELVIN P. SIKES

Racism is any prejudice or discrimination against an individual or a group based on their race, ethnicity, or some other perceived difference. The following reading by Joe R. Feagin and Melvin P. Sikes documents the common and everyday discrimination experienced by middle-class African Americans. Utilizing research based on over two hundred interviews, Feagin and Sikes find that their respondents encounter a disturbing and extensive amount of both individual and institutional discrimination. Moreover, Feagin and Sikes report that since discrimination often involves racial stereotyping, verbal harassment, and even the threat or occurrence of violence, the consequences of discrimination on the individual are enormous. This excerpt is from Feagin and Sikes' 1994 book *Living with Racism: The Black Middle Class Experience*.

Title II of the most important civil rights act of this century, the 1964 Civil Rights Act, stipulates that "all persons shall be entitled to the full and equal enjoyment of the goods, services, facilities, privileges, advantages, and accommodations of any place of public accommodation . . . without discrimination or segregation on the ground of race, color, religion, or national origin." Yet, as we approach the twenty-first century, this promise of full and equal enjoyment of the public places and accommodations of the United States is far from reality for African Americans.

Not long ago Debbie Allen, a movie star and television producer, recounted a painful experience with discrimination at a Beverly Hills jewelry store. A white clerk, possibly stereotyping Allen as poor or criminal, refused to show her some jewelry. Allen was so incensed that she used the incident as the basis for an episode on a television show. Across the country in Tamarac, Florida, a 20-year-old black man, wearing a Syracuse University cap and hoping to invest his savings, visited a branch of Great Western Bank seeking information. After stopping at other banks, he returned to Great Western, got more information, and then went to his car to review the materials. There he was surrounded by sheriff's deputies with guns drawn, handcuffed, and read his rights. The deputies questioned him for some time before dismissing the report of white bank employees that the black man looked like a bank robber.[1]

Discrimination in Public Accommodations

In this chapter the middle-class respondents challenge us to reflect on their experiences with discrimination as they move into traditionally white public accommodations, such as upscale restaurants and department stores, and through public streets once the territory only of whites. They frequently report that their middle-class resources and status provide little protection against overt discrimination. Although there are, at least in principle, some social restraints on hostile white behavior in public accommodations, African Americans often experience hostility and mistreatment when they venture into spaces where many whites question the presence of a black person.

In the authors' experience many middle-class African Americans can relate several recent stories of being treated poorly by whites in public accommodations officially made hospitable by decades of civil rights laws. In our respondents' accounts restaurants are one site of hostile treatment, as are stores, hotels, and places of amusement. A black minister in a predominantly white denomination described his experience at a restaurant near a southern religious camp:

> *We were refused service, because they said they didn't serve black folk. It was suggested that if we stayed there any longer, that there was a possibility that our tires would be slashed. We finally stayed long enough for them to say, "Well,*

*I'll tell you what. We will serve you something to go, but you cannot come in-
side. We refuse that." And it was a situation that—I was not prepared for that.
I was angry. I was humiliated, and I wanted to do something. I wanted to kick
some ass.*[2]

Given the threat of violence, he did not respond aggressively to this exclusion, but internalized his anger. Such encounters are not isolated events for
many middle-class black Americans. The minister described yet another incident in a southern metropolis:

*I was at this place called Joe's restaurant. I had to go into Joe's because I came up
in that community. Joe's is a barbecue place that is right by the auto plant, so all
of the executives from the plant would come there for lunch. I went there with a
guy who was successful. [I] thought I was a decent black person, came in wearing a suit and tie, sat down, and I noticed that, you know, these white boys kept
coming in, and the waitress kept on looking over me. And I eventually said to
her, "Ma'am, I'd like to order." She said, "Well, you're going to have to wait."
And I complained to the owner and he proceeded to cuss me out. Told me that I
didn't have "no goddamn business" in that restaurant telling them who they
ought to serve and when they ought to serve them. Told me that. I came up in
the neighborhood, been eating there for years, and it suddenly dawned on me that
white folk will take your money, but to them in their minds you're still a nigger.
They're able to separate economics from dealing with relationships between them
and black folk. He challenged me to a fight, and this was another source of humiliation. I said to myself, "If I fought this man in his restaurant with there being a hundred white boys that'll substantiate whatever story he told, they could
lynch me and say that I hung myself, you know." I left. I've never gone back to
that place. But I've always thought about burning it down.*

In spite of the 1964 Civil Rights Act black customers today encounter poor
service or are refused service. Even with the growth of black economic resources, there seems to be some conflict within many white business owners
between taking the dollars blacks can spend and recoiling from dealing with
blacks.

In such events the person being rudely treated or ignored is usually quite
conscious of the historical context of the interaction, as can be seen in the
minister's allusion to lynching. In another account, a black news director at a
television station described an incident in which she and her boyfriend responded very differently to an act of discrimination and the anger it pro-
voked in them:

*He was waiting to be seated. . . . He said, "You go to the bathroom and I'll get
the table. . . ." He was standing there when I came back; he continued to stand
there. The restaurant was almost empty. There were waiters, waitresses, and no
one seated. And when I got back to him, he was ready to leave, and said, "Let's
go." I said, "What happened to our table?" He wasn't seated. So I said, "No,
we're not leaving, please." And he said, "No, I'm leaving." So we went outside,*

and we talked about it. And what I said to him was, you have to be aware of the possibilities that this is not the first time that this has happened at this restaurant or at other restaurants, but this is the first time it has happened to a black news director here or someone who could make an issue of it, or someone who is prepared to make an issue of it.

So we went back inside after I talked him into it and, to make a long story short, I had the manager come. I made most of the people who were there (while conducting myself professionally the whole time) aware that I was incensed at being treated this way. . . . I said, "Why do you think we weren't seated?" And the manager said, "Well, I don't really know." And I said, "Guess." He said, "Well, I don't know, because you're black?" I said, "Bingo. Now isn't it funny that you didn't guess that I didn't have any money (and I opened up my purse and I said, because I certainly have money). And isn't it odd that you didn't guess that it's because I couldn't pay for it because I've got two American Express cards and a Master Card right here. I think it's just funny that you would have assumed that it's because I'm black." . . . And then I took out my [business] card and gave it to him and said, "If this happens again, or if I hear of this happening again, I will bring the full wrath of an entire news department down on this restaurant." And he just kind of looked at me. "Not [just] because I am personally offended. I am. But because you have no right to do what you did, and as a people we have lived a long time with having our rights abridged."

There were probably three or four sets of diners in the restaurant and maybe five waiters/waitresses. They watched him [her boyfriend] standing there waiting to be seated. His reaction to it was that he wanted to leave. I understood why he would have reacted that way, because he felt that he was in no condition to be civil. He was ready to take the place apart and . . . sometimes it's appropriate to behave that way. We hadn't gone the first step before going on to the next step. He didn't feel that he could comfortably and calmly take the first step, and I did. So I just asked him to please get back in the restaurant with me, and then you don't have to say a word, and let me handle it from there. It took some convincing, but I had to appeal to his sense of, this is not just you, this is not just for you. We are finally in a position as black people where there are some of us who can genuinely get their attention. And if they don't want to do this because it's right for them to do it, then they'd better do it because they're afraid to do otherwise. If it's fear, then fine, instill the fear.

Discrimination here was not the "No Negroes" exclusion of the recent past, but rejection in the form of poor service. Again a black person's skin color took precedence over money. The black response has changed too, since the 1950s and 1960s, from deference to indignant, vigorous confrontation. Here the assertive black response and the white backtracking are typical of "negotiation" that can occur in racial confrontations today.

In recounting this incident this black professional mentions black "rights" several times. Clearly imbedded in her response is a theory of rights that she, like many African Americans, holds as a part of her worldview. Her response signals the impact of the tradition of civil rights struggle, and civil rights laws, on the life perspective of African Americans. Also of interest here is her mention of her credit cards and other middle-class resources. A quick reading of her statement, and that of other black middle-class people who mention similar trappings of success, might lead to the conclusion that middle-class blacks expect to be treated better than poorer blacks because they have worked hard and have money. But this does not seem to be the meaning of such references. Instead, this woman is outraged that the obvious evidence of hard work and achievements does not protect her from racial discrimination. She has achieved certain elements of the American dream, but they are not sufficient.

A close look at the experience of middle-class African Americans is important to understand the racial backwardness of contemporary U.S. society, for it confirms that no amount of hard work, money, and success can protect a black person from the destructive impact of racial stereotyping and discrimination. In this [article] we show that middle-class black Americans, just like other black Americans, have terrible experiences with everyday racism. But we show much more than that. We also demonstrate that racial stereotyping and discrimination operate independently of the real identities and achievements of specifically targeted black individuals.

The ability of middle-class African Americans to act forcefully against discrimination by whites marks a change from a few decades ago when very few had the resources to fight back successfully. Black Americans have always fought against discrimination, but in earlier decades such fights were usually doomed to failure if not injury. In this account, the woman's ability as a professional to bring a television news team to the restaurant enabled her to take assertive action. This example also underscores the complexity of the interaction in some situations of discrimination, for not only is there a confrontation with a white manager over mistreatment but also a negotiation between the black individuals over how to respond.

It is an effective antidiscrimination strategy on the part of black Americans to make the confrontations public. An executive at a financial institution in an East Coast city recounted his experience with a pattern of poor service in a restaurant, explaining his decision to confront the discriminators:

I took the staff here to a restaurant that had recently opened in the prestigious section of the city, and we waited while other people got waited on, and decided that after about a half hour that these people don't want to wait on us. I happened to have been in the same restaurant a couple of evenings earlier, and it took them about 45 minutes before they came to wait on me and my guest. So, on the second incident, I said, this is not an isolated incident, this is a pattern, because I had spoken with some other people who had not been warmly received in the restaurant. So, I wrote a letter to the owners . . . and sent copies to the city papers. That's my way of expressing myself and letting the world know. You have to let people, other than you and the owner know. You have to let others know you're expressing your dismay at the discrimination or the barrier that's presented to you. I met with the owners. Of course, they wanted to meet with their attorneys with me, because they wanted to sue me. I told them they're welcome to do so. I don't have a thing, but fine they can do it. It just happens that I knew their white attorney. And he more or less vouched that if I had some concern that it must have been legitimate in some form. When the principals came in, one of the people who didn't wait on me was one of the owners who happened to be waiting on everybody else. We resolved the issue by them inviting me to come again, and if I was fairly treated, or if I would come on several occasions and if I was fairly treated I would write a statement of retraction. I told them I would not write a retraction, I would write a statement with regard to how I was treated. Which I ultimately did. And I still go there today, and they speak to me, and I think the pattern is changed to a great degree.

The time- and energy-consuming aspects of publicly confronting discrimination are apparent in this account. The respondent invested much of himself in a considered response to a recurring problem. Forcing whites to renegotiate, especially by using negative publicity, can bring about changes. The arrival on the restaurant scene of middle-class black Americans with substantial resources has at least created situations that force whites into explicit negotiating.

Whites often enter into this "bargaining" situation with tacit assumptions and cultural expectations about black powerlessness. In the two previous examples we see the black professionals establishing "power credibility," as the whites decide that they are not bluffing. It is important to note that the whites here are not just the blue-collar whites often said to be the primary source of whatever bigotry remains in the United States. Those doing the discrimination include middle-class whites, a fact that signals the importance of race over class in much racial interaction.

That discrimination against black customers and employees in white-owned restaurants is widespread has become evident in several court suits filed since 1990 against national chains, including Denny's, Shoney's, and the International House of Pancakes (IHOP). In December 1991, for example, several groups of black college students were reportedly turned away from a Milwaukee IHOP restaurant and told that it was closed, while white customers were allowed in. In 1993 a federal judge ordered the restaurant to pay a settlement for the discrimination. Also in 1993, the Denny's chain, found to have a pattern of discrimination by the U.S. Justice Department, reached an agreement with the Department in which executives promised to train employees in nondiscriminatory behavior and to include more minorities in its advertising. This settlement did not affect a class-action discrimination suit by 32 black customers who reportedly had suffered discrimination in several Denny's restaurants in California. Moreover, in mid-1993 six black secret service agents also sued the chain, alleging discrimination at a Denny's in Annapolis, Maryland. The black agents reported that while they waited for service for nearly an hour, white agents and other white patrons were promptly served.[3] After much bad publicity, Denny's joined in an important agreement with the NAACP to work to end discrimination in its restaurants.[4]

As revealed in the court cases, restaurant discrimination has recently included long waits while whites are served, special cover fees applied only to blacks, and prepayment requirements only for black customers.[5] In the Shoney's case, the chain was sued over discrimination against black employees. According to the *St. Petersburg Times,* top officers in the white-run firm were well known for their antiblack views, and local managers were discouraged from hiring black employees. In a 1992 landmark agreement the company agreed to pay $115 million, the most ever, to employees who could prove racial discrimination.[6]

Restaurants are only one site of discrimination. Daily life inevitably involves contact with clerks and managers in various retail and grocery stores. A utility company executive in an eastern city described how her family was treated in a small store:

> *I can remember one time my husband had picked up our son . . . from camp; and he'd stopped at a little store in the neighborhood near the camp. It was hot, and he was going to buy him a snowball. . . . This was a very old, white neighborhood, and it was just a little sundry store. But the proprietor had a little window where people could come up and order things. Well, my husband and son had gone into the store. And he told them, "Well, I can't give it to you here, but if you go outside to the window, I'll give it to you." And there were other people in the store who'd been served [inside]. So, they just left and didn't buy anything.*

The old white neighborhood in which this episode occurred exemplifies the racial-territorial character of many cities even today. The poor service here seems a throwback to the South of the 1950s, where deferential blacks were served only at the back of a store. This man chose not to confront the white person nor to acquiesce abjectly but rather to leave. Here the effect on the white man was probably inconsequential because there was no confrontation and interracial negotiation. The long-run importance of a service site may well affect a black person's choice of how to respond to such discrimination. The store in this example was not important to the black family just passing through the area. The possibility of returning might have generated a more confrontational response.

Another problem that black shoppers face, especially in department and grocery stores, is the common white assumption that they are likely shoplifters. This is true in spite of the fact that national crime statistics show that most shoplifters are white. For several months in late 1991 a news team at KSTP-TV in Minneapolis conducted a field study of discrimination against black shoppers in several local department stores. Members of the team took jobs as security personnel in the stores, and black and white shoppers were sent into the stores in order to observe the reactions of white security personnel. The ensuing television report, "Who's Minding the Store?" showed how many black customers became the targets of intensive surveillance from white security guards, who neglected white shoppers when black shoppers were in the stores. As a result of the documentary, local black leaders called for a boycott of one of the store chains. Soon a number of the local stores changed their surveillance and security procedures.[7] Excessive surveillance of black customers in department and other stores was reported by some we interviewed. A black professional in the North commented on how she deals with whites who harass her with excessive surveillance and other acts of rejection:

> *[I have faced] harassment in stores, being followed around, being questioned about what are you going to purchase here. . . . I was in an elite department store just this past Saturday and felt that I was being observed while I was window shopping. I in fact actually ended up purchasing something, but felt the entire time I was there—I was in blue jeans and sneakers, that's how I dress on a Saturday—I felt that I was being watched in the store as I was walking through the store—what business did I have there, what was I going to purchase, that kind of thing. . . . There are a few of those white people that won't put change in your hand, touch your skin. That doesn't need to go on. [Do you tell them that?] Oh, I do, I do. That is just so obvious. I usually [speak to them] if they're rude in the manner in which they deal with people. [What do they say about that?] Oh, stuff like, "Oh, excuse me," and some who are really unconscious about it, say "Excuse me," and put the change in your hand. That's happened. But I've watched other people be rude, and I've been told to mind my own business. [But you still do it?] Oh, sure, because for the most part I think that people do have to learn to think for themselves, and demand respect for themselves. . . . I find my best weapon of defense is to educate them, whether it's in the store, in a line, at the bank, any situation, I teach them. And you take them by surprise because you tell them and show them what they should be doing, and what they should be saying, and how they should be thinking. And they look at you because they don't know how to process you. They can't process it because you've just shown them how they should be living, and the fact that they are cheating themselves, really, because the racism is from fear. The racism is from lack of education.*

A number of racial stereotypes are evident in this account. Whites with images of black criminality engage in excessive surveillance, and whites with images of black dirtiness will not touch black hands or skin. Black shoppers at all income levels report being ignored when in need of service and the unwillingness of some whites even to touch their hands. Why such a reaction to black bodies? In a speculative Freudian analysis of white racism, Joel Kovel has argued that for centuries whites have irrationally connected blackness, and black bodies, with fecal matter and dirt. In his view, whites are somehow projecting onto the darkness of the black outgroup personal inclinations, desires, and fears that cannot be openly and honestly acknowledged.[8]

A common black response to contemporary discrimination is evident here. Rather than withdrawing when facing such discrimination, this professional sometimes protracts the interaction with verbal confrontation. She notes the surprise effect of calling whites on the carpet for discrimination, which she sees as grounded in fear and ignorance. Interrupting the normal flow of an interaction to change a one-way experience into a two-way experience forces whites into unaccustomed situations in which they are unsure how to respond.

Middle-class African Americans enter many settings where few blacks have been before. A news anchorperson for an East Coast television station reported on an incident at a luxury automobile dealer:

> I knew I wanted to buy a Porsche, but I didn't know which model. So, on my day off, I went into a Porsche dealership in the city I used to work in. . . . And I was dressed like I normally do when I'm off. I'm into working out a lot, so I'm in sweatsuits, baseball caps, sunglasses quite a bit. So I dashed into this place dressed like that, and I must have walked around the show room floor for 20 minutes. No salesperson ever walked up to me and asked me, "Can I help you? Can I give you some information?" Nothing. I got the impression, the opinion, that they generally thought that this person, being black, being dressed in a sweatsuit, cannot hardly afford to be in here buying a Porsche. He's wasting my time, so I'm not even going to bother. And I knew that. So I specifically, the next day on my lunch hour, dressed in my work clothes, having just come off the air, I walked into that showroom. And I said, "Can I see the general manager?" And they got the general manager for me. And I said to the general manager, "I was in here yesterday." Well, I said, "First of all, I want to buy that Porsche there, the most expensive one on the floor." And I also told him, "Just yesterday I was in here, I was looking in, and I was hoping I could get some information, and oddly none of your sales people ever asked me if they could help me." . . . And there is prejudice, discrimination and racism, and things like that go on. Once they found out who I was, they bent over backward [to wait on me].

White salespeople apparently took the cue from this man's color and clothing and stereotyped him as moneyless, an assumption that the victim challenged the next day when he engaged in an unexpected confrontation. This chronic mistreatment by white salespeople, while white shoppers are generally treated with greater respect, is infuriating for black customers. It is clear from our interviews that African Americans must prepare themselves for this sort of encounter, for they never know when they will be shown normal respect and courtesy as customers or when they must "front" (dress in a certain way, talk in a certain way) in order to receive the treatment accorded a comparable white customer.

Among several respondents who discussed discrimination at retail stores, the manager of a career development organization, who found that discrimination by clerks is common, had a repertoire of responses for dealing with it:

If you're in a store—and let's say the person behind the counter is white—and you walk up to the counter, and a white person walks up to the counter, and you know you were there before the white customer, the person behind the counter knows you were there first, and it never fails, they always go, "Who's next." OK. And what I've done, if they go ahead and serve the white person first, then I will immediately say, "Excuse me, I was here first, and we both know I was here first." . . . If they get away with it once, they're going to get away with it more than once, and then it's going to become something else. And you want to make sure that folks know that you're not being naive, that you really see through what's happening. Or if it's a job opportunity or something like that, too, same thing. You first try to get a clear assessment of what's really going on and sift through that information, and then . . . go from there.

In discussions with middle-class black Americans across the nation, both our respondents and a variety of informants and journalists, we heard many similar accounts of white clerks "looking through" black customers and only "seeing" whites farther back in line. Such incidents suggest that much of the hostility manifest in white actions is based on a deep-lying, perhaps even subconscious or half-conscious, aversion to black color and persona. This executive also spoke of her coping process, one that begins with sifting information before deciding on action. Frequently choosing immediate action, she forces whites to face the reality of their behavior.

The dean of a black college who travels in various parts of the United States described the often complex process of evaluating and responding to the mistreatment that has plagued him in public accommodations:

When you're in a restaurant and . . . you notice that blacks get seated near the kitchen. You notice that if it's a hotel, your room is near the elevator, or your room is always way down in a corner somewhere. You find that you are getting the undesirable rooms. And you come there early in the day and you don't see very many cars on the lot and they'll tell you that this is all we've got. Or you get the room that's got a bad television set. You know that you're being discriminated against. And of course you have to act accordingly. You have to tell them, "Okay, the room is fine, [but] this television set has got to go. Bring me another television set." So in my personal experience, I simply cannot sit and let them get away with it and not let them know that I know that that's what they are doing. . . .

When I face discrimination, first I take a long look at myself and try to determine whether or not I am seeing what I think I'm seeing in 1989, and if it's something that I have an option [about]. In other words, if I'm at a store making a purchase, I'll simply walk away from it. If it's at a restaurant where I'm not getting good service, I first of all let the people know that I'm not getting good service, then I [may] walk away from it. But the thing that I have to do is to let people know that I know that I'm being singled out for separate treatment. And then I might react in any number of ways—depending on where I am and how badly I want whatever it is that I'm there for.

These recurring incidents in public accommodations illustrate the cumulative nature of discrimination. The dean first takes care to assess the incident and avoid jumping to conclusions. One must be constantly prepared on everyday excursions to assess accurately what is happening and then to decide on an appropriate response. What is less obvious here is the degree of pain and emotional drain that such a constant defensive stance involves.

NOTES

1. Lena Williams, "When Blacks Shop, Bias Often Accompanies a Sale," *New York Times,* April 30, 1991, pp. A1, A9.
2. Names and places in interview quotes have been disguised or eliminated to protect anonymity. Some quotes have been lightly edited for grammar and to delete excessive pause phrases like "you know" and "uh."
3. National Public Radio, "Weekend Edition," May 29, 1993.
4. Associated Press, "Denny's to Monitor Treatment of Blacks," *Gainesville Sun,* May 30, 1993, p. 7A.
5. Judy Pasternak, "Service Still Skin Deep for Blacks," *Los Angeles Times,* April 1, 1993, p. A1.
6. Martin Dyckman, "Lawyers Can Be Heroes Too," *St. Petersburg Times,* April 11, 1993, p. 3D.
7. Bill McAuliffe, "Black Leaders Call for Boycott of Local Carsons Stores," *Star Tribune,* December 10, 1991, p. 1B.
8. Joel Kovel, *White Racism,* rev. ed. (New York: Columbia University Press, 1984).

PART VII

Social Institutions

35

THE POWER ELITE

C. WRIGHT MILLS

Who really governs in the United States? In this selection, C. Wright Mills argues that the most important decisions in this country are made by a cohesive "power elite." This power elite consists of the top leaders in three areas: The corporate elite is made up of the executives from large companies; the military elite is the senior officers; and the small political elite includes the president and top officials in the executive and legislative branches. According to Mills' argument, this group of elite officials all know each other and act in unison when critical decisions must be made. This selection, originally published in 1956, is the first of three that address power and politics.

The powers of ordinary men are circumscribed by the everyday worlds in which they live, yet even in these rounds of job, family, and neighborhood they often seem driven by forces they can neither understand nor govern. "Great changes" are beyond their control, but affect their conduct and outlook nonetheless. The very framework of modern society confines them to projects not their own, but from every side, such changes now press upon the men and women of the mass society, who accordingly feel that they are without purpose in an epoch in which they are without power.

But not all men are in this sense ordinary. As the means of information and of power are centralized, some men come to occupy positions in American society from which they can look down upon, so to speak, and by their decisions mightily affect, the everyday worlds of ordinary men and women. They are not made by their jobs; they set up and break down jobs for thousands of others; they are not confined by simple family responsibilities; they can escape. They may live in many hotels and houses, but they are bound by no one community. They need not merely "meet the demands of the day and hour"; in some part, they create these demands, and cause others to meet them. Whether or not they profess their power, their technical and political experience of it far transcends that of the underlying population. What Jacob Burckhardt said of "great men," most Americans might well say of their elite: "They are all that we are not."

The power elite is composed of men whose positions enable them to transcend the ordinary environments of ordinary men and women; they are in positions to make decisions having major consequences. Whether they do or do not make such decisions is less important than the fact that they do occupy such pivotal positions: Their failure to act, their failure to make decisions, is itself an act that is often of greater consequence than the decisions they do make. For they are in command of the major hierarchies and organizations of modern society. They rule the big corporations. They run the machinery of the state and claim its prerogatives. They direct the military establishment. They occupy the strategic command posts of the social structure, in which are now centered the effective means of the power and the wealth and the celebrity which they enjoy.

The power elite are not solitary rulers. Advisers and consultants, spokesmen and opinion makers are often the captains of their higher thought and decision. Immediately below the elite are the professional politicians of the middle levels of power, in the Congress and in the pressure groups, as well as among the new and old upper classes of town and city and region. Mingling with them, in curious ways which we shall explore, are those professional celebrities who live by being continually displayed but are never, so long as they remain celebrities, displayed enough. If such celebrities are not at the head of any dominating hierarchy, they do often have the power to distract the attention of the public or afford sensations to the masses, or, more directly, to gain the ear of those who do occupy positions of direct power. More or less unattached, as critics of morality and technicians of power, as spokesmen of God and creators of mass sensibility, such celebrities and consultants are part of the immediate scene in which the drama of the elite is enacted. But that drama itself is centered in the command posts of the major institutional hierarchies.

The truth about the nature and the power of the elite is not some secret which men of affairs know but will not tell. Such men hold quite various theories about their own roles in the sequence of event and decision. Often they are uncertain about their roles, and even more often they allow their fears and their hopes to affect their assessment of their own power. No matter how great their actual power, they tend to be less acutely aware of it than of the resistances of others to its use. Moreover, most American men of affairs have learned well the rhetoric of public relations, in some cases even to the point of using it when they are alone, and thus coming to believe it. The personal awareness of the actors is only one of the several sources one must examine in order to understand the higher circles. Yet many who believe that there is no elite, or at any rate none of any consequence, rest their argument upon what men of affairs believe about themselves, or at least assert in public.

There is, however, another view: Those who feel, even if vaguely, that a compact and powerful elite of great importance does now prevail in America often base that feeling upon the historical trend of our time. They have felt, for example, the domination of the military event, and from this they infer that generals and admirals, as well as other men of decision influenced by them, must be enormously powerful. They hear that the Congress has again abdicated to a handful of men decisions clearly related to the issue of war or peace. They know that the bomb was dropped over Japan in the name of the United States of America, although they were at no time consulted about the matter. They feel that they live in a time of big decisions; they know that they are not making any. Accordingly, as they consider the present as history, they infer that at its center, making decisions or failing to make them, there must be an elite of power.

On the one hand, those who share this feeling about big historical events assume that there is an elite and that its power is great. On the other hand, those who listen carefully to the reports of men apparently involved in the great decisions often do not believe that there is an elite whose powers are of decisive consequence.

Both views must be taken into account, but neither is adequate. The way to understand the power of the American elite lies neither solely in recognizing the historic scale of events nor in accepting the personal awareness reported by men of apparent decision. Behind such men and behind the events of history, linking the two, are the major institutions of modern society. These hierarchies of state and corporation and army constitute the means of power; as such they are now of a consequence not before equaled in human history— and at their summits, there are now those command posts of modern society which offer us the sociological key to an understanding of the role of the higher circles in America.

Within American society, major national power now resides in the economic, the political, and the military domains. Other institutions seem off to the side of modern history, and, on occasion, duly subordinated to these. No family is as directly powerful in national affairs as any major corporation; no church is as directly powerful in the external biographies of young men in America today as the military establishment; no college is as powerful in the shaping of momentous events as the National Security Council. Religious, educational, and family institutions are not autonomous centers of national power; on the contrary, these decentralized areas are increasingly shaped by the big three, in which developments of decisive and immediate consequence now occur.

Families and churches and schools adapt to modern life; governments and armies and corporations shape it; and, as they do so, they turn these lesser institutions into means for their ends. Religious institutions provide chaplains to the armed forces where they are used as a means of increasing the effectiveness of its morale to kill. Schools select and train men for their jobs in corporations and their specialized tasks in the armed forces. The extended family has, of course, long been broken up by the industrial revolution, and now the son and the father are removed from the family, by compulsion if need be, whenever the army of the state sends out the call. And the symbols of all these lesser institutions are used to legitimate the power and the decisions of the big three.

The life-fate of the modern individual depends not only upon the family into which he was born or which he enters by marriage, but increasingly upon the corporation in which he spends the most alert hours of his best years; not only upon the school where he is educated as a child and adolescent, but also upon the state which touches him throughout his life; not only upon the church in which on occasion he hears the word of God, but also upon the army in which he is disciplined.

If the centralized state could not rely upon the inculcation of nationalist loyalties in public and private schools, its leaders would promptly seek to modify the decentralized educational system. If the bankruptcy rate among the top 500 corporations were as high as the general divorce rate among the 37 million married couples, there would be economic catastrophe on an international scale. If members of armies gave to them no more of their lives than do believers to the churches to which they belong, there would be a military crisis.

Within each of the big three, the typical institutional unit has become enlarged, has become administrative, and, in the power of its decisions, has become centralized. Behind these developments there is a fabulous technology, for as institutions, they have incorporated this technology and guide it, even as it shapes and paces their developments.

The economy—once a great scatter of small productive units in autonomous balance—has become dominated by two or three hundred giant corporations, administratively and politically interrelated, which together hold the keys to economic decisions.

The political order, once a decentralized set of several dozen states with a weak spinal cord, has become a centralized, executive establishment which has taken up into itself many powers previously scattered, and now enters into each and every cranny of the social structure.

The military order, once a slim establishment in a context of distrust fed by state militia, has become the largest and most expensive feature of government, and, although well-versed in smiling public relations, now has all the grim and clumsy efficiency of a sprawling bureaucratic domain.

In each of these institutional areas, the means of power at the disposal of decision makers have increased enormously; their central executive powers have been enhanced; within each of them modern administrative routines have been elaborated and tightened up.

As each of these domains becomes enlarged and centralized, the consequences of its activities become greater, and its traffic with the others increases. The decisions of a handful of corporations bear upon military and political as well as upon economic developments around the world. The decisions of the military establishment rest upon and grievously affect political life as well as the very level of economic activity. The decisions made within the political domain determine economic activities and military programs. There is no longer, on the one hand, an economy, and, on the other hand, a political order containing a military establishment unimportant to politics and to money making. There is a political economy linked, in a thousand ways, with military institutions and decisions. On each side of the world-split running through central Europe and around the Asiatic rimlands, there is an ever-increasing interlocking of economic, military, and political structures. If there is government intervention in the corporate economy, so is there corporate intervention in the governmental process. In the structural sense, this triangle of power is the source of the interlocking directorate that is most important for the historical structure of the present.

The fact of the interlocking is clearly revealed at each of the points of crisis of modern capitalist society—slump, war, and boom. In each, men of decision are led to an awareness of the interdependence of the major institutional orders. In the nineteenth century, when the scale of all institutions was smaller, their liberal integration was achieved in the automatic economy, by an autonomous play of market forces, and in the automatic political domain, by the bargain and the vote. It was then assumed that out of the imbalance and friction that followed the limited decisions then possible a new equilibrium would in due course emerge. That can no longer be assumed, and it is not assumed by the men at the top of each of the three dominant hierarchies.

For given the scope of their consequences, decisions—and indecisions—in any one of these ramify into the others, and hence top decisions tend either to become coordinated or to lead to a commanding indecision. It has not always been like this. When numerous small entrepreneurs made up the economy, for example, many of them could fail and the consequences still remain local; political and military authorities did not intervene. But now, given political expectations and military commitments, can they afford to allow key units of the private corporate economy to break down in slump? Increasingly, they do intervene in economic affairs, and as they do so, the controlling decisions in each order are inspected by agents of the other two, and economic, military, and political structures are interlocked.

At the pinnacle of each of the three enlarged and centralized domains, there have arisen those higher circles which make up the economic, the political, and the military elites. At the top of the economy, among the corporate rich, there are the chief executives; at the top of the political order, the members of the political directorate; at the top of the military establishment, the elite of soldier-statesmen clustered in and around the Joint Chiefs of Staff and the upper echelon. As each of these domains has coincided with the others, as decisions tend to become total in their consequence, the leading men in each of the three domains of power—the warlords, the corporation chieftains, the political directorate—tend to come together, to form the power elite of America.

The higher circles in and around these command posts are often thought of in terms of what their members possess: They have a greater share than other people of the things and experiences that are most highly valued. From this point of view, the elite are simply those who have the most of what there is to have, which is generally held to include money, power, and prestige—as well as all the ways of life to which these lead. But the elite are not simply those who have the most, for they could not "have the most" were it not for their positions in the great institutions. For such institutions are the necessary bases of power, of wealth, and of prestige, and at the same time, the chief means of exercising power, of acquiring and retaining wealth, and of cashing in the higher claims for prestige.

By the powerful we mean, of course, those who are able to realize their will, even if others resist it. No one, accordingly, can be truly powerful unless he has access to the command of major institutions, for it is over these institutional means of power that the truly powerful are, in the first instance, powerful. Higher politicians and key officials of government command such institutional power; so do admirals and generals, and so do the major owners and executives of the larger corporations. Not all power, it is true, is anchored in and exercised by means of such institutions, but only within and through them can power be more or less continuous and important.

Wealth also is acquired and held in and through institutions. The pyramid of wealth cannot be understood merely in terms of the very rich; for the great inheriting families, as we shall see, are now supplemented by the corporate institutions of modern society: Every one of the very rich families has been and is closely connected—always legally and frequently managerially as well—with one of the multimillion-dollar corporations.

The modern corporation is the prime source of wealth, but, in latter-day capitalism, the political apparatus also opens and closes many avenues to wealth. The amount as well as the source of income, the power over consumer's goods as well as over productive capital, are determined by position within the political economy. If our interest in the very rich goes beyond their lavish or their miserly consumption, we must examine their relations to modern forms of corporate property as well as to the state; for such relations now determine the chances of men to secure big property and to receive high income.

Great prestige increasingly follows the major institutional units of the social structure. It is obvious that prestige depends, often quite decisively, upon access to the publicity machines that are now a central and normal feature of all the big institutions of modern America. Moreover, one feature of these hierarchies of corporation, state, and military establishment is that their top positions are increasingly interchangeable. One result of this is the accumulative nature of prestige. Claims for prestige, for example, may be initially based on military roles, then expressed in and augmented by an educational institution run by corporate executives, and cashed in, finally, in the political order, where, for General Eisenhower and those he represents, power and prestige finally meet at the very peak. Like wealth and power, prestige tends to be cumulative: The more of it you have, the more you can get. These values also tend to be translatable into one another: The wealthy find it easier than the poor to gain power; those with status find it easier than those without it to control opportunities for wealth.

If we took the one hundred most powerful men in America, the one hundred wealthiest, and the one hundred most celebrated away from the institutional positions they now occupy, away from their resources of men and women and money, away from the media of mass communication that are now focused upon them—then they would be powerless and poor and uncelebrated. For power is not of a man. Wealth does not center in the person of the wealthy. Celebrity is not inherent in any personality. To be celebrated, to be wealthy, to have power requires access to major institutions, for the institutional positions men occupy determine in large part their chances to have and to hold these valued experiences.

The people of the higher circles may also be conceived as members of a top social stratum, as a set of groups whose members know one another, see one another socially and at business, and so, in making decisions, take one another into account. The elite, according to this conception, feel themselves to be, and are felt by others to be, the inner circle of "the upper social classes." They form a more or less compact social and psychological entity; they have become self-conscious members of a social class. People are either accepted into this class or they are not, and there is a qualitative split, rather than merely a numerical scale, separating them from those who are not elite. They are more or less aware of themselves as a social class and they behave toward one another differently from the way they do toward members of other classes. They accept one another, understand one another, marry one another, tend to work and to think if not together at least alike.

Now, we do not want by our definition to prejudge whether the elite of the command posts are conscious members of such a socially recognized class, or whether considerable proportions of the elite derive from such a clear and distinct class. These are matters to be investigated. Yet in order to be able to recognize what we intend to investigate, we must note something that all biographies and memoirs of the wealthy and the powerful and the eminent make clear: No matter what else they may be, the people of these higher circles are involved in a set of overlapping "crowds" and intricately connected "cliques." There is a kind of mutual attraction among those who "sit on the same terrace"—although this often becomes clear to them, as well as to others, only at the point at which they feel the need to draw the line; only when, in their common defense, they come to understand what they have in common, and so close their ranks against outsiders.

The idea of such ruling stratum implies that most of its members have similar social origins, that throughout their lives they maintain a network of informal connections, and that to some degree there is an interchangeability of position between the various hierarchies of money and power and celebrity. We must, of course, note at once that if such an elite stratum does exist, its social visibility and its form, for very solid historical reasons, are quite different from those of the noble cousinhoods that once ruled various European nations.

That American society has never passed through a feudal epoch is of decisive importance to the nature of the American elite, as well as to American society as a historic whole. For it means that no nobility or aristocracy, established before the capitalist era, has stood in tense opposition to the higher bourgeoisie. It means that this bourgeoisie has monopolized not only wealth but prestige and power as well. It means that no set of noble families has commanded the top positions and monopolized the values that are generally held in high esteem; and certainly that no set has done so explicitly by inherited right. It means that no high church dignitaries or court nobilities, no entrenched landlords with honorific accouterments, no monopolists of high army posts have opposed the enriched bourgeoisie and in the name of birth and prerogative successfully resisted its self-making.

But this does *not* mean that there are no upper strata in the United States. That they emerged from a "middle class" that had no recognized aristocratic superiors does not mean they remained middle class when enormous increases in wealth made their own superiority possible. Their origins and their newness may have made the upper strata less visible in America than elsewhere. But in America today there are in fact tiers and ranges of wealth and power of which people in the middle and lower ranks know very little and may not even dream. There are families who, in their well-being, are quite insulated from the economic jolts and lurches felt by the merely prosperous and those farther down the scale. There are also men of power who in quite small groups make decisions of enormous consequence for the underlying population.

36

MONEY TALKS
Corporate PACs and Political Influence

DAN CLAWSON • ALAN NEUSTADTL • DENISE SCOTT

Sociological research supports the thesis that a power elite exists in this country. A point of debate is the degree of interconnection among the three groups—the corporate, military, and political elites. Nonetheless, current social research still indicates that power is concentrated among a few social groups and institutions, as shown in a recent study (1992) discussed in this selection by Dan Clawson, Alan Neustadtl, and Denise Scott. After investigating 309 corporate political action committees (PACs), the authors conclude that PACs, which represent corporate interests, ensure that the concerns of Big Business are heard on Capitol Hill.

In the past 20 years, political action committees, or PACs, have transformed campaign finance. The chair of the PAC at one of the 25 largest manufacturing companies in the United States explained to us why his corporation has a PAC:

The PAC gives you access. It makes you a player. These congressmen, in particular, are constantly fundraising. Their elections are very expensive and getting increasingly expensive each year. So they have an on-going need for funds.

It profits us in a sense to be able to provide some funds because in the provision of it you get to know people, you help them out. There's no real quid pro quo. There is nobody whose vote you can count on, not with the kind of money we are talking about here. But the PAC gives you access, puts you in the game.

You know, some congressman has got X number of ergs of energy, and here's a person or a company who wants to come see him and give him a thousand dollars, and here's another one who wants to just stop by and say hello. And he only has time to see one. Which one? So the PAC's an attention getter.

Most analyses of campaign finance focus on the candidates who receive the money, not on the people and political action committees that give it. PACs are entities that collect money from many contributors, pool it, and then make donations to candidates. Donors may give to a PAC because they are in basic agreement with its aims, but once they have donated they lose

From *Money Talks: Corporate PACS and Political Influence*, pp. 1–14. Reprinted by permission from Professor Dan Clawson.

direct control over their money, trusting the PAC to decide which candidates should receive contributions.

Corporate PACs have unusual power that has been largely unexamined. In this [reading] we begin the process of giving corporate PACs, and business–government relations in general, the scrutiny they deserve. By far the most important source for our analysis is a set of in-depth interviews we conducted with corporate executives who direct and control their corporations' political activity. The insight these interviews provide into the way corporate executives think, the goals they pursue, and the methods they use to achieve those goals are far more revealing than most analyses made by outside critics. We think most readers will be troubled, as we are, by the worldview and activities of corporate PAC directors. . . .

Why Does the Air Stink?

Everybody wants clean air. Who could oppose it? "I spent seven years of my life trying to stop the Clean Air Act," explained the PAC director for a major corporation that is a heavy-duty polluter. Nonetheless, he was perfectly willing to use his corporation's PAC to contribute to members of Congress who voted for the act:

> How a person votes on the final piece of legislation often is not representative of what they have done. Somebody will do a lot of things during the process. How many guys voted against the Clean Air Act? But during the process some of them were very sympathetic to some of our concerns.

In the world of Congress and political action committees things are not always what they seem. Members of Congress want to vote for clean air, but they also want to receive campaign contributions from corporate PACs and pass a law that business accepts as "reasonable." The compromise solution to this dilemma is to gut the bill by crafting dozens of loopholes inserted in private meetings or in subcommittee hearings that don't receive much (if any) attention in the press. Then the public vote on the final bill can be nearly unanimous: Members of Congress can assure their constituents that they voted for the final bill and their corporate PAC contributors that they helped weaken the bill in private. We can use the Clean Air Act of 1990 to introduce and explain this process.

The public strongly supports clean air and is unimpressed when corporate officials and apologists trot out their normal arguments: "Corporations are already doing all they reasonably can to improve environmental quality"; "we need to balance the costs against the benefits"; "people will lose their jobs if we make controls any stricter." The original Clean Air Act was passed in 1970, revised in 1977, and not revised again until 1990. Although the initial goal of its supporters was to have us breathing clean air by 1975, the dead-line for compliance has been repeatedly extended—and the 1990 legislation provides a new set of deadlines to be reached sometime far in the future.

Because corporations control the production process unless the government specifically intervenes, any delay in government action leaves corporations free to do as they choose. Not only have laws been slow to come, but corporations have fought to delay or subvert implementation. The 1970 law ordered the Environmental Protection Agency (EPA) to regulate the hundreds of poisonous chemicals that are emitted by corporations, but as William Greider notes, "In 20 years of stalling, dodging, and fighting off court orders, the EPA has managed to issue regulatory standards for a total of seven toxics."[1]

Corporations have done exceptionally well politically, given the problem they face: The interests of business often are diametrically opposed to those of the public. Clean air laws and amendments have been few and far between, enforcement is ineffective, and the penalties for infractions are minimal. On the one hand, corporations have had to pay billions; on the other hand, the costs to date are a small fraction of what would be needed to clean up the environment.

This corporate struggle for the right to pollute takes place on many fronts. One front is public relations: The Chemical Manufacturers Association took out a two-page Earth Day ad in the *Washington Post* to demonstrate its concern for the environment; coincidentally many of the corporate signers are also on the EPA's list of high-risk producers.[2] Another front is research: Expert studies delay action while more information is gathered. The federally funded National Acid Precipitation Assessment Program (NAPAP) took 10 years and $600 million to figure out whether acid rain was a problem. Both business and the Reagan administration argued that no action should be taken until the study was completed.[3] The study was discredited when its summary of findings minimized the impact of acid rain—even though this did not accurately represent the expert research in the report. But the key site of struggle has been Congress, where for years corporations have succeeded in defeating environmental legislation. In 1987, utility companies were offered a compromise bill on acid rain, but they "were very adamant that they had beat the thing since 1981 and they could always beat it," according to Representative Edward Madigan (R–Ill.).[4] Throughout the 1980s the utilities defeated all efforts at change, but their intransigence probably hurt them when revisions finally were made.

The stage was set for a revision of the Clean Air Act when George Bush was elected as "the environmental president" and George Mitchell, a strong supporter of environmentalism, became the Senate majority leader. But what sort of clean air bill would it be? "What we wanted," said Richard Ayres, head of the environmentalists' Clean Air Coalition, "is a health-based standard—one-in-1-million cancer risk." Such a standard would require corporations to clean up their plants until the cancer risk from their operations was reduced to one in a million. "The Senate bill still has the requirement," Ayres said, "but there are 40 pages of extensions and exceptions and qualifications and loopholes that largely render the health standard a nullity."[5] Greider reports, for example, that "according to the EPA, there are now 26 coke ovens that pose a cancer risk greater than 1 in 1,000 and six where the risk is greater than 1 in 100. Yet the new clean-air bill will give the steel industry another 30 years to deal with the problem."[6]

This change from what the bill was supposed to do to what it did do came about through what corporate executives like to call the "access" process. The main aim of most corporate political action committee contributions is to help corporate executives attain "access" to key members of Congress and their staffs. Corporate executives (and corporate PAC money) work to persuade the member of Congress to accept a carefully predesigned loophole that sounds innocent but effectively undercuts the stated intention of the bill. Representative Dingell (D–Mich.), chair of the House Committee on Energy and Commerce, is a strong industry supporter; one of the people we interviewed called him "the point man for the Business Roundtable on clean air." Representative Waxman (D–Calif.), chair of the Subcommittee on Health and the Environment, is an environmentalist. Observers of the Clean Air Act legislative process expected a confrontation and contested votes on the floor of the Congress.

The problem for corporations was that, as one Republican staff aide said, "If any bill has the blessing of Waxman and the environmental groups, unless it is totally in outer space, who's going to vote against it?"[7] But corporations successfully minimized public votes. Somehow Waxman was persuaded to make behind-the-scenes compromises with Dingell so members didn't have to publicly side with business against the environment during an election year.[8] Often the access process leads to loopholes that protect a single corporation; but for "clean" air, most special deals targeted entire industries, not specific companies. The initial bill, for example, required cars to be able to use strictly specified cleaner fuels. But the auto industry wanted the rules loosened, and Congress eventually modified the bill by incorporating a variant of a formula suggested by the head of General Motors' fuels and lubricants department.

Nor did corporations stop fighting after they gutted the bill through amendments. Business pressed the EPA for favorable regulations to implement the law: "The cost of this legislation could vary dramatically, depending on how EPA interprets it," said William D. Fay, vice president of the National Coal Association, who headed the hilariously misnamed Clean Air Working Group, an industry coalition that fought to weaken the legislation.[9] An EPA aide working on acid rain regulations reported, "We're having a hard time getting our work done because of the number of phone calls we're getting" from corporations and their lawyers.

Corporations trying to convince federal regulators to adopt the "right" regulations don't rely exclusively on the cogency of their arguments. They often exert pressure on a member of Congress to intervene for them at the EPA or other agency. Senators and representatives regularly intervene on behalf of constituents and contributors by doing everything from straightening out a Social Security problem to asking a regulatory agency to explain why it is pressuring a company. This process—like campaign finance—usually follows accepted etiquette. In addressing a regulatory agency the senator does not say, "Lay off my campaign contributors, or I'll cut your budget." One standard phrasing for letters asks regulators to resolve the problem "as quickly as possible within applicable rules and regulations." [10] No matter how mild and careful the inquiry, the agency receiving the request is certain to give it extra attention; only after careful consideration will they refuse to make any accommodation.

The power disparity between business and environmentalists is enormous during the legislative process but even larger thereafter. When the Clean Air Act passed, corporations and industry groups offered positions, typically with large pay increases, to congressional staff members who wrote the law. The former congressional staff members who work for corporations know how to evade the law and can persuasively claim to EPA that they know what Congress intended. Environmental organizations pay substantially less than Congress and can't afford large staffs. They are rarely able to become involved in the details of the administrative process or influence implementation and enforcement.[11]

Having pushed Congress for a law, and the Environmental Protection Agency for regulations, allowing as much pollution as possible, business then went to the Quayle Council for rules allowing even more pollution. Vice President J. Danforth Quayle's Council, technically the Council on Competitiveness, was created by President Bush specifically to help reduce regulations on business. Quayle told the *Boston Globe* "that this council has an 'open door' to business groups and that he has a bias against regulations." [12] The Council reviews, and can override, all federal regulations, including those by the EPA setting the limits at which a chemical is subject to regulation. The council also recommended that corporations be allowed to increase their polluting emissions if a state did not object within seven days of the proposed increase. Corporations thus have multiple opportunities to win. If they lose in Congress, they can win at the regulatory agency; if they lose there, they can try again at the Quayle Council. If they lose there, they can try to reduce the money available to enforce regulations, tie up the issue in the courts, or accept a minimal fine.

The operation of the Quayle Council probably would have received little publicity, but reporters discovered that the executive director of the Council, Allan Hubbard, had a clear conflict of interest. Hubbard chaired the biweekly White House meetings on the Clean Air Act. He owns half of World Wide

Chemical, received an average of more than a million dollars a year in profits from it while directing the Council, and continues to attend quarterly stockholder meetings. According to the *Boston Globe,* "Records on file with the Indianapolis Air Pollution Control Board show that World Wide Chemical emitted 17,000 to 19,000 pounds of chemicals into the air last year."[13] The company "does not have the permit required to release the emissions," "is putting out nearly four times the allowable emissions without a permit, and could be subject to a $2,500-a-day penalty," according to David Jordan, director of the Indianapolis Air Pollution Board.[14]

In business-government relations attention focuses on scandal. It is outrageous that Hubbard will personally benefit by eliminating regulations that his own company is violating, but the key issue here is not this obvious conflict of interest. The real issue is the *system* of business-government relations, and especially of campaign finance, that offers business so many opportunities to craft loopholes, undermine regulations, and subvert enforcement. Still worse, many of these actions take place outside of public scrutiny. If the Quayle Council were headed by a Boy Scout we'd still object to giving business yet another way to use backroom deals to increase our risk of getting cancer. In *Money Talks* we try to analyze not just the exceptional cases, but the day-to-day reality of corporate-government relations. . . .

Myth One: Key Votes Are the Issue

Many critics of PACs and campaign finance seem to feel that a corporate PAC officer walks into a member's office and says, "Senator, I want you to vote against the Clean Air Act. Here's $5,000 to do so." This view, in this crude form, is simply wrong. The (liberal) critics who hold this view seem to reason as follows: (1) we know that PAC money gives corporations power in relation to Congress; (2) power is the ability to make someone do something against their will; (3) therefore campaign money must force members to switch their votes on key issues. We come to the same conclusion about the outcome—corporate power in relation to Congress—but differ from conventional critics on both the understanding of power and the nature of the process through which campaign money exercises its influence.

The debate over campaign finance is frequently posed as, "Did special interests buy the member's vote on a key issue?" Media accounts as well as most academic analyses in practice adopt this approach.[15] With the question framed in this way, we have to agree with the corporate political action committee directors we interviewed, who answered, "No, they didn't." But they believed it followed that they have no power and maybe not even any influence, and we certainly don't agree with that. If power means the ability to force a member of Congress to vote a certain way on a major bill, corporate PACs rarely have power. However, corporations and their PACs have a great deal of power if power means the ability to exercise a field of influence that shapes the behavior of other social actors. In fact, corporations have effective hegemony: Some alternatives are never seriously considered, and others seem natural and inevitable; some alternatives generate enormous controversy and costs, and others are minor and involve noncontroversial favors. Members of Congress meet regularly with some people, share trust, discuss the issues honestly off the record, and become friends, while other people have a hard time getting in the door much less getting any help. Members don't have to be forced; most of them are eager to do favors for corporations and do so without the public's knowledge. If citizens did understand what was happening their outrage might put an end to the behavior, but even if the favors are brought to light the media will probably present them as at least arguably good public policy.

High-Visibility Issues

Corporate PAC officers could stress two key facts: First, on important highly visible issues they cannot determine the way a member of Congress votes; second, even for low-visibility issues the entire process is loose and uncertain. The more visible an issue, the less likely that a member's vote will be determined by campaign contributions. If the whole world is watching, a member from an environmentally conscious district can't vote against the Clean Air Act because it is simply too popular. An April 1990 poll by Louis Harris and Associates reported that when asked, "Should Congress make the 1970 Clean Air Act stricter than it is now, keep it about the same, or make it less strict?" 73 percent of respondents answered, "Make it stricter"; 23 percent, "Keep it about the same"; and only 2 percent, "Make it less strict" (with 2 percent not sure).[16] Few members could risk openly voting against such sentiments. To oppose the bill they'd have to have a very good reason—perhaps that it would cost their district several hundred jobs, perhaps that the bill was fatally flawed, but never, never, never that they had been promised $5,000, $10,000, or $50,000 for doing so.

The PAC officers we interviewed understood this point, although they weren't always careful to distinguish between high- and low-visibility issues. (As we discuss below, we believe low-visibility issues are an entirely different story.) Virtually all access-oriented PACs went out of their way at some point in the interview to make it clear that they do not and could not buy a member's vote on any significant issue. No corporate official felt otherwise; moreover, these opinions seemed genuine and not merely for public consumption. They pointed out that the maximum legal donation by a PAC is $5,000 per candidate per election. Given that in 1988 the cost of an average winning House campaign was $388,000 and for the Senate $3,745,000,[17] no individual company can provide the financial margin of victory in any but the closest of races. A member of Congress would be a fool to trade 5 percent of the district's votes for the maximum donation an individual PAC can make ($5,000) or even for 10 times that amount. Most PACs therefore feel they have little influence. Even the one person who conceded possible influence in some rare circumstances considered it unlikely:

> You certainly aren't going to be able to buy anybody for $500 or $1,000 or $10,000. It's a joke. Occasionally something will happen where everybody in one industry will be for one specific solution to a problem, and they may then also pour money to one guy. And he suddenly looks out and says, "I haven't got $7,000 coming in from this group, I've got $70,000." That might get his attention: "I've got to support what they want." But that's a rarity, and it doesn't happen too often. Most likely, after the election he's going to rationalize that it wasn't that important and they would have supported him anyway. I just don't think that PACs are that important.

This statement by a senior vice president at a large *Fortune* 500 company probably reflects one part of the reality: Most of the time members' votes can't be bought; occasionally a group of corporations support the same position and combine resources to influence a member's vote even on a major contested issue. Even if that happens, the member's behavior is far from certain.

Low-Visibility Issues and Nonissues

This is true only if we limit our attention to highly visible, publicly contested issues. Most corporate PACs, and most government relations units, focus only a small fraction of their time, money, and energy on the final votes on such issues. So-called access-oriented PACs have a different purpose and style. Their aim is not to influence the member's public vote on the final piece of legislation, but rather to be sure that the bill's wording exempts their company from the bill's most costly or damaging provisions. If tax law is going to be changed, the aim of the company's government relations unit, and its associated PAC, is to be sure that the law has built-in loopholes that protect the company. The law may say that corporate tax rates are increased, and that's what the media and the public think, but section 739, subsection J, paragraph iii, contains a hard-to-decipher phrase. No ordinary mortal can figure out what it means or to whom it applies, but the consequence is that the company doesn't pay the taxes you'd think it would. For example, the 1986 Tax "Reform" Act contained a provision limited to a single company, identified as a "corporation incorporated on June 13, 1917, which has its principal place of business in Bartlesville, Oklahoma."[18] With that provision in the bill, Philips Petroleum didn't mind at all if Congress wanted to "reform" the tax laws.

Two characteristics of such provisions structure the way they are produced. First, by their very nature such provisions, targeted at one (or at most a few) corporations or industries, are unlikely to mobilize widespread business support. Other businesses may not want to oppose these provisions, but neither are they likely to make them a priority, though the broader the scope the broader the support. Business as a whole is somewhat uneasy about very narrow provisions, although most corporations and industry trade associations feel they must fight for their own. Peak business associations such as the Business Roundtable generally prefer a "clean" bill with clear provisions favoring business in general rather than a "Christmas tree" with thousands of special-interest provisions. Most corporations play the game, however, and part of playing the game is not to object to or publicize what other corporations are doing. But they don't feel good about what they do, and if general-interest business associations took a stand they would probably speak against, rather than in favor of, these provisions.

Second, however, these are low-visibility issues; in fact, most of them are not "issues" at all in that they are never examined or contested. The corporation's field of power both makes the member willing to cooperate and gets the media and public to in practice accept these loopholes as noncontroversial. Members don't usually have to take a stand on these matters or be willing to face public scrutiny. If the proposal does become contested, the member probably can back off and drop the issue with few consequences, and the corporation probably can go down the hall and try again with another member. . . .

What Is Power?

Our analysis is based on an understanding of power that differs from that usually articulated by both business and politicians. The corporate PAC directors we interviewed insisted that they have no power:

> If you were to ask me what kind of access and influence do we have, being roughly the 150th largest PAC, I would have to tell you that on the basis of our money we have zero. . . . If you look at the level of our contributions, we know we're not going to buy anybody's vote, we're not going to rent anybody, or whatever the cliches have been over the years. We know that.

The executives who expressed these views[19] used the word *power* in roughly the same sense that it is usually used within political science, which is also the way the term was defined by Max Weber, the classical sociological theorist. Power, according to this common conception, is the ability to make someone do something against his or her will. If that is what power means, then corporations rarely have power in relation to members of Congress. . . . In this regard we agree with the corporate officials we interviewed: A PAC is not in a position to say to a member of Congress, "Either you vote for this bill, or we will defeat your bid for reelection." Rarely do they even say, "Vote for this bill, or you won't get any money from us." Therefore, if power is the ability to make someone do something against his or her will, then PAC donations rarely give corporations power over members of Congress.

This definition of power as the ability to make someone do something against his or her will is what Steven Lukes[20] calls a *one-dimensional view of power*. A *two-dimensional view* recognizes the existence of nondecisions: A potential issue never gets articulated or, if articulated by someone somewhere, never receives serious consideration. In 1989 and 1990 one of the major political battles, and a focus of great effort by corporate PACs, was the Clean Air Act. Yet 20 or 30 years earlier, before the rise of the environmental movement, pollution was a nonissue: It simply didn't get considered, although its effects were, in retrospect, of great importance. In one Sherlock Holmes story the key clue is that the dog didn't bark.[21] A two-dimensional view of power makes the same point: In some situations no one notices power is being exercised—because there is no overt conflict.

Even this model of power is too restrictive, however, because it still focuses on discrete decisions and nondecisions. Tom Wartenberg . . . argues instead for a *field theory of power* that analyzes social power as similar to a magnetic field. A magnetic field alters the motion of objects susceptible to magnetism. Similarly, the mere presence of a powerful social agent alters social space for others and causes them to orient to the powerful agent.[22] One of the executives we interviewed took it for granted that "if we go see the congressman who represents [a city where the company has a major plant], where 10,000 of our employees are also his constituents, we don't need a PAC to go see him." The corporation is so important in that area that the member has to orient himself or herself in relation to the corporation and its concerns. In a different sense, the mere act of accepting a campaign contribution changes the way a member relates to a PAC, creating a sense of obligation and need to reciprocate. The PAC contribution has altered the member's social space, his or her awareness of the company and wish to help it, even if no explicit commitments have been made.

Business Is Different

Power therefore is not just the ability to force people to do something against their will; it is most effective (and least recognized) when it shapes the field of action. Moreover, business's vast resources, influence on the economy, and general legitimacy place it on a different footing from other so-called special interests. Business donors are often treated differently from other campaign contributors. When a member of Congress accepts a $1,000 donation from a corporate PAC, goes to a committee hearing, and proposes "minor" changes in a bill's wording, those changes are often accepted without discussion or examination. The changes "clarify" the language of the bill, perhaps legalizing higher levels of pollution for a specific pollutant or exempting the company from some tax. The media do not report on this change, and no one speaks against it. . . .

Even groups with great social legitimacy encounter more opposition and controversy than business faces for proposals that are virtually without public support. Contrast the largely unopposed commitment of more than $500 billion for the bailout of savings and loan associations with the sharp debate, close votes, and defeats for the rights of men and women to take *unpaid* parental leaves. Although the classic phrase for something noncontroversial that everyone must support is to call it a "motherhood" issue, and it would cost little to guarantee every woman the right to an unpaid parental leave, nonetheless this measure generated intense scrutiny and controversy, ultimately going down to defeat. Few people are prepared to publicly defend pollution or tax evasion, but business is routinely able to win pollution exemptions and tax loopholes. Although cumulatively these provisions may trouble people, individually most are allowed to pass without scrutiny. *No analysis of corporate political activity makes sense unless it begins with a recognition that the PAC is a vital element of corporate power, but it does not operate by itself. The PAC donation is always backed by the wider range of business power and influence.*

Corporations are different from other special-interest groups not only because business has far more resources, but also because of this acceptance and legitimacy. When people feel that "the system" is screwing them, they tend to blame politicians, the government, the media—but rarely business. Although much of the public is outraged at the way money influences elections and public policy, the issue is almost always posed in terms of what politicians do or don't do. This pervasive double standard largely exempts business from criticism. We, on the other hand, believe it is vital to scrutinize business as well. . . .

The Limits to Business Power

We have argued that power is more than winning an open conflict, and business is different from other groups because of its pervasive influence on our society—the way it shapes the social space for all other actors. These two arguments, however, are joined with a third: a recognition of, in fact an insistence on, the limits to business power. We stress the power of business, but business does not feel powerful. As one executive said to us,

> I really wish that our PAC in particular, and our lobbyists, had the influence that is generally perceived by the general population. If you see it written in the press, and you talk to people, they tell you about all that influence that you've got, and frankly I think that's far overplayed, as far as the influence goes. Certainly you can get access to a candidate, and certainly you can get your position known; but as far as influencing that decision, the only way you influence it is by the providing of information.

Executives believe that corporations are constantly under attack, primarily because government simply doesn't understand that business is crucial to everything society does but can easily be crippled by well-intentioned but unrealistic government policies. A widespread view among the people we interviewed is that "far and away the vast majority of things that we do are literally to protect ourselves from public policy that is poorly crafted and nonresponsive to the needs and realities and circumstances of our company." These misguided policies, they feel, can come from many sources— labor unions, environmentalists, the pressure of unrealistic public-interest groups, the government's constant need for money, or the weight of its oppressive bureaucracy. Simply maintaining equilibrium requires a pervasive effort: If attention slips for even a minute, an onerous regulation will be imposed or a precious resource taken away. To some extent such a view is an obvious consequence of the position of the people we interviewed: If business could be sure of always winning, the government relations unit (and thus their jobs) would be unnecessary; if it is easy to win, they deserve little credit for their victories and much blame for defeats. But evidently the corporation agrees with them, since it devotes significant resources to political action of many kinds, including the awareness and involvement of top officials. Chief executive officers and members of the board of directors repeatedly express similar views. . . .

Like the rest of us, business executives can usually think of other things they'd like to have but know they can't get at this time or that they could win but wouldn't consider worth the price that would have to be paid. More important, the odds may be very much in their favor, their opponents may be hobbled with one hand tied behind their back, but it is still a contest requiring pervasive effort. Perhaps once upon a time business could simply make its wishes known and receive what it wanted; today corporations must form PACs, lobby actively, make their case to the public, run advocacy ads, and engage in a multitude of behaviors that they wish were unnecessary. From the outside we are impressed with the high success rates over a wide range of issues and with the lack of a credible challenge to the general authority of business. From the inside they are impressed with the serious consequences of occasional losses and with the continuing effort needed to maintain their privileged position.

NOTES

1. William Greider, "Whitewash: Is Congress Conning Us on Clean Air?" *Rolling Stone,* June 14, 1990, pp. 37–39, 146.
2. Ibid.
3. Margaret E. Kriz, "Dunning the Midwest," *National Journal* (April 14, 1990), pp. 893–97.
4. Ibid., p. 41.
5. Quoted in Greider, "Whitewash," p. 40.
6. Ibid.
7. Margaret E. Kriz, "Politics at the Pump," *National Journal* (June 2, 1990), p. 1328.
8. Information in this paragraph is from Kriz, "Politics at the Pump," pp. 1328–29.
9. Why can't industry just come out and name its groups "Polluters for Profit" or the "Coalition for Acid Rain Preservation" (CARP)? All quotes in this paragraph

are from Carol Matlack, "It's Round Two in Clean Air Fight," *National Journal* (January 26, 1991), p. 226.

10. Charles R. Babcock and Helen Dewar, "Keating Fallout: Senators Draw Own Lines on When to Intervene," *Washington Post,* January 16, 1991, p. A17.

11. Matlack, "It's Round Two in Clean Air Fight," p. 227.

12. Michael Kranish, "House Panel to Probe Waiver for Quayle Aide," *Boston Globe,* November 21, 1991, p. 17.

13. Ibid.

14. Michael Kranish, "Quayle Aide's Firm Is Linked to Pollution: Official Works on Emission Rules," *Boston Globe,* November 20, 1991, p. 4.

15. Janet M. Grenzke, "PACs and the Congressional Supermarket: The Currency Is Complex," *American Journal of Political Science* 33 (1989):1–24; James B. Kau and Paul H. Rubin, *Congressmen, Constituents, and Contributors* (Boston: Martinus Nijhoff, 1982); Alan Neustadtl, "Interest-Group PACsmanship: An Analysis of Campaign Contributions, Issue Visibility, and Legislative Impact," *Social Forces* 69 (1991):549–64.

16. "Opinion Outlook: Views on the American Scene," *National Journal* 22 (April 28, 1990), p. 1052.

17. David B. Magleby and Candice J. Nelson, *The Money Chase: Congressional Campaign Finance Reform* (Washington, DC: Brookings Institution, 1990), p. 36.

18. Gary Klott, "Senators Won Many Exceptions in Bill to Aid Specific Taxpayers," *New York Times,* June 6, 1986, pp. D1–D2.

19. Their views on this, as on other issues, are sometimes complicated and contradictory, and at other points in the same interview the person might take a different position.

20. Steven Lukes, *Power: A Radical View* (New York: Macmillan, 1974).

21. Theodore J. Eismeier and Philip H. Pollock III, "The Retreat from Partisanship: Why the Dog Didn't Bark in the 1984 Election," *Business Strategy and Public Policy,* edited by Alfred A. Marcus, Allen M. Kaufman, and David R. Beam (Westport, CT: Quorum Books, 1987), pp. 137–47.

22. Thomas Wartenberg, *The Forms of Power: From Domination to Transformation* (Philadelphia: Temple University Press, 1990), pp. 66–67, 74.

37

ONE WORLD, READY OR NOT
The Manic Logic of Global Capitalism

WILLIAM GREIDER

This reading by William Greider is an excerpt from his recent book, *One World, Ready or Not: The Manic Logic of Global Capitalism* (1997). Greider explores how the global economic revolution is reshaping international politics and the daily realities of millions of lives. The growth of multinational corporations and the inability of nation-states to regulate them has numerous consequences for capitalists and workers. In the selection following, Greider discusses the rise of global capitalism and the legacy of social problems it is creating for both developed and developing countries.

Imagine a wondrous new machine, strong and supple, a machine that reaps as it destroys. It is huge and mobile, something like the machines of modern agriculture but vastly more complicated and powerful. Think of this awesome machine running over open terrain and ignoring familiar boundaries. It plows across fields and fencerows with a fierce momentum that is exhilarating to behold and also frightening. As it goes, the machine throws off enormous mows of wealth and bounty while it leaves behind great furrows of wreckage.

Now imagine that there are skillful hands on board, but no one is at the wheel. In fact, this machine has no wheel nor any internal governor to control the speed and direction. It is sustained by its own forward motion, guided mainly by its own appetites. And it is accelerating.

The machine is modern capitalism driven by the imperatives of global industrial revolution. The metaphor is imperfect, but it offers a simplified way to visualize what is dauntingly complex and abstract and impossibly diffuse—the drama of a free-running economic system that is reordering the world.

The logic of commerce and capital has overpowered the inertia of politics and launched an epoch of great social transformations. Settled facts of material life are being revised for rich and poor nations alike. Social understandings that were formed by the hard political struggles of the twentieth century are put in doubt. Old verities about the rank ordering of nations are revised and a new map of the world is gradually being drawn. These great changes sweep over the affairs of mere governments and destabilize the established political orders in both advanced and primitive societies. Everything seems new and strange. Nothing seems certain.

Economic revolution, similar to the impulse of political revolution, liberates masses of people and at the same time projects new aspects of tyranny. Old worlds are destroyed and new ones emerge. The past is upended and new social values are created alongside the fabulous new wealth. Marvelous inventions are made plentiful. Great fortunes are accumulated. Millions of peasants find ways to escape from muddy poverty.

Yet masses of people are also tangibly deprived of their claims to self-sufficiency, the independent means of sustaining hearth and home. People and communities, even nations, find themselves losing control over their own destinies, ensnared by the revolutionary demands of commerce.

The great paradox of this economic revolution is that its new technologies enable people and nations to take sudden leaps into modernity, while at the same time they promote the renewal of once-forbidden barbarisms. Amid the newness of things, exploitation of the weak by the strong also flourishes again.

The present economic revolution, like revolutions of the past, is fueled by invention and human ingenuity and a universal aspiration to build and accumulate. But it is also driven by a palpable sense of insecurity. No one can be said to control the energies of unfettered capital, not important governments or financiers, not dictators or democrats.

And, in the race to the future, no one dares to fall a step behind, not nations or major corporations. Even the most effective leaders of business and finance share in the uncertainty, knowing as they do that the uncompromising dynamics can someday turn on the revolutionaries themselves.

As history confirms, every revolution gradually accumulates its own tensions and instabilities, the unresolved contradictions that deepen and eventually lead it to falter or break down. Likewise, this revolution is steadily creating the predicate for its own collapse. The imperatives driving enterprise and finance and leading to great social transformations reveal, in turn, the inherent contradictions that are also propelling the world toward some new version of breakdown, the prospect of an economic or political cataclysm of unknowable dimensions.

Our wondrous machine, with all its great power and creativity, appears to be running out of control toward some sort of abyss. Amid revolutionary fervor, such warnings may sound far-fetched and, as history tells us, usually go unheeded until one day, sometimes quite suddenly, they are confirmed by reality.

. . .

Before the machine can be understood, one must first be able to see it. The daunting shape and scope of the global system are usually described by opaque statistics from business and economics, but only the most sophisticated can grasp the explosive dynamics in those numbers. To visualize this great drama in its full dimensions, one must also see the people.

When I visited Bangkok, in Thailand, the newspapers were preoccupied with the melancholy saga of Honey, a work elephant who was severely injured when a truck sideswiped her on the highway. As doctors tried to mend the elephant's smashed hip, contributions poured in from heartsick citizens, including the king. Elephants have been the emblem of Thai culture for at least seven centuries, but are now gradually dying out. Honey's death prompted editorial reflections on the price of prosperity.

The new national symbol of Thailand, one could say, is the traffic jam. Bangkok's are the worst in Asia, citizens remark with an air of disgusted pride. Their daily commuting routines are the longest in developing Asia and Thais manipulate schedules endlessly to try to avoid the hours of steaming in tropical congestions of cars. The problem is that Thais are buying cars much faster than the government is building a modern transportation system. Thailand may emerge as Toyota's biggest overseas market aside from the United States.[1]

In Poland, the newly chartered Warsaw Stock Exchange was under way in a stately old pre-Communist building on Aleje Jeroszolimskie. Trading was quite thin since only two dozen companies had their shares listed and Poles were already experiencing the turbulence of Adam Smith's *niewidzialna ręka rynku,* "the invisible hand of the market." Stock prices rose fabulously in 1993, and many of the pioneer investors became instantly wealthy, zloty millionaires, at least on paper. The stock market crashed the following spring. As shares fell 40 to 70 percent in ten days, the Polish traders adopted the style of gallows humor familiar to mature financial markets around the world. Watching stocks plunge 27 percent in a single day, a broker observed: "The Warsaw Stock Exchange still awaits its first suicide."[2]

The lobby of Warsaw's Victoria Intercontinental Hotel, a favorite of foreign business travelers, was filled with hopeful plungers. Each morning Polish entrepreneurs would spread their business prospectuses across the broad coffee tables and sit back, a bit fidgety, while visiting investors from Frankfurt or New York or Milan inspected the numbers.

On the city's industrial outskirts, meanwhile, workers at the Huta Luchini steelworks were on strike. They closed down the mill to demand a share of the ownership. These steelworkers had once been revolutionaries themselves, among the militant members of Solidarity, the free trade union that arose to confront the Polish Communist regime in the early 1980s and had campaigned for the autonomy of workers and enterprises organized on principles of self-management. The Warsaw steelworks is now owned by an Italian conglomerate.

In China, as the November days turned crisp and cold, the citizens of

Beijing shopped at sidewalk markets for the traditional supplies of winter cabbage. High, squared-off mounds of cabbages attended by merchants in blue smocks with white kerchiefs on their heads were stacked at street corners along Chang An—Avenue of Eternal Peace—the mainstream boulevard. Farmers hauled cabbages into the city every day, stacked on trucks, bicycle-powered wagons and overloaded handcarts. The ritual reflects a national memory of poverty and famine. Every autumn a family acquires its store of winter cabbages as insurance against the ancient threat of scarcity. One can see the cabbages hanging atop communal walls or outside apartment windows, their outer leaves blackened by Beijing's sooty air.

Meanwhile, traffic on the boulevard was abruptly interrupted to make way for a caravan of important personages—a fleet of limousines and police escorts racing down the center lanes, with blue lights flashing. It was Jean Chrètien, the Canadian prime minister, and a trade delegation from Ottawa and the provinces. Kohl, Mitterand, Major, Balladur, Bentsen, Brown, Christopher—visiting political leaders from the most advanced economies, statesmen seeking contracts for home companies and access to China's explosive market, have become a commonplace.

As usual, McDonald's was already there, selling burgers to consumers. From Kuala Lumpur to Moscow, the company acts like an advanced scout for the global revolution, somehow able to detect the emergence of disposable incomes before other firms see it. Chinese buy their winter cabbages and also fast food. McDonald's measures its market potential with numbers like these: In the United States, there is a McDonald's restaurant for every 29,000 Americans. In China, despite rapid expansion, there is one McDonald's for every 40 million Chinese.

In Tokyo, the Sony Corporation, an authentic symbol of Japan's manufacturing excellence, is on the verge of becoming an un-Japanese company. The human resources manager, Yasunori Kirihara, lamented the prospect but explained it as an inevitable consequence of global economic integration. At present, he said, Sony's employees are split roughly fifty-fifty between Japanese and foreigners. As Sony continues to relocate its factories elsewhere, from Southeast Asia to Mexico, the substantial majority of its workforce, about 60 percent, will soon be outside Japan.

A new Japanese word, *kudoka*, has been popularized in business and political circles to describe this phenomenon. *Kudoka*, I was told, did not exist in the language before the 1980s. Its meaning should be familiar to American industrial workers who have seen their manufacturing jobs disappear. In English, it means "hollowing out."

In Everett, Washington, just north of Seattle, workers on the assembly line for Boeing's new 777, the company's latest addition to its line of large-body aircraft, gossiped that they might be shut down by the earthquake in Kobe, Japan. The main body section of the "Triple Seven," as Boeing people call their new plane, is manufactured by Mitsubishi Heavy Industries, though its plant, as it turned out, was not damaged by the quake. The

777 is a brilliant expression of America's productive prowess in advanced technologies, but their aircraft is manufactured, piece by piece, in twelve different countries.

As these scattered glimpses suggest, the symptoms of upheaval can be found most anywhere, since people in distant places are now connected by powerful strands of the same marketplace. The convergence has no fixed center, no reliable boundaries or settled outcomes. As enterprise opens up new territories, the maps keep changing—changing so rapidly that it has already become commonplace to speak of "one world" markets for everything from cars to capital. The earth's diverse societies are being rearranged and united in complicated ways by global capitalism. The idea evokes benumbed resignation among many. The complexity of it overwhelms. The enormity makes people feel small and helpless.

The essence of this industrial revolution, like others before it, is that commerce and finance have leapt inventively beyond the existing order and existing consciousness of peoples and societies. The global system of trade and production is fast constructing a new functional reality for most everyone's life, a new order based upon its own dynamics and not confined by the traditional social understandings. People may wish to turn away from that fact, but there is essentially no place to hide, not if one lives in any of the industrialized nations.

The only option people really have is to catch up with the reality. The only way to escape a sense of helplessness is to confront this new world on its own terms and try to understand its larger implications. The actual system, as we shall see, does not conform to the economic theory it presumes to follow. Nor are people and nations actually powerless to influence its behavior, as conventional wisdom asserts. But people and nations may restore a sense of control over their own destinies only if they are willing to face the complexity, only by grasping the operating imperatives that drive the global system and the full scope of human consequences that it yields.

Grasping the meaning of this new order requires one to set aside reflexive national loyalties in order to see the system whole. I have tried at least to do that. Above all, I avoid the standard nationalist complaints (most often aimed at Japan) that preoccupy so many books about the global economy, especially books written by Americans. (While I have tried to stand outside national identity and see things in a spirit of universality, I do not imagine for a moment that I have succeeded fully. Like most people, I am bound by culture and personal experience, by limitations of language and native biases, to one nation.)

The usual question—is America winning or losing?—can be disposed of quickly. The answer is yes. America is winning, and yes, it is losing. Some sectors of Americans are triumphant and other sectors are devastated, but not in equal measures. The same rough answer applies in differing degrees throughout most of the world, especially among the wealthiest nations— Germany, France or Britain, even Japan.

Books that nominate one country or another as "the winner" of global competition have a very short shelf life since these things change so rapidly. In 1992, a best-selling author heralded Europe, led by Germany, as the likely champion for its superior economic system; eighteen months later Europe and Germany were mired in gloomy forecasts from their own business leaders, complaining about their failure to keep up with American flexibility. Likewise, the United States has been written off and revived a number of times. Even Japan, so wealthy that many thought it had already won the race, is now experiencing its own tangible crisis of self-doubt.[3]

The obsession with nations in competition misses the point of what is happening: The global economy divides every society into new camps of conflicting economic interests. It undermines every nation's ability to maintain social cohesion. It mocks the assumption of shared political values that supposedly unite people in the nation-state.

That is the fundamental reason politics has become so muddled in the leading capitalist democracies. In recent years voters have turned on established parties and leaders, sometimes quite brutally, in the United States, Canada, Italy, France, Sweden and Japan, to name the most spectacular cases. Nor is there any ideological consistency to these voter rebellions. Socialists were tossed out in socialist Sweden, then restored to power a few years later. In a single election, the Conservative Party of Canada was reduced from governing majority to a remnant of two parliamentary seats. The business party that ruled Japan without interruption for four decades, the Liberal Democrats, was ousted by dissident reformers, then regained power in an unstable coalition of its own, this time led by a socialist.

Deeper political instability lies ahead for these societies because the global economy has put a different political question on the table: What exactly is the national interest in these new circumstances? No elected government in the richest countries, neither right nor left, has produced a definition that convinces its own electorate. Indeed, some important governments, clinging to the inherited postwar orthodoxy, are pursuing economic strategies that arguably do injury to majorities of their own citizens. This reflects not only the heavy hand of defunct theory, but also that insecure politicians do not know what else to do.

Political confusion in the dominant economies is set against a fundamental countervailing reality: For most people living in most parts of the world, the global economy began in 1492. In their history, the centuries of conquest and economic colonization were integral to the rise of industrial capitalism in Europe and North America, but the returns were never really shared with them. Books by Americans proclaiming "one world" may seem quite precious and self-centered to those people. For them, the global economy long ago consigned most regions of the world to lowly status as commodity producers—the hewers and haulers, the rubber tappers, tin miners and cane cutters. What William Faulkner said of the American South applies as well to those colonialized nations that used to be known as the Third

World: the past is never dead, it is not even past. (The global economy has a language problem: The old labels for categories of nations are confused or obsolete. "Third World," a condescending term coined for the Cold War, is not meaningless. Even the "West" is useless if it is meant to designate the advanced economies, since Japan is among them and booming Asia lies west of the United States, not east. We are reduced to cruder terms like rich and poor nations, advanced and primitive economies.)

From the perspective of most of these countries, the present industrial revolution is a rare opening in history, a chance to get out from under. Some of them are succeeding, climbing rapidly in wealth and establishing at least a fragile basis for national self-sufficiency. Dozens of others are trying to do the same. All of them approach the present with deep historical skepticism, the memory of how many times their aspirations were thwarted by the leading economic powers, how many previous openings turned out to be illusory.

When all the larger economic and political questions are exhausted, the heaviest legacy of this new "one world" may be the psychological blow to national arrogance. Americans reflexively think of themselves as without any real peers. Number One. In their own racialist ways so do the Japanese and the Germans. Tribal assumptions of inherited superiority are embedded in the cultures of the French and Chinese and Muslims, among many others. These folk illusions are now under vigorous assault, contradicted by the emerging economic reality.

During my travels I experienced certain small epiphanies: The amazement of watching a great modern industrial factory at work. The anguish of encountering exploited young people, peasant children turned into low-wage industrial workers, struggling to understand their own condition. The simple delight any tourist feels at glimpsing the weird variety of human life and also the underlying sameness.

The most powerful moments, however, were the recurring experience of witnessing poor people who dwell in marginal backwaters doing industrial work of the most advanced order. People of color, people who are black, yellow, red, brown, who exist in surroundings of primitive scarcity, are making complex things of world-class quality, mastering modern technologies that used to be confined to a select few. The tools of advanced civilization are being shared with other tribes. Multinational corporations, awesomely powerful and imperiously aloof, are the ironic vehicle for accomplishing this generous act of history.

The confident presumption that certain high-caliber work can be done only by certain people (mainly, it is assumed, by well-educated white people in a few chosen countries) is mistaken. Observing these scenes of industrial activity, I thought first of the explosive implications for the future of work and prosperity in the advanced economies, including America. The portents are stark and threatening. Yet the meaning also has to be understood in the broader sweep of human history. Watching former peasants making high-tech goods for the global market, I eventually reached a simpler, more nourishing understanding. Of course, I thought. People are capable, everywhere in the world.

Is it conceivable that commerce, pursuing narrow self-interested ends, might accomplish what idealistic politics has never been able to achieve—defeating stubborn ideas of racial superiority? I returned from my travels imagining it might someday be possible. Certainly, enormous conflicts lie ahead for the peoples of the world, political and economic collisions, possibly including the violence of wars between rival economies. Nevertheless, the process of globalization is visibly dismantling enduring stereotypes of race and culture, ancient assumptions of supremacy. This transformation will someday be understood as the most radical dimension of the revolution.

. . .

The raw energies of the global system, its power of excitement, can be glimpsed in the daily headlines about important business deals. Anheuser-Busch buys a stake in Kirin, Japan's biggest brewery, also a 5 percent share of China's Tsingtao, then acquires 10 percent of Antarctica, the leading beer of Brazil. Siemens of Germany forms a partnership with Skoda Plzen to manufacture steam turbines in the Czech Republic. Volvo opens an assembly line near Xian, China, with Chinese machinists making Swedish tour buses. Switzerland's Roche bids $5.3 billion for the U.S. pharmaceutical Syntex, while Smith-Kline Beecham buys another American company for $2.3 billion. NEC, the Japanese electronics giant, agrees to collaborate with Samsung, the Korean multinational, to make DRAM memory chips, probably at a plant in Portugal, to supply the $5 billion European market.

The problem, of course, is that the stories are too diverse and plentiful to make the motivating principles very clear. As the announcements of new ventures accumulate in breathtaking number, the effect is like the blur of a major blizzard. IBM announces quarterly losses of $8 billion and plans to cut 35,000 jobs. Bausch & Lomb begins making contact lenses and Ray-Ban sunglasses in India. Colgate-Palmolive opens a toothbrush factory in Colombia. AT&T forms an alliance with the national telephone companies of Sweden, Switzerland and the Netherlands; its American rival MCI pairs off with British Telecommunications.

Coca-Cola returns to Vietnam, this time without the U.S. military forces. Toyota picks Kentucky to make automobiles, BMW picks South Carolina, Mercedes picks Alabama. Ford and General Motors hope the Chinese government will pick them to make cars in China.[4]

John F. Welch, Jr., CEO of General Electric and widely admired for hardheaded corporate strategies, has warned fellow executives not to be lulled by self-congratulations or press clippings about how American companies have regained an edge over foreign competitors. "These things are going to get tougher," he predicted in mid-1994. "The shakeouts will be more brutal. The pace of change is more rapid." What lies ahead, Welch said, is "a hurricane."[5]

The accumulating evidence supports this warning. After two decades of dramatic changes the revolutionary pressures are not abating or leveling off into familiar patterns. The dynamics appear to be accelerating. What is the nature of the storm upon us? A new structure of power is gradually emerging in the world, forcing great changes everywhere it asserts itself. The broad dimensions are defined by a baseline of unsettling facts:

1. During the last generation the world's 500 largest multinational corporations have grown sevenfold in sales. Yet the worldwide employment of these global firms has remained virtually flat since the early 1970s, hovering around 26 million people. The major multinationals grew in sales from $721 billion in 1971 to $5.2 trillion in 1991, claiming a steadily growing share of commerce (one third of all manufacturing exports, three fourths of commodity trade, four fifths of the trade in technology and management services). Yet the human labor required for each unit of their output is diminished dramatically.

While this galaxy of major global firms grew in size, its center of gravity also shifted. America's flagship companies, from du Pont and IBM to GE and General Motors, were the modern progenitors of globalized manufacturing after World War II, but the United States has lost its dominance. In 1971, 280 of the largest 500 multinationals were American-based. By 1991, the United States had only 157 on the list.

Europe's largest companies surpassed America's in number and sales volume during the last half of the 1980s. By 1991, Europe had 168 of the largest 500. Japan, meanwhile, had risen in twenty years from 53 to 119. A few important multinational corporations have even emerged in countries that were once very poor—Korea, Taiwan, even Thailand. The corporate girth of nations is gradually dispersing, leveling out.[6]

2. The basic mechanism of globalization—companies investing capital in foreign countries, buying existing assets or building new factories—has accelerated explosively during the last fifteen years. The volume of direct foreign investment nearly quadrupled during the 1980s, reaching $2 trillion in the 1990s. The largest portion of that capital flow, about 25 percent, actually went into the United States during the 1980s, reversing the historic pattern. The United States became a debtor nation and sold off domestic assets to foreign investors; Japanese auto companies, among others, prudently located assembly plants in the States.[7]

Direct investing across borders cooled off for several years amid the major recessions of the early 1990s, but as it resumed the heaviest flows of capital were aimed in a different direction—building new production in the so-called emerging markets of Asia and selected nations in Latin America and Eastern Europe. Indeed, another historic relationship seemed broken: the utter dependence of poor nations on the prosperous. This time around, while the advanced economies remained stagnant or mired in recession, a league of poorer economies was enjoying a spectacular investment boom.

The growth of transnational corporate investments, the steady dispersal of production elements across many nations, has nearly obliterated the traditional understanding of trade. Though many of them know better, economists and politicians continue to portray the global trading system in terms that the public can understand—that is, as a collection of nations buying and selling things to each other. However, as the volume of world trade has grown, the traditional role of national markets is increasingly eclipsed by an alternative system: trade generated within the multinational companies themselves as they export and import among their own foreign-based subsidiaries.

According to one scholarly estimate, more than 40 percent of U.S. exports and nearly 50 percent of its imports are actually goods that travel not in the open marketplace, but through these intrafirm channels. A U.S. computer company ships design components to its assembly plant in Malaysia, then distributes the finished hardware back to the United States and to other buyers in Asia and Europe. A typical Japanese plant located in America "imports" most of its components from its parent corporation and allied suppliers, then "exports" products back to the parent in Japan or sister affiliates in other countries.[8]

All of this intrafirm traffic is counted in the national trade statistics, but national identities are increasingly irrelevant to the buyers and sellers. Nation-to-nation trade flows are driven more and more by the proprietary strategies of the multinational corporations organizing their own diversified production, less and less by traditional concepts of comparative advantage among nations or the economic policies of home governments.

The shifting content of trade has led many leading governments, including the one in Washington, to embrace a strategy that might confound some citizens (if it were explained to them clearly) because it seems to offend nationalist intuition. The governments are actively promoting the dispersal of capital investment and production to foreign locations on the assumption that this will lead to increased exports for home-based production (and more jobs for domestic workers). As the flagship multinationals make more things overseas, they will presumably ship more homemade goods to their overseas affiliates. That, anyway, is the logic governments embrace.

3. Finance capital—the trading of stocks, bonds, currencies, and more exotic forms of financial paper—has accelerated its movements around the world at an astonishing pace. International bank loans more than quadrupled from 1980 to 1991, reaching \$3.6 trillion. Global bond financing expanded likewise. Cross-border stockholdings in the so-called Triad—Europe, Japan and the United States—nearly doubled in a few years in the late 1980s.

The global exchange markets in national currencies—swapping dollars for yen or deutschemarks for francs or scores of other such trades—are moving faster still. Foreign-exchange trading totaled more than \$1.2 trillion a day by the early 1990s, compared to only \$640 billion a day as recently as 1989.

Since financial traders usually move in and out of different currencies in order to buy or sell a nation's stocks or bonds, this furious pace of currency exchange reflects the magnifying presence of borderless finance.

The entire global volume of publicly traded financial assets (about $24 trillion) turns over every twenty-four days. The International Monetary Fund, which attempts to monitor such matters, claims that this quickening pace is unexceptional since, it points out, the trading in U.S. government bonds is even faster. The entire traded volume of U.S. treasury debt ($2.6 trillion) turns over every eight days.[9]

Despite the staggering volume the financial trading across borders is mostly transacted by a very small community: the world's largest thirty to fifty banks and a handful of major brokerages that do the actual trades in behalf of investor clients—wealthy individuals and the various pools of private capital, smaller banks and brokerages, pension funds, mutual funds and so on—as well as the banks' own portfolios.

As the volume has swelled, the global financial markets have become much more powerful—and much more erratic. Sentiment and prices can shift suddenly and sharply, cascading losses across innocent bystanders like the multinational corporations that depend on predictable currency values for their cross-border trade or national governments that watch helplessly as global finance raises their domestic interest rates or devalues their currencies. "Crisis" has become an overworked word. Market economists speak more politely of "disturbances." These are the decisive breaks in prices that occur when global investors suddenly lose confidence in one investment sector or an entire country and abruptly shift huge amounts of capital elsewhere quick as the electronic impulses of modern banking.

To make sense out of these bewildering facts, it helps to think of the global system in cruder terms, as a galaxy of four broad, competing power blocs—each losing or gaining influence over events. The biggest, most obvious loser in these terms is labor, both the organized union workers and wage earners in general. Wages are both rising and falling around the world, but workers at both ends of the global economy have lost substantial control over their labor markets and the terms of employment. "Now capital has wings," as New York financier Robert A. Johnson explained succinctly. "Capital can deal with twenty labor markets at once and pick and choose among them. Labor is fixed in one place. So power has shifted."

National governments, likewise, have lost ground on the whole, partly because many have retreated from trying to exercise their power over commerce and finance, implicitly ceding to the revolutionary spirit. In the advanced economies, most governments have become mere salesmen, promoting the fortunes of their own multinationals in the hope that this will provide a core prosperity that keeps everyone afloat. The clearest evidence that this strategy is not working is the condition of labor markets in the wealthiest nations: either mass unemployment or declining real wages (nominal pay adjusted for inflation), and, in some cases, both of these deleterious effects.

The more subtle evidence of the dilemma of leading governments is their deteriorating fiscal condition: most are threatened by rising, seemingly permanent budget deficits and accumulating debt. The swollen fiscal deficits of the United States are the largest in size, but far from the worst in relative terms. The general fiscal crisis of rich nations is driven by the same fundamental—disappointing economic growth that, year after year, fails to generate the tax revenues needed to keep up with the public obligations established in more prosperous times. The modern welfare state, the social protections that rich nations enacted to ameliorate the harsh inequalities of industrial capitalism, is now in peril. Some would say it is already obsolete.

Ironically, the governments of developing countries, at least the most successful ones, are less enthralled by the global system's theory and rhetoric and more willing to impose their own terms on capital and trade. Given their own historical memory, poor countries attempt, if they can, to bargain with the system—making nationalistic trade-offs with global firms and investors. Some succeed; many are overwhelmed.

The multinational corporations are, collectively, the muscle and brains of this new system, the engineers who are designing the brilliant networks of new relationships. It is their success at globalization that has inevitably weakened labor and degraded the control of governments. Some smart organizations are even reconfiguring themselves into what business futurists have dubbed "the virtual corporation," a quick-witted company so dispersed that it resembles the ganglia of a nervous system, a brain attached to many distant nodes but without much bodily substance at the center.[10]

Despite their supple strengths the great multinationals are, one by one, insecure themselves. Even the most muscular industrial giants are quite vulnerable if they fail to adapt to the imperatives of reducing costs and improving rates of return. Critics who focus on the awesome size and sprawl of the global corporations find this point difficult to accept, but the executives of Volkswagen, GM, Volvo, IBM, Eastman Kodak and Pan American Airlines can attest to it. Those well-known firms, among many others, have experienced the harsh consequences of straying from the path of revolution. Their stocks were hammered, their managements ousted, tens of thousands of employees discarded. Behind corporate facades, the anxiety is genuine.

The Robespierre of this revolution is finance capital. Its principles are transparent and pure: maximizing the return on capital without regard to national identity or political and social consequences. Global finance collectively acts as the disinterested enforcer of these imperatives, like a Committee of Public Safety presiding over the Terror (though historians would note that Robespierre's revolutionaries pursued the opposite objective of reducing the great inequalities of wealth).

Financial investors monitor and punish corporations or whole industrial

sectors if their returns weaken. Finance disciplines governments or even entire regions of the globe if those places appear to be creating impediments to
profitable enterprise or unpleasant surprises for capital. If this sounds dicta-
torial, the global financiers also adhere to their own rough version of egalitarian values: they will turn on anyone, even their own home country's
industry and government, if the defense of free capital seems to require it.

As the Jacobins learned during the French Revolution, it is the most zealous, principled advocates of new values who are ultimately most at risk in a
revolutionary environment. Master financiers seem to appreciate this, too.
George Soros, the Hungarian-American billionaire who became fabulously
wealthy by grasping the new principles of global investing before others,
often emphasizes his own fallibility. In early 1994, when Soros got things
wrong, he lost $600 million during two days of brisk disturbance in global
bond markets. When Robespierre got things wrong, he was guillotined before a cheering mob in the Place de la Révolution.

Even the most powerful players—titans of finance or the multinationals
regularly demonized in popular lore—are themselves dwarfed by the system and subject to its harsh, overwhelming consequences. To describe the
power structure of the global system does not imply that anyone is in charge
of the revolution. The revolution runs itself. This point is critical to understanding its anarchic energies and oblivious disregard for parochial victims
or, for that matter, the seeming impotence of enterprises themselves to
control things. This revolution is following historical patterns of behavior
that industrial capitalism has reiterated across the centuries—an explosive
cycle of renewal, migration and destruction that is typically ignited by human invention.

NOTES

Author's Note: As these notes reflect, I have relied on many diverse sources, but none
was more valuable than the *Financial Times* of London. The *Financial Times* provides
an authoritative snapshot of action in the global economy every day, with superb reporting and analysis, much more comprehensive than anything published in the
United States.

1. The elephant population of Thailand has declined to 1,975 in the wild and 2,938
   domesticated animals, according to Rodney Tasker, *Far Eastern Economic Review,*
   April 29, 1993. Daily commuting time in Thailand is the longest in Asia, according
   to a survey of affluent consumers: *Far Eastern Economic Review,* August 27, 1992.
   Thai auto sales and traffic jams: Victor Mallet, *Financial Times,* November 27, 1993.
2. The Warsaw stock market crash: *Warsaw Voice,* April 24, 1994.
3. Economist Lester Thurow wrote as recently as 1992: "History and human nature
   tells us that it will be far easier for the Americans and the Japanese to avoid doing
   what they must do if they are to win. Future historians will record that the twenty-
   first century belonged to the House of Europe!" *Head to Head: Coming Economic
   Battles among Japan, Europe, and America* (New York: Morrow, 1992).
4. Anheuser-Busch: *Financial Times,* June 29 and July 30, 1993, and February 23, 1995;
   Siemens: *Financial Times,* July 21, 1993; Taiwan Aerospace: *Financial Times,* July 24,

1993; drug company mergers: *Financial Times,* May 4, 1994; NEC-Samsung: *Financial Times,* February 7, 1995; IBM losses: *Wall Street Journal,* July 28, 1993; Bausch & Lomb, Colgate-Palmolive: *Wall Street Journal,* August 4, 1993; AT&T: *Financial Times,* June 24, 1994; Coca-Cola: *Financial Times,* July 22, 1993.

5. John F. Welch, Jr., *Wall Street Journal,* June 21, 1994.

6. The 500 largest global firms are described in *Multinationals and the National Interest: Playing by Different Rules,* Office of Technology Assessment, U.S. Congress, September 1993. American firms still dominate among the largest, accounting for 7 of the 20 biggest multinationals, as ranked by foreign assets.

   The top 20 are, in order: Royal Dutch Shell (UK/Netherlands), Ford, GM, Exxon, IBM (U.S.), British Petroleum (UK), Asea Brown Boveri (Switzerland/Sweden), Nestlé (Switzerland), Philips Electronics (Netherlands), Mobil (U.S.), Unilever (UK, Netherlands), Matsushita Electric (Japan), Fiat (Italy), Siemens (Germany), Sony (Japan), Volkswagen (Germany), Elf Aquitaine (France), Mitsubishi (Japan), GE and du Pont (U.S.). Cited in "World Investment Report 1993: Transnational Corporations and Integrated International Production," United Nations, from *Financial Times,* July 21, 1993.

7. *Multinationals and National Interest,* OTA. The biggest owners of the $2 trillion in foreign productive assets continue to be U.S. firms, with a total of $474 billion, followed by Britain, $259 billion, and Japan, $251 billion: *Financial Times,* July 21, 1993.

8. The intrafirm trade patterns vary from country to country. For Japanese manufacturing, 51 percent of all exports from affiliates were to the parent companies or other sister affiliates in 1989, according to John H. Dunning, *Multinational Enterprises and the Global Economy* (Reading, MA: Addison-Wesley, 1993).

9. Bank lending growth is from the annual reports of the Bank for International Settlements. Other financial data is from "International Capital Markets, Part I," International Monetary Fund, 1993.

10. William H. Davidow and Michael S. Malone, *The Virtual Corporation: Structuring and Revitalizing the Corporation for the 21st Century* (New York: HarperCollins, 1992).

THE ECONOMY AND WORK

38

MANIFESTO OF THE COMMUNIST PARTY

KARL MARX • FRIEDRICH ENGELS

The economy and work are the focus of the next three readings. The first selection in this group is an excerpt from the classic "Manifesto of the Communist Party," written by Karl Marx and Friedrich Engels in 1848. Students often are surprised to discover the currency of many of the topics discussed by Marx and Engels. Specifically, Marx and Engels foresaw the rise of global capitalism. They also accurately described exploitive industrial conditions and the oppositional interests of workers and capitalists. Even though Marx and Engels are criticized for not foreseeing the rise of other social agents (such as the middle class, the government, and unions) in mediating the conflict between capitalists and workers, their theory of class struggle and revolution is still provocative and a source for worldwide social change.

The history of all hitherto existing society is the history of class struggles.

Freeman and slave, patrician and plebeian, lord and serf, guild-master and journeyman, in a word, oppressor and oppressed, stood in constant opposition to one another, carried on an uninterrupted, now hidden, now open fight, a fight that each time ended, either in a revolutionary reconstitution of society at large, or in the common ruin of the contending classes.

In the earlier epochs of history, we find almost everywhere a complicated arrangement of society into various orders, a manifold gradation of social rank. In ancient Rome we have patricians, knights, plebeians, slaves; in the Middle Ages, feudal lords, vassals, guild-masters, journeymen, apprentices, serfs; in almost all of these classes, again, subordinate gradations.

The modern bourgeois society that has sprouted from the ruins of feudal society has not done away with class antagonisms. It has but established new classes, new conditions of oppression, new forms of struggle in place of the old ones.

Our epoch, the epoch of the bourgeoisie, possesses, however, this distinctive feature: It has simplified the class antagonisms. Society as a whole is more

---

English translation by Friedrich Engels, 1888.

and more splitting up into two great hostile camps, into two great classes directly facing each other: Bourgeoisie and Proletariat.

From the serfs of the Middle Ages sprang the chartered burghers of the earliest towns. From these burgesses the first elements of the bourgeoisie were developed.

The discovery of America, the rounding of the Cape, opened up fresh ground for the rising bourgeoisie. The East-Indian and Chinese markets, the colonization of America, trade with the colonies, the increase in the means of exchange and in commodities generally, gave to commerce, to navigation, to industry, an impulse never before known, and thereby, to the revolutionary element in the tottering feudal society, a rapid development.

The feudal system of industry, under which industrial production was monopolized by closed guilds, now no longer sufficed for the growing wants of the new markets. The manufacturing system took its place. The guild-masters were pushed on one side by the manufacturing middle class; division of labour between the different corporate guilds vanished in the face of division of labour in each single workshop.

Meantime the markets kept ever growing, the demand ever rising. Even manufacture no longer sufficed. Thereupon, steam and machinery revolutionized industrial production. The place of manufacture was taken by the giant, Modern Industry, the place of the industrial middle class, by industrial millionaires, the leaders of whole industrial armies, the modern bourgeois.

Modern industry has established the world-market, for which the discovery of America paved the way. This market has given an immense development to commerce, to navigation, to communication by land. This development has, in its turn, reacted on the extension of industry; and in proportion as industry, commerce, navigation, railways extended, in the same proportion the bourgeoisie developed, increased its capital, and pushed into the background every class handed down from the Middle Ages.

We see, therefore, how the modern bourgeoisie is itself the product of a long course of development, of a series of revolutions in the modes of production and of exchange.

Each step in the development of the bourgeoisie was accompanied by a corresponding political advance of that class. An oppressed class under the sway of the feudal nobility, an armed and self-governing association in the mediaeval commune; here independent urban republic (as in Italy and Germany), there taxable "third estate" of the monarchy (as in France), afterwards, in the period of manufacture proper, serving either the semi-feudal or the absolute monarchy as a counterpoise against the nobility, and, in fact, corner-stone of the great monarchies in general, the bourgeoisie has at last, since the establishment of Modern Industry and of the world-market, conquered for itself, in the modern representative State, exclusive political sway. The execution of the modern State is but a committee for managing the common affairs of the whole bourgeoisie.

The bourgeoisie, historically, has played a most revolutionary part.

The bourgeoisie, wherever it has got the upper hand, has put an end to all feudal, patriarchal, idyllic relations. It has pitilessly torn asunder the motley feudal ties that bound man to his "natural superiors," and has left remaining no other nexus between man and man than naked self-interest, than callous "cash payment." It has drowned the most heavenly ecstasies of religious fervor, of chivalrous enthusiasm, of philistine sentimentalism, in the icy water of egotistical calculation. It has resolved personal worth into exchange value, and in place of the numberless indefeasible chartered freedoms, has set up that single, unconscionable freedom—Free Trade. In one word, for exploitation, veiled by religious and political illusions, it has substituted naked, shameless, direct, brutal exploitation.

The bourgeoisie has stripped of its halo every occupation hitherto honored and looked up to with reverent awe. It has converted the physician, the lawyer, the priest, the poet, the man of science, into its paid wage-labourers.

The bourgeoisie has torn away from the family its sentimental veil, and has reduced the family relation to a mere money relation.

The bourgeoisie has disclosed how it came to pass that the brutal display of vigor in the Middle Ages, which Reactionists so much admire, found its fitting complement in the most slothful indolence. It has been the first to show what man's activity can bring about. It has accomplished wonders far surpassing Egyptian pyramids, Roman aqueducts, and Gothic cathedrals; it has conducted expeditions that put in the shade all former Exoduses of nations and crusades.

The bourgeoisie cannot exist without constantly revolutionizing the instruments of production, and thereby the relations of production, and with them the whole relations of society. Conservation of the old modes of production in unaltered form, was, on the contrary, the first condition of existence for all earlier industrial classes. Constant revolutionizing of production, uninterrupted disturbance of all social conditions, everlasting uncertainty and agitation distinguish the bourgeois epoch from all earlier ones. All fixed, fast-frozen relations, with their train of ancient and venerable prejudices and opinions, are swept away, all new-formed ones become antiquated before they can ossify. All that is solid melts into air, all that is holy is profaned, and man is at last compelled to face with sober senses, his real conditions of life, and his relations with his kind.

The need of a constantly expanding market for its products chases the bourgeoisie over the whole surface of the globe. It must nestle everywhere, settle everywhere, establish connexions everywhere.

The bourgeoisie has through its exploitation of the world-market given a cosmopolitan character to production and consumption in every country. To the great chagrin of Reactionists, it has drawn from under the feet of industry the national ground on which it stood. All old-established national industries have been destroyed or are daily being destroyed. They are dislodged by new industries, whose introduction becomes a life and death question for all civilized nations, by industries that no longer work up indigenous raw material, but raw material drawn from the remotest zones; industries whose products are consumed, not only at home, but in every quarter of the globe. In place of the old wants, satisfied by the productions of the country, we find new wants, requiring for their satisfaction the products of distant lands and climes. In place of the old local and national seclusion and self-sufficiency, we have intercourse in every direction, universal inter-dependence of nations. And as in material, so also in intellectual production. The intellectual creations of individual nations become common property. National one-sidedness and narrow-mindedness become more and more impossible, and from the numerous national and local literatures, there arises a world literature.

The bourgeoisie, by the rapid improvement of all instruments of production, by the immensely facilitated means of communication, draws all, even the most barbarian, nations into civilization. The cheap prices of its commodities are the heavy artillery with which it batters down all Chinese walls, with which it forces the barbarians' intensely obstinate hatred of foreigners to capitulate. It compels all nations, on pain of extinction, to adopt the bourgeois mode of production; it compels them to introduce what it calls civilization into their midst, *i.e.*, to become bourgeois themselves. In one word, it creates a world after its own image.

The bourgeoisie has subjected the country to the rule of the towns. It has created enormous cities, has greatly increased the urban population as compared with the rural, and has thus rescued a considerable part of the population from the idiocy of rural life. Just as it has made the country dependent on the towns, so it has made barbarian and semi-barbarian countries dependent on the civilized ones, nations of peasants on nations of bourgeois, the East on the West.

The bourgeoisie keeps more and more doing away with the scattered state of the population, of the means of production, and of property. It has agglomerated population, centralized means of production, and has concentrated property in a few hands. The necessary consequence of this was political centralization. Independent, or but loosely connected provinces, with separate interests, laws, governments and systems of taxation, became lumped together into one nation, with one government, one code of laws, one national class-interest, one frontier and one customs-tariff.

The bourgeoisie, during its rule of scarce one hundred years, has created more massive and more colossal productive forces than have all preceding generations together. Subjection of Nature's forces to man, machinery, application of chemistry to industry and agriculture, steam-navigation, railways, electric telegraphs, clearing of whole continents for cultivation, canalization of rivers, whole populations conjured out of the ground—what earlier century had even a presentiment that such productive forces slumbered in the lap of social labour?

We see then: the means of production and of exchange, on whose foundation the bourgeoisie built itself up, were generated in feudal society. At a certain stage in the development of these means of production and of exchange, the conditions under which feudal society produced and exchanged, the feudal organization of agriculture and manufacturing industry, in one word, the feudal relations of property became no longer compatible with the already developed productive forces; they became so many fetters. They had to be burst asunder; they were burst asunder.

Into their place stepped free competition, accompanied by a social and political constitution adapted to it, and by the economical and political sway of the bourgeois class.

A similar movement is going on before our own eyes. Modern bourgeois society with its relations of production, of exchange and of property, a society that has conjured up such gigantic means of production and of exchange, is like the sorcerer, who is no longer able to control the powers of the nether world whom he has called up by his spells. For many a decade past the history of industry and commerce is but the history of the revolt of modern productive forces against modern conditions of production, against the property relations that are the conditions for the existence of the bourgeoisie and of its rule. It is enough to mention the commercial crises that by their periodical return put on its trial, each time more threateningly, the existence of the entire bourgeois society. In these crises a great part not only of the existing products, but also of the previously created productive forces, are periodically destroyed. In these crises there breaks out an epidemic that, in all earlier epochs, would have seemed an absurdity—the epidemic of overproduction. Society suddenly finds itself put back into a state of momentary barbarism; it appears as if a famine, a universal war of devastation had cut off the supply of every means of subsistence; industry and commerce seem to be destroyed; and why? Because there is too much civilization, too much means of subsistence, too much industry, too much commerce. The productive forces at the disposal of society no longer tend to further the development of the conditions of bourgeois property; on the contrary, they have become too powerful for these conditions, by which they are fettered, and so soon as they overcome these fetters, they bring disorder into the whole of bourgeois society, endanger the existence of bourgeois property. The conditions of bourgeois society are too narrow to comprise the wealth created by them. And how does the bourgeoisie get over these crises? On the one hand by enforced destruction of a mass of productive forces; on the other, by the conquest of new markets, and by the more thorough exploitation of the old ones. That is to say, by paving the way for more extensive and more destructive crises, and by diminishing the means whereby crises are prevented.

The weapons with which the bourgeoisie felled feudalism to the ground are now turned against the bourgeoisie itself.

But not only has the bourgeoisie forged the weapons that bring death to itself; it has also called into existence the men who are to wield those weapons—the modern working class—the proletarians.

In proportion as the bourgeoisie, *i.e.,* capital, is developed, in the same proportion is the proletariat, the modern working class, developed—a class of labourers, who live only so long as they find work, and who find work only so long as their labour increases capital. These labourers, who must sell themselves piece-meal, are a commodity, like every other article of commerce, and are consequently exposed to all the vicissitudes of competition, to all the fluctuations of the market.

Owing to the extensive use of machinery and to division of labour, the work of the proletarians has lost all individual character, and consequently, all charm for the workman. He becomes an appendage of the machine, and it is only the most simple, most monotonous, and most easily acquired knack, that is required of him. Hence, the cost of production of a workman is restricted, almost entirely, to the means of subsistence that he requires for his maintenance, and for the propagation of his race. But the price of a commodity, and therefore also of labour, is equal to its cost of production. In proportion, therefore, as the repulsiveness of the work increases, the wage decreases. Nay more, in proportion as the use of machinery and division of labour increases, in the same proportion the burden of toil also increases, whether by prolongation of the working hours, by increase of the work exacted in a given time or by increased speed of the machinery, etc.

Modern industry has converted the little workshop of the patriarchal master into the great factory of the industrial capitalist. Masses of labourers, crowded into the factory, are organised like soldiers. As privates of the industrial army they are placed under the command of a perfect hierarchy of officers and sergeants. Not only are they slaves of the bourgeois class, and of the bourgeois State; they are daily and hourly enslaved by the machine, by the over-looker, and, above all, by the individual bourgeois manufacturer himself. The more openly this despotism proclaims gain to be its end and aim, the more petty, the more hateful and the more embittering it is.

The less the skill and exertion of strength implied in manual labour, in other words, the more modern industry becomes developed, the more is the labour of men superseded by that of women. Differences of age and sex have no longer any distinctive social validity for the working class. All are instruments of labour, more or less expensive to use, according to their age and sex.

No sooner is the exploitation of the labourer by the manufacturer, so far, at an end, that he receives his wages in cash, than he is set upon by the other portions of the bourgeoisie, the landlord, the shopkeeper, the pawnbroker, etc.

39

WHEN WORK DISAPPEARS
The World of the New Urban Poor

WILLIAM JULIUS WILSON

This reading is an excerpt from William Julius Wilson's 1996 book, *When Work Disappears: The World of the New Urban Poor*. Here Wilson examines the effects joblessness and declining wages have had on inner-city neighborhoods in Chicago. Economic changes related to deindustrialization, the globalization of capitalism, and especially the decline of blue-collar jobs have contributed to the concentration of poverty in urban ghettos. In addition, Wilson analyzes other structural factors, such as residential segregation, demographic changes in the population, and local and federal policies that have contributed to the ghettoization of inner-city neighborhoods.

The disappearance of work in many inner-city neighborhoods is partly related to the nationwide decline in the fortunes of low-skilled workers. Although the growing wage inequality has hurt both low-skilled men and women, the problem of declining employment has been concentrated among low-skilled men. In 1987–89, a low-skilled male worker was jobless eight and a half weeks longer than he would have been in 1967–69. Moreover, the proportion of men who "permanently" dropped out of the labor force was more than twice as high in the late 1980s than it had been in the late 1960s. A precipitous drop in real wages—that is, wages adjusted for inflation—has accompanied the increases in joblessness among low-income workers. If you arrange all wages into five groups according to wage percentile (from highest to lowest), you see that men in the bottom fifth of this income distribution experienced more than a 30 percent drop in real wages between 1970 and 1989.

Even the low-skilled workers who are consistently employed face problems of economic advancement. Job ladders—opportunities for promotion within firms—have eroded, and many less-skilled workers stagnate in dead-end, low-paying positions. This suggests that the chances of improving one's earnings by changing jobs have declined: if jobs inside a firm have become less available to the experienced workers in that firm, they are probably even more difficult for outsiders to obtain.

But there is a paradox here. Despite the increasing economic marginality of low-wage workers, unemployment dipped below 6 percent in 1994 and early 1995, many workers are holding more than one job, and overtime work has reached a record high. Yet while tens of millions of new jobs have been created in the past two decades, men who are well below retirement age are working less than they did two decades ago—and a growing percentage are neither working nor looking for work. The proportion of male workers in the prime of their life (between the ages of 22 and 58) who worked in a given decade full-time, year-round, in at least eight out of ten years declined from 79 percent during the 1970s to 71 percent in the 1980s. While the American economy saw a rapid expansion in high technology and services, especially advanced services, growth in blue-collar factory, transportation, and con-struction jobs, traditionally held by men, has not kept pace with the rise in the working-age population. These men are working less as a result.

The growth of a nonworking class of prime-age males along with a larger number of those who are often unemployed, who work part-time, or who work in temporary jobs is concentrated among the poorly educated, the school dropouts, and minorities. In the 1970s, two-thirds of prime-age male workers with less than a high school education worked full-time, year-round, in eight out of ten years. During the 1980s, only half did so. Prime-age black men experienced a similar sharp decline. Seven out of ten of all black men worked full-time, year-round, in eight out of ten years in the 1970s, but only half did so in the 1980s. The figures for those who reside in the inner city are obviously even lower. . . .

Joblessness and declining wages are . . . related to the recent growth in ghetto poverty. The most dramatic increases in ghetto poverty occurred be-tween 1970 and 1980, and they were mostly confined to the large industrial metropolises of the Northeast and Midwest, regions that experienced mas-sive industrial restructuring and loss of blue-collar jobs during that decade. But the rise in ghetto poverty was not the only problem. Industrial restruc-turing had devastating effects on the social organization of many inner-city neighborhoods in these regions. The fate of the West Side black community of North Lawndale vividly exemplifies the cumulative process of economic and social dislocation that has swept through Chicago's inner city.

After more than a quarter century of continuous deterioration, North Lawndale resembles a war zone. Since 1960, nearly half of its housing stock has disappeared; the remaining units are mostly run-down or dilapidated. Two large factories anchored the economy of this West Side neighborhood in its good days—the Hawthorne plant of Western Electric, which employed over 43,000 workers; and an International Harvester plant with 14,000 work-ers. The world headquarters for Sears, Roebuck and Company was located there, providing another 10,000 jobs. The neighborhood also had a Copen-hagen snuff plant, a Sunbeam factory, and a Zenith factory, a Dell Farm food market, an Alden's catalog store, and a U.S. Post Office bulk station. But conditions rapidly changed. Harvester closed its doors in the late 1960s. Sears moved most of its offices to the Loop in downtown Chicago in 1973; a catalog distribution center with a workforce of 3,000 initially remained in the neighborhood but was relocated outside of the state of Illinois in 1987. The Hawthorne plant gradually phased out its operations and finally shut down in 1984.

The departure of the big plants triggered the demise or exodus of the smaller stores, the banks, and other businesses that relied on the wages paid by the large employers. "To make matters worse, scores of stores were forced out of business or pushed out of the neighborhoods by insurance companies in the wake of the 1968 riots that swept through Chicago's West Side after the assassination of Dr. Martin Luther King, Jr. Others were simply burned or abandoned. It has been estimated that the community lost 75 percent of its business establishments from 1960 to 1970 alone." In 1986, North Lawndale, with a population of over 66,000, had only one bank and one supermarket; but it was also home to forty-eight state lottery agents, fifty currency exchanges, and ninety-nine licensed liquor stores and bars.

The impact of industrial restructuring on inner-city employment is clearly apparent to urban blacks. The UPFLS [Chicago Urban Poverty and Family Life Survey] survey posed the following question: "Over the past five or ten years, how many friends of yours have lost their jobs because the place where they worked shut down—would you say none, a few, some, or most?" Only 26 percent of the black residents in our sample reported that none of their friends had lost jobs because their workplace shut down. Indeed, both black men and black women were more likely to report that their friends had lost jobs because of plant closings than were the Mexicans and the other ethnic groups in our study. Moreover, nearly half of the employed black fathers and mothers in the UPFLS survey stated that they considered themselves to be at high risk of losing their jobs because of plant shutdowns. Significantly fewer Hispanic and white parents felt this way.

Some of the inner-city neighborhoods have experienced more visible job losses than others. But residents of the inner city are keenly aware of the rapid depletion of job opportunities. A 33-year-old unmarried black male of North Lawndale who is employed as a clerical worker stated: "Because of the way the economy is structured, we're losing more jobs. Chicago is losing jobs by the thousands. There just aren't any starting companies here and it's harder to find a job compared to what it was years ago."

A similar view was expressed by a 41-year-old black female, also from North Lawndale, who works as a nurse's aide:

> *Chicago is really full of peoples. Everybody can't get a good job. They don't have enough good jobs to provide for everybody. I don't think they have enough jobs period. . . . And all the factories and the places, they closed up and moved out of the city and stuff like that, you know. I guess it's one of the reasons they haven't*

got too many jobs now, 'cause a lot of the jobs now, factories and business, they're done moved out. So that way it's less jobs for lot of peoples.

Respondents from other neighborhoods also reported on the impact of industrial restructuring. According to a 33-year-old South Side janitor:

The machines are putting a lot of people out of jobs. I worked for Time *magazine for seven years on a videograph printer and they come along with the Abedic printer, it cost them half a million dollars: they did what we did in half the time, eliminated two shifts.*

"Jobs were plentiful in the past," stated a 29-year-old unemployed black male who lives in one of the poorest neighborhoods on the South Side.

You could walk out of the house and get a job. Maybe not what you want but you could get a job. Now, you can't find anything. A lot of people in this neighborhood, they want ot work but they can't get work. A few, but a very few, they just don't want to work. The majority they want to work but they can't find work.

Finally, a 41-year-old hospital worker from another impoverished South Side neighborhood associated declining employment opportunities with decreasing skill levels:

Well, most of the jobs have moved out of Chicago. Factory jobs have moved out. There are no jobs here. Not like it was 20, 30 years ago. And people aren't skilled enough for the jobs that are here. You don't have enough skilled and educated people to fill them.

The increasing suburbanization of employment has accompanied industrial restructuring and has further exacerbated the problems of inner-city joblessness and restricted access to jobs. "Metropolitan areas captured nearly 90 percent of the nation's employment growth; much of this growth occurred in booming 'edge cities' at the metropolitan periphery. By 1990, many of these 'edge cities' had more office space and retail sales than the metropolitan downtowns." Over the last two decades, 60 percent of the new jobs created in the Chicago metropolitan area have been located in the northwest suburbs of Cook and Du Page counties. African-Americans constitute less than 2 percent of the population in these areas.

In *The Truly Disadvantaged* (1987), I maintained that one result of these changes for many urban blacks has been a growing mismatch between the suburban location of employment and minorities' residence in the inner city. Although studies based on data collected before 1970 showed no consistent or convincing effects on black employment as a consequence of this spatial mismatch, the employment of inner-city blacks relative to suburban blacks has clearly deteriorated since then. Recent research, conducted mainly by urban and labor economists, strongly shows that the decentralization of employment is continuing and that employment in manufacturing, most of which is already suburbanized, has decreased in central cities, particularly in the Northeast and Midwest. As Farrell Bloch, an economic and statistical consultant, points out, "Not only has the number of manufacturing jobs been decreasing, but new plants now tend to locate in the suburbs to take advantage of cheap land, access to highways, and low crime rates; in addition, businesses shun urban locations to avoid buying land from several different owners, paying high demolition costs for old buildings, and arranging parking for employees and customers."

Blacks living in central cities have less access to employment, as measured by the ratio of jobs to people and the average travel time to and from work, than do central-city whites. Moreover, unlike most other groups of workers across the urban/suburban divide, less educated central-city blacks receive lower wages than suburban blacks who have similar levels of education. And the decline in earnings of central-city blacks is related to the decentralization of employment—that is, the movement of jobs from the cities to the suburbs—in metropolitan areas.

But are the differences in employment between city and suburban blacks mainly the result of changes in the location of jobs? It is possible that in recent years the migration of blacks to the suburbs has become much more selective than in earlier years, so much so that the changes attributed to job location are actually caused by this selective migration. The pattern of black migration to the suburbs in the 1970s was similar to that of whites during the 1950s and 1960s in the sense that it was concentrated among the better-educated and younger city residents. However, in the 1970s this was even more true for blacks, creating a situation in which the education and income gaps between city and suburban blacks seemed to expand at the same time that the differences between city and suburban whites seemed to contract. Accordingly, if one were to take into account differences in education, family background, and so on, how much of the employment gap between city and suburbs would remain?

This question was addressed in a study of the Gautreaux program in Chicago. The Gautreaux program was created under a 1976 court order resulting from a judicial finding of widespread discrimination in the public housing projects of Chicago. The program has relocated more than 4,000 residents from public housing into subsidized housing in neighborhoods throughout the Greater Chicago area. The design of the program permitted the researchers, James E. Rosenbaum and Susan J. Popkin, to contrast systematically the employment experiences of a group of low-income blacks who had been assigned private apartments in the suburbs with the experience of a control group with similar characteristics and histories who had been assigned private apartments in the city. Their findings support the spatial mismatch hypothesis. After taking into account the personal characteristics of the respondents (including family background, family circumstances, levels of human capital, motivation, length of time since the respondent first enrolled in the Gautreaux program), Rosenbaum and Popkin found that those who moved to apartments in the suburbs were significantly more likely to have a job after the move than those placed in the city. When asked what makes it easier to obtain employment in the suburbs, nearly all the suburban respondents mentioned the high availability of jobs.

The African-Americans surveyed in the UPFLS clearly recognized a spatial mismatch of jobs. Both black men and black women saw greater job prospects outside the city. For example, only one-third of black fathers from areas with poverty rates of at least 30 percent reported that their best opportunities for employment were to be found in the city. Nearly two-thirds of whites and Puerto Ricans and over half of Mexicans living in similar neighborhoods felt this way. Getting to suburban jobs is especially problematic for the jobless individuals in the UPFLS because only 28 percent have access to an automobile. This rate falls even further to 18 percent for those living in the ghetto areas.

Among two-car middle-class and affluent families, commuting is accepted as a fact of life; but it occurs in a context of safe school environments for children, more available and accessible day care, and higher incomes to support mobile, away-from-home lifestyles. In a multitiered job market that requires substantial resources for participation, most inner-city minorities must rely on public transportation systems that rarely provide easy and quick access to suburban locations. A 32-year-old unemployed South Side welfare mother described the problem this way:

> There's not enough jobs. I thinks Chicago's the only city that does not have a lot of opportunities opening in it. There's not enough factories, there's not enough work. Most all the good jobs are in the suburbs. Sometimes it's hard for the people in the city to get to the suburbs, because everybody don't own a car. Everybody don't drive.

After commenting on the lack of jobs in his area, a 29-year-old unemployed South Side black male continued:

> You gotta go out in the suburbs, but I can't get out there. The bus go out there but you don't want to catch the bus out there, going two hours each ways. If you have to be at work at eight that mean you have to leave for work at six, that mean you have to get up at five to be at work at eight. Then when wintertime come you be in trouble.

Another unemployed South Side black male had this to say: "Most of the time . . . the places be too far and you need transportation and I don't have none right now. If I had some I'd probably be able to get one [a job]. If I had a car and went way into the suburbs, 'cause there ain't none in the city." This perception was echoed by an 18-year-old unemployed West Side black male:

> They are most likely hiring in the suburbs. Recently, I think about two years ago, I had a job but they say that I need some transportation and they say that the bus out in the suburbs run at a certain time. So I had to pass that job up because I did not have no transport.

An unemployed unmarried welfare mother of two from the West Side likewise stated:

> *Well, I'm goin' to tell you: most jobs, more jobs are in the suburbs. It's where the good jobs and stuff is but you gotta have transportation to get there and it's hard to be gettin' out there in the suburbs. Some people don't know where the suburbs is, some people get lost out there. It is really hard, but some make a way.*

One employed factory worker from the West Side who works a night shift described the situation this way:

> *From what I, I see, you know, it's hard to find a good job in the inner city 'cause so many people moving, you know, west to the suburbs and out of state. . . . Some people turn jobs down because they don't have no way of getting out there. . . . I just see some people just going to work—and they seem like they the type who just used to—they coming all the way from the city and go on all the way to the suburbs and, you know, you can see 'em all bundled and—catching one bus and the next bus. They just used to doing that.*

But the problem is not simply one of transportation and the length of commuting time. There is also the problem of the travel expense and of whether the long trek to the suburbs is actually worth it in terms of the income earned—after all, owning a car creates expenses far beyond the purchase price, including insurance, which is much more costly for city dwellers than it is for suburban motorists. "If you work in the suburbs you gotta have a car," stated an unmarried welfare mother of three children who lives on Chicago's West Side, "then you gotta buy gas. You spending more getting to the suburbs to work, than you is getting paid, so you still ain't getting nowhere."

Indeed, one unemployed 36-year-old black man from the West Side of Chicago actually quit his suburban job because of the transportation problem. "It was more expensive going to work in Naperville, transportation and all, and it wasn't worth it. . . . I was spending more money going to work than I earned working."

If transportation poses a problem for those who have to commute to work from the inner city to the suburbs, it can also hinder poor ghetto residents' ability to travel to the suburbs just to seek employment. For example, one unemployed man who lives on the South Side had just gone to O'Hare Airport looking for work with no luck. His complaint: "The money I spent yesterday, I coulda kept that in my pocket—I coulda kept that. 'Cause you know I musta spent $7 or somethin'. I coulda kept that."

Finally, in addition to enduring the search-and-travel costs, inner-city black workers often confront racial harassment when they enter suburban communities. A 38-year-old South Side divorced mother of two children who works as a hotel cashier described the problems experienced by her son and his coworker in one of Chicago's suburbs:

My son, who works in Caral Stream, an all-white community, they've been stopped by a policeman two or three times asking them why they're in the community. And they're trying to go to work. They want everyone to stay in their own place. That's what society wants. And they followed them all the way to work to make sure. 'Cause it's an all-white neighborhood. But there're no jobs in the black neighborhoods. They got to go way out there to get a job.

These informal observations on the difficulties and cost of travel to suburban employment are consistent with the results of a recent study by the labor economists Harry J. Holzer, Keith R. Ihlandfeldt, and David L. Sjoquist (1994). In addition to finding that the lack of automobile ownership among inner-city blacks contributed significantly to their lower wages and lower rate of employment, these authors also reported that African-Americans "spend more time traveling to work than whites," that "the time cost per mile traveled is . . . significantly higher for blacks," and that the resulting gains are relatively small. Overall, their results suggest that the amount of time and money spent in commuting, when compared with the actual income that accrues to inner-city blacks in low-skill jobs in the suburbs, acts to discourage poor people from seeking employment far from their own neighborhoods. Holzer and his colleagues concluded that it was quite rational for blacks to reject these search-and-travel choices when assessing their position in the job market.

Changes in the industrial and occupational mix, including the removal of jobs from urban centers to suburban corridors, represent external factors that have helped to elevate joblessness among inner-city blacks. But important social and demographic changes within the inner city are also associated with the escalating rates of neighborhood joblessness, and we shall consider these next.

The increase in the proportion of jobless adults in the inner city is also related to changes in the class, racial, and age composition of such neighborhoods—changes that have led to greater concentrations of poverty. Concentrated poverty is positively associated with joblessness. That is, when the former appears, the latter is found as well. As stated previously, poor people today are far more likely to be unemployed or out of the labor force than in previous years. In *The Truly Disadvantaged* (1987), I argue that in addition to the effects of joblessness, inner-city neighborhoods have experienced a growing concentration of poverty for several other reasons, including (1) the out-migration of nonpoor black families; (2) the exodus of nonpoor white and other nonblack families; and (3) the rise in the number of residents who have become poor while living in these areas. Additional research on the growth of concentrated poverty suggests another factor: the movement of poor people into a neighborhood (inmigration). And one more factor should be added to this mix: changes in the age structure of the community.

I believe that the extent to which any one factor is significant in explain-

ing the decrease in the proportion of nonpoor individuals and families depends on the poverty level and racial or ethnic makeup of the neighborhood
at a given time. . . .

One of the important demographic shifts that had an impact on the up-
turn in the jobless rate has been the change in the age structure of inner-city
ghetto neighborhoods. Let us . . . examine the three Bronzeville neighborhoods of Douglas, Grand Boulevard, and Washington Park. . . . [T]he proportion of those in the age categories (20–64) that roughly approximate the
prime-age workforce has declined in all three neighborhoods since 1950,
whereas the proportion in the age category 65 and over has increased. Of the
adults aged 20 and over, the proportion in the prime-age categories declined
by 17 percent in Grand Boulevard, 16 percent in Douglas, and 12 percent in
Washington Park between 1950 and 1990. The smaller the percentage of
prime-age adults in a population, the lower the proportion of residents who
are likely to be employed. The proportion of residents in the age category
5–19 increased sharply in each neighborhood from 1950 to 1990, suggesting
that the growth in the proportion of teenagers also contributed to the rise in
the jobless rate. However, if we consider the fact that male employment in
these neighborhoods declined by a phenomenal 46 percent between 1950 and
1960, these demographic changes obviously can account for only a fraction,
albeit a significant fraction, of the high proportion of the area's jobless adults.

The rise in the proportion of jobless adults in the Bronzeville neighborhoods has been accompanied by an incredible depopulation—a decline of
66 percent in the three neighborhoods combined—that magnifies the problems of the new poverty neighborhoods. As the population drops and the
proportion of nonworking adults rises, basic neighborhood institutions are
more difficult to maintain: stores, banks, credit institutions, restaurants, dry
cleaners, gas stations, medical doctors, and so on lose regular and potential
patrons. Churches experience dwindling numbers of parishioners and shrink-
ing resources; recreational facilities, block clubs, community groups, and
other informal organizations also suffer. As these organizations decline, the
means of formal and informal social control in the neighborhood become
weaker. Levels of crime and street violence increase as a result, leading to
further deterioration of the neighborhood.

The more rapid the neighborhood deterioration, the greater the institutional disinvestment. In the 1960s and 1970s, neighborhoods plagued by
heavy abandonment were frequently "redlined" (identified as areas that
should not receive or be recommended for mortgage loans or insurance);
this paralyzed the housing market, lowered property values, and further
encouraged landlord abandonment. The enactment of federal and state community reinvestment legislation in the 1970s curbed the practice of open redlining. Nonetheless, "prudent lenders will exercise increased caution in
advancing mortgages, particularly in neighborhoods marked by strong indication of owner disinvestment and early abandonment."

As the neighborhood disintegrates, those who are able to leave depart in increasing numbers; among these are many working- and middle-class families. The lower population density in turn creates additional problems. Abandoned buildings increase and often serve as havens for crack use and other illegal enterprises that give criminals footholds in the community. Precipitous declines in density also make it even more difficult to sustain or develop a sense of community. The feeling of safety in numbers is completely lacking in such neighborhoods.

Although changes in the economy (industrial restructuring and reorganization) and changes in the class, racial, and demographic composition of inner-city ghetto neighborhoods are important factors in the shift from institutional to jobless ghettos since 1970, we ought not to lose sight of the fact that this process actually began immediately following World War II.

The federal government contributed to the early decay of inner-city neighborhoods by withholding mortgage capital and by making it difficult for urban areas to retain or attract families able to purchase their own homes. Spurred on by massive mortgage foreclosures during the Great Depression, the federal government in the 1940s began underwriting mortgages in an effort to enable citizens to become homeowners. But the mortgage program was selectively administered by the Federal Housing Administration (FHA), and urban neighborhoods considered poor risks were redlined—an action that excluded virtually all the black neighborhoods and many neighborhoods with a considerable number of European immigrants. It was not until the 1960s that the FHA discontinued its racial restrictions on mortgages.

By manipulating market incentives, the federal government drew middle-class whites to the suburbs and, in effect, trapped blacks in the inner cities. Beginning in the 1950s, the suburbanization of the middle class was also facilitated by a federal transportation and highway policy, including the building of freeway networks through the hearts of many cities, mortgages for veterans, mortgage-interest tax exemptions, and the quick, cheap production of massive amounts of tract housing.

In the nineteenth and early twentieth centuries, with the offer of municipal services as an inducement, cities tended to annex their suburbs. But the relations between cities and suburbs in the United States began to change following a century-long influx of poor migrants who required expensive services and paid relatively little in taxes. Annexation largely ended in the mid-twentieth century as suburbs began to resist incorporation successfully. Suburban communities also drew tighter boundaries through the manipulation of zoning laws and discriminatory land-use controls and site-selection practices, making it difficult for inner-city racial minorities to penetrate.

As separate political jurisdictions, suburbs exercised a great deal of autonomy in their use of zoning, land-use policies, covenants, and deed restrictions. In the face of mounting pressures calling for integration in the 1960s, "suburbs chose to diversify by race rather than class. They retained zoning and other restrictions that allowed only affluent blacks (and in some instances Jews) to enter, thereby intensifying the concentration and isolation of the urban poor."

Other government policies also contributed to the growth of jobless ghettos, both directly and indirectly. Many black communities were uprooted by urban renewal and forced migration. The construction of freeway and highway networks through the hearts of many cities in the 1950s produced the most dramatic changes, as many viable low-income communities were destroyed. These networks not only encouraged relocation from the cities to the suburbs, "they also created barriers between the sections of the cities, walling off poor and minority neighborhoods from central business districts. Like urban renewal, highway and expressway construction also displaced many poor people from their homes."

Federal housing policy also contributed to the gradual shift to jobless ghettos. Indeed, the lack of federal action to fight extensive segregation against African-Americans in urban housing markets and acquiescence to the opposition of organized neighborhood groups to the construction of public housing in their communities have resulted in massive segregated housing projects. The federal public housing program evolved in two policy stages that represented two distinct styles. The Wagner Housing Act of 1937 initiated the first stage. Concerned that the construction of public housing might depress private rent levels, groups such as the U.S. Building and Loan League and the National Association of Real Estate Boards successfully lobbied Congress to require, by law, that for each new unit of public housing one "unsafe or unsanitary" unit of public housing be destroyed. As Mark Condon (1991) points out, "This policy increased employment in the urban construction market while insulating private rent levels by barring the expansion of the housing stock available to low-income families."

The early years of the public housing program produced positive results. Initially, the program mainly served intact families temporarily displaced by the Depression or in need of housing after the end of World War II. For many of these families, public housing was the first step on the road toward economic recovery. Their stay in the projects was relatively brief. The economic mobility of these families "contributed to the sociological stability of the first public housing communities, and explains the program's initial success."

The passage of the Housing Act of 1949 marked the beginning of the second policy stage. It instituted and funded the urban renewal program designed to eradicate urban slums. "Public housing was now meant to collect the ghetto residents left homeless by the urban renewal bulldozers." A new, lower-income ceiling for public housing residency was established by the federal Public Housing Authority, and families with incomes above that ceiling were evicted, thereby restricting access to public housing to the most economically disadvantaged segments of the population.

This change in federal housing policy coincided with the mass migration of African-Americans from the rural South to the cities of the Northeast and Midwest. Since smaller suburban communities refused to permit the construction of public housing, the units were overwhelmingly concentrated in the overcrowded and deteriorating inner city ghettos—the poorest and least socially organized sections of the city and the metropolitan area. "This growing population of politically weak urban poor was unable to counteract the desires of vocal middle- and working-class whites for segregated housing," housing that would keep blacks out of white neighborhoods. In short, public housing represents a federally funded institution that has isolated families by race and class for decades, and has therefore contributed to the growing concentration of jobless families in the inner-city ghettos in recent years.

Also, since 1980, a fundamental shift in the federal government's support for basic urban programs has aggravated the problems of joblessness and social organization in the new poverty neighborhoods. The Reagan and Bush administrations—proponents of the New Federalism—sharply cut spending on direct aid to cities, including general revenue sharing, urban mass transit, public service jobs and job training, compensatory education, social service block grants, local public works, economic development assistance, and urban development action grants. In 1980, the federal contribution to city budgets was 18 percent; by 1990 it had dropped to 6.4 percent. In addition, the economic recession which began in the Northeast in 1989 and lasted until the early 1990s sharply reduced those revenues that the cities themselves generated, thereby creating budget deficits that resulted in further cutbacks in basic services and programs along with increases in local taxes.

For many cities, especially the older cities of the East and Midwest, the combination of the New Federalism and the recession led to the worst fiscal and service crisis since the Depression. Cities have become increasingly underserviced, and many have been on the brink of bankruptcy. They have therefore not been in a position to combat effectively three unhealthy social conditions that have emerged or become prominent since 1980: (1) the prevalence of crack-cocaine addiction and the violent crime associated with it; (2) the AIDS epidemic and its escalating public health costs; and (3) the sharp rise in the homeless population not only for individuals but for whole families as well.

Although drug addiction and its attendant violence, AIDS and its toll on public health resources, and homelessness are found in many American communities, their impact on the ghetto is profound. These communities, whose residents have been pushed to the margins of society, have few resources with which to combat these social ills that arose in the 1980s. Fiscally strapped cities have watched helplessly as these problems—exacerbated by the new poverty, the decline of social organization in the jobless neighborhoods, and the reduction of social services—have made the city at large seem a dangerous and threatening place in which to live. Accordingly, working- and middle-class urban residents continue to relocate in the suburbs. Thus, while joblessness and related social problems are on the rise in inner-city neighborhoods, especially in those that represent the new poverty areas, the larger city has fewer and fewer resources with which to combat them.

Finally, policymakers indirectly contributed to the emergence of jobless ghettos by making decisions that have decreased the attractiveness of low-paying jobs and accelerated the relative decline in wages for low-income workers. In particular, in the absence of an effective labor-market policy, they have tolerated industry practices that undermine worker security, such as the reduction in benefits and the rise of involuntary part-time employment, and they have "allowed the minimum wage to erode to its second-lowest level in purchasing power in 40 years." After adjusting for inflation, "the minimum wage is 26 percent below its average level in the 1970s." Moreover, they virtually eliminated AFDC benefits for families in which a mother is employed at least half-time. In the early 1970s, a working mother with two children whose wages equaled 75 percent of the amount designated as the poverty line could receive AFDC benefits as a wage supplement in forty-nine states; in 1995 only those in three states could. . . . [E]ven with the expansion of the earned income tax credit (a wage subsidy for the working poor) such policies make it difficult for poor workers to support their families and protect their children. The erosion of wages and benefits forces many low-income workers in the inner city to move or remain on welfare.

REFERENCES

Condon, Mark. 1991. "Public Housing, Crime, and the Urban Labor Market: A Study of Black Youths in Chicago." Working paper series, Malcom Wiener Center for Social Policy, John F. Kennedy School of Government, Harvard University, March, no. H-91-3.

Holzer, Harry J., Keith R. Ihlanfeldt, and David L. Sjoquist. 1994. "Work, Search and Travel among White and Black Youth." *Journal of Urban Economics* 35:320–45.

Wilson, William Julius. 1987. *The Truly Disadvantaged: The Inner City, the Underclass, and Public Policy.* Chicago: University of Chicago Press.

40

OVER THE COUNTER
McDonald's

ROBIN LEIDNER

Robin Leidner's 1993 case study, "Over the Counter: McDonald's," takes us inside one employment organization and reveals what it is like to work there. Leidner shows how McDonald's employees are intensively socialized. She also illustrates how the work is reduced to simple steps, and therefore, routinized, so that managers and owners can maintain the most control over their product and over their employees. This process of increased routinization in the work place has a long history in industrialization, especially within factory work. Many social analysts, including Karl Marx (1818–1883), have argued that the routinization of work leads to workers feeling alienated from their products and from their sense of selves.

O rganizations have many ways of obtaining the cooperation of participants, ranging from persuasion and enticement to force and curtailment of options. All organizations "hope to make people want to do what the organization needs done" (Biggart 1989:128), but when they cannot count on success in manipulating people's desires they can do their best to compel people to act in the organization's interests.

Organizations choose strategies that rely on socialization and social control in varying mixtures that are determined by the aims of the organization, the constraints set by the organizational environment and the nature of the work, and the interests and resources of the parties involved. In service-providing organizations, upper-level management must concern itself with the wishes and behavior of service recipients and various groups of workers.[1] For each group, service organizations try to find the most effective and least costly ways to get people to act in the organizations' interests, proffering various carrots and sticks, making efforts to win hearts and minds, closing off choices.

Organizations that routinize work exert control primarily by closing off choices. There is much room for variation, however, in what aspects of the work organizations will choose to routinize, how they go about it, and how much freedom of decision making remains. Moreover, even when routines

From *Fast Food, Fast Talk: Service Work and the Routinization of Everyday Life*, pp. 44–46, 47–48, 49–52, 53–55, 57–58, 60, 65, 72–76, 82–85. Copyright © 1993 by The Regents of the University of California. Reprinted with the permission of University of California Press.

radically constrain choice, organizations still must socialize participants and set up systems of incentives and disincentives to ensure the compliance of workers and customers.

. . . McDonald's . . . take[s] routinization to extremes . . . includ[ing] predetermination of action and transformation of character . . . McDonald's stresses minute specification of procedures, eliminating most decision making for most workers, although it does make some efforts to standardize operations by transforming the characters of its store-level managers. . . .

This . . . [selection] show[s] how the compan[y's] approaches to routinizing the work of those who interact with customers depend largely on the predictability of service recipients' behavior, which in turn depends on the kinds of resources the organizations have available to channel consumer behavior. . . . At McDonald's . . . the routines sharply limit the workers' autonomy without giving them much leverage over customers.

McDonald's

No one ever walks into a McDonald's and asks, "So, what's good today?" except satirically. The heart of McDonald's success is its uniformity and predictability. Not only is the food supposed to taste the same every day everywhere in the world, but McDonald's promises that every meal will be served quickly, courteously, and with a smile. Delivering on that promise over 20 million times a day in 54 countries is the company's colossal challenge (*McDonald's Annual Report* for 1990:2). Its strategy for meeting that challenge draws on scientific management's most basic tenets: Find the One Best Way to do every task and see that the work is conducted accordingly.[2]

To ensure that all McDonald's restaurants serve products of uniform quality, the company uses centralized planning, centrally designed training programs, centrally approved and supervised suppliers, automated machinery and other specially designed equipment, meticulous specifications, and systematic inspections. To provide its customers with a uniformly pleasant "McDonald's experience," the company also tries to mass produce friendliness, deference, diligence, and good cheer through a variety of socialization and social control techniques. Despite sneers from those who equate uniformity with mediocrity, the success of McDonald's has been spectacular.

McFacts

By far the world's largest fast-food company, McDonald's has over 11,800 stores worldwide (*McDonald's Annual Report* for 1990:1), and its 1990 international sales surpassed those of its three largest competitors combined (Berg 1991 sec. 3:6).[3] In the United States, consumer familiarity with Mc-

Donald's is virtually universal: The company estimates that 95 percent of U.S. consumers eat at a McDonald's at least once a year (Koepp 1987:58). McDonald's 1990 profits were $802.3 million, the third highest profits of any retailing company in the world (*Fortune* 1991:179). At a time when the ability of many U.S. businesses to compete on the world market is in question, McDonald's continues to expand around the globe—most recently to Morocco—everywhere remaking consumer demand in its own image.

As politicians, union leaders, and others concerned with the effects of the shift to a service economy are quick to point out, McDonald's is a major employer. McDonald's restaurants in the United States employ about half a million people (Bertagnoli 1989:33), including one out of 15 first-time job seekers (Wildavsky 1989:30). The company claims that 7 percent of all current U.S. workers have worked for McDonald's at some time (Koepp 1987:59). Not only has McDonald's directly influenced the lives of millions of workers, but its impact has also been extended by the efforts of many kinds of organizations, especially in the service sector, to imitate the organizational features they see as central to McDonald's success.

. . .

The relentless standardization and infinite replication that inspire both horror and admiration are the legacy of Ray Kroc, a salesman who got into the hamburger business in 1954, when he was 52 years old, and created a worldwide phenomenon.[4] His inspiration was a phenomenally successful hamburger stand owned by the McDonald brothers of San Bernardino, California. He believed that their success could be reproduced consistently through carefully controlled franchises, and his hamburger business succeeded on an unprecedented scale. The basic idea was to serve a very few items of strictly uniform quality at low prices. Over the years, the menu has expanded somewhat and prices have risen, but the emphasis on strict, detailed standardization has never varied.

. . .

Enforcement of McDonald's standards has been made easier over the years by the introduction of highly specialized equipment. Every company-owned store in the United States now has an "in-store processor," a computer system that calculates yields and food costs, keeps track of inventory and cash, schedules labor, and breaks down sales by time of day, product, and worker (*McDonald's Annual Report* for 1989:29). In today's McDonald's, lights and buzzers tell workers exactly when to turn burgers or take fries out of the fat, and technologically advanced cash registers, linked to the computer system, do much of the thinking for window workers. Specially designed ketchup dispensers squirt exactly the right amount of ketchup on each burger in the approved flower pattern. The french-fry scoops let workers fill a bag and set it down in one continuous motion and help them gauge the proper serving size.

The extreme standardization of McDonald's products, and its workers, is closely tied to its marketing. The company advertises on a massive scale— in 1989, McDonald's spent $1.1 billion systemwide on advertising and promotions (*McDonald's Annual Report* for 1989:32). In fact, McDonald's is the single most advertised brand in the world (*Advertising Age* 1990:6).[5] The national advertising assures the public that it will find high standards of quality, service, and cleanliness at every McDonald's store. The intent of the strict quality-control standards applied to every aspect of running a McDonald's outlet, from proper cleaning of the bathrooms to making sure the hamburgers are served hot, is to help franchise owners keep the promises made in the company's advertising.[6]

The image of McDonald's outlets promoted in the company's advertising is one of fun, wholesomeness, and family orientation. Kroc was particularly concerned that his stores not become teenage hangouts, since that would discourage families' patronage. To minimize their attractiveness to teenage loiterers, McDonald's stores do not have jukeboxes, video games, or even telephones. Kroc initially decided not to hire young women to work behind McDonald's counters for the same reason: "They attracted the wrong kind of boys" (Boas and Chain 1976:19).

You Deserve a Break Today: Conditions of Employment

Although McDonald's does not want teenagers to hang out on its premises, it certainly does want them to work in the stores. Almost half of its U.S. employees are under 20 years old (Wildavsky 1989:30). In recent years, as the McDonald's chain has grown faster than the supply of teenagers, the company has also tried to attract senior citizens and housewives as workers. What people in these groups have in common is a preference or need for part-time work, and therefore a dearth of alternative employment options. Because of this lack of good alternatives, and because they may have other means of support for themselves and their dependents, many people in these groups are willing to accept jobs that provide less than subsistence wages.

Traditionally, McDonald's has paid most of its employees the minimum wage, although labor shortages have now forced wages up in some parts of the country, raising the average hourly pay of crew people to $4.60 by 1989 (Gibson and Johnson 1989:B1). Benefits such as health insurance and sick days are entirely lacking for crew people at most franchises. In fact, when the topic of employee benefits was introduced in a class lecture at McDonald's management training center, it turned out to refer to crew meetings, individual work-evaluation sessions, and similar programs to make McDonald's management seem accessible and fair.

The lack of more tangible benefits is linked to the organization of employment at McDonald's as part-time work. According to the manager of the franchise I studied, all McDonald's hourly employees are officially part-time workers, in that no one is guaranteed a full work week. The company's labor practices are designed to make workers bear the costs of uncertainty based on fluctuation in demand. McDonald's places great emphasis on having no more crew people at work at any time than are required by customer flow at that period, as measured in half-hour increments. Most workers therefore have fluctuating schedules, and they are expected to be flexible about working late or leaving early depending on the volume of business.

Not surprisingly, McDonald's employee-turnover rates are extremely high. Turnover averaged 153 percent in 1984, and 205 percent in 1985 (training center lecture). These high rates are partly attributable to the large percentage of teenage workers, many of whom took the job with the intention of working for only a short time. However, the limited job rewards, both financial and personal, of working at McDonald's are certainly crucial contributing factors.

Some argue that the conditions of employment at McDonald's are unproblematic to the workers who take them. If we assume that most McDonald's workers are teenagers who are in school and are not responsible for supporting themselves or others, then many of the features of McDonald's work do not seem so bad. Fringe benefits and employment security are relatively unimportant to them, and the limited and irregular hours of work may actually be attractive (see Greenberger and Steinberg 1986). These arguments are less persuasive when applied to other McDonald's employees, such as mothers of young children, and retirees, although those workers might similarly appreciate the part-time hours, and access to other forms of income and benefits could make McDonald's employment conditions acceptable, if not desirable. Employment security would not be important to the many people who choose to work at McDonald's as a stopgap or for a limited period.[7] Many of the workers at the franchise I studied had taken their jobs with the intention of holding them only temporarily, and many were being supported by their parents. However, other workers there were trying to support themselves and their dependents on earnings from McDonald's, sometimes in combination with other low-paying jobs.

. . .

McDonald's wants both managers and workers to dedicate themselves to the values summed up in its three-letter corporate credo, "QSC." Quality, service, and cleanliness are the ends that the company's thousands of rules and specifications are intended to achieve. Kroc promised his customers QSC,[8] and he believed firmly that if, at every level of the organization, McDonald's workers were committed to providing higher-quality food, speedier service, and cleaner surroundings than the competition, the success of the enterprise was assured. McDonald's extraordinarily elaborate training programs are designed both to teach McDonald's procedures and standards and to instill and enforce corporate values.

Kroc approached his business with a zeal and dedication that even he regarded as religious: "I've often said that *I believe in God, family, and McDonald's—and in the office that order is reversed*" (Kroc with Anderson 1977:124 [emphasis in the original]). Throughout the organization, Kroc is still frequently quoted and held up as a model, and nowhere is his ongoing influence more apparent than at Hamburger University.

Taking Hamburgers Seriously: Training Managers

McDonald's main management training facility is located on 80 beautifully landscaped acres in Oak Brook, Illinois, a suburb of Chicago. Its name, Hamburger University, captures the thoroughness and intensity with which McDonald's approaches management training, and it also suggests the comic possibilities of immersion in McDonald's corporate world.[9] The company tries to produce managers "with ketchup in their veins," a common McDonald's phrase for people who love their work, take pride in it, and are extraordinarily hardworking, competitive, and loyal to McDonald's. A line I heard frequently at Hamburger U. was, "We take hamburgers very seriously here." Nothing I saw called this fixity of purpose into doubt.

Ensuring uniformity of service and products in its far-flung empire is a major challenge for McDonald's. In each McDonald's store, in regional training centers, and at Hamburger University, crew people, managers, and franchisees learn that there is a McDonald's way to handle virtually every detail of the business, and that doing things differently means doing things wrong. Training begins in the stores, where crew people are instructed using materials provided by the corporation, and where managers prepare for more advanced training. Management trainees and managers seeking promotion work with their store managers to learn materials in manuals and workbooks provided by the corporation. When they have completed the manual for the appropriate level, they are eligible for courses taught in regional training centers and at Hamburger University: the Basic Operations Course, the Intermediate Operations Course, the Applied Equipment Course, and, finally, the Advanced Operations Course, taught only at Hamburger University. Altogether, the full training program requires approximately six hundred to one thousand hours of work. It is required of everyone who wishes to own a McDonald's store, and it is strongly recommended for all store managers. By the time trainees get to Hamburger University for the Advanced Operations Course, they have already put in considerable time working in a McDonald's store—two to three and a half years, on average—and have acquired much detailed knowledge about McDonald's workings.

Hamburger University sometimes offers special programs and seminars in addition to the regular training courses. For example, a group of McDonald's office workers attended Hamburger University during my visit; a training manager told me that they had been brought in to get "a little shot of ketchup and mustard." [10]

The zeal and competence of franchisees and managers are of special concern to McDonald's, since they are the people responsible for daily enforcement of corporate standards. Their training therefore focuses as much on building commitment and motivation as on extending knowledge of company procedures. In teaching management skills, McDonald's also works on the personalities of its managers, encouraging both rigid adherence to routines and, somewhat paradoxically, personal flexibility. Flexibility is presented as a virtue both because the company wants to minimize resistance to adopting McDonald's ways of doing things and to frequent revision of procedures, and because managers must provide whatever responsiveness to special circumstances the system has, since crew people are allowed virtually no discretion. Hamburger University therefore provides a large dose of personal-growth cheerleading along with more prosaic skills training.

. . .

The curriculum of the Advanced Operating Course includes inculcation with pride in McDonald's. Sessions are devoted to McDonald's history and McDonald's dedication to ever-improving QSC. Lectures are sprinkled with statistics attesting to McDonald's phenomenal success. Students hear the story of Ray Kroc's rise to wealth and prominence, based on his strength of character and willingness to work hard, and are assigned his autobiography, *Grinding It Out* (Kroc with Anderson 1977). Kroc is quoted frequently in lectures, and students are encouraged to model themselves on him. They are told repeatedly that they have all proven themselves "winners" by getting as far as they have at McDonald's. The theme throughout is, "We're the best in the world, we know exactly what we're doing, but our success depends on the best efforts of every one of you." [11]

About 3,500 students from all over the world attend classes at Hamburger University each year, most of them taking the Advanced Operations Course (Rosenthal 1989). Those who complete the course receive diplomas proclaiming them Doctors of Hamburgerology. As late as 1978 or 1979, a training manager told me, most classes included only one or two women, but women now comprise 40 – 60 percent of the students, and women and minorities now make up 54 percent of McDonald's franchisees (Bertagnoli 1989:33). In my homeroom, however, the proportion of women was much smaller, and there was just a handful of minority students.

The course lasts two weeks and is extremely rigorous. Class time is about evenly divided between work in the labs and lectures on store operations and personnel management. In the labs, trainees learn the mechanics of ensuring that McDonald's food is of consistent quality and its stores in good working order. They learn to check the equipment and maintain it properly so that fries cook at precisely the right temperature, shakes are mixed to just the right consistency, and ice cubes are uniform. "Taste of Quality" labs reinforce McDonald's standards for food quality. For instance, in a Condiments Lab, trainees are taught exactly how to store vegetables and sauces, what the shelf lives of these products are, and how they should look and taste. Samples of "McDonald's quality" Big Mac Special Sauce are contrasted with samples that have been left too long unrefrigerated and should be discarded. The importance of serving only food that meets McDonald's standards is constantly emphasized and, a trainer pointed out, "McDonald's has standards for everything, down to the width of the pickle slices."

. . .

The training at Hamburger University combines a sense of fun with dead seriousness about keeping McDonald's on top in the hamburger business through relentless quality control and effective management of workers and customers. It is up to the owners and managers of individual McDonald's stores to make that happen.

. . .

Learning the Job

As a manager at Hamburger University explained to me, the crew training process is how McDonald's standardization is maintained, how the company ensures that Big Macs are the same everywhere in the world. The McDonald's central administration supplies franchisees with videotapes and other materials for use in training workers to meet the company's exacting specifications. The company produces a separate videotape for each job in the store, and it encourages franchisees to keep their tape libraries up-to-date as product specifications change. The Hamburger University professor who taught the Advanced Operating Course session on training said that, to keep current, franchisees should be buying 10 or 12 tapes a year. For each work station in the store McDonald's also has a "Station Operation Checklist" (SOC), a short but highly detailed job description that lays out exactly how the job should be done: how much ketchup and mustard go on each kind of hamburger, in what sequence the products customers order are to be gathered, what arm motion is to be used in salting a batch of fries, and so on.

. . .

The Routine

McDonald's had routinized the work of its crews so thoroughly that decision making had practically been eliminated from the jobs. As one window worker told me, "They've tried to break it down so that it's almost idiot-proof." Most of the workers agreed that there was little call for them to use their own judgment on the job, since there were rules about everything. If an unusual problem arose, the workers were supposed to turn it over to a manager.

Many of the noninteractive parts of the window workers' job had been made idiot-proof through automation.[12] The soda machines, for example, automatically dispensed the proper amount of beverage for regular, medium, and large cups. Computerized cash registers performed a variety of functions handled elsewhere by human waitresses, waiters, and cashiers, making some kinds of skill and knowledge unnecessary. As a customer gave an order, the window worker simply pressed the cash register button labeled with the name of the selected product. There was no need to write the orders down, because the buttons lit up to indicate which products had been selected. Nor was there any need to remember prices, because the prices were programmed into the machines. Like most new cash registers, these added the tax automatically and told workers how much change customers were owed, so the window crew did not need to know how to do those calculations. The cash registers also helped regulate some of the crew's interactive work by reminding them to try to increase the size of each sale. For example, when a customer ordered a Big Mac, large fries, and a regular Coke, the cash register buttons for cookies, hot apple pies, ice cream cones, and ice cream sundaes would light up, prompting the worker to suggest dessert. It took some skill to operate the relatively complicated cash register, as my difficulties during my first work shift made clear, but this organizationally specific skill could soon be acquired on the job.

In addition to doing much of the workers' thinking for them, the computerized cash registers made it possible for managers to monitor the crew members' work and the store's inventory very closely.[13] For example, if the number of Quarter Pounder with Cheese boxes gone did not match the number of Quarter Pounders with Cheese sold or accounted for as waste, managers might suspect that workers were giving away or taking food. Managers could easily tell which workers had brought in the most money during a given interval and who was doing the best job of persuading customers to buy a particular item. The computerized system could also complicate what would otherwise have been simple customer requests, however. For example, when a man who had not realized the benefit of ordering his son's food as a Happy Meal came back to the counter to ask whether his little boy could have one of the plastic beach pails the Happy Meals were served in, I had to ask a manager what to do, since fulfilling the request would produce a discrepancy between the inventory and the receipts.[14] Sometimes the extreme systematization can induce rather than prevent idiocy, as when a window worker says she cannot serve a cup of coffee that is half decaffeinated and half regular because she would not know how to ring up the sale.[15]

The interactive part of window work is routinized through the Six Steps of Window Service and also through rules aimed at standardizing attitudes and demeanors as well as words and actions. The window workers were taught that they represented McDonald's to the public and that their attitudes were therefore an important component of service quality. Crew people could be reprimanded for not smiling, and often were. The window workers were supposed to be cheerful and polite at all times, but they were also told to be themselves while on the job. McDonald's does not want its workers to seem like robots, so part of the emotion work asked of the window crew is that they act naturally. "Being yourself" in this situation meant behaving in a way that did not seem stilted. Although workers had some latitude to go beyond the script, the short, highly schematic routine obviously did not allow much room for genuine self-expression.

Workers were not the only ones constrained by McDonald's routines, of course. The cooperation of service recipients was crucial to the smooth functioning of the operation. In many kinds of interactive service work . . . constructing the compliance of service recipients is an important part of the service worker's job. The routines such workers use may be designed to maximize the control each worker has over customers. McDonald's window workers' routines were not intended to give them much leverage over customers' behavior, however. The window workers interacted only with people who had already decided to do business with McDonald's and who therefore did not need to be persuaded to take part in the service interaction. Furthermore, almost all customers were familiar enough with McDonald's routines to know how they were expected to behave. For instance, I never saw a customer who did not know that she or he was supposed to come up to the counter rather than sit down and wait to be served. This customer training was accomplished through advertising, spatial design, customer experience, and the example of other customers, making it unnecessary for the window crew to put much effort into getting customers to fit into their work routines.[16]

McDonald's ubiquitous advertising trains consumers at the same time that it tries to attract them to McDonald's. Television commercials demonstrate how the service system is supposed to work and familiarize customers with new products. Additional cues about expected customer behavior are provided by the design of the restaurants. For example, the entrances usually lead to the service counter, not to the dining area, making it unlikely that customers will fail to realize that they should get in line, and the placement of waste cans makes clear that customers are expected to throw out their own trash. Most important, the majority of customers have had years of experience with McDonald's, as well as with other fast-food restaurants that have similar arrangements. The company estimates that the average customer visits a McDonald's 20 times a year (Koepp 1987:58), and it is not uncommon for a customer to come in several times per week. For many customers, then, ordering at McDonald's is as routine an interaction as it is for the window worker. Indeed, because employee turnover is so high, steady customers may be more familiar with the work routines than the workers serving them are.

Customers who are new to McDonald's can take their cue from more experienced customers.[17]

Not surprisingly, then, most customers at the McDonald's I studied knew what was expected of them and tried to play their part well. They sorted themselves into lines and gazed up at the menu boards while waiting to be served. They usually gave their orders in the conventional sequence: burgers or other entrees, french fries or other side orders, drinks, and desserts. Hurried customers with savvy might order an item "only if it's in the bin," that is, ready to be served. Many customers prepared carefully so that they could give their orders promptly when they got to the counter. This preparation sometimes became apparent when a worker interrupted to ask, "What kind of dressing?" or "Cream and sugar?", flustering customers who could not deliver their orders as planned.

McDonald's routines, like those of other interactive service businesses, depend on the predictability of customers, but these businesses must not grind to a halt if customers are not completely cooperative. Some types of deviations from standard customer behavior are so common that they become routine themselves, and these can be handled through subroutines (Stinchcombe 1990:39). McDonald's routines work most efficiently when all customers accept their products exactly as they are usually prepared; indeed, the whole business is based on this premise. Since, however, some people give special instructions for customized products, such as "no onions," the routine allows for these exceptions.[18] At the franchise I studied, workers could key the special requests into their cash registers, which automatically printed out "grill slips" with the instructions for the grill workers to follow. Under this system, the customer making the special order had to wait for it to be prepared, but the smooth flow of service for other customers was not interrupted. Another type of routine difficulty was customer dissatisfaction with food quality. Whenever a customer had a complaint about the food—cold fries, dried-out burger—window workers were authorized to supply a new product immediately without consulting a supervisor.[19]

These two kinds of difficulties—special orders and complaints about food—were the only irregularities window workers were authorized to handle. The subroutines increased the flexibility of the service system, but they did not increase the workers' discretion, since procedures were in place for dealing with both situations. All other kinds of demands fell outside the window crew's purview. If they were faced with a dispute about money, an extraordinary request, or a furious customer, workers were instructed to call a manager; the crew had no authority to handle such problems.

Given the almost complete regimentation of tasks and preemption of decision making, does McDonald's need the flexibility and thoughtfulness of human workers? As the declining supply of teenagers and legislated increases in the minimum wage drive up labor costs, it is not surprising that McDonald's is experimenting with electronic replacements. So far, the only robot in use handles behind-the-scenes work rather than customer interactions. ARCH (Automated Restaurant Crew Helper) works in a Minnesota McDonald's where it does all the frying and lets workers know when to prepare sandwich buns, when supplies are running low, and when fries are no longer fresh enough to sell. Other McDonald's stores (along with Arby's and Burger King units) are experimenting with a touch-screen computer system that lets customers order their meals themselves, further curtailing the role of the window worker. Although it requires increased customer socialization and cooperation, early reports are that the system cuts service time by 30 seconds and increases sales per window worker 10–20 percent (Chaudhry 1989:F61).

Overview

McDonald's pioneered the routinization of interactive service work and remains an exemplar of extreme standardization. Innovation is not discouraged at McDonald's; the company favors experimentation, at least among managers and franchisees. Ironically, though, "the object is to look for new, innovative ways to create an experience that is exactly the same no matter what McDonald's you walk into, no matter where it is in the world" (Rosenthal 1989:12). Thus, when someone in the field comes up with a good idea— and such McDonald's success stories as the Egg McMuffin and the Big Mac were store-level inspirations (Koepp 1987:60)—the corporation experiments, tests, and refines the idea and finally implements it in a uniform way systemwide. One distinctive feature of McDonald's-style routinization is that there, to a great extent, uniformity is a goal in itself.

. . .

McDonald's . . . does promise uniform products and consistent service, and to provide them the company has broken down virtually every task required to run a store into detailed routines with clear instructions and standards. For those routines to run smoothly, conditions must be relatively predictable, so McDonald's tries to control as many contingencies as possible, including the attitudes and behavior of workers, managers, and customers. The company uses a wide array of socialization and control techniques to ensure that these people are familiar with McDonald's procedures and willing to comply with them.

Most McDonald's work is organized as low-paying, low-status, part-time jobs that give workers little autonomy. Almost every decision about how to do crew people's tasks has been made in advance by the corporation, and many of the decisions have been built into the stores' technology. Why use human workers at all, if not to take advantage of the human capacity to respond to circumstances flexibly? McDonald's does want to provide at least a simulacrum of the human attributes of warmth, friendliness, and recognition. For that reason, not only workers' movements but also their words, demeanor, and attitudes are subject to managerial control.

Although predictability is McDonald's hallmark, not all factors can be controlled by management. One of the most serious irregularities that store management must deal with is fluctuation in the flow of customers, both expected and unexpected. Since personnel costs are the most manipulable variable affecting a store's profitability, managers want to match labor power to consumer demand as exactly as possible. They do so by paying all crew people by the hour, giving them highly irregular hours based on expected sales—sometimes including split shifts—and sending workers home early or keeping them late as conditions require. In other words, the costs of uneven demand are shifted to workers whenever possible. Since most McDonald's crew people cannot count on working a particular number of hours at precisely scheduled times, it is hard for them to make plans based on how much money they will earn or exactly what times they will be free. Workers are pressured to be flexible in order to maximize the organization's own flexibility in staffing levels. In contrast, of course, flexibility in the work process itself is minimized.

Routinization has not made the crew people's work easy. Their jobs, although highly structured and repetitive, are often demanding and stressful. Under these working conditions, the organization's limited commitment to workers, as reflected in job security, wages, and benefits, makes the task of maintaining worker motivation and discipline even more challenging. A variety of factors, many orchestrated by the corporation, keeps McDonald's crew people hard at work despite the limited rewards. Socialization into McDonald's norms, extremely close supervision (both human and electronic), individual and group incentives, peer pressure, and pressure from customers all play their part in getting workers to do things the McDonald's way.

Because franchisees and store-level managers are responsible for enforcing standardization throughout the McDonald's system, their socialization includes a more intensive focus on building commitment to and pride in the organization than does crew training. In fact, it is the corporate attempt at transforming these higher-level McDonald's people by making them more loyal, confident, flexible, and sensitive to others, as well as more knowledgeable about company procedures, that makes the extreme rigidity of the crew training workable. The crew people do not have to be trusted with decision-making authority, because all unusual problems are referred to managers. Their more extensive training gives them the knowledge and attitudes to make the kinds of decisions the corporation would approve. . . . In addition to thorough socialization, McDonald's managers and franchisees are subjected to close corporate oversight. Every aspect of their stores' operations is rated by corporate staff, and they are sanctioned accordingly.

Despite elaborate socialization and social controls, McDonald's stores do not, of course, carry out every corporate directive exactly as recommended. In the store I studied, managers did not always provide their workers with the mandated support and encouragement, crew trainers did not always follow the four-step training system, and window workers did not always carry out the Six Steps of Window Service with the required eye contact and smile. There were many kinds of pressures to deviate from corporate standards. Nonetheless, the benefits of standardization should not be underestimated. As every Durkheimian knows, clear rules and shared standards provide support and coherence as well as constraint. Although some aspects of the routines did strike the participants as overly constraining, undignified, or silly, the approved routines largely worked. In all of these examples of deviation, the routines would have produced more efficient and pleasant service, and those that apply to management and training would have benefited workers as well as customers.

Obtaining the cooperation of workers and managers is not enough to ensure the smooth functioning of McDonald's relatively inflexible routines. Customers must be routinized as well. Not only do customers have to understand the service routine and accept the limited range of choices the company offers, they also must be willing to do some kinds of work that are done for them in conventional restaurants, including carrying food to the table and throwing out their trash. Experience, advertising, the example set by other customers, and clear environmental cues familiarize customers with McDonald's routines, and most want to cooperate in order to speed service. For these reasons, McDonald's interactive service workers do not have to direct most customers, and window workers' routines are therefore not designed to give them power over customers.

NOTES

1. Suppliers, competitors, and other parties outside of the organization are also relevant actors, but organizational efforts to control their behavior will not be considered here (see Prus 1989).
2. The 1990s may bring unprecedented changes to McDonald's. Although its overseas business continues to thrive, domestic sales have been declining. To overcome the challenges to profitability presented by the economic recession, lower-priced competitors, and changes in consumer tastes, CEO Michael Quinlan has instituted experimental changes in the menu, in pricing strategy, and even in the degree of flexibility granted to franchisees (see *Advertising Age* 1991; Berg 1991; *McDonald's Annual Report* for 1990; Therrien 1991).
3. McDonald's restaurants are generally referred to as "stores" by McDonald's staff. The company's share of the domestic fast-food market has declined from 18.7 percent in 1985 to 16.6 percent in 1990 (Therrien 1991).
4. Information about McDonald's history comes primarily from Boas and Chain 1976; Kroc with Anderson 1977; Love 1986; Luxenberg 1985; and McDonald's training materials. Reiter's (1991) description of Burger King reveals numerous parallels in the operation of the two companies, although Burger King, unlike McDonald's, is a subsidiary of a multinational conglomerate.

5. In addition to paid advertising, McDonald's bolsters its public image with pro-motional and philanthropic activities such as an All-American High School Bas-ketball Game, essay contests and scholarship programs for black and Hispanic students, and Ronald McDonald Houses where outpatient children and their families and the parents of hospitalized children can stay at minimal cost.

6. Conversely, details of the routines are designed with marketing in mind. The bags that hold the regular-size portions of french fries are shorter than the french fries are, so that when workers fill them with their regulation french-fry scoops, the servings seem generous, overflowing the packaging. The names of the serv-ing sizes also are intended to give customers the impression that they are getting a lot for their money: French fries come in regular and large sizes, sodas in regu-lar, medium, and large cups. I was quickly corrected during a work shift when I inadvertently referred to an order for a "small" drink.

7. Some commentators fall into the trap of assuming that workers' preferences are determinative of working conditions, a mistake they do not make when dis-cussing higher-status workers such as faculty who must rely on a string of tem-porary appointments.

8. Actually, Kroc usually spoke of QSCV—quality, service, cleanliness, and value (see Kroc with Anderson 1977)—but QSC was the term used in most McDonald's training and motivational materials at the time of my research. The company cannot enforce "value" because antitrust restrictions prevent McDonald's from dictating prices to its franchisees (Love 1986:145). Nevertheless, recent materials return to the original four-part pledge of QSC & V (see, e.g., *McDonald's Annual Report* for 1989:i).

9. Branches of Hamburger University now operate in London, Munich, and Tokyo (*McDonald's Annual Report* for 1989:28). Burger King University is similar in many respects (Reiter 1991).

10. The effort to involve corporate employees in the central mission of the organiza-tion extends beyond such special programs. McDonald's prides itself on keeping its corporate focus firmly on store-level operations, and it wants all its employees to have a clear idea of what it takes to make a McDonald's restaurant work. There-fore, all McDonald's employees, from attorneys to data-entry clerks, spend time working in a McDonald's restaurant.

11. Biggart (1989:143–47) shows that both adulation of a charismatic founder and re-peated characterization of participants as winners are common in direct-sales or-ganizations. Like McDonald's, such organizations face the problem of motivating people who are widely dispersed geographically and who are not corporate em-ployees.

12. The in-store processors similarly affected managers' work. A disaffected McDon-ald's manager told Garson, "There is no such thing as a McDonald's manager. The computer manages the store" (Garson 1988:39).

13. Garson (1988) provides an extended discussion of this point.

14. The manager gave him the pail but had to ring it up on the machine as if he had given away a whole Happy Meal.

15. Thanks to Charles Bosk for this story.

16. Mills (1986) elaborates on "customer socialization." Environmental design as a factor in service provision is discussed by Wener (1985) and Normann (1984).

17. The importance of customer socialization becomes apparent when people with very different consumer experiences are introduced to a service system. When the first McDonald's opened in the Soviet Union in 1990, Moscow's citizens did not find the system immediately comprehensible. They had to be persuaded to get

on the shortest lines at the counter, since they had learned from experience that desirable goods were available only where there are long lines (Goldman 1990).

18. Burger King's "Have it your way" campaign virtually forced McDonald's to allow such customized service.

19. The defective food or its container was put into a special waste bin. Each shift, one worker or manager had the unenviable task of counting the items in the waste bin so that the inventory could be reconciled with the cash intake.

REFERENCES

Advertising Age. 1990. "Adman of the Decade: McDonald's Fred Turner: Making All the Right Moves." (January 1): 6.

———. 1991. "100 Leading National Advertisers: McDonald's." (September 25): 49–50.

Berg, Eric N. May 12, 1991. "An American Icon Wrestles with a Troubled Future." *New York Times* sec. 3, pp. 1, 6.

Bertagnoli, Lisa. July 10, 1989. "McDonald's: Company of the Quarter Century." *Restaurants and Institutions* pp. 32–60.

Biggart, Nicole Woolsey. 1989. *Charismatic Capitalism: Direct Selling Organizations in America.* Chicago: University of Chicago Press, pp. 128, 143–47.

Boas, Max and Steve Chain. 1976. *Big Mac: The Unauthorized Story of McDonald's.* New York: New American Library, p. 19.

Chaudhry, Rajan. August 7, 1989. "Burger Giants Singed by Battle." *Nation's Restaurant News,* p. F61.

"Fortune Global Service 500: The 50 Largest Retailing Companies." *Fortune* (August 26, 1991), p. 179.

Garson, Barbara. 1988. *The Electronic Sweatshop: How Computers Are Transforming the Office of the Future into the Factory of the Past.* New York: Simon and Schuster, p. 39.

Gibson, Richard and Robert Johnson. September 29, 1989. "Big Mac Plots Strategy to Regain Sizzle." *Wall Street Journal,* p. B1.

Goldman, Marshall. May 17, 1990. Presentation at colloquium on Reforming the Soviet Economy, University of Pennsylvania.

Greenberger, Ellen and Laurence Steinberg. 1986. *When Teenagers Work: The Psychological and Social Costs of Adolescent Employment.* New York: Basic Books.

Koepp, Stephen. April 13, 1987. "Big Mac Strikes Back." *Time,* p. 60.

Kroc, Ray with Robert Anderson. 1977. *Grinding It Out: The Making of McDonald's.* Chicago: Contemporary Books, p. 124.

Love, John F. 1986. *McDonald's: Behind the Arches.* New York: Bantam Books, p. 145.

Luxenberg, Stan. 1985. *Roadside Empires: How the Chains Franchised America.* New York: Viking.

McDonald's Annual Report. 1989. Oak Brook, Illinois, pp. i, 28, 29, 32.

———. 1990. Oak Brook, Illinois, pp. 1–2.

Mills, Peter K. 1986. *Managing Service Industries: Organizational Practices in a Post-Industrial Economy.* Cambridge, MA: Ballinger.

Normann, Richard. 1984. *Service Management: Strategy and Leadership in Service Businesses.* Chichester: Wiley.

Prus, Robert. 1989. *Pursuing Customers: An Ethnography of Marketing Activities.* Newbury Park, CA: Sage.

Reiter, Ester. 1991. *Making Fast Food: From the Frying Pan into the Fryer.* Montreal: McGill-Queen's University Press.

Rosenthal, Herman M. June 4, 1989. "Inside Big Mac's World." *Newsday,* p. 12.

Stinchcombe, Arthur L. 1990. *Information and Organizations.* Berkeley: University of California Press, p. 39.

Therrien, Lois. October 21, 1991. "McRisky." *Business Week,* pp. 114–22.

Wener, Richard E. 1985. "The Environmental Psychology of Service Encounters." Pp. 101–12 in *The Service Encounter: Managing Employee/Customer Interaction in Service Businesses,* edited by John A. Czepiel, Michael R. Solomon, and Carol F. Surprenant. Lexington, MA: Lexington Books.

Wildavsky, Ben. 1989. "McJobs: Inside America's Largest Youth Training Program." *Policy Review* 49:30–37.

RELIGION

41

THE PROTESTANT ETHIC AND THE SPIRIT OF CAPITALISM

MAX WEBER

The institution of religion is the topic of the following three selections. Sociologists have long studied how religion affects the social structure and the personal experience of individuals in society. Max Weber (1858–1917), for example, often placed the institution of religion at the center of his social analyses. Weber was particularly concerned with how changes in the institution of religion influenced changes in other social institutions, especially the economy. The selection excerpted here is from Weber's definitive and most famous study, *The Protestant Ethic and the Spirit of Capitalism* (1905). In his analysis of capitalism, Weber argues that the early Protestant worldviews of Calvinism and Puritanism were the primary factors in influencing the development of a capitalist economic system. Without the Protestant Reformation and a change in societal values toward rationality, capitalism would not have evolved as we know it today.

A product of modern European civilization, studying any problem of universal history, is bound to ask himself to what combination of circumstances the fact should be attributed that in Western civilization, and in Western civilization only, cultural phenomena have appeared which (as we like to think) lie in a line of development having *universal* significance

---

and value. . . . All over the world there have been merchants, wholesale and retail, local and engaged in foreign trade. . . .

But in modern times the Occident has developed, in addition to this, a very different form of capitalism which has appeared nowhere else: the rational capitalistic organization of (formally) free labour. Only suggestions of it are found elsewhere. Even the organization of unfree labour reached a considerable degree of rationality only on plantations and to a very limited extent in the *Ergasteria* of antiquity. In the manors, manorial workshops, and domestic industries on estates with serf labour it was probably somewhat less developed. Even real domestic industries with free labour have definitely been proved to have existed in only a few isolated cases outside the Occident. . . .

Rational industrial organization, attuned to a regular market, and neither to political nor irrationally speculative opportunities for profit, is not, however, the only peculiarity of Western capitalism. The modern rational organization of the capitalistic enterprise would not have been possible without two other important factors in its development: the separation of business from the household, which completely dominates modern economic life, and closely connected with it, rational bookkeeping. . . .

Hence in a universal history of culture the central problem for us is not, in the last analysis, even from a purely economic view-point, the development of capitalistic activity as such, differing in different cultures only in form: the adventurer type, or capitalism in trade, war, politics, or administration as sources of gain. It is rather the origin of this sober bourgeois capitalism with its rational organization of free labour. Or in terms of cultural history, the problem is that of the origin of the Western bourgeois class and of its peculiarities, a problem which is certainly closely connected with that of the origin of the capitalistic organization of labour, but is not quite the same thing. For the bourgeois as a class existed prior to the development of the peculiar modern form of capitalism, though, it is true, only in the Western hemisphere.

Now the peculiar modern Western form of capitalism has been, at first sight, strongly influenced by the development of technical possibilities. Its rationality is today essentially dependent on the calculability of the most important technical factors. But this means fundamentally that it is dependent on the peculiarities of modern science, especially the natural sciences based on mathematics and exact and rational experiment. On the other hand, the development of these sciences and of the technique resting upon them now receives important stimulation from these capitalistic interests in its practical economic application. It is true that the origin of Western science cannot be attributed to such interests. Calculation, even with decimals, and algebra have been carried on in India, where the decimal system was invented. But it was only made use of by developing capitalism in the West, while in India it led to no modern arithmetic or book-keeping. Neither was the origin of mathematics and mechanics determined by capitalistic interests. But the *technical* utilization of scientific knowledge, so important for the living conditions of the mass of people, was certainly encouraged by economic considerations, which were extremely favourable to it in the Occident. But this encouragement was derived from the peculiarities of the social structure of the Occident. We must hence ask, from *what* parts of that structure was it derived, since not all of them have been of equal importance?

Among those of undoubted importance are the rational structures of law and of administration. For modern rational capitalism has need, not only of the technical means of production, but of a calculable legal system and of administration in terms of formal rules. Without it adventurous and speculative trading capitalism and all sorts of politically determined capitalisms are possible, but no rational enterprise under individual initiative, with fixed capital and certainty of calculations. Such a legal system and such administration have been available for economic activity in a comparative state of legal and formalistic perfection only in the Occident. We must hence inquire where that law came from. Among other circumstances, capitalistic interest have in turn undoubtedly also helped, but by no means alone nor even principally, to prepare the way for the predominance in law and administration of a class of jurists specially trained in rational law. But these interests did not themselves create that law. Quite different forces were at work in this development. And why did not the capitalistic interests do the same in China or India? Why did not the scientific, the artistic, the political, or the economic development there enter upon that path of rationalization which is peculiar to the Occident?

For in all the above cases it is a question of the specific and peculiar rationalism of Western culture. . . . It is hence our first concern to work out and to explain genetically the special peculiarity of Occidental rationalism, and within this field that of the modern Occidental form. Every such attempt at explanation must, recognizing the fundamental importance of the economic factor, above all take account of the economic conditions. But at the same time the opposite correlation must not be left out of consideration. For though the development of economic rationalism is partly dependent on rational technique and law, it is at the same time determined by the ability and disposition of men to adopt certain types of practical rational conduct. When these types have been obstructed by spiritual obstacles, the development of rational economic conduct has also met serious inner resistance. The magical and religious forces, and the ethical ideas of duty based upon them, have in the past always been among the most important formative influences on conduct. In the studies collected here we shall be concerned with these forces.

Two older essays have been placed at the beginning which attempt, at one important point, to approach the side of the problem which is generally most difficult to grasp: the influence of certain religious ideas on the development of an economic spirit, or the *ethos* of an economic system. In this case we are dealing with the connection of the spirit of modern economic life with the rational ethics of ascetic Protestantism. Thus we treat here only one side of the causal chain. . . .

. . . [T]hat side of English Puritanism which was derived from Calvinism gives the most consistent religious basis for the idea of the calling. . . . For the saints' everlasting rest is in the next world; on earth man must, to be certain of his state of grace, "do the works of him who sent him, as long as it is yet day." Not leisure and enjoyment, but only activity serves to increase the glory of God according to the definite manifestations of His will.

Waste of time is thus the first and in principle the deadliest of sins. The span of human life is infinitely short and precious to make sure of one's own election. Loss of time through sociability, idle talk, luxury, even more sleep than is necessary for health, six to at most eight hours, is worthy of absolute moral condemnation. It does not yet hold, with Franklin, that time is money, but the proposition is true in a certain spiritual sense. It is infinitely valuable because every hour lost is lost to labour for the glory of God. Thus inactive contemplation is also valueless, or even directly reprehensible if it is at the expense of one's daily work. . . .

[T]he same prescription is given for all sexual temptation as is used against religious doubts and a sense of moral unworthiness: "Work hard in your calling." But the most important thing was that even beyond that labour came to be considered in itself the end of life, ordained as such by God. St. Paul's "He who will not work shall not eat" holds unconditionally for everyone. Unwillingness to work is symptomatic of the lack of grace.

Here the difference from the mediæval viewpoint becomes quite evident. Thomas Aquinas also gave an interpretation of that statement of St. Paul. But for him labour is only necessary *naturali ratione* for the maintenance of individual and community. Where this end is achieved, the precept ceases to have any meaning. Moreover, it holds only for the race, not for every individual. It does not apply to anyone who can live without labour on his possessions, and of course contemplation, as a spiritual form of action in the Kingdom of God, takes precedence over the commandment in its literal sense. Moreover, for the popular theology of the time, the highest form of monastic productivity lay in the increase of the *Thesaurus ecclesliæ* through prayer and chant.

. . . For everyone without exception God's Providence has prepared a calling, which he should profess and in which he should labour. And this calling is not, as it was for the Lutheran, a fate to which he must submit and which he must make the best of, but God's commandment to the individual to work for the divine glory. This seemingly subtle difference had far-reaching psychological consequences, and became connected with a further development of the providential interpretation of the economic order which had begun in scholasticism.

It is true that the usefulness of a calling, and thus its favour in the sight of God, is measured primarily in moral terms, and thus in terms of the importance of the goods produced in it for the community. But a further, and, above all, in practice the most important, criterion is found in private profitableness. For if that God, whose hand the Puritan sees in all the occurrences of life, shows one of His elect a chance of profit, he must do it with a purpose. Hence the faithful Christian must follow the call by taking advantage of the opportunity. "If God show you a way in which you may lawfully get more than in another way (without wrong to your soul or to any other), if you refuse this, and choose the less gainful way, you cross one of the ends of your calling, and you refuse to be God's steward, and to accept His gifts and use them for Him when He requireth it: you may labour to be rich for God, though not for the flesh and sin.". . .

The superior indulgence of the *seigneur* and the parvenu ostentation of the *nouveau riche* are equally detestable to asceticism. But, on the other hand, it has the highest ethical appreciation of the sober, middle-class, self-made man. "God blesseth His trade" is a stock remark about those good men who had successfully followed the divine hints. The whole power of the God of the Old Testament, who rewards His people for their obedience in this life, necessarily exercised a similar influence on the Puritan who . . . compared his own state of grace with that of the heroes of the Bible. . . .

Although we cannot here enter upon a discussion of the influence of Puritanism in all . . . directions, we should call attention to the fact that the toleration of pleasure in cultural goods, which contributed to purely aesthetic or athletic enjoyment, certainly always ran up against one characteristic limitation: They must not cost anything. Man is only a trustee of the goods which have come to him through God's grace. He must, like the servant in the parable, give an account of every penny entrusted to him, and it is at least hazardous to spend any of it for a purpose which does not serve the glory of God but only one's own enjoyment. What person, who keeps his eyes open, has not met representatives of this viewpoint even in the present? The idea of a man's duty to his possessions, to which he subordinates himself as an obedient steward, or even as an acquisitive machine, bears with chilling weight on his life. The greater the possessions the heavier, if the ascetic attitude toward life stands the test, the feeling of responsibility for them, for holding them undiminished for the glory of God and increasing them by restless effort. The origin of this type of life also extends in certain roots, like so many aspects of the spirit of capitalism, back into the Middle Ages. But it was in the ethic of ascetic Protestantism that it first found a consistent ethical foundation. Its significance for the development of capitalism is obvious.

This worldly Protestant asceticism, as we may recapitulate up to this point, acted powerfully against the spontaneous enjoyment of possessions; it restricted consumption, especially of luxuries. On the other hand, it had the psychological effect of freeing the acquisition of goods from the inhibitions of traditionalistic ethics. It broke the bonds of the impulse of acquisition in that it not only legalized it, but (in the sense discussed) looked upon it as directly willed by God. . . .

As far as the influence of the Puritan outlook extended, under all circumstances—and this is, of course, much more important than the mere encouragement of capital accumulation—it favoured the development of a rational bourgeois economic life; it was the most important, and above all the only consistent influence in the development of that life. It stood at the cradle of the modern economic man.

To be sure, these Puritanical ideals tended to give way under excessive pressure from the temptations of wealth, as the Puritans themselves knew very well. With great regularity we find the most genuine adherents of Puritanism among the classes which were rising from a lowly status, the small bourgeois and farmers while the *beati possidentes,* even among Quakers, are often found tending to repudiate the old ideals. It was the same fate which again and again befell the predecessor of this worldly asceticism, the monastic asceticism of the Middle Ages. In the latter case, when rational economic activity had worked out its full effects by strict regulation of conduct and limitation of consumption, the wealth accumulated either succumbed directly to the nobility, as in the time before the Reformation, or monastic discipline threatened to break down, and one of the numerous reformations became necessary.

In fact the whole history of monasticism is in a certain sense the history of a continual struggle with the problem of the secularizing influence of wealth. The same is true on a grand scale of the worldly asceticism of Puritanism. The great revival of Methodism, which preceded the expansion of English industry toward the end of the eighteenth century, may well be compared with such a monastic reform. We may hence quote here a passage from John Wesley himself which might well serve as a motto for everything which has been said above. For it shows that the leaders of these ascetic movements understood the seemingly paradoxical relationships which we have here analysed perfectly well, and in the same sense that we have given them. He wrote:

> I fear, wherever riches have increased, the essence of religion has decreased in the same proportion. Therefore I do not see how it is possible, in the nature of things, for any revival of true religion to continue long. For religion must necessarily produce both industry and frugality, and these cannot but produce riches. But as riches increase, so will pride, anger, and love of the world in all its branches. How then is it possible that Methodism, that is, a religion of the heart, though it flourishes now as a green bay tree, should continue in this state? For the Methodists in every place grow diligent and frugal; consequently they increase in goods. Hence they proportionately increase in pride, in anger, in the desire of the flesh, the desire of the eyes, and the pride of life. So, although the form of religion remains, the spirit is swiftly vanishing away. Is there no way to prevent this—this continual decay of pure religion? We ought not to prevent people from being diligent and frugal; *we must exhort all Christians to gain all they can, and to save all they can; that is, in effect, to grow rich.*

As Wesley here says, the full economic effect of those great religious movements, whose significance for economic development lay above all in their ascetic educative influence, generally came only after the peak of the purely religious enthusiasm was past. Then the intensity of the search for the Kingdom of God commenced gradually to pass over into sober economic virtue; the religious roots died out slowly, giving way to utilitarian worldliness. Then, as Dowden puts it, as in *Robinson Crusoe,* the isolated economic man who carries on missionary activities on the side takes the place of the lonely spiritual search for the Kingdom of Heaven of Bunyan's pilgrim, hurrying through the market-place of Vanity. . . .

A specifically bourgeois economic ethic had grown up. With the consciousness of standing in the fullness of God's grace and being visibly blessed by Him, the bourgeois business man, as long as he remained within the bounds of formal correctness, as long as his moral conduct was spotless and the use to which he put his wealth was not objectionable, could follow his pecuniary interests as he would and feel that he was fulfilling a duty in doing so. The power of religious asceticism provided him in addition with sober, conscientious, and unusually industrious workmen, who clung to their work as to a life purpose willed by God.

Finally, it gave him the comforting assurance that the unequal distribution of the goods of this world was a special dispensation of Divine Providence, which in these differences, as in particular grace, pursued secret ends unknown to men. . . .

One of the fundamental elements of the spirit of modern capitalism, and not only of that but of all modern culture: Rational conduct on the basis of the idea of the calling, was born—that is what this discussion has sought to demonstrate—from the spirit of Christian asceticism. One has only to reread the passage from Franklin, quoted at the beginning of this essay, in order to see that the essential elements of the attitude which was there called the spirit of capitalism are the same as what we have just shown to be the content of the Puritan worldly asceticism, only without the religious basis, which by Franklin's time had died away. . . .

Since asceticism undertook to remodel the world and to work out its ideals in the world, material goods have gained an increasing and finally an inexorable power over the lives of men as at no previous period in history. Today the spirit of religious asceticism—whether finally, who knows?—has escaped from the cage. But victorious capitalism, since it rests on mechanical foundations, needs its support no longer. The rosy blush of its laughing heir, the Enlightenment, seems also to be irretrievably fading, and the idea of duty in one's calling prowls about in our lives like the ghost of dead religious beliefs. Where the fulfilment of the calling cannot directly be related to the highest spiritual and cultural values, or when, on the other hand, it need not be felt simply as economic compulsion, the individual generally abandons the attempt to justify it at all. In the field of its highest development, in the United States, the pursuit of wealth, stripped of its religious and ethical meaning, tends to become associated with purely mundane passions, which often actually give it the character of sport.

No one knows who will live in this cage in the future, or whether at the end of this tremendous development entirely new prophets will arise, or there will be a great rebirth of old ideas and ideals, or, if neither, mechanized petrification, embellished with a sort of convulsive self-importance. For of the last stage of this cultural development, it might well be truly said: "Specialists without spirit, sensualists without heart; this nullity imagines that it has attained a level of civilization never before achieved."

But this brings us to the world of judgments of value and of faith, with which this purely historical discussion need not be burdened. . . .

Here we have only attempted to trace the fact and the direction of its influence to their motives in one, though a very important point. But it would also further be necessary to investigate how Protestant Asceticism was in turn influenced in its development and its character by the totality of social conditions, especially economic. The modern man is in general, even with the best will, unable to give religious ideas a significance for culture and national character which they deserve. But it is, of course, not my aim to substitute for a one-sided materialistic an equally one-sided spiritualistic causal interpretation of culture and of history. Each is equally possible, but each, if it does not serve as the preparation, but as the conclusion of an investigation, accomplishes equally little in the interest of historical truth.

42

WHAT THE POLLS DON'T SHOW
A Closer Look at U.S. Church Attendance

C. KIRK HADAWAY

PENNY LONG MARLER • MARK CHAVES

Sociologists who study the institution of religion are documenting the changes occurring within this social institution. One current debate is whether religiosity is growing in the United States or if it is declining due to increasing secularization. In this reading, C. Kirk Hadaway, Penny Long Marler, and Mark Chaves investigate whether the high levels of U.S. church attendance commonly reported are truly correct, given that other evidence indicates a decline in strength among religious institutions. Their study illustrates well the gaps between what individuals say they do (their attitudes), and what individuals actually do (their behavior). To measure this gap effectively, Hadaway, Marler, and Chaves employ numerous types of data collection methods, including analyses of poll data and actual observations of church attendance. Their findings, reported here, were first published in the journal, the *American Sociological Review* (1993).

With respect to religion, the United States is an anomaly. Although thoroughly secular in many ways, religious participation and affiliation remain much higher in America than in other Western industrialized nations (Wald 1987; Bruce 1990:178). Rates of religious activity also exhibit remarkable stability. Current self-reports of church attendance among Protestants do not differ significantly from levels recorded in the 1940s, and attendance among Catholics stabilized almost two decades ago after declining in the 1960s and early 1970s (Hout and Greeley 1987).[1]

Approximately 40 percent of the population of the United States is said to attend church weekly. This statistic is based on extraordinarily stable results from social surveys in which respondents report church attendance. Gallup polls, for example, ask respondents. "Did you, yourself, happen to attend church or synagogue in the last seven days?" In 1991, 42 percent of adult Americans (45 percent of Protestants and 51 percent of Catholics) re-

---

From *American Sociological Review*, 58, 741–752. Copyright © 1993 by the American Sociological Association. Reprinted with permission from ASA and the authors.

sponded affirmatively to this question (Princeton Religion Research Center 1992:4).[2]

In the sociological literature, this high participation rate is prominently and widely cited to bolster attacks against the secularization hypothesis (Hout and Greeley 1987; Greeley 1989; Warner 1993). The rate undergirds Warner's (1993) "new paradigm" of religious adaptability—a proposed replacement for the older secularization paradigm (also see Finke and Stark 1992). Moreover, the attendance rate is appropriated freely by historians and the mass media. The following excerpt from an award-winning book on American religious history illustrates a typical use of this "social fact" outside sociology:

> On any given Sunday morning, over 40 percent of the population of the United States attends religious services. In Canada and Australia this number tails off to about 25 percent; in England to about 10 percent; and in Scandinavia to around 4 percent. . . . Statistically, at least, the United States is God's country. (Hatch 1989:210–11)

Similarly, a June 15, 1991 *New York Times* "Religion Notes" column began: "Nearly all surveys of American churchgoing habits show that roughly 40 percent of Americans attend church once a week" (Goldman 1991). Perhaps the best indicator of the "hardness" of this social fact is that it is a standard feature in the religion chapters of introductory sociology textbooks (Johnson 1992:548; Kornblum 1991:514; Thio 1992:393). It also appears in the most widely used research methods text (Babbie 1992:398).

Still, the characterization of American religious participation as strong and stable is not uniformly accepted. Many social scientists, as well as church leaders, are skeptical about consistently high rates of church attendance. Membership losses among "old-line" Protestant denominations and slowing growth rates among large conservative denominations raise serious questions about such claims (Marler and Hadaway 1992). If Americans are going to church at the rate they report, the churches would be full on Sunday mornings and denominations would be growing. Yet they are not. Is it any wonder that "regular reports . . . that 70% claim church membership and 40% attend weekly" are met with "incredulity" (Warner 1993:1046)?

We present evidence that church attendance rates based on respondents' self-reports substantially *overstate* actual church attendance in the United States. Our empirical strategy is to compare church attendance rates based on counts of actual attenders to rates based on random samples of respondents who are asked to report their own attendance. Using a variety of data sources and data collection strategies, we estimate count-based church attendance rates among Protestants in a rural Ohio county and among Catholics in 18 dioceses. The results are dramatic: Church attendance rates for Protestants and Catholics are approximately *one-half* the generally accepted levels.

Contradictions and Implications

The contradiction between poll-based reports of church participation and denominational reality prompted this research. Consistently high levels of church attendance and a growing U.S. population suggest that most major denominations should be thriving and growing (Glenn 1987:S116–17). Yet most are not. Claims that losses in old-line denominations are more than offset by gains in evangelical denominations and nondenominational churches do not suffice. In addition to the fact that evangelical gains simply are not numerically large enough, Americans *in declining denominations* still claim high levels of membership and attendance.

The Episcopal Church illustrates the contradiction. This denomination should have grown in membership by more than 13 percent from 1967 to 1990, given the percentage of Americans who claim to be Episcopalians (and church members) on social surveys.[3] Instead, membership in the Episcopal Church *declined* by 28 percent. Moreover, attendance figures from Episcopal parishes are far below what would be expected if self-defined Episcopalians attended church in the numbers they claim. Based on Gallup surveys and other poll data, about 35 percent of Episcopalians say they attended church during the last seven days. If 2.5 percent of Americans claim to be Episcopalian and 35 percent of Episcopalians attend worship, total attendance during an average week should exceed 2 million (Johnson 1993:5). Instead, average weekly attendance was less than 900,000 in 1991.[4] Rather than 35 percent, it seems that approximately 16 percent of self-defined Episcopalians attend worship at an Episcopal church during a typical week.[5]

These data *suggest* that many Episcopalians claim to have attended church when in fact they did not. And if Episcopalians overreport their church attendance, perhaps persons who identify with other denominations also overreport their church attendance. This assumption led to our hypothesis that the percentage of Americans who attend church worship during an average week is considerably lower than the 40 percent level that is accepted as a "social fact" in the United States.

We rely on survey data and church statistics. We recognize the tendency in sociology to ignore church statistics because they are presumed to be inflated (Demerath 1974; Hadaway 1989). This is a valid point, but we argue that inflation errors are more serious for membership statistics than for attendance counts. Membership statistics are inflated because many denominations have no accepted procedure for deciding when to purge inactive members from church rolls. Denominations also differ in the meaning of membership. Accurate, consistent attendance data, on the other hand, require only that someone periodically count the persons attending church worship. Some inflation may occur here as well, but the bias is minimal and is not a problem for this research. Our purpose is to establish the *difference* between self-reported behavior and actual behavior, and because such a bias in the count would *decrease* that difference, the fact that the count-based rates are probably overestimates of actual attendance does not threaten our argument.

Data and Results

Protestants

The first step in our research strategy was to compare actual counts of church attendance to self-reported church attendance. We collected three types of data in a circumscribed area: (1) poll-based estimates of religious preferences for residents of the area; (2) poll-based estimates of church attendance for Protestants; and (3) actual counts of church attendance for all Protestant churches in the area.

We selected Ashtabula County, located in extreme northeastern Ohio, because of its manageable-sized population (100,000 persons) and the location of its population centers. The two largest towns in the county are situated near its center, and there are no large towns near the county line. Thus, the number of persons from Ashtabula County who attend church in other counties should be offset by persons from other counties attending church in Ashtabula.

The Protestant population of Ashtabula County was determined through a telephone poll of 602 county residents in the Spring and Fall of 1992. Phone numbers were randomly generated from among all active telephone exchanges. Thus, the sample included listed and unlisted numbers.[6] Survey results indicated that 66.4 percent of the respondents claimed a Protestant identity. Catholics made up 24.8 percent of the population, "nones" 8.0 percent and "others" 0.8 percent. These percentages were comparable to other data for the East North Central census region, the state of Ohio, and Ashtabula County (Davis and Smith 1990: Bradley, Green, Jones, Lynn, and McNeil 1992). Applying the proportion Protestant to the 1990 census population count for Ashtabula County, we estimated the Protestant population of Ashtabula County at 66,565.

The Ashtabula survey also asked respondents if they attended church or synagogue in the last seven days. We found that 35.8 percent of Protestant respondents and 37.2 percent of all respondents claimed to have attended church. This figure is considerably lower than Gallup estimates of 45 percent for Protestants nationally and 45 percent for all respondents in the Midwest. However, a 1991 telephone sample drawn from all Ohio residents and the 1992 Greater Cincinnati Survey (Bishop 1992) yielded results similar to our Ashtabula poll: 36 percent of Protestants in Ohio and 37 percent of Protestants in the Cincinnati area said they attended church in the last seven days.

Based on these data, we estimated the number of Protestants in Ashtabula County claiming church attendance at 22,830 in an average week.

The next step in the research process was to obtain average attendance counts from all Protestant churches in Ashtabula County. No countywide church list existed, so through exhaustive procedures we located every church in the county. We began with the countywide telephone directory, denominational yearbooks, and newspaper advertisements. Then we examined tax-exempt property listings in township plat books. One of the authors visited every church-owned site that contained a structure that was not already identified as a church. The final step was to drive the length of every paved road (and many unpaved roads) in the county searching for churches and posted signs for churches. This process identified 159 Protestant churches located in Ashtabula County. We also located 13 Catholic churches and two spiritualist congregations. Our total of 172 Christian churches can be contrasted to the 128 total for Ashtabula County in *Churches and Church Membership in the United States 1990* (Bradley et al. 1992). We found 44 churches that were not included in this compilation of county-by-county reports from 133 religious denominations or fellowships.

Average attendance figures were obtained through denominational yearbooks, telephone interviews, letters, and church visits. We requested membership totals, definitions of membership, and average attendance estimates (including young children who were not in the worship service) from each church in the county. Average attendance counts were received from 137 Protestant churches. For the remaining 22 (mostly small) Protestant churches, attendance was estimated using the number of cars in the parking lots or actually counting persons attending Sunday services in February and March 1992. Estimates were based on persons-per-car ratios taken from similar churches whose attendance was known.[7] The attendance total for all Protestant churches was 13,080. This total probably overestimates attendance in Ashtabula County.

Based on our estimate of Protestants and our attendance count, we calculate that only 19.6 percent of Protestants attend church during an average week in Ashtabula County. Poll-based attendance estimates for Protestants from the Gallup Organization were 130 percent higher; estimates from our Ashtabula survey were 83 percent higher.

. . .

Catholics

The Catholic churches in Ashtabula County did not collect church attendance data nor could they give reliable estimates of Mass attendance. Thus, we were unable to investigate the possibility that Catholics in this rural county also overstated their attendance (53 percent of Catholic respondents

TABLE 42.1   Count of Total Church Attendance and Percentage Attending Church: Selected Catholic Dioceses in the United States, 1990.

Diocese	Total Church Attendance (1)	Corrected Church Attendance (2)	Total Population (3)	Proportion Catholic (4)	Estimated Catholic Population (5)	Percent Attending Church (6)
Baltimore	173,609	182,289	2,722,904	.259	705,232	25.8
Boston	455,837	455,837[a]	3,754,239	.530	1,989,747	22.9
Chicago	600,350	600,350[a]	5,621,485	.392	2,203,622	27.2
Cincinnati	234,562	246,290	2,805,557	.227	636,861	38.7
Fort Worth	65,618	70,042[a]	2,060,943	.129	265,862	26.3
Harrisburg	115,844	121,636	1,867,124	.159	296,873	41.0
Indianapolis	99,069[b]	108,471[a]	2,201,503	.169	372,054	29.2
La Crosse	132,030[b]	136,894[a]	781,763	.408	318,959	42.9
Milwaukee	310,933[b]	326,480	2,080,883	.408	849,000	38.5
Newark	306,374	307,651[a]	2,650,504	.454	1,203,329	25.6
New York	453,861	453,861[a]	5,096,274	.437	2,227,072	20.4
Omaha	122,719	128,855	775,037	.351	272,038	47.4
Philadelphia	409,946	427,593[a]	3,728,909	.379	1,413,257	30.3
Pittsburgh	295,662	303,629[a]	2,014,935	.415	836,198	36.3
Rockford	95,553	95,553[a]	1,089,576	.288	313,798	30.5
Saginaw	70,896	70,896[a]	685,082	.329	225,392	31.5
San Francisco	115,312	120,414[a]	1,603,678	.341	546,854	22.0
Seattle	131,596	133,905[a]	3,776,852	.177	668,503	20.0
Total	—	4,290,646	—	—	15,344,651	28.0

[a] Count inflated by the known proportion of congregations not reporting.
[b] Count for Indianapolis is for 1989; for La Crosse, 1991; for Milwaukee, 1992.

in our survey reported church attendance in the last seven days). However, many Catholic dioceses in the United States conduct a diocese-wide count of all individuals who attend a religious service on a given Fall weekend.

Table 42.1 lists the dioceses for which we obtained attendance data.[8] Although not a random sample of dioceses, this list includes dioceses from every region of the country except the Southeast, where Catholics constitute only between five and eight percent of the population. The list also includes counts from two of the three largest dioceses in the country, New York and Chicago.

In most of these dioceses, Mass attendance is counted each weekend in October. These counts are then averaged to arrive at a single estimate of weekly attendance. In our judgment, the overall quality of these counts is quite high, even though there are differences in quality control.[9] Column 1 of Table 42.1 presents these counts for 1990 or, in three cases, a year near 1990.[10]

Column 2 presents a "corrected" attendance count that represents our effort to give the counts every possible chance to match survey-based estimates of attendance. First, for the four dioceses that interpolated in order to estimate counts for parishes that did not report a count in 1990, the "corrected attendance" is identical to the number in column 1. Second, for dioceses that did not interpolate, but for which we knew the proportion of parishes that did not report in 1990, we inflated the count in column 1 by this proportion. Third, for dioceses that did not interpolate and did not provide parish-level data, we inflated the count by 5 percent, which is slightly *higher* than the average percent missing data we observed (4 percent).

The attendance data provide the numerator of a count-based attendance rate. The denominator is more difficult to obtain because the U.S. Census does not ask religious affiliation.[11] Fortunately, there was a 1990 nationally representative survey of religious affiliation with a sample size large enough ($N = 113,000$) to reliably estimate, for each diocese, the proportion of the total adult population that is Catholic (Kosmin 1991). Because these data contained county codes, and because dioceses are usually coextensive with a set of counties, we were able to calculate the proportion Catholic for each diocese (column 4).[12]

Calculating count-based church attendance rates then is straightforward. Total population data for each diocese were taken from county-level 1990 U.S. Census reports (column 3). Next, we estimated the total number of Catholics in each diocese by multiplying the total population by the proportion Catholic (column 5).[13] Finally, we calculated a count-based church attendance percentage by dividing the "corrected attendance" figures by the number of Catholics in each diocese (column 6).

The results are clear: With the exception of Omaha, in every diocese for which we have good data the church attendance rate based on actual counts is significantly below the 51 percent rate reported by Gallup and a similar figure computed from General Social Survey data (Smith 1991).[14] Most dramatic, when the data are aggregated the weekly church attendance rate for Catholics is only 28 percent. Recalling the various upward biases operating on the count data (e.g., the tendency for priests to overreport attendance, our overinflation of reported counts, etc.), it is difficult to avoid the conclusion that the actual church attendance rate for Catholics is *substantially* below 51 percent.

· · ·

Table 42.2 presents, for selected dioceses, direct comparisons between self-reported attendance rates and attendance rates based on actual counts. For four dioceses, we located surveys that permit a more direct comparison between survey-based and count-based rates of attendance.[15] In three cases, the self-reported attendance rate for Catholics is similar to or higher than the national rate (44.8 percent in New York, 48.5 percent in Chicago, and 59.3 percent in Cincinnati), while the count-based rate is substantially lower. These results increase our confidence that the observed gap between self-reported

TABLE 42.2   **Percent Attending Mass Weekly, Based on Self-Reports and Actual Counts of Attendance: Selected Dioceses, 1990**

	Percent Attending Mass Weekly	
Diocese	Self-Report[a] (95% Confidence Interval)	Actual Count[b] (Range from Figure 1)
Chicago	45.7 —— 51.3	25.7 —— 28.9
New York	37.8 —— 51.8	19.4 —— 21.5
Cincinnati	54.0 —— 64.6	35.5 —— 42.4
San Francisco	33.2 —— 44.6	29.9 —— 36.5

[a] *Sources:* The Chicago Survey (Taylor 1991); The New York Daily News Easter Season Poll (New York Daily News 1986); The Greater Cincinnati Survey (Bishop 1992); and The Bay Area Survey II (Shanks 1972).

[b] The ranges for Chicago, New York, and Cincinnati are from . . . 1990. . . . The Bay Area Survey, however, is for 1972. Fortunately, the archdiocese of San Francisco has conducted attendance counts since 1961. The ranges for San Francisco draw on population data from the 1970 Census, estimates of the Catholic population based on the proportion Catholic in the 1972 survey, and the 1972 count data in this diocese to calculate the rates.

church attendance and actual church attendance is not an artifact of local variation.

Only in San Francisco do the survey-based and count-based attendance rates overlap. However, the survey-based rates for San Francisco are from 20 years ago. This suggests that the gap between self-reported and actual church attendance may have *increased* over time.

Our conclusion, then, is straightforward: Weekly church attendance by Catholics in the United States is approximately one-half what conventional wisdom takes it to be; the true rate is closer to 25 percent rather than 51 percent.

Objections   Why is the attendance rate for Omaha so high? Many parishes in the Archdiocese of Omaha grossly overstate attendance at Mass in their annual reports. We attended Saturday and Sunday Masses in five parishes where overcounting was suspected and, in each case, found attendance to be significantly lower than that reported to the diocese.[16] One urban parish reported 750 persons attending on average, whereas we counted only 280 in all Masses on a sunny weekend five days before Christmas. A rural parish reported 1,150 persons attending—we counted only 595. A suburban parish reported attendance of almost 4,700—we counted 2,900.[17] The attendance rate for Catholics in Omaha may be above the 28 percent norm presented in Table 42.1, but it is much lower than 47 percent.

What about members of the various Orthodox Catholic churches? Our attendance counts do not include such persons, even though many probably identify their religious preference as "Catholic" rather than "Orthodox" on social surveys. Data from the *Yearbook of American and Canadian Churches* (Bedell and Jones 1992) indicate that approximately 93 percent of American Catholics are Roman Catholics, and the figure may be even higher owing to possible overlap in reports from various Orthodox dioceses. Adjusting for Orthodox attenders increases our estimate of the percent of Catholics who attended church weekly by only a few percentage points.

Discussion

Our results suggest that Protestant and Catholic church attendance is roughly one-half the levels reported by Gallup. What accounts for this gap? One interpretation pertains to the problem of nonresponse in survey sampling. Since the mid-1960s, changing lifestyles and other demographic factors have resulted in increasing nonresponse rates on telephone surveys (Frankel and Frankel 1987). Hard-to-reach populations include single persons and two-career, married-couple households—persons who are also less likely to attend church (Marler forthcoming). If these less religiously active persons are underrepresented in survey results, then self-reported church attendance would be artificially high. While nonresponse bias may contribute to high attendance rates, it is unlikely that sampling problems alone explain the levels of disparity found in this study.

A second possibility is that survey respondents really *do* overreport their church attendance. Research frequently attributes overreporting (or underreporting) to "social desirability" factors. For example, a 1988 study found that youths underreported deviant behavior like substance abuse (Mensch and Kandel 1988). Numerous studies of voting behavior have found that more people say they voted than actually voted (Parry and Crossley 1950; Traugott and Katosh 1979, 1981; Silver, Anderson, and Abramson 1986; Presser and Traugott 1992). In a New York sample, for instance, the gap between those who claimed to have voted and those who actually voted was 16 percentage points (Presser 1990). The interpretation is that people like to see themselves (or present themselves) as "better" than they are, based on a traditionally accepted social or moral norm. Indeed, in the case of voting behavior, nearly all the error is in the socially desirable direction (Presser and Traugott 1992:78). If survey respondents view regular church attendance as normative or view infrequent church attendance as deviant, they may be inclined to overreport their attendance. This tendency may be greater for persons who think they "ought" to attend church (Presser and Traugott 1992:85).

Even with the pressures of social desirability it could be argued that Gallup's time-specific question about church attendance, "in the last seven days" provides a corrective. After all, respondents are not asked to reveal annual patterns of church attendance—only last week's participation. Still, errors in recall are possible because people often remember events and behaviors as occurring more recently than they really did, a response problem called "telescoping" (Sudman and Bradburn 1982; Bradburn, Rips, and Shevell 1987:160).

Furthermore, evidence from cognitive studies of survey responses indicates that much more is involved in answering questions about the frequency of particular behaviors than simple recall of events (Blair and Burton 1987:280). Burton and Blair (1991:51) found that survey respondents answer such questions using information stored in long-term memory. Relevant information includes data about specific episodes or events (e.g., when they occurred, how enjoyable or salient they were, their frequency) as well as nonepisodic information like *rules* (e.g., "I go to church every Sunday"). Such information colors survey responses whether the episode in question occurred last week or last year. What is added to the social desirability thesis is *personal desirability* based on the "quality" of past episodes. In the case of church attendance, a combination of positive episodes and strong internalized rules about church attendance could result in inflated reports.

Whatever the reasons for overreporting, overreporting is a fact. If the gap between reported attendance and actual attendance is real, the implications for religion in America are profound. For instance, is America still uniquely "God's country" among industrialized nations? Although a 20 to 25 percent attendance figure puts the United States at about the same reported levels as Australians, Canadians, Belgians, and the Dutch (Kaldor 1987; Dobberlaere 1988; Lechner 1989; Bibby 1993), survey-based rates in other countries may also be inflated. Indeed, data from the United Kingdom suggest that a small gap exists between poll estimates and attendance counts. A 1989 census of church attendance in England revealed that 10 percent of the adult population actually attended church on "Census Sunday." This percentage is lower than a 1989 pollbased estimate of 14 percent (using General Social Survey-style response categories), but is identical to findings from a 1963 survey that asked about church attendance in the last week (Hastings and Hastings 1989; Brierly 1991).[18] If individuals in other countries are less likely to overreport their church attendance than are Americans, then a different sort of "American exceptionalism" is at work. Americans may not differ much in terms of behavior but rather in how they *report* that behavior.[19]

A striking feature of survey-based church attendance rates is their stability since World War II (Hout and Greeley 1987). Our research raises an intriguing question: Are behavioral patterns truly stable over the last 50 years, or has there been a decline in actual rates of church attendance? That is, has the gap between self-reported and actual attendance remained constant, or has it increased in recent decades? Our results cast considerable doubt on the cross-sectional accuracy of the survey rates, but *changes* in that accuracy are another matter. We suspect that the actual attendance rate has declined since World War II, despite the fact that the survey rate remained basically stable.

Trend data for various denominations suggest a decline in the attendance rate. Although old-line Protestant denominations have recorded declines in membership and church attendance, the *number* of Americans who call themselves Methodist, Lutheran, Episcopalian, Disciple, or Presbyterian has increased over the last 30 years.[20] Declining attendance, coupled with an increasing constituency, results in a decline in the percentage of self-identified Protestants who are counted as attending Protestant churches. For instance, we estimate that the percentage of self-identified Presbyterians who attended Presbyterian churches declined from approximately 26 percent in the mid-1960s to around 16 percent in the late 1980s. Yet throughout this period, poll data indicated that Presbyterian church attendance averaged around 34 percent (Gallup Organization 1981). If self-reported church attendance was stable and actual church attendance declined, it would appear that the gap between what people do and what they say they do increased.[21]

These findings have important ramifications for the interpretation of poll data—especially poll data that attempt to measure behavior rather than attitudes. Although some gap between behavior and perceptions of behavior has always been assumed, we suggest that the gap, at least for church attendance, is substantial. Further, we suggest that the gap may not be constant—that perceptions of behavior are subject to change. If this is true, then poll data, particularly time-series poll data, should not be taken at face value. Clearly, social surveys measure perceptions of behavior; they do not measure actual behavior. To understand behavior and the norms that interpret behavior, attention should focus on the *relationship* between perception and reality.[22]

Conclusion

We have shown that the church attendance rate is probably one-half what everyone thinks it is. But the practical difficulties involved with this research limited our data collection efforts. Although the evidence is compelling because it is so uniform, the fact remains that our data pertain to fewer than 20 Catholic dioceses and to Protestants in only one Ohio county. To confirm the existence of this "gap" and to determine if it has widened in recent decades, researchers should examine existing time-series data from local churches, denominations, regional polls, and religious censuses—any data that permit a comparison of poll-based and count-based measures of religious activity.

In addition, the *meaning* of the gap should be explored at three levels. At the individual level, the roles of social norms and personal "rules" in answers to value-laden questions about behaviors like church attendance require additional investigation. At the group or congregation level, research should explore the processes of regular assembling for corporate worship. Church attendance occurs in group settings, and such settings resemble "regularly organized crowds." We need to know more about the intentions of people who frequent such gatherings and how characteristics of the group affect the behavior of individuals (e.g., see Schelling 1968; McPhail and Tucker 1990). Finally, at the societal level, comparisons of poll-based and count-based measures of church attendance from other nations would be valuable. If changing cultural norms and social contexts affect the gap, we would expect substantial cross-national variation.

These findings undoubtedly will stimulate the ongoing debate over secularization, particularly whether the cultural norm for churchgoing has persisted while the behavior has diminished. Strong religious expression continues in the United States, to be sure, but these data show that it is not as strong as previously thought. Meanwhile, perhaps there should be a moratorium on claims about the singularity of the United States in terms of church attendance.

NOTES

Acknowledgments: This research was supported by grants from the Lilly Endowment, Inc. (#900754) and the University of Notre Dame. Additional financial support was provided by the United Church Board for Homeland Ministries. We are grateful to the diocesan researchers who supplied information on Catholic attendance. We also thank Lara Boucher, James Cavendish, Min Liu, and Ami Nagle for their assistance in data collection and proofing. Robert K. Shelly and three anonymous reviewers gave helpful comments on an earlier version of this [article].

1. Glenn (1987) noted that, during the 1930s and 1940s, Gallup's samples were designed to represent voters rather than the entire adult population. Women, Southerners, blacks, and people at low socioeconomic levels were underrepresented. The exclusion of several high-attendance groups may have lowered the percentage of attenders in the 1930s and 1940s. Our primary concern, however, is with stability in the polls during the last 30 years—a period when this sampling issue is not relevant.

2. The overall attendance figure is lower than the attendance figures for Protestants and Catholics because of the inclusion in the former of persons who express no religious preference (the "nones"). Smith (1991) reported similar rates from the General Social Survey. He converted NORC categories into probabilities of attending church in a given week. For Protestants, attendance estimates ranged from 41 percent to 46 percent, but there was no trend from 1972 to 1989. The converted NORC rate for Catholics was 50 percent in 1989.

3. These figures are based on aggregated General Social Survey data (NORC), Gallup (AIPO) data, our 1992 Marginal Member poll, and U.S. population estimates (U.S. Bureau of the Census 1992). Actual membership figures are from the *Yearbook of American and Canadian Churches* (Bedell and Jones 1992; also earlier volumes) and from information supplied to the authors by the Episcopal Church. The Episcopal Church baptizes infants, and all baptized persons are counted as members. These definitions have not changed during the period of study. Thus, our estimates of self-identified Episcopalians pertain to the entire population rather than adults.

4. The attendance count from Episcopal parishes includes all persons attending (even non-Episcopalians). Of course, Episcopalians may also attend non-Episcopal churches.

5. The attendance rate estimate for self-defined Episcopalians varies according to the

proportion of Episcopalians in the population. Depending on the survey used, the attendance rate varies from 14 percent to 18 percent.

6. The response rate for persons contacted was relatively high for a telephone survey (71 percent). Working phone numbers were discarded after eight unsuccessful attempts to contact someone.

7. The maximum ratio from a church whose attendance was known was three persons per car. This persons-per-car ratio was used to estimate attendance for all nonreporting churches, even though it was clearly too high in some cases.

8. These 18 dioceses represent all dioceses that the Catholic Research Forum knew to be conducting the attendance count and for which we were able to obtain reliable data.

9. In most of these dioceses, the counting and reporting procedure is highly institutionalized with standard forms and computer programs for aggregating the data. Some dioceses have even instituted quality-control systems in which a representative of the diocese attends Mass on an appointed weekend to confirm participation in the count. All of the dioceses ask parish priests to count rather than estimate attendance. The majority appear to comply with this request, particularly in dioceses where this has been a standard procedure for years. As was true for Protestants, however, the institutional politics of the attendance counts is such that a parish pastor has every incentive to *inflate* rather than deflate the actual count.

10. The three exceptions are Indianapolis, La Crosse, and Milwaukee, for which we report 1989, 1991, 1992 counts, respectively. Most of the diocesan counts include parish attendance only. However, when dioceses counted attendance in nonparish settings (e.g., hospitals, campuses), we included those numbers in the count.

11. The Official Catholic Directory provides an estimate of the number of Catholics in each diocese. For some dioceses, the reported number is based on a demographic method that compares the number of births and deaths in the relevant counties with the number of baptisms and funerals conducted by the church. For many dioceses, however, the number in the Directory represents the *registered* Catholics in the diocese, which usually is considerably smaller than the number of individuals who self-identify as Catholic (Celio 1993). The demographic method produces a better estimate, but still underestimates the population of self-identified Catholics.

12. These proportions are based on data weighted so that county samples matched census distributions by age, sex, and education.

13. The census figures refer to *total* population while the surveys are samples of *adults.* However, applying the proportion of Catholic adults to the total population will overestimate the Catholic population only if Catholic fertility is *lower* than non-Catholic fertility. Because only an overestimate of the Catholic population would bias the attendance rate in favor of our argument (by driving the rate down), this discrepancy from ideal demographic calculations is not a cause for concern.

14. The national survey rates pertain to *adults,* while the rates in column 6 pertain to the total population. This difference would increase the gap between the survey-based rate and the count-based rate only in the unlikely event that the attendance rate among those under age 18 is substantially lower than that among those 18 and over.

15. The authors commissioned the inclusion of worship attendance and church membership items on the 1992 Greater Cincinnati Survey.

16. We visited parishes where the ratio of attendees to the number of registered members was high or where attendance was reported in large even numbers (e.g., 500, 750, 2500).

17. The other two parishes overestimated attendance by 20 to 25 percent. Both were unusual in that many persons attending Mass were from other parishes in the city (according to priests and Archdiocese staff). One parish was known for its "quick" Mass (no more than 30 minutes), whereas the other had a heavily attended and lively "gospel Mass." We found no parishes that undercounted attendance. We met with four members of the Archdiocese staff to discuss problems of overestimation. They acknowledged that many priests probably estimated attendance rather than counting attenders. No verification procedures were used in the Archdiocese. There was some financial incentive for accurate reporting of registered members because of per member assessments by the diocese, but there were no incentives for restricting attendance estimates.

18. The 14 percent estimate was computed from the eight response categories using a formula similar to Smith's (1991) translation of General Social Survey data on church attendance.

19. Kaldor (1987:20) also reported a gap between poll-based and count-based measures of church attendance for several denominations in Australia. Unfortunately, he gave no estimate of the size of the gap.

20. Attendance as a percentage of membership among old-line denominations and the Southern Baptist Convention is a remarkably constant 35 to 40 percent. Smaller evangelical, Pentecostal, and Fundamentalist groups typically exhibit higher average attendance rates. Time-series data for a variety of denominations (from old-line to Pentecostal) indicate substantial stability in church attendance as a percent of membership from the early 1970s to the present.

21. This increasing gap is paralleled by changes in another traditional institution—the family. A large gap exists between what Americans say about their families and what they actually do—a gap that has widened in recent decades (Glenn 1992). In surveys over the last 30 years, traditional family relationships are consistently identified as the most important aspect of life. Yet during this period, the proportion of Americans who were satisfied with their marriages declined and the divorce rate rose.

22. A possible interpretation for such gaps is provided by Swidler's (1986:280) description of cultural periods during which norms and values achieve a taken-for-granted quality and people live with "great discontinuity between talk and action." Norms remain the same, but behavior changes. As the gap between norms and behavior widens, tensions to bring values and behavior back in line increase.

REFERENCES

Babbie, Earl. 1992. *Practicing Social Research.* 6th ed. Belmont, CA: Wadsworth.

Bedell, Kenneth B. and Alice M. Jones, eds. 1992. *Yearbook of American and Canadian Churches 1992.* Nashville, TN: Abingdon Press.

Bibby, Reginald W. 1993. "Religion in the Canadian 90s: The Paradox of Poverty and Potential." Pp. 278–92 in *Church and Denominational Growth,* edited by D. A. Roozen and C. K. Hadaway. Nashville, TN: Abingdon Press.

Bishop, George F. 1992. *The Greater Cincinnati Survey* [MRDF]. Cincinnati, OH: Institute for Policy Research, University of Cincinnati [producer, distributor].

Blair, Edward and Scot Burton. 1987. "Cognitive Processes Used by Survey Respondents to Answer Behavioral Frequency Questions." *Journal of Consumer Research* 14:280–88.

Bradburn, Norman M., Lance J. Rips, and Steven K. Shevell. 1987. "Answering Autobiographical Questions: The Impact of Memory and Inference on Surveys." *Science* 236:157–61.

Bradley, Martin, Norman M. Green, Jr., Dale E. Jones, Mac Lynn, and Lou McNeil. 1992. *Churches and Church Membership in the United States 1990.* Atlanta, GA: Glenmary Research Center.

Brierly, Peter. 1991. *'Christian' England.* London, England: MARC Europe.

Bruce, Steve. 1990. *A House Divided: Protestantism, Schism, and Secularization.* London, England: Routledge.

Burton, Scot and Edward Blair. 1991. "Task Conditions, Response Formulation Processes, and Response Accuracy for Behavioral Frequency Questions in Surveys." *Public Opinion Quarterly* 55:50–79.

Celio, Mary Beth. 1993. "Catholics: Who, How Many and Where?" *America,* 9 Jan., pp. 10–14.

Davis, James A. and Tom W. Smith. 1990. *General Social Surveys, 1972–1990* [MRDF]. Principal Investigator, James A. Davis; Director and Co-Principal Investigator, Tom W. Smith. NORC ed. Chicago: National Opinion Research Center [producer]. Storrs, CT: The Roper Center for Public Opinion Research, University of Connecticut [distributor].

Demerath, N. J., III. 1974. *A Tottering Transcendence: Civil vs. Cultic Aspects of the Sacred.* Indianapolis: Bobbs-Merrill Company.

Dobbelaere, Karel. 1988. "Secularization, Polarization, Religious Involvement, and Religious Change in the Low Countries." Pp. 80–115 in *World Catholicism in Transition,* edited by T. M. Gannon. New York: Macmillan.

Finke, Roger and Rodney Stark. 1992. *The Churching of America, 1776–1990.* New Brunswick, NJ: Rutgers University Press.

Frankel, Martin R. and Lester R. Frankel. 1987. "Fifty Years of Survey Sampling in the United States." *Public Opinion Quarterly* 51:S127–S138.

Gallup Organization. 1981. *Religion in America.* Princeton, NJ: Princeton Religion Research Center.

Glenn, Norval D. 1987. "Social Trends in the U.S.: Evidence from Sample Surveys." *Public Opinion Quarterly* 51:S109–S126.

———. 1992. "What Does Family Mean?" *American Demographics* 14(6):30–37.

Goldman, Ari L. 1991. "Religion Notes." *New York Times,* 15 June, p. L10.

Greeley, Andrew M. 1989. *Religious Change in America.* Cambridge, MA: Harvard University Press.

Hadaway, C. Kirk. 1989. "Will the Real Southern Baptist Please Stand Up: Methodological Problems in Surveying Southern Baptist Congregations and Members." *Review of Religious Research* 31:149–61.

Hastings, Elizabeth and Phillip Hastings. 1989. *Index to International Public Opinion, 1988–1989.* New York: Greenwood Press.

Hatch, Nathan O. 1989. *The Democratization of American Christianity.* New Haven, CT: Yale University Press.

Hout, Michael and Andrew M. Greeley. 1987. "The Center Doesn't Hold: Church Attendance in the United States, 1940–1984." *American Sociological Review* 52:325–45.

Johnson, Allan G. 1992. *Human Arrangements: An Introduction to Sociology.* 3d ed. Fort Worth, TX: Harcourt Brace Jovanovich.

Johnson, Benton. 1993. "The Denominations: The Changing Map of Religious America." *The Public Perspective* 4(3):3–6.

Kaldor, Peter. 1987. *Who Goes Where? Who Doesn't Care: Going to Church in Australia.* Homebush West, NSW Australia: Lancer Books.

Kornblum, William. 1991. *Sociology in a Changing World.* 2d ed. Fort Worth, TX: Holt, Rinehart and Winston.

Kosmin, Barry A. 1991. *The National Survey of Religious Identification 1989–90* [MRDF]. New York: The Graduate School and University Center of the City University of New York [producer, distributor].

Lechner, Frank J. 1989. "Catholicism and Social Change in the Netherlands: A Case of Radical Secularization?" *Journal for the Scientific Study of Religion* 28:136–47.

Marler, Penny Long. Forthcoming. "Lost in the Fifties: The Changing Family and the Nostalgic Church." In *Work, Family and Faith: New Patterns among Old Institutions,* edited by N. T. Ammerman and W. C. Roof.

Marler, Penny Long and C. Kirk Hadaway. 1992. "New Church Development and Denominational Growth (1950–1988): Symptom or Cause?" Pp. 29–72 in *Research in the Social Scientific Study of Religion,* vol. 4, edited by M. L. Lynn and D. O. Moberg. Greenwich, CT: JAI Press.

McPhail, Clark and Charles W. Tucker. 1990. "Purposive Collective Action." *American Behavioral Scientists* 34:81–94.

Mensch, Barbara S. and Denise B. Kandel. 1988. "Underreporting of Substance Use in a National Longitudinal Youth Cohort: Individual and Interviewer Effects." *Public Opinion Quarterly* 52:100–24.

New York Daily News. 1986. *New York Daily News Easter Season Poll, 1986* [MRDF #8584]. New York: New York Daily News [producer]. Ann Arbor, MI: Inter-University Consortium for Political and Social Research [distributor].

Parry, Hugh and Helen Crossley. 1950. "Validity of Responses to Survey Questions." *Public Opinion Quarterly* 14:61–80.

Presser, Stanley. 1990. "Can Changes in Context Reduce Overreporting in Surveys?" *Public Opinion Quarterly* 54:586–93.

Presser, Stanley and Michael Traugott. 1992. "Little White Lies and Social Science Models." *Public Opinion Quarterly* 56:77–86.

Princeton Religion Research Center. 1992. "Church Attendance Constant." *Emerging Trends* 14(3):4.

Schelling, Thomas C. 1968. *Micromotives and Macrobehavior.* New York: W. W. Norton.

Shanks, J. Merrill. 1972. *Social Indicators: Bay Area Survey II* [MRDF]. Ann Arbor, MI: Inter-University Consortium for Political and Social Research #8540 [distributor].

Silver, Brian D., Barbara A. Anderson, and Paul R. Abramson. 1986. "Who Overreports Voting?" *American Political Science Review* 80:613–24.

Smith, Tom. 1991. "Counting Flocks and Lost Sheep: Trends in Religious Preference since World War II." *GSS Social Change Report No. 26.* (Revised Jan. 1991). Chicago, IL: National Opinion Research Center.

Sudman, Seymour and Norman M. Bradburn. 1982. *Asking Questions.* San Francisco, CA: Jossey-Bass.

Swidler, Ann. 1986. "Culture in Action: Symbols and Strategies." *American Sociological Review* 51:273–86.

Taylor, D. Garth. 1991. *The Chicago Survey* [MRDF]. Chicago, IL: Metropolitan Chicago Information Center [distributor].

Thio, Alex. 1992. *Sociology: An Introduction.* 3d ed. New York: HarperCollins.

Traugott, Michael and John P. Katosh. 1979. "Response Validity in Surveys of Voting Behavior." *Public Opinion Quarterly* 43:359–77.

———. 1981. "The Consequences of Validated and Self-Reported Voting Measures." *Public Opinion Quarterly* 45:519–35.

Wald, Kenneth D. 1987. *Religion and Politics in the United States.* New York: St. Martin's Press.

Warner, R. Stephen. 1993. "Work in Progress toward a New Paradigm for the Sociological Study of Religion in the United States." *American Journal of Sociology* 98:1044–93.

43

THE ANTI-ABORTION MOVEMENT
AND THE RISE OF THE RELIGIOUS RIGHT

DALLAS A. BLANCHARD

Dallas Blanchard is interested in the social change characteristics of religion, especially the history and growth of religious fundamentalism in the United States. In this reading, taken from his 1994 book of the same title, Blanchard examines how religious fundamentalism has impacted other current social issues, especially the debates concerning abortion and the influence of the Moral Majority on American politics.

For the nearly three decades in which the anti-abortion movement has been active, a variety of individuals and organizations have influenced both the form and the intensity of its protest. This [reading] looks at some of the determining factors in movement participation, particularly at what have become perhaps the most important influences in the 1980s and early 1990s—religious and cultural fundamentalism.

Why and How People Join the Anti-Abortion Movement

Researchers have posited a variety of explanations for what motivates people to join the anti-abortion movement. As with any other social movement, the anti-abortion movement has within it various subgroups, or organizations, each of which attracts different kinds of participants and expects different levels of participation. It might in fact be more appropriate to speak of anti-abortion *movements*.

Those opposing abortion are not unified. Some organizations have a single-issue orientation, opposing abortion alone, while others take what they consider to be a "pro-life" stance on many issues, opposing abortion as well as euthanasia, capital punishment, and the use of nuclear and chemical arms. The importance of abortion varies among the latter groups. There are also paper organizations, having virtually no real membership beyond a single organizer and perhaps several persons willing to lend their names to a letterhead. These are usually front groups for other organizations, designed to address topical issues; Defenders of the Defenders of Life, for instance, served the sole purpose of issuing press releases in defense of persons being tried for arsons and bombings. Some organizations arise and die, wax and wane over time as the climate surrounding an issue—in this case, abortion—changes. The rise, demise, and multiplication of various movement organizations can indicate the overall state of the movement: from growing public support and strength to desperation arising from a lack of support. Organizations also differ on goals, tactics, and strategies. The result of all of this differentiation is that various organizations may distance themselves from one another, depending on the disparities between their missions and their means of fulfilling those missions.

Just as the organizations within a movement differ, so do individuals vary in their motivations for joining it. Some anti-abortion activists are clearly anti-feminist, while others act out of communitarian, familistic, or even feminist concerns. Some are motivated by personal history, while others act on the basis of philosophical principle. A combination of factors in an individual's life history and social background contributes to the decision to join the movement in general and to participate in one organization in particular.

Researchers have identified a number of pathways for joining the anti-abortion movement. Luker, in her 1984 study of the early California movement, found that activists in the initial stages of the movement found their way to it through professional associations. The earliest opponents of abortion liberalization were primarily physicians and attorneys who disagreed with their professional associations' endorsement of abortion reform. It is my hypothesis that membership in organizations that concentrate on the education of the public or religious constituencies and on political lobbying is orchestrated primarily through professional networks. With the passage of the California reform bill and the increase in abortion rates several years later, many recruits to the movement fell into the category Luker refers to as "self-selected"; that is, they were not recruited through existing networks but sought out or sometimes formed organizations through which to express their opposition.

Himmelstein (1984), in summarizing the research on the anti-abortion movement available in the 10 years following *Roe v. Wade,* concluded that religious networks were the primary source of recruitment. Religious networks appear to be more crucial in the recruitment of persons into high-profile and/or violence prone groups (Blanchard and Prewitt 1993)—of which Operation Rescue is an example—than into the earlier, milder activist groups (although such networks are generally important throughout the movement). Such networks were also important, apparently, in recruitment into local Right to Life Committees, sponsored by the National Right to Life Committee and the Catholic church. The National Right to Life Committee, for example, is 72 percent Roman Catholic (Granberg 1981). It appears that the earliest anti-abortion organizations were essentially Catholic and dependent on church networks for their members; the recruitment of Protestants later on has also been dependent on religious networks (Cuneo 1989; Maxwell 1992).

Other avenues for participation in the anti-abortion movement opened up through association with other issues. Feminists for Life, for example, was founded by women involved in the feminist movement. Sojourners, a socially conscious evangelical group concerned with issues such as poverty and racism, has an anti-abortion position. Some anti-nuclear and anti-death penalty groups have also been the basis for the organization for anti-abortion efforts.

Clearly, preexisting networks and organizational memberships are crucial in initial enlistment into the movement. Hall (1993) maintains that individual mobilization into a social movement requires the conditions of attitudinal, network, and biographical availability. My conclusions regarding the anti-abortion movement support this contention. Indeed, biographical availability—the interaction of social class, occupation, familial status, sex, and age—is particularly related to the type of organization with which and the level of activism at which an individual will engage.

General social movement theory places the motivation to join the anti-abortion movement into four basic categories: status defense; anti-feminism; moral commitment; and cultural fundamentalism, or defense.

The earliest explanation for the movement was that participants were members of the working class attempting to shore up, or defend, their declining social status. Clarke, in his 1987 study of English anti-abortionists, finds this explanation to be inadequate, as do Wood and Hughes in their 1984 investigation of an anti-pornography movement group.

Petchesky (1984) concludes that the movement is basically anti-feminist—against the changing status of women. From this position, the primary goal of the movement is to "keep women in their place" and, in particular, to make them suffer for sexual "libertinism." Statements by some anti-abortion activists support this theory. Cuneo (1989), for example, finds what he calls "sexual puritans" on the fringe of the anti-abortion movement in Toronto. Abortion opponent and long-time right-wing activist Phyllis Schlaffley states this position: "It's very healthy for a young girl to be deterred from promiscuity by fear of contracting a painful, incurable disease, or cervical cancer, or sterility, or the likelihood of giving birth to a dead, blind or brain-damaged baby (even ten years later when she may be happily married)" (Planned Parenthood pamphlet [1990]).

Judie Brown, president of the American Life League, offers this judgment in "The Human Life Amendment" (n.d.:18):

The woman who is raped has a right to resist her attacker. But the pre-born child is an innocent non-aggressor who should not be killed because of the crime of the father. More to the point, since a woman has a right to resist the rapist, she also has the right to resist his sperm. . . . However, once the innocent third party to a rape, the preborn child, is conceived, he should not be killed. . . . Incest is a voluntary act on the woman's part. If it were not, it would be rape. And to kill a child because of the identity of his father is no more proper in the case of incest than it is in the case of rape.

A number of researchers have concluded that sexual moralism is the strongest predictor of anti-abortion attitudes.

The theory of moral commitment proposes that movement participants are motivated by concern for the human status of the fetus. It is probably as close as any explanation comes to "pure altruism." Although there is a growing body of research on altruism, researchers on the abortion issue have tended to ignore this as a possible draw to the movement, while movement participants almost exclusively claim this position: that since the fetus is incapable of defending itself, they must act on its behalf.

In examining and categorizing the motivations of participants in the anti-abortion movement in Toronto, Cuneo (1989: 85ff) found only one category—civil rights—that might be considered altruistic. The people in this category tend to be nonreligious and embarrassed by the activities of religious activists; they feel that fetuses have a right to exist but cannot speak for themselves. Cuneo's other primary categories of motivation are characterized by concerns related to the "traditional" family, the status of women in the family, and religion. He also finds an activist fringe composed of what he calls religious seekers; sexual therapeutics, "plagued by guilt and fear of female sexual power" (p. 115); and punitive puritans, who want to punish women for sexual transgressions. All of Cuneo's categories of participant, with the exception of the civil rights category, seek to maintain traditional male/female hierarchies and statuses. If we can generalize Cuneo's Toronto sample to the U.S. anti-abortion movement, I conclude that the majority, but by no means all, of those involved in the movement act out of self-interest, particularly out of defense of a cultural fundamentalist position.

The theory of cultural fundamentalism, or defense, proposes that the anti-abortion movement is largely an expression of the desire to return to what its proponents perceive to be "traditional culture." This theory incorporates elements of the status defense and anti-feminist theories.

It is important to note that a number of researchers at different points in time (Cuneo 1989; Ginsburg 1990; Luker 1984; Maxwell 1991, 1992) have indicated that (1) there have been changes over time in who gets recruited into the movement and why, (2) different motivations tend to bring different kinds of people into different types of activism, and (3) even particular movement organizations draw different kinds of people with quite different motivations. At this point in the history of the anti-abortion movement, the dominant motivation, particularly in the more activist organizations such as Operation Rescue, appears to be cultural fundamentalism. Closely informing cultural fundamentalism are the tenets of religious fundamentalism, usually associated with certain Protestant denominations but also evident in the Catholic and Mormon faiths. It is to the topics of religious and cultural fundamentalism as they relate to the anti-abortion movement that . . . we now turn.

Religious and Cultural Fundamentalism Defined

Cultural fundamentalism is in large part a protest against cultural change: against the rising status of women; against the greater acceptance of "deviant" lifestyles such as homosexuality; against the loss of prayer and Bible reading in the schools; and against the increase in sexual openness and freedom. Wood and Hughes (1984) describe cultural fundamentalism as "adherence to traditional norms, respect for family and religious authority, asceticism and control of impulse. Above all, it is an unflinching and thoroughgoing moralistic outlook on the world; moralism provides a common orientation and common discourse for concerns with the use of alcohol and pornography, the rights for homosexuals, 'pro-family' and 'decency' issues" (p. 89). The theologies of Protestants and Catholics active in the anti-abortion movement—many of whom could also be termed fundamentalists—reflect these concerns.

Protestant fundamentalism arose in the 1880s as a response to the use by Protestant scholars of the relatively new linguistic techniques of text and form criticism in their study of the Bible. These scholars determined that the Pentateuch was a compilation of at least five separate documents written from differing religious perspectives. Similar techniques applied to the New Testament questioned the traditionally assigned authorship of many of its books. The "mainline" denominations of the time (Episcopalian, Congregational, Methodist, Unitarian, and some Presbyterian) began to teach these new insights in their seminaries. With these approaches tended to go a general acceptance of other new and expanding scientific findings, such as evolution.

By 1900 the urbanization and industrialization of the United States were well under way, with their attendant social dislocations. One response to this upheaval was the Social Gospel movement, which strove to enact humanitarian laws regulating such things as child labor, unions, old-age benefits, and guaranteed living wages. With the Social Gospel movement and the acceptance of new scientific discoveries tended to go an optimism about the perfectibility of human nature and society.

Fundamentalism solidified its positions in opposition to these trends as well as in response to social change and the loss of the religious consensus, which came with the influx of European Jewish and Catholic immigrants to America. While fundamentalism was a growing movement prior to 1900, its trumpet was significantly sounded with the publication in 1910 of the first volume of a 12-volume series titled *The Fundamentals*. Prior to the 1920s and

1930s, it was primarily a movement of the North; growth in the South came mostly after 1950.

There are divisions within Protestant fundamentalism, but there is a general common basis of belief. Customary beliefs include a personal experience of salvation; verbal inspiration and literal interpretation of scriptures as worded in the King James Bible; the divinity of Jesus; the literal, physical resurrection of Jesus; special creation of the world in six days, as opposed to the theory of evolution; the virgin birth of Jesus; and the substitutionary atonement (Jesus' death on the cross as a substitution for each of the "saved"). The heart of Protestant fundamentalism is the literal interpretation of the Bible; secondary to this is the belief in substitutionary atonement.

Fundamentalists have also shown a strong tendency toward separatism—separation from the secular world as much as possible and separation from "apostates" (liberals and nonfundamentalist denominations). They are also united in their views on "traditional" family issues: opposing abortion, divorce, the Equal Rights Amendment, and civil rights for homosexuals. While their separatism was expressed prior to the 1970s in extreme hostilities toward Roman Catholicism, fundamentalists and Catholics share a large set of family values, which has led to their pragmatic cooperation in the anti-abortion movement.

Another tie between some Protestant fundamentalists and some Catholics lies in the Charismatic Renewal Movement. This movement, which coalesced in the 1920s, emphasized glossolalia (speaking in tongues) and faith healing. Charismatics were denied admission to the World's Christian Fundamental Association in 1928 because of these emphases. By the 1960s charismaticism began spreading to some mainline denominations and Catholic churches. While Presbyterians, United Methodists, Disciples of Christ, Episcopalians, and Lutherans sometimes reluctantly accepted this new charismatic movement, Southern Baptists and Churches of Christ adamantly opposed it, especially the speaking in tongues. But the Catholic charismatics have tended to be quite conservative both theologically and socially, giving them ideological ties with the charismatic Protestant fundamentalists and fostering cooperation between the two in interdenominational charismatic conferences, a prelude to cooperation in the anti-abortion movement.

There is also a Catholic "fundamentalism," which may or may not be charismatic and which centers on church dogma rather than biblical literalism, the Protestant a priori dogma. Catholic fundamentalists accept virtually unquestioningly the teachings of the church. They share with Protestant fundamentalists the assumption that dogma precedes and supersedes analytical reason, while in liberal Catholic and Protestant thought and in the nation's law reason supersedes dogma. Similar to Catholic fundamentalism is the Mormon faith (or the Church of Jesus Christ of Latter Day Saints), which also takes church dogma at face value.

There are at least six basic commonalities to what can be called Protestant, Catholic, and Mormon fundamentalisms: (1) an attitude of certitude—that one may know the final truth, which includes antagonism to ambiguity; (2) an external source for that certitude—the Bible or church dogma; (3) a belief system that is at root dualistic; (4) an ethic based on the "traditional" family; (5) a justification for violence; and therefore, (6) a rejection of modernism (secularization).

Taking those six commonalities point by point:

1. The certitude of fundamentalism rests on dependence on an external authority. That attitude correlates with authoritarianism which includes obedience to an external authority, and, on that basis, the willingness to assert authority over others.

2. While the Protestant fundamentalists accept their particular interpretation of the King James Version of the Bible as the authoritative source, Mormon and Catholic fundamentalists tend to view church dogma as authoritative.

3. The dualism of Catholics, Protestants, and Mormons includes those of body/soul, body/mind, physical/spiritual. More basically, they see a distinction between God and Satan, the forces of good and evil. In the fundamentalist worldview, Satan is limited and finite; he can be in only one place at one time. He has servants, however, demons who are constantly working his will, trying to deceive believers. A most important gift of the Spirit is the ability to distinguish between the activities of God and those of Satan and his demons.

4. The "traditional" family in the fundamentalist view of things has the father as head of the household, making the basic decisions, with the wife and children subject to his wishes. Obedience is stressed for both wives and children. Physical punishment is generally approved for use against both wives and children.

   This "traditional" family with the father as breadwinner and the mother as homemaker, together rearing a large family, is really not all that traditional. It arose on the family farm, prior to 1900, where large numbers of children were an economic asset. Even then, women were essential in the work of the farm. . . . in the urban environment, the "traditional" family structure was an option primarily for the middle and upper classes, and they limited their family size even prior to the development of efficient birth control methods. Throughout human history women have usually been breadwinners themselves, and the "traditional" family structure was not an option.

5. The justification for violence lies in the substitutionary theory of the atonement theology of both Protestants and Catholics. In this theory, the justice of God demands punishment for human sin. This God also supervises a literal hell, the images of which come more from Dante's *Inferno* than from the pages of the Bible. Fundamentalism, then, wor-

ships a violent God and offers a rationale for human violence (such as Old Testament demands for death when adultery, murder, and other sins are committed). The fundamentalist mindset espouses physical punishment of children, the death penalty, and the use of nuclear weapons; fundamentalists are more frequently wife abusers, committers of incest, and child abusers (Brinkerhoff and Pupri 1988).

6. Modernism entails a general acceptance of ambiguity, contingency, probability (versus certitude), and a unitary view of the universe; that is, the view that there is no separation between body and soul, physical and spiritual, body and mind (when the body dies, the self is thought to die with it). Rejection of modernism and postmodernism is inherent in the rejection of a unitary worldview in favor of a dualistic worldview. The classic fundamentalist position embraces a return to religion as the central social institution, with education, the family, economics, and politics serving religious ends, fashioned after the social structure characteristic of medieval times.

Also characteristic of Catholic, Protestant, and Mormon fundamentalists are a belief in individualism (which supports a naive capitalism); pietism; a chauvinistic Americanism (among some fundamentalists) that sees the United States as the New Israel and its inhabitants as God's new chosen people; and a general opposition to intellectualism, modern science, the tenets of the Social Gospel, and communism. . . . Amid this complex of beliefs and alongside the opposition to evolution, interestingly, is an underlying espousal of social Darwinism, the "survival of the fittest" ethos that presumes American society to be truly civilized, the pinnacle of social progress. This nineteenth-century American neocolonialism dominates the contemporary political views held by the religious right. It is also inherent in their belief in individualism and opposition to social welfare programs.

Particular personality characteristics also correlate with the fundamentalist syndrome: authoritarianism, self-righteousness, prejudice against minorities, moral absolutism (a refusal to compromise on perceived moral issues), and anti-analytical, anti-critical thinking. Many fundamentalists refuse to accept ambiguity as a given in moral decision making and tend to arrive at simplistic solutions to complex problems. For example, many hold that the solution to changes in the contemporary family can be answered by fathers' reasserting their primacy, by forcing their children and wives into blind obedience. Or, they say, premarital sex can be prevented by promoting abstinence. One popular spokesman, Tim LaHaye (1980), asserts that the antidote to sexual desire, especially on the part of teenagers, lies in censoring reading materials. Strict parental discipline automatically engenders self-discipline in children, he asserts. The implication is that enforced other-directedness by parents produces inner-directed children, while the evidence indicates that they are more likely to exchange parental authoritarianism for that of another parental figure. To develop inner direction under such circumstances requires, as a first step, rebellion against and rejection of parental authority—the opposite of parental intent.

One aspect of fundamentalism, particularly the Protestant variety, is its insistence on the subservient role of women. The wife is expected to be subject to the direction of her husband, children to their father. While Luker (1984) found that anti-abortionists in California supported this position and that proponents of choice generally favored equal status for women, recent research has shown that reasons for involvement in the anti-abortion movement vary by denomination. That is, some Catholics tend to be involved in the movement more from a "right to life" position, while Protestants and other Catholics are more concerned with sexual morality. The broader right to life position is consistent with the official Catholic position against the death penalty and nuclear arms, while Protestant fundamentalists generally support the death penalty and a strong military. Thus, Protestant fundamentalists, and some Catholic activists, appear to be more concerned with premarital sexual behavior than with the life of the fetus.

Protestants and Catholics (especially traditional, ethnic Catholics), however, are both concerned with the "proper," or subordinate, role of women and the dominant role of men. Wives should obey their husbands, and unmarried women should refrain from sexual intercourse. Abortion, for the Protestants in particular, is an indication of sexual licentiousness. Therefore, the total abolition of abortion would be a strong deterrent to such behavior, helping to reestablish traditional morality in women. Contemporary, more liberal views of sexual morality cast the virgin female as deviant. The male virgin has long been regarded as deviant. The fundamentalist ethic appears to accept this traditional double standard with its relative silence on male virginity.

Another aspect of this gender role ethic lies in the home-related roles of females. Women are expected to remain at home, to bear children, and to care for them, while also serving the needs of their husbands. Again, this is also related to social class and the social role expectations of the lower and working classes, who tend to expect women to "stay in their place."

Luker's (1984) research reveals that some women in the anti-abortion movement are motivated by a concern for maintaining their ability to rely on men (husbands) to support their social roles as mothers, while pro-choice women tend to want to maintain their independent status. Some of the men involved in anti-abortion violence are clearly acting out of a desire to maintain the dependent status of women and the dominant roles of men. Some of those violent males reveal an inability to establish "normal" relationships with women, which indicates that their violence may arise from a basic insecurity with the performance of normal male roles in relationships with women. This does not mean that these men do not have relationships with women. Indeed, it is in the context of relationships with women that dominance-related tendencies become more manifest. It is likely that insecurity-driven behaviors are characteristic of violent males generally, but psychiatric data are not available to confirm this, even for the population in question.

The Complex of Fundamentalist Issues

The values and beliefs inherent to religious and cultural fundamentalism are expressed in a number of issues other than abortion. Those issues bear some discussion here, particularly as they relate to the abortion question.

1. *Contraception.* Fundamentalists, Catholic, Protestant, and Mormon, generally oppose the use of contraceptives since they limit family size and the intentions of God in sexuality. They especially oppose sex education in the schools and the availability of contraceptives to minors without the approval of their parents. This is because control of women and sexuality are intertwined. If a girl has knowledge of birth control, she is potentially freed of the threat of pregnancy if she becomes sexually active. This frees her from parental control and discovery of illegitimate sexual intercourse.

2. *Prenatal testing, pregnancies from rape or incest, or those endangering a woman's life.* Since every pregnancy is divinely intended, opposition to prenatal testing arises from its use to abort severely defective fetuses and, in some cases, for sex selection. Abortion is wrong regardless of the origins of the pregnancy or the consequences of it.

3. *In vitro fertilization, artificial fertilization, surrogate motherhood.* These are opposed because they interfere with the "natural" fertilization process and because they may mean the destruction of some fertilized embryos.

4. *Homosexuality.* Homophobia is characteristic of fundamentalism, because homosexual behavior is viewed as being "unnatural" and is prohibited in the Bible.

5. *Uses of fetal tissue.* The use of fetal tissue in research and in the treatment of medical conditions such as Parkinson's disease is opposed, because it is thought to encourage abortion.

6. *Foreign relations issues.* Fundamentalists generally support aid to Israel and military funding (Diamond 1989). Indeed, as previously mentioned, they commonly view the United States as the New Israel. Protestant fundamentalists tend to be pre-millenialists, who maintain that biblical prophecies ordain that the reestablishment of the State of Israel will precede the Second Coming of Christ. Thus, they support aid to Israel to hasten the Second Coming, which actually, then, has an element of anti-Semitism to it, since Jews will not be among the saved.

7. *Euthanasia.* So-called right to life groups have frequently intervened in cases where relatives have sought to remove a patient from life-

support systems. Most see a connection with abortion in that both abortion and the removal of life support interfere with God's decision as to when life should begin and end.

The most radical expression of cultural fundamentalism is that of Christian Reconstructionism, to which Randall Terry, former director of Operation Rescue, subscribes. The adherents of Christian Reconstructionism, while a distinct minority, have some congregations of up to 12,000 members and count among their number Methodists, Presbyterians, Lutherans, Baptists, Catholics, and former Jews. They are unabashed theocratists. They believe every area of life—law, politics, the arts, education, medicine, the media, business, and especially morality—should be governed in accordance with the tenets of Christian Reconstructionism. Some, such as Gary North, a prominent reconstructionist and son-in-law of Rousas John Rushdoony, considered the father of reconstructionism, would deny religious liberty—the freedom of religious expression—to "the enemies of God," whom the reconstructionists, of course, would identify.

The reconstructionists want to establish a "God-centered government," a Kingdom of God on Earth, instituting the Old Testament as the Law of the Land. The goal of reconstructionism is to reestablish biblical, Jerusalemic society. Their program is quite specific. Those criminals which the Old Testament condemned to death would be executed, including homosexuals, sodomites, rapists, adulterers, and "incorrigible" youths. Jails would become primarily holding tanks for those awaiting execution or assignment as servants indentured to those whom they wronged as one form of restitution. The media would be censored extensively to reflect the views of the church. Public education and welfare would be abolished (only those who work should eat), and taxes would be limited to the tithe, 10 percent of income, regardless of income level, most of it paid to the church. Property, Social Security, and inheritance taxes would be eliminated. Church elders would serve as judges in courts overseeing moral issues, while "civil" courts would handle other issues. The country would return to the gold standard. Debts, including, for example, 30-year mortgages, would be limited to six years. In short, Christian Reconstructionists see democracy as being opposed to Christianity, as placing the rule of man above the rule of God. They also believe that "true" Christianity has its earthly rewards. They see it as the road to economic prosperity, with God blessing the faithful.

REFERENCES

Editor's Note: The original chapter from which this selection was taken has extensive footnotes and references that could not be listed in their entirety here. For more explanation and documentation of sources, please see Dallas A. Blanchard. 1994. *The Anti-Abortion Movement and the Rise of the Religious Right: From Polite to Fiery Protest.* New York: Twayne Publishers.

Blanchard, Dallas A. and Terry J. Prewitt. 1993. *Religious Violence and Abortion: The Gideon Project.* Gainesville: University Press of Florida.

Brinkerhoff, Merlin B. and Eugene Pupri. 1988. "Religious Involvement and Spousal Abuse: The Canadian Case." Paper presented at the Society of the Scientific Study of Religion.

Clarke, Alan. 1987. "Collective Action against Abortion Represents a Display of, and Concern for, Cultural Values, Rather than an Expression of Status Discontent." *British Journal of Sociology* 38:235–53.

Cuneo, Michael. 1989. *Catholics against the Church: Anti-Abortion Protest in Toronto, 1969–1985.* Toronto: University of Toronto Press.

Diamond, Sara. 1989. *Spiritual Warfare: The Politics of the Christian Right.* Boston: South End Press.

Ginsburg, Faye. 1990. *Contested Lives: The Abortion Debate in an American Community.* Berkeley: University of California Press.

Granberg, Donald. 1978. "Pro-Life or Reflection of Conservative Ideology? An Analysis of Opposition to Legalized Abortion." *Sociology and Social Research* 62:421–23.

———. 1981. "The Abortion Activists." *Family Planning Perspectives* 18:158–61.

Hall, Charles. 1993. "Social Networks and Availability Factors: Mobilizing Adherents for Social Movement Participation" (Ph.D. dissertation, Purdue University).

Himmelstein, Jerome L. 1984. "The Social Basis of Anti-Feminism: Religious Networks and Culture." *Journal for the Scientific Study of Religion* 25:1–25.

LaHaye, Tim. 1980. *The Battle for the Mind.* Old Tappan, NJ: Fleming H. Revell Co.

Luker, Kristin. 1984. *Abortion and the Politics of Motherhood.* Berkeley: University of California Press.

Maxwell, Carol. 1991. "Where's the Land of Happy? Individual Meanings in Pro-Life Direct Action." Paper presented at the Society for the Scientific Study of Religion.

———. 1992. "Denomination, Meaning, and Persistence: Difference in Individual Motivation to Obstruct Abortion Practice." Paper presented at the Society for the Scientific Study of Religion.

Petchesky, Rosalind P. 1984. *Abortion and Woman's Choice: The State, Sexuality, and Reproductive Freedom.* New York: Longman.

Planned Parenthood Federation of America. 1990. Public Affairs Action Letter. (No title, no date.)

Wood, M. and M. Hughes. 1984. "The Moral Basis of Moral Reform: Status Discontent vs. Culture and Socialization As Explanations of Anti-Pornography Social Movement Adherence." *American Sociological Review* 44:86–99.

44

THE SOCIAL STRUCTURE OF MEDICINE

TALCOTT PARSONS

Medical sociology is one of the largest and fastest growing subspecialties within the discipline of sociology. Medical sociologists are concerned with all aspects of the social institution of medicine, including the socialization of doctors, the social construction of health and illness, and the social structure of hospitals and the health care system. The following three readings illustrate different perspectives within the field of medical sociology, beginning with an excerpt from Talcott Parsons' classic 1951 book, *The Social System*. Parsons (1902–1979) was well known for his contributions to the theoretical perspective of structural functionalism. In this selection, Parsons utilizes this perspective to explain how health and illness are significant within a social system, including how they influence the complimentary social roles of patients and physicians.

A little reflection will show immediately that the problem of health is intimately involved in the functional prerequisites of the social system. . . . Certainly by almost any definition health is included in the functional needs of the individual member of the society so that from the point of view of functioning of the social system, too low a general level of health, too high an incidence of illness, is dysfunctional. This is in the first instance because illness incapacitates for the effective performance of social roles. It could of course be that this incidence was completely uncontrollable by social action, an independently given condition of social life. But insofar as it is controllable, through rational action or otherwise, it is clear that there is a functional interest of the society in its control, broadly in the minimization of illness. As one special aspect of this, attention may be called to premature death. From a variety of points of view, the birth and rearing of a child constitute a "cost" to the society, through pregnancy, child care, socialization, formal training, and many other channels. Premature death, before the individual has had the opportunity to play out his full quota of social roles, means that only a partial "return" for this cost has been received.

All this would be true were illness purely a "natural phenomenon" in the sense that, like the vagaries of the weather, it was not, to our knowledge, reciprocally involved in the motivated interactions of human beings. In this case illness would be something which merely "happened to" people, which involved consequences which had to be dealt with and conditions which might or might not be controllable but was in no way an expression of motivated behavior.

This is in fact the case for a very important part of illness, but it has become increasingly clear, by no means for all. In a variety of ways motivational factors accessible to analysis in action terms are involved in the etiology of many illnesses, and conversely, though without exact correspondence, many conditions are open to therapeutic influence through motivational channels. To take the simplest kind of case, differential exposure, to injuries or to infection, is certainly motivated, and the role of unconscious wishes to be injured or to fall ill in such cases has been clearly demonstrated. Then there is the whole range of "psychosomatic" illness about which knowledge has been rapidly accumulating in recent years. Finally, there is the field of "mental disease," the symptoms of which occur mainly on the behavioral level. . . .

Summing up, we may say that illness is a state of disturbance in the "normal" functioning of the total human individual, including both the state of the organism as a biological system and of his personal and social adjustments. It is thus partly biologically and partly socially defined. . . .

Medical practice . . . is a "mechanism" in the social system for coping with the illnesses of its members. It involves a set of institutionalized roles. . . . The immediately relevant social structures consist in the patterning of the role of the medical practitioner himself and, though to common sense it may seem superfluous to analyze it, that of the "sick person" himself. . . .

The role of the medical practitioner belongs to the general class of "professional" roles, a subclass of the larger group of occupational roles. Caring for the sick is thus not an incidental activity of other roles though, for example, mothers do a good deal of it—but has become functionally specialized as a full-time "job." This, of course, is by no means true of all societies. As an occupational role it is institutionalized about the technical content of the function which is given a high degree of primacy relative to other status-determinants. It is thus inevitable both that incumbency of the role should be achieved and that performance criteria by standards of technical competence should be prominent. Selection for it and the context of its performance are to a high degree segregated from other bases of social status and solidarities. . . . Unlike the role of the businessman, however, it is collectivity-oriented not self-oriented.

The importance of this patterning is, in one context, strongly emphasized by its relation to the cultural tradition. One basis for the division of labor is the specialization of technical competence. The role of physician is far along the continuum of increasingly high levels of technical competence re-

quired for performance. Because of the complexity and subtlety of the knowledge and skill required and the consequent length and intensity of training,
it is difficult to see how the functions could, under modern conditions, be ascribed to people occupying a prior status as one of their activities in that
status, following the pattern by which, to a degree, responsibility for the
health of her children is ascribed to the mother-status. There is an intrinsic
connection between achieved statuses and the requirements of high technical competence. . . .

High technical competence also implies specificity of function. Such intensive devotion to expertness in matters of health and disease precludes
comparable expertness in other fields. The physician is not, by virtue of his
modern role, a generalized "wise man" or sage—though there is considerable folklore to that effect—but a specialist whose superiority to his fellows
is confined to the specific sphere of his technical training and experience. For
example one does not expect the physician as such to have better judgment
about foreign policy or tax legislation than any other comparably intelligent
and well-educated citizen. There are of course elaborate subdivisions of specialization within the profession. . . . The physician is [also] expected to treat
an objective problem in objective, scientifically justifiable terms. For example, whether he likes or dislikes the particular patient as a person is supposed to be irrelevant, as indeed it is to most purely objective problems of
how to handle a particular disease.

. . . The "ideology" of the profession lays great emphasis on the obligation of the physician to put the "welfare of the patient" above his personal
interests, and regards "commercialism" as the most serious and insidious
evil with which it has to contend. The line, therefore, is drawn primarily vis-
à-vis "business." The "profit motive" is supposed to be drastically excluded
from the medical world. This attitude is, of course, shared with the other
professions, but it is perhaps more pronounced in the medical case than in
any single one except perhaps the clergy. . . .

An increasing proportion of medical practice is now taking place in the
context of organization. To a large extent this is necessitated by the technological development of medicine itself, above all the need for technical facilities beyond the reach of the individual practitioner, and the fact that
treating the same case often involves the complex cooperation of several different kinds of physicians as well as of auxiliary personnel. This greatly alters the relation of the physician to the rest of the instrumental complex. He
tends to be relieved of much responsibility and hence necessarily of freedom, in relation to his patients other than in his technical role. Even if a hospital executive is a physician himself he is not in the usual sense engaged in
the "practice of medicine" in performing his functions any more than the
president of the Miners' Union is engaged in mining coal.

As was noted, for common sense there may be some question of whether
"being sick" constitutes a social role at all—isn't it simply a state of fact, a
"condition"? Things are not quite so simple as this. The test is the existence

of a set of institutionalized expectations and the corresponding sentiments and sanctions.

There seem to be four aspects of the institutionalized expectation system relative to the sick role. First is the exemption from normal social role responsibilities, which of course is relative to the nature and severity of the illness. This exemption requires legitimation by and to the various alters involved and the physician often serves as a court of appeal as well as a direct legitimatizing agent. It is noteworthy that like all institutionalized patterns the legitimation of being sick enough to avoid obligations can not only be a right of the sick person but an obligation upon him. People are often resistant to admitting they are sick and it is not uncommon for others to tell them that they *ought* to stay in bed. The word generally has a moral connotation. It goes almost without saying that this legitimation has the social function of protection against "malingering."

The second closely related aspect is the institutionalized definition that the sick person cannot be expected by "pulling himself together" to get well by an act of decision or will. In this sense also he is exempted from responsibility—he is in a condition that must "be taken care of." His "condition" must be changed, not merely his "attitude." Of course the process of recovery may be spontaneous but while the illness lasts he can't "help it." This element in the definition of the state of illness is obviously crucial as a bridge to the acceptance of "help."

The third element is the definition of the state of being ill as itself undesirable with its obligation to want to "get well." The first two elements of legitimation of the sick role thus are conditional in a highly important sense. It is a relative legitimation so long as he is in this unfortunate state which both he and alter hope he can get out of as expeditiously as possible.

Finally, the fourth closely related element is the obligation—in proportion to the severity of the condition, of course—to seek *technically competent* help, namely, in the most usual case, that of a physician and to *cooperate* with him in the process of trying to get well. It is here, of course, that the role of the sick person as patient becomes articulated with that of the physician in a complementary role structure.

It is evident from the above that the role of motivational factors in illness immensely broadens the scope and increases the importance of the institutionalized role aspect of being sick. For then the problem of social control becomes much more than one of ascertaining facts and drawing lines. The privileges and exemptions of the sick role may become objects of a "secondary gain" which the patient is positively motivated, usually unconsciously, to secure or to retain. The problem, therefore, of the balance of motivations to recover becomes of first importance. In general motivational balances of great functional significance to the social system are institutionally controlled, and it should, therefore, not be surprising that this is no exception.

A few further points may be made about the specific patterning of the sick role and its relation to social structure. It is, in the first place, a "contingent" role into which anyone, regardless of his status in other respects, may come. It is, furthermore, in the type case temporary. One may say that it is in a certain sense a "negatively achieved" role, through failure to "keep well," though, of course, positive motivations also operate, which by that very token must be motivations to deviance. . . .

The orientation of the sick role vis-à-vis the physician is also defined as collectively-oriented. It is true that the patient has a very obvious self-interest in getting well in most cases, though this point may not always be so simple. But once he has called in a physician the attitude is clearly marked, that he has assumed the obligation to cooperate with that physician in what is regarded as a common task. The obverse of the physician's obligation to be guided by the welfare of the patient is the latter's obligation to "do his part" to the best of his ability. This point is clearly brought out, for example, in the attitudes of the profession toward what is called "shopping around." By that is meant the practice of a patient "checking" the advice of one physician against that of another without telling physician A that he intends to consult physician B, or if he comes back to A that he has done so or who B is. The medical view is that if the patient is not satisfied with the advice his physician gives him he may properly do one of two things, first he may request a consultation, even naming the physician he wishes called in, but in that case it is physician A not the patient who must call B in, the patient may not see B independently, and above all not without A's knowledge. The other proper recourse is to terminate the relation with A and become "B's patient." The notable fact here is that a pattern of behavior on the part not only of the physician but also of the patient, is expected which is in sharp contrast to perfectly legitimate behavior in a commercial relationship. If he is buying a car there is no objection to the customer going to a number of dealers before making up his mind, and there is no obligation for him to inform any one dealer what others he is consulting, to say nothing of approaching the Chevrolet dealer only through the Ford dealer.

The doctor-patient relationship is thus focused on these pattern elements. The patient has a need for technical services because he doesn't—nor do his lay associates, family members, etc.—"know" what is the matter or what to do about it, nor does he control the necessary facilities. The physician is a technical expert who by special training and experience, and by an institutionally validated status, is qualified to "help" the patient in a situation institutionally defined as legitimate in a relative sense but as needing help. . . .

45

IMPURE SCIENCE
AIDS, Activism, and the Politics of Knowledge

STEVEN EPSTEIN

One aspect of sociological research is the study of how social activists can influence and change social institutions and social policy. In this reading, taken from the award-winning book, *Impure Science: AIDS, Activism, and the Politics of Knowledge* (1997), Steven Epstein examines how AIDS activists, such as ACT UP and other groups, have influenced the powerful agendas of AIDS researchers, drug companies, and governmental agencies. In the excerpt that follows, Epstein investigates how, during the first fifteen years of the epidemic, AIDS activists have shaped the construction of medical and scientific knowledge surrounding the causation of and treatments for HIV/AIDS.

Two sets of controversies demonstrate with particular force the centrality of credibility struggles in the constitution of scientific knowledge about AIDS: debates about the *causes* of the syndrome and debates about *treatments*. These debates strike at some of the central questions that confront biomedical science: What is AIDS and what causes it? How can its effects be curtailed?

The Politics of Causation

Who could doubt that HIV, the human immunodeficiency virus, causes AIDS? That proposition has been the accepted scientific wisdom since the mid-1980s, after several groups of researchers reported finding a previously unknown virus in the blood of AIDS patients.[1] It is a conclusion endorsed by preeminent virologists, immunologists, epidemiologists, and clinicians; by the World Health Organization and the Centers for Disease Control and Prevention (CDC); and by prominent AIDS service and advocacy organizations. In the mainstream media, HIV is casually referred to as the "AIDS virus"; among insiders, AIDS is increasingly understood as simply the end stage of "HIV disease." The claim that HIV is the etiological agent in the Acquired

Immunodeficiency Syndrome is the guiding assumption behind billion-dollar programs for HIV antibody testing, antiviral drug development and treatment, and vaccine research around the world. It is the cornerstone of "what science knows about AIDS."[2]

Yet the search for the cause of AIDS took many twists and turns before settling on HIV. Indeed, the notion that AIDS might be caused by a previously unknown virus was initially a relatively *unpopular* one. Beginning with a zero point of near-total uncertainty, competing groups of scientific claims-makers, under the watchful gaze of interested segments of the public who sought to establish "ownership" over the epidemic, advanced various hypotheses. Then, between 1984 and 1986, a bandwagon formed behind the proposal that a particular virus, eventually named HIV, was the causal agent.

Nevertheless, in the late 1980s and early 1990s, some years after the discovery of HIV and the large-scale implementation of social policy based on it, the markers of controversy abounded. Symptomatic were debates about "cofactors" needed to cause disease, investigations into the mysteries of "pathogenesis" (Just *how* does HIV cause disease?), and scares about cases of an "AIDS-like" illness in HIV-negative people. Most astounding of all have been the claims of Peter Duesberg, a molecular biologist at the University of California at Berkeley and a member of the elite National Academy of Sciences. Beginning in 1987 in an article in *Cancer Research* and subsequently in articles in publications such as *Science* and the *Proceedings of the National Academy of Sciences*, Duesberg has maintained that HIV is a harmless passenger in the AIDS epidemic, "just the most common among the occupational viral infections of AIDS patients and those at risk for AIDS, rather than the cause of AIDS."[3] He argues that there is no solid evidence establishing a causal role for the virus and, furthermore, that a retrovirus such as HIV simply cannot cause a syndrome like AIDS. Instead, Duesberg's current alternative hypothesis is that "the American AIDS epidemic is a subset of the drug epidemic,"[4] attributable primarily to long-term consumption of recreational drugs and secondarily to what Duesberg calls "AIDS by prescription"—the toxic effects of the medication azidothymidine (AZT), widely prescribed to fight HIV infection.

Duesberg is only one of a number of researchers, doctors, and activists who have cast doubt on the "HIV hypothesis," but he has attracted by far the most attention. Duesberg's claims have prompted dozens of articles and communications in scientific journals and several hundred articles and letters in the mainstream English-language press. In 1994, *Science,* one of the most important general science journals in the world, devoted eight pages to the "Duesberg phenomenon."[5] The story has found its way into *Naturwissenschaften* and the *Gaceta Médica de México;*[6] the *Los Angeles Times*, the *New York Times*, and the *Times* of London;[7] National Public Radio and *Penthouse;*[8] the position papers of an AIDS advocacy organization and the columns of a pop music magazine;[9] and perhaps every gay and lesbian news source in the

United States. Reporters are quick to stress Duesberg's impressive credentials. He is frequently cast as a "heretic" who, like Galileo, has been excommunicated by dogmatic proponents of "orthodoxy" less interested in truth than in their hold on the faithful.[10] And reporters are often quick to mention that Duesberg has declared himself in principle "quite happy to [be] publicly injected with HIV."[11] Many scientists who think Duesberg is dead wrong are made apoplectic by the mention of his name. "I'm so tired of hearing the Peter Duesberg crap about HIV," said Donald Francis, a prominent AIDS researcher formerly with the CDC, to an audience of one thousand at a 1992 public forum on AIDS in San Francisco. "News reporters looking for an AIDS angle should look for another story. . . . The disease is caused by the virus, dammit, and the press should understand that.[12]

To describe the construction of facts such as "HIV causes AIDS," sociologists of scientific knowledge have adopted the phrase "black box."[13] As Bruno Latour explains, the concept is borrowed from cybernetics, where black boxes are used in diagrams as a quick way of alluding to some complex process or piece of machinery: if it's not necessary to get into the details, one just draws a box and shows the input and the output. Then no one has to worry about what goes on inside the box itself, and the nonexpert may never even realize just how messy the inside really is. Scientific facts are similar: masked beneath their hard exterior is an entire social history of actions and decisions, experiments and arguments, claims and counterclaims—often enough, a *disorderly* history of contingency, controversy, and uncertainty.

Scientists strive to "close" black boxes: they take *observations* ("The radioactive isotope count that indicates the presence of reverse transcriptase, an enzyme associated with retroviruses, rises over time in specially prepared lymph tissue from a person with an illness believed to be AIDS-related"), present them as *discoveries* ("A novel human retrovirus has been grown in T-lymphocytes of AIDS patients"), and turn them into *claims* ("The probable cause of AIDS has been found") which are accepted by others ("HIV, the putative cause of AIDS, . . .") and may eventually become *facts* ("HIV, the virus that causes AIDS, . . .") and, finally, *common knowledge,* too obvious even to merit a footnote. Fact-making—the process of closing a black box—is successful when contingency is forgotten, controversy is smoothed over, and uncertainty is bracketed. Before a black box has been closed, it remains possible to glimpse human actors performing various kinds of work—examining and interpreting, inventing and guessing, persuading and debating. Once the fact-making process is complete and the relevant controversies are closed, human agency fades from view; and the farther one is from the research front, the harder it is to catch glimpses of underlying uncertainties.[14] It then becomes difficult to ask, Was the examination accurate? Was the interpretation defensible? Was the persuasion logical? Those who want to challenge a claim that has been accepted as fact must effectively "reopen" the black box.

What are the dynamics of fact making when science is closely scrutinized by attentive spectators? What are the processes by which black boxes are closed and reopened when scientific arguments become the stuff of news reports and street conversations? There are examples of important controversies in science—the debate over continental drift is one[15]—that barely get any airplay in the "outside" world. AIDS is something else again. With millions of people around the world believed to be infected with HIV, the human stake in the causation controversy is gigantic, immediate, and inescapable. It should therefore come as no surprise that the cast of characters in AIDS debates is diverse. A full-fledged inquiry into the controversy immediately bursts us out of the "scientific field" narrowly construed. It forces an examination of the ensemble of social actors, with varying and conflicting social interests, who at different points have struggled to assert credible knowledge about the epidemic or to assert their capability to weigh and evaluate such knowledge.

At a different level, the causation controversy reflects a struggle for "ownership of" and "democracy within" science. An agenda has emerged, well expressed in the words of writer Jad Adams, one of the "HIV dissidents" and author of *AIDS: The HIV Myth:* "Ultimately, expert advice must be evaluated by the people who are not experts—politicians, journalists, and the public. This is part of democratic life and a scientist has no more right to exclusion from public scrutiny than a treasury official." [16] In the intervention of laypeople in debates about the causes of AIDS, claims about causes are interwoven with claims about the very right to intervene. It makes sense that the opponents of the orthodox position on causation so frequently take aim at what they call the premature "rush to judgment" in 1984 on the question of causation: from their perspective, this moment represented the stifling of democratic openness of opinion and the authoritarian imposition of closure. In many ways the debate has become a *debate about closure*—that is, a debate about when and how scientific controversies end.[17] But concerns about closure in this case break down into a number of important dimensions: *epistemological* (When is causation proven?), *methodological* (How should rival theories be weighed and compared?), *empirical* (Was closure arrived at too early? What conclusions did the evidence permit in 1984 and what conclusions are reasonable today?), and most notably, *political* (Who decides? Which social actors are qualified or entitled to participate in the process of establishing the scientific knowledge about AIDS?). In other words, the controversies about what causes AIDS are simultaneously *controversies about scientific controversies* and how they should be adjudicated— controversies about power and responsibility, about expertise and the right to speak. As frames of knowledge and belief about AIDS have become fixed in place, a range of social actors have engaged in credibility struggles to defend, refine, subvert, overturn, or reconstruct those frames.

It is not just that the controversy extends across a range of scientific disciplines—virology, epidemiology, immunology, molecular biology, pharmacology, toxicology, and clinical medicine. The controversy also spins off into a series of more general debates about the nature of disease and the methods of scientific reasoning: Do diseases typically have a single cause or multiple causes? Are established rules of scientific proof inviolable, or are they subject to revision as scientific knowledge changes and technologies improve? When anomalies are found that appear to falsify an existing hypothesis, when should the hypothesis be scrapped and when is it proper scientific procedure to work with the hypothesis, tinkering with it so that it can account for the anomalies? Does normal, peer-reviewed "establishment science" produce the best results in the end, or do the truly revolutionary findings come from the mavericks and iconoclasts who challenge, or work outside of, the system?

And finally, as the controversy has expanded from one social arena to the next, it has never been articulated in a vacuum, separate from other social concerns. On the contrary, a variety of apparently tangential beliefs and values have spilled over into (indeed, partially constitute) the AIDS etiology debates. These beliefs and values include divergent attitudes toward homosexuality, promiscuity, and drug use; inferences that link the causes or origins of a disease with theories of social blame; and assumptions about whether illnesses are attributable primarily to microbes, lifestyles, or societies. In short, the AIDS causation controversy is inexplicable outside of the larger context of how AIDS has been constructed as a social problem against the backdrop of contested attitudes about scientific medicine.

The Politics of Treatment

Find the cause, then find the cure: this is the mission of biomedicine in a nutshell. But how does it work in practice? What are the social processes that bring a therapy from laboratory bench to medicine cabinet? Who decides what treatment strategies to pursue or how to develop and test medications? Exactly what does it mean to say that a treatment "works"? Like debates about the causes of AIDS, claims and counterclaims about treatments involve frequent struggles for credibility—struggles waged in the shadow of towering uncertainty and driven by urgent need. Progress, and power, derive from the ability to submit credible answers—to push back the bounds of uncertainty, to offer something that "helps," to voice what is "known."

The actors in this drama are as varied as the interests that motivate them and the values that animate them—the researchers hoping to hit on breakthroughs in the basic or applied sciences of AIDS research; the pharmaceutical and biotechnology companies whose stock values might fluctuate by millions of dollars, depending on the latest reports about the successes or failures of their products; the medical professionals who must translate inconclusive and contradictory research findings into workable, day-to-day clinical judgments; the regulatory agencies and advisory bodies that serve as "gatekeepers," ruling on the safety and efficacy of new therapies; the patients who consume the drugs and populate the clinical trials; the reporters and journalists who interpret scientific research findings to various segments of the public; and, of course, the activists who police the whole process and offer their own interpretations of the methods and the outcomes. In the late 1980s, "treatment activism" emerged as the forward wedge of the multifocal AIDS activist movement in the United States, widely hailed—and sometimes damned—for its ingenuity, brashness, aptitude, and muscle.

"There's no doubt that they've had an enormous effect," commented Dr. Stephen Joseph in 1990, soon after leaving the post of New York City health commissioner. "We've basically changed the way we make drugs available in the last year." [18] While the activist impact on the regulatory procedures of the Food and Drug Administration (FDA) has been widely publicized, this remains just one of many items on treatment activists' agenda for the reformation of biomedical science. As the National Research Council of the National Academy of Sciences put it (in a 1993 report otherwise noteworthy for its *skepticism* about the transformative effects of the AIDS epidemic on U.S. society): "Every aspect of the process by which new pharmacologic agents [are] identified, evaluated, regulated, and allocated [has been] tested by the exigencies of [this] epidemic disease. Questions basic to the epistemologic foundations of biomedicine—questions of verifiability, reproducibility, proof, variability, safety, and efficacy—[have all been] subject to debate and reevaluation." [19]

Treatment activists have been pivotal in this rethinking of biomedical truth-making. They have challenged the formal procedures by which clinical drug trials are designed, conducted, and interpreted; confronted the vested interests of the pharmaceutical companies and the research establishment; demanded rapid access to scientific data; insisted on their right to assign priorities in AIDS research; and even organized research on their own, with the cooperation of allied professionals. Starting out on the margins of the system, treatment activists have pushed their way inside, taking their seats at the table of power. Activists now sit as full voting members of the NIH committees that oversee AIDS drug development, as invited participants at the FDA advisory committee meetings where drugs are considered for approval, as members of federal review panels that consider proposals for research grants, and, at local levels, as representatives on the review boards that approve clinical research at hospitals and academic centers.

In addition to moving inward, they have pursued an evolution "backward," as treatment activists themselves have noted. Beginning with a focus on the end stage of the drug development process, they have worked their way back toward earlier and earlier moments—"from drug approval at the regulatory level of [the FDA], to expanded access for drugs still under study . . . , to the design and conduct of the controlled clinical trials themselves. . . ." [20] Most recently, several prominent treatment groups have pushed back even further, to promote, monitor, and criticize the directions of basic AIDS research—the "pure science" investigations in immunology, virology, and molecular biology that are considered the necessary prelude to the applied work of developing and testing specific therapies.[21]

The vigorous participation of self-educated activists—and more broadly, the rise of knowledge-empowered communities that monitor the course of biomedical research—has had momentous effects on the development of AIDS treatments. These developments have transformed the procedures by which drugs are tested, the ways in which test results are interpreted, and the processes by which those interpretations are then used in the licensing of drugs for sale.

The Conduct of Clinical Research

In the postwar era, the assessment of therapies has been linked to the techniques of the randomized clinical trial. Such trials provide crucial "hard data" about treatment effects, but also obscure political decisions about how to measure the risks and benefits of a drug, cloaking them in the aura and mystery of objective science. Widely considered the pathway to objectivity in modern biomedical research, clinical trial results in practice can be subject to enormous amounts of interpretative flexibility. Precisely because the stakes are often high—both in human lives and in stock market values—deciphering clinical trial findings can prove not only a contentious process, but also a highly public one.[22]

Clinical trials are also a form of experimentation that requires the consistent and persistent cooperation of tens, hundreds, or thousands of human beings—"subjects," in both senses of the word, who must ingest substances on schedule, present their bodies on a regular basis for invasive laboratory procedures, and otherwise play by the rules, known more formally as the study protocols. From the standpoint of the researcher, ensuring the cooperation of research subjects is a complicated endeavor because these "bodies" talk back: subjects participate or don't participate and comply with the study protocols or not, depending on their own perceptions of what works and what doesn't, how desperate their own health situation is, and what options are open to them.[23]

It has recently been argued that the history of clinical trials needs to be rewritten to, in effect, "bring the patient back in"—to demonstrate how the capacity to construct knowledge through this particular technique is both enabled and constrained by the research subjects and the resistance they present to the epistemic goals of the clinical investigators.[24] In fact, the AIDS epidemic should be considered a decisive turning point in this revisionist history. AIDS trials are distinctive not only because of the militancy of many of the patients, but because their representatives have mobilized to develop effective social movement organizations that evaluate knowledge claims, disseminate information, and insert laypeople into the process of knowledge construction. The activist representatives of AIDS patients not only facilitate the flow of information to and among them, but also press demands about what should be studied in the first place and how the research protocols should be worded. Highly technical details such as the entry requirements for trials, the types of controls employed, and the endpoints to be used in studies have all been the subject of vociferous debate. Such developments pose substantial complications for the "politics of therapeutic evaluation."[25]

The Interpretation of Studies

"You can't reproduce the real world in a . . . clinical study," acknowledges Dr. Douglas Richman, a prominent AIDS researcher at the University of California at San Diego. "The hope is that you can define things in such a way that you can get some interpretable data in which the bias is sufficiently limited [so] that it's meaningful and it's applicable to other situations. . . ."[26] As Steven Shapin expresses it, any laboratory experiment has credibility only insofar as it is taken to "stand for" some actual conditions in the "real world": for example, "when Robert Boyle put a barometer in an air-pump and then exhausted the air, its behavior was meant to stand for what would happen were one to walk a barometer up to the top of the atmosphere." But the *extent* to which the experiment adequately represents reality is always subject to negotiation—and open to deconstruction.[27] The effect of activist interventions into questions of research design and interpretation has been precisely to "denaturalize" clinical trials—to call the objectivity of the methods into question, to reveal their "artificial and conventional" status, and to make the results of given trials more open to question.[28]

Few people, including practicing physicians and many academic researchers who conduct clinical trials, can entirely follow all the statistical arguments that constitute the formal evidence invoked in favor of, or in opposition to, a given treatment.[29] Most players therefore become adept at reading the signposts: Where was the study published? Who conducted it? Was it peer reviewed? Is anyone criticizing it? Are there any methodological flaws or "gray areas" that have been pointed out? Has the FDA acted on it? Has the NIH issued treatment guidelines? Do I know of doctors who are prescribing this drug? How are their patients doing? The social power of a study depends considerably on these markers of credibility, and their absence can cause problems for the acceptance of the study's findings.

Into this complex field of claims and counterclaims, markers and precedents, signals and responses, enter the AIDS activists. Activist participation has done nothing less than change the ground rules for the *social construction of belief*—the varied processes by which different groups and institutions in society come to believe that a given treatment is "promising" or "disappointing," "effective" or "junk," "state of the art" or "passé." Activists have become proficient at interpreting the credibility of AIDS trials, and they have educated their base communities about how to scrutinize newspaper reports of "miracle cures" and journal articles about the "definitive" clinical trial. Activists in turn have promoted their own assessments: *that* study makes sense;

this drug seems to be working. They have argued for rethinking the risk-benefit calculus for life-threatening illnesses, and they have pushed for the rights of patients to accept greater risk in deciding whether to try experimental treatments.

The Politics of Risk and Regulation

In a world that depends heavily on specialized expertise, decisions about risks increasingly are adjudicated by impersonal organizations and institutions. But particularly in cases of controversy and politicization, it becomes harder to "contain" such decisions within normal organizational routines. Thus the regulatory hearings that consider evidence from clinical trials in order to license pharmaceutical products for sale are often heated sites for the negotiation for credibility, risk, and trust.[30] "Regulatory science," as Sheila Jasanoff calls it in her study of agencies such as the FDA and the Environmental Protective Agency, is indeed a legitimate variety of scientific enterprise, but it is a very particular variety—and at least in the United States, a particularly adversarial one at that. Regulatory science differs from research science in its goals, its institutional locus, its formal products, its time frame, and its accountability.[31]

A distinctive difficulty of regulatory science is that everyone involved in making assessments speaks a somewhat different language. The statistician wants to know if the "null hypothesis" of "no treatment effect" has been disconfirmed to a sufficient degree of statistical certainty. The clinician wants to know if her patients' syndromes show improvement. The pharmaceutical manufacturer is concerned with liability and profit margins. And the regulatory official assesses "safety and efficacy" by measuring compliance with statutory and administrative requirements. Patients and their activist representatives want to know if a drug "works": at times they may demand certainty from institutions ill-equipped to provide it; at other moments they may insist on their willingness—indeed, their *right*—to freely assume the risks of uncertainty and ingest substances about which researchers and regulators have doubts. Should the social priority be "access" or "answers"—rapid approval of experimental therapies or careful consideration of the accumulation of evidence? Are these goals in conflict or can they be advanced simultaneously? Regulators, researchers, doctors, patients, and activists have all held different opinions on these questions—opinions that in some cases have shifted markedly over the course of the past decade.

A small number of drugs, many of them chemical cousins of AZT, have been licensed in the United States as antiviral agents effective against HIV infection or AIDS. (Other drugs have been licensed to fight opportunistic infections and neoplasms that are characteristic of AIDS—the infections and cancers that afflict people with weakened immune systems.) It is universally agreed that none of these drugs is a cure for AIDS. Beyond that, the drugs are shrouded in controversy, and AZT, the drug most widely prescribed throughout the late 1980s and early to mid-1990s, has seen its star rise and then fall. What is "known" and "believed" about these drugs, by whom, and where?

In the debates surrounding treatments, just as in those concerning causation, we see participants engaged in disputes about the *meaning* of evidence that simultaneously are disputes about the *standards* of evidence—about what counts as proof and, crucially, who decides. At the same time, the causation and treatment controversies are in certain respects quite different, and they reveal distinct mechanisms for the establishment of credibility in science. In both cases, the AIDS movement, broadly construed, has played an important and visible role. But in the causation controversies, the most publicized challenges to mainstream views have come from highly credentialed researchers, and representatives of the AIDS movement have enjoyed more success in *assessing* the claims of others than in *asserting* their own. By contrast, the crucial voices of heterodoxy in the treatment controversies have been those of lay activists.

Given the nature of scientific research, there is a certain logic to this difference. The investigation of the etiology and pathogenesis of illness is closer to the realm of "pure science"—the heavily-defended "core" of scientific practice to which few outsiders can successfully gain entry. By contrast, the investigation of treatments—and in particular the establishment of treatment efficacy through the mechanism of the clinical trial—is in part an "applied" science, located more on the "periphery" of scientific practice. It is more easily accessible to members of the patient community, whose participation in the process is indeed essential and who therefore have an immediate claim to a stake in the process and a basis for the development and assertion of their own expertise. A comparison of AIDS causation controversies and treatment controversies is therefore instructive, for it demonstrates how different kinds of scientific debates generate different possibilities for the manufacture of scientific expertise and credibility.

NOTES

1. F. Barré-Sinoussi et al., "Isolation of a T-Lymphotropic Retrovirus from a Patient at Risk for Acquired Immune Deficiency Syndrome (AIDS)," *Science* 220 (20 May 1983):868–70; Robert C. Gallo et al., "Frequent Detection and Isolation of Cytopathic Retroviruses (HTLV-III) from Patients with AIDS and at Risk for AIDS," *Science* 224 (4 May 1984):500–502; Jay A. Levy et al., "Isolation of Lymphocytopathic Retroviruses from San Francisco Patients with AIDS," *Science* 225 (24 August 1984):840–42.

2. The phrase is from Cindy Patton, *Inventing AIDS* (New York: Routledge, 1990), chapter 3.

3. Peter Duesberg, "Retroviruses As Carcinogens and Pathogens: Expectations and Reality," *Cancer Research* 47 (1 March 1987):1119–20; quote from 1215.

4. P. H. Duesberg, "The Role of Drugs in the Origin of AIDS," *Biomedicine & Pharmacotherapy* 46 (January 1992):10.

5. Jon Cohen, "The Duesberg Phenomenon," *Science* 266 (9 December 1994):1642–9.

6. Manfred Eigen, "The AIDS Debate," *Naturwissenschaften* 76 (August 1989):341–50; Luis Benitez Bribiesca, "¿Son En Verdad Los VIH Los Agentes Causales Del SIDA?" *Gaceta Médica de México* 127 (January-February 1991):75–84.

7. Joel N. Shurkin, "The AIDS Debate: Another View," *Los Angeles Times,* 18 January 1988, II-4; Philip M. Boffey, "A Solitary Dissenter Disputes Cause of AIDS," *New York Times,* 12 January 1988, C-3; Neville Hodgkinson, "Experts Mount Startling Challenge to Aids Orthodoxy," *Sunday Times* (London), 26 April 1992, 1.

8. National Public Radio (segment reported by Mike Hornwick, Canadian Broadcasting Corporation), *NPR Weekend Edition,* 16 May 1992; Gary Null, "AIDS: A Man-Made Plague?" *Penthouse,* January 1989, 160.

9. "Who Are the HIV Heretics? Discussion Paper #5" (Project Inform, San Francisco, 3 June, 1992, photocopy); Celia Farber, "AIDS: Words from the Front." *Spin,* January 1988, 43–44, 73.

10. See, for instance, Tom Bethell, "Heretic," *American Spectator,* May 1992, 18–19.

11. Peter H. Duesberg and Bryan J. Ellison, "Peter H. Duesberg and Bryan J. Ellison Respond," *Heritage Foundation Policy Review,* fall 1990, 81–83 (letter to the editor).

12. From the public forum at the VIII International Conference on AIDS Update, San Francisco, 10 August 1992 (author's field notes).

13. Latour, *Science in Action,* chapter 1.

14. Collins, *Changing Order,* 162.

15. See Henry Frankel, "The Continental Drift Debate," in *Scientific Controversies: Case Studies in the Resolution and Closure of Disputes in Science and Technology,* ed. H. Tristram Engelhardt Jr. and Arthur L. Caplan (Cambridge, England: Cambridge Univ. Press, 1987), 203–48.

16. Jad Adams, "Paradigm Unvisited," *Heritage Foundation Policy Review,* fall 1990, 75–76 (letter to the editor).

17. On closure in scientific controversies, see H. Tristram Engelhardt Jr. and Arthur L. Caplan, eds., *Scientific Controversies: Case Studies in the Resolution and Closure of Disputes in Science and Technology* (Cambridge, England: Cambridge Univ. Press, 1987); Harry Collins, "The Seven Sexes: A Study in the Sociology of a Phenomenon, or the Replication of Experiments in Physics," *Sociology* 9 (May 1975): 205–24; Peter Galison, *How Experiments End* (Chicago: Univ. of Chicago Press, 1987).

18. Jason DeParle, "Rush, Rash, Effective, Act-Up Shifts AIDS Policy," *New York Times,* 3 January 1990, B-1.

19. Albert R. Jonsen and Jeff Stryker, eds., *The Social Impact of AIDS in the United States* (Washington, DC: National Academy Press, 1993), 89–90.

20. Gregg Gonsalves and Mark Harrington, "AIDS Research at the NIH: A Critical Review. Part I: Summary" (Treatment Action Group, New York, 1992, photocopy), 1.

21. See Gregg Gonsalves, "Basic Research on HIV Infection: A Report from the Front" (Treatment Action Group, New York, 1993, photocopy); Martin Delaney, "The Evolution of Community-Based Research" (Plenary Address at the IX International Conference on AIDS), Berlin, 8 June 1993.

22. There is an emergent literature in science studies on the history, functions, and controversies surrounding the randomized clinical trial. See Harry Milton Marks, "Ideas As Reforms: Therapeutic Experiments and Medical Practice, 1900–1980" (Ph.D. diss., Massachusetts Institute of Technology, 1987); Evelleen Richards, "The Politics of Therapeutic Evaluation: The Vitamin C and Cancer Controversy," *Social Studies of Science* 18 (1988), 653–701; Evelleen Richards, *Vitamin C*

and Cancer; Medicine or Politics? (New York: St. Martin's, 1991); Anni Dugdale, "Devices and Desires: Constructing the Intrauterine Device, 1908–1988" (Ph.D. diss., Univ. of Wollongong, Australia, 1995); Marcia Lynn Meldrum, "'Departing from the Design': The Randomized Clinical Trial in Historical Context, 1946–1970" (Ph.D. diss., State University of New York at Stony Brook, 1994); J. Rosser Matthews, *Quantification and the Quest for Medical Certainty* (Princeton: Princeton Univ. Press, 1995); Caroline Jean Acker, "Addiction and the Laboratory: The Work of the National Research Council's Committee on Drug Addiction, 1928–1939," *Isis* 86 (June 1995): 167–93; Alan Yoshioka, "British Clinical Trials of Streptomycin, 1946–51" (Ph.D. diss., Imperial College, forthcoming).

23. See Robert M. Veatch, *The Patient As Partner: A Theory of Human-Experimentation Ethics* (Bloomington: Indiana Univ. Press, 1987), 6–7, 211.

24. Meldrum, "Departing from the Design," 384–386.

25. The latter phrase is borrowed from Richards, "Politics of Therapeutic Evaluation."

26. Douglas Richman, interview by author, tape recording, San Diego, 1 June 1994.

27. Shapin, "Cordelia's Love," 262.

28. On the denaturalization of research materials, see Adele E. Clarke, "Research Materials and Reproductive Science in the United States, 1910–1940," in *Physiology in the American Context, 1850–1940,* ed. Gerald L. Geison (Bethesda, MD: American Physiological Society, 1987), 323–350. On the destabilization of technologies, see Ronald Kline and Trevor Pinch, "Taking the Black Box Off Its Wheels: The Social Construction of the Car in the Rural United States" (manuscript, Cornell University, 2 February 1995). On the tactic of revealing the "artifactual and conventional" status of the beliefs of one's opponents in scientific controversies, see Shapin and Schaffer, *Leviathan and the Air-Pump,* 7.

29. See Jack P. Lipton and Alan M. Hershaft, "On the Widespread Acceptance of Dubious Medical Findings," *Journal of Health and Social Behavior* 26 (December 1985):336–51.

30. Sheila Jasanoff, *The Fifth Branch: Science Advisers As Policymakers* (Cambridge, MA: Harvard Univ. Press, 1990), chapter 8; Henk J. H. W. Bodewitz, Henk Buurma, and Gerard H. de Vries, "Regulatory Science and the Social Management of Trust in Medicine," in *The Social Construction of Technological Systems: New Directions in the Sociology and History of Technology,* ed. Wiebe E. Bijker, Thomas P. Hughes, and Trevor J. Pinch (Cambridge, MA: Massachusetts Institute of Technology Press, 1987), 243–59; John Abraham, "Distributing the Benefit of the Doubt: Scientists, Regulators, and Drug Safety," *Science, Technology, & Human Values* 19 (autumn 1994): 493–522; Brian Wynne, "Unruly Technology: Practical Rules, Impractical Discourses and Public Understanding," *Social Studies of Science,* 18 (1988), 147–67, esp. 162–63; Theodore M. Porter, *Trust in Numbers: The Pursuit of Objectivity in Science and Public Life* (Princeton, NJ: Princeton Univ. Press, 1995), 203–16.

31. Jasanoff, *The Fifth Branch,* 76–83. On the adversarial culture of regulation in the United States, see Sheila Jasanoff, "Cross-National Differences in Policy Implementation," *Evaluation Review* 15 (February 1991): 103–119.

46

SPEAKING OF SADNESS
Taking Anti-Depressant Drugs

DAVID A. KARP

How should a society treat the mentally ill? For decades, sociologists have researched this question, resulting in such classic studies as Erving Goffman's *Asylums* (1961) or David L. Rosenhan's "On Being Sane in Insane Places" (included in this volume as reading 19). Today, the deinstitutionalization movement has meant that fewer mentally ill people are hospitalized, and instead, they are more likely to be treated with psychotropic drugs on an outpatient basis. The patient's experience of mental illness is the focus of this reading, taken from David Karp's award winning book, *Speaking of Sadness: Depression, Disconnection, and the Meanings of Illness* (1996). Here, Karp examines how clinically depressed people experience and interpret the medications they take for their illnesses and their altered senses of self.

The purpose of this paper is to explore the symbolic meanings attached to taking anti-depressant medications. The decision to embark on a course of drug taking is not a simple matter of unthinkingly following a doctor's orders. In fact, a patient's willingness to begin a drug regimen and stick with it involves an extensive interpretive process that includes consideration of such issues as the connection between drug use and illness self definitions, the meanings of drug side effects, attitudes towards physicians, evaluations of professional expertise, and ambiguity about the causes of one's problem. As Conrad (1985) points out, available studies rarely deal with such issues and so explain noncompliance only from a doctor-centered perspective. This view improperly slights the range of responses patients make to drug use.

The perspective taken in this study fits with a general literature in social psychology arguing that the subjective experience of taking drugs is deeply connected with individual and collective interpretations about the drug taken. . . .

The case of anti-depressant medications is especially valuable for analysis because these drugs are linked with the meaning of emotional experience. They are designed to alter "abnormal" moods and emotions. If there is

David A. Karp, "Taking Anti-Depressant Medications: Resistance, Trial Commitment, Conversion, Disenchantment," from *Qualitative Sociology*, Vol. 16, pp. 337–359. © 1993 by Plenum Publishing Corporation. Reprinted by permission.

a question in patients' minds about the value of taking medications for such clearly physiological problems as epilepsy and diabetes, decisions about taking drugs for "emotional illness" are still more problematic. Despite the psychiatric profession's clear adoption in recent years of a biochemical paradigm for understanding emotional problems, it is, we shall see, far from clear to patients whether their emotional problems warrant designation as an illness requiring biochemical intervention. . . .

Although prior research [has] clarified how patients understood and legitimated their use of psychotropic drugs in a global way (for example, as a resource for helping them to fulfill family and work roles), this research did not explore how the meanings attached to psychotropic drugs change over the period of their use. An important premise of symbolic interaction theory is that the meanings of objects, events, and situations are constantly being renegotiated and reinterpreted (Blumer 1969). Correspondingly, this paper argues that the use of anti-depressant medications articulates with a more general depression "career" path characterized by ongoing redefinitions of self, illness, and, here, the meaning of medication itself.

In an earlier paper (Karp 1992) I identified clear stages in the evolution of an illness consciousness among depressed persons. Certain events in the course of an illness become critical identity markers that reflect a profound shift in how persons see themselves. . . . At such junctures persons are transformed in a way that requires a redefinition of who they were, are, and might be. The data to follow illustrate that the eventual decision to take medications was a major benchmark in the way my respondents came to see themselves, the nature of their problem, and their images of the future. The consequent decisions to continue and then eventually to stop a drug regimen are complicated and sometimes the product of years of confusion, evaluation, and experimentation.

Although it would do violence to the complexity of persons' responses to drug treatment to say that everyone moved through absolutely determined stages of interpretation, the stories I heard suggest clear regularities. These "moments" in the way respondents simultaneously tried to make sense out of drugs and their illness include an initial *resistance* stage during which they were unwilling to take anti-depressant medications. However, despite their ideological and psychological opposition, those interviewed eventually became desperate enough to try medication and thus capitulated to the advice of medical experts. During a second period of *trial commitment,* individuals express a willingness to experiment with drugs for a short period of time only. Having made the decision to try medications, they begin to accept biochemical definitions of depression's etiology. Such a redefinition is critical in becoming committed to a medical treatment model. For several, taking the drugs has a marginal or even negative impact on their problem. However, by now even these individuals have become *converted* to a belief in biochemical explanations of depression and begin a search to find the "right" drug. Finally, even those who experienced a "miracle" and felt "saved" by medication eventually have other episodes of depression and become *disenchanted* with drugs. They feel a need to get off the drugs "to see what happens," to see whether they can "go it alone.". . .

Method

Between August, 1991 and May, 1992, I conducted the 20 in-depth interviews which constitute the basis for this paper. A number of avenues were used to solicit interviewees. Initial interviews were done with personal acquaintances whom I knew had long histories with depression (10 cases). In addition, advertisements were placed in local newspapers and this strategy yielded a number of responses (6 cases). Finally, after each interview respondents were asked to describe my study to friends whom they knew had histories of depression and to refer names of willing participants (4 cases). In all instances, only those who had been officially diagnosed and treated by mental health professionals were included in the study. . . .

Although it is impossible to know what information persons might have withheld, I found it remarkable how candidly most of those interviewed appeared to speak about their experiences, including such difficult topics as child abuse, drug addiction, work failures, broken relationships, and suicide attempts. Several times interviews were punctuated by tears as persons recounted especially painful incidents. In every case, I reserved time at the end of the interview for respondents to "process" our conversation and to communicate how they felt about the experience. Nearly everyone expressed gratitude for the chance to tell their story, often saying that doing the interview gave them new perspectives on their life. . . .

Interpreting the Drug Experience

There is considerable variability in the time persons take to move through their individual depression careers. In large measure these variations related to how early in life trouble with depression begins and then whether bouts with depression are chronic or intermittent. Several of the persons interviewed realized, in retrospect, that they were deeply troubled from ages as young as four or five, and others did not experience "serious" depression until early adulthood. Consequently, some of those interviewed move into the therapeutic worlds of counselors, therapists, psychiatrists, and drugs by their teenage years, or even earlier. Others go for years before their trouble is diagnosed as depression and only then embark upon a course of therapy. However long it took the respondents to recognize and label their difficulty as depression, their eventual treatment by physicians involved use of prescribed medications. As indicated earlier, an individual's response to medication can be described as a process of unfolding consciousness and identity change consisting of four broad stages: resistance, trial commitment, conversion, and disenchantment.

Resistance

On rare occasions persons with whom I spoke sought out physicians explicitly to obtain anti-depressant medications. Perhaps this will increasingly be the case as both psychiatry and pharmaceutical companies "educate" the public about the nature of depression and as drugs like Prozac are touted in the media as revolutionary cures for depressive "illness." Normally, however, the idea to take medications is first raised by a therapist or doctor, a suggestion that is met with considerable resistance. Typically, respondents offered a number of reasons for initially resisting drugs. Some described themselves nearly identically by saying "I'm the kind of person who doesn't even believe in taking aspirin for a headache." Others were appropriately concerned about the unknown and possibly long-term effects of powerful medication. It is interesting that even respondents who had earlier in their lives experimented with all kinds of drugs (for example, marihuana, cocaine, and LSD) were opposed to taking these drugs. Without denying their stated reasons, there appears to be a central underlying dynamic to their resistance. Taking anti-depressant medication would require a dramatic redefinition of self. Taking the drug would be a clear affirmation that they were a person with a stigmatized emotional disorder. In this respect, a willingness to begin a regimen of psychiatric medications is far from a simple medical decision. It is a decisive juncture in one's self redefinition as an emotionally ill rather than merely a troubled person.

> I didn't want to be told that I had something that was going to affect the rest of my life, and that could only be solved by taking pills. It was sort of definitive. I had a label and it was a label that I thought was pejorative. I didn't want to be this quietly depressed person, that there was something wrong with me. And it was sort of a rebellion in that [I said] "No it isn't, I'm not like that. I don't need you and your pills."

. . .

> My internist said, "You're depressed. You need an anti-depressant." I mean, I didn't understand the word exactly. She sent me to (names a psychiatrist) for anti-depressants. I went to (names psychiatrist) and said "I don't need anti-depressants, but I do need somebody to talk to." Drugs, I was against drugs. I didn't understand them either. But if he would talk to me, maybe we could work our way out of it. . . .

For several respondents the first clear communication that they needed medications followed a crisis that pushed them into a psychiatrist's office or, sometimes, into a hospital. New patients often perceived doctors as unwilling to pay significant attention to their feelings and were, as they saw it, altogether too eager to prescribe medications. Especially in hospitals, respondents sometimes acutely experienced the paradox that psychiatrists didn't want to spend much time hearing about their feelings despite the fact it was their bad feelings that forced them into the hospital. As individuals often saw it, their problems were situational and their souls were wounded. Such a perspective on the causes of their misery did not seem to square with the assessment that they had a disease in the form of unbalanced brain chemicals and should be treated with medication.

While persons suffering from depression often express anger towards those whom they view as implicated in the creation of their problem, I was surprised throughout these interviews by the virulence of the animosity expressed toward psychiatrists. Eventually, many of the persons interviewed found psychiatrists whom they trusted and from whom they benefitted. However, early in their treatment, individuals saw psychiatrists as oppressively evangelistic "true believers" in biochemical causes of depression, a view that they did not then hold. Their initial negative evaluation of psychiatry and psychiatrists I caught in the frequency and regularity with which respondents angrily labeled their doctors as "pill pushers."

> *This particular doctor was such an asshole. He sounded like a used-car salesman for anti-depressants. He was just like so gung-ho. "Oh yuh, you're the typical depressed [person], here's the drug that will cure you. Let me know if you go home and just want to kill yourself or something. We'll try something different for you." And I hated him. I just really hated him. . . .*

> . . .

> *Everything can be cured with a drug. Everything. They've got a drug for everything. Most [psychiatrists], they like to tinker with the body through these drugs, rather than trying to, you know, have people express what they're feeling. They just took one look at me, and pronounced me depressed, and wanted to put me on a battery of anti-depressants.*

> . . .

> *[I feel] a real disenchantment with the traditional psychiatrists like the one that I had, and the ones who resort very quickly to pills. And I certainly have doubts about the degree to which the doctors are hooked up with the drug companies.*

By the time patients arrive for treatment in doctors' offices or hospitals they have already moved through a number of changes in self definition. When asked about the unfolding of the recognition that they were depressed, individuals ordinarily describe an early time of inchoate feelings of distress, followed by feeling that "something is really wrong with me," and then to some variant of "I can't continue to live like this." Even after a crisis severe enough to precipitate hospitalization, individuals are, as we have seen, still resistant to taking medications. Resisting medication is a way of resisting categorization as a mentally ill person. However, the depth and persistence of their misery proves great enough that, under the proddings of physicians and sometimes other patients and family members, individuals begin to waver in their resolve not to take medication. Several persons described themselves as eventually "coming around" to the decision to take drugs because they became willing to try anything to diminish their suffering. Over and again respondents described their capitulation to medications as a consequence of the desperation they felt.

But I also didn't want to do it [take drugs] because I felt such shame. I felt like, "Well I'm not depressed, someone else is depressed." Like I couldn't believe it was me. It was like some wonder drug or something. And I was thinking, "No way, I don't want to jump on this bandwagon." I was so scared of it. I felt like five years from now they'd find out that it gave me cancer or something. I just didn't want to take medication at all. But then at the same time I wanted so desperately for something to fix me. So I was just willing to try anything. He just said, "Give it a week, think about it."

. . .

I was very leery of it [taking medications]. I mean I was concerned about what the effects might be and I didn't like the idea of putting myself on some sort of medication, but at a certain point it just seemed to me that I had to try it and the problem was so great that I really wanted to do anything that would alleviate it. . . .

. . .

I couldn't drag myself around any more. I couldn't sleep. I didn't eat. . . . I just felt physically like there was something wrong with me, and that I had to stop and I think there is a physical component, because now that I've been on medication long enough I think it has helped.

In an especially evocative comment a respondent equated taking the medication with "swallowing" her will.

I have a hard time taking medication . . . I don't like taking pills. I didn't like taking aspirin. I mean, I've generally been very conservative at that, so I kind of swallowed, you know, my will and that's when I took Prozac.

The moment individuals decide to try medications is decisive in beginning a reorientation in their thinking about the nature of their difficulty and of their "selves." Putting the first pill into one's mouth begins both a revision of one's biochemistry and one's self. Social psychologists have long understood that embarking upon a new life direction, especially one that departs from earlier held views of reality, requires the construction of a new "vocabulary of motives" (Mills 1972) and new "accounts" (Lyman and Scott 1968) for behavior. . . . Rather than understanding behaviors as always being propelled by clear motives, we know that behavioral changes often precede motive productions. Taking the medication is the beginning of a process of commitment to biochemical explanations of affective disorders.

Trial Commitment

In his well-known paper entitled "Notes on the Concept of Commitment," Howard Becker (1960) illuminates the idea that commitments to new ways of life do not happen suddenly, all at once. Commitments are built up slowly, gradually, and often imperceptibly through a series of "side bets" or personal decisions, each of which seems of little consequence. Persons, for example, may become committed to work organizations through a series of side bets such as paying into a pension plan, accepting a promotion and new responsibilities, buying a home based on current income, and so on. As Becker explains, each of these apparently independent decisions is like putting individual bricks into a wall until one day it suddenly becomes clear that the wall has grown to such a height that one cannot climb over it—a commitment has been made that is not easily reversed.

The decision to take a medication is sometimes preceded by a *negotiation* with doctors about how long one is willing to try it. . . . Negotiations reflect patients' ambivalence that they have not yet accepted doctors' definitions of them as having a biochemically based illness.

> And so then I started taking this Prozac. And the only reason I would take it is that he promised I would only be on it for three months. I ended up being on it for nine months, probably longer, nine or ten months. If I had known that, I don't think I'd ever gone on it because I just didn't want to put any kind of substance in my body.
> The psychiatrist . . . said, "Look, I just think you should stay on it through the end of this year, you know, and then you can go off it." So I decided . . . I wasn't thinking of it quite so blatantly, but I was sort of thinking, "All right, I'll just take this eight months and see what happens."

Negotiations aside, taking medications coincides with a growing acceptance of official medical versions about the causes of depression. Everyone who suffers from depression feels obliged to construct theories of causation in order to impose some coherence onto an especially hazy, ambiguous life circumstance and to evaluate the extent to which they are responsible for their condition. Although it is impossible ever to fully resolve whether nature or nurture, or some combination, is responsible for depression, every person I interviewed eventually accepted in greater or lesser degree a biochemical explanation of depression.

Adoption of the view that one is victimized by a biochemically sick self constitutes a comfortable "account" for a history of difficulties and failures and absolves one of responsibility. On the negative side, however, acceptance of a victim role, while diminishing a sense of personal responsibility, is also enfeebling. To be a victim of biochemical forces beyond one's control gives force to others' definition of oneself as a helpless, passive object of injury. Holstein and Miller (1990:120) comment that "victimization . . . provides an interpretive framework and a discourse that relieves victims of responsibility for their fates, but at a cost. The cost involves the myriad ways that the victim image debilitates those to whom it is applied." The interpretative dilemma was to navigate between rhetorics of biochemical determinism and a sense of personal efficacy. However, everyone with whom I talked eventually adopted some version of biological causation of depression, as the following representative comments illustrate.

Well, do you feel like a victim?

I would say that uh in me, [it is] my brain chemistry that is prone to depression and that, given like the amount of trauma in [my life], it really added up and had no way to pass or flow and really built up. And like the drug helps it to flow or something. And then the way that I understand I'm no longer on it [medications] is that it's [the brain chemistry] kind of working OK on its own right now.

You seem to doubt the psychiatric model of illness.

I don't doubt it. I don't know. You know, I'm not a psychopharmacologist and I'm not going to say "It's a problem with serotonin uptake in my brain," and I'm not a psychoanalyst and I'm not going to say, "It's you know, the Oedipal whatever." But I feel that it's an illness because it's something you don't have any control over. . . .

There was a sense of relief to a certain extent when I started finding out that the medication was helpful, because then I could say that this certainly partly is a chemical problem, and that I'm not a looney tunes, and I'm not, you know, it's not a mental illness, which really sounds bad to me. I think I'm much less negative about it than I was, even in 1982. But at that time the fact that there might be a chemical imbalance that was being rectified by medication was of great comfort to me.

Well, you know, as a result of that more recent one, more recent depression, I've kind of come around more to the biochemical explanation. . . .

Conversion: Muddle or Miracle

Once patients have accepted and internalized a rhetoric of biochemical causation, they become committed to a process of finding the "right" medication. Such a discovery often proves elusive as persons enter upon a protracted process of trial and error with multiple drugs. This process is often extremely confusing as persons deal with a variety of side effects ranging from such relatively benign problems as dry mouth, constipation, and weight gain to more dramatic experiences like fainting in public places. In several interviews drug "horror stories" were a prominent theme, as in the case of a hospitalized woman whose therapy, along with drugs, consisted of physical exercise.

I was on every drug under the sun. Just everything (said with exasperation). It was like a cocktail. I mean I was really out of control . . . I'll never forget this little vignette where they would drug me and say, "Well, you've got to get out there and be more active . . . I'll never forget—tennis . . . I was so drugged up I could barely see my fingers and this therapist took us out to the tennis courts. He was hitting balls and I couldn't even see the ball. This asshole, I couldn't even see and he's worried about my backhand. It's stupid. You know, at the time I don't think I thought it was too funny. I thought, "What's wrong with me." So things went from bad to worse.

Sometimes individuals stayed on a medication for months that had no discernible positive effect or which they perceived only modestly influenced their condition. The search for the "right" drug seems analogous to a process of serial monogamy in which individuals move through a series of unsatisfying, bad, or even destructive relationships, always with the hope that the right person will eventually be found. Just as individuals internalize the notion of romantic love with its attendant ideology that one's perfect mate is somewhere in the world, respondents maintained their faith, in spite of a series of disappointments, that they would find the right medication.

Anyway I think I continued on the imipramine, but they gave me other drugs. Out of all the drugs that I had I can't say that any one really made me feel better. You know and I can only say that when you find the right drug you really know. "Oh, this is what it means to be better." But I do remember it wasn't imipramine.

. . .

It's [names drug] been effective and I haven't felt the need for anything else. But I also have the feeling, "I wonder if there is something better that I could take a lower dose of that would be effective." Or, "Isn't there something else now that might be better." I always feel that way (laughs).

. . .

I'm feeling very hopeless [right now]. I'm still taking the Trazadone. I'm also taking an anti-anxiety drug once in a while and I feel like I'm treading water. I'm waking up at five o'clock in the morning even with the Trazadone. I wake up in horror that, you know, I'll be a bag lady, that I'm not going to be able to get through my work day today. Every once in a while I wonder "Have I tried enough stuff. Is there something that would work better?"

Many of those interviewed never find a drug that dramatically influences things for the better. These people continue to take the medications, but remain only partial believers in biochemical explanations. However, equal numbers among the respondents interviewed describe the "miracle" of medication. It is among these persons that the metaphor to religious conversion is most apparent. For them, the drug truly provides a "revelation" because it makes them feel "normal," often for the first time in their lives. In these instances, any trace of uncertainty about the biochemical basis for their problem disappears. Finding the right medication is, in fact, described as a spiritual awakening, as an ecstatic experience.

All I can tell you is, "Oh my God, you know when you're on the right medica-
tion." It was the most incredible thing. And I would say that I had a spiritual
experience.

. . .

So I started taking this Trazadone. It may have been a week or two. I had never
experienced such a magical effect in my whole life. It was just magical. Thoughts
that I had been having . . . I had been having these horrible, tortured depressed
thoughts and the only thing I can say is that they just stopped being in my head
and it was like they had run around in my blood and I just didn't think that way
any more. And I started thinking better thoughts, happier thoughts. It was very
clear to me that it wasn't the same as being high. Astonishing. It was wonder-
ful. . . . After two weeks. I mean, it was just magical. My life began to change
profoundly at that point.

. . .

And then I start seeing this therapist last September twice a week and he recom-
mends going to see a psychiatrist. I go to him and he recommends Doxepin and
I start taking that. And then at the end of November it just kind of kicked in. It
was a miracle. It really was. Quite extraordinary.

. . .

Well, I'd had a headache for four months and they treated that with Amitripty-
line. And then I changed doctors. I went to the (names a university) health plan.
Anyway, I saw a psychiatrist and had been seeing her for a while and I guess
probably giving all the classic symptoms that I didn't know existed. And finally
she said, "Well, you know, I think one of the problems here is that you're depressed
and I'm putting you on Imipramine and see if that's going to work." And when
it started working it was like a miracle. It was just like "wow." I know speci-
fically of other times I was very depressed and then when I got out of it I would
describe to people "I feel like I've come out of a tunnel."

While there is a danger in relying too heavily on one biography, it seems worthwhile to present in some detail the dialogue I had with a respondent whose words express particularly well the complexity of depression, the powerful effects of a medication in providing new and plausible realities, and even the uncertainty about "giving up" depression. Although it is not within the province of this paper to offer a full discussion of the "positive" features of depression, several respondents claim that the agony of depression has been instrumental in their spiritual growth. One unanticipated aspect of depression revealed in the interviews is the connection between depression and spiritual life. Several persons in my sample have seriously experimented with Buddhist teachings which they claim, more satisfactorily than Western religions, understand the place of human pain and suffering. Others connect their depression with creativity and insight. The following woman, quoted at length, is a writer. Her comments illuminate the breath-taking impact of feeling normal after years of non-stop pain, the religious-like dimensions of the drug conversion experience, and the uncertainty attached to giving up any long held identity, even one that has been deeply troublesome. Our conversation went like this:

> How would you describe the experience of Prozac?
>
> *I went on Prozac. I was like, cracking up, a couple of years ago, and sort of got back to the mental hospital—time number five. And I think the psychiatrist I was seeing, she didn't know what to do with me, so she sent me to this . . . psychopharmacologist, and he prescribed Prozac for me, and within five days, it was very, very strange. . . . I mean, it was hard to explain, but, I was just incredibly fearful and anxious, and I really at that point was going to kill myself, because I just was like, "Forget it." You know, "I've worked too hard and tried to conquer this thing too much, and I can't do it." And there was a tremendous amount of anger. But within five days of going on the Prozac it was like the obsessions reduced, and it was a very weird feeling. What was strange about it was that it took away the feeling of depression that I've had in my stomach for years, ever since I was a little girl. It was gone. And I remember not wanting to tell anybody about it, because I thought, this is really strange.*
>
> Not wanting to tell anybody because?
>
> *Like, "I think this is working." I was kind of like, "Jesus Christ, what's going on here." Because I'd been on medications that never had done anything for me, and this was so dramatic. . . . It was very dramatic because I was on the brink of really cracking up, and then within five days I wasn't anywhere near cracking up. And actually it's interesting, because I loved it, but I also wanted to go off of it, because I was sure it was going to take away my creativity.*
>
> So, its back to the pain/creativity link.
>
> *Oh, because I couldn't write. I was used to being in an anxious state all of the time, and suddenly I didn't care as much about my writing any more. That was what the weird thing was. It [writing] didn't mean as much to me. Nothing meant as much to me. In a way that was incredibly freeing. And at the same time, I built my whole identity around being a person who was, you know, driven, intense, and I tried sort of whipping myself up into an intense state, you know, and it didn't work.*
>
> You mean, something that you had no trouble with before. . . .
>
> *It [the intensity] wasn't there and as much as I hated it before. I also felt like it was who I was, and the Prozac took it away, and I remember thinking, "This is very nice. I should take this when I go on vacation, you know, and [otherwise] get me off of this stuff, because this is going to make a moron out of me."*

So what's the end of the story? Still taking it?

Well I remained on it, but the course is kind of rocky because then I was a convert to Prozac, and I was like, "This stuff is incredible." I was thinking, "This stuff is just the greatest stuff I've ever taken in the world." I mean, "this is a miracle." And I would think, "This is a miracle." And it was a miracle, it really was a miracle to me. For that one year, I was so happy. . . . And at this point the Prozac has become so intertwined with the millions of meanings that I've given it. Even a God [meaning] for a while.

. . . Persons' commitment and conversion to drugs is completed when those drugs become a routine part of their daily life. The process of adopting the medical version of depression's proper treatment is accomplished when the respondent's initial resistance to drugs completely vanishes. What normally started out as a tentative and ambivalent experiment with medications typically becomes a taken-for-granted way of life. In effect, the persons interviewed have undergone a socialization process that has transformed the meanings to them of medication. The negotiated experiment begun with trepidation has become institutionalized, habitualized, and ritualized. To use the vocabulary offered by Peter Berger and Thomas Luckmann (1967), a once alternative and alien "symbolic universe" has become an accepted and seemingly immutable reality. That is, taking medications now appears as an absolutely unquestioned feature of daily reality. Consider the casualness with which those initially opposed to drugs sometimes come to regard them.

What's interesting to me about the drug now, or at least my attitude toward it, is that I regard it almost as a food supplement. It's just something I eat that's going to have a certain effect. So I don't quite see it as unnatural the way I used to.

. . .

And then I decided, "Hey, this stuff's pretty good, you know? I can be happy or be less anxious and do productive work." So I thought, "OK, I'll stay on it forever." So it was a total turnaround.

. . .

[Now] taking medication is pretty much just a reflex.

. . .

I'm convinced maybe I have to take it for the rest of my life. I'd certainly rather feel like this than like that, and if it's two little pills I've got in my mouth every day that makes me stay this way, then so be it.

Disenchantment and Deconversion

Those who study conversions must include in their analysis the factors that sometimes account for the disenchantment, defection, and deconversion of large numbers of persons from their respective groups or belief systems.

Some persons, of course, retain their commitments to alternative realities over the long term. Equally, though, are those who come to question the utility and correctness of the explanatory schemas with which they had experimented and then fully embraced. Of course, even converts stand at different places on a continuum of commitment. Some are never fully convinced of the value of new behaviors and beliefs, are easily disenchanted with new problem-solving perspectives, and return relatively quickly to old perspectives and identities. A few among those studied stayed on drugs for only a short time, deciding that they were not sufficiently effective to put up with noxious side effects. After experimenting with medications, these persons were easily able to return to the view that their problems were environmentally based and that drugs would not be their salvation. The failure of a belief system is much more devastating, of course, when persons had embraced it unreservedly. This was certainly the case for those who had experienced a drug miracle, but who subsequently suffered a relapse. The young woman writer quoted earlier described her response to the eventual failure of the drug after her ecstatic revelatory experience.

> *Then I decided I was going to go away to Kentucky and live in Appalachia for two months and do an internship in interviewing women down there. And then again I thought, this is the kind of thing I can do, because now I'm on Prozac and I won't freak out, whereas before that kind of change would have freaked me out. And I went, and I freaked out, and that's when I completely like, relapsed. . . . Now I have a somewhat more balanced view of the Prozac in that I can become obsessive, anxious, depressed on it, even very obsessive and anxious and depressed. It's not a miracle drug. It hasn't saved me. And it's been a long time coming to terms with that. It helps somewhat, sometimes, and that's where it's at. And, I did for a while think, I am going to be cured. . . . It was the ultimate disappointment. You know, it was connected with an intense sense of loss and a sense of redemption, and I do not overstate [things]. It really was that.*

The complexity of stopping medications is evident in the fact that even when they do not appear to fundamentally alter depressive feelings, respondents sometimes become psychologically dependent upon them. Once having experimented with the drugs and having accepted biochemical definitions of their condition, persons feel uncertain about stopping. Whatever their current problems, several individuals were afraid that things might deteriorate if they stopped taking the medications.

> *I'm afraid to not take it, but it really hasn't done much of anything.*

> . . .

> *I mean, it's almost to the point now where I take it sometimes but like I really don't feel like I have the need for it. But I'm sort of afraid not to take it . . . I'm on*

such a low dosage [now]. He's (doctor) got me on one pill a night. And it's taken, you know, ten years [to get to that point].

. . .

If I had listened to myself I would have just said "Screw the medications." But also I think I was probably afraid, afraid that if I went off them completely that I would get worse, and I guess there is some evidence for that. . . .

And sometimes persons are afraid to stop the medication because they believe their systems have become physiologically dependent on them.

I'm on anti-depressant medicine right now, have been since '83, around there, and I wanted to go off them and I can't. There's no way I can go off them. There is just no way. I would have to spend six months to a year pretty much in a very controlled environment, as my body, my nervous system reacted to not having the stuff.

Ultimately, the respondents in this study, like the epilepsy patients interviewed by Conrad (1985), become, at the least, ambivalent about the role of medications in dealing with their difficulty. They may feel dependent on the drugs and worry about the consequences of stopping, but they also begin to question the wisdom of staying on the medications. Just as Conrad's epilepsy patients eventually discover that the medications are not the "ticket to normality," it eventually becomes apparent to sufferers of depression that a medical "cure" is not forthcoming. In both instances, patients become disenchanted with the side effects of the drugs, begin to question their efficacy, experiment with dosage levels and sometimes decide even to stop taking them. Conrad describes a number of noncompliance responses of epilepsy patients which reflect efforts to regain control over their illness. He notes (1985:36) that "[self] regulating medication represents an attempt to assert some degree of control over a condition that appears at times to be completely out of control." His findings certainly seem generalizable to the case of depression, as the following comments illustrate.

I guess I myself was curious to see what would happen if I were to stop taking it. Partly my wife didn't like the idea that I was on a drug. She's concerned about long range effects and I guess I was a little concerned about that too.

. . .

I wanted to go off it all along and it started giving me headaches. I wanted to get off it already.

. . .

I had gained a lot of weight on the pills. I was always a very thin person and here I was carrying forty more pounds. My sense of physical identity was damaged and I wanted out.

In other cases individuals finally rebel against taking medications as a way of reclaiming selves that they believe have been lost because of their involvement with anti-depressant medications. These persons who vow never to go on the drugs again have plainly had a deconversion experience.

> *Now in between the new and the old [medications] there would be a period when they would take me off the thing. And my friends during that stretch without fail would say "You seem like yourself again." And if I had listened closely I would have said, "Gee, the implication of this is that these pills are fucking me up." [Finally] I would go in and say "Can I get off it? Can I get off it?" And he would say, "Try it longer." Finally I thought "I'm not going to ask this son of a bitch any longer. I'm just going to take myself off it." And I did and he either forgot about it or didn't raise it. I just took myself off. . . . [And] I will never take another fucking pill in my life. And I'm not generalizing to other people. . . . but for me, I had gotten so fucked up with this stuff that I will never do it again.*

. . .

> *I mean, I put my foot down about the Trazadone. I was at the point where I could say, "I'm just going to stop."*

Discussion

Although the persons quoted in this paper may stand at different points in their drug taking careers, most commonly move through a socialization process which involves overcoming initial resistance to drug taking, negotiating the terms of their treatment, adopting new rhetorics about the cause of depression, experiencing a conversion to medical realities, and eventually becoming disenchanted with the value of medications for solving their problems. This process bears a strong similarity to descriptions of religious conversion and deconversion. That is, one's willingness to begin, sustain, and sometimes stop a doctor-prescribed regimen of anti-depressant medications must be understood in the broader context of adopting a new, identity-altering view of reality; namely; that one suffers from a biochemically based emotional illness. For this reason, the experience of taking anti-depressant medication involves a complex and emotionally charged interpretive process in which nothing less than one's view of self is at stake.

The process described in this paper helps in thinking about some of the social psychological dynamics that are part of the "medicalization" (Conrad and Schneider 1980) of society more broadly. . . . The medical model begins with the easily accepted assertion that normalcy is preferable to abnormalcy. However, normalcy then becomes a synonym for health and abnormalcy a synonym for pathology. Health and pathology, in turn, are defined in terms of the presumed scientific, objective, unbiased standards originating from experimentation and laboratory research. Because it is better to be healthy than to be sick, the medical model supports physicians' decisions, whether requested or not, to provide health for the patient. By defining certain characteristics of the human condition as "illness," and therefore in need of cure, physicians also provide themselves the right to explore every part of the human anatomy, to prescribe a myriad of curative agents, and frequently, to compel treatment.

The medical model is used to support the political reality created by a coalition of physicians, teachers, judges, and other health professionals. Peter Berger and Thomas Luckmann (1967) refer to this coalition as "universe maintenance specialists." These specialists from different disciplines set the norms defining proper and improper behavior, deviant and conforming behavior, normal and pathological behavior, sick and healthy behavior. Thus, therapy "entails the application of conceptual machinery to ensure that actual or potential deviants stay within the institutionalized definitions of reality. . . . This requires a body of knowledge that includes a theory of deviance, a diagnostic apparatus and a conceptual system for the 'cure of souls'" (1967:112).

Nowhere, of course, is the struggle over definitions of illness reality and, literally, the mind of the patient more apparent than in psychiatry. The materials presented earlier illustrate that acceptance of medical versions of reality is not an automatic thing. Psychiatric patients are initially resistant to illness definitions of their problem and "come around" to prescribed medical treatments only with great difficulty. Although everyone described in this paper eventually capitulates to medical versions of reality, their conversion is incomplete as they lose faith in the efficacy of drug treatment and sometimes rebel against it altogether. It seems reasonable to speculate that as part of a general and increasing "democratization" of professional/client relationships, resistance to medical authority will become more intense. Moreover, the terrain of this struggle over reality is most likely to be in the psychiatric arena where the legitimacy of a purely medical model is most suspect. . . .

The persons interviewed eventually realize that doctors, despite their best efforts, will not clear away their confusions about depression. The socialization process described in this paper involves hope that medication will provide the solution to their problem. In most cases, however, this optimistic attitude was replaced with disillusionment and sometimes anger. The failure of medical treatments for depression provides fertile soil for the emergence of self help groups which offer the view of affective disorders as troubles that must ultimately be remedied by the individuals who suffer from them (Karp 1992). Such a definition suggests an anti-psychiatry ideology that demands, at the very least, a greater democracy between doctor and patient in efforts to treat the problem. . . .

REFERENCES

Becker, H. (1960). "Notes on the Concept of Commitment." *American Journal of Sociology* 66:32–40.

Berger, P. and Luckmann, T. (1967). *The Social Construction of Reality.* Garden City, NY: Doubleday.

Blumer, H. (1969). *Symbolic Interaction: Perspective and Method.* Englewood Cliffs, NJ: Prentice-Hall.

Conrad, P. (1985). "The Meaning of Medications: Another Look at Compliance." *Social Science and Medicine* 20:29–37.

Conrad, P., and Schneider, J. (1980). *Deviance and Medicalization.* St. Louis: Mosby.

Holstein, J., and Miller, G. (1990). "Rethinking Victimization: An Interactional Approach to Victimology." *Symbolic Interaction* 13:103–22.

Karp, D. (1992). "Illness Ambiguity and the Search for Meaning." *Journal of Contemporary Ethnography* 21:139–70.

Lyman, S., and Scott, M. (1968). "Accounts." *American Sociological Review* 33 (December):46–62.

Mills, C. W. (1972). "Situated Actions and Vocabularies of Motive." In *Symbolic Interaction,* ed. by J. Manis and B. Meltzer. Boston: Allyn & Bacon.

EDUCATION

47

CIVILIZE THEM WITH A STICK

MARY CROW DOG • RICHARD ERDOES

Few students are aware of our nation's policies toward Native Americans, which included the separation of Indian children from their families and cultures so that these children could be "civilized" into the dominant society. Consequently, thousands of Native American children were forced to leave the reservation to attend boarding schools, day schools, or schools in converted Army posts. These total institutions used tactics similar to those used by the military to resocialize the young Native Americans. In the following selection, taken from *Lakota Woman* (1990), Mary Crow Dog and Richard Erdoes reveal how the institution of education can be an agent of social control whose purpose is to assimilate racial-ethnic populations, such as Native Americans, into the dominate culture.

> *. . . Gathered from the cabin, the wickiup, and the tepee,*
> *partly by cajolery and partly by threats;*
> *partly by bribery and partly by force,*
> *they are induced to leave their kindred*
> *to enter these schools and take upon themselves*
> *the outward appearance of civilized life.*
>
> —ANNUAL REPORT OF THE DEPARTMENT OF INTERIOR, 1901

It is almost impossible to explain to a sympathetic white person what a typical old Indian boarding school was like; how it affected the Indian child suddenly dumped into it like a small creature from another world, helpless, defenseless, bewildered, trying desperately and instinctively to survive and sometimes not surviving at all. I think such children were like the victims of Nazi concentration camps trying to tell average, middle-class Americans what their experience had been like. Even now, when these schools are much improved, when the buildings are new, all gleaming steel and glass, the food tolerable, the teachers well trained and well intentioned, even trained in child psychology—unfortunately the psychology of white children, which is different from ours—the shock to the child upon arrival is still tremendous. Some just seem to shrivel up, don't speak for days on end, and have an empty look in their eyes. I know of an 11-year-old on another reservation who hanged herself, and in our school, while I was there, a girl jumped out of the window, trying to kill herself to escape an unbearable situation. That first shock is always there.

Although the old tiyospaye has been destroyed, in the traditional Sioux families, especially in those where there is no drinking, the child is never left alone. It is always surrounded by relatives, carried around, enveloped in warmth. It is treated with the respect due to any human being, even a small one. It is seldom forced to do anything against its will, seldom screamed at, and never beaten. That much, at least, is left of the old family group among full-bloods. And then suddenly a bus or car arrives, full of strangers, usually white strangers, who yank the child out of the arms of those who love it, taking it screaming to the boarding school. The only word I can think of for what is done to these children is kidnapping.

Even now, in a good school, there is impersonality instead of close human contact; a sterile, cold atmosphere, an unfamiliar routine, language problems, and above all the maza-skan-skan, that damn clock—white man's time as opposed to Indian time, which is natural time. Like eating when you are hungry and sleeping when you are tired, not when that damn clock says you must. But I was not taken to one of the better, modern schools. I was taken to the old-fashioned mission school at St. Francis, run by the nuns and Catholic fathers, built sometime around the turn of the century and not improved a bit when I arrived, not improved as far as the buildings, the food, the teachers, or their methods were concerned.

In the old days, nature was our people's only school and they needed no other. Girls had their toy tipis and dolls, boys their toy bows and arrows. Both rode and swam and played the rough Indian games together. Kids watched their peers and elders and naturally grew from children into adults. Life in the tipi circle was harmonious—until the whiskey peddlers arrived with their wagons and barrels of "Injun whiskey." I often wished I could have grown up in the old, before-whiskey days.

Oddly enough, we owed our unspeakable boarding schools to the do-gooders, the white Indian-lovers. The schools were intended as an alternative to the outright extermination seriously advocated by generals Sherman and Sheridan, as well as by most settlers and prospectors overrunning our land. "You don't have to kill those poor benighted heathen," the do-gooders said, "in order to solve the Indian Problem. Just give us a chance to turn them into useful farmhands, laborers, and chambermaids who will break their backs for you at low wages." In that way the boarding schools were born. The kids were taken away from their villages and pueblos, in their blankets and moccasins, kept completely isolated from their families—sometimes for as long as ten years—suddenly coming back, their short hair slick with pomade, their necks raw from stiff, high collars, their thick jackets always short in the sleeves and pinching under the arms, their tight patent leather shoes giving them corns, the girls in starched white blouses and clumsy, high-buttoned boots—caricatures of white people. When they found out—and they found out quickly—that they were neither wanted by whites nor by Indians, they got good and drunk, many of them staying drunk for the rest of their lives. I still have a poster I found among my grandfather's stuff, given to him by the missionaries to tack up on his wall. It reads:

1. Let Jesus save you.
2. Come out of your blanket, cut your hair, and dress like a white man.
3. Have a Christian family with one wife for life only.
4. Live in a house like your white brother. Work hard and wash often.
5. Learn the value of a hard-earned dollar. Do not waste your money on giveaways. Be punctual.
6. Believe that property and wealth are signs of divine approval.
7. Keep away from saloons and strong spirits.
8. Speak the language of your white brother. Send your children to school to do likewise.
9. Go to church often and regularly.
10. Do not go to Indian dances or to the medicine men.

The people who were stuck upon "solving the Indian Problem" by making us into whites retreated from this position only step by step in the wake of Indian protests.

The mission school at St. Francis was a curse for our family for generations. My grandmother went there, then my mother, then my sisters and I. At one time or other every one of us tried to run away. Grandma told me once about the bad times she had experienced at St. Francis. In those days they let students go home only for one week every year. Two days were used up for transportation, which meant spending just five days out of 365 with her family. And that was an improvement. Before grandma's time, on many reservations they did not let the students go home at all until they had finished school. Anybody who disobeyed the nuns was severely punished. The building in which my grandmother stayed had three floors, for girls only. Way up in the attic were little cells, about five by five by ten feet. One time she was in church and instead of praying she was playing jacks. As punishment they took her to one of those little cubicles where she stayed in darkness because the windows had been boarded up. They left her there for a whole week with only bread and water for nourishment. After she came out she promptly ran away, together with three other girls. They were found and brought back. The nuns stripped them naked and whipped them. They used a horse buggy whip on my grandmother. Then she was put back into the attic—for two weeks.

My mother had much the same experiences but never wanted to talk about them, and then there I was, in the same place. The school is now run by the BIA—the Bureau of Indian Affairs—but only since about 15 years ago. When I was there, during the 1960s, it was still run by the Church. The Jesuit fathers ran the boys' wing and the Sisters of the Sacred Heart ran us— with the help of the strap. Nothing had changed since my grandmother's days. I have been told recently that even in the '70s they were still beating children at that school. All I got out of school was being taught how to pray. I learned quickly that I would be beaten if I failed in my devotions or, God forbid, prayed the wrong way, especially prayed in Indian to Wakan Tanka, the Indian Creator.

The girls' wing was built like an F and was run like a penal institution. Every morning at five o'clock the sisters would come into our large dormitory to wake us up, and immediately we had to kneel down at the sides of our beds and recite the prayers. At six o'clock we were herded into the church for more of the same. I did not take kindly to the discipline and to marching by the clock, left-right, left-right. I was never one to like being forced to do something. I do something because I feel like doing it. I felt this way always, as far as I can remember, and my sister Barbara felt the same way. An old medicine man once told me: "Us Lakotas are not like dogs who can be trained, who can be beaten and keep on wagging their tails, licking the hand that whipped them. We are like cats, little cats, big cats, wildcats, bobcats, mountain lions. It doesn't matter what kind, but cats who can't be tamed, who scratch if you step on their tails." But I was only a kitten and my claws were still small.

Barbara was still in the school when I arrived and during my first year or two she could still protect me a little bit. When Barb was a seventh grader she ran away together with five other girls, early in the morning before sunrise. They brought them back in the evening. The girls had to wait for two hours in front of the mother superior's office. They were hungry and cold, frozen through. It was wintertime and they had been running the whole day without food, trying to make good their escape. The mother superior asked each girl, "Would you do this again?" She told them that as punishment they would not be allowed to visit home for a month and that she'd keep them busy on work details until the skin on their knees and elbows had worn off. At the end of her speech she told each girl, "Get up from this chair and lean over it." She then lifted the girls' skirts and pulled down their underpants. Not little girls either, but teenagers. She had a leather strap about a foot long and four inches wide fastened to a stick, and beat the girls, one after another, until they cried. Barb did not give her that satisfaction but just clenched her teeth. There was one girl, Barb told me, the nun kept on beating and beating until her arm got tired.

I did not escape my share of the strap. Once, when I was 13 years old, I refused to go to Mass. I did not want to go to church because I did not feel well. A nun grabbed me by the hair, dragged me upstairs, made me stoop over, pulled my dress up (we were not allowed at the time to wear jeans), pulled my panties down, and gave me what they called "swats"—25 swats with a board around which Scotch tape had been wound. She hurt me badly.

My classroom was right next to the principal's office and almost every day I could hear him swatting the boys. Beating was the common punishment for not doing one's homework, or for being late to school. It had such a bad effect upon me that I hated and mistrusted every white person on sight, because I met only one kind. It was not until much later that I met sincere white people I could relate to and be friends with. Racism breeds racism in reverse.

The routine at St. Francis was dreary. Six A.M., kneeling in church for an hour or so; seven o'clock, breakfast; eight o'clock, scrub the floor, peel spuds, make classes. We had to mop the dining room twice every day and scrub the tables. If you were caught taking a rest, doodling on the bench with a fingernail or knife, or just rapping, the nun would come up with a dish towel and just slap it across your face, saying, "You're not supposed to be talking, you're supposed to be working!" Monday mornings we had cornmeal mush, Tuesday oatmeal, Wednesday rice and raisins, Thursday cornflakes, and Friday all the leftovers mixed together or sometimes fish. Frequently the food had bugs or rocks in it. We were eating hot dogs that were weeks old, while the nuns were dining on ham, whipped potatoes, sweet peas, and cranberry sauce. In winter our dorm was icy cold while the nuns' rooms were always warm.

I have seen little girls arrive at the school, first graders, just fresh from home and totally unprepared for what awaited them, little girls with pretty braids, and the first thing the nuns did was chop their hair off and tie up what was left behind their ears. Next they would dump the children into tubs of alcohol, a sort of rubbing alcohol, "to get the germs off." Many of the nuns were German immigrants, some from Bavaria, so that we sometimes speculated whether Bavaria was some sort of Dracula country inhabited by monsters. For the sake of objectivity I ought to mention that two of the German fathers were great linguists and that the only Lakota-English dictionaries and grammars which are worth anything were put together by them.

At night some of the girls would huddle in bed together for comfort and reassurance. Then the nun in charge of the dorm would come in and say, "What are the two of you doing in bed together? I smell evil in this room. You girls are evil incarnate. You are sinning. You are going to hell and burn forever. You can act that way in the devil's frying pan." She would get them out of bed in the middle of the night, making them kneel and pray until morning. We had not the slightest idea what it was all about. At home we slept two and three in a bed for animal warmth and a feeling of security.

The nuns and the girls in the two top grades were constantly battling it out physically with fists, nails, and hair-pulling. I myself was growing from a kitten into an undersized cat. My claws were getting bigger and were itching for action. About 1969 or 1970 a strange young white girl appeared on the reservation. She looked about 18 or 20 years old. She was pretty and had long, blond hair down to her waist, patched jeans, boots, and a backpack. She was different from any other white person we had met before. I think her name was Wise. I do not know how she managed to overcome our reluctance and distrust, getting us into a corner, making us listen to her, asking us how we were treated. She told us that she was from New York. She was the first real hippie or Yippie we had come across. She told us of people called the Black Panthers, Young Lords, and Weathermen. She said, "Black people are getting it on. Indians are getting it on in St. Paul and California. How about you?" She also said, "Why don't you put out an underground paper, mimeograph it. It's easy. Tell it like it is. Let it all hang out." She spoke a strange lingo but we caught on fast.

Charlene Left Hand Bull and Gina One Star were two full-blood girls I used to hang out with. We did everything together. They were willing to join me in a Sioux uprising. We put together a newspaper which we called the *Red Panther*. In it we wrote how bad the school was, what kind of slop we had to eat—slimy, rotten, blackened potatoes for two weeks—the way we were beaten. I think I was the one who wrote the worst article about our principal of the moment, Father Keeler. I put all my anger and venom into it. I called him a goddam wasičun son of a bitch. I wrote that he knew nothing about Indians and should go back to where he came from, teaching white children whom he could relate to. I wrote that we knew which priests slept with which nuns and that all they ever could think about was filling their bellies and buying a new car. It was the kind of writing which foamed at the mouth, but which also lifted a great deal of weight from one's soul.

On Saint Patrick's Day, when everybody was at the big powwow, we distributed our newspapers. We put them on windshields and bulletin boards, in desks and pews, in dorms and toilets. But someone saw us and snitched on us. The shit hit the fan. The three of us were taken before a board meeting.

Our parents, in my case my mother, had to come. They were told that ours was a most serious matter, the worst thing that had ever happened in the school's long history. One of the nuns told my mother, "Your daughter really needs to be talked to." "What's wrong with my daughter?" my mother asked. She was given one of our *Red Panther* newspapers. The nun pointed out its name to her and then my piece, waiting for mom's reaction. After a while she asked, "Well, what have you got to say to this? What do you think?"

My mother said, "Well, when I went to school here, some years back, I was treated a lot worse than these kids are. I really can't see how they can have any complaints, because we was treated a lot stricter. We could not even wear skirts halfway up our knees. These girls have it made. But you should forgive them because they are young. And it's supposed to be a free country, free speech and all that. I don't believe what they done is wrong." So all I got out of it was scrubbing six flights of stairs on my hands and knees, every day. And no boy-side privileges.

The boys and girls were still pretty much separated. The only time one could meet a member of the opposite sex was during free time, between 4 and 5:30, in the study hall or on benches or the volleyball court outside, and that was strictly supervised. One day Charlene and I went over to the boys' side. We were on the ball team and they had to let us practice. We played three extra minutes, only three minutes more than we were supposed to. Here was the nuns' opportunity for revenge. We got 25 swats. I told Charlene, "We are getting too old to have our bare asses whipped that way. We are old enough to have babies. Enough of this shit. Next time we fight back." Charlene only said, "Hoka-hay!"

. . .

In a school like this there is always a lot of favoritism. At St. Francis it was strongly tinged with racism. Girls who were near-white, who came from what the nuns called "nice families," got preferential treatment. They waited on the faculty and got to eat ham or eggs and bacon in the morning. They got the easy jobs while the skins, who did not have the right kind of background—myself among them—always wound up in the laundry room sorting out 10-bushel baskets of dirty boys' socks every day. Or we wound up scrubbing the floors and doing all the dishes. The school therefore fostered fights and antagonism between whites and breeds, and between breeds and skins. At one time Charlene and I had to iron all the robes and vestments the priests wore when saying Mass. We had to fold them up and put them into a chest in the back of the church. In a corner, looking over our shoulders, was a statue of the crucified Savior, all bloody and beaten up. Charlene looked up and said, "Look at that poor Indian. The pigs sure worked him over." That was the closest I ever came to seeing Jesus.

I was held up as a bad example and didn't mind. I was old enough to have a boyfriend and promptly got one. At the school we had an hour and a half for ourselves. Between the boys' and the girls' wings were some benches where one could sit. My boyfriend and I used to go there just to hold hands and talk. The nuns were very uptight about any boy-girl stuff. They had an exaggerated fear of anything having even the faintest connection with sex. One day in religion class, an all-girl class, Sister Bernard singled me out for some remarks, pointing me out as a bad example, an example that should be shown. She said that I was too free with my body. That I was holding hands which meant that I was not a good example to follow. She also said that I wore unchaste dresses, skirts which were too short, too suggestive, shorter than regulations permitted, and for that I would be punished. She dressed me down before the whole class, carrying on and on about my unchastity.

. . .

We got a new priest in English. During one of his first classes he asked one of the boys a certain question. The boy was shy. He spoke poor English, but he had the right answer. The priest told him, "You did not say it right. Correct yourself. Say it over again." The boy got flustered and stammered. He could hardly get out a word. But the priest kept after him: "Didn't you hear? I told you to do the whole thing over. Get it right this time." He kept on and on.

I stood up and said, "Father, don't be doing that. If you go into an Indian's home and try to talk Indian, they might laugh at you and say, 'Do it over correctly. Get it right this time!'"

He shouted at me, "Mary, you stay after class. Sit down right now!"

I stayed after class, until after the bell. He told me, "Get over here!" He grabbed me by the arm, pushing me against the blackboard, shouting, "Why are you always mocking us? You have no reason to do this."

I said, "Sure I do. You were making fun of him. You embarrassed him. He needs strengthening, not weakening. You hurt him. I did not hurt you."

He twisted my arm and pushed real hard. I turned around and hit him in the face, giving him a bloody nose. After that I ran out of the room, slamming the door behind me. He and I went to Sister Bernard's office. I told her, "Today I quit school. I'm not taking any more of this, none of this shit anymore. None of this treatment. Better give me my diploma. I can't waste any more time on you people."

Sister Bernard looked at me for a long, long time. She said, "All right, Mary Ellen, go home today. Come back in a few days and get your diploma." And that was that. Oddly enough, that priest turned out okay. He taught a class in grammar, orthography, composition, things like that. I think he wanted more respect in class. He was still young and unsure of himself. But I was in there too long. I didn't feel like hearing it. Later he became a good friend of the Indians, a personal friend of myself and my husband. He stood up for us during Wounded Knee and after. He stood up to his superiors, stuck his neck way out, became a real people's priest. He even learned our language. He died prematurely of cancer. It is not only the good Indians

who die young, but the good whites, too. It is the timid ones who know how
to take care of themselves who grow old. I am still grateful to that priest for
what he did for us later and for the quarrel he picked with me—or did I pick
it with him?—because it ended a situation which had become unendurable
for me. The day of my fight with him was my last day in school.

48

PREPARING FOR POWER
Cultural Capital and Curricula
in America's Elite Boarding Schools

PETER W. COOKSON, JR.
CAROLINE HODGES PERSELL

In addition to teaching individuals life skills, such as reading, writing, and
critical thinking, another important function of education is to help select
the future employment of students. Thus, education tracks and trains people
for certain jobs. Many jobs in society are based on *credentialing* or the requirement of certain educational degrees in order to be hired and promoted.
Schools also provide the valued *cultural capital* of the middle and upper
classes. This knowledge of cultural background, norms, and skills of the
upper classes enables students to obtain higher socioeconomic statuses.
This reading by Peter W. Cookson, Jr., and Caroline Hodges Persell is taken
from their 1985 book of the same title, and it examines the cultural capital
students gain in elite boarding schools.

Borrowing from the British, early American headmasters and teachers
advocated a boarding school curriculum that was classical, conservative, and disciplined. It wasn't until the latter part of the nineteenth
century that such "soft" subjects as English, history, and mathematics were
given a place beside Latin, Greek, rhetoric, and logic in the syllabus. It was the
early schoolmasters' belief that young minds, especially boys' minds, if left
to their own devices, were undisciplined, even anarchic. The only reliable
antidote to mental flabbiness was a rigorous, regular regime of mental calis-
thenics. A boy who could not flawlessly recite long Latin passages was re-

From *Preparing for Power: America's Elite Boarding Schools*, pp. 73–84. Copyright ©
1985 by Peter W. Cookson, Jr. and Caroline Hodges Persell. Reprinted with the permission of BasicBooks, A Division of HarperCollins Publishers, Inc.

quired to increase his mental workouts. Classical languages were to the mind what cold showers were to the body: tonics against waywardness.

Girls, with some exceptions, were not thought of as needing much mental preparation for their future roles as wives and mothers. Their heads were best left uncluttered by thought; too much book learning could give a girl ideas about independence. Besides, the great majority of them were not going on to college, where even more classical languages were required.

As an intellectual status symbol, the classical curriculum helped distinguish gentlemen from virtually everyone else and thus defined the difference between an "educated" man and an untutored one, as well as the difference between high culture and popular culture. Such a division is critical to exclude nonmembers from groups seeking status. For a long time a classical curriculum was the only path to admission to a university, as Harvard and many others required candidates to demonstrate proficiency in Latin and Greek (Levine 1980). Thus, the curriculum of boarding schools has long served both social and practical functions.

Culture, much like real estate or stocks, can be considered a form of capital. As the French scholars Pierre Bourdieu and Jean-Claude Passeron (1977) have indicated, the accumulation of cultural capital can be used to reinforce class differences. Cultural capital is socially created: What constitutes the "best in western civilization" is not arrived at by happenstance, nor was it decided upon by public election. The more deeply embedded the values, the more likely they will be perceived as value free and universal.

Thus curriculum is the nursery of culture and the classical curriculum is the cradle of high culture. The definition of what is a classical course of study has evolved, of course, since the nineteenth century. Greek and Latin are no longer required subjects in most schools—electives abound. But the disciplined and trained mind is still the major objective of the boarding school curriculum.

> The Groton curriculum is predicated on the belief that certain qualities of mind are of major importance: precise and articulate communication; the ability to compute accurately and to reason quantitatively; a grasp of scientific approaches to problem-solving; an understanding of the cultural, social, scientific, and political background of Western civilization; and the ability to reason carefully and logically and to think imaginatively and sensitively. Consequently the School puts considerable emphasis on language, mathematics, science, history, and the arts. (*Groton School* 1981–82:15)

The contrast between the relatively lean curricula of many public schools and the abundant courses offered by boarding schools is apparent. In catalogues of the boarding school's academic requirements, courses are usually grouped by subject matter, and at the larger schools course listings and descriptions can go on for several dozen pages. Far from sounding dreary, the courses described in most catalogues are designed to whet the intellectual appetite. Elective subjects in particular have intriguing titles such as "Hemingway: The Man and His Work," "Varieties of the Poetic Experience," "Effecting Political Change," "Rendezvous with Armageddon," and for those with a scientific bent, "Vertebrate Zoology" and "Mammalian Anatomy and Physiology."

Boarding school students are urged to read deeply and widely. A term course on modern American literature may include works from as many as 10 authors, ranging from William Faulkner to Jack Kerouac. Almost all schools offer a course in Shakespeare in which six or seven plays will be read.

In history, original works are far more likely to be assigned than excerpts from a textbook. A course on the presidency at one school included the following required readings: Rossiter, *The American Presidency;* Hofstadter, *The American Political Tradition;* Hargrove, *Presidential Leadership;* Schlesinger, *A Thousand Days;* Kearns, *Lyndon Johnson and the American Dream;* and White, *Breach of Faith.* Courses often use a college-level text, such as Garraty's *The American Nation* or Palmer's *A History of the Modern World.* Economic history is taught as well—in one school we observed a discussion of the interplay between politics and the depression of 1837—and the idea that there are multiple viewpoints in history is stressed. It is little wonder that many prep school graduates find their first year of college relatively easy.

An advanced-placement English class uses a collection of *The Canterbury Tales* by Geoffrey Chaucer that includes the original middle English on the left page and a modern English translation on the right. An advanced third-year French course includes three or four novels as well as two books of grammar and readings. Even social science courses require a great deal of reading. In a course called "An Introduction to Human Behavior" students are assigned 11 texts including works from B. F. Skinner, Sigmund Freud, Erich Fromm, Jean Piaget, and Rollo May.

Diploma requirements usually include: four years of English, three years of math, three years in one foreign language, two years of history or social science, two years of laboratory science, and one year of art. Many schools require a year of philosophy or religion and also may have such noncredit diploma requirements as four years of physical education, a library skills course, introduction to computers, and a seminar on human sexuality. On average, American public high school seniors take one year less English and math, and more than a year less foreign language than boarding school students (Coleman, Hoffer, and Kilgore 1982:90). Moreover, in the past two decades there has been a historical decline in the number of academic subjects taken by students in the public schools (Adleman 1983).

Because success on the Scholastic Aptitude Test is so critical for admission to a selective college, it is not uncommon for schools to offer English review classes that are specifically designed to help students prepare for the tests. Most schools also offer tutorials and remedial opportunities for students who are weak in a particular subject. For foreign students there is often a course in English as a second language.

As the arts will be part of the future roles of boarding school students, the music, art, and theater programs at many schools are enriching, with special courses such as "The Sound and Sense of Music," "Advanced Drawing," and "The Creative Eye in Film." Student art work is usually on display, and almost every school will produce several full-length plays each year, for example, *Arsenic and Old Lace, A Thurber Carnival, Dracula,* and *The Mousetrap.*

Music is a cherished tradition in many boarding schools, in keeping with their British ancestry. The long-standing "Songs" at Harrow, made famous because Winston Churchill liked to return to them for solace during World War II, are a remarkable display of school solidarity. All 750 boys participate, wearing identical morning coats with tails. Every seat is filled in the circular, sharply tiered replica of Shakespeare's Globe Theater as the boys rise in unison, their voices resonating in the rotunda.

The belief that a well-rounded education includes some "hands-on" experience and travel runs deep in the prep view of learning. Virtually every boarding school provides opportunities for its students to study and work off campus. As volunteers, Taft students, for instance, can "tutor on a one-to-one basis in inner-city schools in Waterbury, act as teachers' helpers in Waterbury Public Schools and work with retarded children at Southbury Training School." They can also work in convalescent homes, hospitals, and day-care centers, and act as "apprentices to veterinarians and help with Girl Scout troops" (*Taft* 1981–82:21). At the Ethel Walker School in Connecticut, girls can go on whale watches, trips to the theater, or work in the office of a local politician. The Madeira School in Virginia has a co-curriculum program requiring students to spend every Wednesday participating in volunteer or internship situations.

Generally speaking, the schools that take the position that manual labor and firsthand experience are good for the soul as well as the mind and body, are more progressive in orientation than other schools. At the Putney School every student has to take a tour of duty at the cow barn, starting at 5:30 A.M. In their own words, "Putney's work program is ambitious. We grow much of our own food, mill our own lumber, pick up our own trash, and have a large part in building our buildings. . . . Stoves won't heat until wood is cut and split" (*The Putney School* 1982:3).

Various styles of student-built structures dot the campus of the Colorado Rocky Mountain School, and at the tiny Midland School in California, there is no service staff, except for one cook. When the water pump breaks, faculty and students fix it, and when buildings are to be built, faculty and students pitch in. "We choose to live simply, to distinguish between our needs and our wants, to do without many of the comforts which often obscure the significant things in life" (*Midland School* 1983:1). The creed of self-reliance is reenacted every day at Midland. When a trustee offered to buy the school a swimming pool, he was turned down. Lounging around a pool is not part of the Midland philosophy.

Travel is very much part of the prep way of life and is continued right through the school year. Not only are semesters or a year abroad (usually in France or Spain) offered, but at some of the smaller schools, everyone goes on an extensive field trip. Every March at the Verde Valley School in Arizona the students travel to "Hopi, Navajo and Zuni reservations, to small villages in northern Mexico, to isolated Spanish-American communities in northern New Mexico and to ethnic neighborhoods of Southwestern cities. They live with native families, attend and teach in schools, work on ranches, and participate in the lives of the host families and their communities" (*Verde Valley School* 1982–83:9). Not all boarding schools, of course, place such a high value on rubbing shoulders with the outside world. At most of the academies, entrepreneurial, and girls' schools the emphasis is on service rather than sharing.

While boarding schools may vary in their general philosophy, the actual curricula do not widely differ. The pressures exerted on prep schools to get their students into good colleges means that virtually all students must study the same core subjects. Although not quick to embrace educational innovation, many boarding schools have added computers to their curricula. This has no doubt been encouraged by announcements by a number of Ivy League and other elite colleges that they want their future applicants to be "computer literate." While people at most boarding schools, or anywhere else for that matter, are not quite sure what is meant by computer literate, they are trying to provide well-equipped computer rooms and teachers who can move their students toward computer proficiency.

For students who have particular interests that cannot be met by the formal curriculum, almost all schools offer independent study, which gives students and teachers at boarding schools a great deal of intellectual flexibility. At Groton, for example, independent study can cover a diverse set of topics including listening to the works of Wagner, conducting a scientific experiment, or studying a special aspect of history.

The boarding school curriculum offers students an abundant buffet of regular course work, electives, volunteer opportunities, travel, and independent study, from which to choose a course of study. By encouraging students to treat academic work as an exciting challenge rather than just a job to be done, the prep schools not only pass on culture but increase their students' competitive edge in the scramble for admission to selective colleges.

The Importance of Sports

Even the most diligent student cannot sit in classrooms all day, and because the prep philosophy emphasizes the whole person, boarding schools offer an impressive array of extracurricular activities, the most important of which is athletics. At progressive schools, the competitive nature of sport is deemphasized. The "afternoon out-of-door program" at Putney, for example, allows for a wide variety of outdoor activities that are noncompetitive; in fact, "skiing is the ideal sport for Putney as one may ski chiefly to enjoy himself, the air, the snow" (*The Putney School* 1982:15).

Putney's sense that sport should be part of a communion with nature is not shared by most other schools, however. At most prep schools sport is about competition, and even more important, about winning. An athletically powerful prep school will field varsity, junior varsity, and third-string teams in most major sports. A typical coed or boys' school will offer football, soccer, cross-country, water polo, ice hockey, swimming, squash, basketball, wrestling, winter track, gymnastics, tennis, golf, baseball, track, and lacrosse. For the faint-hearted there are alternative activities such as modern dance, cycling, tai chi, yoga, ballet, and for the hopelessly unathletic, a "fitness" class. A truly traditional prep school will also have crew like their English forebears at Eton and Harrow. Certain schools have retained such British games as "Fives," but most stop short of the mayhem masquerading as a game called rugby.

Prep teams compete with college freshmen teams, other prep teams, and occasionally with public schools, although public school competitors are picked with care. Not only is there the possible problem of humiliation on the field, there is the even more explosive problem of fraternization in the stands when prep meets townie. Some schools, known as "jock" schools, act essentially as farm teams for Ivy League colleges, consistently providing them with athletes who have been polished by the prep experience. Many prep schools take public high school graduates for a postgraduate year, as a way of adding some size and weight to their football teams.

Prep girls also love sports; they participate as much as the boys, often in the same sports, and with as much vigor. A girls' field hockey game between Exeter and Andover is as intense as when the varsity football teams clash. Horseback riding at girls' schools is still popular; a number of the girls go on to ride in the show or hunt circuit. Unlike many of the girls in public schools, the boarding-school girl is discouraged from being a spectator. Loafing is considered to be almost as bad for girls as it is for boys.

During the school year the halls of nearly all prep schools are decorated with either bulletins of sporting outcomes or posters urging victory in some upcoming game. Pep rallies are common, as are assemblies when awards are given and competitive spirit is eulogized. Often the whole school will be bussed to an opponent's campus if the game is considered to be crucial or if the rivalry is long-standing.

Alumni return to see games, and there are frequent contests between alumni and varsity teams. Because preps retain the love of fitness and sports, it is not uncommon for the old warriors to give the young warriors a thrashing. Similarly, the prep life also invariably includes ritual competitions between, say, the girls' field hockey team and a pick-up faculty team.

Nowhere is the spirit of victory more pronounced than on the ice of the hockey rink. Few public schools can afford a hockey rink so prep schools can attract the best players without much competition. Some prep schools import a few Canadians each year to fill out the roster. Speed, strength, endurance, and fearlessness are the qualities that produce winning hockey and more than one freshman team from an Ivy League college has found itself out-skated by a prep team. Whatever else may be, in Holden Caulfield's term, "phony" about prep schools, sports are for real. This emphasis on sport is not without its critics. At the Harrow School in London, the new headmaster, who was an all-England rugby player, has begun a program to reward artistic and musical prowess as well as athletic and academic skills.

The athletic facilities at prep schools are impressive, and at the larger schools, lavish. Acres and acres of playing fields, scores of tennis courts, one or more gyms, a hockey rink, a golf course, swimming pools, squash courts, workout rooms—all can be found on many prep school campuses. Generally, the facilities are extremely well maintained. The equipment most preps use is the best, as are the uniforms. One boy described how "when your gym clothes get dirty, you simply turn them in at the locker room for a fresh set." The cost of all this, of course, is extraordinary, but considered necessary, because excellence in sport is part of the definition of a gentleman or gentlewoman.

The pressure for athletic success is intense on many campuses, and a student's, as well as a school's, social standing can ride on the narrow margin between victory and defeat. Perhaps because of this, schools generally take great pains to play schools of their own size and social eliteness. A study of who plays whom among prep schools reveals that schools will travel great distances, at considerable expense, to play other prep schools whose students and traditions are similar to their own.

Extracurriculars and Preparation for Life

Not all prep school extracurricular activities require sweating, however. Like public school students, preps can work on the school newspaper or yearbook, help to organize a dance, or be part of a blood donor drive, and are much more likely than their public school counterparts to be involved in such activities. For example, one in three boarding school students is involved in student government compared to one in five public school students, and two in five are involved in the school newspaper or yearbook compared to one in five. This evidence is consistent with other research. Coleman, Hoffer, and Kilgore (1982) found that private school students participate more in extracurricular activities than do public school students. The fact that more boarding school students than public school students are involved in activities provides additional opportunities for them to practice their verbal, interpersonal, and leadership skills.

The catalogue of clubs at prep schools is nearly endless. The opportunity for students to develop special nonacademic interests is one of the qualities of life at prep schools that distinguishes them from many public schools.

Special interest clubs for chess, sailing, bowling, or gun clubs are popular at boys' schools. One elite boys' school has a "war games" club. As the boys at this school are feverishly calculating their country's next strategic arms move, the girls in a Connecticut school are attending a meeting of Amnesty International. Girls, in general, tend to spend their off hours studying the gentler arts such as gourmet cooking and art history. One girls' school has a club with a permanent service mission to the governor's office.

At some schools students can learn printing, metalwork, or woodworking. The shop for the latter at Groton is amply equipped and much of the work turned out by the students is of professional quality. The less traditional schools offer clubs for vegetarian cooking, weaving, quilting, folk music, and—in subtle juxtaposition to the Connecticut girls' school—international cooking. At western schools, the horse still reigns supreme and many students spend endless hours riding, training, cleaning, and loving their own horse, or a horse they have leased from the school.

With the prep emphasis on music, choirs, glee clubs, madrigals, chamber music groups, as well as informal ensembles are all given places to practice. Most schools also have individual practice rooms, and like athletic teams, many prep musicians travel to other schools for concerts and performances.

Some schools offer a five-week "Winterim," during which students and faculty propose and organize a variety of off- and on-campus activities and studies. Such a program breaks the monotony of the usual class routine in the middle of winter, a season teachers repeatedly told us was the worst time at boarding school. It also enables students and faculty to explore new areas or interests in a safe way, that is, without grades.

In prep schools there is a perceived need for students to exercise authority as apprentice leaders early in their educational careers. The tradition of delegating real authority to students has British roots, where head boys and prefects have real power within the public schools. Head boys can discipline other boys by setting punishments and are treated by headmaster and housemasters alike as a part of the administration. In the United States, student power is generally more limited, although at the progressive schools students can be quite involved in the administrative decision-making process.

Virtually all prep schools have a student government. The formal structure of government usually includes a student body president, vice president, treasurer, secretary, class presidents, and dorm prefects, representatives, or "whips," as they are called at one school. Clubs also have presidents and there are always committees to be headed. Some schools have student-faculty senates and in schools like Wooster, in Connecticut, students are expected to play a major part in the disciplinary system. An ambitious student can obtain a great deal of experience in committee work, developing transferable skills for later leadership positions in finance, law, management, or politics.

The office of student body president or head prefect is used by the administration primarily as an extension of the official school culture, and most of the students who fill these offices are quite good at advancing the school's best public relations face. A successful student body president, like a good head, is artful in developing an easy leadership style, which is useful because he or she is in a structural political dilemma. Elected by the students but responsible to the school administration, the student politician is a classic go-between, always running the danger of being seen as "selling out" by students and as "uncooperative" by the administration. Occasionally students rebel against too much pandering to the administration and elect a rebel leader, who makes it his or her business to be a thorn in the side of the administration. A number of heads and deans of students watch elections closely, because if elections go "badly" it could mean a difficult year for them.

The actual content of real power varies by school. At some, authority is more apparent than real; at others, student power can affect important school decisions. At Putney, the "Big Committee" is composed of the school director, student leaders, and teachers. The powers of the Big Committee are laid out in the school's constitution, and students at Putney have real input into the decision-making process. At the Thacher School in California, the Student Leadership Council, which is composed of the school chairman, presidents of the three lower classes, and head prefects, is not only responsible for student activities and events, but also grants funds to groups who petition for special allocations. The power of the purse is learned early in the life of a prep school student. At the Westtown School in Pennsylvania, the student council arrives at decisions not by voting yea or nay, "but by following the Quaker custom of arriving at a 'sense of the meeting'" (*Westtown School* 1982–83:25).

Not all students, of course, participate in school politics; it may well be that many of the students most admired by their peers never run, or never would run, for a political position. The guerrilla leaders who emerge and flourish in the student underlife—or counterculture—may have far greater real power than the "superschoolies" that tend to get elected to public office.

In most coeducational schools boys tend to monopolize positions of power. The highest offices are generally held by boys; girls are found in the vice presidential and secretarial positions. Politics can be important to prep families and we suspect that a number of prep boys arrive at boarding school with a good supply of political ambition. One of the reasons advanced in support of all-girls' schools is that girls can gain important leadership experience there.

Some schools try to capture what they see as the best aspects of single-sex and coed schools. They do this by having boys and girls elect distinct school leaders, by having certain customs, places, and events that they share only with members of their own sex, and by having classes, certain other activities, and social events be coeducational. These schools, often called coordinate schools, see themselves as offering the chance to form strong single-sex bonds, to build self-confidence in adolescents, and to provide experience in working and relating to members of both sexes. Girls at coed schools more generally are likely to say they think in 10 years they will find the social skills they learned to be the most valuable part of their boarding-school experience.

Learning by Example

Part of the social learning students obtain is exposure to significant public personalities. Virtually all the schools have guest speaker programs in which well-known people can be seen and heard. Some of the speakers that have appeared at Miss Porter's School in the last several years include Alex Haley, author; Russell Baker, humorist; Arthur Miller, playwright; and Dick Gregory, comedian. At the boys' schools there is a tendency to invite men who are successful in politics and journalism. Recent speakers at the Hill School include James A. Baker III, Secretary of the Treasury (Hill class of 1948); James Reston, columnist; Frank Borman, astronaut and president of Eastern Airlines; and William Proxmire, United States senator (Hill class of 1934).

Inviting successful alumni to return for talks is one of the ways boarding schools can pass on a sense of the school's efficacy. Throughout the year panels, assemblies, and forums are organized for these occasions. Often the alumni speakers will also have informal sessions with students, visit classrooms, and stay for lunch, tea, or supper.

In keeping with cultural environments of prep schools, especially the select 16 schools, professional musicians, actors, and dancers are regularly invited to perform. Art and sculpture exhibits are common and some schools, such as Andover and Exeter, have permanent art galleries. The art at prep schools is generally either original works by artists such as Toulouse-Lautrec, Matisse, or Daumier, or the work of established contemporary artists such as Frank Stella, who graduated from Andover. At a large school there may be so much cultural activity that it is unnecessary to leave campus for any kind of high cultural event.

Those who come to elite boarding schools to talk or perform are the makers of culture. For adolescents seeking to be the best, these successful individuals give them a sense of importance and empowerment. All around them are the symbols of their special importance—in Groton's main hallway hangs a personal letter from Ronald Reagan to the headmaster, reminding the students that Groton "boasts a former President of the United States and some of America's finest statesmen." Five or six books a year will be published by a school's alumni; Exeter in particular has many alumni authors, including James Agee, Nathaniel G. Benchley, John Knowles, Dwight Macdonald, Jr., Arthur M. Schlesinger, Jr., Sloan Wilson, and Gore Vidal. Roger L. Stevens, Alan Jay Lerner, and Edward Albee are all Choate-Rosemary Hall alumni, adding luster to a theater program that trains many professional actresses and actors. A student at an elite school is part of a world where success is expected, and celebrity and power are part of the unfolding of life. Not every school is as culturally rich as the elite eastern prep schools, but in the main, most schools work hard to develop an appreciation for high culture. At the Orme School in Arizona, a week is set aside each year in which the whole school participates in looking at art, watching art being made, and making art.

Nowhere is the drive for athletic, cultural, and academic excellence more apparent than in the awards, honors, and prizes that are given to outstanding teams or students at the end of each year. Sporting trophies are often large silver cups with the names of annual champions engraved on several sides. At some schools the triumphs have come with enough regularity to warrant building several hundred yards of glass casing to hold the dozens of medals, trophies, and other mementos that are the victors' spoils. Pictures of past winning teams, looking directly into the camera, seem frozen in time.

Academic prizes tend to be slightly less flashy but no less important. Much like British schoolmasters, American schoolmasters believe in rewarding excellence, so most schools give a number of cultural, service, and academic prizes at the end of each year. There is usually at least one prize in each academic discipline, as well as prizes for overall achievement and effort. There are service prizes for dedicated volunteers, as well as debating and creative writing prizes. Almost all schools have cum laude and other honor societies.

Sitting through a graduation ceremony at a boarding school can be an endurance test—some schools give so many prizes that one could fly from New York to Boston and back in the time it takes to go from the classics prize to the prize for the best woodworking or weaving project. But of course, the greatest prize of all is graduation, and more than a few schools chisel, paint, etch, or carve the names of the graduates into wood, stone, or metal to immortalize their passage from the total institution into the world.

REFERENCES

Adleman, Clifford. 1983. "Devaluation, Diffusion and the College Connection: A Study of High School Transcripts, 1964–1981. "Washington, DC: National Commission on Excellence in Education.

Bourdieu, Pierre and Jean-Claude Passeron. 1977. *Reproduction: In Education, Society, and Culture.* Beverly Hills, CA: Sage.

Coleman, James S., Thomas Hoffer, and Sally Kilgore. 1982. *High School Achievement.* New York: Basic Books, p. 90.

Levine, Steven B. 1980. "The Rise of American Boarding Schools and the Development of a National Upper Class." *Social Problems* 28:63–94.

49

CON RESPETO
Bridging the Distances between
Culturally Diverse Families and Schools

GUADALUPE VALDÉS

To be an effective socializing agent, the institution of education should help us develop self-confidence and teach us how to get along with others. Unfortunately, many students slip through the school system without ever being acknowledged as unique human beings. Instead, many students are labeled as slow or as not fitting in, because they do not conform to the dominant culture standards. This reading by Guadalupe Valdés examines one such group of children, the children of Mexican-origin families. As newly arrived immigrants from Mexico, many of these children and their families find American schools confusing and disorienting. The following is an excerpt from Valdés' study, *Con Respeto: Bridging the Distance Between Culturally Diverse Families and Schools* (1996).

It is my purpose here to examine what appears to be a disinterest in education by Mexican parents. By bringing to life the everyday worlds of 10 newly arrived Mexican immigrant families, I hope to propose alternative interpretations for behaviors that schools and school personnel interpret as indifference.

. . .

In this [article], I will argue that Mexican working-class parents bring to the United States goals, life plans, and experiences that do not help them make sense of what schools expect of their children. At the same time, schools expect a "standard" family, a family whose "blueprints for living" are based on particular notions of achievement. They have little understanding about other ways of looking at the world and about other definitions of success. I will further argue that in order to understand how school failure comes to be constructed in the United States for and by newly arrived groups, one must have an understanding of the worlds from which these individuals come.

For Mexican-origin children in the United States, the fact is that school success has been elusive. Indeed, to this day, Mexican-origin children continue to fail in American schools in large numbers. By most available measures (e.g., dropout rates, standardized test scores, college enrollment), it is still the case that educational institutions are not meeting the needs of Mexican-origin students.

. . .

The families selected for study were all originally from the borderlands areas of Mexico. They were *Mexican immigrant* families, as opposed to Mexican-American families (families in which the parents are native-born citizens of this country). Selection of families for the study was made using personal networks and the assistance of the city's "barrio" school. In selecting them, we looked for parents who were Mexican-born, who used Spanish at home, who had been in the town of Las Fuentes for at least a year, who planned to remain in the area for the foreseeable future, and who had a four- or five-year-old child.

. . .

The Focal Children and Their School Placement

Of the forty-seven children in the 10 families, we selected 6 4-year-olds and 6 5-year-olds as focal children. For each of the focal children, information was gathered in the school setting during the three-year period of the study. Children were observed in their regular classrooms, in pullout programs, and in the school yard. Teachers, teacher aides, and other school personnel who worked with the children were interviewed at the end of each year.

. . .

As do most children everywhere in this country, the children of the families in the study spent much of their time in school. Some did better than others in their classes, but in general, they did not excel. In fact, in 7 of the 10 families at least one child in the family was retained in grade. Of the 33 school-aged children in the 10 families, only 2 did well in school.

Some of the children were lucky. They were able to blend in well with other children. They were seen by their teachers as making progress, and at the end of the year they were promoted to the next grade. Others were not so lucky. What they brought with them, what their mothers had so carefully taught them, did not prepare them for the world of school. Their teachers viewed them as having communication problems or social development problems or as simply coming from homes where the parents did not really care a great deal about education.

Pamela Sotelo, for example, spent her kindergarten year saying nothing at all. She did not play with other children or respond when they spoke to her. In the play yard she would seek out her sister or her brother or sit quietly observing the other children play. The only times she spoke was to whisper in Spanish to an elderly woman who volunteered in the classroom. And yet she cut and pasted and scribbled and colored. She imitated other children's behavior and appeared to make sense of even difficult instructions given in English.

Cynthia Ornelas was also quiet. She kept mainly to herself and tried to impress the teacher by volunteering to clean up or straighten up what the other children had left in disarray. She did not usually run and play with the other children, and at times she appeared to be much older than her five years. She wore only dresses to school and sat very properly, like a little lady. On very cold days, she wore a large knit shawl that belonged to her mother and that did not look at all like the colorful jackets the other children wore.

. . .

Seen from a mainstream perspective, without an understanding of why children might behave differently, many of the 12 children in the study did seem strange. Some teachers were confused. Some were worried. Some simply felt that it would take the children time to become like their classmates. As Cynthia's teacher pointed out to us in an interview at the end of the kindergarten year, it was possible that these children would "snap out of it." In describing Cynthia and her conclusions about her, however, she nevertheless painted a picture of a very "odd" little girl indeed.

> *Well, at the beginning she would just sit down at the table . . . wouldn't participate even if they had free play. Everybody would be playing around, she would just sit and look at everybody without even trying to participate. . . .*
>
> *Whenever somebody was playing she thought that was like that's not what we're supposed to be doing, you know, we're supposed to be working or sitting down. Somebody else would just get up and play, and she wouldn't. She'd ask permission, or whatever, you know, she wouldn't just go up there. When something was, uh, you know, when I was cleaning a table she'd go up there and she'd ask me do you need some help. . . .*
>
> *I would say, ah, she doesn't look very alert. She seems tired, you know. She's not a very vibrant little girl jumping around, moving around, talking, not laughing, not a very happy joyful little girl, you know, kind of like quiet, reserved. . . .*

During this interview, the teacher went on to say that she predicted that Cynthia would be in the lowest reading group the following year and would need a tutor for reading. She perceived the child as not having enough experience in school-related activities and as being unwilling to try something if she was afraid that she would do it wrong.

To prod her into conjecturing about Cynthia's future, given her experience with teachers at that particular school and the curriculum, we asked the following questions:

> If you looked at her in the next year or so doing first grade work, and you've already predicted that you think she's going to be in the lowest of the reading groups, and so on, do you see her being retained in first grade? Having problems up the road?

As expected, the prognosis was not particularly encouraging, and it was unclear what exactly might help Cynthia. Comparing her to her two older siblings, the teacher responded:

> *She might snap out of it, she's got it in her, all she has to do is realize she can do it, and she can snap out of it, you know. It's just something that hasn't clicked yet, some of the other kids click a lot earlier and they keep going and it doesn't bother them, but I don't think it's something that will stay with her forever, if she just, you know, puts her mind to it, she's got it. . . . She's, I think she has more in her than the other two kids that came in, thinking and logic and everything else.*

In point of fact, this child might indeed "snap out of it" if she happened to be a youngster who could accept and function within the very different expectations of the school and the home context. On the other hand, by the time she began to "act" like the other children, she might already have been identified as "slow"; or she might have been placed in the lowest reading group and pulled out for special instruction several times during the day. She might, in fact, become just another child who didn't make it.

Cynthia and many of the other children in the study appeared very different from other, more "American" children. Indeed, they did not seem to be very "normal." Teachers' efforts to engage them in fantasy or pretend play were often met with discomfort. The children did not want to be silly. They did not want to play at being rabbits or donkeys or chickens. To teachers trained to believe that all young children like such play, the youngsters' refusal to cooperate and participate seemed odd indeed.

Seen, however, from a framework of how the 12 children in the study were being socialized to succeed within their home contexts, their behavior in school made perfect sense. For example, children whose entire world was the extended family, who were raised to distrust outsiders and to play only with siblings, would, of course, seem either extraordinarily shy or socially retarded to teachers. The children who spent the entire kindergarten year standing alone on the playground, refusing to respond when other children spoke to them, and talking only in a whisper to Spanish-speaking senior-citizen volunteers had learned their lessons well. They knew that they should distrust outsiders, and they had learned not to make friends with strange children. At home, however, these same youngsters chattered happily with their siblings and, as familiarity and trust grew, also with us. At school, they did not trust the teachers yet, and they had not yet learned how to enjoy other children. What was sad was that the teachers in our study had no way of making sense of this behavior. They simply believed that all "normal" youngsters naturally interacted with other children and that something was wrong with Pamela, and Cynthia, and other children like them.

There is other evidence that the expectations and assumptions the children made about what their behavior should be in the school environment placed them at a disadvantage. Put simply, they expected school to be like home and for adults to behave the way adults normally did in the home context. As children trained not to be disruptive, not to call attention to themselves, not to interrupt adult speech, and so forth, they behaved appropriately by following familiar rules of interaction. They did not speak out loud, ask for the teacher's attention, volunteer, or call out answers. They generally sat quietly, taking everything in, and when they had a question, they approached the person that most resembled a family member—the grandmother-like figure of the volunteer aid—just as they had been trained to do by their mothers in front of company, and they whispered a question or a remark.

The "odd" deportment continued beyond the kindergarten years. Indeed, most of the children in the study, even by second grade, seemed not to have become comfortable with "displaying information." Coming from a context where performance for the sake of performance was not expected, where "testing-type" interactions did not take place with adults, and where there were no rewards for such behavior, it took them time to "snap out of it" and to catch on to the fact that what was rewarded in the classroom was the ability to display information on request.

If they were going to do well in American schools, however, the children had to "catch on" quickly. To impress teachers favorably, they had to be ready to perform and indeed outperform their peers. In the school context, it was expected that youngsters should want to outshine the others, to be the best, to be selected for certain privileges, and to compete for attention and limited rewards. But the desire to outperform others did not develop overnight. The children in the study, accustomed to their own secure niche in the family structure—for which they did not have to compete—were unskilled at the game. They were used to having allowances made because of their special characteristics, to their parents' saying, for example, *"es muy despacioso"* (he does things slowly) or *"es muy sentido"* (he's very sensitive), and they were surprised when these same characteristics were never taken into account by the teacher.

Indeed, as I observed the children, much of the time I wondered why they were not all hopelessly confused by the school experience. Even when they worked well, started a task that was assigned, and finished it promptly, they were often admonished for not waiting for directions, or for not reciting parts of the directions before beginning the task. They soon found out that in the school context, there were ways of learning that had more to do with telling than with doing. How different this was from being asked to do something at home!

And the evaluation of the work was different, too. Comments from teachers, even when negative, were incredibly vague as compared to the evaluative remarks made about tasks at home. They were told, "You can do neater work than that" or "You have to work harder on your b's," and not the equivalent of "You left egg yolk on three plates," which would be, "Your b's have to start here and end here and look like this."

The examples of mismatch were many. It is equally clear from our data, however, that not all teachers responded to these children's behavior and characteristics in the same way. Teachers' values and beliefs about appropriate school behavior were different, and both Anglos and Hispanics varied in their response to the same children. We found sensitive teachers in both ethnic groups who believed these children could succeed. But we also found very mainstream-oriented teachers in both groups who had little patience with newly arrived Mexican children and their families.

. . .

The parents [also] were of little help. For them, American schools were unfamiliar institutions. They expected them to be like the schools they had known or attended in Mexico, and they were continually surprised and taken aback by the differences. Assumptions that they made about what schools did, about what they expected of children, and about what they expected of parents were undoubtedly wrong. On many occasions, they discovered that they could not help their children even when they were treated unfairly.

All 10 mothers, however, believed that they had prepared their children well for school. They had taught them to be respectful, and they had taught them to behave. They did not know that other, more "American" mothers had also taught their children their colors, letters, and numbers. They naively believed that letters, colors, and numbers were part of what their children would learn at school.

In this [article], it is my intention to describe and examine the mismatches and the differences that appeared to affect the interactions between children, teachers, and parents during the three years of the study. I . . . argue that misunderstandings between parents and school personnel took place at several levels and were due to different factors. Some of the misunderstandings between teachers and parents occurred because the parents were new immigrants who knew very little about schools in general and even less about American schools. They brought old fears, expectations, and assumptions with them; and family networks collected new information that was not always based on a full understanding of how things worked in this country.

Other misunderstandings were more profound and far more serious. These had to do with expectations that teachers had about what families should be, how they should view education, and how they should behave because of these beliefs. Their models of "good" and "supportive" families did not encompass values and beliefs about life and living that failed to place at the center individual achievement and success.

In this [article], then, I . . . focus on the educational backgrounds of the parents in the study and on their lack of familiarity with American schools. I . . . preface this description and discussion with an overview of the attitudes toward education expressed by members of the 10 families. I . . . then examine and describe the many misunderstandings that arose for them because of the suppositions they made about American schools and because of their lack of knowledge about the educational system in this country.

The Educational Experiences of the Adults

With two exceptions, the parents in the study had very little formal education. . . . Only three individuals had finished elementary school in Mexico. Of the two women who attended school in the United States, one did not complete seventh grade, and the other dropped out after ninth grade.

For many of the adults in the study, education was a sensitive topic. I do not know if it was particularly so because I, in my role of *maestra*, was raising the issue or if the sensitivity was due to a general sense that it was important to have gone to school. . . .

Pedro and Velma Soto, for example, were typical of the adults who appeared to be embarrassed when I asked them about the number of years of schooling completed by the adults in the family. Neither had much exposure to formal education, and both were uncomfortable when discussing the subject of schooling. When I asked Pedro in the first interview how many years of schooling he had completed, he responded that he had completed third grade. During the course of the study, however, the number of years claimed to have been completed varied. At one point the number increased to six, and at another it decreased to one. According to Velma, however, Pedro finished only the first grade, a fact that she insisted did not prevent him from learning to read and write. It is difficult to say, however, how true this claim actually was.

. . .

Velma was less sensitive about her educational background and more willing to talk about her experiences with us. For example, when asked specifically if she remembered how she had been taught to read, she responded:

No, porque era muy vaga. Yo me salía de la escuela (laughs with sister who is present) yo me salía de la escuela a jugar con el chavalo de esta . . . (speaks to her mother who is also present) como se nombra, la novia del profesor Salvador, Amá? Me salía por abajo, yo me acuerdo que me salía por abajo de todas las bancas hasta que salía hasta la puerta.

No, because I was very naughty. I used to leave school, I used to leave school to play with what's her name's kid, what's her name, the girlfriend of Salvador the teacher, Ma? I would get out underneath, I remember that I would get out underneath all the desks until I got out to the door.

She insisted, however, that this behavior did not keep her from making progress in school and from learning:

No, pos yo me apliqué mucho porque no pensaba, no quería que me ganaran las demás muchachas. No quería ser más burra que las demás.

Well, I applied myself because I didn't think, I didn't want the other girls to get ahead of me. I didn't want to be dumber than the rest of them.

Velma's responses to questions about how many years of schooling she completed, however, varied. On one occasion she stated that she had finished sixth grade, but on another occasion she impled that she had made it only to third grade. From her comments about other members of the family, it appears that the completion of primary school (grade six) in Mexico marked achievement of a special sort in her mind. Talking about one of her sisters, for example, she said with some pride: *"Ella sí terminó su sexto año. Ella sí lo logró"* (She did finish sixth grade. She was able to do that.)

Given this perception of what constitutes academic success, it is not surprising that Velma (except when schooling was referred to spontaneously and not focused on) always sought to present herself as having completed sixth grade. She could do so with some legitimacy because she could indeed read and write in Spanish and was even able to attempt reading in English.

Regrets about Having Received Little Schooling

Some of the parents who had received very little education expressed regret at not having had the opportunity to stay in school. It is not clear whether they would have had the same feelings had they remained in Mexico, but in the United States they had come to see that going to school was normal and that most young people stayed in school for many years. In several families, it was the case that the children had already gone beyond the level of education of their parents. This made the parents sensitive about the issue and aware of their own limitations in the eyes of their children.

María Elena Ramírez, for example, recalled with some bitterness that her stepfather had not sent her to school because she was needed at home to care for her younger siblings. *"No me quiso mandar. Dijo que pa qué"* (He didn't want to send me. He said what for).

Isela Sotelo was embarrassed at having to admit that she had gone only as far as the second grade. She emphasized the fact, however, that she could still read and write. *"Pero yo sí sé leer y escribir. Bueno, no me hacen tonta"* (But I can read and write. Anyway, they can't fool me).

Overall, the sentiment expressed by those individuals who had not had much schooling was that life circumstances had prevented them from getting a formal education. They were much less precise in their answers when they were asked how their lives might have been different if they had obtained an education in Mexico. Only Velma Soto and Socorro Tinajero gave examples of the kinds of jobs they might have had in Mexico if they had more schooling. Velma stated that she would have gone to nursing school, and Socorro claimed that she would have moved up quickly in hotel management. None of the other individuals had life experiences in which formal education would have made much difference. The most they could offer in response to my questions about what would have been different was, in the words of Rosario Castro, *"No, pos 'hora les ayudara más a los hijos"* (Well, now I could help the children more).

Attitudes toward Education

Without exception, parents expressed very positive views about education. They felt that education was important and that it was their duty as parents to send their children to school. These positive views were communicated to me in a number of forms, and because of this, I am convinced that they were genuine expressions of their feelings and beliefs. Comments about schooling and education came up frequently, and these comments went beyond the responses given to my direct questions about the importance of education.

In the case of Amelia Soto, for example, her views about formal education came into sharp focus when she became angry at her daughter Lorena for dropping out of high school. Lorena . . . married a young man from Juárez and decided to live there with him. Amelia missed her daughter but, more than anything else, she lamented the fact that Lorena had dropped out of school. It was a topic that she returned to frequently with us. She was willing to do anything, she claimed, including putting up with a son-in-law she did not like, if only Lorena returned to school.

. . .

Rosario Castro also made clear what her feelings were about education not only to us, but also to her children in every way that she could. Indeed, we discovered just how important she thought education was when she recounted how she had made both Rebeca and Miguel sit through first and second grade again, rather than have them spend a year without schooling. Apparently, when Rosario first moved to Juárez, she had been unable to get her children into school. In Juárez, public schools are always very crowded and cannot accommodate all the children in the city. It is not unusual for parents to attempt to register their children at several schools only to find out that there is no more room. Rosario was lucky, however, because she located one of her former teachers from the village, who was then teaching in Juárez. She persuaded this teacher to allow her children to enter her combined first and second grade classroom even though Miguel and Rebeca were much older than the other children. It did not matter to Rosario that her children did not want to go. She was determined that they would attend school, and she had no patience with their objections. She answered her children's protests by saying, *"Que grandota ni que nada, tú vas"* (Big or not, you're going). For Rosario, what was important was that her children would attend school. It did not matter that they were repeating work that they had already had in their village school years before. She did not think about it in those terms. What she cared about was that both Miguel and Rebeca saw themselves as still enrolled in school, and that they did not begin to believe that there were reasons for dropping out.

In the United States, Rosario's children were pushed by her same determination and by her commitment to education. Rosario taught her children to respect their teachers and had little tolerance for their complaints about them. In Rosario's words: *"Las maestras están ay pa enseñarles, y ustedes están ay pa aprender"* (Teachers are there to teach you and you're there to learn). However, she was more than willing to do battle with teachers, to talk with high school counselors, and to insist that she be called whenever her children did not show up at school.

. . .

Isela Sotelo was also a strong supporter of education. She spoke several times not only about her ambitions for her daughter Sara, but also about her own ambition to go to school and to learn English. Although it was clear that she had many insecurities about her ability to do well, she hoped classes for adults would be offered soon at the neighborhood school:

Yo estoy esperando que haiga unas clases allí en la escuela. Yo quiero ir pero con alguien que yo tenga confianza. A veces pienso que no voy a decir algo bien. Pero yo pienso que para entrar a la escuela tiene uno que pasar, ¿verdad? por todo. Se van a reir de uno.	I'm waiting for classes to be given at the school. I want to go but with someone that I trust. Sometimes I think that I am not going to say something right. But I think that to enter school one has to go through everything. People are going to laugh at you.

For Isela, going to school involved sacrifices, and she spoke about education in those terms. Her *consejos* to her two older daughters often focused on the importance of making those sacrifices for the future.

. . .

In different ways, parents in the study demonstrated that they valued schooling. They were aware of their own limited opportunities, and they wanted their children to have more. Even in the face of the many competing demands on the family system, children's schooling was still considered important.

. . .

Commitment and interest in education, however, were not enough to make up for the parents' lack of familiarity with U.S. institutions. In spite of their good intentions, there was much that the families did not understand about American schools. There was much confusion about programs, requirements, and grading. There was much misinformation within the family collective experience about what worked and what did not.

. . .

Parental "Involvement" in School

As might be expected, very few of the families had any concept of "involvement" in their children's education as defined by the schools. As was the case for the white working-class families studied by Lareau (1989), parents in the study did not impress teachers with their willingness to "help" the schools educate their children. At the very most, those parents whose family networks had established that it was important for parents to be seen at school by their children's teachers ordinarily went to open house at the beginning of the school year.

Of the eight families whose children attended Lincoln School, one parent in five of the families attended open houses during the first, second, and third years of the study. These families were the Castros, the Gómezes, the Ramírezes, the Leybas, and the Tinajeros. Parents who did not feel confident in English were accompanied by an older child who could serve as translator, if needed.

For the most part, parents viewed their role at open houses as visiting their children's classroom and looking over their papers and drawings. They did not see it as an opportunity to personally meet their children's teacher. With the exception of Federico Gómez and Joaquín Ramírez, none of the parents made it a point to go up and talk to the teacher during any of the three open houses attended. When questioned about their impressions about open

house and about why they believed open houses were held, no one mentioned that it was an opportunity to find out about their children's school
progress or that one of its purposes was to give parents an idea about the nature of the school program. They saw it, rather, as a pleasant social event that
children liked to go to. Since many teachers gave extra points to children
when their parents were present at open house, the older children put pressure on their parents to attend.

Overall, then, open houses were seen as a time in which the principal,
Mr. Vasquez, spoke to all the parents in the auditorium and made it a point
to speak Spanish during a portion of his talk. They saw it as a time in which
they got to see exactly where their children's classrooms were, where they
had lunch, and how far or how near they were to the classrooms of siblings
and cousins. Even the more sophisticated parents (e.g., Federico Gómez and
Joaquín Ramírez) did not have a sense that they could learn a great deal about
how their children spent their time at school or about teacher expectations
from listening to the presentations during open house.

. . .

The families also attended enchilada suppers and Mother's Day celebrations.
Again, usually only one of the parents was in attendance, and there was little
interaction with school personnel.

Parental involvement, then, was limited to ceremonial occasions at which
there was little time for teachers to talk about children's progress. Parents
made an appearance to please the children, to whom those things mattered,
and felt that they had done their duty. None of the families knew about PTA,
about volunteering to work at the school, or about other ways in which they
might become "involved" in their children's education.

Parental Interactions with School Personnel

When parents interacted with school personnel, they did so only on those
occasions in which they felt that their children needed their intervention or
when they had been asked to come to the school by the teacher. Even when
asked to come, however, it was often the case that parents did not respond.
In some instances, the request came at a bad time (e.g., when the father, who
spoke the most English, was away), and in other instances, notes (generally
written in English) asking parents to call and make an appointment were interpreted as invitations that did not have to be accepted. In many families,
however, neither of the two parents felt competent enough to deal with
school personnel. They were embarrassed, and found almost any excuse not
to go to the school and *"ponerse en evidencia"* (show how ignorant or incapable they were).

Even when some parents were as deeply committed to their children doing well in school as was Eulalia Gómez, they hesitated to speak to the teacher herself. Eulalia, for example, spoke only to the teacher's aide, who not only spoke Spanish well, but who also seemed to Eulalia more approachable than the teacher:

A ella es a la que le pregunto, porque como ella era la que siempre me saludaba cuando iba a recoger a Federico, pos se me hacía más fácil.	I always ask her since she was the one that always said hello to me when I went to get Federico, so it seemed easier.

Reina Leyba also spoke only to the aide even when she was very upset about the fact that her daughter, Maya, was being kept after school. Regardless of the fact that it was not acceptable to Reina for Maya to be kept after the regular school dismissal, she did not dare talk to the teacher.

No no sé, hasta le dije a ver si te apuras de salir de esa escuela porque yo no he ido a conocer a esa maestra. No quiero conocerla. Me platicó mi cuñada que es muy caraja, y luego le dije yo voy a hablar, porque yo estoy pagando pa que me los traiga un señor y me los lleve a la escuela. Y me los deja, después de la clase a Maya, y le dije voy ir a hablar con esa maestra y me dice, y no, no me animé.	No, I don't know, I even said, let's see if you hurry up and get out of the school because I haven't gone to meet the teacher. I don't want to meet her. My sister-in-law told me that she's a real mean one and then I said I'm going to go say something because I'm paying so that a man takes them back and forth to school. And she keeps them, keeps Maya after class, and I said, I'm going to go talk to the teacher and she said . . . and no, I didn't have the courage to.

Reina could not describe the teacher, and did not know her name.

. . .

The truth of the matter was that Reina herself had not talked to any of the teachers. It was her husband, who was home in the evenings and who went to open house, who had seen the children's teachers. When both Reina and Héctor did go to school on one occasion, they followed the extended family's advice and chose not to risk antagonizing the teacher. In Reina's case, her apprehensiveness at talking with the teacher reflected a certain degree of *vergüenza* (embarrassment), but more than anything, it reflected caution. She had been warned by the extended family about the dangers of saying the wrong thing to teachers and that much harm could be done by teachers who took a dislike to particular children.

. . .

Parental Involvement in Children's Schoolwork

... The 10 mothers in the study saw themselves as participating actively in their children's *educación,* that is, in raising their children to be good and well-behaved human beings. They did not, however, see themselves as adjunct schoolteachers. They did not see their role as involving the teaching of school subjects. In their own experience in school, this had been the province of the teacher. Mothers, on the other hand, had been responsible for the moral upbringing of their children. Parental teaching involved guiding youngsters, molding them with *consejos,* and supervising them carefully.

When American teachers expected that Mexican working-class mothers would "help" their children with their schoolwork, they were making assumptions about abilities that the mothers did not have. Moreover, they were also making assumptions about the universality of what, in American schools, counts as knowledge. For example, when Mrs. Lockley complained that Velma Soto had not taught Saúl his ABC's, she did not consider that the teaching and the learning of the alphabet might not be equally valued in all school contexts. She could not possibly imagine that there might be very valid reasons why parents might not have prepared their children for school by teaching them the alphabet, and it was difficult for her to consider that parents might not understand, even when told, why learning the ABC's was so important.

Indeed, the learning of the alphabet by children is an example of how parents' experiences did not help them make sense of their new world. In Mexico, the ability to recite the alphabet *per se* is not considered particularly important. Instead, recognition of syllables containing a consonant and a vowel is considered fundamental to reading. A child who can recognize and call out combinations such as *ba, be, bi, bo, bu* and *da, de, di, do, du* containing the five Spanish vowels is considered to be making progress toward reading. And indeed, most reading instruction begins by having children work with such combinations. What is important is the *sound* of the letter combinations and not their names.

Given this experience, the parents in the study could not anticipate that in this country, teachers expected the children to know their ABC's, that is, to be able to recite the alphabet by the time they began first grade. More importantly, the parents were not aware that for many teachers, knowing the alphabet was an indicator of children's abilities and of parents' "involvement" in their education. By not making certain that their children arrived in school with the "right" knowledge, they were, in fact, condemning their children to placement in the lowest reading groups. Unfortunately, as was the case for Saúl, as well as for many of the other children, this placement was the beginning of an endless cycle of academic failure.

The School Context: A Summary

For the children, the teachers, and the parents, the school context presented many challenges. Teachers tried their best and appeared to fail. Children brought with them skills they had learned at home and found them inappropriate. Parents felt helpless, confused, and angry.

Both the schools and the families made assumptions about each other. Schools expected a "standard" family, a family whose members were educated, who were familiar with how schools worked, and who saw their role as complementing the teacher's in developing children's academic abilities. It did not occur to school personnel that parents might not know the appropriate ways to communicate with the teachers, that they might feel embarrassed about writing notes filled with errors, and that they might not even understand how to interpret their children's report cards. When children came to school without certain skills that their families, in good faith, believed the teachers should teach (e.g., the alphabet, the colors, the numbers), school personnel assumed parental indifference, troubled homes, and little interest in education.

The parents, on the other hand, were living lives that required large amounts of energy just to survive. They had little formal schooling and few notions about what schools expected of them and their children. And yet, they valued education. The collective family wisdom had already instilled in them a sense of the importance of high school graduation. They wanted their children to have good jobs, and they wanted them to have whatever education they would need in order to get such jobs.

. . . However, the parents' notions about "good" jobs were not "standard" notions. Education occupied a particular place within their life plans that was not entirely congruent with the place it occupies in the middle-class American world. . . . The misunderstandings, such as those presented in this [article], that are caused by lack of information can be adjusted. Teachers can be informed about what parents do not know, and parents can be taught how American schools work. What is not as easily fixed are values and beliefs that run counter to views held in Western industrialized countries about individual success and school achievement.

REFERENCES

Lareau, Annette. 1989. *Home Advantage.* London: Falmer Press.

THE FAMILY

50

GAY AND LESBIAN FAMILIES ARE HERE

JUDITH STACEY

Some scholars argue that to understand completely the current debate about family, we need to examine the changing definitions of family. For example, many people define *family* only in terms of heterosexual marriage and blood ties. If we delineate family based on only these criteria, think of all the people we leave out, including adopted and foster children, cohabiting couples, gay and lesbian couples, and friends who are often closer than blood relatives. In the following selection, taken from *In the Name of the Family: Rethinking Family Values in the Post Modern Age* (1996), Judith Stacey challenges us to examine our heterosexist and narrow definitions of family. Stacey argues that gay and lesbian families already exist in large numbers; they are not deviant; and many of these families are fighting for the same rights as heterosexual families, including the right to adopt children and the right to marry someone of the same sex.

In 1992 in Houston, I talked about the cultural war going on for the soul of America. And that war is still going on! We cannot worship the false god of gay rights. To put that sort of relationship on the same level as marriage is a moral lie.

—Pat Buchanan, February 10, 1996

Homosexuality is a peculiar and rare human trait that affects only a small percentage of the population and is of little interest to the rest.

—Jonathan Rauch 1994

I came to Beijing to the Fourth World Conference of Women to speak on behalf of lesbian families. We are part of families. We are daughters, we are sisters, we are aunts, nieces, cousins. In addition, many of us are mothers and grandmothers. We share concerns for our families that are the same concerns of women around the world.

—Bonnie Tinker, *Love Makes a Family*, September 1995

Until but a short time ago, gay and lesbian families seemed quite a queer concept, even preposterous, if not oxymoronic, not only to scholars and the general public, but even to most lesbians and gay men. The grass roots movement for gay liberation that exploded into public visibility in 1969, when gays resisted a police raid at the Stonewall bar in New York City, struggled along with the militant feminist movement of that period to liberate gays and women *from* perceived evils and injustices represented by the family, rather than *for* access to its blessings and privileges. During the early 1970s, marches for gay pride and women's liberation flaunted provocative, countercultural banners, like "Smash The Family" and "Smash Monogamy." Their legacy is a lasting public association of gay liberation and feminism with family subversion. Yet how "queer" such antifamily rhetoric sounds today, when gays and lesbians are in the thick of a vigorous profamily movement of their own.

Gay and lesbian families are indisputably here. In June of 1993, police chief Tom Potter joined his lesbian, police officer daughter in a Portland, Oregon, gay pride march for "family values." By the late 1980s an astonishing "gay-by boom" had swelled the ranks of children living with gay and lesbian parents to between six to fourteen million.[1] *Family Values* is the title of a popular 1993 book by and about a lesbian's successful struggle to become a legal second mother to one of these "turkey-baster" babies, the son she and his biological mother have co-parented since his birth.[2] In 1989 Denmark became the first nation in the world to legalize a form of gay marriage, termed "registered partnerships," and its Nordic neighbors, Norway and Sweden, soon followed suit. In 1993, thousands of gay and lesbian couples participated in a mass wedding ceremony on the Washington Mall during the largest demonstration for gay rights in U.S. history. Three years later, on March 25, 1996, Mayor of San Francisco Willie Brown proudly presided over a civic ceremony to celebrate the domestic partnerships of nearly 200 same-sex couples. "We're leading the way here in San Francisco," the mayor declared, "for the rest of the nation to fully embrace the diversity of people in love, regardless of their gender or sexual orientation."[3] By then thousands of gay and lesbian couples across the nation were eagerly awaiting the outcome of *Baehr v. Lewin*, cautiously optimistic that Hawaii's Supreme Court will soon order the state to become the first in the United States, and in the modern world, to grant full legal marriage rights to same-sex couples. As this work went to press in May 1996, the Republican party had just made gay marriage opposition a wedge issue in their presidential campaign.

Gay and lesbian families are undeniably here, yet they are not queer, if one uses the term in the sense of "odd" to signify a marginal or deviant population.[4] It is nearly impossible to define this category of families in a manner that could successfully distinguish all of its members, needs, relationships, or even their values, from those of all other families. In fact, it is almost impossible to define this category in a satisfactory, substantive way at all. What should count as a gay or lesbian family? Even if we bracket the thorny matter of how to define an individual as gay or lesbian and rely on self-identification, we still face a jesuitical challenge. Should we count only families in which every single member is gay? Clearly there are not very many, if even any, of these. Or does the presence of just one gay member color a family gay? Just as clearly, there are very many of these, including those of Ronald Reagan, Colin Powell, Phyllis Schlafly and Newt Gingrich.[5] More to the point, why would we want to designate a family type according to the sexual identity of one or more of its members? No research, as we will see, has ever shown a uniform, distinctive pattern of relationships, structure, or even of "family values," among families that include self-identified gays. Of course, most nongays restrict the term gay family to units that contain one or two gay parents and their children. However, even such families that most commonsensically qualify as gay or lesbian are as diverse as are those which do not.

Gay and lesbian families come in different sizes, shapes, ethnicities, races, religions, resources, creeds, and quirks, and even engage in diverse sexual practices. The more one attempts to arrive at a coherent, defensible sorting principle, the more evident it becomes that the category "gay and lesbian family" signals nothing so much as the consequential social fact of widespread, institutionalized homophobia.[6] The gay and lesbian family label marks the cognitive dissonance, and even emotional threat, that much of the nongay public experiences upon recognizing that gays can participate in family life at all. What unifies such families is their need to contend with the particular array of psychic, social, legal, practical, and even physical challenges to their very existence that institutionalized hostility to homosexuality produces. Paradoxically, the label "gay and lesbian family" would become irrelevant if the nongay population could only "get used to it."

In this [article] I hope to facilitate such a process of normalization, ironically, perhaps, to allow the marker "gay and lesbian" as a family category once again to seem queer—as queer, that is, as it now seems to identify a *family,* rather than an individual or a desire, as heterosexual. . . . Gay and lesbian families represent such a new, embattled, visible and necessarily self-conscious, genre of postmodern kinship, that they more readily expose the widening gap between the complex reality of postmodern family forms and the simplistic modern family ideology that still undergirds most public rhetoric, policy and law concerning families. In short, I hope to demonstrate that, contrary to Jonathan Rauch's well-meaning claim in the second epigraph above, the experience of "homosexuals"[7] should be of immense interest to everyone else. Nongay families, family scholars and policymakers alike can learn a great deal from examining the experience, struggles, conflicts, needs, and achievements of contemporary gay and lesbian families. . . .

A More, or Less, Perfect Union?

Much nearer at hand . . . than most ever dared to imagine has come the momentous prospect of legal gay marriage. The idea of same-sex marriage used to draw nearly as many jeers from gays and lesbians as from nongays. As one lesbian couple recalls, "In 1981, we were a very, very small handful of lesbians who got married. We took a lot of flak from other lesbians, as well as heterosexuals. In 1981, we didn't know any other lesbians, not a single one, who had had a ceremony in Santa Cruz, and a lot of lesbians live in that city. Everybody was on our case about it. They said, What are you doing, How heterosexual. We really had to sell it." [8]

Less than a decade later, gay and lesbian couples could proudly announce their weddings and anniversaries, not only in the gay press, which now includes specialized magazines for gay and lesbian couples, like *Partners Magazine,* but even in such mainstream, Midwestern newspapers as the Minneapolis *Star Tribune.*[9] Jewish rabbis, Protestant ministers, Quaker meetings, and even some Catholic priests regularly perform gay and lesbian wedding or commitment ceremonies. This phenomenon is memorialized in cultural productions within the gay community, like "Chicks In White Satin," a documentary about a Jewish lesbian wedding which won prizes at recent gay film festivals, but it has also become a fashionable pop culture motif. In December 1995, the long-running TV sitcom program "Roseanne" featured a gay male wedding in a much-hyped episode called "December Bride." Even more provocative, however, was a prime-time lesbian wedding that aired one month later on "Friends," the highest rated sitcom of the 1995–1996 television season. Making a cameo appearance on the January 18, 1996 episode, Candice Gingrich, the lesbian half-sister of right-wing Speaker of the House Newt Gingrich, conducted a wedding ceremony which joined the characters who play a lesbian couple on the series "in holy matrimony" and pronounced them "wife and wife."

When the very first social science research collection about gay parents was published in 1987, not even one decade ago, its editor concluded that however desirable such unions might be, "it is highly unlikely that marriages between same-sex individuals will be legalized in any state in the foreseeable future." [10] Yet, almost immediately thereafter, precisely this specter began to exercise imaginations across the political spectrum. A national poll reported by the *San Francisco Examiner* in 1989 found that 86 percent of lesbians and gay men supported legalizing same-sex marriage.[11] However, it is the pending *Baehr v. Lewin* court decision concerning same-sex marriage rights in Hawaii that has thrust this issue into escalating levels of front-page and prime-time prominence. Amidst rampant rumors that thousands of mainland gay and lesbian couples were stocking their hope chests with Hawaiian excursion fares, poised to fly to tropical altars the instant the first gay matrimonial bans falter, right-wing Christian groups began actively mobilizing resistance. Militant antiabortion leader Randall Terry of Operation Rescue flew to Hawaii in February 1996 to fight "queer marriage," and right-wing Christian women's leader and radio broadcast personality Beverly La-Haye urged her "Godly" listeners to fight gay marriage in Hawaii.[12]

Meanwhile, fearing that Hawaii will become a gay marriage mecca, state legislators have rushed to introduce bills that exclude same-sex marriages performed in other states from being recognized in their own, because the "full faith and credit" clause of the U.S. Constitution obligates interstate recognition of legal marriages. While fourteen states had rejected such bills by May 1995, eight others had passed them, and contests were underway in numerous others, including California.[13] On May 8, 1996, gay marriage galloped onto the nation's center political stage when Republicans introduced the Defense of Marriage Act (DOMA) which defines marriage in exclusively heterosexual terms, as "a legal union between one man and one woman as husband and wife."[14] The last legislation that Republican presidential candidate Bob Dole co-sponsored before he resigned from the Senate to pursue his White House bid full throttle, DOMA exploits homophobia to defeat President Clinton and the Democrats in November 1996. With Clinton severely bruised by the political debacle incited by his support for gay rights in the military when he first took office, but still dependent upon the support of his gay constituency, the President indeed found himself "wedged" between a rock and a very hard place. Unsurprisingly, he tried to waffle. Naming this a "time when we need to do things to strengthen the American family," Clinton publicly opposed same-sex marriage at the same time that he tried to reaffirm support for gay rights and to expose the divisive Republican strategy.[15]

Polemics favoring and opposing gay marriage rights now proliferate in editorial pages and legislatures across the nation, and mainstream religious bodies find themselves compelled to confront the issue. In March 1996 the Vatican felt called upon not merely to condemn same-sex marriage and a "moral disorder," but also to warn Catholics that they would themselves risk "moral censure" if they were to support "the election of the candidate who has formally promised to translate into law the homosexual demand."[16] Just one day after the Vatican published this admonition, the Central Conference of American Rabbis, which represents the large, generally liberal wing of Judaism, took a momentous action in direct opposition. The Conference resoundingly endorsed a resolution to "support the right of gay and lesbian couples to share fully and equally in the rights of civil marriage." Unsurprisingly, Orthodox rabbis immediately condemned the action as prohibited in the Bible and "another breakdown in the family unit."[17] One week later, in another historic development, a lead editorial in the *New York Times* strongly endorsed gay marriage.[18]

As with child custody, the campaign for gay marriage clings to legal footholds carved by racial justice pioneers. It is startling to recall how recent it was that the Supreme Court finally struck down antimiscegenation laws. Not until 1967, that is only two years before Stonewall, did the high court, in *Loving v. Virginia,* find state restrictions on interracial marriages to be unconstitutional. (Twenty states still had such restrictions on the books in 1967, only one state fewer than the twenty-one which currently prohibit sodomy.) A handful of gay couples quickly sought to marry in the 1970s through appeals to this precedent, but until three lesbian and gay male couples sued Hawaii in *Baerh v. Lewin* for equal rights to choose marriage partners without restrictions on gender, all U.S. courts had dismissed the analogy. In a historic ruling in 1993, the Hawaiian state Supreme Court remanded this suit to the state, requiring it to demonstrate a "compelling state interest" in prohibiting same-sex marriage, a strict scrutiny standard that few believe the state will be able to meet. Significantly, the case was neither argued nor adjudicated as a gay rights issue. Rather, just as ERA opponents once had warned and advocates had denied, passage of an equal rights amendment to Hawaii's state constitution in 1972 paved the legal foundation for *Baehr.*[19]

Most gay activists and legal scholars anticipate a victory for gay marriage when *Baehr* is finally decided early in 1997, but they do not all look forward to this prospect with great delight. Although most of their constituents desire the right to marry, gay activists and theorists continue to vigorously debate the politics and effects of this campaign. Refining earlier feminist and socialist critiques of the gender and class inequities of marriage, an articulate, vocal minority seeks not to extend the right to marry, but to dismantle an institution they regard as inherently, and irredeemably, hierarchical, unequal, conservative, and repressive. Nancy Polikoff, one of the most articulate lesbian legal activist-scholars opposed to the marriage campaign, argues that

> Advocating lesbian and gay marriage will detract from, and even contradict, efforts to unhook economic benefits from marriage and make basic health care and other necessities available to all. It will also require a rhetorical strategy that emphasizes similarities between our relationships and heterosexual marriages, values long-term monogamous coupling above all other relationships, and denies the potential of lesbian and gay marriage to transform the gendered nature of marriage for all people. I fear that the very process of employing that rhetorical strategy for the years it will take to achieve its objective will lead our movement's public representatives, and the countless lesbians and gay men who hear us, to believe exactly what we say.[20]

A second perspective supports legal marriage as one long-term goal of the gay rights movement, but voices serious strategic objections to making this a priority before there is sufficient public support to sustain a favorable ruling in Hawaii or the nation. Such critics fear that a premature victory will prove pyrrhic, because efforts to defend it against the vehement backlash it has already begun to incite are apt to fail, after sapping resources and time better devoted to other urgent struggles for gay rights. Rather than risk a major setback for the gay movement, they advise an incremental approach to establishing legal family status for gay and lesbian kin ties through a multi-faceted struggle for family diversity.[21]

However, the largest, and most diverse, contingent of gay activist voices now supports the marriage rights campaign, perhaps because gay marriage can be read to harmonize with virtually every hue on the gay ideological spectrum. Pro-gay marriage arguments range from profoundly conservative to liberal humanist to radical and deconstructive. Conservatives, like those radicals who still oppose marriage, view it as an institution that promotes monogamy, commitment and social stability, along with interests in private property, social conformity and mainstream values. They likewise agree that legalizing gay marriage would further marginalize sexual radicals by segregating counter-cultural gays and lesbians from the "whitebread" gay couples who could then choose to marry their way into Middle America. Radicals and conservatives, in other words, envision the same prospect, but regard it with inverse sentiments.[22]

Liberal gays support legal marriage, of course, not only to affirm the legitimacy of their relationships and help sustain them in a hostile world, but as a straightforward matter of equal civil rights. As one long-coupled gay man expresses it: "I resent the fact that married people get lower taxes. But as long as there is this institution of marriage and heterosexuals have that privilege, then gay people should be able to do it too."[23] Liberals also recognize that marriage rights provide access to the social advantages of divorce law. "I used to say, 'Why do we want to get married? It doesn't work for straight people,'" one gay lawyer comments. "But now I say we should care: They have the privilege of divorce and we don't. We're left out there to twirl around in pain."[24]

Less obvious or familiar, however, are cogent arguments in favor of gay marriage that some feminist and other critical gay legal theorists have developed in response to opposition within the gay community. Nan Hunter, for example, rejects feminist legal colleague Nancy Polikoff's belief that marriage is an unalterably sexist and heterosexist institution. Building upon critical theories that reject the notion that social institutions or categories have inherent, fixed meanings apart from their social contexts, Hunter argues that legalized same-sex marriage would have "enormous potential to destabilize the gendered definition of marriage for everyone."[25]

Evan Wolfson, director of the Marriage Project of the gay legal rights organization Lambda Legal Defense, who has submitted a brief in support of *Baehr*, pursues the logic of "anti-essentialism" even more consistently. The institution of marriage is neither inherently equal nor unequal, he argues, but depends upon an everchanging cultural and political context.[26] (Anyone who doubts this need only consider such examples as polygamy, arranged marriages, or the same-sex unions in early Western history documented by the late Princeton historian, John Boswell.) Hoping to use marriage precisely to change its context, gay philosopher Richard Mohr argues that access to legal marriage would provide an opportunity to reconstruct its meaning by serving "as a nurturing ground for social marriage, and not (as now) as that which legally defines and creates marriage and so precludes legal examination of it." For Mohr, social marriage represents "the fused intersection of love's sanctity and necessity's demands," and does not necessarily depend upon sexual monogamy.[27]

Support for gay marriage, not long ago anathema to radicals and conservatives, gays and nongays, alike, now issues forth from ethical and political perspectives as diverse, and even incompatible, as these. The cultural and political context has changed so dramatically since Stonewall that it now seems easier to understand why marriage has come to enjoy overwhelming support in the gay community than to grasp the depth of resistance to the institution that characterized the early movement. Still, I take seriously many of the strategic concerns about the costly political risks posed by a premature campaign. Although surveys and electoral struggles suggest a gradual growth in public support for gay rights, that support is tepid, uneven and fickle, as the debacle over Clinton's attempt to combat legal exclusion of gays from the military made distressingly clear. Thus, while 52 percent of those surveyed in a 1994 *Time* magazine/CNN poll claimed to consider gay lifestyle acceptable, 64 percent did not want to legalize gay marriages or to permit gay couples to adopt children.[28]

Gay marriage, despite its apparent compatibility with mainstream family values sentiment, raises far more threatening questions than does military service about gender relations, sexuality and family life. Few contemporary politicians, irrespective of their personal convictions, display the courage to confront this contradiction, even when urged to do so by gay conservatives. In *Virtually Normal: An Argument about Homosexuality*, *New Republic* editor Andrew Sullivan develops the "conservative case for gay marriage," that he earlier published as an op-ed, which stresses the contribution gay marriage could make to a conservative agenda for family and political life. A review of Sullivan's book in the *New Yorker* points out that, "here is where the advocates of gay rights can steal the conservatives' clothes."[29] The epigraph to this chapter by Jonathan Rauch about the insignificance of the homosexual minority comes from a *Wall Street Journal* op-ed he wrote to persuade Republicans that they should support legal gay marriage, not only because it is consistent with conservative values, but to guard against the possibility that gay rights advocates will exploit the party's inconsistency on this issue to political advantage.[30]

The logic behind the conservative case for gay marriage strikes me as compelling. Most importantly, gay marriage would strengthen the ranks of those endangered two-parent, "intact," married-couples families whose praises conservative, "profamily" enthusiasts never seem to tire of singing. Unsurprisingly, however, the case has won few nongay conservative converts to the cause. After all, homophobia is a matter of passion and politics, not logic. The religious right regards homosexuality as an abomination, and it has effectively consolidated its influence over the Republican Party. For example, in 1994, Republicans in the Montana state senate went so far as to pass a bill that would require anyone convicted of homosexual acts to register for life as a violent offender. They reversed their vote in response to an outpouring of public outrage.[31] It was not long afterward, however, that Republican presidential contender Robert Dole returned the thousand-dollar campaign contribution from the gay Log Cabin Republicans in the name, of course, of family values. Nor have figures prominent in the centrist, secular neo-family-values campaign or the communitarian movement, whose professed values affirm both communal support for marital commitment and for tolerance, displayed much concern for such consistency.[32] And even when, in the 1995 fall preelection season, President Clinton sought to "shore up" his standing among gays and lesbians by announcing his administration's support of a bill to outlaw employment discrimination against gays, he specifically withheld his support from gay marriage.[33] First Lady Hillary Rodham Clinton's recent book, *It Takes a Village,* ostensibly written to challenge "false nostalgia for family values," fails even to mention gay marriage or gay families, let alone to advocate village rights and resources for children whose parents are gay.[34]

Despite my personal political baptism in the heady, anti-family crucible of early second wave feminism, I, for one, have converted to the long-term cause. A "postmodern" ideological stew of discordant convictions enticed me to this table. Like Wolfson, Mohr, and Hunter, I have come to believe that legitimizing gay and lesbian marriages would promote a democratic, pluralistic expansion of the meaning, practice, and politics of family life in the United States. This could help to supplant the destructive sanctity of the *family* with respect for diverse and vibrant *families.*

To begin with, the liberal implications of legal gay marriage are far from trivial, as the current rush by the states and Congress to nullify them should confirm. The Supreme Court is certain to have its docket flooded far into the next century with constitutional conflicts that a favorable decision in Hawaii, or elsewhere, will unleash. Under the "full faith and credit" provision of the Constitution, which requires the 50 states to recognize each other's laws, legal gay marriage in one state could begin to threaten anti-sodomy laws in all the others. Policing marital sex would be difficult to legitimate, and differential prosecution of conjugal sex among same-sex couples could violate equal protection legislation. Likewise, if gay marriages were legalized, the myriad state barriers to child custody, adoption, fertility services, inheritance, and other family rights that lesbians and gay men currently suffer could also become subject to legal challenge. Moreover, it seems hard to overestimate the profound cultural implications for the struggle against the pernicious effects of legally condoned homophobia that would ensue were lesbian and gay relationships to be admitted into the ranks of legitimate kinship. In a society that forbids most public school teachers and counselors even the merest expression of tolerance for homosexuality, while lesbian and gay youth attempt suicide at rates three to five times greater than other youth,[35] granting full recognition to even just whitebread lesbian and gay relationships could have dramatic, and salutary, consequences.

Of course, considerations truer to some of my earlier, more visionary feminist convictions also invite me to join the gay wedding procession. For while I share some of Polikoff's disbelief that same-sex marriage can in itself dismantle the patterned gender and sexual injustices of the institution, I do believe it could make a potent contribution to those projects. . . . Moreover, as Mohr suggests, admitting gays to the wedding banquet invites gays and nongays alike to consider the kinds of place settings that could best accommodate the diverse needs of all contemporary families.

Subjecting the conjugal institution to this sort of heightened democratic scrutiny could help it to assume varied creative forms. If we begin to value the meaning and quality of intimate bonds over their customary forms, there are few limits to the kinds of marriage and kinship patterns people might wish to devise. The "companionate marriage," a much celebrated, but less often realized, ideal of modern sociological lore, could take on new life. Two friends might decide to marry without basing their bond on erotic or romantic attachment, as Dorthe, a prominent Danish lesbian activist who had initially opposed the campaign for gay marriage, fantasized after her nation's parliament approved gay registered partnerships: "If I am going to marry it will be with one of my oldest friends in order to share pensions and things like that. But I'd never marry a lover. That is the advantage of being married to a close friend. Then, you never have to marry a lover!"[36] Or, more radical still, perhaps some might dare to question the dyadic limitations of Western marriage and seek some of the benefits of extended family life through small-group marriages arranged to share resources, nurturance and labor. After all, if it is true that "The Two-Parent Family Is Better"[37] than a single-parent family, as family-values crusaders like David Popenoe tirelessly proclaim, might not three-, four-, or more-parent families be better yet, as many utopian communards have long believed?

While conservative advocates of gay marriage surely would balk at such radical visions, they correctly realize that putative champions of committed relationships and of two-parent families who oppose gay marriage can be charged with gross hypocrisy on this score. For access to legal marriage not only would promote long-term, committed intimacy among gay couples, but also would afford invaluable protection to the children of gay parents, as well as indirect protection to closeted gay youth who reside with nongay parents. Clearly, only through a process of massive denial of the fact that millions of children living in gay and lesbian families are here, and here to stay, can anyone genuinely concerned with the best interests of children deny their parents the right to marry.

In the face of arguments for legalizing gay marriage as compelling and incongruent as these, it is hard to dispute Evan Wolfson's enthusiastic claim that, "The brilliance of our movement's taking on marriage is that marriage is, at once and truly, both conservative and transformative, easily understood in basic human terms of equality and respect, and liberating in its individual and social potential."[38]

NOTES

Epigraph Sources: Buchanan quoted in Susan Yoachum and David Tuller, "Right Makes Might in Iowa," *San Francisco Chronicle,* February 12, 1996: A1, 11; Rauch (see bibliographic entry); Bonnie Tinker, "Love Makes a Family," Presentation to 1995 United Nations International Women's Conference, Beijing, September 14.

1. The estimate that at least six million children were living with a gay parent by 1985 appeared in Schulenberg, *Gay Parenting,* and has been accepted or revised upwards by most scholars since then. See, for example, Bozett, 39; Patterson, "Children of Lesbian and Gay Parents"; Allen and Demo, "The Families of Lesbians and Gay Men: A New Frontier in Family Research."
2. Burke, *Family Values: A Lesbian Mother's Fight for Her Son.*
3. Goldberg, "Virtual Marriages for Same-Sex Couples."
4. Many gay activist groups and scholars, however, have begun to reclaim the term "queer" as a badge of pride, in much the same way that the Black power movement of the 1960s reclaimed the formerly derogatory term of blacks.
5. Reagan and Schlafly both have gay sons, Powell has a lesbian daughter, and Gingrich has a lesbian half-sister.
6. For a sensitive discussion of the definitional difficulties involved in research on gay and lesbian families, see Allen and Demo, "Families of Lesbians and Gay Men," 112–13.
7. Most gay and lesbian scholars and activists reject the term "homosexual" because it originated within a medical model that classified homosexuality as a sexual perversion or disease and because the term emphasizes sexuality as at the core of the individual's identity. In this [article], I follow the generally preferred contemporary practice of using the terms "lesbians" and "gay men," but I also occasionally employ the term "gay" generically to include both women and men. I also play with the multiple, and currently shifting, meanings of the term "queer," by specifying whether I am using the term in its older pejorative sense, in its newer sense of proudly challenging fixed notions of gender and sexuality, or in its more colloquial sense of simply "odd."
8. Quoted in Sherman, ed. *Lesbian and Gay Marriage,* 191.
9. Ibid., 173.
10. Bozett, epilogue to *Gay and Lesbian Parents,* 232.
11. Cited in Sherman, *Lesbian and Gay Marriage,* 9, fn 6. A more recent poll conducted by *The Advocate* suggests that the trend of support for gay marriage is increasing. See Wolfson, "Crossing the Threshold," 583.
12. Terry announced his plans January 24, 1996 on "Randall Terry Live," and LaHaye made her pitch the next day, January 25, 1996 on "Beverly LaHaye Live."
13. Dunlap, "Some States Trying to Stop Gay Marriages before They Start," A18; Dunlap, "Fearing a Toehold for Gay Marriage, Conservative Rush to Bar the Door," A7. Lockhead, "GOP Bill Targets Same-Sex Marriages," *San Francisco Chronicle,* May 9, 1996, A1, 15.
14. Ibid., A1.

15. Press Briefing by Mike McCurry, White House, May 14, 1996, Office of the Press Secretary.
16. "Vatican Denounces Gay-Marriage Idea," *New York Times,* March 29, 1996, A8.
17. Dunlap, "Reform Rabbis Vote to Back Gay Marriage," A8.
18. "The Freedom to Marry," *New York Times,* April 7, 1996, Editorials/ Letters, p. 10.
19. The decision stated that the sexual orientation of the parties was irrelevant, because same-sex spouses could be of any sexual orientation. It was the gender discrimination involved in limiting one's choice of spouse that violated the state constitution. See Wolfson, "Crossing the Threshold," 573.
20. Polikoff, "We Will Get What We Ask For: Why Legalizing Gay and Lesbian Marriage Will Not 'Dismantle the Legal Structure of Gender in Every Marriage.'"
21. Law Professor, Thomas Coleman, who is executive director of the "Family Diversity Project" in California, expresses these views in Sherman, 128–29.
22. Sullivan, "The Conservative Case for Gay Marriage"; Rauch, "A Pro-Gay, Pro-Family Policy."
23. Tede Matthews in Sherman, 57.
24. Kirk Johnson quoted in Wolfson, 567.
25. Hunter, "Marriage, Law and Gender," 12.
26. Wolfson, "Crossing the Threshold."
27. Mohr, *A More Perfect Union,* 48, 41, 50.
28. "Some Progress Found in Poll on Gay Rights," *San Francisco Chronicle,* June 20, 1994.
29. Ryan, "No Easy Way Out," 90. Sullivan, "Here Comes the Groom."
30. Rauch, "Pro-Gay, Pro-Family Policy."
31. Herscher, "After Reconsidering, Montana Junks Gay Sex Bill," A2.
32. See chap. 3, pp. 69–71 above.
33. Clinton, according to his senior adviser George Stephanopoulos, "thinks the proper role for the government is to work on the fight against discrimination, but he does not believe we should support (gay) marriage." Quoted in Sandalow and Tuller, "White House Tells Gays It Backs Them," A2.
34. Clinton, *It Takes a Village,* book jacket copy.
35. Remafedi, *Death by Denial.*
36. Quoted in Miller, *Out in the World,* 350.
37. This is the title and central argument of Popenoe's *New York Times* op-ed discussed above .
38. Wolfson, "Crossing the Threshold," 599.

REFERENCES

Allen, Katherine R., and David H. Demo. 1995. "The Families of Lesbians and Gay Men: A New Frontier in Family Research." *Journal of Marriage and the Family* 57 (February):111–27.
Bozett, Frederick W., ed. 1987. *Gay and Lesbian Parents.* New York: Praeger.
Burke, Phyllis. 1993. *Family Values: A Lesbian Mother's Fight for Her Son.* New York: Random House.
Clinton, Hillary Rodham. 1996. *It Takes a Village: And Other Lessons Children Teach Us.* New York: Simon & Schuster.
Dunlap, David W. 1995. "Some States Trying to Stop Gay Marriages Before They Start," *New York Times,* March 15, A18.

Goldberg, Carey. 1996. "Virtual Marriages for Same-Sex Couples." *New York Times,* March 26, A8.

Herscher, Elaine. 1995. "After Reconsidering, Montana Junks Gay Sex Bill," *San Francisco Chronicle,* March 24.

Hunter, Nan D. 1991. "Marriage, Law, and Gender: A Feminist Inquiry." *Law & Sexuality,* 1(1):9–30.

Miller, Neil. 1992. *Out in the World: Gay and Lesbian Life from Buenos Aires to Bangkok.* New York: Random House.

Mohr, Richard. 1994. *A More Perfect Union: Why Straight America Must Stand Up for Gay Rights.* Boston: Beacon.

Patterson, Charlotte J. 1992. "Children of Lesbian and Gay Parents." *Child Development* 63: 1025–42.

Polikoff, Nancy. 1993. "We Will Get What We Ask For: Why Legalizing Gay and Lesbian Marriage Will Not 'Dismantle the Legal Structure of Gender in Every Marriage,'" *Virginia Law Review* 79:1549–50.

Popenoe, David. 1992. "The Controversial Truth: The Two-Parent Family Is Better." *New York Times,* December 26, 13.

Rauch, Jonathan. 1994. "A Pro-Gay, Pro-Family Policy." *Wall Street Journal,* November 29, A22.

Remafedi, Gary. 1994. *Death by Denial.* Boston: Alyson Publications.

Ryan, Alan, ed. 1995. "No Easy Way Out." *New Yorker,* September 11, 90.

Sandalow, Marc, and David Tuller. 1995. "White House Tells Gays It Backs Them." *San Francisco Chronicle,* October 21, A2.

Sherman, Suzanne, ed. 1992. *Lesbian and Gay Marriage: Private Commitments, Public Ceremonies.* Philadelphia: Temple University Press.

Sullivan, Andrew. 1989. "Here Comes the Groom: A (Conservative) Case for Gay Marriage." *New Republic* 201(9):20–21.

Wolfson, Evan. 1994–95. "Crossing the Threshold: Equal Marriage Rights for Lesbians and Gay Men and the Intra-Community Critique." *Review of Law & Social Change* 21:3.

51

THE MEANING OF MOTHERHOOD
IN BLACK CULTURE

PATRICIA HILL COLLINS

In this selection, taken from *Black Feminist Thought* (1990), Patricia Hill Collins observes how motherhood is socially constructed within the African American community. Collins states that African American children often are raised by othermothers, grandmothers, and extended kin relations. These racial-ethnic differences in family formation patterns and parenting challenge the dominant culture's stereotype of the nuclear family. Moreover, Collins' research illustrates that the family, regardless of its membership or structure, is an institution that primarily socializes children and stabilizes adults.

Bloodmothers, Othermothers, and Women-Centered Networks

In African American communities, the boundaries distinguishing biological mothers of children from other women who care for children are often fluid and changing. Biological mothers or bloodmothers are expected to care for their children. But African and African American communities have also recognized that vesting one person with full responsibility for mothering a child may not be wise or possible. As a result, "othermothers," women who assist bloodmothers by sharing mothering responsibilities, traditionally have been central to the institution of Black motherhood.[1]

The centrality of women in African American extended families is well known.[2] Organized, resilient, women-centered networks of bloodmothers and othermothers are key in understanding this centrality: Grandmothers, sisters, aunts, or cousins acted as othermothers by taking on child care responsibilities for each other's children. When needed, temporary child-care arrangements turned into long-term care or informal adoption.[3]

In African American communities, these women-centered networks of community-based child care often extend beyond the boundaries of biologically related extended families to support "fictive kin."[4] Civil rights activist Ella Baker describes how informal adoption by othermothers functioned in the Southern, rural community of her childhood:

My aunt who had thirteen children of her own raised three more. She had become a midwife, and a child was born who was covered with sores. Nobody was particularly wanting the child, so she took the child and raised him . . . and another mother decided she didn't want to be bothered with two children. So my aunt took one and raised him. . . . They were part of the family.[5]

Even when relationships were not between kin or fictive kin, African American community norms were such that neighbors cared for each other's children. In the following passage, Sara Brooks, a Southern domestic worker, describes the importance of the community-based child care that a neighbor offered her daughter. In doing so, she also shows how the African American cultural value placed on cooperative child care found institutional support in the adverse conditions under which so many Black women mothered.

She kept Vivian and she didn't charge me nothin either. You see, people used to look after each other, but now it's not that way. I reckon it's because we all was poor, and I guess they put theirself in the place of the person that they was helpin.[6]

Othermothers were key not only in supporting children but also in supporting bloodmothers who, for whatever reason, were ill-prepared or had little desire to care for their children. Given the pressures from the larger political economy, the emphasis placed on community-based child care and the respect given to othermothers who assume the responsibilities of child care have served a critical function in African American communities. Children orphaned by sale or death of their parents under slavery; children conceived through rape; children of young mothers; children born into extreme poverty; or children, who for other reasons have been rejected by their bloodmothers, have all been supported by othermothers who, like Ella Baker's aunt, took in additional children, even when they had enough of their own.

Providing As Part of Mothering

The work done by African American women in providing the economic resources essential to Black family well-being affects motherhood in a contradictory fashion. On the one hand, African American women have long integrated their activities as economic providers into their mothering relationships. In contrast to the cult of true womanhood where work is defined as being in opposition to and incompatible with motherhood, work for Black women has been an important and valued dimension of Afro-centric definitions of Black motherhood. On the other hand, African American women's experiences as mothers under oppression were such that the type and purpose of work Black women were forced to do greatly impacted on the type of mothering relationships bloodmothers and othermothers had with Black children.

While slavery both disrupted West African family patterns and exposed enslaved Africans to the gender ideologies and practices of slaveowners, it simultaneously made it impossible, had they wanted to do so, for enslaved Africans to implement slaveowners' ideologies. Thus, the separate spheres of providing as a male domain and affective nurturing as a female domain did not develop within African American families.[7] Providing for Black children's physical survival and attending to their affective, emotional needs continued as interdependent dimensions of an Afrocentric ideology of motherhood. However, by changing the conditions under which Black women worked and the purpose of the work itself, slavery introduced the problem of how best to continue traditional Afrocentric values under oppressive conditions. Institutions of community-based child care, informal adoption, greater reliance on othermothers, all emerge as adaptations to the exigencies of combining exploitative work with nurturing children.

In spite of the change in political status brought on by emancipation, the majority of African American women remained exploited agricultural workers. However, their placement in southern political economies allowed them to combine child care with field labor. Sara Brooks describes how strong the links between providing and caring for others were for her:

> When I was about nine I was nursin my sister Sally—I'm about seven or eight years older than Sally. And when I would put her to sleep, instead of me goin somewhere and sit down and play, I'd get my little old hoe and get out there and work right in the field around the house.[8]

Black women's shift from southern agriculture to domestic work in southern and northern towns and cities represented a change in the type of work done, but not in the meaning of work to women and their families. Whether they wanted to or not, the majority of African American women had to work and could not afford the luxury of motherhood as a noneconomically productive, female "occupation."

Community Othermothers and Social Activism

Black women's experiences as othermothers have provided a foundation for Black women's social activism. Black women's feelings of responsibility for nurturing the children in their own extended family network have stimulated a more generalized ethic of care where Black women feel accountable to all the Black community's children.

This notion of Black women as community othermothers for all Black children traditionally allowed Black women to treat biologically unrelated children as if they were members of their own families. For example, sociologist Karen Fields describes how her grandmother, Mamie Garvin Fields, draws on her power as a community othermother when dealing with unfamiliar children.

> She will say to a child on the street who looks up to no good, picking out a name at random, "Aren't you Miz Pinckney's boy?" in that same reproving tone. If the reply is, "No, *ma'am*, my mother is Miz Gadsden," whatever threat there was dissipates.[9]

The use of family language in referring to members of the Black community also illustrates this dimension of Black motherhood. For example, Mamie Garvin Fields describes how she became active in surveying the poor housing conditions of Black people in Charleston.

> I was one of the volunteers they got to make a survey of the places where we were paying extortious rents for indescribable property. I said "we," although it wasn't Bob and me. We had our own home, and so did many of the Federated Women. Yet we still felt like it really was "we" living in those terrible places, and it was up to us to do something about them.[10]

To take another example, while describing her increasingly successful efforts to teach a boy who had given other teachers problems, my daughter's kindergarten teacher stated, "You know how it can be—the majority of the children in the learning disabled classes are *our children*. I know he didn't belong there, so I volunteered to take him." In these statements, both women invoke the language of family to describe the ties that bind them as Black women to their responsibilities to other members of the Black community as family.

Sociologist Cheryl Gilkes suggests that community othermother relationships are sometimes behind Black women's decisions to become community activists.[11] Gilkes notes that many of the Black women community activists in her study became involved in community organizing in response to the needs of their own children and of those in their communities. The following comment is typical of how many of the Black women in Gilkes' study relate to Black children: "There were a lot of summer programs springing up for kids, but they were exclusive . . . and I found that most of *our kids* (emphasis mine) were excluded."[12] For many women, what began as the daily expression of their obligations as community othermothers, as was the case for the kindergarten teacher, developed into full-fledged roles as community leaders.

NOTES

1. The terms used in this section appear in Rosalie Riegle Troester, "Turbulence and Tenderness: Mothers, Daughters, and Othermothers" in Paule Marshall's *Brown Girl, Brownstones,* and in *SAGE: A Scholarly Journal on Black Women* 1 (Fall 1984): 13–16.

2. See Tanner's discussion of matrifocality, 1974; see also Carrie Allen McCray, "The Black Woman and Family Roles," in *The Black Woman,* ed. LaFrances Rogers-Rose (Beverly Hills, CA: Sage, 1980), pp. 67–78; Elmer Martin and Joanne Mitchell Martin, *The Black Extended Family* (Chicago: University of Chicago, 1978); Joyce Aschenbrenner, *Lifelines, Black Families in Chicago* (Prospect Heights, IL: Waveland, 1975); and Carol B. Stack, *All Our Kin* (New York: Harper & Row, 1974).

3. Martin and Martin, *The Black Extended Family;* Stack, *All Our Kin;* and Virginia Young, "Family and Childhood in a Southern Negro Community," *American Anthropologist* 72 (1970):269–88.

4. Stack, *All Our Kin.*

5. Ellen Cantarow, *Moving the Mountain: Women Working for Social Change* (Old Westbury, NY: Feminist Press, 1980), p. 59.

6. Thordis Simonsen, ed., *You May Plow Here: The Narrative of Sara Brooks* (New York: Touchstone, 1986), p. 81.

7. Deborah White, *Arn't I a Woman? Female Slaves in the Plantation South* (New York: Norton, 1984); Bonnie Thornton Dill, "Our Mothers' Grief: Racial Ethnic Women and the Maintenance of Families," Research Paper 4, Center for Research on Women (Memphis, TN: Memphis State University, 1986); Leith Mullings, "Uneven Development: Class, Race and Gender in the United States before 1900," in *Women's Work, Development and the Division of Labor by Gender,* eds. Eleanor Leacock and Helen Safa (South Hadley, MA: Bergin & Garvey, 1986), pp. 41–57.

8. Simonsen, *You May Plow Here,* p. 86.

9. Mamie Garvin Fields and Karen Fields, *Lemon Swamp and Other Places: A Carolina Memoir* (New York: Free Press, 1983), p. xvii.

10. Ibid, p. 195.

11. Cheryl Gilkes, "'Holding Back the Ocean with a Broom,' Black Women and Community Work," in Rogers-Rose, *The Black Woman,* pp. 217–31; "Going Up for the Oppressed: The Career Mobility of Black Women Community Workers," *Journal of Social Issues* 39 (1983):115–39.

12. Gilkes, "'Holding Back,'" p. 219.

52

THE TIME BIND
When Work Becomes
Home and Home Becomes Work

ARLIE RUSSELL HOCHSCHILD

What are the relationships between work life and family life? How do individuals negotiate the role demands of both social institutions? Arlie Hochschild investigates these questions in her three-year study of a large corporation, called "Amerco." Hochschild interviewed 130 employees, including middle and upper management, clerks and factory workers, most of whom were working parents. Hochschild also talked with human resource specialists, psychologists, child-care workers, and homemakers who were married to Amerco employees. In this selection, adapted from her book, *The Time Bind: When Work Becomes Home and Home Becomes Work* (1997), Hochschild discusses her findings about the changing relationship between work life and home life for many working parents.

It's 7:40 A.M. when Cassie Bell, 4, arrives at the Spotted Deer Child-Care Center, her hair half-combed, a blanket in one hand, a fudge bar in the other. "I'm late," her mother, Gwen, a sturdy young woman whose short-cropped hair frames a pleasant face, explains to the child-care worker in charge. "Cassie wanted the fudge bar so bad, I gave it to her," she adds apologetically.

"*Pleeese,* can't you take me with you?" Cassie pleads.

"You know I can't take you to work," Gwen replies in a tone that suggests that she has been expecting this request. Cassie's shoulders droop. But she has struck a hard bargain—the morning fudge bar—aware of her mother's anxiety about the long day that lies ahead at the center. As Gwen explains later, she continually feels that she owes Cassie more time than she gives her—she has a "time debt."

Arriving at her office just before 8, Gwen finds on her desk a cup of coffee in her personal mug, milk no sugar (exactly as she likes it), prepared by a co-worker who managed to get in ahead of her. As the assistant to the head of public relations at a company I will call Amerco, Gwen has to handle responses to any reports that may appear about the company in the press—a challenging job, but one that gives her satisfaction. As she prepares for her first meeting of the day, she misses her daughter, but she also feels relief; there's a lot to get done at Amerco.

Gwen used to work a straight eight-hour day. But over the last three years, her workday has gradually stretched to eight and a half or nine hours, not counting the E-mail messages and faxes she answers from home. She complains about her hours to her co-workers and listens to their complaints—but she loves her job. Gwen picks up Cassie at 5:45 and gives her a long, affectionate hug.

At home, Gwen's husband, John, a computer programmer, plays with their daughter while Gwen prepares dinner. To protect the dinner "hour"— 8:00–8:30—Gwen checks that the phone machine is on, hears the phone ring during dinner but resists the urge to answer. After Cassie's bath, Gwen and Cassie have "quality time," or "Q.T.," as John affectionately calls it. Half an hour later, at 9:30, Gwen tucks Cassie into bed.

There are, in a sense, two Bell households: the rushed family they actually are and the relaxed family they imagine they might be if only they had time. Gwen and John complain that they are in a time bind. What they say they want seems so modest—time to throw a ball, to read to Cassie, to witness the small dramas of her development, not to speak of having a little fun and romance themselves. Yet even these modest wishes seem strangely out of reach. Before going to bed, Gwen has to E-mail messages to her colleagues in preparation for the next day's meeting; John goes to bed early, exhausted— he's out the door by 7 every morning.

Nationwide, many working parents are in the same boat. More mothers of small children than ever now work outside the home. In 1993, 56 percent of women with children between 6 and 17 worked outside the home full time year round; 43 percent of women with children 6 and under did the same. Meanwhile, fathers of small children are not cutting back hours of work to help out at home. If anything, they have increased their hours at work. According to a 1993 national survey conducted by the Families and Work Institute in New York, American men average 48.8 hours of work a week, and women 41.7 hours, including overtime and commuting. All in all, more women are on the economic train, and for many—men and women alike— that train is going faster.

But Amerco has "family-friendly" policies. If your division head and supervisor agree, you can work part time, share a job with another worker, work some hours at home, take parental leave or use "flex time." But hardly anyone uses these policies. In seven years, only two Amerco fathers have taken formal parental leave. Fewer than 1 percent have taken advantage of the opportunity to work part time. Of all such policies, only flex time— which rearranges but does not shorten work time—has had a significant number of takers (perhaps a third of working parents at Amerco).

Forgoing family-friendly policies is not exclusive to Amerco workers. A

1991 study of 188 companies conducted by the Families and Work Institute found that while a majority offered part-time shifts, fewer than 5 percent of employees made use of them. Thirty-five percent offered "flex place"—work from home—and fewer than 3 percent of their employees took advantage of it. And an earlier Bureau of Labor Statistics survey asked workers whether they preferred a shorter workweek, a longer one or their present schedule. About 62 percent preferred their present schedule; 28 percent would have preferred longer hours. Fewer than 10 percent said they wanted a cut in hours.

Still, I found it hard to believe that people didn't protest their long hours at work. So I contacted Bright Horizons, a company that runs 136 company-based child-care centers associated with corporations, hospitals and Federal agencies in 25 states. Bright Horizons allowed me to add questions to a questionnaire they sent out to 3,000 parents whose children attended the centers. The respondents, mainly middle-class parents in their early 30s, largely confirmed the picture I'd found at Amerco. A third of fathers and a fifth of mothers described themselves as "workaholic," and 1 out of 3 said their partners were.

To be sure, some parents have tried to shorten their hours. Twenty-one percent of the nation's women voluntarily work part time, as do 7 percent of men. A number of others make under-the-table arrangements that don't show up on surveys. But while working parents say they need more time at home, the main story of their lives does not center on a struggle to get it. Why? Given the hours parents are working these days, why aren't they taking advantage of an opportunity to reduce their time at work?

The most widely held explanation is that working parents cannot afford to work shorter hours. Certainly this is true for many. But if money is the whole explanation, why would it be that at places like Amerco, the best-paid employees—upper-level managers and professionals—were the least interested in part-time work or job sharing, while clerical workers who earned less were more interested?

Similarly, if money were the answer, we would expect poorer new mothers to return to work more quickly after giving birth than rich mothers. But among working women nationwide, well-to-do new mothers are not much more likely to stay home after 13 weeks with a new baby than low-income new mothers. When asked what they look for in a job, only a third of respondents in a recent study said salary came first. Money is important, but by itself, money does not explain why many people don't want to cut back hours at work.

A second explanation goes that workers don't dare ask for time off because they are afraid it would make them vulnerable to layoffs. With recent downsizings at many large corporations, and with well-paying, secure jobs being replaced by lower-paying, insecure ones, it occurred to me that perhaps employees are "working scared." But when I asked Amerco employees whether they worked long hours for fear of getting on a layoff list, virtually everyone said no. Even among a particularly vulnerable group—factory workers who were laid off in the downturn of the early 1980s and were later rehired—most did not cite fear for their jobs as the only, or main, reason they worked overtime. For unionized workers, layoffs are assigned by seniority, and for nonunionized workers, layoffs are usually related to the profitability of the division a person works in, not to an individual work schedule.

Were workers uninformed about the company's family-friendly policies? No. Some even mentioned that they were proud to work for a company that offered such enlightened policies. Were rigid middle managers standing in the way of workers using these policies? Sometimes. But when I compared Amerco employees who worked for flexible managers with those who worked for rigid managers, I found that the flexible managers reported only a few more applicants than the rigid ones. The evidence, however counterintuitive, pointed to a paradox: workers at the company I studied weren't protesting the time bind. They were accommodating to it.

Why? I did not anticipate the conclusion I found myself coming to: namely, that work has become a form of "home" and home has become "work." The worlds of home and work have not begun to blur, as the conventional wisdom goes, but to reverse places. We are used to thinking that home is where most people feel the most appreciated, the most truly "themselves," the most secure, the most relaxed. We are used to thinking that work is where most people feel like "just a number" or "a cog in a machine." It is where they have to be "on," have to "act," where they are least secure and most harried.

But new management techniques so pervasive in corporate life have helped transform the workplace into a more appreciative, personal sort of social world. Meanwhile, at home the divorce rate has risen, and the emotional demands have become more baffling and complex. In addition to teething, tantrums and the normal developments of growing children, the needs of elderly parents are creating more tasks for the modern family—as are the blending, unblending, reblending of new stepparents, stepchildren, exes and former in-laws.

This idea began to dawn on me during one of my first interviews with an Amerco worker. Linda Avery, a friendly, 38-year-old mother, is a shift supervisor at an Amerco plant. When I meet her in the factory's coffee-break room over a couple of Cokes, she is wearing blue jeans and a pink jersey, her hair pulled back in a long, blond ponytail. Linda's husband, Bill, is a technician in the same plant. By working different shifts, they manage to share the care of their 2-year-old son and Linda's 16-year-old daughter from a previous marriage. "Bill works the 7 A.M. to 3 P.M. shift while I watch the baby," she explains. "Then I work the 3 P.M. to 11 P.M. shift and he watches the baby. My daughter works at Walgreen's after school."

Linda is working overtime, and so I begin by asking whether Amerco required the overtime, or whether she volunteered for it. "Oh, I put in for it," she replies. I ask her whether, if finances and company policy permitted, she'd be interested in cutting back on the overtime. She takes off her safety glasses, rubs her face and, without answering my question, explains: "I get home, and the minute I turn the key, my daughter is right there. Granted, she needs somebody to talk to about her day. . . . The baby is still up. He should have been in bed two hours ago, and that upsets me. The dishes are piled in the sink. My daughter comes right up to the door and complains about anything her stepfather said or did, and she wants to talk about her job. My husband is in the other room hollering to my daughter, 'Tracy, I don't ever get any time to talk to your mother, because you're always monopolizing her time before I even get a chance!' They all come at me at once."

Linda's description of the urgency of demands and the unarbitrated quarrels that await her homecoming contrast with her account of arriving at her job as a shift supervisor: "I usually come to work early, just to get away from the house. When I arrive, people are there waiting. We sit, we talk, we joke. I let them know what's going on, who has to be where, what changes I've made for the shift that day. We sit and chitchat for 5 or 10 minutes. There's laughing, joking, fun."

For Linda, home has come to feel like work and work has come to feel a bit like home. Indeed, she feels she can get relief from the "work" of being at home only by going to the "home" of work. Why has her life at home come to seem like this? Linda explains it this way: "My husband's a great help watching our baby. But as far as doing housework or even taking the baby when I'm at home, no. He figures he works five days a week; he's not going to come home and clean. But he doesn't stop to think that I work seven days a week. Why should I have to come home and do the housework without help from anybody else? My husband and I have been through this over and over again. Even if he would just pick up from the kitchen table and stack the dishes for me, that would make a big difference. He does nothing. On his weekends off, he goes fishing. If I want any time off, I have to get a sitter. He'll help out if I'm not here, but the minute I am, all the work at home is mine."

With a light laugh, she continues: "So I take a lot of overtime. The more I get out of the house, the better I am. It's a terrible thing to say, but that's the way I feel."

When Bill feels the need for time off, to relax, to have fun, to feel free, he climbs in his truck and takes his free time without his family. Largely in response, Linda grabs what she also calls "free time"—at work. Neither Linda nor Bill Avery wants more time together at home, not as things are arranged now.

How do Linda and Bill Avery fit into the broader picture of American family and work life? Current research suggests that however hectic their lives, women who do paid work feel less depressed, think better of themselves and are more satisfied than women who stay at home. One study reported that women who work outside the home feel more valued at home than housewives do. Meanwhile, work is where many women feel like "good mothers." As Linda reflects: "I'm a good mom at home, but I'm a better mom at work. At home, I get into fights with Tracy. I want her to apply to a junior college, but she's not interested. At work, I think I'm better at seeing the other person's point of view."

Many workers feel more confident they could "get the job done" at work than at home. One study found that only 59 percent of workers feel their "performance" in the family is "good or unusually good," while 86 percent rank their performance on the job this way.

Forces at work and at home are simultaneously reinforcing this "reversal." This lure of work has been enhanced in recent years by the rise of company cultural engineering—in particular, the shift from Frederick Taylor's principles of scientific management to the Total Quality principles originally set out by W. Edwards Deming. Under the influence of a Taylorist world view, the manager's job was to coerce the worker's mind and body, not to appeal to the worker's heart. The Taylorized worker was de-skilled, replaceable and cheap, and as a consequence felt bored, demeaned and unappreciated.

Using modern participative management techniques, many companies now train workers to make their own work decisions, and then set before their newly "empowered" employees moral as well as financial incentives. At Amerco, the Total Quality worker is invited to feel recognized for job accomplishments. Amerco regularly strengthens the familylike ties of co-workers by holding "recognition ceremonies" honoring particular workers or self-managed production teams. Amerco employees speak of "belonging to the Amerco family," and proudly wear their "Total Quality" pins or "High Performance Team" T-shirts, symbols of their loyalty to the company and of its loyalty to them.

The company occasionally decorates a section of the factory and serves refreshments. The production teams, too, have regular get-togethers. In a New Age recasting of an old business slogan—"The Customer Is Always Right"—Amerco proposes that its workers "Value the Internal Customer." This means: Be as polite and considerate to co-workers inside the company as you would be to customers outside it. How many recognition ceremonies for competent performance are being offered at home? Who is valuing the internal customer there?

Amerco also tries to take on the role of a helpful relative with regard to employee problems at work and at home. The education-and-training division offers employees free courses (on company time) in "Dealing With Anger," "How to Give and Accept Criticism," "How to Cope With Difficult People."

At home, of course, people seldom receive anything like this much help on issues basic to family life. There, no courses are being offered on "Dealing With Your Child's Disappointment in You" or "How to Treat Your Spouse Like an Internal Customer."

If Total Quality calls for "re-skilling" the worker in an "enriched" job environment, technological developments have long been de-skilling parents at home. Over the centuries, store-bought goods have replaced homespun cloth, homemade soap and home-baked foods. Day care for children, retirement homes for the elderly, even psychotherapy are, in a way, commercial substitutes for jobs that a mother once did at home. Even family-generated entertainment has, to some extent, been replaced by television, video games and the VCR. I sometimes watched Amerco families sitting together after their dinners, mute but cozy, watching sitcoms in which television mothers, fathers and children related in an animated way to one another while the viewing family engaged in relational loafing.

The one "skill" still required of family members is the hardest one of all—the emotional work of forging, deepening or repairing family relationships. It takes time to develop this skill, and even then things can go awry. Family ties are complicated. People get hurt. Yet as broken homes become more common—and as the sense of belonging to a geographical community grows less and less secure in an age of mobility—the corporate world has created a sense of "neighborhood," of "feminine culture," of family at work. Life at work can be insecure; the company can fire workers. But workers aren't so secure at home, either. Many employees have been working for Amerco for 20 years but are on their second or third marriages or relationships. The shifting balance between these two "divorce rates" may be the most powerful reason why tired parents flee a world of unresolved quarrels and unwashed laundry for the orderliness, harmony and managed cheer of work. People are getting their "pink slips" at home.

Amerco workers have not only turned their offices into "home" and their homes into workplaces; many have also begun to "Taylorize" time at home, where families are succumbing to a cult of efficiency previously associated mainly with the office and factory. Meanwhile, work time, with its ever longer hours, has become more hospitable to sociability—periods of talking with friends on E-mail, patching up quarrels, gossiping. Within the long workday of many Amerco employees are great hidden pockets of inefficiency while, in the far smaller number of waking weekday hours at home, they are, despite themselves, forced to act increasingly time-conscious and efficient.

The Averys respond to their time bind at home by trying to value and protect "quality time." A concept unknown to their parents and grandparents, "quality time" has become a powerful symbol of the struggle against the growing pressures at home. It reflects the extent to which modern parents feel the flow of time to be running against them. The premise behind "quality time" is that the time we devote to relationships can somehow be separated from ordinary time. Relationships go on during quantity time, of course, but then we are only passively, not actively, wholeheartedly, specializing in our emotional ties. We aren't "on." Quality time at home becomes like an office appointment. You don't want to be caught "goofing off around the water cooler" when you are "at work."

Quality time holds out the hope that scheduling intense periods of togetherness can compensate for an overall loss of time in such a way that a relationship will suffer no loss of quality. But this is just another way of transferring the cult of efficiency from office to home. We must now get our relationships in good repair in less time. Instead of nine hours a day with a child, we declare ourselves capable of getting "the same result" with one intensely focused hour.

Parents now more commonly speak of time as if it is a threatened form of personal capital they have no choice but to manage and invest. What's new here is the spread into the home of a financial manager's attitude toward time. Working parents at Amerco owe what they think of as time debts at home. This is because they are, in a sense, inadvertently "Taylorizing" the house—speeding up the pace of home life as Taylor once tried to "scientifically" speed up the pace of factory life.

Advertisers of products aimed at women have recognized that this new reality provides an opportunity to sell products, and have turned the very pressure that threatens to explode the home into a positive attribute. Take, for example, an ad promoting Instant Quaker Oatmeal: it shows a smiling mother ready for the office in her square-shouldered suit, hugging her happy son. A caption reads: "Nicky is a very picky eater. With Instant Quaker Oatmeal, I can give him a terrific hot breakfast in just 90 seconds. And I don't have to spend any time coaxing him to eat it!" Here, the modern mother seems to have absorbed the lessons of Frederick Taylor as she presses for efficiency at home because she is in a hurry to get to work.

Part of modern parenthood seems to include coping with the resistance of real children who are not so eager to get their cereal so fast. Some parents try desperately not to appease their children with special gifts or smooth-talking promises about the future. But when time is scarce, even the best parents find themselves passing a system-wide familial speed-up along to the most vulnerable workers on the line. Parents are then obliged to try to control the damage done by a reversal of worlds. They monitor mealtime, homework time, bedtime, trying to cut out "wasted" time.

In response, children often protest the pace, the deadlines, the grand irrationality of "efficient" family life. Children dawdle. They refuse to leave places when it's time to leave. They insist on leaving places when it's not time to leave. Surely, this is part of the usual stop-and-go of childhood itself, but perhaps, too, it is the plea of children for more family time, and more control over what time there is. This only adds to the feeling that life at home has become hard work.

Instead of trying to arrange shorter or more flexible work schedules, Amerco parents often avoid confronting the reality of the time bind. Some minimize their ideas about how much care a child, a partner or they themselves "really need." They make do with less time, less attention, less understanding and less support at home than they once imagined possible. They *emotionally downsize* life. In essence, they deny the needs of family members, and they themselves become emotional ascetics. If they once "needed" time with each other, they are now increasingly "fine" without it.

Another way that working parents try to evade the time bind is to buy themselves out of it—an approach that puts women in particular at the heart of a contradiction. Like men, women absorb the work-family speed-up far more than they resist it; but unlike men, they still shoulder most of the workload at home. And women still represent in people's minds the heart and soul of family life. They're the ones—especially women of the urban middle and upper-middle classes—who feel most acutely the need to save time, who are the most tempted by the new "time saving" goods and services— and who wind up feeling the most guilty about it. For example, Playgroup Connections, a Washington-area business started by a former executive recruiter, matches playmates to one another. One mother hired the service to find her child a French-speaking playmate.

In several cities, children home alone can call a number for "Grandma, Please!" and reach an adult who has the time to talk with them, sing to them or help them with their homework. An ad for Kindercare Learning Centers, a for-profit child-care chain, pitches its appeal this way: "You want your child to be active, tolerant, smart, loved, emotionally stable, self-aware, artistic and get a two-hour nap. Anything else?" It goes on to note that Kindercare accepts children 6 weeks to 12 years old and provides a number to call for the Kindercare nearest you. Another typical service organizes children's birthday parties, making out invitations ("sure hope you can come") and providing party favors, entertainment, a decorated cake and balloons. Creative Memories is a service that puts ancestral photos into family albums for you.

An overwhelming majority of the working mothers I spoke with recoiled from the idea of buying themselves out of parental duties. A bought birthday party was "too impersonal," a 90-second breakfast "too fast." Yet a surprising amount of lunchtime conversation between female friends at Amerco was devoted to expressing complex, conflicting feelings about the lure of trading time for one service or another. The temptation to order flash-frozen dinners or to call a local number for a homework helper did not come up because such services had not yet appeared at Spotted Deer Child-Care Center. But many women dwelled on the question of how to decide where a mother's job began and ended, especially with regard to baby sitters and television. One mother said to another in the breakroom of an Amerco plant: "Damon doesn't settle down until 10 at night, so he hates me to wake him up in the morning and I hate to do it. He's cranky. He pulls the covers up. I put on cartoons. That way, I can dress him and he doesn't object. I don't like to use TV that way. It's like a drug. But I do it."

The other mother countered: "Well, Todd is up before we are, so that's not a problem. It's after dinner, when I feel like watching a little television, that I feel guilty, because he gets too much TV at the sitter's."

As task after task falls into the realm of time-saving goods and services, questions arise about the moral meanings attached to doing or not doing such tasks. Is it being a good mother to bake a child's birthday cake (alone or together with one's partner)? Or can we gratefully save time by ordering it, and be good mothers by planning the party? Can we save more time by hiring a planning service, and be good mothers simply by watching our children have a good time? "Wouldn't that be nice!" one Amerco mother exclaimed. As the idea of the "good mother" retreats before the pressures of work and the expansion of motherly services, mothers are in fact continually reinventing themselves.

The final way working parents tried to evade the time bind was to develop what I call "potential selves." The potential selves that I discovered in my Amerco interviews were fantasy creations of time-poor parents who dreamed of living as time millionaires.

One man, a gifted 55-year-old engineer in research and development at Amerco, told how he had dreamed of taking his daughters on a camping trip in the Sierra Mountains: "I bought all the gear three years ago when they were 5 and 7, the tent, the sleeping bags, the air mattresses, the backpacks, the ponchos. I got a map of the area. I even got the freeze-dried food. Since then the kids and I have talked about it a lot, and gone over what we're going to do. They've been on me to do it for a long time. I feel bad about it. I keep putting it off, but we'll do it, I just don't know when."

Banished to garages and attics of many Amerco workers were expensive electric saws, cameras, skis and musical instruments, all bought with wages it took time to earn. These items were to their owners what Cassie's fudge bar was to her—a substitute for time, a talisman, a reminder of the potential self.

Obviously, not everyone, not even a majority of Americans, is making a home out of work and a workplace out of home. But in the working world, it is a growing reality, and one we need to face. Increasing numbers of women are discovering a great male secret—that work can be an escape from the pressures of home, pressures that the changing nature of work itself are only intensifying. Neither men nor women are going to take up "family-friendly" policies, whether corporate or governmental, as long as the current realities of work and home remain as they are. For a substantial number of time-bound parents, the stripped-down home and the neighborhood devoid of community are simply losing out to the pull of the workplace.

There are several broader, historical causes of this reversal of realms. The last 30 years have witnessed the rapid rise of women in the workplace. At the same time, job mobility has taken families farther from relatives who might lend a hand, and made it harder to make close friends of neighbors who could help out. Moreover, as women have acquired more education and have joined men at work, they have absorbed the views of an older, male-oriented work world, its views of a "real career," far more than men have taken up their share of the work at home. One reason women have changed more than men is that the world of "male" work seems more honorable and valuable than the "female" world of home and children.

So where do we go from here? There is surely no going back to the mythical 1950s family that confined women to the home. Most women don't wish to return to a full-time role at home—and couldn't afford it even if they did.

But equally troubling is a workaholic culture that strands both men and women outside the home.

For a while now, scholars on work-family issues have pointed to Sweden, Norway and Denmark as better models of work-family balance. Today, for example, almost all Swedish fathers take two paid weeks off from work at the birth of their children, and about half of fathers and most mothers take additional "parental leave" during the child's first or second year. Research shows that men who take family leave when their children are very young are more likely to be involved with their children as they grow older. When I mentioned this Swedish record of paternity leave to a focus group of American male managers, one of them replied, "Right, we've already heard about Sweden." To this executive, paternity leave was a good idea not for the U.S. today, but for some "potential society" in another place and time.

Meanwhile, children are paying the price. In her book *When the Bough Breaks: The Cost of Neglecting Our Children,* the economist Sylvia Hewlett claims that "compared with the previous generation, young people today are more likely to "underperform at school; commit suicide; need psychiatric help; suffer a severe eating disorder; bear a child out of wedlock; take drugs; be the victim of a violent crime." But we needn't dwell on sledgehammer problems like heroin or suicide to realize that children like those at Spotted Deer need more of our time. If other advanced nations with two-job families can give children the time they need, why can't we?

Author's Note: Over three years, I interviewed 130 respondents for a book. They spoke freely and allowed me to follow them through "typical" days, on the understanding that I would protect their anonymity. I have changed the names of the company and of those I interviewed, and altered certain identifying details. Their words appear here as they were spoken.—A.R.H.

PART VIII
Social Change

53

THE HYPOTHESIS OF CULTURAL LAG

WILLIAM F. OGBURN

In this reading, the first of four to focus on social change, William F. Ogburn presents his theory of social change, the hypothesis of the cultural lag. Ogburn (1886—1959) is best known for introducing this concept of *cultural lag,* which has influenced the work and theoretical ideas of numerous twentieth-century scholars. Ironically, Ogburn did not see himself as a theoretician per se, but instead spent most of his time researching the sociology of the family, urban sociology, and the social effects of aviation. The excerpt presented here was originally published in an early work by Ogburn, the 1922 book, *Social Change.*

This rapidity of change in modern times raises the very important question of social adjustment. Problems of social adjustment are of two sorts. One concerns the adaptation of man to culture or perhaps preferably the adapting of culture to man. The other problem is the question of adjustments, occasioned as a result of these rapid social changes, between the different parts of culture, which no doubt means ultimately the adaptation of culture to man. This second problem of adjustment between the different parts of culture is the immediate subject of our inquiry.

The thesis is that the various parts of modern culture are not changing at the same rate, some parts are changing much more rapidly than others; and since there is a correlation and interdependence of parts, a rapid change in one part of our culture requires readjustments through other changes in the various correlated parts of culture. For instance, industry and education are correlated, hence a change in industry makes adjustments necessary through changes in the educational system. Industry and education are two variables, and if the change in industry occurs first and the adjustment through education follows, industry may be referred to as the independent variable and education as the dependent variable. Where one part of culture changes first, through some discovery or invention, and occasions changes in some part of culture dependent upon it, there frequently is a delay in the changes occasioned in the dependent part of culture. The extent of this lag will vary according to the nature of the cultural material, but may exist for a considerable number of years, during which time there may be said to be a maladjustment. It is desirable to reduce the period of maladjustment, to make the cultural adjustments as quickly as possible.

The foregoing account sets forth a problem that occurs when there is a rapid change in a culture of interdependent parts and when the rates of change in the parts are unequal. The discussion will be presented according to the following outlines. First the hypothesis will be presented, then examined and tested by a rather full consideration of the facts of a single instance, to be followed by several illustrations. Next the nature and cause of the phenomenon of cultural maladjustment in general will be analyzed. The extent of such cultural lags will be estimated, and finally the significance for society will be set forth.

A first simple statement of the hypothesis we wish to investigate now follows. A large part of our environment consists of the material conditions of life and a large part of our social heritage is our material culture. These material things consist of houses, factories, machines, raw materials, manufactured products, foodstuffs, and other material objects. In using these material things we employ certain methods. Some of these methods are as simple as the technique of handling a tool. But a good many of the ways of using the material objects of culture involve rather larger usages and adjustments, such as customs, beliefs, philosophies, laws, governments. One important function of government, for instance, is the adjustment of the population to the material conditions of life, although there are other governmental functions. [William Graham] Sumner has called many of these processes of adjustments, mores [see his work, Folkways, 1907]. The cultural adjustments to material conditions, however, include a larger body of processes than the mores; certainly they include the folkways and social institutions. These ways of adjustment may be called, for purposes of this particular analysis, the adaptive culture. The adaptive culture is therefore that portion of the nonmaterial culture which is adjusted or adapted to the material conditions. Some parts of the nonmaterial culture are thoroughly adaptive culture such as certain rules involved in handling technical appliances, and some parts are only indirectly or partially so, as for instance, religion. The family makes some adjustments to fit changed material conditions, while some of its functions remain constant. The family therefore, under the terminology used here is a part of the nonmaterial culture that is only partly adaptive. When the material conditions change, changes are occasioned in the adaptive culture. But these changes in the adaptive culture do not synchronize exactly with the change in the material culture. There is a lag which may last for varying lengths of time, sometimes indeed, for many years.

An illustration will serve to make the hypothesis more clearly understood. One class of material objects to which we adjust ourselves is the forests. The material conditions of forestry have changed a good deal in the United States during the past century. At one time the forests were quite plentiful for the needs of the small population. There was plenty of wood easily accessible for fuel, building and manufacture. The forests were sufficiently extensive to prevent in many large areas the washing of the soil, and the streams were clear. In fact, at one time, the forests seemed to be too plentiful, from the point of view of the needs of the people. Food and agricultural products were at one time the first need of the people and the clearing of land of trees and stumps was a common undertaking of the community in the days of the early settlers. In some places, the quickest procedure was to kill and burn the trees and plant between the stumps. When the material conditions were like these, the method of adjustment to the forests was characterized by a policy which has been called exploitation. Exploitation in regard to the forests was indeed a part of the mores of the time, and describes a part of the adaptive culture in relation to forests.

As time went on, however, the population grew, manufacturing became highly developed, and the need for forests increased. But the forests were being destroyed. This was particularly true in the Appalachian, Great Lakes and Gulf regions. The policy of exploitation continued. Then rather suddenly it began to be realized in certain centres of thought that if the policy of cutting timber continued at the same rate and in the same manner the forests would in a short time be gone and very soon indeed they would be inadequate to supply the needs of the population. It was realized that the custom in regard to using the forests must be changed and a policy of conservation was advocated. The new policy of conservation means not only a restriction in the amount of cutting down of trees, but it means a more scientific method of cutting, and also reforestation. Forests may be cut in such a way, by selecting trees according to their size, age and location, as to yield a large quantity of timber and yet not diminish the forest area. Also by the proper distribution of cutting plots in a particular area, the cutting can be so timed that by the time the last plot is cut the young trees on the plot first cut will be grown. Some areas when cut leave a land which is well adapted to farming, whereas such sections as mountainous regions when denuded of forests are poorly suited to agriculture. There of course are many other methods of conservation of forests. The science of forestry is, indeed, fairly highly developed in principle, though not in practice in the United States. A new adaptive culture, one of conservation, is therefore suited to the changed material conditions.

That the conservation of forests in the United States should have been earlier is quite generally admitted. We may say, therefore, that the old policy of exploitation has hung over longer than it should before the institution of the new policy. In other words, the material conditions in regard to our forests have changed but the old customs of the use of forests which once fitted the material conditions very well have hung over into a period of changed conditions. These old customs are not only not satisfactorily adapted, but are really socially harmful. These customs of course have a utility, since they meet certain human needs; but methods of greater utility are needed. There seems to be a lag in the mores in regard to forestry after the material conditions have changed.

The foregoing discussion of forestry illustrates the hypothesis which it is proposed to discuss. It is desirable to state more clearly and fully the points involved in the analysis. The first point concerns the degree of adjustment or correlation between the material conditions and the adaptive nonmaterial culture. The degree of this adjustment may be only more or less perfect or satisfactory; but we do adjust ourselves to the material conditions through some form of culture; that is, we live, we get along, through this adjustment. The particular culture which is adjusted to the material conditions may be very complex, and, indeed, quite a number of widely different parts of culture may be adjusted to a fairly homogeneous material condition. Of a particular cultural form, such as the family or government, relationship to a particular material culture is only one of its purposes or functions. Not all functions of family organization, as, for instance, the affectional function, are primarily adaptive to material conditions.

Another point to observe is that the changes in the material culture precede changes in the adaptive culture. This statement is not in the form of a universal dictum. Conceivably, forms of adaptation might be worked out prior to a change in the material situation and the adaptation might be applied practically at the same time as the change in the material conditions. But such a situation presumes a very high degree of planning, prediction and control. The collection of data, it is thought, will show that at the present time there are a very large number of cases where the material conditions change and the changes in the adaptive culture follow later. There are certain general theoretical reasons why this is so; but it is not desirable to discuss these until later. For the present, the analysis will only concern those cases where changes in the adaptive culture do not precede changes in the material culture. Furthermore, it is not implied that changes may not occur in nonmaterial culture while the material culture remains the same. Art or education, for instance, may undergo many changes with a constant material culture. Still another point in the analysis is that the old, unchanged, adaptive culture is not adjusted to the new, changed, material conditions. It may be true that the old adaptive culture is never wholly unadjusted to the new conditions. There may be some degree of adjustment. But the thesis is that the unchanged adaptive culture was more harmoniously related to the old than to the new material conditions and that a new adaptive culture will be better suited to the new material conditions than was the old adaptive culture. Adjustment is therefore a relative term, and perhaps only in a few cases would there be a situation which might be called perfect adjustment or perfect lack of adjustment.

It is desirable, however, not to make the analysis too general until there has been a more careful consideration of particular instances. We now propose, therefore, to test the hypothesis by the facts in a definite case of social change. In attempting to verify the hypothesis in a particular case by measurement, the following series of steps will be followed. The old material conditions will be described, that part of the adaptive culture under consideration will be described, and the degree of adjustment between these two parts of culture shown. Then the changed material conditions and the changed adaptive culture will be defined and the degree of adaptation shown. It is necessary also to show that the unchanged adaptive culture is not as harmoniously adjusted to the new conditions as to the old and not as harmoniously adjusted to the new conditions as is a changed adaptive culture.

54

THE McDONALDIZATION OF SOCIETY

GEORGE RITZER

In this reading, originally published in 1983, George Ritzer examines the larger consequences of having an organization, such as McDonald's, in society. Ritzer argues that societies are being transformed by a process he labels "McDonaldization," in which the principles of the fast-food restaurant have come to influence other aspects of the social structure, such as the family, politics, education, travel, and leisure. Ritzer also summarizes the societal costs and benefits of this widespread social change.

A wide-ranging process of *rationalization* is occurring across American society and is having an increasingly powerful impact in many other parts of the world. It encompasses such disparate phenomena as fast-food restaurants, TV dinners, packaged tours, industrial robots, plea bargaining, and open-heart surgery on an assembly-line basis. As widespread and as important as these developments are, it is clear that we have barely begun a process that promises even more extraordinary changes (e.g., genetic engineering) in the years to come. We can think of rationalization as a historical

From *Journal of American Culture* 6, no. 1 (1983):100–107. Reprinted with the permission of the publishers.

process and rationality as the end result of that development. As a historical process, rationalization has distinctive roots in the western world. Writing in the late nineteenth and early twentieth centuries, the great German sociologist Max Weber saw his society as the center of the ongoing process of rationalization and the bureaucracy as its paradigm case. The model of rationalization, at least in contemporary America, is no longer the bureaucracy, but might be better thought of as the fast-food restaurant. As a result, our concern here is with what might be termed the "McDonaldization of Society." While the fast-food restaurant is not the ultimate expression of rationality, it is the current exemplar for future developments in rationalization.

A society characterized by rationality is one which emphasizes *efficiency, predictability, calculability, substitution of nonhuman for human technology,* and *control over uncertainty.* In discussing the various dimensions of rationalization, we will be little concerned with the gains already made, and yet to be realized, by greater rationalization. These advantages are widely discussed in schools and in the mass media. In fact, we are in danger of being seduced by the innumerable advantages already offered, and promised in the future, by rationalization. The glitter of these accomplishments and promises has served to distract most people from the grave dangers posed by progressive rationalization. In other words, we are ultimately concerned here with the irrational consequences that often flow from rational systems. Thus, the second major theme of this essay might be termed "the irrationality of rationality." . . .

Efficiency

The process of rationalization leads to a society in which a great deal of emphasis is placed on finding the best or optimum means to any given end. Whatever a group of people define as an end, and everything they so define, is to be pursued by attempting to find the best means to achieve the end. Thus, in the Germany of Weber's day, the bureaucracy was seen as the most efficient means of handling a wide array of administrative tasks. Somewhat later, the Nazis came to develop the concentration camp, its ovens, and other devices as the optimum method of collecting and murdering millions of Jews and other people. The efficiency that Weber described in turn-of-the-century Germany, and which later came to characterize many Nazi activities, has become a basic principle of life in virtually every sector of a rational society.

The modern American family, often with two wage earners, has little time to prepare elaborate meals. For the relatively few who still cook such meals, there is likely to be great reliance on cookbooks that make cooking from scratch much more efficient. However, such cooking is relatively rare today. Most families take as their objective quickly and easily prepared meals. To this end, much use is made of prepackaged meals and frozen TV dinners.

For many modern families, the TV dinner is no longer efficient enough. To many people, eating out, particularly in a fast-food restaurant, is a far more efficient way of obtaining their meals. Fast-food restaurants capitalize on this by being organized so that diners are fed as efficiently as possible. They offer a limited, simple menu that can be cooked and served in an assembly-line fashion. The latest development in fast-food restaurants, the addition of drive-through windows, constitutes an effort to increase still further the efficiency of the dining experience. The family now can simply drive through, pick up its order, and eat it while driving to the next, undoubtedly efficiently organized, activity. The success of the fast-food restaurant has come full circle with frozen food manufacturers now touting products for the home modeled after those served in fast-food restaurants.

Increasingly, efficiently organized food production and distribution systems lie at the base of the ability of people to eat their food efficiently at home, in the fast-food restaurant, or in their cars. Farms, groves, ranches, slaughterhouses, warehouses, transportation systems, and retailers are all oriented toward increasing efficiency. A notable example is chicken production where they are mass-bred, force-fed (often with many chemicals), slaughtered on an assembly line, iced or fast frozen, and shipped to all parts of the country. Some may argue that such chickens do not taste as good as the fresh-killed, local variety, but their complaints are likely to be drowned in a flood of mass-produced chickens. Then there is bacon which is more efficiently shipped, stored, and sold when it is preserved by sodium nitrate, a chemical which is unfortunately thought by many to be carcinogenic. Whatever one may say about the quality or the danger of the products, the fact remains that they are all shaped by the drive for efficiency. . . .

One of the most interesting and important aspects of efficiency is that it often comes to be not a means but an end in itself. This "displacement of goals" is a major problem in a rationalizing society. We have, for example, the bureaucrats who slavishly follow the rules even though their inflexibility negatively affects the organization's ability to achieve its goals. Then there are the bureaucrats who are so concerned with efficiency that they lose sight of the ultimate goals the means are designed to achieve. A good example was the Nazi concentration camp officers who, in devoting so much attention to maximizing the efficiency of the camps' operation, lost sight of the fact that the ultimate purpose of the camps was the murder of millions of people.

Predictability

A second component of rationalization involves the effort to ensure predictability from one place to another. In a rational society, people want to know what to expect when they enter a given setting or acquire some sort of commodity. They neither want nor expect surprises. They want to know that if they journey to another locale, the setting they enter or the commodity they buy will be essentially the same as the setting they entered or product they purchased earlier. Furthermore, people want to be sure that what they encounter is much like what they encountered at earlier times. In order to ensure predictability over time and place a rational society must emphasize such things as discipline, order, systemization, formalization, routine, consistency, and methodical operation.

One of the attractions of TV dinners for modern families is that they are highly predictable. The TV dinner composed of fried chicken, mashed potatoes, green peas, and peach cobbler is exactly the same from one time to another and one city to another. Home cooking from scratch is, conversely, a notoriously unpredictable enterprise with little assurance that dishes will taste the same time after time. However, the cookbook cannot eliminate all unpredictability. There are often simply too many ingredients and other variables involved. Thus the cookbook dish is far less predictable than the TV dinner or a wide array of other prepared dishes.

Fast-food restaurants rank very high on the dimension of predictability. In order to help ensure consistency, the fast-food restaurant offers only a limited menu. Predictable end products are made possible by the use of similar raw materials, technologies, and preparation and serving techniques. Not only the food is predictable; the physical structures, the logo, the "ambience," and even the personnel are as well.

The food that is shipped to our homes and our fast-food restaurants is itself affected by the process of increasing predictability. Thus our favorite white bread is indistinguishable from one place to another. In fact, food producers have made great efforts to ensure such predictability.

On packaged tours travelers can be fairly sure that the people they travel with will be much like themselves. The planes, buses, hotel accommodations, restaurants, and at least the way in which the sites are visited are very similar from one location to another. Many people go on packaged tours *because* they are far more predictable than travel undertaken on an individual basis.

Amusement parks used to be highly unpredictable affairs. People could never be sure, from one park to another, precisely what sorts of rides, events, foods, visitors, and employees they would encounter. All of that has changed in the era of the theme parks inspired by Disneyland. Such parks seek to ensure predictability in various ways. For example, a specific type of young person is hired in these parks, and they are all trained in much the same way, so that they have a robot-like predictability.

Other leisure-time activities have grown similarly predictable. Camping in the wild is loaded with uncertainties—bugs, bears, rain, cold, and the like. To make camping more predictable, organized grounds have sprung up around the country. Gone are many of the elements of unpredictability replaced by RVs, paved-over parking lots, sanitized campsites, fences and enclosed camp centers that provide laundry and food services, recreational activities, television, and video games. Sporting events, too, have in a variety of ways been made more predictable. The use of artificial turf in baseball makes for a more predictable bounce of a ball. . . .

Calculability or Quantity Rather than Quality

It could easily be argued that the emphasis on quantifiable measures, on things that can be counted, is *the* most defining characteristic of a rational society. Quality is notoriously difficult to evaluate. How do we assess the quality of a hamburger, or a physician, or a student? Instead of even trying, in an increasing number of cases, a rational society seeks to develop a series of quantifiable measures that it takes as surrogates for quality. This urge to quantify has given great impetus to the development of the computer and has, in turn, been spurred by the widespread use and increasing sophistication of the computer.

The fact is that many aspects of modern rational society, especially as far as calculable issues are concerned, are made possible and more widespread by the computer. We need not belabor the ability of the computer to handle large numbers of virtually anything, but somewhat less obvious is the use of the computer to give the illusion of personal attention in a world made increasingly impersonal in large part because of the computer's capacity to turn virtually everything into quantifiable dimensions. We have all now had many experiences where we open a letter personally addressed to us only to find a computer letter. We are aware that the names and addresses of millions of people have been stored on tape and that with the aid of a number of word processors a form letter has been sent to every name on the list. Although the computer is able to give a sense of personal attention, most people are nothing more than an item on a huge mailing list.

Our main concern here, though, is not with the computer, but with the emphasis on quantity rather than quality that it has helped foster. One of the most obvious examples in the university is the emphasis given to grades and cumulative grade point averages. With less and less contact between professor and student, there is little real effort to assess the quality of what students know, let alone the quality of their overall abilities. Instead, the sole measure of the quality of most college students is their grade in a given course and their grade point averages. Another blatant example is the emphasis on a variety of uniform exams such as SATs and GREs in which the essence of an applicant is reduced to a few simple scores and percentiles.

Within the educational institution, the importance of grades is well known, but somewhat less known is the way quantifiable factors have become an essential part of the process of evaluating college professors. For example, teaching ability is very hard to evaluate. Administrators have difficulty assessing teaching quality and thus substitute quantitative scores. Of course each score involves qualitative judgments, but this is conveniently ig-nored. Student opinion polls are taken and the scores are summed, aver-aged, and compared. Those who score well are deemed good teachers while those who don't are seen as poor teachers. There are many problems involved in relying on these scores such as the fact that easy teachers in "gut" courses may well obtain high ratings while rigorous teachers of difficult courses are likely to score poorly. . . .

In the workworld we find many examples of the effort to substitute quantity for quality. Scientific management was heavily oriented to turning everything work-related into quantifiable dimensions. Instead of relying on the "rule of thumb" of the operator, scientific management sought to de-velop precise measures of how much work was to be done by each and every motion of the worker. Everything that could be was reduced to num-bers and all these numbers were then analyzable using a variety of mathe-matical formulae. The assembly line is similarly oriented to a variety of quantifiable dimensions such as optimizing the speed of the line, minimiz-ing time for each task, lowering the price of the finished product, increasing sales and ultimately increasing profits. The divisional system pioneered by General Motors and thought to be one of the major reasons for its past suc-cess was oriented to the reduction of the performance of each division to a few, bottom-line numbers. By monitoring and comparing these numbers, General Motors was able to exercise control over the results without getting involved in the day-to-day activities of each division. . . .

Thus, the third dimension of rationalization, calculability or the em-phasis on quantity rather than quality, has wide applicability to the social world. It is truly central, if not the central, component of a rationalizing society. To return to our favorite example, it is the case that McDonald's ex-pends far more effort telling us how many billions of hamburgers it has sold than it does in telling us about the quality of those burgers. Relatedly, it touts the size of its product (the "Big Mac") more than the quality of the product (it is not the "Good Mac"). The bottom line in many settings is the number of customers processed, the speed with which they are processed, and the profits produced. Quality is secondary, if indeed there is any con-cern at all for it.

Substitution of Nonhuman Technology

In spite of Herculean efforts, there are important limits to the ability to ratio-nalize what human beings think and do. Seemingly no matter what one does, people still retain at least the ultimate capacity to think and act in a va-riety of unanticipated ways. Thus, in spite of great efforts to make human be-havior more efficient, more predictable, more calculable, people continue to act in unforeseen ways. People continue to make home-cooked meals from scratch, to camp in tents in the wild, to eat in old-fashioned diners, and to sabotage the assembly lines. Because of these realities, there is great interest among those who foster increasing rationality in using rational technologies to limit individual independence and ultimately to replace human beings with machines and other technologies that lack the ability to think and act in unpredictable ways.

McDonald's does not yet have robots to serve us food, but it does have teenagers whose ability to act autonomously is almost completely eliminated by techniques, procedures, routines, and machines. There are numerous examples of this including rules which prescribe all the things a counterperson should do in dealing with a customer as well as a large variety of technologies which determine the actions of workers such as drink dispensers which shut themselves off when the cup is full; buzzers, lights, and bells which indicate when food (e.g., french fries) is done; and cash registers which have the prices of each item programmed in. One of the latest attempts to constrain individual action is Denny's use of pre-measured packages of dehydrated food that are "cooked" simply by putting them under the hot water tap. Because of such tools and machines, as well as the elaborate rules dictating worker behavior, people often feel like they are dealing with human robots when they relate to the personnel of a fast-food restaurant. When human robots are found, mechanical robots cannot be far behind. Once people are reduced to a few robot-like actions, it is a relatively easy step to replace them with mechanical robots. Thus, Burgerworld is reportedly opening a prototypical restaurant in which mechanical robots serve the food.

Much of the recent history of work, especially manual work, is a history of efforts to replace human technology with nonhuman technology. Scientific management was oriented to the development of an elaborate and rigid set of rules about how jobs were to be done. The workers were to blindly and obediently follow those rules and not to do the work the way they saw fit. The various skills needed to perform a task were carefully delineated and broken down into a series of routine steps that could be taught to all workers. The skills, in other words, were built into the routines rather than belonging to skilled craftspersons. Similar points can be made about the assembly line which is basically a set of nonhuman technologies that have the needed steps and skills built into them. The human worker is reduced to performing a limited number of simple, repetitive operations. However, the control of this technology over the individual worker is so great and omnipresent that individual workers have reacted negatively manifesting such things as tardiness, absenteeism, turnover, and even sabotage. We are now witnessing a new stage in this technological development with automated processes now totally replacing many workers with robots. With the coming of robots we have reached the ultimate stage in the replacement of humans with nonhuman technology.

Even religion and religious crusades have not been unaffected by the spread of nonhuman technologies. The growth of large religious organizations, the use of Madison Avenue techniques, and even drive-in churches all reflect the incursion of modern technology. But it is in the electronic church, religion through the TV screens, that replacement of human by nonhuman technology in religion is most visible and has its most important manifestation. . . .

Control

This leads us to the fifth major dimension of rationalization — control. Rational systems are oriented toward, and structured to expedite, control in a variety of senses. At the most general level, we can say that rational systems are set up to allow for greater control over the uncertainties of life — birth, death, food production and distribution, housing, religious salvation, and many, many others. More specifically, rational systems are oriented to gaining greater control over the major source of uncertainty in social life — other people. Among other things, this means control over subordinates by superiors and control of clients and customers by workers.

There are many examples of rationalization oriented toward gaining greater control over the uncertainties of life. The burgeoning of the genetic engineering movement can be seen as being aimed at gaining better control over the production of life itself. Similarly, amniocentesis can be seen as a technique which will allow the parents to determine the kind of child they will have. The efforts to rationalize food production and distribution can be seen as being aimed at gaining greater control over the problems of hunger and starvation. A steady and regular supply of food can make life itself more certain for large numbers of people who today live under the threat of death from starvation.

At a more specific level, the rationalization of food preparation and serving at McDonald's gives it great control over its employees. The automobile assembly line has a similar impact. In fact, the vast majority of the structures of a rational society exert extraordinary control over the people who labor in them. But because of the limits that still exist on the degree of control that rational structures can exercise over individuals, many rationalizing employers are driven to seek to more fully rationalize their operations and totally eliminate the worker. The result is an automated, robot-like technology over which, barring some *2001* rebellion, there is almost total control.

In addition to control over employees, rational systems are also interested in controlling the customer/clients they serve. For example, the fast-food restaurant with its counter, the absence of waiters and waitresses, the limited seating, and the drive-through windows all tend to lead customers to do certain things and not to do others.

Irrationality of Rationality

Although not an inherent part of rationalization, the *irrationality of rationality* is a seemingly inevitable byproduct of the process. We can think of the irrationality of rationality in several ways. At the most general level it can simply be seen as an overarching label for all the negative effects of rationalization. More specifically, it can be seen as the opposite of rationality, at least in some of its senses. For example, there are the inefficiencies and unpredictabilities that are often produced by seemingly rational systems. Thus, although bureaucracies are constructed to bring about greater efficiency in organizational work, the fact is that there are notorious inefficiencies such as the "red tape" associated with the operation of most bureaucracies. Or, take the example of the arms race in which a focus on quantifiable aspects of nuclear weapons may well have made the occurrence of nuclear war more, rather than less, unpredictable.

Of greatest importance, however, is the variety of negative effects that rational systems have on the individuals who live, work, and are served by them. We might say that *rational systems are not reasonable systems.* As we've already discussed, rationality brings with it great dehumanization as people are reduced to acting like robots. Among the dehumanizing aspects of a rational society are large lecture classes, computer letters, pray TV, work on the automobile assembly line, and dining at a fast-food restaurant. Rationalization also tends to bring with it disenchantment leaving much of our lives without any mystery or excitement. Production by a hand craftsman is far more mysterious than an assembly-line technology where each worker does a single, very limited operation. Camping in an RV tends to suffer in comparison to the joys to be derived from camping in the wild. Overall a fully rational society would be a very bleak and uninteresting place.

Conclusions

Rationalization, with McDonald's as the paradigm case, is occurring throughout America, and, increasingly, other societies. In virtually every sector of society more and more emphasis is placed on efficiency, predictability, calculability, replacement of human by nonhuman technology, and control over uncertainty. Although progressive rationalization has brought with it innumerable advantages, it has also created a number of problems, the various irrationalities of rationality, which threaten to accelerate in the years to come. These problems, and their acceleration should not be taken as a case for the return to a less rational form of society. Such a return is not only impossible but also undesirable. What is needed is not a less rational society, but greater control over the process of rationalization involving, among other things, efforts to ameliorate its irrational consequences.

55

THE QUEST FOR ENVIRONMENTAL EQUITY
Mobilizing the African American Community
for Social Change

ROBERT D. BULLARD • BEVERLY H. WRIGHT

This selection is a 1989 study of social change written by two sociologists, Robert D. Bullard and Beverly H. Wright. In their research, Bullard and Wright combine analyses of environmental racism, social movement organizations, and social justice issues. Their investigation reveals why African American communities are more active and militant in grassroots environmental movements than in mainstream groups. Moreover, to illustrate their argument, Bullard and Wright present case studies of five African American communities that were involved in environmental disputes.

Much research has been devoted to analyzing environmental movements in the United States. Despite this wide coverage, there is a dearth of material on the convergence of environmentalism and social justice advocacy. Nearly two decades ago, Gale (1972) compared the civil rights movement and the environmental movement. The modern environmental movement has its roots in the civil rights and antiwar movements of the late sixties (Humphrey and Buttel 1982). Student activists who broke away from the civil rights and antiwar movements formed the core of the environmental movement in the early 1970s.

There is a substantial body of literature on grass-roots environmental groups (Freudenberg 1984; Freudenberg and Steinsapir 1990; Gottlieb and Ingram 1988). However, little research has been conducted on African American, Latino, and Native American grassroots environmental groups such as the Gulf Coast Tenants Organization (New Orleans), Mothers of East Los Angeles, Concerned Citizens of South Central Los Angeles, Southwest Organizing Project (Albuquerque), Toxic Avengers of Brooklyn, West Harlem Environmental Action, or Native Americans for a Clean Environment (Oklahoma). A special issue of *Environmental Action* highlighted the fact that the time is long overdue for the nation to move "beyond white environmentalism" (Truax 1990).

From *American Environmentalism: The U.S. Environmental Movement, 1970–1990*, pp. 39–49. Originally presented at the annual meeting of the American Sociological Association, San Francisco, August 9–13, 1989. Copyright © 1992 by Taylor & Francis, Inc. Reprinted with the permission of the publishers.

This paper analyzes environmental activism within five African American communities in the South. The issues that are addressed include (1) factors that shape environmental mobilization, (2) the level of convergence between environmental justice and social equity goals, (3) the source of environmental leadership, and (4) types of dispute resolution strategies used.

The Environmental Justice Movement

The civil rights movement has its roots in the southern United States. Southern racism deprived blacks of "political rights, economic opportunity, social justice, and human dignity" (Bloom 1987:18). However, racism is by no means limited to any one region of the country. The environmental justice movement for African Americans is centered in the South, a region where marked ecological disparities exist between black and white communities. Many of these disparities were institutionalized by laws and public policies during the "Jim Crow" era. African American communities systematically became the "dumping grounds" (Bullard 1990:43) for all kinds of locally unwanted land uses (LULUs).

The literature is replete with studies documenting the disproportionate environmental burden borne by African Americans (Bullard 1990; Bullard and Wright 1986, 1987a; Commission for Racial Justice [United Church of Christ] 1987; Gianessi, Peskin, and Wolff 1979; Jordon 1980; Kazis and Grossman 1983; Kruvant 1975; McCaull 1975; U.S. General Accounting Office 1983). These ecological disparities were highlighted in the 1983 Urban Environment Conference whose theme was "taking back our health." The conference was held in New Orleans and was one of the first national forums that brought together Third World people in this country and progressive whites to talk about environmental justice and coalition building. This broad-based group of civil rights activists, organized labor leaders, and grass-roots environmental activists formed a loose alliance (Urban Environment Conference, Inc. 1985:29). Cooperative action between social justice and environmental groups was seen as one of the best strategies to weaken the hold of "job blackmail"—the threat of job loss or plant closure—on the working class and communities of color (Kazis and Grossman 1983).

A growing number of African American grass-roots environmental groups and their leaders have begun to adopt confrontational strategies (e.g., protests, neighborhood demonstrations, picketing, political pressure, and litigation) similar to those used in earlier civil rights disputes. These activists advocate a brand of environmentalism that attempts to address disparate impact and equity issues. Documentation of civil rights violations has strengthened the move to make environmental quality a basic right of all individuals (Bullard and Wright 1987a, 1987b).

Social justice advocate Reverend Ben Chavis defines many of the ecological inequities within the African American community as direct results of "environmental racism." The privileges of whites (access to a clean environment) are created and institutionalized at the expense of people of color (Commission for Racial Justice 1987:x). Thus the practice of targeting urban ghettos or rural blackbelt communities for noxious facilities (i.e., hazardous waste landfills, incinerators, paper mills, garbage dumps, and other polluting industries) is seen as another expression of institutional racism.

The U.S. General Accounting Office (1983) observed a strong relationship between the locations of off-site hazardous waste landfills and the racial and socioeconomic status of surrounding communities. The GAO looked at eight southern states that comprised the federal Environmental Protection Agency's (EPA's) Region IV (Alabama, Florida, Georgia, Kentucky, Mississippi, North Carolina, South Carolina, and Tennessee). The government study identified four off-site hazardous waste landfills in the region. African Americans made up a majority of the population in three of the four communities where the off-site hazardous waste landfills are located. The fourth site is located in a community where 38 percent of the population is African American. In 1990, only two off-site hazardous waste landfills were operating in Region IV, and both of these sites are located in African American communities. African Americans, who make up only 20 percent of the region's population, continue to shoulder a heavier toxic waste burden than any other group in the region.

The Commission for Racial Justice's (1987) ground-breaking report *Toxic Wastes and Race* clearly shows that African American communities and other communities of color bear a heavier burden than society at large in the disposal of the nation's hazardous waste. Race was the most potent variable in predicting the location of uncontrolled (abandoned) and commercial toxic waste sites in the United States.

The nation's total hazardous waste disposal capacity was 127,989 acre-feet in 1987 (Commission for Racial Justice 1987). In 1987, three of the nation's largest commercial hazardous waste sites were located in African American or Latino communities. These three sites—Chemical Waste Management site in Emelle, Alabama (black); Rollins Environmental Services in Scotlandville, Louisiana (black); and Chemical Waste Management site in Kettleman City, California (Latino)—accounted for 51,070 acre-feet of the disposal capacity, or 40 percent of the nation's total hazardous waste disposal capacity in 1987 (Commission for Racial Justice 1987).

The first national protest by African Americans against environmental racism came in 1982 after the mostly black Warren County, North Carolina, was selected as the burial site for 32,000 cubic yards of soil contaminated with highly toxic polychlorinated biphenyls, or PCBs. The soil was illegally dumped along the roadways in 14 North Carolina counties in 1978. African American civil rights activists, political leaders, and local residents marched in protest demonstrations against the construction of the PCB landfill in their community. More than 400 demonstrators were jailed. Although the protests were unsuccessful in halting the landfill construction, they marked the first time that blacks mobilized a nationally broad-based group to protest environmental inequities and the first time that demonstrators had been sent to jail for protesting against a hazardous waste landfill (Bullard and Wright 1986; Geiser and Waneck 1983:13–17).

. . .

Case Studies from the Southern United States

The African American community is bombarded with all kinds of environmental stressors. Our goal was to select varied noxious facilities—municipal landfill, hazardous waste landfill and incinerator, and lead smelter facilities—and then gauge public opposition to these facilities. On the surface, municipal landfills may seem nonthreatening because they receive household garbage. However, sanitary landfills routinely accept household waste—some of which is highly toxic—and many receive illegally dumped hazardous waste. The threat (whether real or perceived) of living next to a toxic waste dump and incinerator has been well publicized. Similarly, the ill-effects of lead poisoning have been known since the Roman era.

The heightened militancy among African Americans on environmental issues served as a backdrop for studying a special brand of environmentalism. This analysis centered on five African American communities that were involved in environmental disputes during 1979–1987: Houston's Northwood Manor neighborhood (Texas), the West Dallas neighborhood (Texas), Institute (West Virginia), Alsen (Louisiana), and Emelle (Alabama). Although the communities have different histories, they share the common action of challenging the notion that social justice and environmental concern are incompatible goals.

The analysis is based on in-depth interviews conducted with a total of 15 opinion leaders who were identified through the "reputational" approach and who were active in the local environmental disputes. The interviews were conducted in the summer of 1988 and were supplemented with archival documents and newspaper articles, editorials, and feature stories on the disputes. The data addressed the following: (1) issue crystallization (e.g., each opinion leader was asked how he or she defined the local dispute), (2) citizen opposition tactics used, (3) type of leadership that spearheaded the citizen opposition, (4) methods used to resolve the dispute, and (5) outcome of the dispute.

Houston, Texas

Houston in the 1970s was dubbed the "golden buckle" of the Sunbelt. In 1982 it became the nation's fourth largest city, with 1.7 million inhabitants. Houston is the only major U.S. city that does not have zoning, a policy that has contributed to haphazard and irrational land-use planning and infra-structure chaos (Babcock 1982; Bullard 1984, 1987; Feagin 1985, 1987). Discriminatory facility-siting decisions allowed the city's black neighborhoods to become the "dumping grounds" for Houston's municipal garbage (Bullard 1983). From the late 1920s to the late 1970s, more than three-fourths of the city's solid waste sites (incinerators and landfills) were located in black neighborhoods, although African Americans made up only one-fourth of Houston's population.

In 1979 residents of the city's Northwood Manor neighborhood (where African Americans made up more than 84 percent of the total residents) chose to challenge the Browning-Ferris Industries' (one of the world's largest waste disposal firms) selection of their area for a garbage dump. Residents from this middle-income suburban neighborhood (some 83 percent of the residents own their homes) mobilized soon after they discovered the construction was not an expansion of their subdivision but a municipal landfill.

Dallas, Texas

Dallas is the nation's seventh largest city, with a population of 904,078 in 1980. African Americans represent 29.4 percent of the city's population. The African American population remains segregated: eight of every ten blacks live in mostly black neighborhoods. West Dallas is just one of these segregated enclaves, and African Americans make up 85 percent of the neighborhood residents. This low-income neighborhood dates back to the turn of the century. For more than five decades, residents were bombarded with toxic emissions from the nearby RSR Corp. lead smelter facility (Dallas Alliance Environmental Task Force 1983). The smelter routinely pumped more than 269 tons of lead particles each year into the air. After repeated violations and citations, residents from West Dallas in 1981 mobilized to close the plant and get the lead-tainted soil removed from their neighborhood.

Institute, West Virginia

Institute is located in the Kanawha River Valley just six miles west of Charleston, the state capital. It is an unincorporated community where African Americans represent more than 90 percent of the population. The community dates back to 1891 when the state legislature selected the site for West Virginia Colored Institute (later renamed West Virginia State College). The community is also home to the Union Carbide chemical plant that was the prototype for the company's plant in Bhopal, India. The Institute plant was the only plant in the United States that manufactured the same deadly methyl isocyanate (MIC) responsible for the 1985 Bhopal disaster. A leak on August 11, 1985 at the Union Carbide Institute plant sent more than 135 local residents to the hospital. This accident heightened an already uneasy relationship that had existed for years between Union Carbide and Institute residents. People were concerned that another Bhopal incident would happen in Institute (Franklin 1986; Slaughter 1985). Institute residents organized themselves into a group called People Concerned about MIC to combat this toxic threat.

Alsen, Louisiana

Alsen is an unincorporated community located on the Mississippi River several miles north of Baton Rouge, Louisiana's state capital. African Americans make up 98.9 percent of this community, which lies at the beginning of the 85-mile industrial corridor where one-quarter of the nation's petrochemicals are produced. This corridor has been described as a "massive human experiment" and a "national sacrifice zone" (Brown 1987:152–161). The nation's fourth largest hazardous waste landfill is located adjacent to the Alsen community. The landfill opened in the late seventies. The site represented 11.3 percent of the nation's remaining hazardous waste landfill capacity in 1986 (Commission for Racial Justice 1987). Between 1980 and 1985, Rollins, the company operating the site, was cited for more than 100 state and federal toxic emission violations but did not pay any penalties. The community began organizing in late 1981 against the Rollins hazardous waste facility.

Emelle, Alabama

This Sumter County community is located in the heart of west Alabama's economically impoverished "blackbelt." African Americans make up more than 90 percent of the rural community's 626 residents. Emelle is home to Chemical Waste Management's "Cadillac" of hazardous waste landfills, the nation's largest hazardous waste dump (Gunter and Williams 1986:19). The site covers more than 2,400 acres and represented nearly one-fourth of the nation's hazardous waste landfill capacity in 1986. The Emelle landfill opened in 1978 and is one of two hazardous waste landfills located in EPA's Region IV (i.e., the eight states in the southeastern United States). The landfill receives some of the most toxic waste in the country, including waste from cleaned-up "Superfund" sites. Public opposition began after residents discovered the new job-generating industry was not a brick factory (as was rumored) but a toxic waste dump. The initial protest against the facility, led by members of the Minority Peoples' Council, was over worker safety rather than risks to the larger community.

Environmental Conflict Resolution

The environmental disputes explored in this analysis were seen by grassroots leaders as based on unfair treatment and as an expression of racial discrimination. These activists saw their communities sharing a disparate burden and degree of risk associated with the industrial plants. The noxious facility siting disputes were linked to earlier civil rights disputes that centered on racial disparities. Residents in Houston and Dallas, the neighborhoods in the two large cities studied, were able to inject their environmental disputes into the local political elections. Of the five communities studied, Emelle, which is a community heavily dependent upon the millions of industrial dollars pumped into the local economy annually, gave the strongest endorsement of jobs over the environment. However, even residents from this rural community were not willing to sit silent and watch their area turned into a toxic wasteland.

The opposition strategies varied somewhat across the communities. However, several common strategies were used by residents in the affected communities. For example, all five communities used protest demonstrations, petitions, and press lobbying to publicize their plight. Three of the communities (West Dallas, Alsen, and Houston's Northwood Manor neighborhood) were successful in enlisting the assistance of government agencies in their efforts to redress their environmental problem. The West Dallas community was the only one to actually convince the city and state to join them in litigation against the industrial polluter. Houston's city council, after intense pressure from the African American community, passed a resolution opposing the controversial municipal sanitary landfill. Alsen residents convinced state environmental officials to take action against Rollins over its toxic emissions. These same three communities also filed class-action lawsuits against the industrial firms.

Who spearheaded the local opposition against the polluting industries? There is clear evidence that indigenous social action groups and their leaders held the most important and visible roles in mobilizing the opposition to industrial polluters. African American church leaders, community improvement workers, and civil rights activists planned and initiated most of the local opposition strategies. Mainstream environmental leaders and other "outside elites" played only a minor role in mobilizing citizen opposition in these communities. The West Dallas community was able to get a government-sanctioned citizen group, the Dallas Alliance Environmental Task Force, to work on the local lead pollution problem. Institute's People Concerned about MIC was initiated by a white professor from West Virginia State College and included a broad cross-section of the community. In Emelle, African American civil rights activists (e.g., Minority People's Council) and white environmentalists (e.g., Alabamians for a Clean Environment) have forged a loose alliance to work on the local hazardous waste problem. This is not a small point, given the history of race relations in Alabama's blackbelt.

How were the environmental disputes resolved? The disputes in the West Dallas, Alsen, and Houston neighborhoods were resolved by governmental decisions and adjudication. Bargaining and negotiation were the chief tools used to address (though not resolve) the ongoing environmental disputes in Emelle and Institute. Only West Dallas was able to force the polluting industry to completely shut down (but not dismantle and clean up the site), whereas capacity reductions were placed on the industries in Alsen, Houston, and Institute.

Litigation brought by citizens from West Dallas and Alsen resulted in out-of-court settlement agreements in favor of the plaintiffs and fines paid to governmental regulatory agencies for pollution and safety violations. In 1985 the West Dallas plaintiffs (370 children who lived in the nearby public housing project and 40 property owners) won a $20 million settlement against RSR Corp. The Alsen plaintiffs agreed to settle their dispute for an undisclosed amount (it is reported that Rollins awarded each Alsen plaintiff an average of $3,000). Government officials also fined the Institute and Emelle facilities for pollution and safety violations. Citizens in Alsen and Institute were able to extract some concessions from the firms, mainly in the form of technical modifications in the plant operations, updated safety and pollution monitoring systems, and reduced emission levels.

The federal court in 1984 ruled against the Houston plaintiffs (five years after the suit was brought and the site opened), and the landfill was built. The Northwood Manor residents, however, were able to force the city and state to modify their requirements for siting solid waste facilities. The Houston city council passed ordinances that (1) prohibited city-owned solid waste trucks from dumping at the controversial landfill and (2) regulated the distance that future landfills could be placed near public facilities (e.g., schools, parks, and recreation playgrounds). This was not a small concession given the fact that the city has long resisted any move to institute land-use zoning. The Texas Department of Health, which is the state permit agency for municipal landfills, also modified its regulations requiring waste disposal applicants to include socioeconomic information on census tracts contiguous to the proposed sites.

Conclusion

In their search for operating space, industries such as waste disposal and treatment facilities, heavy metals operations, and chemical plants found minority communities to be logical choices for their expansion. These communities and their leaders were seen as having a Third World view of development—that is, any development is better than no development at all. Moreover, many residents in these communities were suspicious of environmentalists, a sentiment that aligned them with the pro-growth advocates.

African Americans have begun to challenge the legitimacy of environment–jobs trade-offs. They are now asking whether the costs borne by their communities are imposed to spare the larger community. Can environmental inequities (resulting from industrial facility siting decisions) be compensated? What are "acceptable" risks? Concern about inequity—the inherent imbalance between localized costs and dispersed benefits—appears to be the driving force around which African American communities are organizing.

A great deal of overlap exists between the leadership of African American social action groups, neighborhood associations, and community-based grass-roots environmental groups that are formed to challenge local environmental problems. Preexisting institutions and their leaders play a pivotal role in the organization, planning, and mobilization stages of the opposition activities.

The Not in My Backyard (NIMBY) syndrome has trickled down to nearly all communities, including African Americans in the suburbs, impoverished ghettos, and rural blackbelt. Few residents want garbage dumps, landfills, incinerators, or other polluting industries in their backyards. The price of siting noxious facilities has skyrocketed in recent years as a result of more stringent federal regulations and the growing militancy among communities of the poor, of the working class, and of color.

African Americans and other people of color are still underrepresented in the mainstream environmental organizations at all levels. This picture must change if the U.S. national environmental movement is to provide leadership in the global environmental movement, i.e., the Third World, where most of the world's population is located. On the other hand, by embracing environmental justice issues, grass-roots environmental groups have been able to make progress toward alliances with African American communities around the toxics issue.

Changing demographics point to a more racially diverse nation. It is time for the environmental movement to diversify and reach out to the "other" United States. This does not mean the Big Ten should swallow up grass-roots efforts. The 1990s offer some challenging opportunities for the environmental movement in the United States to embrace social justice and redistributive policies. African Americans and other people of color must be empowered through their own organizations to address the problems in their communities. Some positive signs indicate that the larger environmental and social justice community is beginning to take the first steps toward reducing the artificial barriers that have kept them apart.

REFERENCES

Authors' Note: Research for this paper was supported by a grant from Resources for the Future Small Grants Program.

Babcock, Richard. 1982. "Houston: Unzoned, Unfettered, and Most Unrepentent." *Planning* 48:21–23.

Bloom, Jack. 1987. *Class, Race and the Civil Rights Movement.* Bloomington: Indiana University Press.

Brown, Michael H. 1987. *The Toxic Cloud: The Poisoning of America's Air.* New York: Harper & Row.

Bullard, Robert D. 1983. "Solid Waste Sites and the Black Houston Community." *Sociological Inquiry* 53:273–88.

————. 1984. "Endangered Environs: The Price of Unplanned Growth in Boomtown Houston." *California Sociologist* 7:84–102.

————. 1990. *Dumping in Dixie: Race, Class, and Environmental Quality.* Boulder, CO: Westview.

Bullard, Robert D. and Beverly H. Wright. 1986. "The Politics of Pollution: Implications for the Black Community." *Phylon* 47:71–78.

————. 1987a. "Blacks and the Environment." *Humboldt Journal of Social Relations* 14:165–84.

————. 1987b. "Environmentalism and the Politics of Equity: Emergent Trends in the Black Community." *Mid-American Review of Sociology* 12:21–37.

Commission for Racial Justice. 1987. *Toxic Wastes and Race: A National Report on the Racial and Socioeconomic Characteristics of Communities with Hazardous Wastes Sites.* New York: United Church of Christ.

Dallas Alliance Environmental Task Force. 1983, June 29. *Final Report.* Dallas, Texas: Author.

Feagin, Joe R. 1985. "The Global Context of Metropolitan Growth: Houston and the Oil Industry." *American Journal of Sociology* 90:1204–30.

————. 1987. *Free Enterprise City: Houston in Political and Economic Perspective.* New Brunswick, NJ: Rutgers University Press.

Franklin, Ben A. 1986. "In the Shadow of the Valley." *Sierra* 71:38–43.

Freudenberg, Nicholas. 1984. "Citizen Action for Environmental Health: Report of a Survey of Community Organizations." *American Journal of Public Health* 74:444–48.

Freudenberg, N. and C. Steinsapir. 1990. February 15–20. "The Grass Roots Environmental Movement: Not in Our Backyards." Paper presented at the annual meeting of the American Association for the Advancement of Science, New Orleans.

Gale, Richard P. 1972. "From Sit-in to Hike-in: A Comparison of the Civil Rights and Environmental Movements." Pp. 280–305 in *Social Behavior, Natural Resources, and the Environment,* eds. W. R. Burch, N. H. Cheek, and L. Taylor. New York: Harper & Row.

————. 1983. "The Environmental Movement and the Left: Antagonists or Allies?" *Sociological Inquiry* 53:179–99.

Geiser, Ken and Gerry Waneck. 1983. "PCBs and Warren County." *Science for the People* 15:13–17.

Gianessi, L. P., H. M. Peskin, and E. Wolff. 1979, May. "The Distributional Effect of Uniform Air Pollution Policy in the U.S." *Quarterly Journal of Economics* 93:281–301.

Gottlieb, Robert and Helen Ingram. 1988. "The New Environmentalists." *The Progressive* 52:14–15.

Gunter, Booth and Mike Williams. 1986. "The Cadillac of Dumps." *Sierra* 71:9–22.

Humphrey, Craig R. and Frederick R. Buttel. 1982. *Environment, Energy and Society.* Belmont, CA: Wadsworth.

Jordon, Vernon. 1980. "Sins of Omission." *Environmental Action* 11:26–30.

Kazis, Richard and Richard Grossman. 1983. *Fear at Work: Job Blackmail, Labor, and the Environment.* New York: The Pilgrim Press.

Kruvant, W. J. 1975. "People, Energy and Pollution." Pp. 125–67 in *The American Energy Consumer,* eds. D. Newman and D. Dawn. Cambridge, MA: Ballinger.

McCaull, Julian. 1975. "Discriminatory Air Pollution: If the Poor Don't Breathe." *Environment* 19:26–32.

Slaughter, Jane. 1985. "Valley of the Shadow of Death." *The Progressive* 49:50.

Truax, Hawley. 1990. "Beyond White Environmentalism: Minorities and the Environment." *Environmental Action* 21:19–30.

Urban Environment Conference, Inc. 1985. *Taking Back Our Health: An Institute on Surviving the Threat to Minority Communities.* Washington, DC: Urban Environment Inc.

U.S. General Accounting Office. 1983. *Siting of Hazardous Waste Landfills and Their Correlation with Racial and Economic Status of Surrounding Communities.* Washington, DC: Government Printing Office.

56

THINK GLOBALLY, ACT POLITICALLY
Some Notes toward New Movement Strategy

RICHARD FLACKS

This last reading is by Richard Flacks, a sociologist who studies the dynamics of social movements. Flacks is especially interested in understanding when social movements are the most effective at causing social change. In this selection, adapted from *Making History: The American Left and the American Mind* (1988), Flacks examines the relationship between social movements and electoral politics of the 1960s in order to learn whether strategies employed then would be successful now. Flacks suggests new directions social movements and activists should take, including the need to "think globally and act politically."

Social movements arise when normal politics fail. The great American movements of labor, women, and blacks expressed the exclusion of their constituencies from the central political processes. Workers had no rights in their workplace to defend their life interests; at the same time, they could not find adequate political representation. Women and blacks could not vote at all, nor did they have institutional power to protect themselves.

The primary victories of these movements were political: the right to vote, the right to organize and strike, the development of electoral constituencies with leverage, the achievement of legislative and judicial acknowledgement of and protection for rights, the establishment of organizational infrastructures that formulate public policies and lobby for them, the achievement of some veto power in the political arena, the capacity to elect representatives in localities where the movement has been strong. In the course of decades of struggle by these movements, the American definition of citizenship rights became more inclusive. Groups previously denied full citizenship achieved legal recognition. Areas of life previously excluded from government intervention became subject to it.

From *Cultural Politics and Social Movements,* edited by Darnovsky, Epstein, and Flack. Reprinted by permission of Temple University.

Movements and Electoral Politics after the Sixties

By the end of the 1960s, movement activists came to see that the achievement of political inclusion and citizenship as defined by the Constitution and mainstream political culture had been accomplished. This achievement, however, was insufficient: Millions of workers—black and white—remained poor and insecure, women remained subordinated, major social needs remained unfulfilled, the quality of urban life was deteriorating, militarism and war remained the first priority of the state.

In short, despite movement gains, normal politics were still not a framework in which the pressing needs and interests of movement constituencies could be fulfilled. Indeed, some groups who had previously felt represented (especially members of the growing intellectual/professional strata) were experiencing the established political framework as irrational and closed. Elite domination of the state and of the political parties frequently thwarted the popular will; at the same time, racial, ethnic, and other organized minorities were necessarily disadvantaged within the electoral process.

A number of movement projects were initiated in that period whose purpose was to restructure electoral and governmental processes:

The Reform of the Democratic Party

Labor activists had sought representation in the Democratic Party since the New Deal days and during the 1940s and 1950s had taken considerable control of particular state and local Democratic Party organizations. Similar representation was one of the main goals of the southern civil rights movement; by the late sixties, black voting blocs in the South became the basis for considerable party realignment. By the early 1970s, a wide range of movement-based activists pressed for party reform that would undermine the power of traditional machine politicians and compel the recognition of women and minorities. The McGovern candidacy in 1972 offered hope that a new national Democratic Party could be created that would be rooted in the mass constituencies mobilized for change in the sixties, combined with the working-class base that formed during the New Deal. It turned out, of course, to be impossible to forge such a coalition, given the racial and cultural barriers among the constituencies and, indeed, among the activist leaderships as well.

Twenty years later, many activists still hope for a progressive national political party as the key to an effective political strategy for change. Each movement has some capacity to advance a particular agenda to protect certain interests and to veto certain threats. But no movement on its own has the potential to achieve the redistribution of wealth, power, and social priorities that would significantly improve the life chances of their constituents or sustain their deepest aspirations. A political party representing the common ground of progressive movements would seem to be the obvious framework for mobilizing the political resources and formulating the programmatic agenda for change. And yet, no leadership has emerged in the last twenty years to work systematically to create such a party. Movements continue to act as pressure groups within the Democratic Party. The Jesse Jackson campaigns created moments in which a "common ground" politics seemed to promise results. Experiments in the creation of third parties have had some local success. But in the climate of the last fifteen years, as mainstream politics moved rightward and movement gains came under attack, prospects for a progressive national force seemed always receding.

Single-Issue Coalitions

Although systematic efforts to create a national electoral coalition did not eventuate, single-issue, ad hoc coalition projects became increasingly evident and effective in the 1980s and 1990s. Some examples: the campaign against Robert Bork's Supreme Court nomination; the campaigns against aid to the contras in Nicaragua; the anti-apartheid disinvestment efforts; the anti-NAFTA campaign; the campaign for national health care reform. In all of these, national and local organizations and activists from diverse movements were able to collaborate on common projects focused on a particular well-defined and short-term objective. Seemingly insurmountable barriers— for example, those between labor unions and the peace movement—were in some cases overcome. New institutional sources for activist energy came into being—for example, liberal religious communities. The ad hoc nature of these efforts meant that they did not seem to build on one another; still, they offered evidence that, despite the fragmentation of the left and the rise of a politics of identity, coalescence, at least under immediate conditions of practical necessity and opportunity, was possible.

Localism

Since the sixties, movement activists have had substantial success in influencing electoral politics and governmental policy at city and state levels. Considerable numbers of New Left activists came to see that the student movement as such was a limited vehicle for advancing far-reaching social change. The university campus, despite its significance in postindustrial society, remained too isolated from the political and cultural mainstream; students, despite their capacity for dramatic and effective disruption, could not achieve their goals without substantial links to potential majorities. And, from a biographical perspective, students had to graduate into a wider world and find new arenas in which to fulfill their political commitments.

Many student activists, accordingly, sought to overcome their political and cultural isolation and searched for activist vocations by settling into particular local communities. What we mean by "new social movements" has much to do with these post-sixties organizing efforts, for it is out of these that feminism, environmentalism, gay liberation, and the anti-nuclear movements emerged.

The localist emphasis of post-sixties activism resulted in part from the limited resources available to the left; most particularly the absence of any central organizational authority that could have directed a national strategy. But localism derived also from the ideological perspectives that dominated the New Left—the emphasis on participatory democracy, on decentralization, on human scale. The feminist critique of patriarchal leadership reinforced these perspectives by encouraging both male and female activists to work in nonhierarchical, face-to-face ways—rather than in the self-promoting top-down manner that seems required by efforts to assert national leadership.

The new movements developed, accordingly, in highly decentralized ways. Although each of them contained national organizational structures, these had relatively little to do with directing the manifold movement activities that emerged out of issues arising in particular regions, communities, neighborhoods, and workplaces.

The environmental movement is a prototypical case. Environmentalism did not become a mass movement because of the initiatives of national organizations; rather, the movement was constructed out of a host of seemingly disparate local protests and projects: struggles over land use, urban development, population growth, toxic waste disposal, nuclear power, neighborhood preservation, defense of traditional culture, occupational hazards and so forth. Typically, members of a local community came together and acted in response to a locally experienced threat—at times, using the resources (language, know-how, material support) made available by the formal organizations of the national movement. In the midst of such local struggles that were often some veteran activists—people whose identities were shaped in the Old or New Left. Over the course of time, the influence of experienced activists was no longer a necessary ingredient for enabling local protest to take off. After twenty-five years, many who don't consider themselves to be activists have acquired the consciousness and skills to act effectively in local protest.

The local creativity of the new social movements was an important, if largely hidden, feature of American social history during the last quarter century. Local protests often succeeded in deflating the particular threats that initially sparked them, or won certain concessions and accommodations from the corporate and state bureaucracies that encroached on community life. Moreover, locally based movement activity rather quickly developed a certain strategic thrust that went beyond the merely reactive. The political aim of grassroots activism was to win a degree of direct voice in the decisions and policies that determine the community's future. This implicit strategy was implemented in a variety of political projects.

Beginning in the early seventies, new social movement activists, especially in towns with sizable university populations, began competing directly for local office. In the eighties this effort widened with the development of local "rainbow" coalition politics in a number of cities, whereby black community activists made electoral alliance with feminist, environmentalist, gay, and peace constituencies. Eventually progressive coalitions came to local power in a variety of places rather different from the progressive university town. Indeed, there is probably no major city in the country whose politics has not been affected by the separate and combined efforts of movement activists to win at least a piece of local power.[1]

In addition to seeking electoral office, locally based movements have pressed for structural reform at the local and state level—reform that would provide movement constituencies with legal bases for intervening in the decision-making process and holding government directly accountable. Decisions previously reserved for specialized or elite arenas were now subject to public scrutiny and voice.

A major example of movement initiatives in this regard is with the Environmental Quality Act in California (CEQA), which requires that all local development be subject to environmental impact review. The EIR process compels a public weighing of social costs and provides an arena for public testimony and an opportunity for public negotiation of "mitigations" with respect to all changes of land use. Governmental procedures such as mandatory public hearings provide community movements with significant opportunities for mobilization, public education, the development of expertise, and the exercise of community leadership. From the perspective of public authority, the process was agreed to in an effort to get community residents "off the streets" and into the bureaucratic structure; in practice, however, it has provided a degree of information and opportunity for public participation not previously available.

In general, in the last twenty-five years, a variety of mechanisms embodying principles of public review and participatory planning have emerged in American community and institutional life. Public mechanisms similar to those provided by the EIR exist in some locales with respect to job hiring and promotion policies, police practices, health service provision, provision of services for the aged, and public education (where local control has, of course, a long tradition in the United States). The development of these mechanisms has meant considerable change in the structure of power at the local level.

But the local democracy achieved during this past quarter century is a limited one: American communities are now places where social movements have some ability to veto or modify unwanted decisions. Largely missing at the community level are institutional mechanisms for promoting economic redistribution, for effectively controlling the flow of capital, or for effectively determining the planning processes that shape their futures. These processes are determined beyond the locality.

Having learned to "act locally while thinking globally," movement activists discovered that the innovative post-sixties political strategies had effective limits: They could not provide a significant way to protect local communities from the incursions of globalized megacorporations nor from the globalizing cultural frameworks provided by the megamedia.

The Failure of Normal Politics

In general, movement activists hope that the outcome of mass protest will be the democratizing of normal politics. Normalcy is necessary in the aftermath of protest. Grassroots movement participants need eventually to go home to raise their families and live in the freer space that their protests have helped open. Meanwhile, committed activists hope to find long-term careers within stable political institutions, representing the grassroots, serving the people as professionals, administrators, politicians.

The sixties generation's hopes for the establishment of a liveable normal politics were exercised through the strategies I have enumerated above. These were, I have suggested, not unsuccessful. The most egregious denials of human rights characteristic of American society prior to the sixties have been removed. Avenues for democratic participation for a variety of previously excluded groups have been opened; arenas of life previously subject to authoritarian control are now less so; daily life and human relations are in many ways more free and cultural expression far less repressed and homogenized.

We do not, however, now have a normal politics in which the relatively disadvantaged groups in society believe that their interests and needs and aspirations can be effectively expressed and addressed. Indeed, the evidence is that millions of Americans who formerly thought themselves to be represented politically are increasingly alienated. Few constituencies feel adequately represented by political leadership; populist mistrust of politicians is pervasive; government is perceived largely as a burden rather than a resource.

Normal politics worked in the aftermath of the thirties. The labor movement and radical ferment of the Depression years helped solidify the Keynesian–welfare state model for sustaining political stability and steady economic growth. After World War II, mass parties, claiming to represent workers and other mobilized constituencies, effectively determined national policies in many countries.

These mass parties established their dominance not only by being a voice for disadvantaged mass constituencies but by maintaining the *silence* of some of these (women, ethnic minorities, the least skilled, for example). The upsurges of the sixties were in large part due to the prior underrepresentation or exclusion of such groups from the normal politics that the labor movement of the thirties had helped create.

Sixties activists in Europe and the United States assumed initially that the established mass parties could be made more inclusive. As we have seen, one of the key strategic projects of activists in the United States in the early seventies was the reform of the Democratic Party so that it could effectively represent the claims of previously marginalized constituencies and thereby establish a new majority coalition. Hopes for a revitalization of the European social democratic parties were also prevalent in the seventies.

Efforts to broaden the mass parties as effective vehicles of economic redistribution and democratization were largely frustrated. Much discussion in Europe and the United States in the seventies envisioned a new social democratic program "beyond the welfare state"—that is, reasserting efforts to promote popular democratic control of planning and investment, workplace democracy, environmentalism, and women's liberation. Programmatic change in these directions did occur in some of the European parties. Once in power, however, European social democratic parties (for example, in France and Spain) reverted to versions of neoliberalism, abandoning even their prior commitment to preserving the welfare state. A similar shift to the right has been evident during the brief periods when the Democratic Party has controlled the White House.

Why did this eminently rational hope for the revitalization of social democracy remain unfulfilled? Part of the problem the mass parties faced was the splintering of their traditional base. The very success of the post–World War II social contract in raising living standards of industrial workers and promoting economic growth meant that large numbers of workers sought to protect their relative advantage, resented taxation that supported the welfare state, and hoped for more opportunity to own things. Against this, traditional party rhetoric about solidarity and equality and the common good seemed stultifying. Just when parts of the working class "bourgeoisified," these parties were, at the same time, compelled to respond to the rising demands of ethnic minorities, women, and the less skilled for recognition, justice, and voice. Class identity, which had undergirded the political strength of these parties, broke into many fragments. No single leadership could claim to speak for these diverse and conflicting parts. Indeed, white male working- and middle-class voters resonated far more to Reaganite and Thatcherite political appeals than to the increasingly hollow rhetoric of their putative party leaderships.

The heart of the problem is that the mass parties no longer can muster the resources within the scope of their domestic political economies to sustain the programs and policies required by Keynesian and welfare-state logics. The globalization of the world economy weakens the capacity of mass parties to use the state as an instrument for allocating resources to benefit their constituencies. Welfare states face intensifying fiscal crisis, capital flow is beyond state control, and Keynesian policies supporting high wages seem to conflict with the need to revitalize national competitiveness. The social-democratic/welfare-state program no longer seems sustainable, and promises made in its name lose credibility.

As a result, the parties find themselves paralyzed, no longer able to offer a credible majoritarian program that meets the needs of both the relatively advantaged and the newly emergent groups that constitute their base. Limited on the one hand by the conservatism of their more advantaged constituents and on the other hand by the fiscal constraints resulting from dependency on global capital flows, these once-dominant parties appear mired in compromise and contradiction. Because state-based strategies of social reform—whether called socialist, capitalist, corporatist, or something else—appear to be politically and economically unviable, the parties whose programs were based on such strategies seem to have had their day as embodiments of popular hope.

The United States has, of course, always lacked a European-style social-democratic party. But after the 1960s, the Democratic Party's dilemmas were quite similar to those experienced by mass parties elsewhere. Many movement activists, either explicitly or implicitly, imagined that a movement coalition on the national level would revitalize the Democratic Party and usher in a scenario of the following sort: A progressive Democrat would enter the White House with the promise of completing the welfare state agenda of the New Deal and the Great Society. The bloated military budget would be redistributed to domestic investment that would create full employment by rebuilding the inner cities, constructing affordable housing, expanding education and other human services, and so on. The social wage would be expanded by providing universal health care, reforming welfare, and establishing entitlements for child care, lifelong education, and the like. In such a climate, the social movements would be institutionalized as frameworks for the advancement of constituencies' rights and interests within the electoral and judicial process. Movement activists would find fruitful vocations as advocates, representatives, and professionals in service to their constituencies.

There was, of course, no such new New Deal in the postwar America of the 1970s and the 1980s. Public policy was moved sharply rightward, and so the hope of a normal politics into which the pursuit of equality and social justice could be incorporated never materialized. The movements did become institutionalized: in the seventies a host of lobbying organizations emerged out of the civil rights, women's, peace, and environmental movements; a vast industry of direct-mail solicitation for such causes largely replaced street-level protest; large numbers of activists entered electoral politics, public service, and academic and professional roles with some continuing commitment to their movement identities guiding their work.

In the eighties, the movements lost much of their will and capacity to mobilize direct-action and anti-institutional protest. But it would be quite wrong to describe the seventies and eighties as a period of popular demobilization. As we have seen, at the level of town and neighborhood and local institution, within workplaces and families, the "abnormal" politics of new social movements continued. It was in this period that environmentalism and feminism became integral to the practices of daily life of millions and were incorporated into the political and social life of communities and institutions. This was the era of gay liberation, of collective action by the disabled, and of the cultural politics of racial identity.

Indeed, in the last few years, there has been a tendency among movement-oriented intellectuals and academics to want to redefine the historical meaning of social movements. Rather than measure movements' impacts in terms of political reform, we increasingly stress their impact on culture, consciousness, and identity. A number of recent efforts to theorize movements are very much in this vein.[2]

This interpretation of social movements is paralleled by the apparently interminable debate within academia about "multiculturalism" and "political correctness." The so-called "culture wars" in higher education derive from the effort by academically rooted movement activists, begun in the 1960s, to make higher education more demographically and intellectually inclusive and from counter-efforts to block or dilute this thrust.

The cultural turn, from one angle, represents an important advance in the theory and practice of democratic social action. A new complex of understandings about social power and about the institutional sources of social change is embedded in efforts consciously to reconstruct identity, redefine the boundaries of social knowledge, and reform education. But certainly there is a dark side to this emphasis: the turn to culture is a turn away from efforts to analyze and strategize economic and state power on the part of movement activists and intellectuals. And the emphasis on "new" social movements focused on racial, ethnic, sexual, and other status-based identities has seemed to invalidate class as a basis for collective action.

The political vacuum left by the decline of socialist organizations and social-democratic parties cannot adequately be filled by the politics of culture and identity. Cultural projects are inherently nonstrategic; they don't redistribute wealth or address state power, they don't require the mobilization of grassroots collective action to challenge institutionalized power structures. Societal reconstruction requires that people organize in their shared interest while also defending and fulfilling their collective identities. Movements must embody material goals and debate strategies for achieving them, even as members engage in re-envisionings of the terms and meanings of their lives.

Elements of a New Movement Strategy

The parties and organizations of the left, for a century, provided the primary space within which questions of strategy, program, and class interest were thrashed out. Such space is now largely gone. Where does such discussion now take place? Primarily in the periodicals and journals of leftward orientation and in the forums provided by the university. Accordingly, public discourse about movement strategy and program is largely the province of intellectuals, whose life situation is likely to be at least somewhat removed from that experienced by movement constituencies. Political discussion under university auspices, moreover, is constrained in a number of ways by canons of academic discourse. Until some organizational format is created to permit university-based intellectuals to connect with movement-based activists and intellectuals, efforts to reconstitute a political strategy and program will be hampered.

Despite the absence of such an organizational format, I think those who are concerned about sustaining democratic action—whether we are housed in universities or in movements—need to carry on strategic discussion where we can and perhaps by so doing begin to open the social space a new politics requires. So, for the sake of discussion, I would like to suggest some possible lines along which movement strategy might develop in the coming period. Such strategy must begin with the fact that the capacities of states to do economic steering, allocate capital, and redistribute income have been largely superseded by global capital flow, transnational corporate organization, and the dynamic of the world market.

The globalization dynamic has ravaging effects on the daily lives of many who once believed themselves to be secure, provoking widening ripples of anxiety in the great majority of people in the apparently affluent regions of the world. The most evident expressions of popular insecurity and grievance take the form of protectionism, expressed in varying degrees of virulence. Alongside resistance to "free trade" policies are demands to exclude immigrants, violent "ethnic cleansing" projects, tax revolts, popular support for xenophobic and demagogic politicians, a general disgust with the political mainstream (a disgust endlessly reinforced by the discovery and mongering of political and personal scandal). The one remaining power clearly controlled by national states—the power to police—becomes, increasingly, the defining political issue.

In this situation, it seems to me, there are several strategic imperatives shared by democratic movements—lines of action required for their common defense that, at the same time, have the potential of advancing the possibilities for democratic alternatives to protectionism. The following strategic directions are applicable, at least, to the American movements:

A New Internationalism

Protectionism resists economic changes that threaten the wages and well-being of relatively well-off sectors of the working class. The alternative is to support improved living standards for workers in the poor countries. How? The most obvious way would be for American unions and labor organizers to provide direct assistance to labor struggles in those countries to which industrial jobs and capital have been and are being exported. Concerted action by Americans in support of such struggles—sympathetic demonstrations, political action, and job action—is necessary. Environmental internationalism (already evident in growing international networks of environmental activists and global environmental conferences) provides a second, equally important, track for strategic internationalism.

Americans have not been averse to mass action that either directly or indirectly expresses cross-national solidarity. Such action was integral to the anti-war and anti-interventionist activity during the Vietnam War, and of course manifested by strong grassroots opposition to U.S. policy in Central America. The most effective and relevant solidarity movement was the anti-apartheid struggle, which made extensive use of economic leverage. The campaign against NAFTA, although labeled as protectionist, undoubtedly raised popular awareness about the plight of Mexican workers and peasants and may well have stimulated movement networks that could be activated for long-term internationalist projects.

Such projects are made more likely by a fundamentally new social reality: Americans increasingly are in the same boat as the rest of the world. If, historically, American living standards were enhanced by imperialism, today the American population is increasingly being colonized by the same supra-national forces that are at work in the rest of the planet. American elites can no longer credibly promise Americans that they will be advantaged in the global economy. The increasing congruence of interests between the peoples of the northern and southern hemispheres provides a material basis for a new internationalist consciousness. The growing popularity of "world music" is a cultural manifestation of this potential.

Community Empowerment

As the nation state declines, the local community becomes the focus of hope for collective power to maintain everyday life. Whenever corporate decisions threaten economic loss and social dislocation, community-based mobilization has been an increasingly frequent—and often surprisingly effective—response. Struggles to prevent or mitigate plant closings and relocations, to oppose corporate pollution or destructive development—or force the mitigation of these—are integral to local scenes everywhere. Increasingly, communities seem to have developed considerable expertise about means of resistance; the need for "outside" organizers seems less than in the past as indigenous leadership grows in sophistication and creativity.

In the United States, as we have seen, a growing body of law has provided some legal foundation for community empowerment. State and national environmental legislation adopted over the last twenty-five years provides rights previously unavailable for local movements to challenge proposed developments because of their environmental impacts. Efforts to win similar legal protection for communities that are threatened with economic disruption—as, for example, the effort to pass plant-closing legislation—have been less successful.

In addition to legal support for community voices in corporate decisions, communities need access to capital for local investment, capital not now available from conventional private sources of finance. Community economic development grounded in democratic planning may be a fundamental strategy for protecting living standards against the ravages of the global market. I refer here not to the commonplace and often disastrous efforts by communities to invite their own rape by corporations and developers, but to efforts to develop community investment and ownership of enterprises that might be job creating and locally beneficial. Moreover, the provision of life necessities—including food, housing, recreation, child care—through community-directed, nonmarket mechanisms can provide social wage substitutions for declining or insecure private wages.

A promising strategic direction for community-based movement activists, therefore, would be to formulate an agenda for national legislation to empower localities. Such an agenda would include establishing national rules requiring the inclusion of community voices in corporate decisions that affect localities, and providing major national resources to support community planning, development, ownership, and control aimed at sustainable local and regional economies.

Participatory Democracy

The global market and the decline of the state compel the restructuring of private and public institutions. Corporate and bureaucratic downsizing, when carried out from above, is designed to protect the incomes and perquisites of those at the top while imposing the costs of economic realism on those with the least leverage. Within each institution, fear, demoralization, and resentment are the result. In the larger society, increasing economic insecurity and dislocation for previously comfortable middle layers accompany the further degradation of the poorest. In the name of efficiency, environmental protections are threatened, previously taken-for-granted fringe benefits are liquidated, all of the institutional "frills" that make up a reasonable varied daily life are abolished. Rearguard resistance to such changes often proves frustratingly ineffective.

The alternative is to enable—and indeed compel—all of the constituencies of a given institution (workplace, school, government bureaucracy) to participate in the planning of institutional change. This means, of course, open books, the diffusion of expert knowledge, the development of institutional mechanisms of representation, voice, and accountability.

There is considerable evidence that demands for participation are a typical response to the threat of retrenchment and downsizing. Cuts are often administered so quickly that the opportunity to mobilize a response from below is short-circuited. But in instances, such as in universities, where retrenchment warnings have happened in advance of implementation, the mobilization of energy and the capacity of affected groups to grasp technical issues and to bargain about these is evident.

652 *Richard Flacks*

Instead of simple resistance to such threats (which often does not materialize because people see cuts as necessary or inevitable, or otherwise become hopeless) movement strategy might focus on demands for the democratic restructuring of institutional life. Such demands are not for self-interested or privileged protection of particular groups. They are in fact quite the opposite: The aspiration to exercise institutional voice is integrally connected with the need to take institutional responsibility.

To conclude: Social movements arise and are revitalized when normal politics fail. We seem to have entered an epoch in which normal politics not only are failing but cannot be restored in the traditional ways. Government based on representation through political parties and capable of steering national economies is now obsolete. Social polarization, tribalistic fragmentation, and cultural despair are looming dangers. Social movements—the semi-spontaneous upsurges of grassroots initiative—have until now been understood as spasmodic moments in which popular intervention revitalized and reformed institutions. Now that the parties are over, the fate of democracy and the chances for social justice will depend on the movements' capacity to take ongoing responsibility for the social future.

NOTES

1. The rise of progressive electoral coalitions has been described in Pierre Clavel, *The Progressive City* (New Brunswick, NJ: Rutgers University Press, 1986). Studies of two key cases include Mark Kann, *Middle Class Radicalism in Santa Monica* (Philadelphia: Temple University Press, 1986); W. J. Conroy, *Challenging the Boundaries of Reform: Socialism in Burlington* (Philadelphia: Temple University Press, 1990); J. M. Berry et al., *The Rebirth of Urban Democracy* (Washington: Brookings Institution, 1993); R. E. DeLeon, *Left Coast City* (Lawrence: University of Kansas Press, 1992). See also J. M. Kling and P. S. Posner, *Dilemmas of Activism* (Philadelphia: Temple University Press, 1990).
2. Important discussion of the impact of movements on culture and consciousness may be found in Alberto Melucci, *Nomads of the Present* (Philadelphia: Temple University Press, 1989); Ron Eyerman and Andrew Jamison, *Social Movements* (University Park: Pennsylvania State University Press, 1991); and Barbara Epstein, *Political Protest and Cultural Revolution* (Berkeley: University of California Press, 1991).